Messiah and the Throne

Jewish Merkabah Mysticism
and Early Christian Exaltation Discourse

Messiah and the Throne

Jewish Merkabah Mysticism
and Early Christian Exaltation Discourse

Timo Eskola

Fontes Press

First published 2001 in Germany by Mohr Siebeck
© 2001 Mohr Siebeck
All rights reserved
Fontes edition published 2019

ISBN-13: 978-1-948048-16-3 (Hardback)
ISBN-13: 978-1-948048-17-0 (Paperback)

All rights reserved. No part of this publication may be reproduced, stored in a retrieval system, or transmitted in any form or by any means—electronic, mechanical, photocopy, recording, or any other—except for brief quotations in printed reviews, without the prior permission of the publisher.

FONTES PRESS
Dallas, TX
www.fontespress.com

Preface

Almost thirty years have passed since the days of my doctoral dissertation on the Christology of Romans 1:3-4, published in Finland 1992. The following years were spent on an investigation on the soteriology of Paul, treating the themes of theodicy and predestination in Pauline teaching on justification (published in WUNT 2. series 1998). After that project I wished to return to the study of Christology, since I had been developing earlier ideas by writing articles and giving lectures on the subject in my capacity as a New Testament scholar at the Theological Institute of Finland (Helsinki), and as a docent at the University of Helsinki. I had never yet published any of that material in English.

When I returned to the subject it soon became apparent, however, that quite much had happened in the field of the study of exaltation Christology. Divine agent theory (Hurtado) was quite new when I wrote my dissertation in 1988-1991. Since then it has gained many adherents in scholarship. Also the angelic interpretation (Fossum, Segal, Gieschen) has become rather popular. Furthermore, several publications on a messianic interpretation, and on the significance of Psalm 110, as well as other books on the divine throne, have moved the discussion to a new level.

All these attempts to explain early exaltation Christology are linked with early Jewish merkabah mysticism. Therefore, I could not escape the challenge of approaching the subject of resurrection theology in Rom. 1:3-4 and in several parallel passages from the point of view of the merkabah-throne. This led me to a new investigation of Jewish merkabah texts, as well as to a new study of New Testament exaltation passages.

The research was once again made possible by a research project of the Institute, and it became a real source of joy in my life. I am especially indebted to my colleague, Rev. Eero Junkkaala, General Secretary of the Theological Institute, who has continuously encouraged me in my work. My thanks also go to the staff of the Institute, our librarian Erkki Hanhikorpi, as well as to our secretary, Mrs. Kirsi Sell, who has taken care of many practical matters.

Already in my dissertation I expressed my deep gratitude both to Prof. Dr. Peter Stuhlmacher and to Prof. Dr. Martin Hengel for their hospitality during my stay in Tübingen when writing my dissertation. Now after several more years of work, I wish to renew my thanks while the years have proven that their instructions have provided for a continuing inspiration in my study of early Christology.

My special thanks go to Prof. Kai Mikkonen at the Faculty of Arts, University of Helsinki. In my studies on literary theory he has patiently guided me through the paths of structuralism, post-structuralism, and intertextual criticism. I hope that the methodological ideas developed in this study will be a credit to this dialogue. I should also like to thank some friends of mine and "fellows" of the Institute: Docent Lauri Thurén (Åbo/Joensuu) for his suggestions and comments, and Prof. Antti Laato (Åbo), with whom I have spent hours discussing new literary methods and their application to biblical study.

Not least, I am deeply indebted to Mr. Michael Cox, Lic. Theol. (Kerava), Mrs. Virpi Hopkins, M.A., and Mr. Michael Hopkins, B.B.A., M.T.S., (Helsinki) for their labours in undertaking the language revision of this manuscript.

Finally, I wish to express my sincere thanks to Professors Martin Hengel and Otfried Hofius of Tübingen for their kind acceptance of my study for publication in this distinguished series, as well as the editorial staff of J.C.B. Mohr (Paul Siebeck) for their highly professional assistance in preparing the manuscript for publication.

Timo Eskola
Theological Institute of Finland
Kaisaniemenkatu 13 A 4. krs
FIN-00100 Helsinki
Finland
e-mail: timo.eskola@teolinst.fi

Unless otherwise indicated, biblical quotations in English are taken from the New Revised Standard Version.

Contents

Preface V
Abbreviations X

I Introduction

§ 1 Jewish Mysticism and New Testament Exegesis 1
   1.1. The relation of merkabah mysticism and early Christology in scholarship 1
      a. Merkabah mysticism in Jewish studies 1
      b. Merkabah mysticism and Christology: early suggestions 6
      c. Angelic interpretation 7
      d. The divine agent theory 9
      e. The theory of messianic enthronement 11
      f. Some later developments of the main theories 13
   1.2. Setting the task 15
   1.3. Problems of methodology: on discourse and meaning 17
      a. The contribution of semiotics and semantics 17
      b. The contribution of structuralism and narratology 29
      c. The contribution of intertextual criticism 34
      d. A linguistic approach and the methodology of Christological study 38

II The Heavenly Throne in the Old Testament, Second Temple Jewish Theology, and the Pseudepigrapha

§ 2 God as King and the Ark of the Covenant as His Throne 43
   2.1. The Lord is King 44
   2.2. The ark as the throne of God in the Old Testament 50
   2.3. The function of the throne in the Temple cult 55
   2.4. The enthronement of the anointed king 58

§ 3 The Throne in Early Jewish Mysticism: the Merkabah 65
   3.1. Throne visions in Old Testament prophetic literature 65
   3.2. The throne in pre-Christian Jewish literature 71
      a. The Book of the Watchers (1 Enoch 14) 72
      b. Jubilees 75
      c. The Testament of Levi 77
      d. Qumran 79
      e. The Exagoge of Ezekiel 86

Contents

3.3. Thrones and enthronements in the literature of the Common Era 91
    a. Similitudes (1 Enoch 37-71) 91
    b. Philo 96
    c. The Fourth Book of Ezra 98
    d. The Testament of Job 100
    e. 2 Enoch 103
    f. The Apocalypse of Abraham 105
    g. The Ladder of Jacob 107
    h. The Ascension of Isaiah 108
    i. The Life of Adam and Eve/The Apocalypse of Moses 111
    j. The Testament of Abraham 113
    k. The Testament of Isaac 115
    l. 3 Baruch 116
    m. Hellenistic synagogue prayer 4 117
    n. The Sibylline Oracles, Book 3 118
    o. Questions of Ezra 119
    p. 3 Enoch 120

§ 4 From Merkabah Mysticism to Christology: Suggestions and Refutations
    4.1. Merkabah mysticism and royal metaphors 124
    4.2. Is there an exalted Messiah in merkabah mysticism? 127
    4.3. Limitations of the angelic interpretation 137
    4.4. Throne in a cultic setting 146
    4.5. Throne in eschatological judgment descriptions 151
    4.6. Conclusions 154

III The Messiah and the Throne in the New Testament Christological Discourses

§ 5 At the Right Hand of God *(enthronement discourse)* 158
    5.1. Psalm 110 and Christology in early Lukan traditions 160
    5.2. Paul and merkabah mysticism 182
    5.3. Reception of early enthronement Christology
        in the letter to the Hebrews and in the Revelation of John 202

§ 6 Resurrection as Enthronement in Rom. 1:3-4 *(resurrection discourse)* 217
    6.1. Early tradition and the kerygmatic formula 217
    6.2. The formula and the symbolic world of Jewish Christianity 227
    6.3. Enthronement theme in the context of resurrection discourse 244

§ 7 Throne as a Place for the Atonement *(cultic discourse)* 251
    7.1. The throne as a mercy seat 251
    7.2. The unity of exaltation and atonement 258
    7.3. The emergence of the cultic interpretation 264

§ 8 The Centre of the Last Judgment *(judicial discourse)* 270
    8.1. Son of Man and his throne 270
    8.2. The reception of early judgment descriptions in Paul 274
    8.3. Judicial discourse and the problem of polarized eschatology 277

§ 9 The History of Influence:
Enthronement in Jewish Christian Pseudepigrapha 285
  9.1. Exalted Christ in the Ascension of Isaiah 285
  9.2. Enthroned Davidide in the Sibyllines 289
  9.3. Paul and merkabah in the Apocalypse of Paul 293

IV The Nature of Early Enthronement Christology

§ 10 Some Problems with the "Theocratic" Theory
     of Adoptionist Christology 295
  10.1. The theory of theocratic adoptionism in scholarship 296
  10.2. Adoptionism and the Ebionite theory 299
  10.3. Defining early Jewish Christianity 309

§ 11 Main Factors in the Emergence of Christology 322
  11.1. Divine agents and angels? 323
  11.2. Possible features of a Christian merkabah tradition 328
  11.3. Merkabah tradition and the search for a "missing link" 331
  11.4. Semiosis in early Christian theology 336

§ 12 Theocracy, Exaltation Discourse, and Christology 338
  12.1. Three enthroned figures 339
     a. Messianic Davidide on the throne of Glory 339
     b. New Melchizedek on the mercy seat 344
     c. Son of Man on the judgment seat 346
  12.2. Four narratives – four ascent stories 347
     a. The heavenly enthronement of the seed of David 348
     b. Prince of life conquers death 351
     c. Eternal high priest enters the debir 356
     d. Eschatological entrée of the messianic judge 359
  12.3. Intertextual aspect: Christ as the reigning God on the throne of Glory 361

Conclusion 375

Bibliography 391

Index of Ancient Sources 415

Index of Authors 429

Index of Subjects 434

Abbreviations

1. Periodicals, Series, Reference Works

AASF	Annales Academiae Scientiarum Fennicae
AGAJU	Arbeiten zur Geschichte des antiken Judentums und des Urchristentums
ALGHJ	Arbeiten zur Literatur und Geschichte des hellenistischen Judentums
AncB	Anchor Bible
ABD	Anchor Bible Dictionary
AGSU	Arbeiten zur Geschichte des Spätjudentums und Urchristentums
AnBib	Analecta Biblica
ANFa	Ante-Nicene Fathers
ANRW	Aufstieg und Niedergang der römischen Welt
ASOR	American Schools of Oriental Research
ATD	Altes Testament Deutsch
AThANT	Abhandlungen zur Theologie des Alten und Neuen Testaments
AThD	Acta Theologica Danica
AzTh	Arbeiten zur Theologie
BA	Biblical Archaeologist
BBB	Bonner Biblische Beiträge
BBR	Bulletin for Biblical Research
BDR	Blass/Debrunner/Rehkopf, Grammatik des neutestamentlichen Griechisch
BEThL	Bibliotheca Ephemeridum Theologicarum Lovaniensium
BEvTh	Beiträge zur Evangelischen Theologie
BHTh	Beiträge zur historischen Theologie
Bib	Biblica
BK	Biblischer Kommentar
BKAT	Biblischer Kommentar. Altes Testament
BNTC	Black's New Testament Commentaries
BZ	Biblische Zeitschrift
BZAW	Beihefte zur Zeitschrift für die alttestamentliche Wissenschaft
BZNW	Beihefte zur Zeitschrift für die neutestamentliche Wissenschaft
CB	Coniectanea Biblica
CB.NT	Coniectanea Biblica. New Testament Series
CB.OT	Coniectanea Biblica. Old Testament Series
CBQ	Catholic Biblical Quarterly
CCWJCW	Cambridge Commentaries on Writings of the Jewish and Christian World 200 BC to AD 200
CJAS	Christianity and Judaism in Antiquity Series
CNT	Coniectanea neotestamentica

DJD	Discoveries in the Judaean Desert (of Jordan)
DMMRS	Duke monographs in medieval and Renaissance studies
EETh	Einführung in die evangelische Theologie
EJ	Encyclopedia Judaica
EJTh	European Journal of Theology
EKK	Evangelisch-Katholischer Kommentar
EQ	Evangelical Quarterly
EvTh	Evangelische Theologie
EWNT	Exegetisches Wörterbuch zum Neuen Testament, ed. H. Balz, G. Schneider
ET	Expository Times
ExpT	Expository Times
FzB	Forschung zur Bibel
FRLANT	Forschungen zur Religion und Literatur des Alten und Neuen Testaments
GCS	Die griechischen christlichen Schriftsteller der ersten drei Jahrhunderte
GNT	Grundrisse zum Neuen Testament
GTA	Göttinger Theologische Arbeiten
HAT	Handbuch zum Alten Testament
HNT	Handbuch zum Neuen Testament
HR	History of Religions
HThK	Herders Theologischer Kommentar
HThS	Harvard Theological Studies
ICC	International Critical Commentary
ICS	Illinois Classical Studies
IntB	The Interpreter's Bible
Interp.	Interpretation
IVP	InterVarsity Press
JBL	Journal of Biblical Literature
JJS	Journal of Jewish Studies
JR	Journal of Religion
JRS	Journal of Religious Studies
JSJ	Journal for the Study of Judaism
JSNT	Journal for the Study of the New Testament
JSNTS	Journal for the Study of the New Testament, Supplement Series
JSOT	Journal for the Study of the Old Testament
JSOTS	Journal for the Study of the Old Testament, Supplement Series
JSS	Journal of Semitic Studies
JThS	Journal of Theological Studies
KAT	Kommentar zum Alten Testament
KEK	Kritisch-Exegetischer Kommentar
LCC	Library of Christian classics
LCL	Loeb Classical Library

MNTC	Moffatt New Testament commentary
MS	Monograph Series
MSSNTS	Monograph Series. Society for New Testament Studies
NAC	New American Commentary
NF	Neue Folge
NIBC	New International Biblical Commentary
NICNT	New international commentary on the New Testament
NIGTC	New International Greek Testament Commentary
NT	Novum Testamentum
NTA	Neutestamentliche Abhandlungen
NTD	Neues Testament Deutsch
NTOA	Novum testamentum et orbis antiquus
NTS	New Testament Studies
NT.S	Novum Testamentum. Supplements
NTTS	New Testament tools and studies
OTL	Old Testament library
OTP	The Old Testament Pseudepigrapha
PVTG	Pseudepigrapha veteris testamenti Graece
RB	Revue biblique
RGG	Religion in Geschichte und Gegenwart
RQ	Revue de Qumran
SBL	Society of Biblical Literature
SBL.DS	SBL Dissertation Series
SBLMS	SBL Monograph Series
SBLSBS	SBL Sources for Biblical Study
SBL.SP	SBL Seminar Papers
SBM	Stuttgarter Biblische Monographien
SBS	Stuttgarter Bibelstudien
SBT	Studies in Biblical Theology
ScEs	Science et esprit
SESJ	Suomen eksegeettisen seuran julkaisuja
SEÅ	Svensk Exegetisk Årsbok
SJLA	Studies in Judaism in Late Antiquity
SJT	Scottish Journal of Theology
SNT	Schriften des Neuen Testaments
SNTS	Society for New Testament Studies
StANT	Studien zum Alten und Neuen Testament
STAT	Suomalaisen tiedeakatemian toimituksia
STKSJ	Suomalaisen teologisen kirjallisuusseuran julkaisuja
StTDJ	Studies on the texts of the desert of Judah
StTh	Studia theologica (Lund)
StUNT	Studien zur Umwelt der Neuen Testaments
SVT	Supplements to Vetus Testamentum
SVTP	Studia in Veteris Testamenti Pseudepigrapha

TANZ	Texte und Arbeiten zum neutestamentlichen Zeitalter
TB	Theologische Bücherei
TBLNT	Theologisches Begriffslexikon zum Neuen Testament
TDNT	Theological Dictionary of the New Testament
TDOT	Theological Dictionary of the Old Testament
TEH	Theologische Existenz heute
THAT	Theologisches Handwörterbuch zum Alten Testament
ThBeitr	Theologische Beiträge
ThLZ	Theologische Literaturzeitung
ThR	Theologische Rundschau
ThSt	Theological Studies
ThW	Theologische Wissenschaft
ThWAT	Theologisches Wörterbuch zum Alten Testament
ThWNT	Theologisches Wörterbuch zum Neuen Testament
ThZ	Theologische Zeitschrift
TRE	Theologische Realenzyklopädie
TPI	Trinity Press International
TS	Theological studies
TSAJ	Texte und Studien zum Antiken Judentum
TToday	Theology Today
TyndB	Tyndale Bulletin
USF	University of South Florida
UTB	Uni-Taschenbücher
VT	Vetus Testamentum
WBC	Word Biblical Commentary
WTJ	Westminster theological journal
WMANT	Wissenschaftliche Monographien zum Alten und Neuen Testament
WUNT	Wissenschaftliche Untersuchungen zum Neuen Testament
ZAW	Zeitschrift für die alttestamentliche Wissenschaft
ZNW	Zeitschrift für die neutestamentliche Wissenschaft
ZThK	Zeitschrift für Theologie und Kirche

2. Technical and Other Abbreviations

AV	Authorized Version
cf.	confer
col.	columna
ed(s).	editor(s)
ET	English Translation
f	fragment
FS	Festschrift (Studies in Honour of, etc.)
H	Hebrew text of Sirach
KJV	King James Version

LXX	Septuagint
m	Mishnah tractate
MS(S)	manuscript(s)
MT	Masoretic text
n	footnote
n.d.	no date
NEB	New English Bible
NIV	New International Version
NRSV	New Revised Standard Version
NT	New Testament
o.c.	opus citatum
OT	Old Testament
RSV	Revised Standard Version
v(v)	verse(s)
vol.	volume

I

Introduction

§ 1 Jewish Mysticism and New Testament Exegesis

The study of New Testament Christology has often learned much from the study of Jewish theology, and especially from the study of Jewish mysticism in the Second Temple period and later traditions. When we are attempting to find a relevant interpretation for exaltation Christology in the New Testament, we need to pay special attention to the exhaustive and inspiring study of Jewish mysticism that has taken place over the last two decades. In this introductory chapter we shall first make a short survey of the history of interpretation concerning the relation between Second Temple Jewish mystical tradition and early Christology. In addition, there are certain necessary methodological questions that need to be answered.

1.1. The relation of merkabah mysticism and early Christology in scholarship

Did merkabah mysticism influence the development of Christology? The relation between Jewish mysticism and the emerging Christology of early Jewish Christianity has interested scholars for a long time. Even though merkabah mysticism itself appears not to be very well known in the area of New Testament studies in general, in the history of scholarship we can already now find several different theories explaining that relation. Before proceeding to the definition of the task of this study we shall first treat the major theories that have been proposed as a solution for the basic problem concerning the aforementioned relationship. As a start we need to see how merkabah mysticism has been considered in the area of Jewish studies.

a. Merkabah mysticism in Jewish studies

The concept of merkabah mysticism itself needs some clarification. It is apparent that exaltation Christology has relevant parallels in several themes of apocalyptic Jewish mysticism, for example in themes such as heavenly journeys, ascensions, throne visions and enthronements. In scholarship such Jewish mysticism has most often been defined as merkabah mysticism, because heavenly journeys and throne visions focus on the heavenly *merkabah*, the throne chariot of God. Throne descriptions have been regarded as a uniting feature for the passages under consideration. In Jewish studies the throne has further been considered as the main feature of such mysticism. Even though merkabah mysticism has often been regarded as a relatively late phenomenon belonging to Hekhalot literature, we are here interested in its pre-Christian origins and early forms in New Testament times.

What is also interesting, is the close relationship of Jewish mysticism to the traditional Temple-centred faith of Israel. *G. Scholem*, the writer of *Major Trends in Jewish Mysticism*, connected Jewish mysticism to the main themes of Jewish faith, i.e. to the worshipping of God the King on his heavenly throne.[1]

"We know that in the period of the Second Temple an esoteric doctrine was already taught in Pharisaic circles. The first chapter of Genesis, the story of Creation (Maaseh Bereshith), and the first chapter of Ezekiel, the vision of God's throne-chariot (the 'Merkabah'), were the favorite subjects of discussion and interpretation which it was apparently considered inadvisable to make public."

Thus it was Scholem who gave the first, and greatly influential, definition of the nature of early Jewish mysticism:[2]

"What was the central theme of these oldest of mystical doctrines within the framework of Judaism? No doubts are possible on this point: the earliest Jewish mysticism is throne-mysticism. Its essence is not absorbed contemplation of God's true nature, but perception of His appearance on the throne, as described by Ezekiel, and cognition of the mysteries of the celestial throne-world. The throne-world is to the Jewish mystic what the pleroma, the 'fullness,' the bright sphere of divinity with its potencies, aeons, archons and dominions is to the Hellenistic and early Christian mystics of the period who appear in the history of religion under the names of Gnostics and Hermetics."

For a time Jewish mysticism was associated with Jewish apocalyptic that was popular in the second and first centuries B.C.E. Therefore the writings and different themes in that tradition were interpreted merely in that rather late context. In his innovative study *The Dawn of Apocalyptic* (1975) *P. D. Hanson*, however, challenged this view. Hanson investigated the relationship between Jewish apocalyptic eschatology and the prophetic tradition of Israel.[3]

"Our point is this: The origins of apocalyptic cannot be explained by a method which juxtaposes seventh- and second-century compositions and then proceeds to account for the features of the latter by reference to its immediate environment. The apocalyptic literature of the second century and after is the result of a long development reaching back to pre-exilic times and beyond, and not the new baby of second-century foreign parents. Not only the sources of origin, but the intrinsic nature of late apocalyptic compositions can be understood

---

[1] Scholem, *Major Trends*, 42.

[2] Scholem, *Major Trends*, 43-44.

[3] Hanson, *The Dawn*, 6.

only by tracing the centuries-long development through which the apocalyptic eschatology developed from prophetic and other even more archaic native roots."

Hanson's conclusion is important for our study of the tradition history of the main ideas of merkabah mysticism. We are not dealing with a peculiar second century B.C.E. phenomenon, but instead with a "centuries-long development" of ideas. Therefore, in the present study, we need to take such a background into consideration.

In apocalyptic writings the throne of God is constantly associated with an ascent structure. Throne visions occur in a context where a privileged pious one is making a heavenly journey under the guidance of an angel. Therefore the study of throne mysticism has often focused on such an ascent structure.

A.F. Segal first treated the ascent structure in his monograph *Two Powers in Heaven* (1977), where he investigated a Jewish heresy of a divine heavenly being beside God. Even though the analyses were centred on rabbinic writings, Segal also made some comments on earlier apocalyptic writings and the New Testament.[4]

In his famous ANRW article, *Heavenly Ascent in Hellenistic Judaism, Early Christianity and their Environment* (1980), Segal then made a detailed survey of the ascent structure in apocalyptic writings. In this paper Segal stated that although apocalyptic literature may have many different functions, an underlying ascent structure behind most writings can be isolated.[5] He paid special attention to angelic figures which performed different functions in heaven. Segal also made some direct suggestions concerning the connection of early Christology to such an ascent structure, and we shall return to these statements later.

Even though the golden era of Jewish mysticism is usually thought to have begun in the first centuries of the Common Era, the data of earlier forms of mysticism have been well known from the very first studies. Segal, for instance, investigates the pre-Christian writings of Qumran, 1 Enoch and the Testament of Levi. Thus the scholarly dating of the earliest phases of Jewish mysticism has not essentially changed over the years.

In the same year, 1980, *I. Gruenwald* published an important study entitled *Apocalyptic and Merkavah Mysticism*. Gruenwald first studied various types of biblical theophany and then listed some of the characteristic features of throne visions (here in a somewhat abbreviated form):[6]

a. God is sitting on a throne;
b. He has the appearance of a man;

---

[4] See e.g. Segal, *Two Powers*, 182ff.
[5] Segal, *ANRW II 23.2.* (1980) 1358.
[6] Gruenwald, *Apocalyptic*, 31.

c. God is sitting in a palace;
d. Fire occupies an important position in the vision;
e. God is accompanied by angels who minister to Him;
f. The angels recite hymns.

It is easy to see that these elements are linked to the Temple theophanies of the prophets, thus revealing a cultic context. Further, as Gruenwald notes, these elements "became major components in the mystical visions found in apocalyptic and later on in the Merkavah visions of *Hekhalot* literature." Gruenwald also investigated apocalyptic writings from 1 Enoch and the Apocalypse of Abraham to the Ascension of Isaiah and the Apocalypse of Paul, detecting the occurrence of those features.

Furthermore, Gruenwald paid attention to the reception of merkabah material in a Christian environment. He noted, for example, that in the Ascension of Isaiah a text that has undergone Christian redaction, several features connected the Christian editorial contribution to the underlying Jewish original. Furthermore he concluded, however, that such features might derive from Gnostic Christianity.[7] In the Apocalypse of John he found a more "traditional" Jewish teaching. "Although the *Apocalypse of John* received its final shape some twenty years after the destruction of the Temple, its Merkavah material is nevertheless typical of its Jewish counterpart before the destruction."[8]

The transcendent nature of Jewish apocalyptic was brought out in the lengthy study *The Open Heaven* (1982) by *Chr. Rowland.*[9]

"By the time we reach the apocalyptic writings of the third and second centuries BC and later, we find that a cosmology has developed in which God is enthroned in glory in heaven, and his activities are carried out among men either by angelic intermediaries or other modes of divine operation like the spirit or shekinah. The cosmological beliefs were such that it often became necessary for anyone who would enter the immediate presence of God to embark on a journey through the heavenly world, in order to reach God himself."

In this transcendent scene, according to Rowland, angelic intermediaries played a significant role. Thus the suggestions of Segal concerning the importance of angelology in the interpretation were taken further. Rowland found evidence that the developing angelology "had produced an angelic figure of considerable status, whose position in the heavenly hierarchy set him apart from the rest of the angels". Such a belief in an exalted angel "owed much to the developments of the throne-theophany already inherent in the book of

---

[7] Gruenwald, *Apocalyptic*, 61f.

[8] Gruenwald, *Apocalyptic*, 62.

[9] Rowland, *Open Heaven*, 80.

Ezekiel itself".[10] In addition, Rowland suggested that there was another development that took a rather different form. In certain apocalyptic writings there appeared an attempt to reinterpret the throne-theophany "by identifying the figure on the throne, not with God but with a man exalted to heaven by God". This was especially the case with the Son of Man ideas of the Similitudes of Enoch.[11]

As the basic features of the "ascent structure" of Jewish mysticism had been investigated, further studies began to make precise the details in this subject. In *The Faces of the Chariot* (1988) *D. J. Halperin* studied early Jewish responses to the prophet's vision in the book of Ezekiel. Halperin was interested in throne visions, and one of his main theses was that on the basis of Ezekiel's vision there emerged a "hymnic tradition". This tradition focused on heavenly worship. The seraphs with other heavenly beings eternally sang "Holy, Holy, Holy" before God's throne.[12] According to Halperin, Jewish mysticism building on such a tradition was of a cultic nature.

Therefore, for example in 1 Enoch, the merkabah was located in a heavenly Temple. Halperin pays attention to the fact that heavenly beings were engaged in a heavenly liturgy.[13]

"Daniel and Enoch share an image, perhaps drawn from the hymnic tradition of merkabah exegesis (think of the Angelic liturgy), of God surrounded by multitudes of angels. But, in the Holy of Holies, God sits alone. Even the priests, as Josephus stresses... may not enter this inner shrine... The angels, barred from the inner house, are the priests of Enoch's heavenly Temple. The high priest must be Enoch himself, who appears in the celestial Holy of Holies to procure forgiveness for holy beings."[14]

Another interesting field of study is naturally the world of the Dead Sea Scrolls. Especially the publication of the Songs of the Sabbath Sacrifice inspired scholars in the study of mysticism.[15] In 1982 *L. Schiffman* suggested in his article that merkabah speculation at Qumran is probably one of the main sources for merkabah mysticism in general. There are similarities in terminology and motifs, even though no mention of a heavenly journey can be

---

[10] Rowland, *Open Heaven*, 94, 111.

[11] Rowland, *Open Heaven*, 104.

[12] Halperin, *Chariot*, 46, 61.

[13] Other detailed studies concerned for example the nature of the heavenly sanctuary in apocalyptic writings, see especially A.J. McNicol's article "The Heavenly Sanctuary in Judaism", *JRS 13* (1987) 66-94.

[14] Halperin, *Chariot*, 81-82.

[15] This can be seen already from the first comments of Strugnell in his article "The Angelic Liturgy at Qumran", *VT suppl.* (1960) 318-345.

found.[16] He also paid attention to the connection between earthly worship and heavenly liturgy.[17]

Finally *C. Newsom's* critical edition of the Songs of the Sabbath Sacrifice (1985) opened the field for scholars in this area. In her analysis Newsom noted the cultic character of these songs which focus on the heavenly Temple and describe the heavenly liturgy of the cherubim in detail.[18]

In sum, Jewish mysticism is "throne mysticism". It is especially interested in throne visions. In these visions one can detect an ascent structure, where privileged persons are escorted before God's throne of glory in heaven. Some writings describe a heavenly worship that is located in the heavenly temple. Furthermore, according to certain passages, angelic intermediaries make services to God both in heaven and on earth.

Even though many Jewish apocalyptic writings derive from the Common Era and have apparently been subjected to Christian redaction, certain writings are clearly pre-Christian. Jewish mysticism seems to have a long tradition history, and many of the relevant themes for our study occur in writings that were written centuries before the New Testament.

b. Merkabah mysticism and Christology: early suggestions

As we have seen above, the scholars working on Jewish mysticism noted certain similarities between merkabah mysticism and New Testament Christology. Especially descriptions of heavenly figures were compared with descriptions of the resurrected Christ in New Testament. Further the idea of exaltation soon became important.

In New Testament scholarship several independent analyses were also made concerning this relation. For example, the idea of heavenly visions was taken under consideration. As early as 1971 *J.W. Bowker* wrote about merkabah visions and the theology of Paul in his JSS article. Bowker focused on Paul's accounts of visions and their similarities with Jewish accounts of ascension.[19] This point of view is important and it poses several important questions. Was Paul a seer himself? What is his relationship to the tradition of merkabah visions? Such questions need to be answered in the investigation later.

In the area of the study of Christology we also need to remember *M. Hengel's* early work *Der Sohn Gottes* (German 1975; in English, *The Son of God*, 1976). In his study Hengel proposed that the Jewish background for a

---

[16] Schiffman, *Mystics*, 45-46.

[17] Schiffman, *Mystics*, 17-18.

[18] See e.g. Newsom, *Songs*, 18ff.

[19] Bowker, *JSS 16* (1971) 157-173. Later the theme was investigated e.g. by Schäfer, *JJS 35* (1984) 19-35.

Christological description of an exalted Son of God can be found in the exalted figures that appear e.g. in 1 Enoch. In addition to such an ascent structure, Psalm 110 appeared to be decisive for early Christology.[20]

Hengel commented further on the angelic interpretation that was held in the area of Jewish studies. Even though there was developed angel Christology e.g. in Gnostic circles, which may have been building on a similar tradition as the Melchizedek text from Qumran, New Testament Christology did not embrace such a view. For example, in the Letter to the Hebrews a fundamental distinction is made between the exalted Christ and the angels. Even though the idea of angel veneration was possible at that time, early Christology "left all these intermediary stages behind in a bold move" in Christological thinking.[21]

In addition to these early attempts to clarify the influence of Jewish mysticism on early Christology, there have been three major theories by which that relation has been explained. The first of these has emphasized the angelology found in merkabah texts.

c. Angelic interpretation

One of the first scholars to suggest the angelic interpretation was *A.F. Segal*, whose analyses were described above. In addition to the interpretation of Jewish mysticism, Segal made some quite direct suggestions concerning the nature of early Christology. He noted, for instance, the special significance of Psalm 110 for Christological descriptions.

"The Easter experience of the church was from the earliest time understood and expressed as the fulfillment of Ps. 110 and Dan. 7:13, seen as prophetic scripture. Jesus is proclaimed as a divine figure on the basis of his ascension to heaven and subsequent identification with the 'Lord' (Kyrios = YHWH) of Ps. 110 and the 'son of man' of Dan. 7:13 and Ps. 8:4."[22]

Segal was quite optimistic as regards angelic interpretation. "Indeed, it is probable that Jesus' identity was very early associated with the angel of YHWH who is superior to all angels in that he represents God's name on earth."[23] This kind of interpretation was unique, however, since the ascension was closely associated with resurrection. Segal noted that, for example, in the Christ-hymn of Philippians 2 the ascension of Jesus in his resurrection was described by exploiting Old Testament enthronement language (cf. Ps. 97:9 LXX). Furthermore, he concluded that "the Pauline predicates of the exalted Christ in Philippians are divine in character, biblical references referring to

---

[20] Hengel, *Son of God*, 60f.
[21] Hengel, *Son of God*, 82-84.
[22] Segal, *ANRW 23.2.* (1980) 1371.
[23] Segal, *ANRW 23.2.* (1980) 1371.

God used in Jewish liturgy as doxologies."[24] According to Segal, the implicit three-fold level of the universe found in the hymn entails further the belief that Christ has surmounted all the various levels to become its ruler.

The enthronement theme was not applied merely to Christology. Segal paid attention to the fact that in Ephesians, for instance, not only Christ is seated at the right hand of God, but believers are enthroned with him. In Christology, however, the enthronement theme found several other lines of interpretation. In Hebrews the enthronement "at the right hand of God" is expressed by the priestly Melchizedek tradition. In the Apocalypse of John, in turn, Segal also found a descent-ascent pattern. Here Christ was a "man-child" who was caught up to God and His throne.[25]

The Apocalypse of John was also of interest to *R. Bauckham,* who wrote on the worship of Jesus in apocalyptic Christianity. Bauckham argued that "the highest Christology, including the direct ascription of the title 'God' to Jesus, seems to have occurred earliest in contexts of worship," even though he did not believe that the heavenly liturgy of the Apocalypse would reflect an earthly liturgy practised in the Johannine churches.[26] After comparing the Apocalypse to the Ascension of Isaiah, Bauckham stated that apocalyptic Christian circles emphasized a traditional motif "designed to rule out angelolatry." While they at the same time depicted the worship of Jesus in the throne-room of heaven, they deliberately placed Christ "on the divine side of the line which monotheism must draw between God and creatures."[27]

C. Rowland, whose aforementioned work bore the subtitle "A Study of Apocalyptic in Judaism and Early Christianity," stressed more the aspect of angelology in the formation of early Christology. He compared the Apocalypse of John with the Apocalypse of Abraham, where the angel Jaoel had a primary status. Since in both of these writings the exalted one possessed a divine name and was described in a somewhat similar manner (sapphire, chrysolite, rainbow), Rowland concluded that it was "not easy to differentiate between this angel and the risen Christ who appears to John on the island of Patmos."[28] "Both of these works clearly think of the angelic figure as one who possesses divine attributes." In the Apocalypse of Abraham the figure is clearly an angel. In the Book of Revelation Christ is not directly described as an angel but, according to Rowland, "his function is not too different from the angelic

---

[24] Segal, *ANRW* 23.2. (1980) 1373. Later in his *Paul the Convert,* Segal applied several themes of the Jewish mystical tradition to the interpretation of Paul's theology. See especially Segal, *Paul,* 40-52.

[25] Segal, *ANRW* 23.2. (1980) 1374-1375.

[26] Bauckham, *NTS* 27 (1980-1) 331, 335.

[27] Bauckham, *NTS* 27 (1980-1) 335.

[28] Rowland, *Open Heaven,* 102.

intermediaries, who guide the apocalypticists on their heavenly journeys and reveal to them the secrets of God."[29]

It is small wonder that Rowland concludes that modern study of Christology fails to note the "extent of the influence of angel-christology on primitive Christian doctrine." According to Rowland, the letter to the Hebrews, for example, indicates that in the community addressed some were having difficulty separating Christ from other angelic beings.[30] This, however, is not self-evident. If Bauckham's conclusions are correct, the matter may be quite the opposite. The earliest Christology may have been expressed by exploiting the difference between the status of Christ and the angels from the very start. In spite of this, Rowland's view confirms the fact that, as we saw already in the writings of Segal, angelology in fact had great influence on the application of merkabah mysticism in the interpretation of early Christology.

d. The divine agent theory

The next of the major theories is the one that speaks of a tradition of divine agency in Jewish mysticism. Previous suggestions and explanations had been based on rather short remarks and even the angelic interpretation in its first stages was not a very comprehensive theory. Such suggestions, however, prepared the way for more extensive analyses.

The study of Christology took a major step forward in 1988 when *L.W. Hurtado* published his monograph *One God, One Lord*. Building on the foundation of new and blossoming Jewish studies Hurtado focused especially on matters related to merkabah mysticism. He highlighted a notion of divine agency in Second Temple Judaism.

"[T]he literature of postexilic Judaism contains many references to various heavenly figures who are described as participating in some way in God's rule of the world and his redemption of the elect. In particular, there are heavenly figures described as occupying a position second only to God and acting on God's behalf in some major capacity. It is these figures which are most relevant for the historical problem of the origin of the cultic veneration of Jesus."[31]

Hurtado argued that many Jews speculated about heavenly beings who were considered to be God's pre-eminent servants and who had a special status in the heavenly hierarchy. He classified three general types of beings who attained this role. There were personified divine attributes such as Wisdom or Logos, exalted patriarchs like Enoch and Moses, and principal angels like Michael. The divine agency category then became crucial for the interpretation of early Christology.

---

[29] Rowland, *Open Heaven*, 103.

[30] Rowland, *Open Heaven*, 112.

[31] Hurtado, *One God*, 17.

"At the earliest stages, Christian experience of and reflection upon the risen Jesus were probably influenced by and drew upon the divine agency category. Jesus was experienced and understood as exalted to the position of God's chief agent. The divine agency tradition was important in providing the resources for accommodating a heavenly figure second only to God in authority and glory."[32]

The content of early Christology was, however, no longer consistent with Jewish conceptions. In what Hurtado calls "the Christian mutation", Jewish monotheistic devotion was altered. The risen Christ came to share in the devotional and cultic attention normally reserved for God: "the early Christian mutation in Jewish monotheism was a religious devotion with a certain binitarian shape."[33]

Hurtado exploited the new areas of Jewish studies, but he did not accept the suggestion of an angel-christology as the only source explaining early Christology. His conclusions continued on the line of Bauckham underlining the devotional character of Christological statements. In the early dating of the devotional exaltation Christology Hurtado followed Hengel, and once again challenged the widely-accepted "Hellenistic" theory about the formation of the so called high Christology.[34]

A few years later *P.G. Davis*, accepting the basic idea of Hurtado's thesis, attempted to improve the understanding of the dynamics of both Jewish theology and early Christology. Davis stated that the mere concentration on the status of divine agents does not sufficiently explain the origin of high Christology. Other factors, and especially that of function should be considered, as well.[35]

In what Davis calls a "triple pattern of mediation" he defined a new pattern for the analysis of the modes of mediation. Precisely when was a particular divine agent acting as a significant mediator? – asked Davis. A neutral distinction between the past, the present, and the future would serve best when searching for an answer to that question.[36] According to Davis' analysis, in Jewish theology the legacy pattern, mediation from the past which shapes the present and future, can be seen in the cases of Abraham, Moses and David. The intervention pattern, according to which active mediation might be expected in the present, is characteristic primarily of angels. The consum-

---

[32] Hurtado, *One God*, 123f.

[33] Hurtado, *One God*, 124.

[34] In the Son of God Hengel had stated that the development in early Christology "progressed *in a very short time*." (italics his). Hengel, *Son of God*, 75. Hengel's work also openly challenges the history of religions school, see pp. 16ff. In this respect Hurtado follows Hengel completely.

[35] Davis, *JTS 45* (1994) 481.

[36] Davis, *JTS 45* (1994) 483.

mation pattern, in which a decisive act of mediation in the future is awaited, describes the expectations associated with various messianic figures.[37]

These three patterns are combined only rarely in Jewish theology. In the Book of Watchers Michael seems to have such a function, in the Dead Sea Scrolls the Spirit of Light has it, and finally Enoch has such a function in the literature associated with him. According to Davis, this triple pattern of mediation is, strikingly, "virtually a constant in the New Testament". It is the pattern with which the function of the "divine agent" was explained.[38] This contribution of Davis has no doubt been necessary. In the interpretation of early Christology excessively narrow approaches should be avoided.

e. The theory of messianic enthronement

The third of the main theories of interpretation emphasizes the messianic feature found in the merkabah tradition. This feature is considered the primary link that unites Jewish mysticism to the Christology of earliest Christianity. At least from the side of Christology such an approach is easily justified, Christ being often described as the Jewish Messiah enthroned in the resurrection.

This theory was explicated at the beginning of the 1990s, especially in Tübingen, where the study of the relationship between merkabah mysticism and New Testament Christology became a major theme. *M. Hengel* developed the ideas that he had introduced earlier in his monograph "Son of God". Now he expanded the investigation on the relation of throne mysticism and early Christian statements of the exaltation of Christ.[39] The title of his article reveals the main intention of his work, " 'Sit at My Right Hand!' The Enthronement of Christ at the Right Hand of God and Psalm 110:1".[40]

Hengel's articles were further accompanied by a couple of books on related themes. The kingship of God and throne-mysticism were leading themes in the collection *Königsherrschaft Gottes und himmlischer Kult im Judentum, Urchristentum und in der hellenistischen Welt*, where e.g. *A.M.* Schwemer wrote about the theme of the kingship of God in the context of the Songs of the Sabbath Sacrifice of Qumran, and *H. Löhr* compared these Sabbath Songs

---

[37] Davis, *JTS* 45 (1994) 502.

[38] Davis, *JTS* 45 (1994) 503.

[39] Hengel first published an article entitled "Psalm 110 und die Erhöhung des Auferstandenen zur Rechten Gottes" in the Festschrift for F. Hahn (1991). This paper was further the basis for his Strasburg colloquium lecture in 1990, which he expanded considerably before the re-publication of the article, see the collection, M. Philonenko (ed.), *Le Trône de Dieu*, 108-194. This version was later published in English (see below). For Tübingen scholarship cf. also Stuhlmacher, *Biblische Theologie*, 165ff., 183ff.

[40] In Hengel, *Studies*, 119-225.

with the Letter to the Hebrews.[41] In a Strasburg collection *E. Trocmé* wrote about the Temple polemic of the Hellenists, and *C. Grappe* about the logion of the "twelve thrones" and its relation to intertestamentical literature.[42]

As we return to Hengel's article, the basic idea in his analysis is the central position of Psalm 110 in early Christology – as the title suggests. He gives a detailed analysis of throne descriptions both in the Old Testament and in Second Temple Jewish literature. Hengel's focus was on the enthronement theme itself. He explored e.g. the Moses figure in the Exagoge of Ezekiel, the Metatron figure in 3 Enoch, the enthronement of David in Tannaitic discussion, and the Qumranic enthronement text 4Q491.

The special contribution of Hengel to the investigation of the relationship between Jewish writings and the New Testament is in the explication of clear differences in the descriptions. Hengel does not accept the theory of an angel-christology, as we saw in the "Son of God" monograph. According to Hengel, the status of the exalted Christ excludes the possibility of such interpretation. In the preaching of the first apostles Jesus was revered as the "one who was exalted to the Merkaba-throne and who shares the throne at the right hand of God – whereby all of the speculation about angels was ignored and remained in the early period excluded."[43]

In Jewish writings there certainly appeared several divine agents who were given a special status in heaven. They acted in the heavenly sphere, however. In the final comparison they could never serve as a complete parallel to Christological statements. The disciples of Jesus, for their part, claimed that "a historical person, who was put to death in a disgraceful fashion in Jerusalem as a leader of the people, was enthroned as the companion of God on the throne in accordance with Ps. 110:1. Here lies the greatest mystery of the origin of the earliest christology."[44]

Therefore the relationship between Jewish merkabah mysticism and early Christology is ambivalent. The writings in question provided for a proper scene according to which the first Christians were able to explicate their belief in the Resurrected One – the one whose exaltation they announced in their commission – but the description of the exalted Christ was unique at the time.

"His resurrection was – as anticipation – the beginning of the general resurrection and the period until his coming to judgement was a period of grace to permit the repentance of the people of God. The 'exaltation to God' could not be better circumscribed than in dependency upon Ps. 110:1 with the formula of 'sitting at the right hand of God', that is, in the language

---

[41] See Schwemer, *Königsherrschaft*, 45-118; Löhr, *Königsherrschaft*, 185-206.
[42] See Trocmé, *Le Trône*, 195-203; Grappe, *Le Trône*, 203-212.
[43] Hengel, *Studies*, 201.
[44] Hengel, *Studies*, 203.

of the time: sharing the 'throne of glory', which is above the divine throne-chariot, with God himself. With that there was connected an eschatological authorization. In terms of content the kingdom of God and the kingdom of the Messiah became practically identical."[45]

Thereafter several scholars have exploited the exalted figures or mediatorial figures of Jewish apocalyptic in their interpretation of early Christology. Different scholars have applied this category to different aspects of Christology and in this respect a rather vast area of study has been covered. *A. Chester*, for example, applied the concept of Jewish mediatorial figures in his messianic interpretation: "for Paul, Jesus is clearly a figure of the heavenly world, and thus fits a messianic category already developed within contemporary Judaism, where the Messiah is a human or angelic figure belonging... in the heavenly world."[46] He concentrated on the messianic aspect, even though he also saw close links with angelological, wisdom and exalted human traditions.

f. Some later developments of the main theories

Later in the 1990s several scholars focused on Jewish mysticism in their Christological research. They mostly attempted to develop one or more of the three main theories presented above. The angelic interpretation has become popular, and the explanations of Hurtado and his theory of divine agency have also been frequently commented upon, even though not many scholars have concentrated exclusively on this theory. We shall begin with the new developments and applications of the theory of messianic enthronement.

C. C. Newman investigated the aspect of "glory" in his monograph *Paul's Glory-Christology* (1992). His subject led him to analyse the occurrence of glory in the context of throne visions. In his conclusions Newman stated that Paul inherited "a symbolic universe with signs already 'full' of signification." In the throne visions of early Jewish apocalypses, "Glory formed part of the characteristic field of signifiers used to describe the heavens."[47] In accordance with his semiotic approach, Newman then interpreted the emergence of Paul's teaching. "The net effect of becoming a Christian rearranged Paul's symbolic world; Paul's world was suffused and transformed by an apocalyptic Christology... Paul also identifies Jesus as the one who mediated the eschatological Glory of God."[48]

According to Newman, Paul further interpreted the Christophany in the light of the tradition-history of Glory. Therefore Paul interpreted the Christophany, for example, "as the Davidic Messiah's exaltation to Glory", and "as an

---

[45] Hengel, *Studies*, 216f.
[46] Chester, *Paulus*, 77.
[47] Newman, *Glory-Christology*, 241-242.
[48] Newman, *Glory-Christology*, 245.

apocalyptic throne vision in which he saw the principal agent of God."[49] *D.B. Capes* also applied some of this methodology in his study *Old Testament Yahweh Texts in Paul's Christology* (1992). His analysis focused on the concept *Kyrios*, and he paid attention to the fact that this title also appears in the context of New Testament throne descriptions.[50] *D.L. Bock*, in turn, investigated the theme of exaltation in his monograph *Blasphemy and Exaltation in Judaism and the Final Examination of Jesus* (1998). In his interpretation Jesus' alleged blasphemy at his trial operated on two levels. Though there were several exalted and enthroned figures in Jewish tradition, a "teacher from Galilee was not among the luminaries for whom such a role might be considered." Secondly, Jesus also attacked the leadership, "by implicitly claiming to be their future judge."[51]

Furthermore, the angelic interpretation has inspired several scholars since Segal and Rowland. *J. Fossum* touched on this subject in his study *The Name of God and the Angel of the Lord* (1985), where he investigated Samaritan and Jewish concepts of intermediation and the origin of Gnosticism, as the sub-title of his work indicates. Fossum attempted to prove that in both Samaritan and Jewish writings, and in agreement with Platonic philosophy, there occurred an idea of a second power in heaven, that was identified as the Angel of the Lord. This angel shared God's name and was considered divine. This was further thought to be the pattern according to which both apocalyptic writers and the first Christians formed their concepts of exalted and enthroned divine beings in heaven.[52] Fossum is thus convinced that even pre-Christian Jewish apocalyptic spoke of a divine angelic intermediary.

C. H. T. Fletcher-Louis followed Fossum, making only some slight adjustments to the pattern in his *Luke-Acts: Angels, Christology and Soteriology* (1997). According to Fletcher-Louis, there is no direct angel-Christology in early Christian thought, but one can detect angelomorphic identity in Christological statements. He seeks a "more versatile application" of the angelic interpretation in the study of early Christology.[53] A similar approach can be found in *C. A. Gieschen's* extensive monograph *Angelomorphic Christology* (1998). As the title reveals, his emphasis is on the alleged angelomorphic aspect of early Christology.[54]

---

[49] Newman, *Glory-Christology*, 245-246.

[50] See e.g. Capes, *Yahweh Texts*, 175ff.; following Segal in particular.

[51] Bock, *Blasphemy*, 236.

[52] Fossum, *Name*, 333; cf. also 292f.

[53] Fletcher-Louis, *Angels*, 251f.

[54] See e.g. Gieschen, *Christology*, 3-6.

L. T. Stuckenbruck gives an exhaustive treatment of angel veneration in his investigation *Angel Veneration and Christology* (1995), but unlike the aforementioned scholars he is not convinced that angelic beings in Jewish writings are actually considered divine.[55] This view is shared by *P. R. Carrell*, who investigated angelology and Christology in the Apocalypse of John in his study *Jesus and the Angels* (1997).[56]

As regards the treatment of the enthronement theme, angelic interpretation thus appears to be one of the most popular theories. Therefore, it must be taken into consideration since different patterns focusing on angelic heavenly figures are applied also to the aspect of enthronement. Angelic interpretation is also related to the speculation over ascent structure, and therefore there are certain features in that study that are also vital for the topic of the present study.

1.2. Setting the task

In sum, we may conclude that the study of Jewish apocalyptic has provided much information on the origins and the nature of Jewish mysticism. The throne mysticism that we meet in Second Temple Jewish writings is a result of a long process of development. Merkabah mysticism is not merely an obscure ideology of sectarian thinkers, but it is often of a cultic nature and belongs to the core of Judaism. Therefore we need to be careful when locating different writings and different ideas in the history of Jewish religion.

Merkabah mysticism is above all throne mysticism, describing a heavenly palace and God sitting on his heavenly throne. This palace is identified as the Temple of God. Most heavenly journeys of the seers end up in this Temple and the journey is highlighted in a meeting with God. Such an ascent structure is typical of several different writings.

The ascent structure is further associated with the enthronement theme. Several apocalyptic writings speak of exalted patriarchs or other heavenly figures enthroned in heaven. According to the angelic interpretation, most exalted figures should be identified as angels or angelic beings, because these have a privileged exalted status in most apocalyptic writings.

But how is one to study early Christology? Should we attempt to form a category of angelic beings or of divine agents and exploit it then in a pattern according to which the emergence of exaltation Christology might be explained? Should we content ourselves with the investigation of the aspect of status, or should we attempt to take the aspect of function into account, as well? There are several question as regards the factual interpretation of the origins of Christology. The history of interpretation surveyed above reveals

---

[55] Stuckenbruck, *Angel Veneration*, 200ff.
[56] See e.g. Carrell, *Jesus*, 224ff.

that it is not an easy matter to define the amount and the manner in which merkabah mysticism influenced the formation of resurrection Christology. It is rather apparent that, in early Christology, the resurrection of Jesus was interpreted as a heavenly enthronement. But the question remains: what is the model or the pattern according to which the Christian formulation has been made – or is there any close relationship at all?

At least two reservations need to be made. Firstly, different scholars have exploited so different heavenly figures in their patterns and in their interpretation that it is not possible to accept an idea of merely one category of divine agents that would cover all figures. Our analysis must concentrate on each different figure separately, and comparisons with Christology must take distinct characters into account – not just a general category.

Secondly, the concentration on distinct figures must be applied to the analysis of their status and function, as well. A "category" as such cannot have a status. Different figures have different positions and there are several eschatological functions in the heavenly hierarchy, or in God's plan about which the writers speak. Therefore, for example in the estimation of the enthronement theme, these differences must be taken into account.

The raising of certain fundamental questions does not mean a denial of the basic relationship between Jewish mysticism and early Christology. On the contrary, the focusing on exalted figures and the ascent structure in Jewish literature, and their comparison with early Christology can be regarded as a complete research programme inside a new paradigm of Christological study. Some have dubbed it the "new history of religions school" and this is no doubt one proper way to define it.

In the sense of scientific research, however, such a new "school" is rather a paradigm, i.e. an approach where new premises have been adopted. Our overview above has shown that several scholars have accepted this kind of research programme. Therefore we can also prove that evident growth of knowledge has taken place in the investigation of this field. Scholars have been able to discern several aspects of exaltation Christology on the basis of the ascent structure, concerning e.g. the enthronement, glory, kingship and heavenly judgment. On the other hand, we may also point out certain less investigated areas and themes, such as the resurrection, the soteriological function of the Davidide, and the distinct nature of the enthronement.

What is lacking, somewhat surprisingly, is a monograph on the enthronement theme itself. This is unexpected since merkabah mysticism in itself focuses on throne visions and the enthronement theme is closely associated with it. These themes have further primary significance both in Jewish mysticism and in early Christology. *Therefore it will be the main purpose of this work to investigate the relationship between Jewish merkabah mysticism and New Testament exaltation Christology by focusing on the central metaphor of the throne.* In this study our interest lies in the occupants of the throne, in enthronements, and in the function of the throne in different contexts.

When the task is carried out, a discussion with the three major theories of interpreting the relation between Jewish mysticism and early Christology must be continued in addition. Therefore they will be commented on throughout the work.

1.3. Problems of methodology: on discourse and meaning

Investigations on the nature of early Christology are deeply engaged in tradition-critical study. One of the basic methodological problems in this area is the fact that traditions may seldom be detected with detailed literal accuracy. Another weakness of historical investigation in biblical studies has further been its insufficient ability to treat the content of religious beliefs. Even though all historical study is tied up with questions of understanding the content, there have not been many methodological tools available.

Problems have been even more difficult as regards the investigation of the theological ideas contained in the different writings. Usually scholars have automatically applied the so called systematic analysis used in the dogmatic study of doctrine, concentrating on the appearance of key expressions and the organization of religious ideas. This rather unreflective procedure may have been proper in some cases, but in respect of the exegetical study of old texts it cannot be considered a very detailed and analytical methodological tool. Historical study obviously needs additional methodological devices. In such a situation modern linguistic theories may help us further.

a. The contribution of semiotics and semantics

The study of Christology needs methodological devices that are able to take into account the ideological world of religious communities. In the present study of biblical texts and ancient writings, more and more weight is given to modern literary theory. Different aspects of this wide field have been exploited in exegetical works.[57]

In New Testament studies one can detect terminology such as discourse,

---

[57] Literary theory in general, and narrative analysis in particular have for a long time been exploited, especially in the study of the Gospels and separate Gospel stories. Pauline theology has also been investigated from this point of view. See e.g. Hays, *The Faith of Jesus Christ* (investigating the narrative substructure of Galatians), and Witherington, *Paul's Narrative Thought World* (searching for the overall pattern of Paul's thought).

narration, deep structure, signs, and symbolic universe. Terms such as these apparently derive from structuralism, narratology, and even rhetorical criticism.

All of those approaches may naturally also be exploited in biblical criticism, where we constantly study different kinds of fantastic stories concerning heavenly events. We are dealing with peculiar symbols that seem to have been well known in the communities in the contexts in which the writers of apocalyptic texts worked. Texts depend on special discourses where, for instance, heavenly court procedures are being described. The object of study in itself demands consultation with literary theory.

In the area of christological study the exploitation of literary methods has not always been very reflective, however. Scholars seldom define the methods they use, or assess the appropriateness of the exploitation of literary methods in exegetical investigation.[58] Therefore, a somewhat more detailed discussion of the methodological standpoint is needed here. First of all, it is necessary to discuss some linguistic themes that concern the nature of language systems. In addition, some reflections on the problem of semantics are appropriate.[59]

From the linguistic point of view, the field of semiotics is indebted to the Swiss linguist Ferdinand de Saussure, whose definition of signs laid the foundation of the whole modern theory of signs. In Saussurean semiotics a sign comprises both the *signifier*, i.e. the acoustic or graphic form of the sign, and the *signified*, i.e. the concept or the message. This distinction was crucial as regards his understanding of the nature of language.[60]

With the aid of this distinction de Saussure attempted to define the object of linguistic study so that investigation would be scientific and objective. The definition was supported by another distinction made between *langue* and *parole*. For de Saussure, *langue* was the abstract language system, 'language'. *Parole*, in turn, was 'speech', i.e. the individual utterances made by speakers

---

[58] Methodological reflection in exegetical writings is often rather short. For instance, in the work of Newman, *Glory-Christology*, 8f., esp. footnote 14, which relies heavily on new methods, one finds merely one footnote on the methods themselves. Newman's work in itself, however, is a fine example of investigation where different new methods, ranging from semiotics to structuralism, have been exploited.

[59] There have been some attempts to apply, for instance, structuralism to exegetical study in general, but the applications have not always been very consistent. For example, Patte, in his 'What is Structural Exegesis?', freely combined Saussurean semiotics with selected structuralist theories and post-structuralist premises, and thereafter joined them with Bultmannian form criticism and the myth-theory of the history-of-religions-school. See e.g. Patte, *What is Structural Exegesis*, 53f. Later, however, Patte presented a more developed view following Greimas, in his *Structural Exegesis for New Testament Critics*; see e.g. pp 3ff.

[60] See de Saussure, *Course*, 65ff.

of the language in everyday life. Only *langue* was formal and could be studied as an objective system of signs.[61] In such a context de Saussure also made his famous suggestion with regard to a science "which studies the role of signs as part of social life", i.e. semiology.[62]

According to de Saussure, therefore, the idea of a language system is the key to linguistic study. Signs live inside a language system. They are conventional ("arbitrary" or unmotivated) inside a system, and therefore the signs themselves must be studied in the context of the respective language system.[63] These are the basic conceptions on which different semiotic theories have later been constructed.

Such a theory of signs has certain peculiar features. On the one hand, de Saussure's theory appears to be a communication theory. He speaks of the role of signs as part of social life. A sign is always a sign for someone. Therefore, words can at the same time be vehicles of communication. On the other hand, there is a strong psychological aspect in his theory. Signs live their own life in the minds of human beings. The system of signs appears to be an autonomous synchronic system that is not dependent on the speakers.[64]

As a system of signs, language is thus, according to de Saussure, an independent object of investigation. This was essentially what he had been searching for. He attempted to define language in such a way that it could be investigated in a scientific sense. For de Saussure, language is not dependent on individual utterances. In this respect his theory actually divorces linguistics from the study of social interaction.[65] This kind of tension in de Saussure's theory has left several questions open, and later investigation has attempted to answer them. With his theory de Saussure has no doubt made a permanent contribution to the theory of signs.

---

[61] For the concepts, see de Saussure, *Course*, 19.

[62] So de Saussure, *Course*, 15.

[63] See de Saussure, *Course*; 71ff. de Saussure's idea of the arbitrariness of the sign has encountered much negative criticism. It is best to speak of conventions instead. Jakobson, for instance, has noted that the relation between the signifier and the signified is in reality a habitual, learned contiguity, which is obligatory for all members of a given language community. Jakobson, *Verbal Art*, 28.

[64] According to Harris, de Saussure accepted a so called translation theory or a speech-circuit model from J. Locke. Communication is a process of transferring thoughts from one human mind to another. What is somewhat surprising, however, is that de Saussure applied such a theory concerning actually discourse (*parole*) merely to the study of the system of language (*langue*). Harris, *Reading Saussure*, 205.

[65] See Harris, *Foundations*, 200. "For all that was necessary for the analysis of the underlying linguistic system was a point by point comparison of linguistic expressions, considered independently of the circumstances of utterance and the disparities between different speakers."

As regards the hermeneutical aspect, i.e. that of meaning, however, his theory has needed some precision. For de Saussure, language as such was a sufficient system of signs expressing ideas. His critics have paid attention to the fact that *langue* as such is merely a system where words are defined in relation to other words. Therefore, *langue* is something like a lexical system of words, for instance the one we find in an English-English lexicon. Speech as well as literature, however, is something else. There we find words that are used for a definite purpose.

As regards meaning, the aspect of human speech becomes necessary. This was noted especially by E. Benveniste who wished to balance Saussurean tradition in this respect.

"When we say that a certain element of a language, long or short, has a meaning, we mean by this a certain property which this element possesses qua signifier: that of forming a unit which is distinctive, contrastive, delimited by other units, and identifiable for native speakers for whom this language is language. This 'meaning' is implicit, inherent in the linguistic system and its parts. But at the same time, all human speech has reference to the world of objects, both as a whole, in its complete utterances in the form of sentences, which refer to concrete and specific situations, and in the form of inferior units that relate to general and particular 'objects' recognized from experience or created by linguistic convention. Each utterance, and each term of the utterance, thus has a referend, a knowledge of which is implied by the native use of the language."[66]

Literature, or speech, is not merely a collection of words. The problem concerning *parole* needs to be approached from a new angle. According to Roman Jakobson, the process of communication must be reconsidered. There is an important phase of encoding that needs to be taken into account. "The addressee perceives that the given utterance (message) is a *combination* of constituent parts (sentences, words, phonemes) *selected* from the repository of all possible constituent parts (the code)."[67] This is where interpretation enters the picture. According to Jakobson, these two operations provide each sign with two sets of interpretants. There are two references, one to the code and the other to the context, which serve to interpret the sign.[68]

Even more emphasis was placed on the aspect of "utterance" in the criticism of Paul Ricoeur, who made a distinction between semiotics and semantics.

---

[66] Benveniste, *Problems*, 108.

[67] Jakobson, commenting on de Saussure in his "Two Aspects of Language", in *Language in Literature*, 99.

[68] Ibid, 99. Jakobson borrowed the concept of interpretant from Peirce. As regards Peirce's semiotics, however, we must be somewhat cautious, because his theory of signs differs from that of de Saussure. Peirce has introduced a triadic theory where sign and object are together constantly related to an interpretant. As de Saussure was not interested in the object (in "things") it is not easy to compare these semiotic theories. For a general introduction to Peirce, see Hawkes, *Structuralism*, 124ff.

According to Ricoeur, de Saussure was able to deal with the language system, but he neglected the aspect of using the language in speech. Following Benveniste, Ricoeur substituted the term "discourse" for that of *parole*.[69] The study of discourse needed a new methodology, because the essential meaning of speech or writing came from the actual use of words. Therefore, when the meaning of "sentences" was studied, a theory of semantics was needed.[70]

In the system of language (*langue*), remarks Ricoeur, there is no problem of reference. Signs only refer to other signs within the system. With the sentence, however, "language is directed beyond itself".[71] Language is not a world of its own. There is always a relation between language and the ontological condition of being in the world. Thus Ricoeur brings experience to language. Language is a postulate that has no immanent justification, but it is one "according to which we presuppose the existence of singular things which we identify".[72]

The meaning of words and concepts of the symbolic world, therefore, are not merely dependent on the language system (the lexical system) to which they belong. Every term may be exploited in different discourses and their meaning is defined by the discourse in which it is used. We must note here, however, that the technical term 'discourse' has several different meanings in different theories. Ricoeur did not yet speak of discourse in the later rather sociological sense that the term is given, for instance, in the context of discourse analysis. We shall return to the problem of defining the term below. At this point suffice it to note that Ricoeur introduced the idea of discourse in the sense of "parole" as regards semantics.

In the study of New Testament semantics the significance of the context has been noted ever since the publication of the books of James Barr. In this respect all aspects of the present approach are not new as such. Barr's criticism was directed especially against the etymological study of meaning that was common in biblical studies.[73] According to modern semantic theory, the precise meaning of a word is defined by its context, i.e. by its use in a sentence.[74]

The first suggestions of the so called semantic shift do not yet rely on a very developed conception of discourse, however. A discourse is not merely a "style" in the context in which a word is being used, such as "cultic style" or

---

[69] On his relation to Benveniste, see Ricoeur, *The Rule of Metaphor*, 67.

[70] See Ricoeur, *Interpretation Theory*, 6f.

[71] Ricoeur, *Interpretation Theory*, 20.

[72] Ricoeur, *Interpretation Theory*, 21.

[73] See Barr, *Semantics*, 256, 263f.

[74] At least in British biblical criticism this kind of approach has become popular; see the evaluation of Barr's theory and its influence in Thiselton, *Interpretation*, 75ff.

"legal style".[75] The term itself refers to a speech event, and therefore Ricoeur understood it as an individual discourse, a speech of one speaker.[76] As such, however, it is at the same time a cultural discourse. The speaker is linked to his tradition and to his environment, and he uses terminology typical of his community when addressing respective themes.

In this respect, in a speech event, a dialogue takes place between the speaker and his tradition. This is something else than merely the exploitation of the language system. In a speech event the speaker himself/herself engages in a cultural discourse and makes his/her contribution to it.

The term 'discourse' has been used in so many contexts that we must actually be rather cautious in its presentation and definition. For Ricoeur it was the way in which language is directed beyond itself, and referring to an object. In the context of narratology, however, discourse is identified as the narration itself, as we shall see later. Following Chatman, narrative discourse may therefore be defined as the "expression, the means by which the content is communicated."[77] We have not yet reached that point, however, and therefore it is necessary to define more closely what the term means in the present study.

In this respect one more aspect is needed for the help of the definition. In a more limited sense discourse may be seen as a means for constructing the topic itself. This will become apparent in what follows.

From the point of view of communication a discourse has to do with social interaction. It is small wonder, therefore, that one of the most quoted definition of discourse comes from the field of sociology.

"A discourse is a group of statements which provide a language for talking about – i.e. a way of representing – a particular kind of knowledge about a topic. When statements about a topic are made within a particular discourse, the discourse makes it possible to construct the topic in a certain way."[78]

Such ideas confirm the assumption that the concept of discourse may be fruitfully exploited in semantics, as Ricoeur suggested. This does not merely mean that words would have different meanings in respect of different speakers. It is also apparent that words have different meanings in different discourses – if we accept the aforementioned sociological approach. According

---

[75] Thiselton's article shows that both Barr and his followers, including Thiselton himself, still accepted the Saussurean dichotomy between *langue* and *parole*. The importance of discourse, as, for instance, Ricoeur presented it, had not yet affected their explanations. See Thiselton, *Interpretation*, 88-89.

[76] This aspect is emphasized especially by Ricoeur, *Interpretation Theory*, 9f.

[77] Chatman, *Story and Discourse*, 19.

[78] Hall, *Formations of Modernity*, 291. Foucault spoke of discursive formations: "We shall call discourse a group of statements in so far as they belong to the same discursive formation." Foucault, *The Archaeology of Knowledge*, 117.

to a standard example, for instance, a drinking glass in its everyday use is a household article. When it is placed on a stand in the museum of modern art, it becomes a piece of art, and people can show their intelligence by discussing about its finesses. However, when somebody takes the same glass and throws it at an unpleasant neighbour, it is a dangerous weapon, and we may read terrifying accounts of such events in the newspapers.[79]

The sociological approach was developed especially by M. Foucault, who studied the so called archaeology of the language of institutions and power structures. According to Foucault, a discourse is not a permanent rhetorical entity that would remain in history for a long time. He locates discourse in a smaller sociological context. Discourse is "made up of a limited number of statements for which a group of conditions of existence can be defined." Therefore, discourse "in this sense is not an ideal, timeless form that also possesses a history."[80] Foucault speaks rather of discursive practice. It is a body of anonymous, historical rules that are determined in the time and space that have defined a given period.

Such rather general principles may be helpful when we attempt to understand how different groups constructed their religious and theological beliefs. It is evident that discourses construct their own objects of knowledge – at least to some extent. They have a system of concepts of their own. Therefore they also use their own logic that concerns the relations of the expressions. According to Foucault, therefore, discourse contributes to the production, transformation, and reproduction of the objects of social life.

In such a theory there are, however, several limitations. As Freundlieb has remarked, Foucault's model "allowed only very limited application of the notion of discourse or discourse analysis to literary texts, since these texts do not in themselves constitute a discursive practice; and Foucault's whole archaeology is plagued, in any case, by its inherent problems of linguistic idealism and relativism."[81] In his theory there is further an evident danger of overemphasizing the determination of discourse by discursive structures. Therefore certain attempts have been made to improve the applicability of the concept of discourse to the interpretation of literature.

Following Foucault in many respects, N. Fairclough has attempted to balance the theory of discourse analysis by returning the social theory to the context of structuralism. Fairclough speaks of a dialectical relationship between discourse and social structure and postulates that discourse is shaped and

---

[79] Cf. Foucault, *The Archaeology of Knowledge*, 107.

[80] Foucault, *The Archaeology of Knowledge*, 117.

[81] See the rather severe criticism by Freundlieb, *Poetics Today 16* (1995) 339, cf. pp. 301f., 317ff.

constrained by social structure. Specific discursive events vary in their structural determination according to the particular social domain or institutional framework in which they are generated.[82]

While discursive practice is manifested in linguistic form, Fairclough concentrated on "texts". "Analysis of a particular discourse as a piece of discursive practice focuses upon processes of text production, distribution and consumption."[83] Therefore textual features are emphasized in his theory.

Foucault's and Fairclough's notions have their advantages. In a discourse a term or expression has been set in the context of an interpretation – just as Jakobson and Ricoeur earlier claimed. Thus the study of discourse is also a matter of hermeneutical work. Therefore, we must take into account the possibility of the development of discourses. In the course of tradition changes take place and therefore we may detect differences between different phases and layers of tradition.

"To say that one discursive formation is substituted for another is not to say that a whole world of absolutely new objects, enunciations, concepts, and theoretical choices emerges fully armed and fully organized in a text that will place that world once and for all; it is to say that a general transformation of relations has occurred, but that it does not necessarily alter all the elements; it is to say that statements are governed by new rules of formation, it is not to say that all objects or concepts, all enunciations or all theoretical choices disappear."[84]

This aspect is especially significant in the study of the relation between Jewish apocalyptic mysticism and early Christian Christology. It is plausible that in them similar discourses have features that differ essentially from each other. What is interesting is the transformation of relations that has evidently occurred in the new context of Christian identity.

In the present study a discourse is thus conceived as a group of statements which provide a language for talking about a topic, in this case especially about Christology. While a discourse has a role in constructing its own objects of knowledge, its analysis focuses on processes of text production. A discourse is further historically and sociologically limited, which produces the problem of interdiscursivity.

When expressions of early Christology are understood as expressions of certain discourses, their relation to earlier descriptions of Second Temple

---

[82] Fairclough, *Discourse*, 64. On the question of his relationship to Foucault, see e.g. pp. 37f., 41ff.

[83] Fairclough, *Discourse*, 71.

[84] Foucault, *The Archaeology of Knowledge*, 173. Fairclough makes a distinction between "manifest intertextuality" and "interdiscursivity", where the latter represents the constitution of texts out of elements of orders of discourse. Fairclough, *Discourse*, 85.

Jewish theology become somewhat problematic. A simple typological interpretation, for instance, no longer seems a self-evident alternative. Therefore the aspect of discursive change provides an interesting challenge for the interpretation of the nature of early Christology.[85]

Further, a distinction between a general discourse and a particular discourse is necessary, even though this kind of distinction is rather self-evident. The distinction is important especially for the reason that it shows that in the world of human communication there are several kinds of discourses. A theological discourse, for instance, is quite a general one. Most of the discussions about the throne, both in Jewish theology and early Christology belong in this category, and only a few of them belong in the category of political discourse.

Descriptions of heavenly journeys and heavenly enthronements, that will be the focus of interest of the present study, belong apparently within the sphere of a certain exaltation discourse. Inside such a general discourse, however, the throne itself may have several different meanings in different contexts. This proves that there must be particular discourses in which the exact meaning of the word is defined. The symbol or metaphor of throne may be studied in the context of enthronement discourse, resurrection discourse, cultic discourse, or judicial discourse, because in New Testament Christology we can detect that ? kind of discourse and the same symbol has been exploited in every one of them. Most of these discourses are linked to respective discourses in Second Temple Jewish theology. What is interesting is the relationship between the discourses of Jewish theology and New Testament Christology. A more detailed methodological approach for the study of such relations will be described below.[86]

The interests of the present study lie in semantic questions. The investigation of the meaning of Christology is largely a matter of investigating the meaning of christological expressions. The point of view of different discourses is important in the search for meaning, but also the expressions themselves demand our attention. The terminology exploited in christological description is not very simple. In fact, as we noted above, many relevant symbols in the area of this study are metaphors referring to God and his world. Therefore we must briefly concentrate also on the nature of metaphors.

Once again we need to remark that the concentration on metaphors is pre-

---

[85] Even though one should probably avoid using difficult terms such as "interdiscursivity", the idea of discursive change is important as regards the point of view of development of ideas and changes in theological thinking. Cf. Fairclough, *Discourse*, 68. This kind of methodology is welcome when the one attempts to explain the relation between Jewish theology and early Christian Christology.

[86] See the chapter on intertextualism below.

sented here as a general tool. The exploitation of this category in the study of Jewish theology does not imply that the investigation should be a traditional semantic analysis (concerning occurrences, semantic fields, and styles etc.). Such analyses are useful, but they are usually not made in the context of historical study. Even though a detailed semantic analysis in not meant here, the concept of metaphor itself needs some clarification.

What is a metaphor? A simple definition is that it is "that figure of speech whereby we speak about one thing in terms which are seen to be suggestive of another."[87] It is like a parable in one expression or even one word. A metaphor brings two separate subjects together and explains the latter with the help of the former.

The interesting dynamics of the metaphor concern these two poles, i.e. the subject itself that is referred to, and the image that is used. They are usually called by the terms given by I. A. Richards. The image used in the metaphor is called a *vehicle*. It is a vehicle that carries a meaning in some special manner. The vehicle, however, is not identical with the thing that is referred to, the *tenor*.[88]

There is a dynamic relation between the vehicle and the tenor. This relation is not merely a matter of association, but rather a connection or intersection of several semantic fields. There is some similarity between the vehicle and the tenor, but there are explicit differences, as well. According to Ricoeur (in his response to Wittgenstein), in the deciphering of a metaphor, "What must be construed is the common element B, the *Gestalt* namely the point of view in which A (the tenor) and C (the vehicle) are similar."[89]

Concerning the aforementioned dynamic relation, M. Black proposed an interactive view of metaphor. The metaphor "selects, emphasizes, suppresses, and organizes features of the principal subject [i.e. the tenor] by implying statements about it that normally apply to the subsidiary subject [i.e. the vehicle]."[90] Moreover, according to Black, this involves "shifts in meaning of words belonging to the same family or system as the metaphorical expression."[91]

Therefore, one is inclined to think that the meaning of a metaphorical expression exceeds the limits of the meaning of the exploited image, the vehicle. When a shopkeeper is "a real fox", or a man is "a wolf", we do not

---

[87] Soskice, *Metaphor*, 15.

[88] For different theories about metaphor, and the view of Richards, see Soskice, *Metaphor*, 39.

[89] See Ricoeur, *The Rule of Metaphor*, 213.

[90] Black, *Models*, 44-45.

[91] Black, *Models*, 45.

really ascribe merely the animal qualities to the subject. The shopkeeper has rather very human fox-like qualities that in this case are certainly more vicious and cunning than the real qualities of foxes.

Ricoeur, assessing the iconic theory of metaphor, remarks that the "seeing as", "activated in reading ensures the joining of verbal meaning with imagistic fullness."[92] There is a positive link between vehicle and tenor, but this does not mean that tenor resembles the vehicle in all possible respects. The metaphor has a limited function and it aims at fulfilling that function, namely seeing the tenor as the vehicle from one selected point of view.[93]

The mention of a "selected point of view" refers implicitly to a speaker, and this reveals another feature of metaphors. Metaphors may be seen to be linked to the idea of discourse. Searle has remarked, "Metaphorical meaning is always the speaker's utterance meaning."[94] Metaphors are meaningful only in the context and in the particular function in which they are used.[95]

Black linked this idea to the concept of discourse:

"A successful metaphor is realized in discourse, is embodied in the given 'text,' and need not be treated as a riddle. So the writer or speaker is employing conventional means to produce a nonstandard effect, while using only the standard syntactic and semantic resources of his speech community."[96]

Assumedly our language is filled with dead metaphors. Soskice speaks of a metaphor-as-myth thesis according to which most of the ordinary metaphors originally refer to metaphysical reality, even though this is no longer recognized as the words are used in everyday speech.[97] Lakoff and Johnson follow the intention but give a simpler explanation. Most of "our normal conceptual system is metaphorically structured; that is, most concepts are partially understood in terms of other concepts."[98] In the study of Jewish literature and early Christology, however, we are interested in "live" metaphors that intentionally describe the object (the tenor).

It is easy to see that the language speaking of theocracy, in both the Old and

---

[92] Ricoeur, *The Rule of Metaphor*, 213.

[93] Lakoff and Johnson speak distinctively of structural similarity. "It involves the way we understand how the individual highlighted expreriences fit together in a coherent way." Lakoff and Johnson, *Metaphors*, 150.

[94] Searle, *Metaphor and Thought*, 93.

[95] In his Rule of Metaphor, Ricoeur emphasized the dependence of word-meaning on the meaning of the sentence, *The Rule of Metaphor*, 128-129.

[96] Black, *Metaphor and Thought*, 23.

[97] Soskice, *Metaphor*, 80-81.

[98] Lakoff and Johnson, *Metaphors*, 56. According to Soskice, there is a danger of confusing word derivation with word meaning, however. The metaphor-as-myth thesis should not be dependent on an etymological approach. Soskice, *Metaphor*, 81.

New Testaments, is full of symbols. The theological scene is built up by using different metaphors that enable the writer to express his message perfectly. In theocratic descriptions these metaphors (the vehicles) are usually taken from an earthly court of the king: the kingship of God, God's palace and His throne. Similar metaphors later build up the scene of New Testament Christology: the Lordship of Christ, his heavenly power and his throne.

Several different metaphors or metaphorical expressions often seem to belong together. According to Brettler, for example, the metaphor 'God is king' "has many associated submetaphors which may be invoked without the explicit use of the root מלכ, 'to reign'."[99] This is a useful notion for the present study, too. Especially in New Testament Christology several submetaphors are used while their meaning is dependent on the basic metaphors of 'king' and 'throne'.

As we have been speaking of Old and New Testament symbols, the concept of the 'symbolic universe' (or 'symbolic world') has been used. Finally, this concept, too, needs some clarification. The term 'symbolic universe' was introduced by Berger and Luckmann, and once again in the context of sociological study. In their theory of the sociology of knowledge it represented "bodies of theoretical tradition that integrate different provinces of meaning and encompass the institutional order in a symbolic totality."[100] The symbolic universe was conceived of as "the matrix of *all* socially objectivated and subjectively real meanings."[101]

The term thus fits well in the social and historical definition of discourse that was outlined above. Even though one would not exploit or even accept Berger's and Luckmann's idea of social legitimation as a primary function of the symbolic universe, the concept itself may well be used in the investigation of the belief-systems of religious communities. The symbolic universe comprises for instance, the symbols, images and concepts that are used in the theological discourses of the Old and New Testaments.

In Jewish writings the symbolic universe of Jewish theologians seems to be dependent on various fixed metaphors that appear in different writings from time to time. This fact connects the categories of symbolic universe and metaphors. It is justified to make a hypothesis that Jewish tradition was dependent on a common symbolic universe which also directed the tradition and the belief system of Jewish theology. Therefore God and the heavenly

---

[99] Brettler, *God is King*, 23. This notion changes his methodology. "[I]n investigating the metaphor 'God is king', we must study phrases such as 'God sits on a throne' or 'the members of the court surround God' or 'the members of the heavenly court are called... (Sons of God)'." ibid.

[100] Berger and Luckmann, *Social Construction*, 113.

[101] Berger and Luckmann, *Social Construction*, 114.

world are described by using similar metaphors even though the context changed from century to century, not least at the time of apocalyptic writings. In other words, the writer was engaged in a cultic and apocalyptic discourse when writing about the heavenly world. This resulted in an interesting dynamic relationship between tradition and new contexts. Theological ideas were applied in new situations and employed for new purposes. The symbolic universe behind the discourse, however, carried old tradition in new contexts.

Semiotics and semantics can thus contribute to the study of New Testament Christology in several ways. It is plausible that both the terminology exploited in christological statements and the discourses in the context of which the final meaning of the expressions used is formulated, are related to Jewish tradition prominent at the time of the early Church. The relation between Jewish theology and early Christology may, however, not be studied merely by investigating similarities and resemblances. In spite of the common terminology and symbolic world, the meaning itself must be studied in the immediate context and in respect of the discourse that is actually used in christological descriptions.

b. The contribution of structuralism and narratology

If we aim to widen the scope of investigation from the semantic dynamics of metaphors to the function of metaphors in religious thinking, certain new aspects in methodology need to be brought to the fore. In the field of literary theory such a task has been carried out by structuralistic methods. In New Testament criticism structuralistic terminology such as 'deep structure' has sometimes been exploited rather freely. In this respect also it is proper here to discuss the methodological contribution that can be gained from structuralistic and narratological approaches.

Structuralism, as we know, is not a single theory. Instead, there are several quite different structuralistic theories, and also the problems that are being treated and investigated under these theories vary significantly. The uniting factor among structuralistic theories is that they are usually based on Saussurean linguistics. In such a tradition some theories treat texts as quite formal and autonomous, while others concentrate on the writing process. Furthermore, there are different definitions about the very "structure" of the text.

On the one hand, under the influence of formalism, structuralism has tended to focus on the formal structure of the text at the expense of the content.[102] On the other hand, in structuralism in general, there is a clear interest in the codes that people use to construct meaning. The word 'structure' itself points in the

---

[102] See Eagleton, *Literary Theory*, 106ff.; Hawkes, *Structuralism*, 59ff.

direction of a rather systematic approach. Therefore, it is logical to maintain that, in structuralism, the proper object of linguistic study is "the system which underlies any particular human signifying practice, not the individual utterance."[103]

Firstly, structuralism has given birth to the study of narrative syntax. In his classical study on Russian folk tales, V. Propp investigated the dynamics of the plot of the story. In his analysis the hero, his assistant, and the villain played significant roles. Propp discerned typical characters and typical actions in these stories.[104] In this respect Propp identified the "subject" and the "predicate" of the story in his analysis.

Later T. Todorov introduced the idea of narrative syntax and investigated its components in detail. Todorov analyzed Boccaccio's *Decameron* and reduced the characters to substantives, their qualities to adjectives, and their actions to verbs. Thus every story could be read as an expanded sentence where the units are interconnected in different ways.[105]

Secondly, the idea of a transformational syntax has been described from the point of view of different narrative levels. According to A. J. Greimas, the discerning of characters concerns only the surface narrative level. On this level he substituted for Propp's categories three pairs of binary oppositions, thus presenting six roles (*actants*): subject-object, sender-receiver, helper-opponent.[106] As an analogy to linguistic levels, however, Greimas proposed that the structure of a narrative also comprises different levels.[107]

In this way Greimas attempted to exploit linguistic categories in structuralist narrative analysis. As Rimmon-Kenan wrote:

"The notions of deep and surface structure come from 'transformational generative grammar', which undertakes to enumerate (characterize) the infinite set of sentences of a language by positing a finite number of deep-structure (phrase-structure) rules and a set of transformational rules which convert deep structures to surface structure. Whereas surface structure is the abstract formulation of the organization of the observable sentence, deep structure – with its simpler and more abstract form – lies beneath it and can only be retrieved through a backward retracing of the transformational process."[108]

Such analysis on narrative levels helps us to specify the use of structuralistic terminology in the study of the New Testament. It is rather obvious that the use

---

[103] Selden-Widdowson-Brooker, *Guide*, 67.

[104] Propp, *Morphology*, 20-22, 88ff.

[105] For a short introduction, see Todorov, *Poetics*, 108ff.

[106] See Greimas, *Structural Semantics*, 198ff.; cf. Hawkes, *Structuralism*, 88.

[107] "To the two linguistic levels 1) surface linguistic structures 2) deep linguistic structures, two other narrative levels are added: 3) surface narrative structures 4) deep narrative structures." Greimas, *Modern Language Notes* 86 (1971) 797.

[108] Rimmon-Kenan, *Narrative Fiction*, 9-10.

of the concept of deep structure in Biblical criticism has been rather vague.[109] One should be quite cautious, for instance, not to call every christological theme a "deep structure". Biblical scholars have apparently not paid much attention to the investigation of a "transformational process" between deep structure and surface structure. Moreover, such a procedure would be rather technical. It is not plausible that a detailed study on that level will become common in New Testament investigations.

In narratology, the so called deep structure refers to the story itself, i.e. to the actual chronological order of events that may be detected on the basis of the narration. Thus a deep structure is not an abstract ideological (or theological) theme that should be discerned, for instance, behind the christological description of the New Testament. The term does not refer to themes but to structures of narration.

There are several ways in which structuralism can make a considerable contribution to the study of Christology. When analysing the nature of Christology we need to pay attention to the figures and their roles, both in Jewish messianology and early Christology. Information will also be acquired from different polarizations that are made between selected oppositions.

New Testament Christology most often has a narrative character. As we noted earlier, there are numerous stories about heavenly journeys and transcendental events. It is also possible to search for a kind of a "syntax of Christology". In these stories there are different subjects with different qualities and performing different actions. Both in Jewish merkabah mysticism and in early Christology there are ascent structures that may be compared with each other when their "syntax" is considered. Structuralistic methodology enables us to discern such structures in apocalyptic descriptions.

In the study of Christology, it is further useful to concentrate on the "codes" employed to construct meaning. In this respect the discussion of intentionalism affects somewhat the application of literary theory in biblical studies. It is well known that structuralism has developed into theories that emphasize the autonomy of the text, such as deconstructionism and reader response theories.[110] We should note, however, that even though structuralism has been text-centred, the theory has at the same time been referring to the writing process. Every structure in the text is intentional. When we analyse the structure, we are simultaneously analyzing the strategies of the writer.

Application of the hermeneutical developments of Saussurean linguistics are

---

[109] For instance, Newman in his study on Pauline Glory-Christology has made a detailed study of the relation between surface symbols and deep structure, see Newman, *Glory-Christology*, 184ff., 194, 218ff.

[110] See e.g. the overview by Culler, *Signs*, 22ff.; 47ff.; 119ff.

also appropriate here. Structuralist theories tend to build on a rather strict Saussurean linguistic dualism, where meaning has merely to do with the language system. "Things" actually have no place in this semantic structure.[111] The classical remark of Hirsch should be remembered when the problem of intention is addressed: "The text does not exist even as a sequence of words until it is construed; until then, it is merely a sequence of signs."[112]

There is evidently an intention in every normal written document. Therefore it is no surprise that a scholar who was strongly engaged in formalism and structuralism, Roman Jakobson, is the one who introduced a communication theory. As we saw in the previous chapter, he considered the text a result of a speech event and studied it as an act of communication. All communication consists of a *message* initiated by an *addresser*, whose destination is an *addressee*. In Jakobson's theory there were three further factors in a speech event. There is a *contact* between addresser and addressee, and the message must be formulated in terms of a *code*. A message must also refer to a *context* understood by both addresser and addressee.[113]

As we noted earlier, in Jakobson's theory the message must be encoded using the signs of the language. It means the selection of words and expressions from the repository of the language. In his theory the poetic function of language concerned the process from selection (all possible constituent parts) to combination (in a sentence).[114]

In modern narratology this kind of approach has produced a detailed theory of the narrative-communication situation. According to the theory, there are several distinct factors in a narrative which all play their roles in the communication process. The most general distinction comprises the real author, implied author, narrator, narratee, implied reader and real reader.[115] Both the narrator and the characters have a rhetorical function in the narrative, while its outer level is constructed and designed by the implied author.[116]

In the application of narratology to biblical studies there is one major problem, however. Narratology was developed as a method for analysing fiction. This point of view raises the well-known problem concerning the difference between fact and fiction in literary theory. A scholar analysing narrative strategies or the roles of characters is dealing with the imagination of the writer. He is investigating merely a role of a real author who is free to act in

---

[111] Cf. Selden-Widdowson-Brooker, *Guide*, 68, 74.

[112] Hirsch, *Validity*, 13.

[113] See Jakobson in his "Linguistics and Poetics", in *Language and Literature*, 66ff.

[114] Jakobson, *Language and Literature*, 99.

[115] Chatman, *Story and Discourse*, 151.

[116] Phelan, *Narrative*, 4.

the way he wishes as the implied author of the work. Cohn speaks of the omniscience of the author. The author is free, for instance, to make the narrator restrict the information that is revealed to the reader. In this way the relation of the story to its reader is easily manipulated.[117]

Fiction is thus merely a story that may be regarded as rather autonomous – as the poststructuralist scholars have done. The story itself does not necessarily give actual evidence of the real author or his/her situation, not to mention his/her beliefs. Also, his/her ideology is often impossible to discover, as the author is free to represent different and even conflicting views in a novel.[118]

Religious writings, and the New Testament in particular, are different in many respects. They are not products of free imagination. They cannot be approached as works of an omniscient implied author. Quite the contrary, the New Testament writings are dependent on several factors that are deeply rooted in the factual world. They have a definite message and they are usually directed by religious tradition and fixed beliefs. Furthermore, the writings attempt to influence the reader and they apparently aim at producing a religious/ideological change in the reader. In this respect the whole theory of narratology as such cannot be applied to the study of the New Testament.

Several ideas of narratological theories can, however, be exploited in the study of Christology. The concepts of narrative syntax and transformational syntax seem to be quite applicable. The aspect of communication is especially useful. Therefore, concentration on an implied reader may also be quite illuminating on many occasions.

Therefore, we must restrict the aims of investigation and remain in the common area where the theoretical presuppositions of narratology fit the material at hand. Nevertheless, there is plenty of room for this kind of study. For instance, Christology, as we have noted above, is often described by exploiting heavenly stories that have a clear narrative character. They comprise both characters that act in a certain way, and a meaningful story.[119] The analysis of the code itself thus demands a knowledge of narratological theory.

---

[117] Cohn, *Fiction*, 175.

[118] Cohn further mentions the problem of focalization that creates difficulties in the assessment of ideological views in a novel. Sometimes the narrator maintains his own vantage point on the fictional world and tells what he/she thinks of it. Sometimes, however, the fictional events are filtered through the experience of a character. In this respect, a novel may contain several conflicting views and no final position is adopted between them. Cohn, *Fiction*, 177f.

[119] Narratology apparently applies even to the epistemological level of human perception. The world is often construed as a narration in our minds. We attempt to understand the real world by creating a story. Meaningful events appear to us as relations between characters. In this respect the difference between fact and fiction is no longer a disturbing one.

In this respect structuralism and narratology can provide indispensable tools for christological investigation.

c. The contribution of intertextual criticism

As we are interested in the function of metaphors in religious thinking, this also means that the investigation focuses on the reception and exploitation of traditions based on the same symbolic world and using the same metaphors in new contexts. In literary theory this kind of approach is usually called 'intertextualism'.

Intertextuality concerns either the relation of two or more writings that have an evident connection, or more widely the relationship between ideas in a certain period. According to the adherents of this approach, no writing can be isolated. All texts belong to a flow of culture and a flow of writings. Every writing is constructed on earlier ideas, terms, and idioms. In the analysis, therefore, we need to focus on the intertextual process where earlier elements and texts have been exploited and merged in new descriptions. The new text may assimilate, echo, re-assess, or even contradict earlier material. The originality of an individual writing can be found in the way it moulds, adapts, and re-interprets earlier texts and gives them a new direction.[120]

In this approach a "text" is not necessarily a written text that can be detected behind the extant writing. It can also be a cultural entity, and in this respect the concepts of 'text' and 'discourse' may be considered complementary. Even though this kind of approach may appear to be somewhat vague, it is nevertheless useful, for instance in the comparison of established beliefs and conceptions.

There have been several ways to introduce this kind of approach in scholarship. We have already earlier seen that scholars interested in the theory of discourse spoke of the discourse change and the relation between different discourses.[121] In addition to this, the so called "Russian (Tartu-Moscow) school" emphasized the immediate context and the relation between actual texts. The French school, however, is known for its "pantextualism". In this theory the "text" is understood as a large cultural system that influences the writer. Further, in American scholarship a reader-based approach has prevailed.

The Russian school focused on different textual surfaces in a writing. In Mikhail Bakhtin's "dialogism" interpretation is interested in the relationship between these textual surfaces. Bakhtin's basic idea was that in a writing one may detect a dialogue between different texts. An analysis must not accept

---

[120] For a general introduction to the subject, see e.g. Culler, *Pursuit of Signs*, 100ff.

[121] See especially Fairclough, *Discourse*, 68.

merely the traditional categories of truth and falsehood, or of good and evil in the interpretation. A writing is rather a combination of a multiplicity of voices from the contemporary world or history.[122] "Each idea belongs to someone; it is situated with respect of a voice that expresses it and to a horizon toward which it is directed. In place of the absolute we find a multiplicity of viewpoints."[123]

The emphasis on actual texts (quoted passages or allusions) was highlighted especially by Kiril Taranovski. Taranovski investigated different *subtexts* that were related to the extant text. For him, intertextuality meant the reciprocal relationship between these texts, as well as the moulding of the subtexts.[124] A similar approach can be found in the works of Gérard Genette, who wished to restrict the use of intertextuality merely to occasions where the existence of another text can be demonstrated. Intertextuality as such, in his theory, is part of a larger theory of transtextuality, where more vague links between the writing and its environment are also taken into account. Thus the significance of the context was emphasized.[125]

The French school, too, learned from Bakhtin. Julia Kristeva, who actually introduced the term "intertextuality", developed the idea of different textual surfaces into the concept of a "mosaic of quotations". Kristeva was no longer interested in the traditional idea of certain sources behind a writing. Instead, in her theory the "text" is understood as a large cultural system that influences every writer. "The term inter-textuality denotes this transposition of one (or several) sign system(s) into another; but since this term has often been understood in the banal sense of 'study of sources,' we prefer the term *transposition* because it specifies that the passage from one signifying system to another demands a new articulation of the thetic – of enunciative and denotative positionality."[126]

A similar polarization between source-intertextualism and pantextualism is proposed by Roland Barthes. He considered the text to be a woven fabric consisting of countless echoes of culture.

"Every text, being itself the intertext of another text, belongs to the intertextual, which must not be confused with a text's origins: to search for the 'sources of' and 'influence upon' a work is to satisfy the myth of filiation."[127]

---

[122] Bakhtin, *Problems of Dostoevsky's Poetics*, 6ff., 185ff., 238f., 251ff.

[123] See the assessment of Bakhtin's work in Todorov, *Literature*, 76.

[124] This can be seen, for instance, in the analytical comments of Taranovski in his *Essays on Mandelstam*, 92, 114.

[125] Genette, *Palimpsestes*, 7ff.

[126] Kristeva, *Revolution*, 59-60.

[127] Barthes, *Textual Strategies*, 77.

In Barthes' poststructural view, the "text" is in fact a product of reading, and it is located between the writing and the reader. It belongs to the process of reading, not to the writing itself.[128] While Bakhtin's influence can still be perceived in Kristeva's conception of transparent layers of textual surfaces, Barthes has departed from this tradition and separated the text from the writing.

Laurent Jenny represents a mediating view between the two aforementioned traditions. Even though he emphasizes that no text is comprehensible without the point of view of intertextuality, intertextuality in itself is not unrelated to source criticism. Sources are the basis on which the work of transformation and assimilation can be done. The intertextual approach is no longer source criticism, however. It is the focal text which keeps control over the meaning that is based on the reworking of the subtexts.[129]

Reader-based idealism has also been strong in the American tradition that has grown out of the works of H. Bloom. In rather psychological and Freudian terms Bloom identified the relation between a poet and his predecessor who serves as a model for him.

"Poetic Influence – when it involves two strong, authentic poets, – always proceeds by a misreading of the prior poet, an act of creative correction that is actually and necessarily a misinterpretation. The history of fruitful poetic influence... is a history of anxiety and self-saving caricature, of distortion, of perverse, wilful revisionism without which modern poetry as such could not exist."[130]

For Bloom the writing of poetry is a matter of individuation. "Initial love for the precursor's poetry is transformed rapidly enough into revisionary strife, without which individuation is not possible."[131] The love and hate situation thus governs the writing process, and new poetry is a result of a struggle against ("paternal") precursors.

It is easy to understand that Bloom's theory has been popular in American poststructuralism, especially in ethnic or feminist interpretations. As a theory of intertextualism in respect of old written documents, however, it does not seem to be very useful. The question concerning the definition of intertextual methodology should therefore be addressed rather on the basis of the aforementioned theories.

What is meant by intertextuality in the present study, is the application and

---

[128] Barthes, *Textual Strategies*, 73ff.

[129] See Jenny, *French literary theory today*, 39-40, 45.

[130] Bloom, *Anxiety*, 30. Cf. the analysis of Selden et al.: "They experience an Oedipal hatred, a desperate desire to deny paternity. The suppression of their aggressive feelings give rise to various defensive strategies." Selden-Widdowson-Brooker, *Guide*, 179.

[131] Bloom, *Map of Misreading*, 10. "The 'tropes' and 'defenses' are interchangeable forms of 'revisionary ratios'. Strong poets cope with the 'anxiety of influence' by adopting separately or successively six psychic defences." Selden-Widdowson-Brooker, *Guide*, 180.

adaptation both of earlier written documents and the "echoes of culture", in this case especially earlier theological discourses. The actual meaning of a text is dependent on the manner in which the writer has used the material that intertextual analysis has revealed. Therefore it is necessary to emphasize that, even though the meaning of symbols etc. is partly dependent on the *present* discourse (and not another previous discourse where the same symbolic world has been exploited), the meaning of a writing is often dependent on the actual use of texts, and subtexts.

In practice, this means, for instance, that in the present study a distinction will be made between messianological discourse in Second Temple Jewish apocalyptic, and exaltation discourse in early Christology. Even though there are several similarities between these two, and the same terms and similar conceptions are used in both of them, the final meaning of Christology in respective passages of the New Testament will be studied in terms of the writing itself and its own intentions. The original feature of early Christology, however, may be detected in the transformation of earlier beliefs and images and their exploitation in the new context.

Furthermore, we need to consider the role of actual, influential sources. Genette and Taranovski wished to restrict the use of the concept of intertextuality. One may naturally reduce intertextualism to the occasions where the existence of another text can be demonstrated, and there would still be much to investigate. We should note, however, that the line between quotation, allusion and more vague transformation is not clear. In addition to this, at least in the New Testament, there are such clear conceptual connections to the Old Testament and Jewish theology that a more general approach is justified. Therefore, both of the extant traditions of intertextuality may be exploited to some extent in New Testament criticism.[132]

As regards the subject of this investigation, i.e. the influence of Jewish merkabah mysticism on early Christology, there are both explicit quotations and more vague allusions that can be studied.[133] In the Jewish apocalyptic discourse, of which early Christology is a part, there are further different modifications of tradition.

---

[132] Cf. Peirce's approach to the intertextuality of biblical texts developed by my friend Antti Laato for the reconstruction of the proclamation of the historical Old Testament prophets. Laato, *History*, 306ff.

[133] Laato emphasizes that "every historical period has its own cultural and other codes which determine the *epistème* or ordering-space within which living, thinking, writing, reading and knowing are possible." Laato, *History*, 307. According to Laato, "intertextual text production should be implemented to describe the changes which the writer of a phenotext made in the intra-, inter- and extratextual levels of the genotext." Laato, *History*, 335.

The relation of different enthronement stories is thus also quite interesting. Moreover, the symbolic world of Jewish apocalyptic itself may be regarded as a "text" (in a pantextualist sense) that is historically and culturally limited. New Testament Christology applies and transforms central images and symbols that were generally known in Jewish culture at that time. The originality of such an intertextual procedure reveals well the intentions of early Christian theologians.

In the study of Christology intertextual criticism may help us define the relation between early Christological statements and contemporary and earlier Jewish descriptions of heavenly figures and heavenly residences. One might ask, though, how this kind of study differs from the customary tradition criticism of the New Testament. In biblical studies the relation of New Testament and earlier Jewish theology, as well as that of the New Testament and the Old Testament, has been a standard subject of study for decades. The answer would probably be that in this area the study of the New Testament has been ahead of its time. Intertextual criticism gives a proper theoretical justification for tradition criticism. Therefore the interest in intertextuality is to be welcomed also in the study of Christology.

d. A linguistic approach and the methodology of Christological study

The linguistic approach descibed above has one further special advantage as regards the study of Christology. Christology has traditionally been studied by concentrating on Christological "titles", such as Lord, Son of Man, and Son of God. A little more than a decade ago one could still remark: "Indeed, it is often assumed that NT christology *is* a matter of the history of titles. Probably no other factor has contributed more to the current aridity of the discipline than this fascination with the palaeontology of christological titles."[134]

This approach has led to complex explanations and has left scholars with more open questions than answers. The contribution of literary theory can help with these problems. When the so called titles are interpreted in their proper contexts, directed by the symbolic world of the writer and constantly linked with different metaphors, we are able to give much more informative explanations for early Christology than the previous theories could.[135]

The study of Christological titles owes probably most to W. Bousset, who in his book *Kyrios Christos* interpreted the development of early Christology by locating different titles in defined contexts. In the old history-of-religions school and especially in the works of Bousset this context was usually

---

[134] Keck, *NTS 32* (1986) 368.

[135] For the methodological problems of Christology on this question, see e.g. Vielhauer, *EvTh 25* (1965) 24ff.; Balz, *Methodische Probleme*, 23ff.; Hurtado, *TS 40* (1979) 306ff.; Osborne, *Semeia 30* (1985) 49ff.; Keck, *NTS 32* (1986) 362ff.

considered Hellenistic.[136] Bousset had accepted the premises of German idealism. Religions were a universal phenomenon, partly or completely based on myths. They were further centred around divine figures who were called by different titles.[137] In the idealistic interpretation of Bousset, therefore, titles represented a universal "idea" of a religious hero who inevitably had to be found in the hierarchy of every religion.[138]

In New Testament Christology Bousset then traced independent titles and attempted to locate them in their proper religious context. He thought that most of the titles had no tradition-historical connection to the Old Testament or Jewish writings. They had been born "in the collective subconscious" of the community. Therefore, for instance, the titles Lord and Son of God necessarily had to derive from divine appellations of Hellenistic cultic heroes. In the Christian community these titles were then applied to Jesus, who only in the Hellenistic communitites was revered as the divine Son of God.[139]

It is rather apparent that Bousset's approach was that of the simple identification of similar or vaguely resembling expressions. Titles were seen as autonomous entities that carry meaning even from one religion to another. Such an approach is far from modern discourse analysis and semantics, where the possible occurrence of similar expressions is but the starting-point in the interpretation process. The expressions themselves must be subjected to the study of respective discourses and the meaning needs to be assessed in respect of the present context.

Bousset's influence has been enormous in biblical studies, however. The old history-of-religions school influenced European scholarship, especially through R. Bultmann's Theology of the New Testament, where the titles have a key role as regards the interpretation of Christology. Later this tradition may be seen in full flower in F. Hahn's *Christologische Hoheitstitel* (1964), probably the most influential work on Christology written after Bousset. Even though Bousset's theory was now developed in certain respects, and, for example, the parties of early Christianity were seen in a somewhat new light in Hahn's work, the basic approach of tracing independent titles did not change.[140]

---

[136] Cf. Hurtado's critique of Bousset's influence on Hurtado, *TS 40* (1979) 306ff.

[137] For a critical analysis, see Colpe, *Die religionsgeschichtliche Schule*, 194ff.

[138] Berger, *Exegese*, 90ff.

[139] See e.g. Bousset, *Kyrios Christos*, 57, 99.

[140] See Hahn, *Hoheitstitel*, 251, 292. Later such an approach is common. Pokorny accepted the basic idea of the theory in his *Christologie*, 12; Dunn still traces "recognized titles" in his *Christology in the Making*, 13,67; and Casey is completely dependent on the old methodology in his *Jewish Prophet*, see e.g. 44, 79.

The problems of this approach, however, are too numerous. In New Testament writings different appellations are naturally attached to Christ. In the Bousset school of scholarship, however, the titles are considered isolated and separated from their consistent tradition-historical background. Also, Hahn is dependent on these flaws implicit in the basic approach, even though he has attempted to present his ideas in a more sophisticated form. This is the reason why his book has encountered quite severe criticism since its publication.[141]

The meaning of a title cannot be separated from the context in which it appears.[142] Titles, which no doubt do occur in christological passages, are integral parts of the whole description. Also, christological formulas have a context that needs to be taken into account.[143] In this respect the christological studies investigating the relation between merkabah mysticism and early Christology referred to in previous chapters, are based on a far more sound methodology than previous general studies on Christology.

There are also other theoretical problems in the title-dominated approach. Firstly, modern scholars are not very conscious of the theoretical connection of that approach with German idealism and the old history-of-religions school. It is hard to believe that all those who investigate christological titles would subscribe to the agenda of the old school today. In Bousset's theory heroic idealism has completely displaced even a general conception of semantic meaning.

Secondly, one of the results of these problems is that the so called titles were too easily exploited in anachronistic or ideologically irrelevant explanations. Bousset's theory was dependent on a strict dichotomy between Jewish Christianity and Hellenistic Christianity, and most titles were interpreted in the context of the latter. Over the past two decades the history-of-religions approach has changed dramatically. Our understanding of the nature of Second Temple Judaism has changed and the Hellenization of the whole area has been acknowledged. Further, in the interpretation, the emphasis of scholarship is now on Second Temple Jewish literature, which is considered

---

[141] Vielhauer, in his lengthy recension, criticized the title-dominated approach, as well as the pattern of history implied in the theory. Vielhauer, *EvTh* 25 (1965) 26; for a similar criticism, see Balz, *Methodische Probleme*, 117-118; Hengel, *Geschichte*, 56; Hurtado, *One God*, 99; Keck, *NTS* 32 (1986) 367ff. Hahn gave his answer some years after Vielhauer's recension and acknowledged the validity of many of the critical claims. He admitted that relevant contexts ("Vorstellungskomplexe") need to be taken into account. Hahn never rejected the actual theory, though. See Hahn, *VuF* 15 (1970) 10-11.

[142] Keck notes that title-dominated study reflects "an inadequate view of language, because it assumes that meaning resides in words like 'Lord'." Keck, *NTS* 32 (1986) 368.

[143] Cf. Hengel: "Nicht die isolierte Betrachtung der einzelnen christologischen Chiffren, sondern ihre Zusammenschau müsste das letzte Ziel einer sinnvollen Darstellung der urchristlichen Christologie sein." Hengel, *Geschichte*, 56.

the proper context for New Testament Christology rather than non-Christian Hellenism.[144]

Thirdly, we must note the problematic conception of semantics in the Boussetian tradition. The old theory is not sensitive at all in respect of the distinction made in modern semantics between lexical meaning and the referential significance of words.[145] The meanings of christological appellations and descriptions are not dependent on the occurrence of similar images in other contexts. The primary meaning of christological expressions depends on the discourse in which they occur.

As regards meaning, christological appellations in their contexts are closely linked to fixed metaphors which add necessary information, giving the final significance (German: "Sinn") to the appellation – or rather to the christological concept to which the appellation refers. These appellations, such as Lord or Son of God, should not be regarded as autonomous "titles", but rather as parts of complex Christological descriptions and expressions. These expressions comprise e.g. royal metaphors, Old Testament allusions and historical references, as we shall see later in the analysis.

In fact, the so called titles as such should not be regarded as methodological keys in christological study at all. Rather, we must concentrate on the narrative world and symbolic universe in the context of which christological descriptions have been constructed. In this respect, in the present study, we shall investigate the exploitation of common metaphors in different descriptions, both Jewish and Christian. The transformation of discourses is an extremely important factor when the relation between Jewish mysticism and early Christology is assessed.

When assessing the contribution of modern literary theory to christological study we have thus reached certain methodological principles for the investigation. First of all, the investigation of the relation between Jewish theology and early Christology is directed by the fruitful tension between a common symbolic universe representing continuity and novel christological discourse representing discontinuity in Second Temple Jewish tradition. There are furthermore certain detailed principles that may be listed here.

1. Christological expressions need to be investigated as parts of relevant discourses.
2. The message of a christological description must be constructed with the aid of central metaphors exploited in the description.

---

[144] For the criticism of patterns of history, see already Balz, *Methodische Probleme*, 175; and Vielhauer, *EvTh 25* (1965) 25.

[145] This has been noted especially by Keck, *NTS 32* (1986) 368f.

3. The narrative character of christological description must be taken into account when the nature of the "story" and its message are investigated.

4. The identity and originality of christological statements will be revealed through the investigation of intertextual transformations and applications that appear in christological descriptions.

II

The Heavenly Throne in the Old Testament, Second Temple Jewish Theology, and the Pseudepigrapha

§ 2 God as King and the Ark of the Covenant as His Throne

In the area of christological study concentrating on exaltation Christology there is always one burning question calling for an answer. What makes enthronement discourse meaningful? Scholars have spent hours and hours studying apocalyptic writings and Jewish throne mysticism, seeking for answers. In the background of the problem there lies a question concerning the symbolic world that has been exploited both in Second Temple Jewish writings and in the New Testament. The first task of the present study, therefore, is to investigate how the idea of heavenly kingship was expressed in the writings of the Old Testament.

Such an enterprise necessarily leads us to the world of "subtexts", as well. In what follows, the Old Testament is surveyed in order to discern either actual passages or a theological "text" that has influenced especially apocalyptic thinkers in the Second Temple period. Intertextuality is a reality already among Jewish writings, not to mention the nature of New Testament christological passages. The discernment of relevant subtexts is an essential task in the search for meaning.

In the Introduction we have already seen that scholars have been quite interested in the background of the mystical tradition. It is apparent, as Hanson pointed out, that there is a "centuries-long development" in Jewish theology during which time certain main images were exploited again and again in new theological contexts. The relation between the Old Testament prophetic writings and Second Temple Jewish mysticism has often been studied in detail. Especially the influence of the Book of Ezekiel has been seen to be significant. As regards the key images of Jewish mysticism we should follow those scholars who wish to go further. The first point of departure is that merkabah mysticism is centred on God's throne. This notion leads us to the Old

Testament, where God is presented as a king who sits enthroned on the throne of Glory.

In the writings of the Old Testament God the King has a palace and there he reigns amidst His divine court. It is this heavenly King who is also worshipped in the Temple liturgy of the chosen people. The idea of the kingship of God is further behind the basic pattern of theocracy seen in the Old Testament.

The kingship of God has naturally been one of the most popular subjects in the field of Old Testament studies.[1] Scholars have fervently discussed the origin of the conception, and about its relation to other Near Eastern religions. The relation between theocracy and human kingship is filled with questions and problems, as well. Such historical questions are beyond the scope of this study. What is relevant, however, is that we remember the enormous significance of this conception to Old Testament religion and, respectively, to Second Temple Jewish theology.

The present study is interested in the narrative tradition that was alive during the Second Temple period. The Old Testament story was really a Jewish legacy that was passed on from one generation to another.[2] Therefore, the basic features concerning the kingship of God form a natural background for Jewish mysticism at that period.

This is further what I would like to call the "remembering of the obvious" in biblical interpretation, which may be – at least among New Testament scholars – one of the most difficult tasks of all. One must not neglect the simplest narrative reality that filled every pious mind during a tumultuous period of apocalyptic interest. Royal depictions and appellations of God are vital in Second Temple Judaism, as well as in the Old Testament. Especially apocalyptic writings from that period are filled with similar metaphors. Here the strength of "the obvious" becomes explicit. The basic features of Jewish theocracy serve as indispensable premises when we are attempting to understand how royal imagery influenced both the descriptions of Jewish mysticism and the formation of early Christian Christology.

2.1. The Lord is King

In the Old Testament the idea of the kingship of God is usually expressed by the formula יהוה מלך ("the Lord is/has become a king"). This formula or

---

[1] For the history of interpretation, see e.g. Hasel, *Old Testament Theology*, 141f.

[2] For instance, the Dead Sea Scrolls have shown that most of the writings of the Tanakh were regarded highly in the second pre-Christian century. There were several commentaries on Scriptures that were regarded as divinely inspired. In this sense we may speak of the Old Testament even when the Second Temple period is referred to.

similar expressions appear in most Old Testament books.³ When we attempt to find a relevant context for throne descriptions in the Old Testament, royal depictions evidently have a key role in the search. Therefore the following survey focuses especially on the metaphor 'king' as well as on certain related metaphors such as the 'throne' itself. These metaphors show that God's kingship in Israel was patterned after human kingship.

A survey of the theme of kingship is invaluable, since it forms the basis on which an analysis of the reception of that theme in Second Temple writings is constructed. Such a survey, however, necessarily remains on a general level and focuses on the conceptions and metaphors extant in the writings available in the intertestamental period.

God is already called king in writings describing the premonarchic period. For instance, according to the Book of Judges, the judges themselves brought Lord's theocratic reign to fulfilment in the politically unorganized Israel (Judg. 8:23; 1 Sam. 8:7).⁴ This is stated, for instance, in Gideon's answer to the Israelites: "I will not rule over you, and my son will not rule over you; the Lord will rule over you" (Judg. 8:23). It is naturally a matter in dispute after which kind of "human kingship" the religious conception was patterned, or was thought to have been patterned, in a situation where Israel did not yet have a king. But should the theocratic conception be premonarchic there evidently were patterns available for it in that religious environment.⁵ What is clear, at least, is that already in the book of Judges human kingship is a vehicle of the crucial metaphor and it was considered suitable for conveying the message concerning the sovereignty of God.⁶

In Exodus 15, in the song of Moses, a similar belief is applied to a Jerusalem-centred situation: "You brought them in and planted them on the mountain of your own possession, the place, O Lord, that you made your abode, the sanctuary, O Lord, that your hands have established. The Lord will

---

³ For the expression, see Seybold, *TDOT 8* (1997) 365ff. Yahweh is qualified with the epithet king 41 times, and occurs 13 times as the subject of מלך. For the problem of translating the expression, see especially pp. 370-371.

⁴ See Szikszai, *IDB 4* (1962) 618.

⁵ As Brettler notes, in a premonarchic situation the Israelite monarchy could not have been the so-called "vehicle" of the metaphor 'king'. Brettler, *God is King*, 14. For recent discussion, see Laato, *Star*, 52, who suggests that the religious outlook of tribal Israel "was modified according to the religious language used in the Canaanite myths".

⁶ "There is no doubt that the phrase 'Yahweh is king' is informed by and linked to political models that were availabe to Israel in the ancient world... Nonetheless, it is important to recognize that Israel's rhetoric is permeated with 'Yahweh as king' and that Israel's preferred mode of theological discourse is political." Brueggeman, *Theology*, 238.

reign forever and ever" (Ex. 15:17-18).[7] The tone of the song is theocratic and no human king is mentioned in the context. This is not to say that such a song could not have been used or even written in a monarchic situation.

In the writings describing the period of the monarchy the metaphor 'king' and also the key formula appear in several different contexts. A semantic analysis reveals that these occurrences paint a colourful picture. God is called 'king', for example in a context where the aspect of God as warrior is emphasized (Psalm 24; Zech. 14). On the other hand, the appellation appears in contexts where God is depicted as a judge (Isa. 41:21; Ps. 5:3). In Micah he is even called a shepherd (Mic. 2:13).

Further, God the king is the creator (Isa. 43:15; Ps. 149:2). In a general sense he is naturally the king of Israel (Isa. 44:6; Zeph. 3:15), the everlasting king (Jer. 10:10) or the king of heaven (Dan. 4:34).[8]

The most majestic descriptions of God as king can be found in the Book of Psalms. For instance, in Psalm 48 Mount Zion is the holy mountain where God dwells. The Temple is a royal palace of God, and Jerusalem is his capital.[9]

"Great is the Lord and greatly to be praised in the city of our God. His holy mountain, beautiful in elevation, is the joy of all the earth, Mount Zion, in the far north, the city of the great King. Within its citadels God has shown himself a sure defence" (Ps. 48:1-3).

Here, actually, the Psalmist exploits a word-play on an ancient mythological tradition. This interpretation is based on a reading that is commonly accepted: "Mount Zion, the Heights of Zaphon, is the city of the Great King!" Mount Zion is first identified as the mythological mountain dwelling of Baal, i.e. Zaphon, which occurs e.g. in the Ugaritic texts. By exploiting such a metaphor the writer simultaneously contrasts Baal with the God of Israel. The Lord on Mount Zion is the only true God and the great King who reigns over the whole earth.[10]

In the so-called kingship-psalms there are several descriptions of the enthronement of God. The famous discussion concerning the liturgical nature of these psalms is of little use here. It may be that there is an association with a theoretical liturgical celebration of Yahweh's kingship in these psalms

---

[7] Actually, the song of Moses has been used as evidence for a rather early dating of the idea of God as king. See e.g. Soggin, *Judges*, 158f.; Brettler, *God is King*, 14. Not all scholars consider it premonarchic, however. For the discussion, see Veijola, *Königtum*, 100-103.

[8] See Brettler, *God is King*, 32.

[9] Cf. e.g. the analysis by Mettinger, *Dethronement*, 25.

[10] See Dahood, *Psalms I*, 289f.; Craigie, *Psalms 1-50*, 353.

(especially Psalms 96-99), as Mowinckel had suggested.[11] From the point of view of the common use of these psalms in the Second Temple period, however, suffice it to say that they are "kingship-of-Yahweh psalms" without a necessary link to enthronement ceremonies as such.[12]

There is a clear liturgical tone in some of the psalms, however.

> "Let us come into his presence with thanksgiving; let us make a joyful noise to him with songs of praise! For the Lord is a great God, and a great King above all gods" (Ps. 95:2-3; cf. Ps. 98:6).

One of the remarkable features of these psalms is no doubt the universal nature of God's reign. In this respect Brueggeman has attempted to revive the liturgical theory and stated that there are several psalms which represent a "Jerusalem liturgy". The purpose of the liturgy, reflected e.g. in Psalm 96, is "to assert and to enact Yahweh's legitimate governance over the nations and the peoples of the world".[13] We need to remember the notion of Kraus, however, than in contrast to the dying and rising gods in the Orient, Israel's God never needed a periodically renewed enthronement in power.[14]

A liturgical element is evident further in the cultic acclamation that appears in several of these "kingship-of-Yahweh psalms". "Say among the nations, 'The Lord is king'!" (Ps. 96:10).[15] The acclamation most probably had a function in worship (cf. 93:1; 97:1; 99:1).[16] Such liturgical features underline the significance of royal metaphors in the description of Jewish faith.

The aspect of the royal reign is also the conviction of other psalmists. God is often depicted as a universal king. "All the ends of the earth shall remember and turn to the Lord; and all the families of the nations shall worship before him. For dominion belongs to the Lord, and he rules over the nations" (Ps. 22:27-28). "God is king over the nations; God sits on his holy throne" (Ps. 47:9; cf. Ps. 96:10). God the King offers protection and He gives salvation.

---

[11] The dating of the enthronement language in Psalms is a subject of a well-known dispute. H. Gunkel and H-J. Kraus date it late, but S. Mowinckel "early in the liturgy and faith of Israel". For the discussion see e.g. Brueggeman, *Theology*, 238, also n. 20. Whatever the final solution for the dating, the Psalms obviously express well the religious ideas of Second Temple Judaism as regards the kingship of God.

[12] See Tate, *Psalms 51-100*, 505. For an overview of the theory of the so-called enthronement festival of Yahweh, see Seybold, *TDOT 8* (1997) 371f.

[13] Brueggeman, *Theology*, 493.

[14] Kraus, *Psalmen I*, LXVII.

[15] "In a quick liturgical utterance, the temple-dynastic establishment in Jerusalem sweeps away all other claims to legitimacy and subsumes all other worldly powers under their theological governance." Brueggeman, *Theology*, 493.

[16] See Kraus, *Psalmen I*, LXVII.

"Yet God my King is from of old, working salvation in the earth" (Ps. 74:12).

There are some further mystical elements in the Psalms that resemble the features of the merkabah mysticism of apocalyptic. In these passages God's throne is not linked with the earthly Temple, but rather with the heavenly realm. We may note, for example, the devout praise of Psalm 93:

"The Lord is king, he is robed in majesty; the Lord is robed, he is girded with strength. He has established the world; it shall never be moved; your throne is established from of old; you are from everlasting" (93:1-2).

The majestic throne of God is everlasting. In a parallel description thunder becomes a metaphor for the heavenly palace. "The Lord is king! Let the earth rejoice; let the many coastlands be glad! Clouds and thick darkness are all around him; righteousness and justice are the foundation of his throne. Fire goes before him, and consumes his adversaries on every side. His lightnings light up the world; the earth sees and trembles" (Ps. 97:1-3).[17]

The theme of the kingship of God also appears frequently in the Book of Isaiah. The idea is clear already in Isaiah's vision, as he sees the Lord "sitting on a throne" in heaven. His eyes have "seen the King, the Lord of hosts" (Isa. 6:1,5). A similar setting "in the Hall of the Heavenly Council" appears further in several Old Testament passages (cf. 1 Kgs 22:17-23; Job 1:6-12; 2:1-6; Zech. 3:1-5).[18] As Wildberger has noted, Isaiah does not describe God himself. Instead, God's throne is referred to and therefore the focus is on God's kingship.[19]

In the eschatological predictions of Isaiah it is God the King who will judge the earth on the Last Day.

"On that day the Lord will punish the host of heaven in heaven, and on earth the kings of the earth... Then the moon will be abashed, and the sun ashamed; for the Lord of hosts will reign (מלך יהוה) on Mount Zion and in Jerusalem, and before his elders he will manifest his glory" (Isa 24:21, 23).

The metaphor of the kingship of the Lord is constantly used when God's universal power is emphasized.[20]

In the comforting message of so-called Second Isaiah the royal reign of God is the basis for the good news from the very beginningt. "Get you up to a high mountain, O Zion, herald of good tidings... say to the cities of Judah, 'Here is

---

[17] According to Seybold, both of these psalms may be interpreted in a similar way. In these psalms, various aspects of Yahweh's rule, i.e. creation, cosmic order, and revelation, are appended to the primary confession. Seybold, *TDOT 8* (1997) 372.

[18] Watts, *Isaiah 1-33*, 72.

[19] Wildberger, *Jesaja I*, 244.

[20] LXX: βασιλεύσει κύριος ἐν Ζιων. Cf. Gray, *Isaiah I-XXVII*, 421.

your God!' See, the Lord God comes with might, and his arm rules for him" (Isa. 40:9-10). The blessing on Israel comes on the basis that the Lord is the only God that exists. "Thus says the Lord, the King of Israel, and his Redeemer, the Lord of hosts: I am the first and I am the last; besides me there is no god" (44:6).[21]

Such a message is evidently the reason why the eschatological hope of this book was centred around the idea of God's kingship and sovereign rule, and the hope of Judah was expressed with theocratic terminology. The final content of the "gospel," the good news, was the restoration of the kingship of the Lord. The hope of Judah was expressed by the proclamation: "Your God reigns" (מלך אלהיך, Isa. 52:7). Israel/Judah had been a kingdom of God in the past, and it would be one again when God would reveal his power and bring salvation to his people.[22] Volz is probably correct when he comments that in this eschatological event the reign of God is renewed in a remarkable way. God enters Zion and he himself will be the king of Israel.[23] Furthermore, this message of good news has probably to do with the "new song" of salvation that is to be sung to the Lord the King. The theme occurs in a somewhat similar context e.g. in Isa. 42:10ff. and Psalm 98:1ff.

These examples show that the kingship of Yahweh was a significant motif in the Old Testament and apparently even in pre-exilic Jewish theology. 'King' was an influential metaphor that expressed the sovereignty of God. The "obvious" thing that we need to remember in the investigation of both Jewish theology and early Christology is the theocratic ideal of Old Testament faith that appears to have been borne by royal metaphors.

The usefulness of the methodological solution of concentrating on metaphors is first of all proven by the fact that central religious beliefs concerning God are expressed by employing metaphors. Royal images seem to form a consistent whole comprising, for instance, a court and a throne. These metaphors may be regarded as symbols which are part of the symbolic universe of the Jewish community. Whenever theologians spoke of God, it was appropriate to speak of him as a heavenly king who sits enthroned in his court.

Such theocratic theological discourse is political by nature, but it is not

---

[21] According to Kraus, the enthronement psalms are dependent on Deutero-Isaiah and thus belong to the same tradition. See, Kraus, *Königsherrschaft*, 107ff., 143. His explanation is dependent on speculation over a possible enthronement feast and its origin. Tate dates the origin of these psalms to the pre-exilic period. Tate, *Psalms 51-100*, 505f. Whatever the case, these psalms must have been significant in the Second Temple cult.

[22] See von Rad, *Theologie II*, 256; Stuhlmacher, *Theologie*, 68.

[23] Volz, *Jesaia II*, 122.

solely theocratic. Already the passages surveyed above indicate that the same symbolic universe with its metaphors was applied to the cult, as well. Royal metaphors appear in a liturgical context. This leads us further and raises the question how the royal imagery is exploited in a cultic context.

2.2. The ark as the throne of God in the Old Testament

As we investigate the crucial metaphor 'throne' we encounter not only passages where God is described as a king, but also passages describing the Temple. In Old Testament descriptions the Temple was in many respects like a palace, and the scene was completed by references to a royal throne. There were also different figures acting as servants, especially the cherubim that constantly served the Lord in the holy place. What is of special interest is that the throne of God was believed to be found on earth – and in a most special and holy place for Israel.

The holiest place in the Old Testament is naturally the Tabernacle/Temple, and in the centre of the Holy of Holies was the ark (Ex. 25:22; Isa. 24:23; Ps. 47:9, etc.).[24]

"The cherubim shall spread out their wings above, overshadowing the mercy seat with their wings... There I will meet with you and from above the mercy seat, from between the two cherubim that are on the ark of the covenant, I will deliver to you all my commands for the Israelites" (Ex. 25:20-22).

This meant simply that theocratic ideology was centred around the Tabernacle. According to the testimony of the Torah, the throne of God the King was located first in the Tabernacle and later in the Temple of Jerusalem.

In 1 Samuel there is a further passage where the idea of Yahweh's kingship is linked to the Sanctuary at Shiloh.[25] According to chapters 4-6, the ark was housed in Shiloh where Samuel served as a priest. Here too we find the conviction that in the Sanctuary God sits on the cherub-throne: "the ark of the covenant of the Lord of hosts, who is enthroned on the cherubim" (1 Sam. 4:4).[26]

The Jerusalem Temple is also referred to in such traditions. In 2 Kings, i.e. in Hezekiah's prayer, the ark is depicted as God's throne, as well. The liturgical nature of the passage is evident, and therefore the verse belongs in the context of Temple theology. "O Lord the God of Israel, who are enthroned above the cherubim, you are God, you alone" (2 Kings 19:15).

---

[24] For this tradition see e.g. Fabry, *TDOT VII* (1995) 253-255; Gese, *Zur biblischen Theologie*, 103-105.

[25] This passage, too, suggests a rather early date. See Fabry, *TDOT VII* (1995) 253.

[26] According to Laato, this may also be one source for anti-monarchism in Israel. See Laato, *Star*, 62.

In several Old Testament passages the throne is usually the traditional cherub-throne. According to the established conception, the two cherubim together formed a throne for the invisible God.[27] In this respect the ark may have been considered the footstool of the enthroned God, as is probably the case in 1 Chron. 28:2 and Ps. 99:5 (cf. Ps. 132:7).[28] On the other hand, however, it may not be proper to set too rigid conditions for the use of metaphors. The ark as such, with its cherubim, may simply have been considered the cherub-throne (cf. Ps. 99:1).[29]

In the Temple the ark/throne was naturally associated with the Temple liturgy. God could be approached and certain members of the community were entitled to come before His throne. In the stories of the wilderness Moses has this privilege. When the day's journey was about to begin he recited a liturgy before the ark. "Arise, O Lord, let your enemies be scattered, and your foes flee before you." And when the ark came to rest: "Return, O Lord of the ten thousand thousands of Israel." (Num. 10:35-36). In this story God is a warrior-king who protects Israel on her journey.

It is further obvious that the ark also enjoyed an exceptional status in the Temple liturgy. In Psalm 24 we have an interesting description of a religious procession where the ark is carried into the Temple. The scene is liturgical. A crowd of pious Jews stand at the gates of the Temple and welcome the Lord as He enters the building. "Lift up your heads, O gates! and be lifted up, O ancient doors! that the King of glory may come in" (Ps. 24:7). God was seated on the ark, and this liturgical hymn, linked perhaps with a ceremony, was a reminder of the entering of the ark into the Temple of Jerusalem.[30]

The liturgy is continued as the procession approaches the gates. The people sing an antiphon to the Lord.

"Who is the King of glory?
  The Lord, strong and mighty,
  the Lord, mighty in battle...
Who is this King of glory?
  The Lord of hosts,
  he is the King of glory" (Ps. 24:8-9).

The enthroned God is a warrior-king who has defeated the forces of chaos (v. 2) and who now enters the Temple as the King of the universe. The belief

---

[27] See Mettinger, *Dethronement*, 19-24.

[28] So Seow, *ABD I* (1992) 389.

[29] For the conception of the throne in Psalm 99, see Seybold, *TDOT 8* (1997) 372f.

[30] So Kraus, *Psalmen I*, 194. Craigie even suggests that the original setting of the liturgical piece may have been the arrival of the ark in Jerusalem in David's time. Craigie, *Psalms 1-50*, 214.

that God is king is not merely a matter of politically oriented theocracy. The final significance of the concept is cultic. As Craigie has noted, "the kingship of the Lord is not merely a religious affirmation – it is a basis of worship and praise."[31]

Tournay suggests that in Psalm 24 there is a setting of a liturgical theophany, like the one in Ps. 27:4. The liturgical procession taking place with the transfer of the ark also reminds the post-exilic singers that the God of glory is a majestic ruler "whose face and presence and manifestation in the Temple the faithful seek."[32]

In some other psalms which mention the kingship of God the setting is clearly the Temple of Jerusalem.

"The Lord is king; let the peoples tremble! He sits enthroned upon the cherubim; let the earth quake! The Lord is great in Zion; he is exalted over all the peoples... Extol the Lord our God; worship at his footstool. Holy is he!" (Ps. 99:1, 2, 5; cf. 80:1-2).

Psalm 102 includes a shorter version: "But you, O Lord, are enthroned forever; your name endures to all generations" (102:12). In these passages the ark of the covenant was considered the throne of God. The basic theocratic imagery attached to the Temple remained intact and was applied in liturgical use whenever necessary.

It is probably worth noting that in the Old Testament the throne is further used as a metaphor for earthly things, and especially as a metaphor for kingship in general. In several Old Testament passages the idea of sitting on the throne is equivalent to reigning (cf. Jer. 22:30). There are also examples from the opposite point of view. Loss of kingship is expressed through the image of overturned thrones (Hag. 2:22; Ps. 89:45). On the other hand, the king's success may be expressed figuratively through a high throne (Isa. 14:13).[33]

What is of special interest for the present study, however, is that the metaphorical use of the throne extends to heavenly things, as well. In the Psalms we find several passages where certain features of merkabah speculation are evident. Firstly, God's throne is located in heaven: "The Lord is in his holy temple; the Lord's throne is in heaven" (Ps. 11:4). It is probable that the close relation between the heavenly temple and the temple of Jerusalem is meant here, but the emphasis is on the heavenly one.[34]

These descriptions do not need any heavenly vision for their justification,

---

[31] Craigie, *Psalms 1-50*, 214.

[32] Tournay, *Hearing God*, 126-127.

[33] See Brettler, *God is King*, 81-82.

[34] Cf. Craigie, *Psalms 1-50*, 133.

but they rest on a metaphorical understanding of the Temple itself.[35] Secondly, there is also heavenly worship being performed before the throne:[36]

"The Lord has established his throne in the heavens, and his kingdom rules over all. Bless the Lord, O you his angels, you mighty ones who do his bidding, obedient to his spoken word. Bless the Lord, all his hosts, his ministers that do his will" (Ps. 103:19-21).

Here too the unity of the heavenly realm and the earthy realm is evident. According to Psalm 22, God is, in fact, "enthroned on the praises of Israel" (22:3). The worship that takes place in the Temple joins the heavenly worship that is conducted before the heavenly throne of God.[37]

Psalm 33 underlines the transcendence of God. "The Lord looks down from heaven; he sees all humankind. From where he sits enthroned he watches all the inhabitants of the earth" (33:13-14). Such a transcendent setting places emphasis on God's universal power. There is not much difference between this description and references to the enthroned God in the Temple of Jerusalem.

The throne is naturally also a sign of God's ultimate power. In Psalm 9 the context is judgment: "But the Lord sits enthroned forever, he has established his throne for judgment" (9:7). God's righteousness will be emphasized. "Your throne, O God, endures forever and ever. Your royal sceptre is a sceptre of equity; you love righteousness and hate wickedness" (Ps. 45:6; cf. 89:14; 93:1-2).

In the visions of the prophet Ezekiel we find a similar conviction, and the prophet makes full use of this belief in his admonitions. In chapters 8-10 the prophet sees the temple of Jerusalem. The glory of God once rested on the throne of the Holy of Holies, but because of the presence of abominations in the temple it departs. "Now the glory of the God of Israel had gone up from the cherub on which it rested to the threshold of the house" (9:3).[38] The Lord rises from his throne in the Temple when passing judgment.[39]

The fire of the enthroned God then becomes a symbol for the destruction of Jerusalem (10:1-2). Finally the Lord leaves the temple. "Then the glory of the

---

[35] "The heavenly and the earthly may not be regarded as two opposed poles in a field of tension; rather, heaven and earth become one in the sacred space of the sanctuary." Mettinger, *Dethronement*, 31.

[36] Kraus, *Psalmen II*, 704.

[37] Brettler in fact thinks that such an idea of God 'sitting' on his throne may be an early concept in Old Testament theology. It is probably mentioned in Exod. 15:17. Brettler, *God is King*, 82.

[38] For example, Cooke identifies the glory mentioned here with the glory of the cherub-throne, i.e. the ark, since it had always existed in the inner sanctuary. Cooke, *Ezekiel*, 105.

[39] See Mettinger, *Dethronement*, 101.

Lord went out from the threshold of the house and stopped above the cherubim" (10:18). At the time of Ezekiel, then, the cherub-throne of the temple was apparently still the very centre of Temple worship, and the judgment of idolaters was pronounced by exploiting that very image.[40]

In Jeremiah 3 the ark of the covenant is acknowledged as the throne of God, but the lost ark is no longer missed, because "Jerusalem shall be called the throne of the Lord" (Jer. 3:16-17). The throne itself is highly esteemed, which can be seen in several passages. In 14:21, for example, Israelites plead for mercy: "Do not spurn us, for your name's sake; do not dishonour your glorious throne; remember and do not break your covenant with us." A similar attitude is found in the vision of judgment in chapter 17. "O glorious throne, exalted from the beginning, shrine of our sanctuary! O hope of Israel! O Lord! All who forsake you shall be put to shame" (Jer. 17:12).[41]

Later in sapiential theology God's throne is called especially the throne of glory. This can be seen, for example, in the Wisdom of Solomon, where Solomon prays for wisdom: "Send her forth from the holy heavens, and from the throne of your glory send her" (SapSol. 9:10).

But what is the relation between the earthly throne and the heavenly throne? One might suggest that in the Temple of Jerusalem heaven touches earth. In some respect this is true, while pious Jews seem to be convinced that God can be met with in the Temple. On the other hand, however, the earthly throne may be seen as an imitation of the heavenly one. In this case the throne in the Holy of Holies is modelled after the heavenly throne of glory. This is surely one way to interpret the nature of the throne. We should remember, though, that in the Temple liturgy this earthly throne factually represented the heavenly one, and God was believed to sit enthroned on the cherubim in the Holy of Holies.[42]

The symbolic world of Old Testament faith presents us with a majestic scene. God is a king and the Temple is his palace. In these descriptions God has no crown or a royal sceptre but he has a throne. God sits enthroned on the

---

[40] "Ezekiel's vision, which depicts the *kabôd* departing from Jerusalem is in reality the mirror-image of the central themes of the theophanic tradition, that is, the coming of God." Mettinger, *Dethronement*, 133. Therefore, God's departure is clearly a sign of judgment. Cf. Zimmerli, *Ezekiel I*, 231.

[41] In this latter passage the sanctuary is identified with the heavenly throne. See Mettinger, *Dethronement*, 25.

[42] For the discussion, see Brettler, *God is King*, 84f., who maintains that the earthly throne was probably a model of the heavenly throne, but that there is a special relation between the two in Old Testament theology. The passages in Jeremiah show that in certain polemical situations God was not believed to be confined to the earthly Temple, and so the special relation between these two thrones left room for speculation.

cherub-throne in the Holy of Holies. Even though the earthly throne is some kind of imitation of the heavenly throne of Glory, God can be met with in the temple. It is apparent that such images provided a metaphorical justification for maintaining the theocratic ideal of Old Testament faith among the people of Judah for centuries.

2.3. The function of the throne in the Temple cult

In the Old Testament the throne was not merely a symbol of divine power. The ark was naturally also a significant element in the description of the Temple cult. Therefore we need to extend the analysis to the cultic realm and investigate what kind of function the throne had in the Temple.

The ark was the place where atonement was provided annually in the Holy of Holies. Thus the throne of God was considered the centre of all Jewish worship. This is one of the "obvious" beliefs that we must not forget when preparing ourselves for the investigation of throne-mysticism both in Second Temple Jewish theology and in the early Christian tradition. Actually, the throne maintained communion between God and his people. The atonement which was achieved on the Day of Atonement was the realization of the heart of Jewish theocratic belief: God was given his proper status as the king of Israel, and no sin, unbelief or unfaithfulness was allowed to hinder his royal dominion.

According to the Old Testament, as we have seen, the mercy seat was a cherub-throne. It was located in the Holy of Holies, in the centre of worship. The detailed instructions for the construction of the ark remind us not only of its form, but also of its function in the Temple.

"Then you shall make a mercy seat of pure gold; two cubits and a half shall be its length, and a cubit and a half its width. You shall make two cherubim of gold; you shall make them of hammered work, at the two end of the mercy seat. Make one cherub at the one end, and one cherub at the other; of one piece with the mercy seat you shall make the cherubim at its two ends. The cherubim shall spread out their wings above, overshadowing the mercy seat... There I will meet with you, and from above the mercy seat, from between the two cherubim that are on the ark of the covenant, I will deliver to you all my commands for the Israelites" (Ex. 25:17-22).

There are several elements in the Temple cult that emphasize the special status of the ark as a throne. The Holy of Holies where the ark was located was considered a restricted area.[43] It was not possible to enter that room without divine sanction. This is one of the first premises in Temple ideology, and we know that it was also carefully upheld in Jewish tradition.

---

[43] Gese, *Zur biblischen Theologie*, 103f. Worship maintained its features even though the ark was actually absent, as far as we know, during the Second Temple period.

The *debir* was further a special place expressing God's holiness, and the cherub-throne was considered a symbol for the presence of God.[44] They were separated from earthly practices and even from daily worship in the Temple. This belief maintained a particular conception of God in Jewish theology. There is a basic difference and a factual opposition between God and human beings. Such tension is the starting-point for a theological understanding of the significance of the Holy of Holies. If believers wish to approach God, they must do it according to certain divine rules and instructions.

This is the context in which the priestly organization of the Temple fits. There was a strict hierarchy among the priests. The office of the high priest possessed the most important functions in Temple worship. The most prominent of these was ministry in the Holy of Holies.[45] Therefore the hierachical organization of the priests expressed the same intention as the "architectural" plan of the Temple. The *debir* was an isolated residence of God, and God could be approached only according to strict instructions.

Also, the ministry of the high priest in the Holy of Holies was limited. Prayers or daily sacrifices were separated from the liturgical act of approaching God in the *debir*. The latter was reserved for the Day of Atonement alone.

"Aaron shall present the bull as a sin offering for himself, and shall make atonement for himself and for his house; he shall slaughter the bull as a sin offering for himself. He shall take a censer full of coals of fire from the altar before the Lord, and two handfuls of crushed sweet incense, and he shall bring it inside the curtain and put the incense on the fire before the Lord, that the cloud of the incense may cover the mercy seat that is upon the covenant, or he will die" (Lev. 16:11-13).

The message of these instructions is clear. The "cloud of the incense" is necessary if the priest wishes to avoid destruction before God's face. It is another curtain between God and the priest protecting the sinful human being before the great Judge and King of Israel. All this emphasizes God's holiness. Therefore, there are several different sacrificial operations in the Temple on the Day of Atonement. They all express the unique character of the event.

"He shall slaughter the goat of the sin offering that is for the people and bring its blood inside the curtain, and do with it as he did with the blood of the bull, sprinkling it upon the mercy seat and before the mercy seat. Thus he shall make atonement for the sanctuary, because of the uncleannesses of the people of Israel, and because of their transgressions, all their sins" (Lev. 16:15-16).

The high priest enters the Holy of Holies bringing the blood of the goat. He sprinkles it upon the mercy seat. Here again the throne plays a significant role.

---

[44] See Janowski, *Sühne*, 328f.

[45] For the priestly organization, see Schürer, *History*, 238ff., 275ff.; Rehm *ABD 4* (1992) 302ff.

Atonement is made before God's throne and the blood is sprinkled on the throne itself.

Why was entering before God's throne so carefully protected and controlled? Why was the throne itself so isolated? It seems that all the separate features that we have considered above aim at one and the same end. God is the King of Israel and he cannot be approached without a sacrifice. If someone were to approach the throne apart from this controlled liturgy, he would die.

However, the ark is both a throne and a mercy seat. The contact between God and human beings has been made possible. The setting is implicitly revelatory, and it is evidently based on the idea of theophany. God has communicated with humankind and declared that he resides in the Holy of Holies. He can be approached if the sacrificial cult is observed. Atonement is provided, and the high priest who enters the Holy of Holies will not die.[46]

Therefore, the cultic ideal is fundamentally in agreement with the covenantal idea that can be seen in the theocratic ideology. The purpose of the cult was to maintain communion between God and Israel. When this purpose was fulfilled, God remained the King of the people. Therefore the sacrifice had the power of fulfilling the most significant purpose of Jewish faith: maintaining belief in the kingship of God.[47]

This means further that communion between Israel and her God is based on covenantal grace. The chosen people will not be destroyed before God's face. There is an atonement for their sins. God's throne is a mercy seat. Holy God is merciful towards sinful humankind. Sin as such does not prevent Israel from approaching her God.[48]

In this respect we may state that in these Old Testament passages *the throne is a metaphor of mediation*. It stands at the crucial point where heavenly holiness and earthly sinfulness meet. God the King sits on his throne, and the high priest enters as a representative of Israel. The throne is both a metaphor of power and a metaphor of mercy.

The blood of the sacrifice is sprinkled on the throne. Thus the place of

---

[46] As Janowski interprets this event: When the High Priest as a representative of Israel enters the Holy of Holies and makes atonement by the rite of blood, he fulfils the intention of the "Urzene" at Sinai (Ex. 24:15ff.). So the presence of God is highlighted on the Day of Atonement. Janowski, *Sühne*, 349. Cf. Lang, *TDOT VII* (1995) 298.

[47] Cf. Gese, *Zur biblischen Theologie*, 104. Seow seems to be too strict in his conclusion: "Thus, P [i.e. in Exod. 25] leaves no room for the interpretation of the ark throne or the footstool of a throne. The ark was a *rendezvous* where God would meet the people, but it was not the locus of a throning presence." Seow, *ABD I* (1992) 392.

[48] We should remember that the ark was also called "the ark of the covenant". "The association of the ark with the covenant is typical of the Deuteronomists; it is their special designation of the ark." Seow, *ABD I* (1992) 387.

divine holiness that would destroy approaching human beings actually becomes a mercy seat.

It is evident that, in the cultic discourse of Temple-centred theology, the concept of God's throne was given connotations that differed from those present in the royal psalms, for instance. Nevertheless, in several writings the Holy of Holies appears to be the basic context that signifies the cherub-throne. From this point of view, it is actually the cultic feature that constitutes the meaning of the throne in Old Testament tradition.

2.4. The enthronement of the anointed king

As regards our topic of "the Messiah and the throne" one question still remains unanswered. What is the relation between God the King and human kings of Israel in the Old Testament? How do the Scriptures describe the enthronement of the anointed king? In the Old Testament there are certain passages that are significant in respect of the enthronement theme, both in Second Temple Jewish theology and in New Testament Christology.

The Old Testament story is not complete without the famous cry: "Give us a king to govern us" (1 Sam. 8:6). The tradition of the earthly kingship which developed into the government of the Davidic dynasty, implies a transition from pure theocracy to another kind of government.

"[A]nd the Lord said to Samuel, 'Listen to the voice of the people in all that they say to you; for they have not rejected you, but they have rejected me from being king over them" (8:7).

There are several alternatives for interpreting this passage. There may even be redactional layers in the text itself, which makes the interpretation more difficult. The most important feature here, however, is found in verse 5. When the Israelites want a king they wish to be "like the other nations". Such a request has several significant implications, as Eslinger has noted: "The request of Yahweh's people (ʿam yhwh) to become like the nations (kekol-haggóyim) in political structure is, therefore, not only a rejection of the theocracy and its judges, but even more it is a rejection of the covenant."[49]

It is naturally possible that these kinds of text express a theological disagreement between different modes of theocracy.[50] We must note, however, that the whole picture is not that simple. In the writings of the Old Testament Davidic kingship is legitimated by theocracy. In this sense these two traditions have actually been brought together and adjusted to fit each other. The kingship of Solomon, for example, is described as a "theocratic" kingship in 1

---

[49] Eslinger, Kingship, 257.

[50] There may naturally be antimonarchic tendencies in different redactional layers of 1 Sam. 8, as Veijola has pointed out. Veijola, Königtum, 119. In spite of this, later dynastic ideology seems to be rather well adjusted to the theocratic ideal.

Chronicles 29: "Then Solomon sat on the throne of the Lord, succeeding his father David as king" (1 Chron. 29:23).

According to Chronicles, the throne of the earthly king was actually the throne of the Lord himself. Solomon, therefore, was completely dependent on God, and his success, too, was dependent on God's actions. "The Lord highly exalted Solomon in the sight of all Israel, and bestowed upon him such royal majesty as had not been on any king before him in Israel" (1 Chron. 29:25). A similar belief is referred to in Psalm 61: "Prolong the life of the king; may his years endure to all generations! May he be enthroned forever before God" (61:6-7).

The intention of theocratic belief was realized in the conviction that the earthly king was merely a representative of the heavenly Ruler. In 2 Samuel 7 this representative office was attributed to the Davidic dynasty. The relationship between God and king, presented in this passage, has often been interpreted as an adoptional relationship.

In the so-called prophecy of Nathan the relationship between God and king is expressed in the terms of sonship.

"I will raise up your offspring [seed (AV)] after you, who shall come forth from your body, and I will establish his kingdom... I will be a father to him, and he shall be a son to me" (2 Sam. 7:12-14 NRSV).

In this passage the Davidide is given a decree according to which he will be transferred to divine sonship. The king will be treated as God's son. If he commits iniquity, he will be punished, but nevertheless the mercy of God will not be taken away from him. There is a firm covenant between the God of Israel and the king.[51]

The concept of sonship and the relationship between God and the king has been interpreted in several ways, however, as we shall see below. The adoptionist interpretation has further been suggested on the grounds of Psalm 2, which too seems to present a description of an act of adoption.

Psalm 2 is a song that most probably reflects the enthronement of a Davidic king. In the psalm God announces: "I have set my king on Zion" (Ps. 2:6). This announcement is followed by a metaphorical statement:

"You are my son, today I have begotten you" (Ps. 2:7).

Many scholars think that this declaration was borrowed from contemporary legal terminology.[52] Through adoption the king is a true son of God, and this

---

[51] See e.g. Duling, *NTS 19* (1973) 56.

[52] So Rengstorf, *NT V* (1962) 234-238; Michel - Betz, *Judentum Urchristentum Kirche*, 5; Cooke, *ZAW 73* (1961) 209; and Kraus, *Psalmen I*, 153.

will not deny the king anything. The Davidide is permitted to make request ("ask of me", verse 8) of God, and he will show his favour.

An adoptionist interpretation is not the only alternative as regards Psalm 2 and 2 Sam. 7. Such language might also be considered as a sign of another kind of legitimation of an illegitimate child, or even as a statement concerning a vassal relationship in a covenantal context.[53] The ideas of formal covenants or vassal treatments, however, do not explain well the basic image of sonship that dominates the enthronement language present in these passages.

The idea of sonship is even more emphasized in Psalm 2, since the idea of begetting is introduced. God "begets" a new king. This theme also occurs in the kingship-of-Yahweh psalms elsewhere. In Psalm 110 (LXX 109:3; now followed in the new Finnish translation) it is God himself who begets the king (Ps. 110:3).[54]

If taken literally, this kind of statement might express a belief in the divine nature of the king. This, of course, is the case with the parallel traditions in Egyptian religion, where the divine birth of the ruler legitimates his divinity. In Israel, however, the king himself is not worshipped as god. The king appears not to be considered divine by nature, as was the case among the neighbouring nations.[55] His relationship to the God of heaven was theocratic. Therefore it is consistent to interpret the sonship of the king in some kind of adoptional terms. The Davidide who reigns is an adopted son of God who receives his authority from the heavenly King.[56]

In spite of all antimonarchic speculations which may well be true as regards different intentions in Old Testament theology, dynastic ideology in these

---

[53] Fohrer sees the "adoption" as a legitimation of the child of a maidservant, not as the adoption of a child from another family. Fohrer, *ThWNT VIII* (1969) 351. Becker speaks of the vassal relationship common in Near-Eastern covenant forms. Becker, *Messianic Expectation,* 28. Dumbrell thinks that there has merely been a theological shift from the Sinaitic covenant to the Davidic covenant. Israel as a son of God became a model for the king. Dumbrell, *Covenant,* 151.

[54] Following the LXX (109:3) we read Ps 110:3 as follows: "On my holy mountains from the bosom of the dawn I have given birth to you like the dew". For the reconstruction, cf. Kraus, *Psalmen II,* 926. For the discussion see Laato, *Immanuel,* 72.

[55] For instance, von Rad has noted that in Egyptian mythology god was considered the physical father of the king. This is never the case in Israel. von Rad, *ThLZ* (1947) 214. Cooke underlines the metaphorical nature of these descriptions: "None of these texts has been found to require more than a metaphorical and adoptional interpretation." Cooke, *ZAW 73* (1961) 225.

[56] According to Mettinger's analysis, the divine sonship of the Israelite king "was not conceived in mythological categories." Mettinger, *King,* 265. Instead divine sonship can be interpreted in adoptionist terms, while it "denotes a filial relationship between the king and his God." ibid. 266.

God as king

passages seems to be quite in agreement with theocratic belief.[57] The intimate relation between God and the king is further confirmed by the enthronement theme.

In Psalm 110 this is expressed by a statement that has become a standard for later Jewish theology and New Testament Christology.

"The Lord says to my lord, 'Sit at my right hand until I make your enemies your footstool" (Ps. 110:1).

This statement is evidently an associated submetaphor for the enthronement theme. Sitting "at the right hand" expresses both the great significance of the throne of God and the special status of the enthroned one. Therefore, this submetaphor proves that God's throne was a living metaphor which was constantly referred to in theological discourse.[58] Here the submetaphor serves the intentions of dynastic ideology, which appear to be of a theocratic nature.

Later in Jewish theology the anticipation of a messianic Davidide was adapted to eschatology. The future king was idealized and many expectations were laid on him. Throne descriptions occur in an apocalyptic context, but the theocratic setting remains the same.

In certain apocalyptic texts the eschatological Messiah is clearly a royal figure. In these texts he is a Davidide, even though he is hardly ever called the Son of David (e.g. PsSol 17:21; 4Qflor.,11; 4Qpatr., 3; 4Q161,8-10, III,18f.; 4. Ezra 12:32f.). In some of these passages the Davidide is associated with the throne, too. The enthronement of the Messiah is seen as a highlight of the eschatological future. This aspect will be treated in detail later.

In Jewish messianological speculation the idea of a priestly Messiah is prominent. This eschatological figure usually has a somewhat different function from the political Messiah. In certain cases these two aspects overlap, however. For example, in the Testament of Levi the idea of eschatological atonement is connected with a priestly Messiah who brings salvation to the faithful. This can be seen especially in chapter 18.

"And then the Lord will raise up a new priest to whom all the words of the Lord will be revealed. He shall effect the judgment of truth over the earth for many days. And his star shall rise in heaven like a king; kindling the light of knowledge as day is illumined by the sun. And he shall be extolled by the whole inhabited world" (TLev. 18:2-3).

The messianic figure here is a priest who brings salvation to Israel. He is not merely a priest, however, as would be the case in the eschatology of

---

[57] As Laato notes in regard to Psalm 2: "The Davidic king does not have this power in and of himself – only if he remains faithful to Yhwh does his authority fall under the Lord's protection. Therefore the Psalm presupposes the king's loyalty to his Lord." Laato, *Star*, 93.

[58] For the definition of submetaphor, see Introduction, and Brettler, *God is King*, 21.

Qumran. We can see that he has the status of a king, as well.[59] The Messiah is considered both a priest and a king. He will be the judge of the nations. Such a function can be attached only to a king, to whom all the people are subject.[60]

In the Testament of Naphtali the rivalry between the tribes of Levi and Judah concerning their messianic role is settled in favour of Judah.[61]

"Command your children that they be in unity with Levi and Judah, for through Judah will salvation arise for Israel, and in him will Jacob be blessed. Through his kingly power God will appear... to save the race of Israel" (TNaph. 8:2-3).

Political kingship in Israel, whether historical or idealist, inevitably influenced the way the appellation 'king' was used of God. Therefore it is important to pay attention to Brettler's notion that human royal appellations such as 'anointed' or 'divine designee' were not appropriate as divine appellations in the Old Testament. "The Bible sees God as the king in the strongest sense of the word, therefore he only is worthy of fullfledged royal appellations." Thus the metaphorical use of such appellations emphasized the qualitative difference between God's kingship and human kingship.[62]

In the Old Testament there is an interesting relationship between human kingship and the kingship of God. On the one hand, human kingship is the vehicle through which we can understand something about God's kingship. On the other hand, however, human kingship appears to be legitimated in several passages exactly by God's divine kingship. We can understand many things about Israel's kingship only through heavenly kingship.

This fact influences our understanding of the enthronement theme, too. According to several passages, Davidic kings or Messiahs are enthroned not merely on a throne of their own but also, at least in a metaphorical sense, on God's throne. Furthermore, the king is called son of God after his enthronement. These features are important as regards the reception of the idea of enthronement in later Jewish theology. In the following chapter we shall

---

[59] Qumran as a priestly community taught more conservatively of a priestly Messiah. The "Messiah of Aaron" was to end the power of the "Wicked Priest" in Jerusalem (1QSa II, 17-21). He was to take over the service of atonement (4QAaronA). At Qumran it would have been a sacrilege to teach that a royal Messiah could have a priestly function. On the origins of priestly messianism, see Collins, *Scepter and the Star*, 83.

[60] In TLev. 18 the royal Messiah has a priestly title but the function of a judge. This dualism might be explained by the fact that the Hasmoneans had attempted to unite the roles of the ruler and the High Priest. Due to historical uncertainty several scholars have concluded, however, that in this text we see evidence of Christian influence. See the discussion in Becker, *Testamente*, 291-293. Christian influence is proposed e.g. in the commentary Hollander - de Jonge, *Testaments*, 76, 179.

[61] van der Woude, *Die messianischen Vorstellungen*, 195, 200f.

[62] Brettler, *God is King*, 48-49.

investigate not only the descriptions of God's throne in Second Temple Jewish writings, but also passages where an act of enthronement, and especially an enthronement on God's throne of Glory, takes place.

As we aim at investigating the relation between Jewish merkabah mysticism and early Christology, a survey of selected Old Testament themes has proven invaluable:

1. The Old Testament presents a colourful picture of theocratic concepts available for Jewish theologians in the Second Temple period. The images and symbols that were significant for Jewish apocalyptic mystics had their rationale in standard Old Testament beliefs. In fact the most important of them, for instance the depiction of God as a heavenly King, or the symbol of the throne, belonged to the very core of Jewish Temple liturgy.

2. In practice the Scriptures must have directed the symbolic world of different Jewish groups, and therefore the key symbols could also be interpreted differently in different contexts. The application of central metaphors in Sadducean groups evidently differed from that in apocalyptic circles. In spite of this, we are entitled to expect that the reception of key metaphors in Jewish theology may reveal something important about the relationship between traditional Old Testament beliefs and new interpretations.

3. The theological language of Israel is political by definition. Israel's God is King. He is a heavenly ruler who sits enthroned in his palace, which is the Temple itself. The word 'theocracy' expresses this idea well. God reigns over his chosen people. He is the highest authority both in political and religious affairs.

4. The kings who ruled Israel in history were also subject to this theocratic scheme. Especially in the tradition of the Davidic dynasty they were considered adopted sons of God who reigned on God's throne. Usually the king was not a priest, even though some leaders such as Moses appear to have all these functions under their power. Cultic theocracy led by the high priest was separated from political theocracy, but the divine metaphors of theocracy remained the same.

5. What is more interesting still, is the double meaning of the throne. The throne itself is a metaphor of power. In the Temple cult it had this meaning, too, because the ark was the throne of God the King. In the cult, however, the

scene was wider because of the prevailing cultic discourse. Through the idea of atonement the throne became a mercy seat, too. This was a theological necessity, since Holy God could not be approached without an atoning sacrifice. Therefore the throne is finally a mediatorial metaphor in which the idea of meeting with God was crystallized.

§ 3 The Throne in Early Jewish Mysticism: the Merkabah

As we proceed to the actual merkabah passages in the writings of Second Temple Judaism the significance of the common symbolic universe soon becomes evident. Essential symbols are exploited in what we might in a general sense call 'apocalyptic discourses'. They also have a special role in such descriptions that are important in respect of later exaltation Christology. In the analysis of Jewish writings we shall focus on stories about different ascensions to a heavenly palace, on descriptions of occupants of heavenly thrones, on different kinds of enthronements, and on the functions of the throne in different descriptions of the heavenly realm.

Royal metaphors themselves were most probably self-evident for Jewish theologians in the Second Temple period. Temple worship in Jerusalem centred around the throne of God in the *debir*. The focus of Jewish faith lay in the Holy of Holies behind the Temple veil. This imagery also inevitably influenced Jewish mysticism.

Thus it is justified to suppose that Jewish mysticism was not living in a vacuum. It centred on the very same focus as the Temple cult. Mysticism was extremely interested in the heavenly palace, i.e. the eternal Temple of glory, God's reign and His kingship. As Scholem stated in his standard study, "the earliest Jewish mysticism is throne-mysticism".[1] Apocalyptic thinking was not directed by free imagination. In Jewish mysticism we can see a strong engagement to Israel's tradition and the history of the people. The transmission of the tradition was not merely conservative preservation, though. Instead, the tradition provided materials for new interpretations which turned out to be rather novel and bold at times.

3.1. Throne visions in Old Testament prophetic literature

Already in the Introduction the point was made that Second Temple throne visions were often modelled on the visions of the Old Testament prophetic writings. Therefore the analysis must begin with a short survey of these passages. Already in the biblical prophetic writings we meet mystical contemplation of the heavens and God's dwellings. Thus the roots of Jewish mysticism can be found in the Old Testament prophetic literature, such as the books of Isaiah and Ezekiel. Later in Second Temple tradition a rich literature was produced. The scene was usually used for apocalyptic purposes.

As Rowland has noted, several of the ideas in the apocalypses were no new innovations in Jewish religion. Already in Genesis we find passages where the

---

[1] Scholem, *Major Trends*, 42.

angel of God was regarded as communicating the appearance of God himself. The angels spoke to certain people, such as Hagar (Gen. 21:18) and Abraham (Gen. 22:11), appeared in the form of a man by the oaks of Mamre (Gen. 18:2), and finally the angel of God appeared to Jacob in a dream, identifying himself as the "God of Bethel" (Gen. 31:11-13).[2] Therefore interest in the form of God can be detected in several Old Testament writings. As regards the idea of a heavenly ascent, one needs only to remember the story of Jacob's ladder (Gen. 28:11-17), where "the angels of God were ascending and descending" on the ladder reaching to heaven.

One of the primary roots for the visions of God is probably the theophany at *Mount Sinai*. On the mountain God revealed himself in a great fire (Ex. 19:16-18; Deut. 4:11-15). Moses, Aaron, Nadab and Abihu and seventy of the elders saw God himself: "and they saw the God of Israel. Under his feet there was something like a pavement of sapphire stone, like the very heaven for clearness" (Ex. 24:10). This was later used in a merkabah speculation over the Temple, in Psalm 68:17, "With mighty chariotry, twice ten thousands upon thousands, the Lord came from Sinai into the holy place." Fire, in turn, was the element which expressed the glory of God, as we see already in the story of the burning bush. The angel of the Lord appeared to Moses "in a flame of fire" (Ex. 3:2).[3]

In 1 Kings we also find a vision of a throne. In the middle of the prophet Micaiah's prediction to King Ahab there is a description of the heavenly throne: "I saw the Lord sitting on his throne, with all the host of heaven standing beside him to the right and to the left of him" (1 Kings 22:19). In the story of Elijah's ascension a "chariot of fire" is mentioned (2 Kings 2:11). This story serves as a natural basis for the idea of ascension. In this story there is no vision of God's throne, though.

Isaiah's vision of God in the Temple has become a typos for a whole tradition of heavenly visions.

"I saw the Lord sitting on a throne, high and lofty; and the hem of his robe filled the temple. Seraphs were in attendance above him; each had six wings; with two they covered their faces, and with two they covered their feet, and with two they flew" (Isa 6:1-2).

First of all, there is a throne in heaven and it is presented in a metaphorical relationship to the Temple itself. The throne is huge. The message of such a magnifying symbolism needs little explanation. There are also several heavenly beings that later appear in mystical tradition.

As Gray notes, the word היכל in Hebrew denotes primarily a palace or a

---

[2] See Rowland, *Open Heaven*, 95.

[3] For the Old Testament examples see e.g. Gruenwald, *Merkavah Mysticism*, 29f.

royal residence. However, he denies that the writer means here any heavenly Temple in the manner of the apocalyptic writings.[4] This seems to be too strict an interpretation. The heavenly palace in Isaiah is rather meant to have some kind of identity with the earthly Temple. The images of the heavenly Temple and the Temple of Jerusalem merge into each other so that the heavenly one is a prototype for the earthly one.[5]

In the vision of Isaiah there is also a strong liturgical element. The seraphs sing the *trishagion*: "Holy, holy, holy is the Lord of hosts; the whole earth is full of his glory" (6:3). The threefold *sanctus* was evidently in constant use in the Temple liturgy.[6] This has further become a typos for a heavenly liturgy that often occurs in apocalyptic visions.

Finally, *Ezekiel* provides the model of the heavenly throne and the worship before that throne. The throne appears in fire and four creatures, the *ḥayyot*, stand in front of it (1:4-5). "A great cloud with brightness around it and fire flashing forth continually, and in the middle of the fire, something like gleaming amber. In the middle of it was something like four living creatures." These creatures have four faces, the faces of a human being, a lion, an ox, and an eagle (1:6-10). Later in Ezek. 10:9-17 the creatures are equated with the cherubim. This confirms that also in Ezekiel the scene is located in the Temple of Jerusalem.[7]

The throne of God is the cherub-throne in the Holy of Holies, even though we meet the version of the throne-chariot in most of the descriptions.[8] The throne is namely described as a chariot with wheels, the *'ofannîm,* (1:15).

"And above the dome over their heads there was something like a throne, in appearance like sapphire; and seated above the likeness of a throne was something that seemed like a human form" (1:26).

The appearance of God in human form is somewhat parallel to the appearances of the angels of God in human form in other Old Testament writings. Later in 8:2-4 a similar figure appears in a new vision, but now independent from the throne itself.[9] Not too much attention should be paid to this independence, since the glory of God was factually in the heavens (v. 4).

Also in Ezekiel God reveals himself in fire: "Upward from what appeared like the loins I saw something like gleaming amber, something that looked like

---

[4] Gray, *Isaiah I-XXVII*, 103.

[5] So Wildberger, *Jesaja I*, 245f.

[6] Wildberger, *Jesaja I*, 248.

[7] Halperin, *Chariot*, 46; Cooke, *Ezekiel*, 20f.

[8] For the chariot, see Greenberg, *Ezekiel 1-20*, 57f.

[9] Rowland, *Open Heaven*, 95.

fire enclosed all around" (1:27). All in all, the prophet is describing the glory of God, as he says in the next sentence: "This was the appearance of the likeness of the glory of the Lord" (1:28).

This description of Ezekiel has become a standard for apocalyptic, and several later writers employ these images in their writings. The wind, the creatures, and the wheels appear constantly in merkabah speculation. They actually even have heuristic value in the investigation of apocalyptic writings and other relevant passages in Jewish theology.

As we have seen in previous chapters, a similar concept of the heavenly throne can be found in the Psalms. "The Lord is in his holy temple; the Lord's throne is in heaven" (Ps. 11:4; ἐν οὐρανῷ ὁ θρόνος αὐτοῦ, LXX Ps. 10:4). Also in the Psalms the throne of God is a metaphor for his universal reign. "The Lord has established his throne in the heavens, and his kingdom rules over all" (Ps. 103:19).

There are other kinds of metaphor that signify the unity between the earthly and the heavenly temple. The key element in these metaphors is the Temple curtain that separates "the holy place from the most holy" (Ex. 26:33). As in the tabernacle, it is often a cloud that covers the place where the glory of God resides (Ex. 40:34). This is how God prevents worshippers from seeing his throne. In Job 26:9 we find a reading, supported by the Septuagint: "He holdeth back the face of his throne, and spreadeth his cloud upon it" (Authorized Version). In Psalm 18 it is again a cloud that covers the *merkabah* in the heavens: "He rode on a cherub, and flew; he came swiftly upon the wings of the wind. He made darkness his covering around him, his canopy thick clouds dark with water" (18:10-11; cf. 2 Sam. 22:12). Clouds and darkness are the metaphors in use further in Psalm 97:2, where the Lord the King is described: "Clouds and thick darkness are all around him; righteousness and justice are the foundations of his throne."

Later in Jewish theology such metaphors evidently inspired a special *pargod* (Aramaic for curtain) speculation.[10] For example, in 3 Enoch there is a curtain separating the Throne of Glory from the other parts of the highest heaven (3 En. 45). The cloud covering the *merkabah* is not simply a projection of the Temple veil, but indeed a metaphor for a necessary curtain before the heavenly Throne of Glory itself. So the heavenly palace is depicted as a Temple, and the throne itself is identified as the mercy seat. Such Temple metaphors are apparent in several apocalyptic works from the Second Temple period.

In the Septuagint text of *Daniel* the God of Israel is an enthroned God. In the "Song of the Three Jews" in the furnace, both the kingship of God and the cherub-throne are emphasized. The tormented men praise God in the furnace.

---

[10] For the interpretations in Jewish theology, see Hofius, *Der Vorhang*, 4ff., 17f.

"Blessed are you who look into the depths from your throne on the cherubim, and to be praised and highly exalted forever. Blessed are you on the throne of your kingdom, and to be extolled and highly exalted forever" (LXX Dan. 3:54-55).

The visions of Daniel are also significant for the prophetic tradition of throne visions. The vision in Daniel 7 has different acts like a drama. The vision of heaven begins by a description of how God himself takes his throne. This is an eschatological act where God takes his throne in order to execute judgment over the whole world. "As I watched, thrones were set in place, and an Ancient One took his throne, his clothing was white as snow, and the hair of his head like pure wool" (7:9).

The throne that Daniel sees is a chariot with wheels, and in addition it is a throne of fire. "[H]is throne was fiery flames, and its wheels were burning fire." (7:9). There are no special creatures worshipping God before the throne, but an innumerable crowd, instead. "A thousand thousand served him" (7:10). The scene is eschatological and leads to the judgment of the earth.

The Book of Daniel is another source for the enthronement theme in apocalyptic, even though the actual text leaves room for discussion in this question, as well. The special feature in Daniel's vision is the ascension of the Son of Man, the "one like a human being".

"I saw one like a human being coming with the clouds of heaven. And he came to the Ancient One and was presented before him. To him was given dominion and glory and kingship, that all peoples, nations, and languages should serve him" (7:14).[11]

No throne is mentioned here, and this makes the intepretation somewhat more difficult. The new status of the Son of Man implies, however, that an enthronement must have taken place.[12] The Son of Man explicitly exercises the office of king in the heavenly world. This view is apparent further in the Septuagint text of Dan. 7:14, (καὶ ἐδόθη αὐτῷ ἐξουσία). Hengel is correct in remarking that this kind of ἐξουσία is the sign of an enthronement to sovereign power.[13] The "giving" of power is thus apparently an act of enthronement to βασιλεία, as is mentioned in the same verse.

On the basis of a Septuagint variant - "he came as the Ancient of Days" - Rowland suggests that the Son of Man may even be the embodiment of the

---

[11] The enigmatic description of the main character has inspired scholars, and an angelic interpretation has been suggested e.g. by Collins, *Daniel*, 310. We shall return to this question later.

[12] The idea of everlasting dominion is not quite sensible without presupposing an enthronement, and the latter is usually referred to in interpretation, see e.g. Montgomery, *Daniel*, 303. Plöger even connects v. 14 with Ps. 110:1. Plöger, *Daniel*, 112.

[13] See Hengel, *Studies*, 183.

person of the Ancient of Days.[14] This, however, does not seem very logical. God and the Son of Man are two separate characters in these passages, and the latter does not appear as a "human form" of God.

Analogous to the enthronement theme, there is in the Old Testament a theme that could be called the "exaltation of the poor". In the so called prayer of Hannah (1 Sam. 2:1-10) we see the features of this theme quite clearly.

"The Lord makes poor and makes rich; he brings low, he also exalts. He raises up the poor from the dust; he lifts the needy from the ash heap, to make them sit with princes and inherit a seat of honour." (1 Sam. 2:7-8)

On the one hand, the granting of a seat of honour is an expression that may indicate the enthronement theme. On the other hand, this may naturally also be a metaphorical expression by which the contrast between the humility of the poor one and his heavenly glory is emphasized. In that case the idea of an actual enthronement does not have much value. It is interesting to note, however, that at the end of the prayer a similar exaltation is granted to the Lord's anointed. In this description an enthronement is not mentioned, though. "The Lord will judge the ends of the earth; he will give strength to his king, and exalt the power of his anointed" (1 Sam. 2:10).

In Job 36 the idea of an enthronement is more clear.

"He does not keep the wicked alive, but gives the afflicted their right. He does not withdraw his eyes from the righteous, but with kings on the throne he sets them forever, and they are exalted" (Job 36:6-7).

This passage in Job is significant because it evidently has a history of influence in Jewish writings. The righteous one in Job 36 is apparently Job himself, and this view has been developed further in later pseudepigrapha associated with the person of Job. We shall return to this question when the Testament of Job will be investigated.

There are certain common features in the visions recorded in the Old Testament. The most characteristic of these is that God is sitting on a throne. This is a heavenly throne and it is located in a heavenly palace. The cultic aspect is evident, however. The throne is often identified as the mercy seat on the ark of the covenant. The throne that is above the ark and which the cherubim cover with their wings is connected with the throne of glory located in the heavenly temple above. It is not merely a symbol of the heavenly throne but its true representative; it is a place where God can be approached. Furthermore, in the visions, God is accompanied by angels who minister to him, singing hymns of praise. There are also certain details which are important for the description of the throne. Several texts mention the throne of

---

[14] Rowland, *Open Heaven*, 98.

fire. This throne is accompanied by four creatures. The throne is furthermore placed on a chariot with wheels. We also find many of these features in the Jewish apocalyptic texts in the apocrypha and pseudepigrapha, and at Qumran. We shall examine them in the following chapters.

3.2. The throne in pre-Christian Jewish literature

In apocalyptic writings most of the stories of heavenly visions describe a journey of a chosen one, who is called to visit the heavens. Such a story may well be treated as an expression of an ascent structure, as some scholars have done. The seer is guided by an angel who explains or reveals heavenly mysteries to him. Usually the climax of the journey is a meeting with God. The visitor is accompanied in front of the heavenly throne and God himself addresses him. He is allowed to hear God's words, and often he is also given the mission of proclaiming God's words to men on earth. God's throne is naturally in the centre of the scene.

Such journeys are not the only descriptions where a heavenly throne plays an essential role. In addition, we find promises or actual descriptions of enthronements. In some cases the enthronement takes place on the throne of glory itself. There are several different characteristics that are attached to the idea of enthronement in apocalyptic writings. In what follows we shall attempt to discern the different functions they have in these ascent stories.

These general notions already explain why the analysis concerns not merely the occurrence of the metaphor of 'throne'. We need to investigate the nature of the royal imagery attached to the heavenly palace and also survey the occurrence of the ascent structure. These areas, as well as descriptions of heavenly enthronements, further reveal the contexts in which the reception of Old Testament metaphors may be detected.

The content of relevant visions is easily investigated, but the study of pseudepigraphic texts as such is a somewhat complex matter. The dating of the writings is a rather difficult matter, and it is not simple to date different features in the texts either. It is not easy to discern between passages written in the Hasmonean period, ideas dependent on Gnostic influence in the third or fourth centuries, or texts subjected to Bogomil editing in the tenth century.[15] The Dead Sea Scrolls have proved, however, that several writings have a long history. The discovery of part of 1 Enoch, for example, or the finding of excerpts from the Testaments of the Patriarchs at Qumran show that the tradition history of these writings goes back to the pre-Christian period, and all

---

[15] The last of these was a sect founded by Pope Bogomil in the 10th century A.D. They were Slavs who claimed, for example, that the God of the Old Testament was the God of evil.

of the writings need not be dated to the later Roman period. In spite of certain problems in dating and in the identification of redaction there is, however, one positive observation to be made. The aspect of the kingship of God hardly ever appears to be the subject of ambivalent speculation.

a. The Book of the Watchers (1 Enoch 14)

Enoch, one of the antediluvian heroes in Gen. 5:21-24, is a legendary figure in whose name a large amount of literature was written. Enoch served as a perfect example for apocalyptic speculation, for several reasons. He was said to have "walked with God". Furthermore, his sudden ascent to heaven ("he was no more, because God took him"; Gen. 5:24) without any report of his death became a model for exaltation. Enoch may be used as an example of a pious one making a heavenly journey. The physical nature of his ascension is unique, however, and it is seldom referred to in later apocalyptic writings.[16]

The Book of the Watchers (1 Enoch 1-36) is important for our study because it comes from the early period and presents one of the oldest visions of a heavenly journey.[17] Parts of the text have been found at Qumran. There seems to be a close connection with the book of Daniel, as well.[18]

In the Book of the Watchers we have a scene which is clearly based on selected Old Testament metaphors. There is a palace and a throne (9:4). We see wheels and the cherubim. The whole scene is theocratic, transcendent, and cultic. All this is supported by an intentional use of temple imagery.

"And behold I saw the clouds: And they were calling me in a vision; and the fogs were calling me; and the course of the stars and the lightnings were rushing me and causing me to desire; and in the vision, the winds were causing me to fly and rushing me high up into heaven" (14:8-9).

Enoch enters a "great house which was built of white marble" (14:10). This heavenly divine palace was built of crystal (cf. Ezekiel 1:22). Inside the building Enoch saw another house, which was within the first one. The second one "excelled (the other) – in glory and great honour – to the extent that it is impossible for me to recount to you concerning its glory and greatness" (14:16).

---

[16] See Segal, *ANRW II 23.2.* (1980) 1359.

[17] Rowland notes that here we have an early account of a mortal taken into the divine presence. Rowland, *Templum*, 192.

[18] The Aramaic manuscript evidence indicates that at least part of the section was already a literary unit in the first half of the second century B.C.E. Nickelsburg dates the compilation of chapters 1-36 to the period before 175 B.C.E. Nickelsburg, *Jewish Literature*, 48. For a general introduction on the compilation of different books in 1 Enoch, see Stone, *Jewish Writings*, 395ff.

These two rooms obviously belong to the heavenly temple. This is confirmed by the fact that the second room appears to be the Holy of Holies. In the second "house" Enoch sees God enthroned. God sits on a fiery throne with brilliant shining wheels (cf. Dan. 7:9-10).[19] Unlike the story in the Testament of Levi, which will be investigated below in detail, here we have a description of a manifestation of God himself.[20]

"And I observed and saw inside it a lofty throne – its appearance was like crystal and its wheels like the shining sun; and (I heard?) the voice of the cherubim; and from beneath the throne were issuing streams of flaming fire. It was difficult to look at it. And the Great Glory was sitting upon it – as for his gown, which was shining more brightly than the sun, it was whiter than any snow" (14:18-20).

The temple imagery is emphasized by the remark that angels could not enter the inner house. "None of the angels was able to come in and see the face of the Excellent and the Glorious One" (14:21).[21] The seer sees the Holy of Holies where – apart from him – no one was allowed to enter. As Halperin says, "in the Holy of Holies, God sits alone".[22]

The temple vision of Enoch is also in some sense a reminder of the visions of Daniel and Isaiah. The seers see a lofty throne and heavenly beings. They are also ashamed to look at the Holy Lord.

"And the Lord called me with his own mouth and said to me, 'Come near to me, Enoch, and to my holy Word.' And he lifted me up and brought me near to the gate, but I (continued) to look down with my face" (14:24-25).

In this vision the setting is reminiscent of the call of a prophet. At the end of the throne vision God reveals to Enoch the secrets concerning fallen angels, the Watchers. Enoch is given a mission to deliver this knowledge to human beings. This was actually stated in the opening lines of the story: "This is the book of the words of righteousness and the chastisement of the eternal Watchers, in accordance with how the Holy and Great One had commanded in

---

[19] Halperin, *Chariot*, 81. Himmelfarb has noted that in biblical Hebrew *hekhal* serves for both the king's palace and the temple. "Thus even in those texts where the idea of temple dominates, the imagery associated with the royal palace never disappears." Himmelfarb, *Ascent*, 14.

[20] See Segal, *Two Powers*, 192; Newman, *Glory-Christology*, 84.

[21] Gruenwald has noted that, "This fact, that Enoch makes this heavenly trip with no angelic accompaniment, is even more emphatically stressed when Enoch himself says (verse 21): 'None of the angels could enter and behold His face'. In this respect Enoch is here more privileged than all the angels, and even more so when he finds himself addressed by God." Gruenwald, *Merkavah Mysticism*, 36-37.

[22] Halperin, *Chariot*, 82. According to Himmelfarb, the mention of the "horror" which overwhelms Enoch when he enters the building reveals that it is actually access to God's heavenly temple that causes Enoch to fear. Himmelfarb, *Ascent*, 16.

this vision." (14:1). Temple imagery, therefore, has here the connotation of the place of judgment.

This is apparently possible because of the throne metaphor that carries such a double meaning.[23] The idea itself fits well with the basic story. As Segal has noted, Enoch's ascent has the primary purpose of explaining some of the great evil on earth while confirming that both the suffering of the righteous and the success of sinners will be put right hereafter.[24]

In addition, it is rather evident that the theocratic ideal of Jewish faith is emphasized in this sequence. The story expresses the core of the faith in one God and the calling of the Chosen People. The elect shall see the glory of God and stand before His throne. In this sense the vision of Enoch is rather conservative and reveals the essential nature of the apocalyptic mysticism of that time.[25]

There are also some short references to the throne of God in the Book of the Watchers. The next section introduces a mountain theme which was later of importance to several writers. In 18:8-9 the throne is not located in a house, but on the peak of a mountain: "the throne of God, which is of alabaster and whose summit is of sapphire; and I saw a flaming fire." Gruenwald is most obviously correct when he comments that "this mountain, again, is the middle one in a series of seven mountains which Enoch is allowed to see, and the theophany which Enoch experiences thereon is obviously reminiscent of the theophany on Mount Sinai."[26]

In 25:3 we find a similar vision, where the vision of a mountain is interpreted: "This tall mountain... is (indeed) his throne, on which the Holy and Great Lord of Glory, the Eternal King, will sit when he descends to visit the earth with goodness." This vision is furthermore special for its description and interpretation of the tree of life, which is clearly connected with the throne. Cf. some verses above: "The seven mountains were (situated) in the midst of these (ravines) and (in respect to) their heights all resembled the seat of a throne (which is) surrounded by fragrant trees" (24:3). And among them was the extraordinary tree of life. This is explained in 24:5: "And the elect will be

---

[23] "While the scene is not specifically a court scene, as in Daniel, it is the setting for the divine condemnation of the Watchers." Collins, *Apocalyptic Imagination*, 42.

[24] Segal, *ANRW II 23.2.* (1980) 1359f. The problem of theodicy is one of the central themes of 1 En. 1-36. See my analysis in Eskola, *Theodicy*, 35ff.

[25] Hartman has noted that chapters 1-5 at the beginning of the book, which exploit traditional cultic (biblical) language, serve as an introduction to the whole Book of the Watchers, thus reflecting features that appear later in the work. Hartman, *Asking for a Meaning*, 116f., 138ff. In this respect there may well be an intentional connection between the "introduction" and chapter 14, which has several cultic features.

[26] Gruenwald, *Merkavah Mysticism*, 37-38.

presented with its fruit for life. He will plant it in the direction of the northeast, upon the holy place – in the direction of the house of the Lord, the Eternal King." (cf. later, 2 Enoch, ApcMos).

There are several metaphors in this description which connect the throne with the Temple of Jerusalem. The mountain appears to be Mount Zion and the house of the Lord is the expected place for the Eternal King to sit "when he descends to visit the earth". A mountain is a significant metaphor in apocalyptic writings, denoting the Temple of Jerusalem, and even Psalm 68 connects these two places (68:17, 24). It is further noteworthy that, according to the writer of 1 En. 25, the throne of the King also becomes the tree of life for the "righteous and the pious" (25:4-5).

In the Book of the Watchers the so called ascent structure is governed by traditional cultic ideology. Enoch, who makes the heavenly journey, is escorted to a heavenly Temple and there he meets God himself. In this passage the throne of God is in the centre of events, but it is worth noting that no enthronement of Enoch or any other character is mentioned. What is interesting, too, is how the description is linked to the classical problem of theodicy. Enoch's ascent has the purpose of explaining the great evil on earth and the suffering of the righteous.[27]

The passages examined provide a significant example of the reception of Old Testament metaphors in a new context. God is still the King of Israel who sits on his holy throne. The images themselves have not changed, but their function is now eschatological. Enoch has a prophetic call through his apocalyptic vision. Royal metaphors guarantee the continuity of tradition in the new situation. God the King whom Enoch sees is the same heavenly King of Israel who called all the prophets.

b. Jubilees

The Book of Jubilees belongs in the same environment as the Enochic writings and the apocryphal works bearing the name of Levi. Both Enoch (Jub. 4:16) and Levi (Jub. 31:11) are mentioned in the book.[28] Enoch has an important

---

[27] Admittedly, there is some justification for the opinion held by Collins: "The symbolic universe of Enoch is expressed in mythological terms although it embraces pseudoscientific cosmology." Collins, *Seers*, 50. Collins, however, has not paid attention to the traditional features that are evident in the very same symbolic universe.

[28] The Book of Jubilees is usually dated to the Maccabaean period (161-140 B.C.E.). There is an explicit citation of the book in Qumran Damascus Document (CD 16:3-4), and therefore it was most probably written before c. 100 B.C.E. If the references to wars in chapters 34-38 refer to the Maccabaean wars, the time of writing might be around 150 B.C.E. For the argumentation, see Eissfeldt, *Old Testament*, 608; Nickelsburg, *Jewish Literature*, 78-79.

role to play at the beginning of the work. In chapter 4 his life is recounted at length. Enoch was "the first who learned writing and knowledge and wisdom," and he also wrote a book of the signs of the heaven, probably a sacral calendar ("their weeks according to jubilees he recounted", 4:18, as well as the sabbaths).[29]

Enoch was also a seer. "And he saw what was and what will be in a vision of his sleep as it will happen among the children of men in their generations until the day of judgment" (4:19). Evidently these kinds of visions are the reason why Enoch was "therefore with the angels of God six jubilees of years." The angels "showed him everything which is on earth and in the heavens, the dominion of the sun" (4:21).[30] There is no direct causality between these visions and Enoch's final ascension, but some kind of similarity is probably intended. "And he was taken from among the children of men, and we led him to the garden of Eden for greatness and honour" (4:23). According to a later passage, Enoch would also "report every deed of each generation in the day of judgment" (10:17).[31]

In heaven Enoch surprisingly exercises a priestly function. "And he offered the incense which is acceptable before the Lord in the evening (at) the holy place on Mount Qater" (4:25).[32] This feature confirms the conception of the cultic nature of early merkabah mysticism. In his ascension Enoch joins in heavenly worship.

Even though the eschatology of Jubilees can be called apocalyptic, the description of ascension is restricted to that of Enoch. This is probably due to the fact that there are only a few stories about visions in the book. As regards the throne, we find traces of sacral mysticism, however. For the writer of Jubilees the garden of Eden was the holy of holies and the dwelling of the Lord.

"And he [i.e. Noah] knew that the garden of Eden was the holy of holies and the dwelling of the Lord. And Mount Sinai (was) in the midst of the desert and Mount Zion (was) in the midst of the navel of the earth. The three of these were created as holy places, one facing the other" (Jub. 8:19; cf. 1QapGen 19:8; 1 Enoch 26:1).

Paradise is naturally an effective metaphor and it is easy to understand why

---

[29] For Enoch traditions in Jubilees, see VanderKam, *From Revelation to Canon*, 305-331.

[30] This has most probably to do with the solar calendar employed in the Book of Jubilees.

[31] Bock thinks that Enoch's ascension "testifies to his qualifications" for the new role in heaven. Bock, *Blasphemy*, 123.

[32] The name Qater may refer to the Hebrew root qtr, that is used to describe the burning of incense. See the comments of Wintermute in *OTP II*, 63; esp. note n.

it is again here, as in 1 Enoch, linked with the "dwelling of the Lord". This dwelling may be both the Holy of Holies and Mount Sinai. All these metaphors refer ultimately to the heavenly Temple, where the glory of God resides. The linking of the garden of Eden and Mount Zion was later of importance in several apocalyptic writings and merkabah speculations.

The ascent structure is vague in Jubilees, but it is clear that Enoch plays an important role in the work. The idea of Enoch's cultic function in the heavenly Temple is strong evidence for the cultic nature of this mystical tradition. The heavenly throne itself is not mentioned in the book, but the occurrence of the Temple imagery confirms the picture that may be drawn on the basis of 1 Enoch, and which will find more colours in the Testament of Levi below.

c. The Testament of Levi

The Testament of Levi belongs to a larger compilation, the Testaments of the Twelve Patriarchs. Apart from certain Christian interpolations the Testaments may be dated to the pre-Christian period.[33] The Testament of Levi itself, however, may have an independent history of its own. Fragments of TLev. have been found at Qumran. This shows that testamentary literature linked with the sons of Jacob was produced in the Second Temple period.

In the Testament of Levi the cultic context of the merkabah is even more emphasized than in the works studied above – but from quite another perspective. Here we have a pseudepigraphic testament of the priestly tribe. This point of departure entitles us to expect to find cultic significance in the text. This testament also meets such expectations. In Levi's vision the temple scene is prominent. The writing concentrates on the priest's role and the justification of the Levite priesthood.

At the beginning of the vision we find a perfect heavenly journey. "And behold, the heavens were opened, and an angel of the Lord spoke to me: 'Levi, Levi, enter!' And I entered the first heaven" (2:6-7). There are three different heavens in ascending order, the heaven of water, the heaven of light, and the heaven of God's dwelling-place.[34]

---

[33] See Kee in *OTP I*, 776ff. Kee favours a rather early date. For the discussion and a case for a later date, however, cf. Eissfeldt, *Old Testament*, 634-636. The disagreement concerns the possibility of making a division between the Jewish original and the Christian redaction. For a critical history of research, see Slingerlander, *Testaments*, especially pp. 60ff. I admit, however, that it is difficult to decide between the two alternatives. Hollander and de Jonge state that "it is practically impossible to answer the question whether there ever existed Jewish Testaments in some form." The author of the Testaments may well have been a Christian writer who merely exploited Jewish traditions and materials. See Hollander and de Jonge, *Testaments*, 84-85.

[34] Cf. Kee, *OTP I*, 779.

In this testament we also find what has been called the apocalyptic idea of the temple in heaven.[35] Such an idea was evidently already implied in the visions of Isaiah and Ezekiel. In the Testament of Levi, however, it became a prominent scene in terms of which the whole heavenly journey is described. In TLev. 3:6 we find a description of the heavenly Temple and a heavenly Holy of Holies where God dwells. Rowland describes this Temple as follows: "There with God are archangels who offer propitiatory sacrifices to the Lord on behalf of the sins of ignorance of the righteous. They present to the Lord a pleasing odour, a rational and bloodless offering."[36]

The description of heaven in TLev. is thus far more developed than, for instance, in early Enochic literature.[37] After the description of two separate heavens there follows a climatic scene in which Levi sees God enthroned:

"At this moment the angel opened for me the gates of heaven and I saw the Holy Most High sitting on the throne. And he said to me, 'Levi, to you I have given the blessing of the priesthood until I shall come and dwell in the midst of Israel'" (5:1-2).[38]

After this Levi is returned back to earth and an angel commands him to execute vengeance on Shechem for the sake of Dinah (5:3-5).[39]

In the context of the Testament of Levi the merkabah tradition is appealed to for the justification of the Levite priesthood.[40] This is why the context is naturally cultic, though it has not been exploited to its full potential. It concentrates on the premises of the priesthood, not on its actual practice (cf. the description of the priesthood later in TLev.) Nevertheless, in 2:10, there is a heavenly dimension to Levi's priestly role. He will "stand near" the Lord and be "his minister."[41]

There is no mention of any enthronement in the Testament of Levi, but in chapter 8:3 the idea of eternal priesthood is apparently referred to. When Levi is clothed in the vestments of the priesthood, the men (angels?) say, "From now on be a priest, you and all your posterity". It has been suggested that this expresses a similar conviction to what we find in Psalm 110. The Levite

---

[35] For the definition, see MacRae, *Semeia 12* (1978) 182-183. This aspect is quite important later in the descriptions of early Christology, for instance in the Letter to the Hebrews. See below e.g. chapter 7.

[36] Rowland, *Templum*, 189.

[37] Segal, *ANRW II 23.2.* (1980) 1361.

[38] According to manuscript β, this is precisely the throne of *glory*.

[39] Cf. Gen 34.

[40] Cf. Collins, *Apocalyptic Imagination*, 109f.

[41] Himmelfarb pays attention to the process of consecration as priest in which Levi is anointed and dressed in priestly garments. She later links such a description to the idea of transformation, even though she does not mean TLev. itself. Himmelfarb, *Ascent*, 37.

priesthood would thus be identified with the eternal priesthood "according to the order of Melchizedek" (Ps. 110:4). Hay suggests that this concept of priesthood developed in the Hasmonaean family.[42] It is possible that the idea of eternal priesthood, which admittedly also appears in 1 Macc. 14:41, is present here.[43] Psalm 110 alone, however, cannot be the only basis for such a conclusion.

It is evident, however, that in TLev. 18 such priestly expectations have became messianic. "And then the Lord will raise up a new priest to whom all the words of the Lord will be revealed" (18:2). This priestly Messiah is the one who brings salvation: "And he shall open the gates of paradise; he shall remove the sword that has threatened since Adam" (18:10). The latter verse, however, bears the marks of Christian editing.[44]

The Testament of Levi also provides a good example of a story about a heavenly journey. The exploitation of the ascent structure is evident, and here the description of heaven is more developed than in early Enochic literature. The apocalyptic idea of the temple in heaven may be clearly seen in the structure of the heavenly realm. Here, as in the Book of the Watchers, the explicit mention of an enthronement is lacking. The reception of royal metaphors in TLev. further confirms the picture that we gain from the Book of the Watchers. The divine throne is the place where God can be met with. The nature of the description is theocratic and also cultic. The ascent story as such is reminiscent of a prophetic call. Like Enoch, Levi is given a special mission on earth.

d. Qumran

In the Dead Sea Scrolls and in the writings of the Qumran community itself there are traces of merkabah speculation and a well-developed sacral mysticism. As Qumran was the centre of a priestly sect, both the Temple and the throne of God were of great significance in the covenanters' thinking. The apocalyptic features in Qumran literature have lately been given much attention and this has helped in defining the nature of merkabah mysticism in the writings used in the community.

Throne visions. Among the writings found in the caves there were several

---

[42] Hay, *Glory*, 24f.

[43] Simon was appointed as a "high priest for ever" – until "a trustworthy prophet should arise."

[44] The question whether these Messianic ideas are of Christian origin or not is difficult and shall not be dealt with in detail here. Suffice it to say, however, that in comparison with the Messianic eschatology of Qumran the teaching of a Messianic High Priest would not be unique in Jewish apocalypticism. For the discussion see e.g. Collins, *Scepter*, 91 f.

texts that speak directly of heavenly visions, such as the fragments of Enoch (4Q204), the Aramaic Testament of Levi (4Q213) and Pseudo-Ezekiel (4Q385): "The vision which Ezekiel saw [...] the gleam of the chariot and four living creatures" (frag. 4, 5-6; Martínez). In this sense apocalyptic was widely present in the literature used by the sect.

The proper scene for Qumranic merkabah mysticism is found especially in devotional and cultic texts. Among the fragments called Daily Prayers (4Q503) we have a prayer where the pious one praises God whose temple is in heaven. God lives in the Holy of Holies and this is the place where prayers reach him. The manuscript is unfortunately rather badly damaged: "(4) [...Blessed be] your name, God of Israel, in all [...] ... (8) [holy of] holies in the heights [...]... (10) [...] and glory in the holy [of holies...]".[45]

Such a devotional attitude may be detected further in the "Angelic Liturgy", where we find a similar scene and the same devotional atmosphere. The Songs of the Sabbath Sacrifice, as the work is now called, is undoubtedly the most interesting liturgical text among the Qumran scrolls. As Halperin notes, the language of the Songs is drawn directly from the Temple.[46] The setting, however, bears the marks of the apocalyptic idea of the temple in heaven.[47]

The scene of the Songs of the Sabbath Sacrifice is quite similar to that of apocalyptic visions. The main source of inspiration is probably the Book of Ezekiel, from which the concepts of throne-chariot and the heavenly sanctuary are taken. The songs describe the heavenly liturgy that is conducted before the heavenly *merkabah*.[48] For example, in 4Q405 the cherubim praise God before the heavenly throne:

"They bless the image of the *merkabah*-throne /
Above the firmament of the cherubim /
And they hymn the splendor of the firmament of light /
Beneath the seat of his glory" (4Q405, 22.8).[49]

---

[45] Frags. 13-16 col VI, 4-10, in the edition by Martínez.

[46] Halperin, *Chariot*, 50.

[47] The songs include nothing that can be dated. On the grounds of internal evidence, for instance, Stegemann is convinced that they were composed in the fourth or third century B.C.E., because the temple terminology fits the situation of the Jerusalem Temple. Stegemann, *Library*, 99. Newsom admits that the problem of provenance cannot be resolved by internal evidence beyond question, but on the grounds of certain points of verbal similarity she prefers to conclude that the scroll is a product of the Qumran community. Newsom, *Songs*, 2-4.

[48] See Schiffman, *Mystics*, 17.

[49] This translation comes from Halperin, and it underlines the heavenly scene well, Halperin, *Chariot*, 52.

This aspect was not unknown to the canonical Psalmists, either.[50] In the Hymns of Qumran, however, this theme is given little space, even though there was a tradition for it in the canonical psalms. The author of the Hodayot, in some cases probably the Teacher of Righteousness himself, seems to have been more interested in the personal experiences of the believer and the uprightness of the righteous ones.

In the Songs of Sabbath Sacrifice, however, heavenly worship and the praises of God occupy a prominent place. Therefore, it is only natural that the kingship of God is a leading theme in these songs. According to the analyses of Schwemer, kingship is actually a key term for the understanding of the work.[51]

Both in the Enochic Book of the Watchers and in the Songs of Sabbath Sacrifice we thus find the inclusion of the cultic aspect of Old Testament throne descriptions. This suggests that it must have been a prominent feature in early merkabah mysticism. The cultic aspect of these songs is so important that we shall return to it later (in chapter 4.4.).

The enthronement theme. The most interesting of the texts concerning the enthronement theme is a 4Q fragment that was initially identified as part of the War Scroll, 4QM^a (4Q491). This identification may be correct, but most scholars consider the passage to be rather independent and designate it a hymn. In line with an early interpretation, it has been called the "Song of Michael (the archangel)", since the singer rejoices in his own heavenly glory.[52]

In the War Scroll itself we do not find any detailed merkabah mysticism, but the scene of the work implies similar points of departure. According to the writing, God's "holy dwelling" is in heaven, and a host of angels perform a liturgy praising God's name (1QM XII,1). This is also the context and scene for the fragment.

In 4Q491 the speaker, however, is not necessarily an angelic figure but rather a human being. The singer rejoices in his extraordinary status in heaven. 4Q491, fr. 11, col. I,12-13a:

---

[50] In Psalm 103:19-21 we find a similar scene of angels blessing the enthroned Lord in heaven. "The Lord has established his throne in the heavens, and his kingdom rules over all. Bless the Lord, O you his angels, you mighty ones who do his bidding, obedient to his spoken word. Bless the Lord, all his hosts, his ministers that do his will."

[51] See the extensive analysis by Schwemer in *Königsherrschaft Gottes*, 45ff., for the aforementioned idea especially 116.

[52] For the discussion, see e.g. Hengel, *Le Trône*, 175; Collins, *Scepter*, 137. Vermes, for example, gives a combined title: "The Song of Michael and the Just", *Dead Sea Scrolls*, 147.

"a throne of strength in the congregation of the gods
above none of the kings of the East shall sit...
my glory [is incomparable] and besides me no-one is exalted"
(Martínez)

The exaltation is then interpreted as an enthronement to the realm of heavenly beings, presumably angels. "For I have taken my seat... in the heavens... I shall be reckoned with gods and established in the holy congregation" (13-14).[53]

The rest of the fragment is rather corrupt, but one can find exclamations such as: "who is comparable to me in my glory?" (15, Martínez); and: "For I am counted among the gods, and my glory is with the sons of the king" (18, Martínez).

Such a description has inspired some scholars to conclude that this text is an example of "speculation on deification by ascent towards or into the heavens".[54] Such a conclusion, however, is not very well rooted either in the eschatology of Qumran or in the apocalyptic character of Second Temple Judaism. Ascension as such does not produce deification. Already in 1QH we find the hope of the righteous of Qumran, anticipating a glorious future in heaven:

"I walk on limitless level ground, and I know there is hope for him whom Thou hast shaped from dust for the everlasting Council. Thou hast cleansed a perverse spirit of great sin that it may stand with the host of the Holy Ones, and that I may enter into community with the congregation of the Sons of Heaven" (1QH 3:21-22, Vermes).

Qumran was a prototypical community for the heavenly congregation, and membership on earth would certainly lead to eternal joy with the "congregation of the Sons of Heaven". Thus the idea of entering into the heavenly congregation, as it appears in 4Q491, is a common theme in Qumran eschatology.

The ideas of exaltation and enthronement, too, conform to the apocalyptic of Second Temple Judaism. As we shall see later in detail, a heavenly enthronement was promised e.g. to Moses in the Exagoge of Ezekiel and to Job in the Testament of Job: "He gave me the sceptre and told me to sit on the great throne" (Ex.Ez. fr. 6, 15); "My throne is in the upper world, and its splendour and majesty come from the right hand of the Father" (TJob 33). These early writings contain a similar scene of enthronement as 4Q491 – not to mention the later examples of the enthronement of several patriarchs from Abraham and Enoch to Isaiah.

The expression "among the gods" is rather rare in Jewish writings in

---

[53] Translation by Collins, *Scepter*, 137.

[54] So Morton Smith, *Dead Sea Scrolls*, 187; cf. *Jesus*, 298.

general, but not at Qumran. In the Old Testament it was an expression used of heavenly beings: "Who is like you, O Lord, among the gods?" (Ex. 15:11). In addition to the reference to false gods, the word may refer to angels, as most probably does the expression "sons of God" in Gen. 6:2-4 and Ps. 89:7. In Qumran writings the idea "I shall be reckoned with gods" is also found in fragments 4Q427 VII and 4Q471b.[55] In the Songs of the Sabbath Sacrifice the title "gods" is given to several heavenly beings. In the seventh song the "august ones" are the "chiefs of the praises of all the gods" (col. I, 31-32). They are further described as the "spirits of the holy of the holies, the living gods, the spirits of everlasting holiness above all the holy ones" (col. I, 44-45).[56]

The exalted character in 4Q491 anticipates a glorious future: "I shall be reckoned with gods". He expects that he will be exalted to the highest rank of heaven and he is given the right to worship God with the "gods" of the Holy of Holies. Who is the one that sings such a song? We have already noted that an angel is not a very convincing option.[57] Instead, the singer in 4Q491 might well be a righteous Jew – in the context of the War Scroll even a high priest reading aloud prayers and hymns before battle (1QM 15:4) – anticipating his own enthronement. Some scholars have suggested that the singer is a teacher, in the Qumran context probably even the Teacher of Righteousness himself.[58]

At the end of the 4Q491 fragment there is a reference to teaching, but the expression used there may also refer to a judge: "And who can deal with the issue of my lips? Who shall summon me to be destroyed by my judgment?" (4Q491 fr. 11, 17). In Second Temple Jewish theology it was a general belief that the righteous would "govern nations and rule over peoples" in the end of days (see e.g. SapSol. 3:8). In apocalyptic writings this idea was often united with the enthronement theme.[59] In this respect the singer is like any patriarch who is enthroned, and who shall "rule over peoples" in the future.

---

[55] See Collins, *Scepter*, 138.

[56] Fletcher-Louis suggests that there is "perhaps specific reference to an angelomorphic identity in line 18." He interprets entering the heavenly realm as a process of transformation. Fletcher-Louis, *Angels*, 189. In the text itself, however, there is nothing to indicate such a change. The use of the term 'angelomorphic' is vague, though, and Fletcher-Louis avoids claiming that the exalted figure actually is an angel.

[57] In the Dead Sea Scrolls the status of the Qumran priests is several times metaphorically compared with the status of the highest angels that worship God in the heavenly sanctuary. See for instance 1QSb 4, 25-26; 4Q511, frag. 35. This metaphorical relationship is missed by Gieschen, who believes that some of the priests were actually identified as angels – "even to the point of deification". Gieschen, *Christology*, 174.

[58] See Collins, *Scepter*, 148.

[59] See e.g. Ex.Ez. fr. 7,9 below.

This is why the singer of the hymn may also be a messianic figure.[60] In Qumran ideology this would be quite natural. In the Blessings 1QSb the messianic High Priest is promised a place in the heavenly palace and the Holy of Holies: "May he [renew] for you the Covenant of the [everlasting] priesthood; may He sanctify you [for the House] of Holiness" (1QSb 3, 25ff.).

"May you be as an Angel of the Presence in the Abode of Holiness to the glory of the God of [hosts]... May you attend upon the service in the Temple of the Kingdom... in common council [with the Holy Ones] for everlasting ages..." (1QSb 4, 25ff).

These passages express a similar interesting relationship between heaven and earth typical of the mystical liturgy of the community. 1QSb is, however, a writing most probably describing a future messianic age. Thus the High Priest is evidently said to attend a heavenly liturgy in the heavenly palace "of the Kingdom".

This leads to another topic of discussion concerning the figure of Melchizedek in 11QMelch. Scholars have usually identified this character as the Archangel Michael. Even though the figure evidently has angelic characteristics, we must not forget that in the Old Testament Melchizedek is a priestly figure, as he is in the New Testament, too. If the theology of the 4Q491 fragment is somehow related to that of 11QMelch., it would be logical to find the priestly interpretation in the latter, too.[61]

In conclusion we may state that 4Q491 does not describe any deification of a human being. As Collins has noted, "The primary interest of this fragment does not lie in the specific identification of the speaker, which can never be certain, but in the notion of a human figure enthroned in heaven, in a Jewish context."[62] The one who "takes his seat" in the heavens is described in a similar way to the messianic High Priest of the Qumran community. At the end of days he will sit enthroned in the holy congregation – in like manner as the enthroned patriarchs according to other apocalyptic Jewish writings from the Second Temple period.

The ascension of the Messiah. The idea of the exaltation of the Messiah is expressed in different ways in different fragments. There are several fragments which speak of the enthronement of the Davidide. They are obviously eschatological, but the idea of a heavenly enthronement is not so evident in these texts. Among the *pesharim* we have e.g. the Isaiah Pesher (4Q161), which is an eschatological interpretation of the prophecy of Isaiah concerning

---

[60] So Hengel, *Studies*, 203; also n. 199.

[61] We shall return to this question in chapter 4 below.

[62] Collins, *Scepter*, 149.

the "shoot" of David.[63] In 4Q161 Isa 11:1-5 is quoted, followed by an interpretation. The idea of a throne is introduced when the power of the Davidic Messiah is described (Frags. 8-10, col. III, 18-21, Vermes):

"[Interpreted, this concerns the Branch] of David who shall arise at the end [of days]... God will uphold him with [the spirit of might, and will give him] a throne of glory and a crown of [holiness]... [He will put a sceptre] in his hand and he shall rule over all the [nations]."

This fragment exploits the rather traditional belief that the Davidide shall rule over nations in the end of days.[64] The Isaiah passage is interpreted as a promise of the enthronement of the Messiah. This does not, however, necessarily mean a heavenly enthronement of the Davidide. Even though the text is eschatological in nature, it does not explicitly speak of the final judgment which the Davidide would execute.[65] The granting of the throne of glory is rather a reference to the coronation day, in the manner of Psalm 110. The conception of the Messianic figure in this fragment is thus similar to the idea of a political Messiah appearing in other Qumran writings. He is an earthly king who would lead Israel to a glorious future.

Such a belief can be found in 4Q285, where the Book of Isaiah is once again interpreted (Isa 10:34-11:1). Here the Davidide is called the Prince of the Congregation, and it is believed that he will destroy his enemies.[66] He is an eschatological prince who will renew the covenant and establish a new kingdom (cf. 1QSb 5, 20ff.). No reference to a heavenly reality is made in this context.[67] The same is true of the Genesis Pesher 4Q252 on Gen. 49:10. In this fragment the awaited Davidide is evidently a political Messiah who is expected to fulfil the political hopes invested in the family of David.[68]

There is also some similarity with e.g. the Messianic Apocalypse (4Q521). The fragment is so corrupt, however, that it is impossible to reach solid conclusions concerning its content. Instead of describing the enthronement of the Davidide the fragment speaks of the glorification of the pious: "And He will glorify the pious on the throne of the eternal Kingdom" (fr. 2,7).

In Florilegium, 4Q174, frags. 1-3, col. I,10-11 there is a Messianic

---

[63] For a general introduction to 4Q161, see van der Woude, *Messianischen Vorstellungen*, 175ff.; VanderKam, *Community*, 216ff.

[64] Cf. Schiffman, *Messiah*, 124.

[65] This was the interpretation by van der Woude. He thought that the Messianic figure would necessarily be exalted in the office of an eschatological judge; van der Woude, *Messianischen Vorstellungen*, 182.

[66] For the details of the corrupted text, see e.g. VanderKam, *Community*, 219.

[67] Cf. Chester, *Paulus*, 24ff.

[68] Thus Laato, *Star*, 294f., VanderKam, *Community*, 217.

interpretation of the traditional key text for the Davidic dynasty, i.e. 2 Sam. 7:12-14. It is exceptional as regards one interesting detail. The exaltation of the Davidide is expressed by using the metaphor of the throne: "I will raise up your seed after you and establish the throne of his kingdom forever... This (refers to the) 'branch of David', who will arise with the Interpreter of the Law..." In this passage, however, we find only the symbol of the throne. There is no mention of an ascension, and the description remains in the sphere of political messianism.[69]

Our survey of the Dead Sea Scrolls shows that the Qumran writings probably contain the most interesting features of early merkabah mysticism in the pre-Christian period. The so called ascent structure is evident in several writings. Texts expressing heavenly worship before the throne of glory open a whole new area of theology before us. Enthronement passages, however, do not appear to exploit the ascent structure in their interpretation. An enthronement discourse seems to be important, but it is applied in the sense of political messianology. The idea of a heavenly enthronement is not attached to the figure of the Davidide. The Qumran writings do know, however, the concept of a heavenly enthronement, as the interesting fragment 4Q491 shows.

The Qumran writings also appear to be dependent on the royal metaphors found in the Old Testament. Their appearance in several different literary genres indicates that the symbolic universe of the Second Temple period was quite influential. Jewish theology centred on fixed metaphors, and they also maintained traditions. Most Qumranic interpretations are very conservative and reveal the same intention as do the books of the Old Testament.

e. The Exagoge of Ezekiel

The Exagoge ("Exodus") of Ezekiel the Dramatist is a drama based on the biblical story of the Exodus. Fragments of the writing are known to us, as they are quoted by Alexander Polyhistor and preserved by Eusebius. The writing derives most probably from the second century B.C. Its origin seems to be in Hellenistic Judaism.[70]

In the Exagoge of Ezekiel the main character is naturally Moses. The writer relates his story, exploiting some extra-canonical midrashic and haggadic traditions. Before the story of the burning bush he adds a unique section of

---

[69] Schiffman, *Messiah*, 125; Laato, *Star*, 297.

[70] On the questions of dating and provenance, see Holladay, *Fragments*, 301ff. The remains of the writing have been preserved in seventeen separate excerpts in Eusebius' *Preparatio Evangelica*, Book IX, 28-29. A useful commentary is provided by Jacobson, *The Exagoge of Ezekiel;* on introductory questions see pp. 5ff.

Moses' vision in the wilderness.[71] Considering the story of Moses, it is only natural that the vision begins with the mountain theme. The throne is evidently the throne of God and it is located at Sinai, as it is in the Book of Jubilees.[72]

"I dreamt there was on the summit of Mount Sinai
A certain great throne (θρόνον μέγαν)
extending up to heaven's cleft,
On which there sat a certain noble man" (frag. 6, lines 8-10).

As regards Moses' vision of God, the theophany at Sinai probably serves here as a starting-point: "and they saw the God of Israel. Under his feet there was something like a pavement of sapphire stone" (Ex. 24:10). No actual dream of Moses is described in the Torah. So there was still room for some kind of vision. Pious imagination easily filled such a gap. In 2 Baruch 59 there is a hint of the heavenly journey of Moses at Sinai: "the heavens which are under the throne of the Mighty One were severely shaken when he took Moses with him. For he showed him many warnings together with the ways of the Law and the end of time" (2 Bar. 59:3-4). This scene then proceeds as an apocalyptic vision. According to Pseudo-Philo, there was an apocalyptic vision at Mount Sinai. God "commanded him many things and showed him the tree of life" (Ps.-Philo 11:15).

In the Exagoge of Ezekiel Moses is naturally not yet placed at Mount Sinai, but only dreams about it. Thus there may be other sources of influence behind the description. A vision of such a lofty throne reaching up to heaven may well be a reminiscence of the vision of Isaiah. On the throne Moses sees someone who resembles a man. This anthropomorphic theophany (ἐν τῷ καθῆσθαι φῶτα γενναῖόν τινα) is one of the features that connect this vision with Daniel 7.[73]

The enthroned one gives Moses a sceptre and invites him to sit on the throne. Moses is also given a diadem, and as he sits on the throne he is shown all the world and the stars under his feet.

"He gave me the sceptre and told me to sit on the great throne.
He gave me the royal crown and he himself left the throne.
I beheld the entire circled earth both beneath the earth
and above the heaven, and a host of stars fell on its knees before me"
(frag. 6, lines 15-19).

---

[71] This story is unique and there are no hints of it in other literature, such as Philo's Vit.Mos.

[72] For the discussion concerning the throne, see e.g. Jacobson, *ICS* 6 (1981) 288; Holladay, *Fragments*, 443f.

[73] Against Jacobson, *ICS* 6 (1981) 278, according to whom φώς means "man", not "God". Anthropomorphic theophany, however, is a commonplace in Jewish apocalyptic. See Hengel, *Le Trône*, 166.

This is an early example of the exploitation of the theme of the enthronement of a patriarch (cf. 4Q491; 1 Enoch 51:3 etc.). Later Jewish writings contain a rich tradition on this theme, and it is applied to several individuals from Adam and Abel to Isaiah and the righteous of Israel.[74]

The story of the dream of Moses is, in a sense, a re-working of the dream of Joseph (Gen 37:9). The stars bow down to Moses as they bowed down to Joseph. Here the stars serve as a metaphor for the nations. The same metaphor is used in Gen. 26:4, where it is promised that the offspring of Abraham will be "as numerous as the stars of heaven", and the people of Israel would have a leading role among "all the nations of the earth". In the Exodus of Ezekiel all nations fall under the rule of Moses (cf. Ex. 32:13; Ps. 146:4 LXX).

In the next scene Moses' father-in-law interprets the dream to him. This interpretation is important for the understanding of the basic purpose of the vision.

"O Friend, that which God has signified to you is good; Might I live until the time when these things happen to you. Then you will raise up a great throne. And it is you who will judge and lead humankind." (frag.7, lines 3-7).[75]

Even though the idea of Moses' enthronement is somewhat symbolic, expressing the unique status of Moses in human history, it is not used as a simple metaphor here. The scene is too apocalyptic to allow merely an earthly interpretation. Moses will be given a great throne and he will be a judge and a leader of the whole of humankind. This must refer to Moses' heavenly status.[76] Furthermore, Moses' cosmic panorama is interpreted as implying his omniscience: "So will you see things present, past, and future" (frag. 7, line 9).[77] One key to the explanation of this section is the theme of heavenly judges.

---

[74] Jacobson suggests that the enthronement tradition might be dependent on Psalm 110:1. Both of these passages continue "with the transmission of the sceptre and the prophecy of future domination." Jacobson, *The Exagoge of Ezekiel*, 90. Such influence is possible, but the tradition of the enthronement of the patriarchs better explains the description.

[75] The verb ἐξανίστημι may be understood either as 'raise up' or 'remove' and even 'overthrow'. See Holladay, *Fragments*, 447. I here follow Jacobson, who chooses the first of these options, Jacobson, *The Exagoge of Ezekiel*, 93. The context, with a description of the transmission of throne and sceptre to Moses, refers to the establishing of the throne.

[76] For later traditions of the enthronement of Moses in rabbinic writings, see Meeks, *Essays*, 357ff.

[77] For Holladay this is a signal of the influence of "mantic imagery". Moses is described as a prophet. Holladay, *Fragments*, 450f. This is too narrow an interpretation, even from the apocalyptic point of view. Thus van der Horst is right in commenting that the mere prophetic function fails to do justice to several elements in the dream-vision, van der Horst, *Essays*, 70.

According to Daniel, the judgment "was given for the holy ones of the Most High" (Dan. 7:22). In the Book of Zechariah the high priest Joshua is promised a heavenly reign: "If you will walk in my ways and keep my requirements, then you shall rule my house and have charge of my courts" (Zech. 3:7). In sapiential theology we find a similar conviction, now applied to all righteous ones. According to the Wisdom of Solomon, the destiny of the righteous is great: "They will govern nations and rule over peoples" (SapSol. 3:8). According to the Sibyllines, the prophets "are judges of men and righteous kings" in the eschatological kingdom (Sib. 3:781-782). The "elect" of Qumran also anticipated such a future destiny: "by means of his chosen ones God will judge all the nations" (1QpHab. V, 4). In the New Testament this is a standard belief (Matt. 19:28; Lk. 22:30; 1 Cor. 6:2; Rev. 20:4).

On the grounds of such evident relations to apocalyptic literature we are justified in concluding that the Exagoge of Ezekiel presents an early example of the enthronement theme. Moses is promised an enthronement in the future. He is a prototype of a righteous patriarch who will be installed as a judge on the throne of glory. He will "govern nations and rule over peoples". This is what sapiential theology had taught at roughly the same period.

But what of the enthronement itself? The cosmic scene has raised interesting questions concerning the nature of Moses. Are we here witnessing the deification of Moses, as van der Horst has suggested?[78]

It is true that the nature of Moses has been a subject of speculation in Hellenistic Judaism. Philo called Moses "god" in his relation to Pharaoh (*VitMos.* I, 155-159). This was based on certain Old Testament passages (Ex. 4:16 and 7:1 LXX). This, however, as Williamson has put it, never threatened Philo's monotheistic conviction.[79] The ascribing of the divine name to a heavenly figure is, however, not unique in Jewish apocalyptic. In the Apocalypse of Abraham, for example, we find an angel "in whom God's name resides", i.e. Jaoel.[80] It seems that in Jewish thought the divine name can also be used as an honorary title which does not refer to deification.

This is even more true of Qumranic angelology. As Newsome has noted, the Songs of the Sabbath Sacrifice contain the two expressions angelic *elim* and angelic *elohim*.[81] The divine epithet for special angels at the summit of the angelic hierarchy is most clearly ascribed to the "angelic spirits" that are associated with the heavenly sanctuary: "The spirits of the holy of holies, the

---

[78] van der Horst, *Essays*, 67.

[79] Williamson, *Philo*, 117f.

[80] Cf. also 3 En. 48D:1.

[81] Newsom, *Songs*, 23f. Cf. also the analysis of Qumran texts above.

living gods, the spirits of everlasting holiness above all the holy ones" (4Q403 1i, 44).[82]

In the Exagoge of Ezekiel Moses also seems to be merely an enthroned righteous man who is installed as a judge in heaven. Ezekiel is not referring to Exodus 4:16 or 7:1.[83] Moses' status no doubt seems to be extraordinary and universal. His enthronement does not defile monotheistic theocracy, however. Quite the contrary, Moses is here an archetype of several similar enthroned judges who are mentioned in later Jewish writings, such as TJob, TIsaac and AscIsa.[84]

This leads finally to one important conclusion. We must be cautious not to identify enthronement with deification. An exalted servant of God is often installed in a high position in heaven, but there is a strict hierarchy. The enthronement theme in Jewish theology certainly expresses the hierarchy that prevails in heaven and the hierarchy that prevails on earth, but in no way can it be interpreted as posing a threat to traditional theocracy.[85]

In sum, the employment of Old Testament metaphors and royal imagery in pre-Christian Second Temple Judaism has certain common features. The use of tradition is rather conservative. Even though old metaphors appear in apocalyptic visions, they are exploited in a rather traditional manner. The seers usually have a prophetic mission and the vision serves that purpose. What is also typical of these visions and of the sight of God's throne is that the setting is often cultic. This feature confirms that pre-Christian Jewish mysticism seems to be completely dependent on the central premises of Old Testament beliefs.

Royal metaphors guarantee continuity between the past and the present. An ascent structure may be detected behind several descriptions. In some cases, at least as regards 4Q491, enthronement discourse is applied to this pattern. Traditional messianology, however, is never presented in terms of the ascent structure. Therefore, in pre-Christian writings, the concept of Messiah is not yet associated with the idea of a heavenly throne.

---

[82] Cf. the comments of Newsom concerning line 44 in Newsom, *Songs*, 223.

[83] Hengel, *Studies*, 191.

[84] This is what Jacobson fails to recognize, as he maintains that there is actually a "conscious rejection on Ezekiel's part" of the legend of the ascension and enthronement of Moses. Jacobson, *ICS 6* (1981) 277-278.

[85] Holladay resolves the disagreement of van der Horst and Jacobson as follows: "If this scene is interpreted as an elevation of Moses to divine status, it should be balanced with God's reminder to Moses later in the poem that he is θνητός (Frg. 9, line 8 = v 102)". Holladay, *Fragments*, 438.

3.3. Thrones and enthronements in the literature of the Common Era

In Jewish literature from the Common Era the cultic aspect diminishes in apocalyptic descriptions, and the descriptions of heavenly ascent are more often associated with the enthronement theme. Works dated to the Common Era have some peculiar features of their own. Most of the extant Jewish writings from this period have been preserved by the Christian Church. This reveals an interesting relationship between Judaism and Christianity. Some of the writings examined below have undergone Christian redaction and even rewriting. There also exists literature reflecting post-70 attitudes following the destruction of the Temple.

a. Similitudes (1 Enoch 37-71)

One of the main figures in the "divine agency" interpretation is the Son of Man or the Elect One of 1 Enoch. This is a character who acts in heaven and who is also granted an enthronement. He is also a heavenly judge, and as an eschatological figure he exercises a significant function in the final judgment of the earth. Similitudes is generally regarded as a Jewish work, even though some scholars claim to find Christian influence in it.[86]

The Similitudes shows several features of the merkabah tradition. We find both a description of a heavenly journey and several throne visions describing an enthronement. For example, in chapter 45 the Elect One is enthroned on the throne of glory: "On that day, my Elect One shall sit on the seat of glory and make a selection of their deeds" (45:3). He is an eschatological judge, and his position seems to be extraordinary. The identification of such a figure is not an easy matter, however.

It is true that in the next chapter the Elect One is most probably described as the Son of Man, and an angelomorphic description is given of him. "His countenance was full of grace like that of one among the holy angels" (46:1). The character himself, however, remains completely human. He is identified as "the One who was born of human beings" (46:2).[87] Therefore, in this text, he is not an angelic figure. He is rather a hero like the exalted patriarchs. Like the

---

[86] See Hengel, *Studies*, 185f. On the other hand, e.g. Segal considers Similitudes a post-Christian work that should probably be seen as a Christian document. Segal, *ANRW II 23.2.* (1980) 1377f. In his analysis, however, he does not define specific Christian features or base his interpretation on them. On the grounds of internal evidence Nickelsburg considers Similitudes a Jewish work, dating it to "around the turn of the era." Nickelsburg, *Jewish Literature*, 223.

[87] Fletcher-Louis, in his angelomorphic/angelic interpretation, concludes that the figure "transcends earthly categories". Fletcher-Louis, *Angels*, 150. This, however, is an overstatement. In Jewish apocalyptic there are several human figures who are placed high in the heavenly hierarchy.

patriarchs, he too will be exalted on a heavenly throne and act as a judge in the end of days.

The eschatological aspect is emphasized in chapter 51. Here the enthronement of the Elect One is described as an eschatological entrée. After the resurrection of the dead the Elect One as a heavenly judge will separate the righteous ones from sinners.

"In those days, Sheol will return all the deposits which she had received and hell give back all that which it owes. And he shall choose the righteous and the holy ones from among (the risen dead), for the day when they shall be selected and saved has arrived. In those days, (the Elect One) shall sit on my throne, and from the conscience of his mouth shall come out all the secrets of wisdom, for the Lord of the Spirits has given them to him and glorified him" (51:1-3).

This scene seems to be a reminiscence of Daniel 7. The Elect One is a figure who is not obviously an ordinary human being, and his identity seems to be messianic.[88] But even here the analysis of earlier Jewish writings has tempered enthusiasm for these texts. The heroic figure in the Similitudes does not differ very much from Moses in the Exagoge of Ezekiel, or from the righteous Jew in 4Q491. His enthronement is a majestic one, as is to be expected. God even announces that he shall sit on "my" divine throne. We are further told that God is the Lord of the Spirits. This probably means that the Lord is worshipped by his creatures and the cherubim in heaven.

But what of the messianic nature of the passage? Hurtado suggests that the association of this figure with God's throne is similar to the conception of the Davidic king in some Old Testament passages.[89] There is some evidence to support such a conclusion. It is possible that the Davidide who sits "on the throne of the Lord" is like Solomon, who was described in the same terms (1 Chron. 29:23). In Sirach 47 David is praised in a similar manner: "The Lord took away his sins, and exalted his power forever, he gave him a covenant of kingship and a glorious throne (καὶ θρόνον δόξης) in Israel" (Sir. 47:11). It is obvious that in Similitudes the titles the 'Elect One', the 'Son of Man', the 'Righteous One' and 'Messiah' are related.[90]

Does this mean that as a king, and even as a heavenly king, the Messiah, the Elect One is a Davidide who has been given universal rule? At Qumran we find the idea of the eschatological enthronement of the Davidide. The description of Daniel 7 may be in line with this tradition. One should be rather

---

[88] Stone emphasizes this background: "The origins of the figure doubtless lie largely in exegesis of Dan 7, as well as in existing traditions of expectation of a cosmic redeemer." Stone, *Jewish Writings*, 402.

[89] Hurtado, *One God*, 53f.

[90] See Hengel, *Studies*, 185.

cautious, however, when identifying the figure on the throne.[91] Even if the exalted one is not actually Enoch himself (see below, and 1 En. 71:14-17), he is more likely to be an enthroned patriarch like Moses or Abraham than a "divine" agent.[92] An angelic interpretation has also been suggested, but there is no evidence for this in the texts themselves.[93]

The passage in 1 En. 51 is also special because of the occurrence of the theme of resurrection. The judgment of the Elect One will take place after the resurrection, and in this way the righteous will be separated from the wicked. Through resurrection the holy ones will attain salvation. With an interest in New Testament Christology one is naturally eager to investigate the relation of the Elect One to the resurrection. In this matter nothing new is introduced. 1 Enoch does not state that the enthronement of the Elect One will take place in his resurrection. In this respect the passage reveals no Christian influence but relies on Jewish tradition and especially on that of Daniel 7.[94]

Later in 55:4 the act of enthronement is referred to again. Here the "sapiential" feature is prominent, and the Elect One is installed as a judge. "Kings, potentates, dwellers upon the earth: You would have to see my Elect One, how he sits on the throne of glory and judges Azaz'el and all his company, and his army, in the name of the Lord of the Spirits!" This message is repeated in 61:8: "He placed the Elect One on the throne of glory; and he shall judge all the works of the holy ones in heaven above, weighing their deeds in the balance." In both of these passages the throne is a throne of glory, which is obviously the throne of God. In the latter passage the Elect One

---

[91] Hurtado is perhaps a little too optimistic when he states that the Similitudes blend together features of the manlike figure from Daniel, the "Servant" of Isaiah 40-55, and the Davidic Messiah. Hurtado, *One God*, 54. The features of a royal enthronement are not to be denied, however. In addition, Collins has remarked that the identity of the Son of Man figure does not depend entirely on its association with Daniel. It must be connected with the figure of the Chosen One, and even with the Righteous One of 38:2 and 53:6. Collins, *Apocalyptic Imagination*, 148.

[92] Bock claims that the Son of Man is a highly exalted figure, given "almost unprecedented authority." Bock, *Blasphemy*, 126. It is noteworthy, though, that in this respect the figure does not differ essentially from the exalted patriarchs. They too are presented as enthroned judges in heaven.

[93] Newman suggests that the concept of glory might refer to the appearance of an angel. Glory "marks the throne as a divine possession", and God shares this honour "with his special, chosen angel." Newman, *Glory-Christology*, 88. There is no reference to an angel in the text, however.

[94] It is true that the characteristic functions of such a figure "extend beyond those normally attributed to the Davidic Messiah", as Stone has noted; Stone, *Jewish Writings*, 402. The remaining differences with respect to Christological descriptions are remarkable, however.

judges "the works of the holy ones". It is somewhat striking that they too need to be judged and not only the unbelieving world below.[95]

1 Enoch 62 is a great description of the last judgment, and it opens with a scene where God sits upon the throne of glory.

"The Lord of the Spirits has sat down on the throne of his glory, and the spirit of righteousness has been poured out upon him. The word of his mouth will slay sinners; and all oppressors shall be eliminated from before his face" (62:2).

It is necessary to note that in analyzing an eschatological description we must discern between an enthronement and sitting upon a throne for the execution of judgement. In Enoch 62 we see an eschatological entrée. God assumes the role of judge and sits down "on the throne of his glory". This does not, of course, indicate his enthronement. We should interpret "sitting on the throne" in New Testament eschatology in a similar way. In the mind of the writers the phrase in question does not necessarily mean the "enthronement" of Christ, but rather the inauguration of the judgment. This is a rather important observation for our later evaluation of the nature of early Christian eschatology.

The Son of Man too is sitting on the throne: "and pain shall seize them when they see that Son of Man sitting on the throne of his glory" (1 En. 62:5b; cf. Matth. 24:30). Even though we find a parallel to this in Jesus' words, we must resist the temptation to conclude hastily that here we have an interpolation. In Matthew 24 "pain" is expressed by wailing when the Son of Man appears. The Son of Man comes on a cloud, though, not sitting "on the throne of his glory" as in Similitudes. This is evidence for the conclusion that this is not a direct quotation. Therefore it is probable that the statement in the Similitudes is independent – and Jewish. There is nothing in this statement that a Jew could not say based on the Enochic tradition.

The similarities with the New Testament are striking in many respects, but it is not necessary to posit a direct causal relation. In the soteriological section salvation is described in a way that is well known e.g. from Qumran.[96]

"The righteous and elect ones shall be saved on that day; and thenceforth they shall never see the faces of the sinners and the oppressors. The Lord of the Spirits will abide over them; they shall eat and rest and rise with that Son of Man for ever and ever" (1 En. 62:13-14).

In the Similitudes we even find a similar messianic banquet to the one that forms the highlight of the eschatology of Qumran (1QSa, II). According to the Similitudes, those who attain salvation are the "elect ones", and this is what

---

[95] According to Bock, these texts present the main figure as an eschatological judge. Therefore, the image is that "of a shared judgment". Bock, *Blasphemy*, 126.

[96] Cf. chapter 3.2.b. above.

they are called at Qumran, too. Why, then, is the Son of Man figure connected with this kind of soteriology? It is probable that in the Enochic tradition the Son of Man was identified with the Davidic Messiah through Daniel 7. At Qumran it is the Davidic Messiah who conducts the messianic banquet on the day of salvation.

This speculation is important since it suggests that the Son of Man eschatology of the Similitudes is an independent tradition and not one dependent on the New Testament.[97] In this case, too, the throne visions concerning the Son of Man may be authentic and independent.

In the Similitudes we also find a perfect description of a heavenly journey and a *merkabah* vision. The introduction is traditional: "And the angel Michael, one of the archangels, seizing me by my right hand and lifting me up, led me out into all the secrets of mercy..." (71:3). In heaven Enoch sees the throne of glory. The story repeats the features of the vision in 1 Enoch 14.

"He carried off my spirit, and I, Enoch, was in the heaven of heavens. There I saw – in the midst of that light – a structure built of crystals; and between those crystals tongues of living fire... Moreover, seraphim, cherubim, and ophanim – the sleepless ones who guard the throne of his glory – also encircled it" (71:5-7).

The heavenly court is further described exploiting the traditions of Daniel 7: "With them is the Antecedent of Time: His head is white and pure like wool and his garment is indescribable" (71:10).

Some scholars have concluded that in this chapter Enoch himself is identified as the Son of Man. This common hypothesis is well expounded by Alexander, who speaks of a metamorphosis in the Books of Enoch. "Enoch is exalted to the heaven of heavens and by some mysterious process ends up as the Son of man (1 En. 71:14). This may perhaps be compared with the metamorphosis of Enoch into the archangel Metatron in 3 Enoch 3-15."[98]

Such a conclusion is not necessary, however, if we read the passage carefully. Chapter 71 does not give a description of an enthronement but speaks of a heavenly journey. It is explicitly said that it is the spirit of Enoch that ascends to heaven. Enoch is called a 'son of man', a human being, in verse 14,[99] but here a different word is used from that in the expression 'Son of Man' elsewhere.

---

[97] Cf. Nickelsburg, *Jewish Literature*, 215, 222.

[98] Alexander, *OTP I*, 247. For the basic arguments in support of such a view, see Sjöberg, *Menschensohn*, 159-172. The position is accepted e.g. by Hurtado, *One God*, 54, and Bock, *Blasphemy*, 125f. According to Gieschen, Enoch is transformed into an exalted angel. Gieschen, *Christology*, 156.

[99] This is noted in the OTP translation by using small letters in the former expression. See the comments of Isaac in *OTP I*, 50, n. *s*.

In chapter 71 Enoch is finally described as a pious servant of God, "upon whom righteousness has dwelt", and therefore his future life and salvation is secured. He is granted new life in the kingdom of the Son of Man in heaven (71:17).[100]

In sum, the Enochic traditions in Similitudes are very interesting. The scene of the section is similar to that of the Book of the Watchers, but several details are quite different. The theocratic ideal is confirmed and God's heavenly throne is still the centre of history. The setting, however, is no longer cultic. The key character in these chapters is "the Elect One" who is enthroned on the throne of glory. He is further described as the embodiment of wisdom and a ruler who reigns in glory. Even though his identification is not completely clear, royal features are on several occasions visible.

b. Philo

As Segal has stated, it is typical of Philo to allegorize the mind of human beings as the likeness of god. Therefore, by "the power of the mind, man ascends, first to the atmosphere then to the heavens." Such an interpretation of the ascension is evident, for example, in Philo's commentary on Genesis 1:26.[101]

Furthermore, Philo refers to the mystical ascension of certain patriarchs, such as Abraham and Jacob and Moses, as well as Melchizedek and Levi. There are two ways that lead to such an ascension. One of them belongs within the sphere of Philo's concept of "the power of the mind". The other takes place "without the co-operation of any reasoning process."

> "These no doubt are truly admirable persons and superior to the other classes. They have, as I said, advanced from down to up by a sort of heavenly ladder and by reason and reflection happily inferred the creator from his works. But those, if such there be, who have had the power to apprehend Him through Himself without the co-operation of any reasoning process to lead them to the sight, must be recorded as holy and genuine worshippers and friends of God in truth. In their company is he who in the Hebrew is called Israel but in our tongue, the God-seer who sees not His real nature, for that, as I said, is impossible – but that He is."[102]

According to Philo, Moses occupies a special place in the history of Israel. Moses is the chief model of a heavenly ascension. When Moses ascended Mount Sinai, he had a vision of God. Philo's description is not, however, a traditional ascension story, but expresses the allegorized ascension of a soul, as Philo writes elsewhere.

---

[100] Collins, *NTS* 38 (1992) 454, makes a clear distinction between Enoch and the Son of Man in 1 En. 71.

[101] See Segal, *ANRW* II 23.2. (1980) 1357.

[102] *De Praemiis et poenis,* 43f. (Loeb edition VIII, 337).

"Ex. 24. 12a: What is the meaning of the words, "Come up to me to the mountain and be there?" This signifies that a holy soul is divinized by ascending not to the air or to the ether or to heaven (which is) higher than all but to (a region) above the heavens. And beyond the world there is no place but God. And He determines the stability of the removal by saying "be there" (thus) demonstrating the placelessness and the unchanging habitation of the divine palace. For those who have a quickly satiated passion for reflexion fly upward for only a short distance under divine inspiration and then they immediately return. They do not fly so much as they are drawn downwards, I mean, to the depths of Tartarus. But those who do not return from the holy and divine city, to which they have migrated, have God as their chief leader in the migration."[103]

We do not find in Philo any description of an enthronement like the one in the Exagoge of Ezekiel. For him, Moses is not the prototype of a righteous patriarch who is installed as a judge on the throne of glory. Moses' vision apparently has the nature of the ascension of a soul. The allegorical nature of the description also plays down the idea of the "divinization" of the soul in ascension. An actual, ontological deification of Moses is not at issue.

It is true that Philo called Moses "god" in relation to Pharaoh (*VitMos.* I, 155-159), as we noted above, but this never threatened his monotheistic convictions. Moses was a truly God-inspired soul and a sinless "divine" man, even in a somewhat "docetic" way but, nevertheless, a human being.[104] Scholars are, however, divided as to whether Philo really meant the deification of Moses, at least to some extent.[105]

Philo was not interested in enthronement traditions, but he did pay some attention to the ark as the throne of God. He exploits or even invents a special cultic discourse. In *Vita Mosis* he speculated on the cherubim that stood above the ark. Philo gave an allegorical interpretation of these creatures.

"I should myself say that they are allegorical representations of the two most august and highest potencies of Him that is, the creative and the kingly. His creative potency is called God, because through it He placed and made and ordered this universe, and the kingly is called Lord (ἡ δὲ βασιλικὴ κύριος), being that with which He governs what has come into being and rules it steadfastly with justice" (Vit.Mos. II, 99-100.).

---

[103] *Questions on Exodus,* 40, (Loeb edition, Supplement II, 82).

[104] Meeks maintains, however, that such an analogy "approaches consubstantiality", Meeks, *The Prophet-King,* 104f. He speaks further of a "cluster of traditions" of Moses' heavenly enthronement, and ascribes the aspect of deification to the "usual" Hellenistic conception of the "divine man". Meeks, *Essays,* 370f. I believe that arguing for such a causality (without clear evidence) is no longer so "usual".

[105] For example, Hurtado, who is inclined to interpret several works in accordance with the divine agency theory. accepts the idea only with reservations. He thinks that the language of divinity was applied to Moses "the paradigmatic leader" only in an ethicized sense, and that this was governed by Philo's fundamental refusal to attribute real divinity to any human being. Hurtado, *One God.* 63.

There are two special features in this interpretation. The kingly power of God is considered to be the basic signification of the cherub-throne. Furthermore, 'Lord' is used as a royal title. All this emphasizes the significance of the throne ideology in Jewish theology.

Chester has further suggested that Philo employed certain "mediatorial concepts" in his theology. The most prominent of these is Logos. Philo no doubt made use of developed Jewish angelological traditions in his thinking. He calls the Logos "archangel" and thus gives it "an extremely elevated status in the heavenly realm."[106]

"But if there be any as yet unfit to be called a Son of God, let him press to take his place under God's First-born, the Word (Logos), who holds the eldership among the angels, their ruler (archangel) as it were. And many names are his, for he is called 'the Beginning,' and the Name of God, and His Word (Logos), and the Man after His image, and 'he that sees,' that is Israel."[107]

This passage contains several interesting features, such as the identification of Logos the archangel as the Name of God and "he that sees" (Israel).[108] This confirms the fact that angelic beings enjoyed a special status in Jewish mysticism. In Philo's case, however, the statements are always directed by the allegorical interpretation. Therefore his freedom in seeing connections is unparalleled. The negative point is unfortunately that this also diminishes the possibility of using Philo as an example of a wider tradition of interpretation. What is important, however, is that Philo does not present these ideas in the context of any special ascent structure. There is no mention of any enthronement either.

Even though Philo's writings employ the allegorical method and he often emphasizes the sphere of "the power of the mind" or the ascension of the soul, his theology reveals a dependency on several themes in Jewish apocalyptic. In this sense too his works confirm the fact that several themes of early merkabah mysticism were known in Jewish communities in New Testament times. Special attention should be paid to the "allegorical representations of the two most august and highest potencies", i.e. Philo's interpretation of the cherub-throne.

c. The Fourth Book of Ezra

The Fourth Book of Ezra comes from the period after the fall of Jerusalem, and is a good representative of the Jewish theology of crisis in the first century

---

[106] Chester, *Paulus*, 48.

[107] *De Confusione Linguarum*, 146.

[108] In the Prayer of Joseph we find also the tradition where Israel, "a man seeing God", is an archangel, PrJos. A, 2-3.

C.E. As is well known, this apocalypse is one of the main sources that discuss the problem of theodicy. The problem of theodicy has already appeared several times in our analysis of apocalyptic writings and we are to see many more examples below. It often provides a basic context for apocalyptic speculation. This has not so much to do with the ascent structure itself, but it is rather dependent on the fact that most of these writings attempt to provide a solution to the theology of crisis which is typical of the theology of the Chosen People in the Second Temple period and also after the destruction of the Temple.[109]

4 Ezra contains speculation that is typical of this theological tradition. The fear that God might abandon Israel brings up the problem of theodicy. Is God unable to help his people, or has he rejected them? The writer shows no unbelief. He remains humbly before his God. In this respect we meet the traditional conception of God the King in 4 Ezra. God rules and he is able to help his own. The problem in question is to be found elsewhere.

For example, the prayer of Ezra in chapter 8 begins with praise of the heavenly God who sits on his throne of glory:

"He said, 'O Lord who inhabits eternity, whose eyes are exalted and whose upper chambers are in the air, whose throne is beyond measure and whose glory is beyond comprehension, before whom the hosts of angels stand trembling and at whose command they are changed to wind and fire, whose word is sure and whose utterances are certain, whose ordinance is strong and whose command is terrible, whose look dries up the depths and whose indignation makes the mountains melt away, and whose truth is established forever – hear, O Lord, the prayer of your servant" (8:20-25).

The setting of this prayer is devotional, cultic and transcendent. In this respect it repeats the traditional conceptions of both Temple piety and apocalyptic mysticism. Ezra exploits the visionary tradition of the prophets. The throne is "beyond measure," and it is also the throne of glory. It is also probable that with his prayer Ezra joins in the heavenly worship before the throne.

The ascent structure differs from that of other apocalypses to some degree. As the burning question of the work concerns the fate of souls after death, the writer states that everyone is rewarded according to his actions on earth. When the soul departs from the body, it either wanders without rest or goes to God.

The righteous who have kept "the Law of the Lawgiver perfectly" shall see "with great joy the glory of him who receives them" (7:89-91). The writer does not mention a special heavenly journey, but the idea of the ascension of the soul to God implies such a structure.[110] This, however, is almost all that is

---

[109] I have studied the Jewish theology of crisis and the problem of theodicy elsewhere; see Eskola, *Theodicy*, 29ff.; comments on 4 Ezra, pp. 69ff.

[110] Cf. Segal, *ANRW II 23.2.* (1980) 1366.

said of the ascension. There are seven "orders" of salvation described in 4 Ezra 7, and in accordance with them saved souls "are to be made like the light of the stars, being incorruptible from then on" (7:97).

The throne of God in 4 Ezra is also an eschatological throne of judgment: "And the Most High shall be revealed upon the seat of judgment, and compassion shall pass away... judgment alone shall remain" (7:33-34). Souls are judged in the eschatological climax. An interesting feature in this event is that, according to chapter 12, the Davidic Messiah will join God in that judgment: "he will set them living before his judgment seat, and when he has reproved them, then he will destroy them" (12:32-33).

Here again we meet the eschatological act of sitting upon the throne of judgment for the last judgment. The setting is similar to that of the Similitudes of 1 Enoch. The judgment will take place after the general resurrection. In 4 Ezra the salvation of the righteous ones is also connected with the resurrection, i.e. with the event in which "the treasure of immortality is made manifest".[111] The enthronement of the Messiah, however, is not linked with his own resurrection. Such a theme appears to be absent from Jewish apocalyptic.

The ascent structure in 4 Ezra differs somewhat from other descriptions, but there are similar features, as well. The enthronement theme is eschatological, and the main scene of the throne of God concerns the last judgment. In the work there is also an evident application of the prophetic tradition concerning the vision of God's throne.

d. The Testament of Job

The Testament of Job is a first century C.E. work that elaborates in an interesting way on the great themes of wisdom literature and the problem of theodicy. The author exceeds the limits of traditional wisdom speculation, however. The Testament of Job belongs in the eschatological tradition of Second Temple Jewish theology and develops characteristic themes of apocalyptic. As the biblical book of Job provides the point of departure for speculation in this apocryphal testament, it is only natural that here too the apocalyptic description appears in the context of the problem of theodicy.[112]

The enthronement theme is introduced at the climax of the work, when Job answers his friends. In chapter 32 the lament of Eliphas concludes with the question that has been repeated several times throughout the lament: "Now

---

[111] Cf. 4 Ezra 8:48-55.

[112] According to Nickelsburg, the place and date of the work cannot be fixed with certainty. The description of Job as king of Egypt connects the writing with that country, however. A first century C.E. dating is suggested, but this is uncertain. Nickelsburg, *Jewish Literature*, 247.

where is the splendour of your throne?" Job's answer exploits the metaphor of the throne and reveals a connection with merkabah speculation.

In spite of the misfortune that Job has suffered down on earth, he is certain that he has a reward up in heaven. Job is convinced of his future exaltation and informs his friends that he has been promised a throne "at the right hand" of God.

"After Eliphas finished wailing while his fellow kings responded to him all in a great commotion, when the uproar died down, I said to them, 'Quiet! Now I will show you my throne with the splendour of its majesty, which is among the holy ones. My throne is in the upper world, and its splendour and majesty come from the right hand of the Father. The whole world shall pass away and its splendour shall fade. And those who heed it shall share in its overthrow. But my throne is in the holy land, and its splendour is in the world of the changeless one. Rivers will dry up (Job 14:11), and the arrogance of their waves goes down into the depths of the abyss. But the rivers of my land, where my throne is, do not dry up nor will they disappear, but they will exist forever. These kings will pass away, and rulers come and go; but their splendour and boast shall be as in a mirror. But my kingdom is for ever and ever, and its splendour and majesty are in the chariots of the Father" (TJob 33).

Firstly, the throne of God is given prominence. At the end of the above passage, God's throne is identified as the "chariots of the Father".[113] Thus the scene of the work is clearly apocalyptic and the passage displays merkabah speculation. Small wonder that there appear to be several thrones in heaven.

Secondly, the ascension of Job is the premise behind the whole train of thought. This theme seems to elaborate on the idea that was introduced in (the biblical) Job 36, "He does not withdraw his eyes from the righteous, but with kings on the throne he sets them forever, and they are exalted" (Job 36:7). Later in TJob, in chapter 39, there is a further reference to the ascension of Job's children. Their burial is refused permission because the heavenly King has already taken them up: "Do not trouble yourselves in vain. For you will not find my children, since they were taken up into heaven by the Creator their King" (TJob 39:11-12).

The enthronement theme itself belongs in the tradition of the enthronement of the patriarchs and pious Jews. It bears the marks that we have seen above, and which recur e.g. in TBenj 10:6. The distinctive feature of the description of the enthronement is the reference to Ps. 110. The "splendour and majesty" of Job's throne comes "from the right hand (ἐκ δεξιῶν) of the Father".[114]

A similar feature appears in TBenj. 10:3, "And then you will see Enoch and

---

[113] See Hengel, *Studies*, 206.

[114] Cf. Hay, *Glory*, 23. According to Hengel, there may even be Christian influence in this description, where the glory of Job's throne comes "from the right hand" of God. The passage does not say, however, that Job would sit "at the right hand" of God. Hengel, *Studies*, 207.

Seth and Abraham and Isaac and Jacob being raised up at the right hand in great joy." This passage, however, places the exalted patriarchs "at the right hand" of God. This particular feature is lacking in TJob 33.

As we think of Job's destiny, the tradition of the ascension of martyrs may also have influenced the writer in including the enthronement theme in his story. In 4 Maccabees the honorary place beside God's throne is the prize of the martyrs: "The tyrant himself and his whole council were astonished at their endurance, on account of which they now stand beside the divine throne and live the life of the age of blessing" (4 Macc. 17:18).[115]

The role of resurrection is not clear in TJob. Job's ascension is not clearly linked with his own resurrection. Actually the scene is rather different. As in several other apocalyptic Jewish writings, here too Job's soul ascends to heaven after his death (52:8). There is a separation of body and soul. A great chariot comes and takes Job's soul to heaven, but his body was "borne to the tomb" (52:11; 53:8).

It is probable that, according to the writer, Job's final enthronement would take place after the last events and after the general resurrection. For instance, in *ApcMos.* this kind of future is promised to Adam, whose soul appears to function even though his body is buried in Paradise (*ApcMos.* 41:3; cf. *TAbr.* 20:11-12).[116] A somewhat similar pattern may be seen in the Testament of Isaac, where the souls of men are said to await their final exaltation in the resurrection.[117]

The theme of the exaltation of the patriarchs is here exploited for the purpose of underlining Job's enduring faith in the One God who is the King of the heavens. Therefore, TJob appears to be an apologetic work providing a justification for the monotheistic theocracy of Israel. Such a work is necessary when the circumstances of the readers raise the problem of theodicy.

The Testament of Job reveals how flexible the use of merkabah traditions was. They suit the processing of different problems perpetually in new contexts. As the main theme of the work is the problem of theodicy, merkabah description is exploited to the end of resolving that problem. It provides a suitable description of God's majesty in the heavens. The exaltation of Job verifies that a reward awaits the faithful in the end.[118]

The enthronement theme, however, became irreplaceable for the author, as it enabled him to connect Job's fate with the fate of other suffering righteous persons in apocalyptic writings. Job's throne is in heaven and it is

---

[115] Cf. later Eph. 2:4-6; Rev. 7:13-15.

[116] See section i. below.

[117] This work will be studied in section k. below.

[118] So Segal, *ANRW II 23.2.* (1980) 1368.

imperishable. It is also contrasted with the "rotted" throne of the bad friend Elihu, in 43:7. His throne lies in Hades. Therefore, we are justified in concluding that the enthronement theme has a positive value throughout the writing and that it expresses the true basis of Job's hope during his suffering. Job's throne is legitimated by God's throne, and the location "at the right hand" is essential for such legitimation.

e. 2 Enoch

In the second book of Enoch we find, once again, a full description of a heavenly journey.[119] The hero is naturally Enoch, whose ascension is speculated upon in a somewhat different manner from in 1 Enoch, but the differences are not significant: "The story of Enoch: how the Lord took him to heaven" (2 En. 1:1).

First of all we should note the section where the third heaven is described as Paradise.

"And those men took me from there, and they brought me up to the third heaven, and set me down (there). Then I looked downward, and I saw Paradise... And I saw the trees in full flower... And in the midst (of them was) the tree of life, at that place where the Lord takes a rest when he goes into Paradise... And there are 300 angels, very bright, who look after Paradise; and with never-ceasing voice and pleasant singing they worship the Lord every day and hour" (J 8:1-3, 8).

It seems clear that 2 Enoch exploits the Jubilees tradition of the Garden of Eden. The connection need not be direct, though. The description of Paradise is well developed and dynamic. One of the similarities is that in 2 Enoch, too, the centre of Paradise, i.e. the tree of life, is the place where the Lord rests.

One should pay attention to the theme of never-ceasing worship, which is a clear indicator of merkabah speculation. The tree of life is here a submetaphor of the throne itself.[120] It is not clear, however, whether the notion of the worshipping angels necessarily refers to worship in Paradise or not. The writer may merely mean that even the angels are fascinated with Paradise. In 8:8 they declare, "How very pleasant is this place!" Furthermore, Enoch is told that this place was prepared for the righteous as an eternal inheritance (9:1).

In chapter 20 the heavenly journey proceeds finally to the seventh heaven.

---

[119] The dating of 2 Enoch is difficult and the work is dealt with here only for the sake of its content. The manuscripts of the work are late and datings range from pre-Christian times to the late Middle Ages. A long and complex process of editing must be assumed for the work. See the introduction of Andersen, *OTP I*, 91ff., esp. 95.

[120] Cf. Gruenwald, *Merkavah Mysticism*, 50-51: "Wherever this Paradise is located, either on earth or in heaven, the Tree of Life could be the place on which God rests, and God's theophany on the Tree of Life is, thus, a counterpart to His theophanies in the Temple and on His Throne of Glory."

Enoch first sees the fiery armies of the great archangels, and the cherubim, and the seraphim. Then he is led to a place where he can see the throne of God. "And they showed (me) the Lord, from a distance, sitting on his exceedingly high throne" (20:3). The peculiar feature of the J-text is the conviction that God's throne is located in the 10th heaven (20:3; 22:1; lacking in the A-text). There worship of him is performed gloriously (20:4).

In 2 Enoch we can also find the enthronement theme, and here we also have a rather rare description of an angelic enthronement. In chapter 24 the Lord tells Enoch, "Enoch, sit to the left of me with Gabriel" (J 24:1). In the A-text this is specified - "closer than Gabriel." Gabriel appears to be seated in an honorary place beside God, even though he must make room for Enoch.[121] On the other hand, the fact that Gabriel is required to move may indicate that his seating is temporary. Therefore the angel may in fact be merely escorting Enoch to the throne. His position is not permanent and therefore this passage reveals much about the relation of the angels to heavenly thrones.[122]

Because of the problems involved in the dating of the work it is not possible to decide in what context such angelology belongs. It may be a rather late feature, and in this case its "uniqueness" is no argument for an early date. Therefore the evidence of 2 Enoch is not sufficient to reach strong conclusions as regards the interpretation of the angels.

In chapter 22 there is, however, a reference to some kind of transformation. Here, too, we find a description of a heavenly consecration. Enoch is anointed and clothed in glorious garments. After this he declares, "And I looked at myself, and I had become like one of his glorious ones, and there was no observable difference" (J 22:10). It is not clear, however, whether an actual ontological transformation is meant here.[123]

Some scholars have further referred to two figures in 2 Enoch - Melchizedek and Adam - who have been interpreted as exalted agents of God. However, such an explanation exhibits severe weaknesses. The description of Melchizedek has been influenced by some kind of Christian, probably sectarian, tradition (2 En. 71:33-34).[124] Adam, in turn, who appears in chapter 30, is not at all an exalted figure. In a late sectarian account of creation Adam

---

[121] See Rowland, *Open Heaven*, 94.

[122] On the temporary feature, see Bock, *Blasphemy*, 164f.

[123] Himmelfarb thinks, however, that there is a transformation and that this is linked to the act of clothing. "The combination of clothing and anointing suggests that the process by which Enoch becomes an angel is a heavenly version of priestly investiture." Himmelfarb, *Ascent*, 40.

[124] This passage will be dealt with later. Some scholars have regarded this section as Jewish, however. See e.g. Chester, *Paulus*, 60.

is described as a "second angel, honoured and great and glorious" (30:11), but he remains on earth. He is assigned to be a king, "to reign on the earth" and to possess divine wisdom. We have seen similar descriptions of Adam in other apocalyptic works and in these descriptions no ascent structure can be detected.[125]

In sum, in 2 Enoch the enthronement itself does not display standard features. Enoch is not enthroned as a judge or in order to reign in heaven. Instead, to him are revealed God's secrets and God's wisdom. Here the atmosphere is similar to the Enoch tradition in Jubilees, even though the final version of 2 Enoch is quite late. All this demonstrates how difficult it is to deal with the different traditions and redactional stages in the work. The ascent structure is evident, however. 2 Enoch passes on the tradition in which God's heavenly throne is the centre of Jewish mysticism. In this respect the work is a fine example of the exposition of key ideas of mystical contemplation.

f. The Apocalypse of Abraham

Even though the Apocalypse of Abraham is important for our study of merkabah mysticism, the text of the work is problematic. Halperin is correct in his remark that this is in some ways "the most uncertain and problematic of the texts with which we have to deal".[126] We only possess the Slavonic version, which has been read for centuries in Russia and has been re-worked repeatedly. Nevertheless, the story itself is interesting and it presents a detailed vision of an ascension. In addition, we should note that the *merkabah* description has not been considered a late redaction.[127]

The Apocalypse of Abraham concentrates first on the retelling of the making of the Covenant (Gen. 15). Quite soon, however, the scene changes and Abraham begins to see visions. There is a description of an ascension and Abraham's heavenly journey (15).[128]

Abraham is guided by the angel Jaoel. Jaoel himself declares that he possesses God's "ineffable name" (10:8; cf. 10:3). Gruenwald suggests that the name combines the first three root-letters of the Tetragrammaton (YHW)

---

[125] Chester, who places emphasis on the angelic status of Adam but ignores the lack of ascent structure, also admits the late date of this recension. Chester, *Paulus*, 60.

[126] Halperin, *Chariot*, 103.

[127] As Segal puts it, "there is nothing in the ascension tradition per se that is characteristic of a Bogomil invention"; Segal, *ANRW II 23.2.* (1980) 1362, n. 100.

[128] In Pseudo-Philo, too, we have a short reference to the heavenly journey of Abraham. "Is it not regarding this people that I spoke to Abraham in a vision, saying, '*Your seed will be like the stars of the heaven,*' when I lifted him above the firmament and showed him the arrangements of the stars" (Ps.-Philo 18:5).

with the usual "el" ending indicating 'God' (*Yhwel*, to be pronounced Yahoel), and this suggestion seems plausible. The divine name of the angel does not indicate deification *per se* but merely the especially high status of the angel Jaoel. A similar pattern can be seen later in 3 Enoch (cf. 3 Enoch 48D:1). Jewish mysticism evidently included speculation concerning an archangel in whom God's name resides (cf. Ex. 23:21; 32:20-21).[129]

The status of the angel with a theophoric name should not be exaggerated. It is noteworthy that he worships God with Abraham and sings songs of praise to the Enthroned One (esp. 17:1-21). He has priestly status in the heavenly liturgy. In this respect one cannot speak of a shared authority status.[130] Rather, Jaoel bears a resemblance to Metatron in Hekalot literature.[131]

Up in heaven the angel first advises Abraham to recite a hymn which the angel has taught him. Here we meet an exceptional hymn that is also the longest merkabah hymn in apocalyptic literature. The hymn concentrates on the names and qualities of God. "Eternal One, Mighty One, Holy El, God autocrat self-originate, incorruptible, immaculate" (17:8-9a). Here we also find the names that reside in the guiding angel: "Eli, eternal, mighty one, holy, Sabaoth, most glorious El, El, El, El, Iaoel" (17:13).[132]

A throne vision follows and it exploits the features of Ezekiel's vision:

"And as the fire rose up, soaring to the highest point, I saw under the fire a throne of fire and the many-eyed ones round about, reciting the song, under the throne four fiery living creatures, singing" (ApAbr. 18:3; cf. Ezek. 1:6-12, 23).

The description of the heavenly throne is quite complete since there is also a throne-chariot in heaven.

"And while I was still standing and watching, I saw behind the living creatures a chariot with fiery wheels. Each wheel was full of eyes round about. And above the wheels was the throne which I had seen. And it was covered with fire and the fire encircled it round about, and an indescribable light surrounded the fiery crowd" (18:12-13).

The Apocalypse of Abraham seems to exploit the standard images of merkabah mysticism in their rather early form.[133] The vision of God's throne has a primary function in the story, and the ascension pattern is simple. The writer of the text is further interested in the heavenly reward of the faithful, of

---

[129] See Gruenwald, *Merkavah Mysticism*, 53f.; cf. Segal, *ANRW II 23.2*. (1980) 1362.

[130] In agreement with Stuckenbruck, *Angel Veneration*, 219. See also Bock, *Blasphemy*, 174.

[131] Thus Collins, *Apocalyptic Imagination*, 183. This would mean that the work should be dated rather late after all.

[132] See e.g. Halperin, *Chariot*, 106f.

[133] Segal, *ANRW II 23.2*. (1980) 1363.

which Abraham is a perfect example. These will be taken to the heavenly paradise when they die (21:6-7).

This work has been considered important by the proponents of the angelic interpretation. However, even Rowland admits that there is no mention of Jaoel's enthronement: "there is no explicit evidence from the Apocalypse of Abraham to suggest that Jaoel was the one whose seat was on the throne of God."[134] Therefore, we must separate the idea of ascent structure from the angelic interpretation and consider Jaoel's status on its own. In the Apocalypse of Abraham, Abraham's heavenly journey is the key issue and we must keep to the evidence when interpreting it.

In the Apocalypse of Abraham the hymnic tradition of the prophetic books of the Old Testament is exploited. The setting is cultic in the sense that there is a Temple in heaven. Abraham joins in the heavenly liturgy and worships the enthroned God. The idea of the ascent is thus exploited in a cultic discourse.

g. The Ladder of Jacob

The Ladder of Jacob is a late apocalyptical work that is probably related to the Apocalypse of Abraham, and therefore it is proper to consider it next.[135] Here again the treatment of the text must be thematic, because such a late writing may reflect mystical ideas that developed centuries after the Second Temple period. The reason for the investigation of this kind of writing, however, is its evident dependence on much earlier traditions.

The Ladder of Jacob is an elaboration of Jacob's dream at Bethel (Gen. 28:11-22). It is to be expected that this story has inspired Jewish mystics. In the biblical story of the dream Jacob saw a ladder reaching from the earth to heaven. In the new vision Jacob sees "the house of God" and everything else that is in the heavens. At the top of the ladder he saw a "face as of a man, carved out of fire" (1:4). So the ascension (and the ladder) led directly to heaven.

The description of the merkabah is a rather traditional one.

"You who sit firmly on the cherubim and the fiery throne of glory... and the many-eyed (ones) just as I saw in my dream, holding the four-faced cherubim, bearing also the many-eyed seraphim, carrying the whole world under your arm" (2:7-9).

Reminiscences of the visions of Ezekiel are here connected with the so

---

[134] See Rowland, *Open Heaven*, 103. This is quite important, since Rowland wished to be able to connect these passages with the more explicit angelic descriptions: "it is not impossible that we have a theological description here which reflects that found in Ezekiel 1 and 8, where the human figure on the throne leaves the throne to function as the agent of the divine will."

[135] On the provenance of the work, see Lunt, *OTP II*, 401.

called hymnic tradition. In front of the throne the six-winged seraphim unceasingly sing a hymn (2:15), which includes the *trishagion*, accompanied by a list of transliterated Hebrew divine names. "Holy, Holy, Holy, Yao, Yaova, Yaoil, Yao, Kados, Chavod, Savaoth" (2:17-18).[136]

The vision in the Ladder of Jacob is a good example of how the traditional merkabah description was revived in eschatological writings. The influence of Ezekiel is evident here as it is in the Apocalypse of Abraham. These pseudepigraphical works interpret the experience of the patriarchs in the context of merkabah mysticism. There are several different works bearing the names of different biblical characters, but the scene is similar in all of them.

The name Jacob also occurs in a fragment associated with the unknown work called the Prayer of Joseph, extant merely in the writings of Origen. There the figure "Jacob" is quite exceptional: "I, Jacob, who is speaking to you, am also Israel, an angel of God and a ruling spirit" (*PrJos.* fragment A, 1). In this writing "Jacob" should, however, be regarded as an angelic figure, and he has nothing to do with other Jacob traditions.[137]

The writer of the Ladder of Jacob comforted his Jewish readers with his conviction that, despite all external threats, it is God who reigns. Already the descendants of Jacob were "exiles in a strange land", but the Lord rescued them. Moreover, "the Lord will judge the people for whom they slave" (5:16-17). In such a context the merkabah vision once again serves to resolve the problem of theodicy by appealing to the reign of God and offering readers eschatological hope.

h. *The Ascension of Isaiah*

The Ascension of Isaiah is a composite work where different testamentary writings concerning the prophet Isaiah are joined together. In general, the work is divided into two main parts. The writing begins with "the Martyrdom of Isaiah," which is the story of the prophet's execution (chapters 1-5). Chapters 6-11 form an entity of their own, usually called "the Vision of Isaiah," but the text itself is not very uniform.[138]

The basic nature of the Martyrdom of Isaiah is Jewish, but in 3:13-4:18 a

---

[136] Cf. the comments of Lunt in *OTP II*, 408, especially footnotes h and i.

[137] Bock suggests that this figure has a "transcendent-human mix", as does the Enochic Son of Man. Bock, *Blasphemy*, 132. This, however, does not seem to be the case. In apocalyptic works angelic figures have been given peculiar names, but these do not imply very much concerning the nature of the figures, especially in the contexts where the figures are identified clearly.

[138] For a general introduction, see Knibb, *OTP I*, 147f. For a discussion of the problems of dating and providence, see Hall, *JBL 109* (1990) 289ff.

Christian redactor has added a lengthy prophecy of Christ.[139] The question of the Vision of Isaiah is a more complicated one. On even a superficial reading one gains the picture that the Vision begins with a traditional Jewish ascent story that later changes into a description of Christ's actions in the heavenly realm. This kind of change can be explained in several ways. On the one hand, it may be that here, too, a Christian redactor has added to an apocalyptic Jewish writing a story about Christ's ascension.[140] On the other hand, however, the whole story may come from the hand of a Jewish-Christian writer exploiting traditional themes in his work.[141]

Most scholars note that it is difficult to date the different sections of the Ascension with any precision. Jewish sources may be pre-Christian, but it is not easy to make a distinction between them and possible Jewish traditions that may have been exploited in the compilation of the work. The work as a whole is obviously Christian and evidently reflects the situation at the end of the first century C.E. or the beginning of the second.[142]

The Vision of Isaiah begins as a normal Jewish description of a heavenly journey. Christian features in the first chapters of the Vision can be found merely in short interpolations at the end of thematic sections. The ascension passes all seven heavens. One exception in respect of other apocalypses may be detected, however. Each heaven seems to have a throne, except the sixth one, since it is directed by the "power of the seventh heaven" (8:7). This is probably the only occurrence in Jewish apocalyptic of the idea of different thrones in different heavens.[143]

In the seventh heaven we do not actually see a throne. It is evident, though, that there, too, God's throne of glory is the centre of the highest heaven.[144] In the story, however, the description of separate heavens is in fact interrupted

---

[139] Cf. Eissfeldt, *Old Testament*, 609-610.

[140] For instance, Gruenwald thinks that the book as a whole is of Jewish origin and that all obviously Christian references come from a later editor. Gruenwald, *Merkavah Mysticism*, 61-62, especially footnote 119.

[141] Eissfeldt considers the whole Vision of Isaiah to be Christian. Eissfeldt, *Old Testament*, 610. According to Hall, "nothing interrupts the flow of narrative" in the work. Therefore he rejects the idea of the existence of a Jewish source behind the Vision. Hall, *JBL* 113 (1994) 475, 483. Cf. Gieschen, *Christology*, 229.

[142] For different possible datings, see especially Knibb, *OTP I*, 149f. A reference has been made, for instance, to the figure of Antichrist in 4:2f., which presumably means Nero. Therefore, a date before 68 C.E. is not possible.

[143] See Gruenwald, *Merkavah Mysticism*, 59.

[144] Hall states that the narrative "builds evenly to the climatic vision of God." Hall, *JBL* 113 (1994) 475. In respect of traditional Jewish ascent stories this is hardly the case.

when Isaiah reaches the seventh heaven (9:6ff.). It seems probable that a traditional merkabah vision has been left out and replaced by a Christian message. Instead of a vision of God's throne the manuscript contains several sporadic descriptions of the story of Christ. Later in chapter 9 there is a description of the worship of God (9:27ff.). This, of course, is typical of all the stories we have examined so far. Even though the throne is not mentioned, we see angels praising God and singing hymns to Him.

Angels have a prominent place in the ascension story of the Vision of Isaiah. One of the interesting features is that here the worship of angels is explicitly prohibited. "Worship neither throne, nor angel from the six heavens, from where I was sent to lead you, before I tell you in the seventh heaven" (7:21). Such a prohibition can also be found in the Book of Revelation (19:10; 22:9).[145]

Finally, the merkabah vision proper seems to have been replaced by a vision of the enthronement of Christ. It seems evident that a redactor wished to introduce the glorified Lord of his own faith into the traditional Jewish description of a heavenly throne. This is a remarkable feature, and we shall return to an analysis of it later, in chapter 3.[146]

In *AscIsa* the enthronement of Christ is naturally linked to his resurrection. This, however, is described by exploiting the terminology of early Christology, where these themes were inseparable. Therefore, we know nothing of the relation of the ascent structure to resurrection in the original Jewish story, where the ascension of a messianic figure may well have occurred – as in Enochic literature.

Furthermore, it is important to note that the traditional enthronement theme occurs in an implicit way in this work, too. Isaiah himself has a throne awaiting him in the seventh heaven. "For above all the heavens and their angels is placed your throne, and also your robes and your crown which you are to see" (7:22). Isaiah is one of the faithful righteous ones who will, like the patriarchs, be enthroned in the end of days.[147]

In the seventh heaven there are further thrones for the righteous, but the righteous ones "from the time of Adam onwards", such as Abel and Enoch,

---

[145] Gruenwald, *Merkavah Mysticism*, 59; Bauckham, *NTS 27* (1980) 323.

[146] Bock states that the portrait of the Isaiah 6 event in *AscIsa* is most probably Christian, not Jewish. Bock, *Blasphemy*, 147. This appears to be an over-statement, however. The basic content of the work is completely in line with other Jewish apocalyptic writings.

[147] Hall also pays attention to the idea of Isaiah's enthronement: "the Vision of Isaiah is a book about how Isaiah attains a heavenly throne." Hall, *JBL 113* (1994) 477. Nevertheless he does not recognize the fundamentally Jewish character of such a theme.

whom Isaiah saw in heaven, were not sitting on them (9:7-10).[148] Only the righteous ones who will ascend with Christ will receive their thrones once Christ has ascended into the seventh heaven (9:17-18). In addition, *AscIsa* mentions thrones that will be given to all believers (9:24-26). It is obvious that the theme of the enthronement of the patriarchs has been altered to the theme of enthroned believers.[149]

This is a novel interpretation of the theme of the enthronement of the pious. It shows that even Christian mysticism elaborated on these profoundly Jewish traditions. It is easy to suggest that this kind of eschatology emerged especially among Jewish Christians. The new interpretation, of course, can already be seen in the Book of Revelation, where the enthronement theme plays a significant role, as we shall see later.

According to the author, some kind of transformation takes place in heaven. When Isaiah sees Abel and Enoch and all the righteous in heaven, they are "like the angels who stand there in great glory" (9:9). This, however, may be merely a reference to their new status, similar to that of the angels.[150]

Even though the Ascension of Isaiah is basically a (Jewish) Christian work, it is so clearly based on earlier Jewish material and sources that parts of the work can be used as evidence for Jewish thinking. In this respect especially the Vision of Isaiah appears to exploit the ideas of rather traditional Jewish mysticism. Its cosmology is based on the idea of seven heavens. The number of thrones, however, is original. An ascent structure can be discerned behind the story up to the point of Isaiah's own enthronement. The writer of the original Jewish Vision of Isaiah was presumably quite familiar with the idea of the enthronement of the patriarchs.

i. The Life of Adam and Eve/The Apocalypse of Moses

This late apocryphal story about the Fall displays several features of throne mysticism. Relevant terminology is exploited for example in the story about the eating of the fruit. At the beginning of the story the serpent and Eve enter

---

[148] Abel and Enoch are described as "like the angels who stand there in great glory" (9:9). Chester concludes that this confirms an angelic interpretation. Chester, *Paulus*, 59. This, however, is not the case. These patriarchs are not identifies as angels, but only compared to them.

[149] This suggests that *AscIsa* originally contained an explicit description of the enthronement of the patriarchs. One cannot prove this, however, based on the extant evidence.

[150] Himmelfarb suggests that in 9:30 there is a reference to Isaiah's own transformation. Himmelfarb, *Ascent*, 56. Knibb is probably correct, however, when he comments that the transformation of the appearance of Jesus is meant here. See his comment o2. on *AscIsa* 9:30 in *OTP II*.

Paradise. The serpent demands that Eve swear to him that she will give the fruit to her husband too. "I do not know by what sort of oath I should swear to you; however, that which I do know I tell you: By the throne of the Lord and the cherubim and the tree of life, I shall give (it) also to my husband to eat" (*ApcMos.* 19:2).[151]

Later, when God heard of the transgression he descended to Paradise on a cherub-throne: "And as we heard the archangel sounding the trumpet, we said, 'Behold, God is coming into Paradise to judge us.' We were afraid and hid. And God returned to Paradise, seated on a chariot of cherubim, and the angels were praising him" (*ApcMos.* 22:3). In this story the location of the throne is by the tree of life: "And the throne of God was made ready where the tree of life was" (22:4).

The repentance of Eve expresses true faith in God the heavenly King: "I have sinned, O God... I have sinned against you, I have sinned against your chosen angels, I have sinned against the cherubim, I have sinned against your steadfast throne" (*ApcMos.* 32:2). Here the scene is evidently cultic. It is right and proper that the sins of righteous Jews were confessed before the throne, where the atonement was made for them.

Despite the fact that Adam was punished, in the story God finally takes him up to the heavenly Paradise.

"Blessed be the glory of the Lord over his works; he has had mercy on Adam... and so the Lord of all, sitting on his holy throne, stretched out his hands and took Adam and handed him over to the archangel Michael, saying to him, 'Take him up into Paradise, to the third heaven, and leave (him) there until that great and fearful day which I am about to establish for the world" (ApcMos. 39:2-5).

In *Vita* the scene is somewhat different. Adam is carried up to God's *merkabah* so that God can judge him.[152] This is the context of the particular heavenly journey. Adam tells that after the expulsion from Paradise he was taken to heaven where he worshipped God in repentance. Later he was promised a merciful exaltation.

"After your mother and I had been driven out of Paradise, while we were praying, Michael the archangel and messenger of God came to me. And I saw a chariot like the wind and its wheels were fiery. I was carried off into the Paradise of righteousness, and I saw the Lord sitting and his appearance was unbearable flaming fire. And many thousands of angels were at the right and at the left of the chariot" (LAE 25:2-3).

Finally, in the Apocalypse of Moses, the enthronement theme forms the climax of the story of Adam. Adam's dead body is taken up to Paradise, and Adam is promised a throne in heaven and his glory is thus renewed.

---

[151] On the dating of the work see e.g. Halperin, *Chariot*, 96.

[152] Cf. Halperin, *Chariot*, 100.

"Adam, why did you do this? If you had kept my commandment, those who brought you down into this place would not have rejoiced. Yet now I tell you that their joy shall be turned into sorrow, but your sorrow shall be turned into joy; and when that happens, I will establish you in your dominion on the throne of your seducer... and they shall greatly mourn and weep when they see you sitting on his glorious throne" (ApcMos. 39:1-3; cf. LAE 47:3).[153]

Adam's body is then prepared for burial, and later buried in a tomb in Paradise. In *ApcMos.* 28:4 Adam is promised a resurrection to life. This is consistent with the idea that Adam's exaltation and enthronement would take place in the resurrection on the last day (*ApcMos.* 41:3). There is also a comforting message included. Segal notes: "Immortality is within grasp for all the true sons of Adam who can repent of their sins."[154]

The interpretation of this story is somewhat difficult since it may have been affected to a great extent by Christian traditions. The basic features of mysticism contained in it, however, seem to be quite similar to those occurring in Jewish apocalyptic literature. In part, the Apocalypse of Moses appears to belong to the same tradition with Jubilees and 2 Enoch. In addition, the description of a heavenly journey and the enthronement theme, for example, reveal a close connection with the vast apocalyptic tradition of the first and second centuries C.E. Adam is here the prototype of the exalted patriarch and his enthronement is placed within the great panorama of salvation history. The power of evil will finally be destroyed and Adam will be given a throne in heaven.

j. The Testament of Abraham

It is commonly assumed that the Testament of Abraham, with two other testaments, springs from an apocryphal book written in the first century C.E. These rather similar works are usually called the Testaments of the Three Patriarchs.[155] The Testament of Abraham, presumably, was originally a Jewish work written in Greek. The other two are the Testament of Isaac and the Testament of Jacob. All of these testaments later underwent Christian redaction.

The Testament of Abraham and the Testament of Isaac appear to belong to a

---

[153] Chester refers on this point to the beginning of LAE, where the devil tells the story of his expulsion from heaven (12-17). In this story Michael commands all the angels to worship Adam. To Chester this is an indication of "the very high position accorded Adam". Chester, *Paulus*, 60. The text, however, does not speak of Adam's enthronement, but of his creation. The angels are made to worship Adam as being the image of God in Paradise. This should not be confused with the worship of angels before a heavenly throne. For a similar problematic interpretation, see Fossum, *Name*, 266ff.

[154] Segal, *ANRW II 23.2.* (1980) 1364.

[155] See the introduction of Sanders in *OTP I*, 869ff.

tradition where the theme of enthronement plays a significant role. In both of these works we find exalted patriarchs, and their heavenly status is described in a glorious manner.

First of all, there is a traditional heavenly journey in *TAbr.* 10: "And the archangel Michael went down and took Abraham on a chariot of cherubim and lifted him up into the air of heaven" (recension A, 10:1). On his journey Abraham saw the entire inhabited earth as well as the heavens.

In heaven Abraham saw two roads and two gates, a broad one and a narrow one. Near the gates there was a throne, and on it a distinguished character sat enthroned.

"And outside the two gates of that place, they saw a man seated on a golden throne. And the appearance of that man was terrifying, like the Master's" (11:4).

The enthroned one rejoiced when he saw souls entering through the narrow gate, because it led to life. When he saw souls entering the broad gate he cast himself on the ground crying and wailing, for the broad gate was the gate of sinners (*TAbr.* 11:5-11).[156]

Even though the setting of the story is of a Christian nature and the recensions have clearly been influenced by the New Testament, the description has been constructed on the basis of Jewish traditions. The enthroned one in chapter 11 is identified as Adam, "the first-formed Adam" (11:9). He, however, is not the only patriarch sitting enthroned in heaven.[157]

Between the two gates "there stood a terrifying throne with the appearance of terrifying crystal, flashing like fire" (12:4). This patriarch is identified as Abel (13:2), and his appearance is majestic. "And upon it sat a wondrous man, bright as the sun, like unto a son of God" (12:5). Abel is appointed a heavenly judge and he will "judge the entire creation" (13:3).

The descriptions of these figures are extraordinary, but their status should not be exaggerated. Abel is a heavenly judge, "an all-wondrous judge", as the work itself announces (13:1).[158] In this respect he is a common character in the tradition of the exalted patriarchs.

---

[156] All references here are to recension A.

[157] According to Bock, this text shows "that one cannot simply assume that the mention of a throne in heaven or a reference to someone sitting on such a throne automatically indicates the honoree is seated next to God or that the honor is uniquely his." Bock, *Blasphemy*, 117-118.

[158] Cf. Bock, *Blasphemy*, 121. This fits the general message of the Testament of Abraham. The writing especially focuses on judgment. See Collins, *Apocalyptic Imagination*, 202f.

Adam no doubt is described as a heavenly luminary, but in the story there is actually nothing particular that might refer to any kind of divinization.[159]

At the end of the book Abraham's death is described. The Archangel Michael is present on that occasion. Here again a peculiar dualism is introduced. Abraham's body is buried, but his soul is taken to heaven. It does not appear to have an independent life in heaven without the body, however.

"And they buried him in the promised land at the oak of Mamre, while the angels escorted his precious soul and ascended into heaven singing the thrice-holy hymn to God, the master of all, and they set it (down) for the worship of the God and Father" (20:11-12).

After this the testament describes great praise and Abraham's worship in heaven, in the manner of apocalyptic tradition. God also commands the angels to bring Abraham to paradise. The thrice-holy hymn usually serves as an allusion to the vision of Isaiah.

The Testament of Abraham contains both a description of a heavenly journey and representative examples of enthroned patriarchs. Even though we cannot decide the dating of such descriptions with any certainty, it seems evident that these passages are dependent on Jewish traditions, not merely on the resurrection theology of the New Testament. The testament adds little to the picture that we gain from early merkabah mysticism. The enthroned ones have a special status in heaven, but, for example, the ministry of Abel is similar to that of exalted patriarchs in other apocalyptic writings. The aspect of heavenly worship connects the work to prophetic traditions, and may reveal dependence on cultic features, as well.

k. The Testament of Isaac

In the Testament of Isaac the traditional features of merkabah mysticism are even clearer than in the Testament of Abraham.[160] In the story an angel first takes Isaac for a preliminary visit to the heavens. There Isaac sees Abraham and other saints. The throne vision itself is placed in the heavenly Temple.

"Then they took me by the hand and led me to the curtain before the throne of the Father. So I prostrated myself before him and worshipped him with my father and all the saints, while we uttered praises and cried aloud, saying, 'Most holy, most holy, most holy is the Lord Sabaoth! Heaven and earth are filled with your sanctified glory'" (6:4-5).

---

[159] Chester seems to be too optimistic when he comments that "the description of him seems very close to that of a divine figure." Chester, *Paulus*, 57. We must note, however, that there is no evidence whatever for deification in the work itself.

[160] The dating of *TIsaac* is difficult, however. Extant writings are late and none of them is in Greek, even though the originals are assumed to have been written in Greek. The work is evidently dependent on *TAbr*. See Stinespring, *OTP I*, 903f.

Later the praises are repeated.[161] God calls his angels and moves with his chariot-throne. "Then he mounted the chariot of the seraphim, while the cherubim went before [with the angels. And when they had come to the couch of our father Isaac, our father Isaac immediately beheld the face of our Lord, full of joy toward him]" (6:26-27).

The enthronement theme is also explicit in the Testament of Isaac. Like Abraham, Isaac is a righteous patriarch who is promised a throne in heaven.

"For your father Abraham is awaiting you; he himself is about to come for you, but now he is resting. There has been prepared for you the throne beside your father Abraham; likewise for your beloved son Jacob" (2:7).

Even though there is no description of an actual enthronement at the end of the book, it is indirectly alluded to, since it is God himself who carries Isaac's soul to heaven upon his holy chariot (7:1). Such a description of God's own actions in the event of the ascent is rather unique.[162] The carrying of the soul to heaven has a special purpose, however. As we have seen, in Jewish apocalyptic this was the way how the interim period between death and resurrection was described. The soul was separated from the body and awaited its final exaltation.

In the Testament of Isaac we find traditional merkabah terminology. God sits on a chariot of seraphim and the hosts of heaven worship him in front of the throne. There is no description of different heavens, but the cultic feature is prominent. In the heavenly Temple there is a curtain and God's throne is behind that curtain, as it was in the Temple of Jerusalem.

In these testaments ascension has primarily to do with the theme of life after death. In the Testament of Isaac we have a "preliminary" ascension, though, but it serves the description of the final ascension of Isaac's soul. The actual story of ascension is in the service of the enthronement theme, i.e. the enthronement of the patriarchs themselves.

l. 3 Baruch

In addition to extensive and evident merkabah visions and descriptions of heavenly ascent, it is useful to make some comments on shorter occurrences, as well. For example, in 3 Baruch we find once again a detailed description of a heavenly journey. Baruch enters five separate heavens.[163] The peculiarity of

---

[161] There seems to be a *trishagion* in the text, even though in a somewhat altered form.

[162] Even though God appears to be active e.g. in the ascension of Adam in *ApcMos* 39, it is the Archangel Michael who escorts Adam to heaven.

[163] In this respect the book is rare among Jewish writings. See Stone, *Jewish Writings*, 411.

the work is that each heaven has doors.[164] "And the angel of hosts took me and carried me where the firmament of heaven is. And it was the first heaven, and in that heaven he showed me very large doors" (Slavonic version, 2:1-2).[165]

The manuscript of the book has probably been corrupted, since only five heavens are mentioned, and there is no clear description of God's throne. Chariots as such are mentioned on different occasions. In chapter 6, for example, we read about chariots of the sun: "And the sun entered (the chariot) and a voice came" (Slavonic version, 6:14). Later in the book a vision of a moon, in turn, is explained accordingly: "It is like a woman, sitting on a chariot, and twenty angels are leading the chariot..." (Slavonic version, 9:3).

The composition of the book implies, though, that a theophany could be expected in the future. In the fifth heaven Baruch already sees Michael, who has keys to the higher heavens. All he is told now is, however: "Wait and you will see the glory of God" (Slavonic version, 11:2).

The end of the book is a torso. Baruch is simply returned to where he was "at the beginning". We can only guess that in the original manuscript there was also a description of the sixth and seventh heavens, and most probably a merkabah vision, as well. As a description of a heavenly journey 3 Baruch is, in spite of everything, a work that is clearly based on merkabah mysticism. It shows us that speculation concerning the divine court did not diminish over the years.

m. Hellenistic synagogue prayer 4

The prayers included in the Apostolic Constitutions contain interesting remnants of Jewish synagogue prayers. Even though the constitutions themselves come directly from a Christian environment, these prayers have a Jewish content. They are based on the general theme of praising God, but the prayers also contain numerous allusions to the Psalms. Christian additions are few in number and easily detected. The dating of these prayers is dependent on how we assess the relationship between church and synagogue. The Apostolic Constitutions were compiled in 380 C.E., but the prayers may derive from a period when Christians still felt free to borrow from the synagogue liturgy. This may even take us back to the first part of the second century.

---

[164] It is naturally possible that there were seven heavens in the author's view, and only due to the incompleteness of the book can this no longer be seen in the work but, nevertheless, such a claim is unprovable.

[165] Here, too, there is a problem of dating. A Slavonic version of the work must be used, and the tradition history of the work is only hypothetical. See the introduction of Gaylord, *OTP I*, 653ff.

The most important of these prayers for the present study is number 4 (*AposCon* 7.35.1-0). It is a song of praise to God, and begins: "Great are you, O Lord, Almighty One, and great is your strength" (4:1). The worship itself is strikingly transcendent and exploits the themes of Ezekiel and Isaiah.

"There is one Holy One! And holy seraphim, together with the six-winged cherubim, singing to you the triumphal song, with never-silent voices cry out, 'Holy, holy holy, Lord Sabaoth, the heaven and the earth are full of your glory' " (4:8-10; cf. Isa 6:3).[166]

The description of the prayer is cultic and resembles the milieu of the Qumranic Songs of the Sabbath Sacrifice. Here, too, heavenly worship seems to justify earthly prayers. "And the other throngs of the hosts, archangels, thrones, dominions, sovereignties, authorities, powers, crying out, say, 'Blessed be the glory of the Lord from its place!'" (4:11-12).

Israel too sings: "The chariot of God is ten thousands multiplied by thousands of thriving ones; the Lord is among them in Sinai, in the holy place!" (4:15; cf. LXX Ps 67:18). The Lord appeared in his chariot at Sinai. Sinai is here again a holy place, especially due to God's theophany.[167]

This synagogue prayer continues the sacral tradition of Jewish mysticism. The employment of traditional themes has not produced considerable alterations to them. Worship on earth is connected with heavenly worship. "Wherefore also all men ought, from their very breasts, to send up to you *through Christ* the hymn on behalf of all" (4:22). This tradition was important for synagogue liturgy, but evidently was also fascinating for early Christian devotion.

n. The Sibylline Oracles, Book 3

One might expect that merkabah speculation would have found its way into the Sibyllines, but this does not seem to be the case. There are merely some vague references to this tradition in the collection, and furthermore, some of these are clearly of Christian origin, as we shall see later.[168] In the third book of the Sibyllines there are some traits of Jewish mysticism, however. The third book has been considered rather old. It is possible that the Jewish original should be dated even to the Hasmonaean period.[169]

There is no clear merkabah vision in the Jewish stratum of the Sibyllines, but book 3 begins with an interesting opening line. "Blessed, heavenly one, who thunders on high, who have the cherubim as your throne" (3:1). Thunder

---

[166] Cf. also Dan. 8:13.

[167] This might refer to a similar tradition as in Jubilees 8:19.

[168] See the analyses in chapter 3.

[169] Collins, *OTP I*, 354ff.

is here again a metaphor for the heavenly temple, as the *pargod*, i.e. the Temple veil (see Psalms 11:4; 18:10; 103:19).[170]

The short line at the beginning of the work is astonishingly rich in content. With just a few characterizations it presents several features of the mystical tradition. The divine residence is a heavenly Temple. There is an ark in the sanctuary. The praise is focused on the cherub-throne upon which God sits.

After the blessing, and after the wailing of the prophet over his calling, there follows praise of God and denunciation of idolatry. Here the theocratic ideal of the opening line is placed in the service of apology. "There is one God, sole ruler, ineffable, who lives in the sky, self-begotten, invisible, who himself sees all things" (3,11-12).[171]

The brief description at the beginning of book three of the Sibyllines introduces several themes that were considered significant in the Jewish merkabah tradition. Even the context of the description is traditional. The reminder of a heavenly vision serves the purpose of confirming monotheism and denouncing idolatry.

o. Questions of Ezra

One of the brief but interesting passages comes from the fragmentary work Questions of Ezra.[172] It also contains some clear features of merkabah speculation. The setting of the work is simple: "Ezra the prophet saw the angel of God and asked him one question after another" (A, 1). The angel is once again a mediator who will escort the righteous prophet on his heavenly journey.

In this work the ascent structure is clear. Ezra sets outs on a mystical journey under angelic guidance. According to the work, there are seven steps to the Divinity. "To that way there are seven camps and seven steps to the Divinity, if I can make (someone) pass along it" (A, 19). The journey climaxes naturally on the seventh step, where a theophany takes place.

"[I]n the seventh, then, having brought (him)
I make him approach the great throne of the Divinity,
opposite the garden facing the glory of God where the sublime light is" (A, 21).

Some other features of merkabah tradition are contained in the writing.

---

[170] Cf. the *pargod* speculation examined above in chapter 3.1.

[171] The approach differs only slightly from that of apocalyptic writings that exploit a similar tradition in resolving the problem of theodicy, as we saw earlier.

[172] The Questions of Ezra is interesting merely from the point of view of the so called history of influence. The text is known only from late Armenian manuscripts, see Stone, *OTP I*, 591f.

Especially the prophetic tradition is emphasized. The cultic worship in heaven climaxes in the singing of the *trishagion*.

"Around him are incorporeal seraphim, six-winged cherubim; With two wings they cover their face, and with two wings their feet, and flying with two, they cry, 'Holy, Holy, (Holy) Lord of Hosts, the heaven and earth are full of your glory'" (A, 29).

Such short passages confirm that merkabah speculation had great influence on several different lines of tradition. The basic features of Jewish mysticism are applied in new contexts and adapted to meet new needs. The message does not alter significantly, though. The theocratic ideal, the sovereign kingship of the enthroned God, remains in the centre of these writings.

p. 3 Enoch

Finally, we must briefly examine the employment of the Enochic tradition in the late work called the Third Book of Enoch, which is probably the most famous of the writings of merkabah mysticism. It is a work that is dated rather late, perhaps to the seventh or eighth century, but it is dependent on traditions that we know from at least the Roman period.[173]

The main features of early merkabah mysticism appear in a developed form in 3 Enoch. The cosmology of the work is quite complete. There are seven heavens above the earth (17:1-3; 18:1-2). In the seventh heaven we find a series of seven palaces arranged concentrically (1:1-2; 7; 18:3). In the heavens there are hundreds and thousands of angels who are ordered in hierarchies. The highest angels are called princes (see e.g. chapter 18) and the highest of them all is Metatron.

The metamorphosis of Enoch into Metatron is most evidently one of the main characteristics of the work. At the beginning the famous passage from Gen. 5 is quoted:

"Enoch walked with God. Then he vanished because God took him."[174]

After this Metatron is the main character in the work. In 4:3 Metatron then reveals that he is Enoch. In this respect he is not a pure angelic figure, but an exalted human being.[175] We cannot deny that he is a person who has been

---

[173] The problems of dating are properly presented in the extensive introduction by Alexander in *OTP I*, 225-229. For the book's relation to late Jewish mysticism, see also Alexander, *ABD 2* (1992) 522-526. A critical edition of the text has been provided by Schäfer and Herrmann. In their work the final redaction of the text is located in Babylonia. See Schäfer-Herrmann, *Hekhalot-Literatur*, LIV.

[174] Gen. 5:24.

[175] Cf. Bock, *Blasphemy*, 177. In hekhalot speculation the human aspect of Metatron remained a subject of discussion, however. See Halperin, *Faces*, 423f.

transformed and awarded an angelic status, even though the idea of a transformation in 1 Enoch appeared to be a false interpretation.[176]

The significance and status of Metatron is evident in 3 Enoch. In 4:5 he is appointed a ruler of angels: "And the Holy One, blessed be he, appointed me in the height as a prince and a ruler among the ministering angels." Later a similar statement is repeated and expanded with a cultic function: "I set him as a prince over all the princes, and made him a minister of the throne of glory" (48C:4).[177] He is even given a theophoric name and called "the lesser YHWH" (12:5), and he is honoured more than any other angel.[178]

The meaning of the name Metatron is enigmatic, but it is tempting to explain it by its somewhat interpretative Greek etymology, μετάθρονος meaning σύνθρονος, "(the one) next to the throne".[179] The throne of God's vice-regent Metatron is next to God's throne of glory. This would underline the significance of the enthronement theme, which is important in the work.

The status of Metatron reminds one of the status of the angelic figures of the Holy of Holies that appear in the Qumranic Songs of the Sabbath Sacrifice. As the latter were called "gods", it is easy to understand that Metatron is called the "lesser YHWH". In addition, in 3 Enoch, eight "terrible" heavenly princes are called YHWH "by the name of their King" (3 En. 10:3). The analogous status of Metatron and the angels confirms the suggestion that the name Metatron actually means "next to the throne". Metatron is the highest figure in the celestial hierarchy. This status places him unquestionably in the closest possible vicinity to God, i.e. in the Holy of Holies, before the face of God, where his ministry is exercised.

The theocratic and monotheistic nature of the work is uncontested. Heaven is the temple of God, and his throne of glory is separated by a curtain from the rest of the heavens (chapter 45). Heavenly beings worship God before the

---

[176] In a study of transformational mysticism, Morray-Jones concludes: "There is evidence, then, of the early existence of a tradition concerning the ascent to heaven of an exceptionally righteous man who beholds the vision of the divine *kabod* upon the Merkabah, is transformed into an angelic being and enthroned as celestial vice-regent, thereby becoming identified with the Name-bearing angel who either is or is closely associated with the *kabod* itself and functions as a second, intermediary power in heaven." Morray-Jones, *JSJ 43* (1992) 10. As far as the problems in dating the writings are considered, the evidence of "early existence" must, however, be doubted.

[177] Cf. Schäfer-Herrmann, *Hekhalot-Literatur*, 166 (§72).

[178] Segal suggests that this theme has to do with Jewish speculation about the name of God as a mediator in creation, connected further with the idea that this mediation could be portrayed by a principal angel. Segal, *Two Powers*, 197.

[179] This is suggested e.g. by Lieberman in an appendix in Gruenwald, *Merkavah Mysticism*, 235f. Hengel considers it plausible, but not certain, Hengel, *Studies*, 191.

throne, which of course is typical of merkabah mysticism. The enthronement theme has its place alongside the throne mysticism, however. The highlight of this tradition is the enthronement of Metatron in chapter 10. Metatron relates that the Holy One "made for me a throne like the throne of glory" (10:1).

The enthronement of Metatron is a majestic occasion and it is confirmed by God's statement: "I have appointed Metatron my servant as a prince and a ruler over all the denizens of the heights" (10:3). The status of Metatron is thus similar to that of Moses in the Exagoge of Ezekiel and Enoch in the Similitudes – perhaps even greater. Metatron is probably thought of as the highest being possible in heaven, apart from God.

The enthronement theme is highlighted at the end of the work, where there is a brief account of the ascension of Enoch and how he was made "the minister of the throne of glory" (3 Enoch 48C:4). This is where the enthronement is explained by the new status of Enoch/Metatron. As the "lesser YHWH" he has become the "minister of the throne" *par excellence*. He is evidently an angelic being, as we saw above. His high status in the heavenly hierarchy and his theophoric name prove that he is "next to God" and an angel of the Holy of Holies.[180] We shall later deal with the question how this relates to the idea of "two powers in heaven" (16:3-4) and to the question of the divinization of angelic beings.

The late mystical writing 3 Enoch is a good example of the employment and development of throne mysticism in the Jewish tradition. In this work the concept of the heavenly Temple is exploited in detail. Both cosmology and angelology are developed and serve the presentation of the heavenly world. Also, the story of this work is based on an ascent structure. Furthermore, the idea of enthronement appears to be significant for the author. Even though the description of the heavenly world and its inhabitants is extraordinary rich in such an example of later Hekalot literature, several features comprising both the description of God's divine Temple and the angelic hosts are quite similar to those found, for instance, in 1 Enoch or in the Dead Sea Scrolls. Therefore, we may conclude that the mystical tradition has deep roots. It has had enormous impact on Jewish theology from the Second Temple period onwards.

The investigation of various apocalyptic writings has revealed a wide spectrum of colours in the exploitation of the ascent structure. Throne visions are described in different contexts and the idea of enthronement serves several purposes.

---

[180] Therefore, this writing fits well with the interpretation of Himmelfarb, where the idea of transformation is emphasized, see Himmelfarb, *Ascension*, 44-45.

There are common features in these writings, as well. The idea of a heavenly journey appears constantly in different texts. The ascent story usually climaxes in seeing God's throne in the highest heaven. The heavenly world is described by using traditional terminology in most cases. Early Jewish mysticism is, above all, throne mysticism, as Scholem stated.

Furthermore, the apocalyptic idea of a heavenly Temple seems to be significant for several writers. Temple terminology has been transferred to the celestial realm. This feature, however, could be seen already in certain biblical writings, such as the Psalms. The cultic aspect is sometimes expressed in terms of *pargod* speculation, where the Temple veil serves as a significant symbol and indicator of the heavenly Holy of Holies that lies behind the veil.

There are several different descriptions of heavenly enthronements in these writings. There seems to be a special relationship between God's throne of Glory and other heavenly thrones. The throne in Jewish apocalyptic may be a place of judgment, and different characters are exalted to the status of heavenly judges. The throne is also an honorary place that is promised to several righteous people, especially to patriarchs and prophets.

All this shows that the symbolic universe of traditional Old Testament religion maintained its relevance in the literature of Jewish mysticism. Heavenly journeys are described in terms of theocratic theology, and the cultic nature of the encounter with God is evident. Communication with God is constantly linked to heavenly liturgy. This gives reason to expect that similar symbols are significant for the enthusiastic Jews who constructed early Christology at the turn of the era – even though the discourses in which those symbols were exploited may have changed.

It was in the interests of this study first to investigate different writings separately in order to avoid making too hasty identifications and generalizations. In what follows we need to make a thematic summary, however. Constructive approaches are necessary if we are later on to make justifiable comparisons with early Christian descriptions.

§ 4 From Merkabah Mysticism to Christology: Suggestions and Refutations

After a detailed analysis of relevant merkabah passages we are now able to approach the question concerning the relation between merkabah mysticism and Christology from another point of view. What kind of features in merkabah mysticism could serve as links between Jewish mysticism and early Christology? When answering this question we must interact critically with the three theories of interpretation presented in the Introduction. In particular, the premises on which different theories have been constructed needs to be investigated. Can the angelic interpretation cross the bridge that leads to Christology? Is the divine agency category sufficient in the interpretation? Are there enough materials for a messianic interpretation?

The analysis has shown that there is considerable diversity among merkabah texts as regards different heavenly figures that are associated with some kind of heavenly throne. There are several different patterns for exaltation and the characters in the visions of heavenly journeys have different status and function in the heavenly court. There are also, however, some common elements. The main scene for the stories of heavenly ascent is the heavenly Temple, and metaphors used in the descriptions derive from the cultic environment. Therefore, there is a throne in the Temple, in the Holy of Holies, and according to most writings it is a signal of the kingship of God who rules the heavens and earth. Key elements of the symbolic universe are essential for the present investigation. The visions, in turn, are usually simple stories where the plot and the main characters are easily detected. Thus, the discerning of distinct elements in these stories helps in the interpretation of recurring themes and the reconstuction of the main ideas of Jewish writers of that period.

4.1. Merkabah mysticism and royal metaphors

At first we must consider shortly the basic nature of merkabah mysticism. It is apparent that the occurrence of merkabah speculation is well attested throughout Second Temple Jewish literature and later apocalyptic writings. The dating of the writings justifies such a conclusion. We are not dealing merely with texts that were later than the New Testament, even though many of the writings themselves derive from the period after the destruction of the Temple. For instance several Qumran writings belong to the Hasmonean period, as does the Exagoge of Ezekiel. Also parts of the first book of Enoch must be regarded as quite old.

Furthermore, there is a logical link between such Jewish writings and canonical prophets, especially Ezekiel and Daniel. All this proves that the basic question is justified. Merkabah mysticism predates New Testament Christology and may well have had influence on it.

In Second Temple period, and also later on, merkabah mysticism was rather conservative. God's throne remained in the centre of the thoughts of Jewish writers. There are several features which recur from time to time, and they also serve as a basis for continuity between earlier beliefs and merkabah traditions.

First of all, the nature of the visions and their interpretations is intentionally theocratic. Jewish mystics completely preserve the core of the temple ideology of prophetic tradition. The writings of both Isaiah and Ezekiel serve as models for the description of the heavenly Temple and the heavenly throne. They provide the scene on which different characters appear also in later apocalyptic works. God's throne is transcendent and, according to the writers, it can be approached by the help of God's messengers, the angels.

This means that the theocratic ideal of First Temple Judaism is preserved. God is still the King of Israel. The eschatological hope of righteous Jews has not been altered. The adoration of the enthroned God in the Jerusalem Temple is identical with the adoration of the heavenly God on the *merkabah*-throne.[1]

Therefore, the theocratic ideology appears in a rather simple form in apocalyptic writings. seers are escorted to heaven, before God's throne. The purpose of the writers is crystal-clear. The identity of Jewish faith is preserved only as far as the Enthroned One is praised and worshiped as heavenly King. It is no wonder that some of the visitors are then given a message which they should deliver to the fallen Israel after their return to the earth.[2]

The throne itself, naturally, is a fundamental metaphor in most of the investigated visions. The throne not only expresses power but also serves as a metaphor for the Lordship of God. Even earthly kings performed sovereign reign over their subservients. Much more then does God as a heavenly King reign over the whole world. This is an example where we see how a metaphor works in practice.[3]

Apocalyptic writings provide further an obvious context for the emphasizing of divine power. Quite many of the writings investigated above concentrate on

---

[1] This conclusion merely confirms what Scholem already stated about Jewish mysticism. He emphasized the difference between Jewish mysticism and Catholic mysticism or Moslem Sufism. Jewish mysticism is based on traditional beliefs, such as the belief in the unity of God, and in the revelation as laid down in the Torah. Scholem, *Major Trendds,* 10. The Jewish mystic expressed his vision in termos of his own religious background. "God's pre-existing throne, which embodies and exemplifies all forms of creation, is at once the goal and the theme of his mystical vision." ibid. 44.

[2] Cf. Dean-Otting, *Heavenly Journeys,* 264f., 278f.

[3] According to the metaphor theory the significance of the metaphor exceeds the factual significance of the used image itself. See Introduction.

the problem of theodicy. The chosen people is in danger and God is silent. In such a situation a solution is desperately needed. One basic solution was to remind the readers of God's universal and eschatological power. seers have seen the Lord who reigns. The heavenly King has got the last word.

As we consider the descriptions of heavenly journeys, they seem to express, in particular, the transcendence of God. In Jewish writings these journeys may be short, through three heavens (1 Enoch; TLev.), or long and filled with interesting details of even seven or ten separate heavens (e.g. AscIsa; ApAbr; 3 Baruch). The emphasis on transcendence as such is not necessarily a sign of Temple criticism, but may as well express the "transcendent" justification of Temple cult.[4] This should be borne in mind later when we examine the cultic nature of Jewish apocalyptic. Rowland writes:

"Indeed, as we have seen, the apocalyptic literature cannot readily be identified as the repository of the ideas of the marginalized when only occasionally do we find critical or deviant ideas in them. The language of revelation can be used by the powerful just as much as the weak and marginalized as a way of cloaking their positions of power with the mantle of divine authority."[5]

When we compare the function of the throne in Old Testament descriptions with that of apocalyptic writings we note that, in the latter, the throne is no longer a mediatorial metaphor. It is rather a revelatorial metaphor. It serves the new revelation gained through heavenly journeys. The revelatorial aspect was evidently one feature in Old Testament theology, too, but in the apocalyptic it seems to be especially emphasized.

But why is the revelatorial aspect primary in stories about heavenly journeys? Should we, in spite of our hesitation above, conclude that apocalypticism was founded on Temple criticism where the mediatorial function of the Temple had been rejected? This, most probably, is not the case. It seems rather that the sacrificial cult was only associated with the earthly realm. Visions concern the heavenly realm, however, and there the communion with God was direct – mediated at most by angels.

It is rather important to notice that the apocalyptic speaks of visions. Usually all humans involved, the seers, still belonged to the earthly realm. In their every-day life they still needed the mediatorial cult. This aspect cannot be rejected merely on the grounds of the fact that the seers are often identified as patriarchal heroes. Therefore the relation between these two realms was

---

[4] Himmelfarb remarks that in the Second Temple there was no longer a throne. Therefore, it was easy for those who were unhappy with the priests to see that the Temple was merely a copy of the true Temple located in heaven. Himmelfarb, *Ascent*, 13.

[5] Rowland, *Templum*, 196.

especially close.⁶ We could even speak of a mystical unity. This is true as regards cult. Earthly worship was connected and united with heavenly worship. We should not forget that the most magnificent examples of cultic mysticism, found at Qumran, were songs of the Sabbath sacrifice. In these songs the mediatorial, sacrificial cult had been planted into a revelatorial setting.⁷

Even though the nature of merkabah mysticism remains thoroughly theocratic, there are several active characters acting in heaven. They are also associated with a throne, or even with the throne of glory itself. We shall now turn to this question and consider their status in heaven and their function in merkabah passages.

4.2. Is there an exalted Messiah in merkabah mysticism?

As we search for the points of contact between merkabah mysticism and Christology the messianic aspect appears to be highly relevant. Is there a direct channel through which Jewish ideas could have influenced the emergence of Christology? Do merkabah writings speak of an exalted and enthroned Messiah?

The problem concerning the exaltation and enthronement of heavenly figures in Jewish writings is not simple. Once again one is confronted with a diversity of descriptions. We have seen above that, according to apocalyptic writings, there are several different thrones in the heavens. God's throne is naturally at the centre of all events, but in addition to this patriarchs and even some righteous ones are said to have thrones of their own. Furthermore, in the case of multiple heavens, each heaven may have a throne of its own that is occupied by an angel (AscIsa). There is a difference between God's throne and other thrones.⁸ However, certain exalted ones are said to sit on the throne of glory itself, i.e. on the throne of God.

We should also consider the fact that descriptions of heavenly journeys differ from each other. It is justified to speak of an ascent structure that may be discerned from the writings, but there is not one sole ascent story.⁹ In some cases the seer is taken on a heavenly journey, in others the exaltation of a

---

⁶ As Halperin notes: "The *merkabah* and its attendants can hardly have interested anyone unless they seemed to communicate something important to earthly folk." Halperin, *Chariot*, 61.

⁷ Cf. the discussion in chapter 4.2. below.

⁸ Cf. Dean-Otting, *Heavenly Journeys*, 286f.

⁹ The general idea of an ascent structure, as Segal suggested, is a rather useful category in this respect. As we shall see later, exalted figures themselves are not identical. They cannot be treated as merely one type when further conclusions are made. Cf. Introduction above.

remarkable person is described or just promised. Some writings describe a heavenly liturgy, and lastly there are also stories of heavenly enthronements. Such descriptions may be treated as different narratives derived from a general ascent structure. Later, in the investigation of New Testament Christology, the idea of different "christological narratives" will be exploited. This will entail the reconstruction of hypothetical ascent narratives behind christological statements that apparently have been implied in the construction of Christology.

In Jewish writings there are also several exalted figures who are often associated with a throne. How should we consider these characters and especially the enthroned figures that appear in those descriptions? Is it justified to speak of "divine agents" of God? Is it possible to define a category that sufficiently covers all separate features and also suits the interpretation of early Christology? In order to answer these questions we must first consider the different characters separately.

First of all, we have different traditions of exalted patriarchs. According to these traditions God has exalted several pious Jews in the course of history, or will exalt them in the end of days. These figures are usually given or promised a throne, and they will judge the world with God in the last judgment. In the Exagoge of Ezekiel the chosen one was Moses. In the Testament of Isaac the enthronement was promised to Abraham, Isaac and Jacob (TIsaac 2:7). Testament of Benjamin adds Enoch, Noah, and Shem to this list (TBenj. 10:6). When all the investigated writings are considered together, we get an impressive list of patriarchs who are said to be enthroned in heaven, such as Adam, Abel, Enoch, Noah, Shem, Abraham, Isaac, Jacob, Moses, Isaiah and Job.

These figures or persons cannot exactly be called "divine agents," because they are not actually helping God in his works. Instead of that, they are privileged to get a high status in the heavenly hierarchy and to take part in some of the functions of the last judgment. Their ministry is more like a honorary office than an independent soteriological function concerning the last events. This tradition is similar to the description of the "Richterkollegium" of the 12 disciples in Matthew 19:28.[10] According to Gospel tradition they will function as judges in heaven, but they are always subject to the Lord himself.[11]

Secondly, in Jewish apocalyptic, there are certain priestly figures that act in

---

[10] See below; cf. the thrones of the "elders" in Revelation.

[11] Actually Hurtado, who was the one to introduce the idea of divine agents, himself separates the function of exalted patriarchs from that of other exalted figures. He considers the former representative figures who, for some Jews, served "as assurance of the eschatological reward for which they themselves hoped." Hurtado, *One God,* 66.

heaven. In 11QMelch., Melchizedek is an exceptional character who has a special role in the end of the world, in the "latter days". His function is twofold. "For the Sons of Light, Melchizedek will proclaim release and make expiation; for Belial and those of his lot, Melchizedek will exact the vengeance of the judgments of God."[12] The eschatology of this fragment resembles that of 1 En. 91-93, where angels execute the last judgment in the seventh part of the tenth week. In 11QMelch. the era when Melchizedek will bring peace on earth is described as the last year of Jubilee in Israel (11QMelch. 1-5).

In 11QMelch., there is also a messianic figure who precedes Melchizedek and brings good news about God's intervention.[13] This presentation refers to Isa 52:7. Melchizedek himself is apparently a remarkable angel.[14] He is designed as *elohim* (11QMelch. 25), as were the extraordingary angels in the Songs of the Sabbath Sacrifice, and here Psalm 82:2 is directly referred to. The Psalm quotation emphasizes that the last judgment is executed by a special angelic illuminary.[15]

On the grounds of the judgment descriptions Melchizedek has been identified as the archangel Michael.[16] This view is confirmed by the fact that he also has a priestly function before God in the heavenly Temple. The "jubilee" that Melchizedek brings is put into effect with priestly service. "And the day [of atonem]ent is the end of the tenth jubilee in which atonement will be made for all the sons of [God] and for the men of the lot of Melchizedek." (11QMelch., lines 7-8).

Melchizedek's soteriological role is quite understandable, even though it cannot be identified with Christian theology of atonement. At Qumran the salvation of Zion concerned the chosen of the community who kept the covenant of God (11QMelch. 15-16).[17] Melchizedek, who provides a priestly atonement, actually restores the temple cult that had been broken by the "ungodly" Jerusalem priests.

---

[12] Brooke, *ABD IV* (1992) 687. For the dualism, see Kobelski, *Melchizedek*, 84ff.

[13] This character is an eschatological prophet, as Kobelski has noted, rather than the Davidic Messiah (Fitzmyer). See Kobelski, *Melchizedek*, 61-62; Fitzmyer, *Semitic Background*, 253.

[14] The messianic figure and Melchizedek are distinct characters. Among the proponents of the angelic interpretation Gieschen identifies Melchizedek as the king of Isa 52. Gieschen, *Christology*, 172. Fletcher-Louis is more cautious and speaks merely of an angelomorphic nature of the figure. Fletcher-Louis, *Angels*, 155.

[15] There is evident parallelism with 1 En. 10:12 where the archangel Michael executes the judgment.

[16] For the generality of this view, see Brooke, *ABD IV* (1992) 687.

[17] For the soteriology of Qumran community and the significance of obedience, cf. Ringgren, *Faith*, 110; Garnet, *Pauline studies*, 20f.

Melchizedek assists God so that the theocratic ideal may once again come true in Israel. No enthronement is mentioned in the Melchizedek fragment. It may be implied, though, since the judgment is usually associated with a throne. In this respect the status of Melchizedek resembles that of the exalted patriarchs. However, Melchizedek's soteriological function is different. What is of special interest is the exploitation of the appellation Melchizedek. If we have here the archangel Michael with royal and high priestly characteristics, why is he called Melchizedek? It is probable that Psalm 110 has been exploited in this interpretation. Therefore, 11QMelch. may be regarded as one of the earliest examples of exploiting Psalm 110 in an apocalyptic Jewish writing.

In Qumran writings we also have the interesting hero of the fragment 4Q491. Here the exalted figure anticipated a glorious future: "I shall be reckoned with gods". He expected that he would be exalted to the highest rank of heaven where he would worship God with the "gods" of the Holy of Holies. Even though the character might be identified as a religious teacher or a messianic figure, the best arguments are in favor of a priestly interpretation. The hero of 4Q491 may well be a messianic High Priest, who will be exalted when the future events begin to take place. In Qumran ideology there was also a parallel to this. In the Blessings 1QSb the messianic High Priest was promised a place in the heavenly palace and Holy of Holies: "May he [renew] for you the Covenant of the [everlasting] priesthood; may He sanctify you [for the House] of Holiness" (1QSb 3, 25ff.).

According to this interpretation the hero of 4Q491 is an eschatological priest.[18] The sect believed that the Temple cult would be purified when the decisive events took place, i.e. when the holy war would broke out. Therefore it is quite natural that the fragment in question would belong to the War Scroll. The scene of the fragment is transcendent, however. The status of the eschatological priest is justified with the authority of the heavenly Temple. He will minister in the heavenly Holy of Holies, where he is placed among the "gods" of the *debir*.

Such an eschatological figure has little to do with the exalted patriarchs that are described in other writings. There is a close link to the description of Melchizedek in 11QMelch., but here the figure does not seem to be of angelic nature. The variety of heavenly figures makes it increasingly more difficult to assume that all these figures could fit in merely under one category of divine agents.

In Enochic writings, and especially in the Parables, the "chosen one", or the Son of Man, appears to be a messianic figure in a somewhat more traditional way. The enthronement scenes (51:3; 61:8) as such refer to the enthronement

---

[18] Cf. Hengel, *Studies*, 203.

of a "political" Messiah. The startling feature in such description is, however, that the enthronement is considered transcendent.[19] The Son of Man also conducts a messianic banquet at the end of days. In this respect he resembles the Davidide that appears in the Qumran writings. The identity of the character is vague, though, and perhaps it is proper to leave the final interpretation open. He may even be a heavenly figure like the Son of Man in Daniel, and in this case he may have been regarded as some kind of heavenly being.[20] As the idea of a metamorphosis in the first book of Enoch has been abandoned above, the interpretation where the Son of Man would actually be an exalted patriarch is not accepted.[21]

What is evident, though, is the exalted status of the enthroned Son of Man. He is a heavenly judge as most of the exalted figures in the apocalyptic writings are. He is even said to sit on the throne of Glory. His position is extraordinary. This fact does not seem to threathen monotheism, though. All these figures are servants of God and remain in a theocratic relation to him.

Messiah, however, in a traditional sense is a kingly figure. He is a son of David and as an eschatological figure he fulfils the hopes of Davidic dynasty. The abovementioned "agents" do not actually fit in this role. They are heavenly actors who have significant functions in heaven, but they are not exactly royal princes anticipating their enthronement. In our search for a heavenly messianic figure we must lastly turn to those passages where the basic messianic figure of the Davidide appears.

We have seen above that even an earthly Davidide was believed to sit "on the throne of the Lord" like Solomon did (1 Chron. 29:23). In the Old Testament kingship ideology Psalm 110 has naturally also had a significant function. The earthly Davidide was considered the adopted son of God, and he ruled "at the right hand" of God on the heavenly throne. This motif was important in the so called Davidic promise tradition – and naturally in New

---

[19] Nickelsburg has argued that Enochic Parables present an essential transformation of traditional themes. Political messianology is transformed into a belief in heavenly kingship. The messianic figure is a compilation of the figures of Davidic Messiah, Danielic Son of Man, and the Isaianic Chosen One. The most crucial one of the transformations is that theophany is replaced by "huiophany". "The righteous Son of Man appears to judge and is seated on God's glorious throne." Nickelsburg, *Judaisms*, 62.

[20] Collins has suggested an angelic interpretation in one of his commentaries, see Collins, *Daniel*, 310f. That conclusion, however, rests on hypotheses like all the other theories. Rather, the texts suggest a transformation like Nickelsburg stated: "Three traditional figures of exalted status have become one figure who is both similar to, and notably different from, the prototypes. Nickelsburg, *Judaisms*, 63.

[21] Alexander, in *OTP I*, 247. This interpretation has probably been made under the influence of 3 Enoch, where a metamorphosis most evidently takes place.

Testament Christology.[22] In certain eschatologial passages of the apocalyptic writings the enthronement of a Davidic Messiah is described. The Isaiah Pesher of Qumran (4Q161) is one of the rare occurrences of such a belief. The writer is describing an enthronement of the "shoot" of David (Frags. 8-10, col. III, 18-21, Vermes):

> "[Interpreted, this concerns the Branch] of David who shall arise at the end [of days]... God will uphold him with [the spirit of might, and will give him] a throne of glory and a crown of [holiness]... [He will put a sceptre] in his hand and he shall rule over all the [nations]."

According to this fragment the Davidide shall rule over nations in the end. The Isaiah passage is interpreted as a promise of the enthronement of the Messiah. But should we consider the scene transcendent? Is the fragment describing the heavenly enthronement of the Davidide? This is not evident. The passage seems to describe rather the enthronement of a political Messiah who shall conduct the holy war in the eschatological climax of Israel's history.[23] The idea of ruling all the nations is a typical description of Davidic rulers. Therefore, this passage does not yet transform the eschatological enthronement to the heavenly realm.[24]

The Davidide in this fragment also brings salvation, but this is understood in the manner of the traditional theocratic pattern. Under the leadership of the new Davidic Messiah true Israel, i.e. the righteous ones, will renew the theocratic ideal in the eschatological congregation. This was one of the basic beliefs in Qumran eschatology. According to the Rule of the Congregation a Messiah-king (a Davidide?) would lead a messianic banquet with the priest and this would take place at the inauguration of the time of grace (1QSa II, 17-22).[25]

As regards Davidic messianology there are also certain other classical passages where this tradition is explicit. In the Testament of Judah, which is one of the most obvious writings to mention this theme, the Messiah will fulfill the promises given to Judah. "With an oath the Lord swore to me that the rule

---

[22] In this respect Duling has grounds for his reconstruction of the so called promise tradition in Jewish theology. See Duling, *NTS 19* (1973) 56ff.

[23] Cf. Schiffman: "The author or authors of the Pesarim on Isaiah clearly expected the sect to be led in the end of days by the prince of the congregation and/or the Davidic Messiah." Schiffman, *Messiah*, 124.

[24] For instance Collins notes that the Davidide is associated with the eschatological war, and at least in this respect the passage is rather political and historical. See Collins, *Scepter*, 57-58. Cf. the extensive analysis of Talmon, *Judaisms*, 123-128.

[25] In spite of these notions we must agree with Charlesworth who remarks that messianology was not a major concern of the community. For instance, biblical Psalms were not exploited in the presentation of messianology, and even other psalms, written as Davidic Pseudepigrapha, were not messianic. Charlesworth, *Messiah*, 25.

would not cease for my posterity." (TJud. 22:3). The Messiah is a Star from Jacob, and a Sun of righteousness. He is the Shoot of God, i.e. the Davidide that was promised in Isa. 11:1.[26] Even though there is evident Christian redaction in this passage, the basic messianology is in agreement with Jewish beliefs. No explicit enthronement is mentioned, but it must be presumed, though. The new Davidide shall reign as a king and his kingdom is a kingdom of salvation.

In the Psalms of Solomon the Davidide is also a political Messiah who acts as a righteous king in Israel:[27]

"See, Lord, and raise up for them their king, the son of David, to rule over your servant Israel in the time known to you, O God. Undergrid him with the strength to destroy the unrighteous rulers, who trample her to destruction... He will gather a holy people whom he will lead in righteousness; and he will judge the tribes of the people that have been made holy by the Lord their God." (PsSol. 17:21, 26).

The writer mentions the "raising up" of the son of David, but a factual enthronement has to be inferred from the context. A throne must naturally exist, since the Davidide shall reign as a king. The throne is not given primary significance, though, and therefore the eschatology of this passage is not explicitly transcendent.

In 4. Ezra 12:32f. we find a rather similar conception of a Davidic king:

"And as for the lion that you saw... this is the Messiah whom the Most High has kept until the end of days, who will arise from the posterity of David, and will come and speak to them; he will denounce them for their ungodliness and for their wickedness, and will cast up before them their contemptuous dealings. For first he will set them living before his judgment seat, and when he has reproved them, then he will destroy them. But he will deliver in mercy the remnant of my people..."

Here the throne of the Davidide is a judgment seat. This scene is thoroughly eschatological and resembles the descriptions of the enthronement of the Son of Man in 1 Enoch.[28] These passages prove that there was some kind of tradition of the enthronement of the Messiah, the son of David, in Jewish writings.[29] According to these texts he is both an eschatological judge and an ideal king under whose leadership a glorious era will begin.

---

[26] Cf. Jer. 23:5; 33:15; Zech. 3:8; 6:12.

[27] For the political connotations, see Collins, *Scepter*, 55.

[28] This passage of 4 Ezra has naturally also been considered a Christian interpolation, but this is not evident at all. The message of the writer is quite similar to that of the righteous ones of Qumran.

[29] Stone remarks, however, that the royal features are vague in 4 Ezra. "Moreover, in spite of the title 'Messiah,' the Davidic descent, and the lion symbol by which he is represented, the Messiah is nowhere talked of in the language of kingship." Stone, *Judaisms*, 215.

The examples investigated above show that it is not so easy to speak of Jewish "messianology" of the Second Temple period. One might rather admit with Charlesworth that, "Jews did not profess a coherent and normative messianology" at all.[30] There is further uncertainty whether there ever existed factual descriptions of the heavenly enthronement of the Davidide – even though certain writings admittedly speak of his throne. Davidic Messiah usually maintains the rather political features that are attached to the historical dynasty. This is probably the reason why eschatological features are not prominent in these descriptions.[31]

According to our analysis the descriptions of a heavenly enthronement vary significantly in different writings. Visions that speak of the enthronement of prominent figures are usually eschatological. The enthronement will take place in the eschatological future, in the end of days. This is true also as regards the enthronement of the patriarchs. The stories of their exaltation usually mention their death and the departure of the soul from the body. A throne is promised to these significant persons, but the enthronement itself will be an eschatological event.[32]

This leads us to an interesting question concerning the role of resurrection in exaltation and enthronement descriptions. This is a question posed by New Testament materials, since there the exaltation and resurrection are identical. In Jewish writings the situation is somewhat different, even though there are similarities, as well.

Resurrection as such is not a prominent feature in Old Testament theology, but even there it is linked with the idea of a last judgment.[33] This is its context also in Jewish theology. For instance, certain passages in 2 Maccabeans serve as examples of this. The Maccabean martyrs face their death calmly, being convinced of their resurrection to life in the end:

"the King of the universe will raise us up to an everlasting renewal of life" (2 Macc. 7:9).

---

[30] Charlesworth, *Messiah*, 35.

[31] Hengel notes that the messianic interpretation of Psalm 110, which was certainly present in New Testament times and was directly attached to the idea of the enthronement of a Davidic Messiah, was suppressed in Jewish theology. Later in Tannaitic discussion it appear again. Hengel, *Studies*, 194-196.

[32] As this notion is combined with Charlesworth's claim concerning the vagueness of Jewish beliefs of that time, the problem concerning the emergence of earliest Christology is no longer so easy. The combining of messianic beliefs and exaltation descriptions is not automatically motivated by "standard" Jewish conceptions. Therefore, there are several open questions to be answered in later chapters. For Charlesworth's conclusions, see especially Charlesworth, *Judaisms*, 251ff.

[33] See e.g. Isa. 26:19; Ezek. 37:12; Dan. 12:2.

The oppressor will not escape God's punishment: "But for you there will be no resurrection to life!" (2 Macc. 7:14.)

According to the Wisdom of Solomon the persecuted righteous ones will be resurrected to life (2:19-20; 4:7-11; 5:15-16) and they will be present when the judgment of the wicked takes place (5:1ff.).[34] They will receive a status like that of the enthroned patriarchs: "They will govern nations and rule over peoples, and the Lord will reign over them forever".[35]

In Daniel the judgment is linked with the resurrection. Some shall be taken to everlasting life, others to everlasting contempt (Dan. 12:2). In the Psalms of Solomon the resurrection of the righteous ones means their salvation to eternal life (2:30-31; 3:11-12; 14:6-10; 15:12-13). A similar belief is explicit in 4 Ezra 8:48. Resurrection is promised to the righteous.

The enthronement theme is connected to this motif for example in the Apocalypse of Moses. There the enthronement of Adam is described as an eschatological enthronement that takes place in the eschatological resurrection (ApcMos. 39:3; 41:3). Adam's resurrection means also his final salvation and he is allowed to eat from the tree of life (ApcMos. 28:4). A similar motif is found in TLev. 18:10-11, where the Messiah leads his own to Paradise where they may eat from the tree of life.

This much can be concluded on the basis of apocalyptic writings. Most writers believe in the resurrection of the dead. It is considered a crucial eschatological event which leads to the last judgment. For righteous Jews it will be a "resurrection to life". This is how, for example, the writer of the Testament of Judah understands the event. "And after this Abraham, Isaac, and Jacob will be resurrected to life and I and my brothers will be chiefs (wielding) our scepters in Israel." (TJud. 25:1).

This is a feature that also connects the resurrection with the idea of enthronement. The resurrection of the dead is the unique event that precedes the exaltation and enthronement of patriarchs. This is the closest relation that we can find between resurrection and enthronement. It is also quite logical since we are speaking of dead patriarchs whose souls have been taken to rest and who await their personal resurrection and exaltation.

As regards other heavenly figures, however, no writer speaks of their personal resurrection as a significant eschatological event. Their enthronement is often an event of an eschatological entering upon the throne, and only as such an event does it occur in the context of the general resurrection. These

---

[34] See especially the analysis of Nickelsburg, *Resurrection*, 48ff.

[35] There is a parallel to this in Sirach 4:12, even though in Sirach the eschatological redaction does not remove the basic sapiential conviction that from the dead "thanksgiving has ceased" (Sirach 17:28).

other figures, however, appear to be in heaven already. They themselves are not part of the resurrection. For example in TJud. 24 there was a description of the exaltation of the Messiah, but it was completely separated from the resurrection mentioned in TJud. 25, which was further applied to the exaltation of the patriarchs.[36]

The most obvious question that arises on the basis of New Testament Christology concerns the resurrection of a Davidide. Is there anything in apocalyptic Jewish writings that would resemble such an idea? The answer is negative. In no writing is the resurrection considered a premise for the enthronement of the Shoot of David.

The description of the exaltation of the Davidide on the throne of glory remains on such a metaphorical level that almost nothing is said about the person itself. Usually his kingship can be understood in earthly terms. Even if his reign could be interpreted as an eschatological reign, as in the case of the Qumran passage, the Son of David is not presented as an earthly person who would ascend to heaven before his enthronement. This fact leaves us with a puzzle that we must attempt to solve later when New Testament Christology is investigated.

On the one hand, our analysis has clarified certain aspects and details in the merkabah tradition of Jewish mysticism. On the other hand, new questions have arisen and certain problems have become more difficult. This is partly the case with the enthronement theme. It has not turned out to be as clear as some scholars have suggested. Also the question concerning the messianology of Second Temple Judaism as such has turned out to be difficult. It is not at all apparent that there prevailed any clearly defined conception of an eschatological Messiah. In this respect one needs to ask anew, where did the first Christians get their convictions and how did they justify them.

Another difficulty concerns the theory of divine agents. The figures paralleled in that theory are too diverse to be identified with merely one category.[37] It is true that, as far as the ascent structure is concerned, all these different figures ascend to heaven. In some way or another they make a heavenly journey. In heaven, though, they have different functions and

---

[36] This is notable since, due to the Christian redaction in the passage, one could expect a clear description of an enthronement of the Resurrected One in the manner of AscIsa.

[37] Hurtado pays attention to such variation, but his conclusion is that it justifies the construction of a general category. "The variation shows that a number of Jewish groups worked with the idea of God having such a chief agent who was second only to God in rank." Hurtado, *One God*, 18. I am not convinced that Jewish apocalypticists had a research programme where they attempted to work out a concept of a chief agent. Instead, apocalyptical descriptions seem to include several different heavenly figures which have little in common.

different status. It is not justified to reduce all these functions to merely one pattern and make that pattern the prototype of early Christology.

4.3. Limitations of the angelic interpretation

In the chapter on the history of investigation the angelic interpretation appeared to be popular both in the interpretation of Jewish mysticism and in the interpretation of early Christology. Could angelic figures serve as models with which certain key elements of early Christology could be explained? There were some good arguments behind this theory, but as regards the main question concerning the enthronement of a Messiah we confront similar problems as we did above when the messianic aspect was investigated.

Many of the recent monographs investigating the relation between Jewish apocalyptic and early Christology attempt to develop the insights of Segal, Rowland and Fossum.[38] There are naturally several factors which seem to serve as evidence for the theory. If the angelic figure, exploited in the theory, is defined only on a general level, this theory is often rather suitable for interpretation. Rowland, for example, spoke of an "angelic figure of considerable status". Such a concept was easily applied in the interpretation and explanation of both the descriptions of Jewish mysticism and early Christology. There are no doubt angelic figures of considerable status in apocalyptic writings and they have a special function in heaven. According to our analysis, however, the status of these angelic figures has in some degree been over-estimated in scholarship.

Such general statements concerning the relation between Jewish mysticism and early Christology are not, however, very useful in a detailed analysis. This is probably the reason why both Rowland himself and his followers were forced to redefine such a point of departure. As regards Christology they have made a new distinction between *angel* Christology and *angelomorphic* Christology. Angel Christology means here an explicit identification of Christ as an angel.[39] This was considered too strong an interpretation since, according to these scholars, angelic form, function, or terminology do not necessarily imply created ontology. The occurrence of these features does not prove that Christ was identified entirely with the created order. Therefore Christology was defined merely as "angelomorphic".

One must ask, however, whether such distinction alters the situation. It evidently helps one to use angelic interpretation without a necessary commitment to an ontological principle. But once the ontology is rejected, the whole theory seems to vanish. It is obvious that if Christ in early Christology

---

[38] See chapter 1.1. above.

[39] See Gieschen, *Christology*, 28; following Rowland, *JSNT* 24 (1985), 100.

has features of angelic form and function, he has merely been described by using such metaphors.

This kind of interpretation is no longer "angelic", since Christ is not identified as an angel. The latter has naturally also been suggested, as we saw earlier e.g. in the interpretation of Segal, but this kind of interpretation is exactly what these scholars have attempted to redefine.[40] In later studies certain angelic features were merely exploited in the interpretation of early Christology, and usually they concerned the high status of a heavenly being. Therefore the conclusions were bound to remain on a general level.

These problems concern also the analysis of Jewish mysticism. An angelic interpretation in its strict form appears to have been used in the interpretation of Jewish writings. In many of the extensive monographs investigating angelic figures no distinction has been made between proper angels and exalted human beings or other kinds of mediatorial heavenly figures. This reveals that the concept of angelomorphy has in fact been used as a heuristic tool for the identification of angelic beings.[41] In fact, this too has produced certain confusion.

For example in Gieschen's analysis the criteria of divinity seem to have a primary significance for the results he gets. In the beginning of his investigation he has first defined these criteria in detail. They comprise divine position, divine appearance, divine functions, divine name and divine veneration.[42] Later in the analysis he uses them constantly when attempting to prove the identity of high angelic beings. Therefore, for example as regards Adam in the Life of Adam and Eve (13:1-15:3), he speaks of the "veneration of an angelomorphic figure in a Jewish context," even though the text gives little evidence for such a feature.[43]

For Gieschen, the criterion of veneration seems to prove the exceptional divine nature of Adam in this passage. Therefore Adam is defined as angelomorphic. The angelic interpretation has emerged here as a secondary conclusion, and we must note that it is subordinated to the five criteria that Gieschen has chosen for his interpretation.

Such conclusions appear to ignore certain basic notions. Exalted patriarchs in Jewish mysticism do not appear to be angelic figures. Their exaltation is

---

[40] In the Introduction (1.1.) we saw that for example Segal and Rowland in their earlier works suggested a straightforward angel Christology.

[41] This can be seen for example in Fletcher-Louis, *Angels*, 145ff., who is rather cautious in the matter, though, and in Gieschen, *Christology*, 152ff., who makes quite definite conclusions.

[42] Gieschen, *Christology*, 31-33.

[43] Gieschen, *Christology*, 154.

extraordinary, but they have a special function of their own in heaven. Usually they act as heavenly judges, which expresses their high status in the heavenly hierarchy. However, one is not entitled to conclude that a position merely would express something about the ontological nature of the being, whether concerning divinity or angelic nature. Hierarchical status is functional. In the description of certain patriarchs, such as Abel or Enoch one does detect angelomorphic features, but it would be a methodological error to conclude that the occurrence of such features would imply an ontological change in the patriarchs themselves.

Certain exceptions must be admitted, though. For example, in the late writing of 2 Enoch, Adam is called "a second angel" (30:11), and also some kind of transformation of Enoch (21:1-22:10) is described further on.[44] In the Prayer of Joseph Jacob was identified as the angel of God.[45] These late passages are exceptions, however, and they have little in common with other passages speaking of the exaltation of patriarchs.

While Gieschen has presented detailed criteria in this question, some further comments may be made on his theory. The appearance of exalted beings does not give us information about their ontological nature. One may detect similarities between the descriptions of exalted figures and the descriptions of angels or even theophanies. We should note, however, that such descriptions never alter the relationship of the exalted one and God. This concerns the criterion of "divine" functions as well. Exalted patriarchs act as heavenly judges, but their status in the heavenly hierarchy is strictly defined. Only the theme of creating the world, and probably that of absolving sins – even though this may also be a priestly function – appear to reveal certain divine aspect in heavenly functions. The problem of investigation in these matters, however, is that these aspects do not occur in the passages related to the angelic interpretation.[46]

What is special about angels in Jewish mysticism are their names. According to Gieschen names, too, may imply divinity. Even here we must express our doubts, though. Angels no doubt have divine names in several writings. This fact, however, is rather similar to the occurrence of theophoric names in Jewish culture in general.

As we have seen above, scholars have paid a lot of attention, for example, to the angel Jaoel in the Apocalypse of Abraham. Jaoel was the angel who

---

[44] Cf. Fletcher-Louis, *Angels*, 153f.; Gieschen, *Christology*, 153.

[45] Fletcher-Louis is correct when noting that here Jacob/Israel is not merely angelomorphic, but an angel, see *Angels*, 160. The problem of the transformation of Enoch is speculative, however, as we have seen above in chapter 3.3.

[46] For the definition of such criteria, see Gieschen, *Christology*, 32.

possessed God's "ineffable name" (ApAbr. 10:8; cf. 10:3). In the Old Testament we found passages where an angel was said to bear God's name. For example in the story where the conquest of Canaan was promised God also promised to "send an angel" before Israel in order to guard the people. About this angel God said: "my name is in him." (Ex. 23:21).[47]

An extraordinary example of an angelic figure possessing a theophoric name is found in the Qumran fragment 11QMelch. There the figure of Melchizedek was described as an eschatological saviour who will bring peace on earth. Melchizedek was also called *Elohim* (11QMelch. 25).[48] The divine name of the angel here does not necessarily mean deification in itself, but rather the especially high status of the angel. A similar pattern can be seen later in 3 Enoch. Metatron is called "the lesser YHWH" (12:5), and he is honored more than any other angel (cf. 3 Enoch 48D:1).[49]

In the Qumran fragment the character of Melchizedek was evidently Michael the archangel, as we have seen before. He will act as a judge at the end of days. We must remember, though, that in Jewish apocalyptic there were several different exalted figures who had the status of a heavenly judge. Melchizedek is apparently quite special, since he will also be the one who saves people from the power of Belial. He must be regarded as an important heavenly being, because the scriptural proof of Isa. 52:7 actually talks about the Lordship of God.[50] The relation of angels to God is not very clear in Jewish writings. They represent God, but simultaneously they almost seem to incarnate God in some manner – at least if our western mind is not leading us astray in our interpretation. The scene is confusing and does not become much clearer when we consider the ideas of Philo in what follows.

In Philo we find the most revealing passage where he explains the allegorical meaning of the cherubim above the ark in the Holy of Holies. The first one of the cherubim was called "God" and it represented God's "creative potency". The second one was called Lord, and this one was a kingly cherub.

---

[47] Gieschen, too, calls Jaoel's name theophoric, and in his interpretation he actually admits that, in spite of "some veneration" of Jaoel in the passage, this angel joins Abraham in worshipping God (ApAbr. 17:1-21). Gieschen, *Christology*, 143f.

[48] Hurtado thinks that the divine title is used because "this figure was so highly exalted and so closely identified with divine purposes that the community could see him referred to in quite exalted terms such as 'Elohim' and in passages where one could more easily see God himself as the referent." Hurtado, *One God, one Lord*, 79.

[49] Gieschen defines Melchizedek divine due to his function as a judge and the application of divine names. Gieschen, *Christology*, 172. This, however, is not evident in the passage. Fletcher-Louis, for example, speaks merely of an "angelomorphic view of kingship and priesthood." Fletcher-Louis, *Angels*, 155.

[50] Hurtado, *One God, one Lord*, 77ff.; Collins, *Scepter and the Star*, 162.

It represented God's just government (Vit.Mos. II, 99-100). Philo's interpretation is simultaneously very traditional and also novel as regards Jewish mysticism. It is traditional, since the kingly power of God is considered the basic meaning of the cherub-throne. On the other hand, however, Philo's interpretation presupposes that there are special *cherubim* beside God's heavenly throne.

It seems that Jewish theology in general held a belief that in heaven there are special angels who possess theophoric names. Their status is high and they are often connected with God's throne. The most interesting one of those theophoric names is "god". Angels in general may have been called sons of God (Gen. 6:2-4; Ps. 89:7), as is also the case e.g. in the Prayer of Joseph (fr. A, 6). In Qumran writings, however, the special title "god" seemed to belong to the highest angels.

In the Qumran fragment 4Q491 we have seen the startling statement of the exalted figure: "I am counted among the gods, and my glory is with the sons of the king" (line 18). A similar idea was further found in fragments 4Q427 VII and 4Q471b. In the Songs of the Sabbath Sacrifice the title "gods" is given to several heavenly beings. In the seventh song the "august ones" are the "chiefs of the praises of all the gods" (col. I, 31-32). They are further described as the "spirits of the holy of the holies, the living gods, the spirits of everlasting holiness above all the holy ones" (col. I, 44-45).

It seems evident that in the mysticism of the Songs of the Sabbath Sacrifice the heavenly beings that worshiped in the heavenly Holy of Holies, before the face of God, were called "gods". In this sense the scene is somewhat different than in 1 Enoch, where God is said to sit alone in the Holy of Holies (1 Enoch 14:21). This kind of conviction is somewhat extraordinary in itself, however, since in the descriptions of the divine throne the cherubim usually always accompany the throne.[51]

These angels of the Holy of Holies had got theophoric names due to their extraordinary status in heavenly hierarchy. A similar logic can be found behind the theophoric name Jaoel, the angel "in whom God's name resides" (ApcAbr. 10:8). And when we recall the exalted figure in the Qumran fragment 4Q491, i.e. the one who anticipated a glorious future, it is only natural that he expressed his expectation by referring to the angels of the *debir*: "I shall be reckoned with gods". He expected that he will be exalted to the highest rank of heaven and he will be given the right to worship God with the "gods" of the Holy of Holies.[52]

---

[51] Cf. the analysis of the Songs of the Sabbath Sacrifice below in chapter 4.2.

[52] Therefore it is not possible to accept Gieschen's criterion, according to which a theophoric name alone would express divinity. Gieschen, *Christology*, 33.

In addition to this we must note that in several writings angels served as priests in the heavenly Temple. As early as 1 Enoch 14 they had this ministry, even though they were barred from the inner house.[53] In the Qumran Songs of the Sabbath Sacrifice this theme forms the basic line of the whole collection. Furthermore, in 11QMelch. Melchizedek ministers in the Temple on the Day of Atonement, and most probably a heavenly Temple is referred to here. In this respect these passages evidence an assimilation of the angelic interpretation with the priestly interpretation.

Theophoric names appear to reveal the status of certain angels. Names probably also refer to the priestly function of these angels. Divinity in a proper sense, however, is not meant when they are used. This is the reason why names cannot be regarded as a criterion of divinity.

Furthermore, angelic interpretation has little to contribute to the investigation of the enthronement theme. In the Qumran fragment 4Q491 the enthronement of the hero is evident, but there is no mention of any enthronement of the angels. According to AscIsa the angels had thrones in separate heavens. There was no mention of any angel's throne in the highest heaven, however. The late writing of 2 Enoch is the only document where we can find the idea that an angel is associated with God's throne as regards the status of the angel. In chapter 24 the Lord told Enoch: "Enoch, sit to the left of me with Gabriel." (2 Enoch, J 24:1; the A-text: "closer than Gabriel."). Gabriel appears to be seated in an honorary place beside God, even though he must make room for Enoch.[54]

Finally we need to consider the question of angel veneration and the problem of deification in Jewish mysticism. As we have seen in the Introduction, there are actually two schools opposing each other in these questions. One is convinced that there can be found descriptions of a divine angelic intermediary in pre-Christian Jewish apocalyptic.[55] The other argues that in no passage under consideration the divinity of the heavenly figure is explicit.[56]

As several scholars have pointed out, there are passages in Jewish writings where exalted beings are revered. There are, for example, expressions of thanksgiving in response to various functions or activities attributed to angels (e.g. Jos.Asen. 15:12; TLev. 5:5-6). In Qumran (11QBer) angels are placed

---

[53] So Halperin, *Chariot*, 82.

[54] Bock, *Blasphemy*, 164f., 183.

[55] This was the line of Rowland and Fossum, accepted later e.g. by Fletcher-Louis, *Angels*, 211f.; Gieschen, *Christology*, 183.

[56] This was the conclusion of Hurtado, followed later e.g. by Stuckenbruck, *Angel Veneration*, 180, 200f.; and Carrell, *Jesus*, 224f.

alongside God in blessing formulae.[57] However, passages such as that in the Life of Adam and Eve, where Satan is told to venerate and worship the "image of God" (LAE 14:2), are not evidence for the divine nature of Adam.[58]

On the other hand there are passages where the worship of angels is prohibited. In the Ascension of Isaiah, for example, where separate heavens had thrones of their own, the worship of the thrones and the angels on them was strictly prohibited. "Worship neither throne, nor angel from the six heavens" (7:21). In 3 Enoch, in turn, Metatron no doubt has a special status in heaven, but even there the famous cry: "There are indeed two powers in heaven!", awakens a reaction (3 En. 16:3-4), causing the dethronement of Metatron.

How does all this affect our estimation of the angelic interpretation? In several Jewish writings it is clear we find an "angelic figure of considerable status". These angels have theophoric names, and are granted even the titles "elohim", "Lord", and "god". In these passages, however, the focus is on the throne of God. The task of these angels is to worship God. They are naturally on the top of the heavenly hierarchy, but their function is to praise God before the throne of glory.

Angel veneration has apparently had a place at least in sectarian Jewish theology, but the beliefs that may be detected by the help of extant materials seem to depend on a concept of heavenly hierarchy. There are passages where the veneration of angels is a necessary premise for the understanding of the warnings of the writer. The factual evidence for angel worship in Jewish writings is problematic, though.[59] As Stuckenbruck has concluded, there is no clear evidence of a cultic devotion to angels. Angel veneration occurs in certain writings, but even here the sources do not allow to speak of a common practice.[60]

The speculative nature of the evidence makes it difficult to draw conclusions and the significance of research programmes and schools of interpretation increases in the explanation of the texts. It is no wonder that the final question of the problem of deification is treated differently in the two schools of interpretation mentioned above. Some scholars are convinced that in certain Jewish writings the aspect of deification can be detected. There are others, however, who consider such interpretation exaggerated.

---

[57] See Stuckenbruck, *Angel Veneration*, 201.

[58] Against Gieschen, *Christology*, 154.

[59] Scholars often refer for instance to Col. 2:18 and to Paul's Jewish opponents in this connection, but even that passage is problematic. It is probable that it speaks merely about heavenly liturgy and angelic visions. See chapter 5.2. below.

[60] Stuckenbruck, *Angel Veneration*, 201.

The problem of deification concerned particularly Moses traditions. For example, Meeks suggested that Philo speaks of the deification of Moses, and van den Horst maintained that, in the Exagoge of Ezekiel, the theme of the deification of Moses is explicit, as well.[61] We have already stated above that enthronement as such should not be identified as deification. If one wishes to argue for deification, it should be done on other grounds.

This is, of course, what Meeks has attempted to do. He stated that in Philo the concept of Moses' implicit or even explicit deity, or at least a divine status, originates in a "usual" Hellenistic conception of the "divine man".[62] This, however, is no longer a valid argument, as it may have been during the period when the history-of-religions school prevailed. Firstly, the argument concerning "divine men" is anachronistic. And secondly, in accordance with the first notion, there are no clear signs of such conception in Jewish or Christian literature in the first century A.D.

Philo, as we stated earlier, has a theocratic tendency. He calls Moses "god", but similar terminology has been found also elsewhere in Jewish writings (e.g. Qumran Songs of the Sabbath Sacrifice), and the exploitation of the term as such is no proof for deification. Also the connections between the abovementioned passages of Philo and Exagoge of Ezekiel have turned out to be hypothetical. In these writings there is no evidence for the kind of argumentation of which van den Horst was speaking.

In the ascent stories of Jewish writings several figures are enthroned on the throne of Glory, and this feature has been taken as a further justification for the idea of deification. In the significant passages of the Similitudes Enoch sits on the throne of Glory itself. This is also what Moses does in the dream vision of the Exagoge of Ezekiel. There is, however, no logical causality between enthronement and deification. Enthronement as such means simply that the chosen one gains an extraordinary status in heaven. This fact emphasizes that according to the apocalyptics there was a strict hierarchy in the palaces of the heavenly court.[63] The relationship, however, between God and the enthroned ones is not defined by such a status. It speaks merely of the relationship between the enthroned one and other heavenly beings (or even human beings). In the writings that we have examined the scene is constantly theocratic. The enthroned one rules only in God's name and under God's authority. According to most stories, his main task in the heavenly court is to worship God. This aspect is most significant when defining the relationship between God and his "agents".

---

[61] van den Horst, *Essays*, 67.

[62] Meeks, *Essays*, 369ff.

[63] Cf. Hengel, *Studies*, 191.

Certain scholars have treated Moses traditions in the context of angelomorphic interpretation.[64] There is speculation of this interpretation, however, since these Mosaic texts do not always bear traditional marks of angelomorphy.[65] Angelomorphic interpretation has little in common with the questions posed at Moses traditions. Also the problem of deification is different in these two. Therefore we must make the conclucions mostly in the area of angelic interpretation itself.

The criteria for divinity, treated above, have turned out to be quite insufficient. As we have seen, divine position, divine appearance, divine functions, and divine name are not sufficient categories to be used as proper criteria for the divinity of a heavenly being. The criterion of divine veneration might have been helpful in this question, but there were no relevant passages that could have been used as evidence in this question. In Jewish writings cultic devotion to angels or other kinds of exalted figures is not explicit.

It may naturally be that scholars mean different things with the word divine. All scholars do not actually use it to mean deity as such, but merely heavenly functions prescribed by God. Therefore the discussion over the criteria may be somewhat confusing. It is apparent that, according to many of the investigated texts, exalted figures do have a special status and they do have extraordinary eschatological functions in heaven. However, writers do not treat them as Gods and they do not worship them as Gods. Quite the contrary, all high angels and most of the exalted figures themselves worship God in heaven. They all remain under the theocratic pattern of Jewish theology. The picture differs dramatically from the pantheons of the polytheistic religions prevailing at the time. Therefore it is important to note that negative results in the search for the aspect of deification in Jewish apocalyptic do not grow out of a desire to fit these traditions into the monotheistic faith of mainstream Judaism. The message of apocalyptic writers is not that of deification.

The theory lacks evidence. The message of these writers is rather that heaven is a whole new world. There are lots of different beings in heaven and they all are organized into a hierarchical order. Those sitting high in the hierarchical organization are revered more than those sitting below them.[66] In the highest heaven, however, in the Holy of Holies, there is always God the King sitting on his throne of glory, the Omnipotent ruler of everything.

---

[64] See Gieschen, *Christology*, 164.

[65] Fletcher-Louis comments that "strictly speaking" Moses is not angelomorphic in the Exagoge. Therefore it must be interpreted separately. In spite of that he considers it consistent with the angelomorphic Moses tradition. Fletcher-Louis, *Angels*, 179f.

[66] Stuckenbruck concludes that even the intermediary functions of angels cannot be harmonized into one concept of angelic intercession. Stuckenbruck, *Angel Veneration*, 179.

It is no doubt of interest to the present study to investigate the "angelic figures of considerable status" in Jewish writings. There are several exceptional figures mentioned in different writings and they perform functions that separately may be paralleled with certain New Testament passages or themes. However, the problem concerning the very essence of the angelic interpretation is difficult. The theme of angelic existence does not seem to be fruitful in the interpretation of early Christology. The same must be said of the idea of transformation into an angelic being. Therefore, the aspect of analogy is the only relevant approach when the relationship between merkabah mysticism and early Christology is investigated. In this respect certain scholars have been speaking of angelomorphic relation. This, however, must be regarded as a rather limited method, because it can refer merely to certain analoguous features between different expressions. What is more problematic, still, is that angelomorphic interpretation has no relevant link to essential royal themes of early Christology.

4.4. Throne in a cultic setting

Throne descriptions do not comprise merely the instances of the enthronement theme. Throne appears in several contexts in merkabah mysticism, and these other descriptions too have relevance when the relation between merkabah mysticism and early Christology is considered. Sacral features of apocalyptic mysticism in the Second Temple period are quite interesting and deserve more attention. In the writings that we have investigated descriptions of throne visions and passages indicating merkabah mysticism often occur in a cultic context. The heavenly temple serves as a scene for the visions in those cases. Furthermore, the *merkabah,* i.e. God's throne, is located in the Holy of Holies in heaven. It is tempting to conclude that all this is closely connected with the earthly Temple of Jerusalem. In the following we attempt to find some explanations how the cultic discourse affects the descriptions of the heavenly throne.

It is not very easy to identify the proper context for sacral mysticism. Apocalyptic mysticism in the Second Temple period was often critical towards the Temple. For example, at Qumran the attitude towards the earthly temple cult of Jerusalem was hostile. In such a context it would be expected that the nature of the cult was considered transcendental and proper worship was considered to be mystical worship before the heavenly throne.

This, however, does not yet explain the birth and the basic nature of cultic mysticism. It is also possible that the heavenly liturgy found in writings such as the First Book of Enoch, the Qumran Songs of the Sabbath Sacrifice and the Testament of Levi reflects the priestly mysticism of Second Temple mainstream

Judaism. For example in 1 Enoch it was quite clear that the heavenly journey aimed at the heavenly temple. The seer was like a priest who was allowed to walk into the Holy of Holies (1 En. 14).[67]

In this respect it is understandable that some decades after the writing of 1 Enoch 14 elsewhere, namely at Qumran, the priestly sect claiming to be a new temple in the wilderness exploited such mysticism for the justification of its own worship.[68] We need to remember that at Qumran even the sacrifices were considered spiritual and understood in a metaphorical way (1QS IX, 3-6). Also atonement was produced without the help of whole burnt offerings.[69]

It is well known that the theology of Qumran was developed in the context of Second Temple apocalypticism in a number of ways. Historical dualism was strong in their eschatology and formed a basis for their antagonistic attitude towards the Jerusalem Temple. Thus it was convenient to exploit themes of Jewish mysticism. However, the content of the most important writing in this question, i.e. the Songs of the Sabbath Sacrifice, is not a result of the historical situation of the sect.

The title of the Songs themselves connects them to the Sabbath sacrifices of the Temple. In the Qumranian context this already is somewhat astonishing. As sacrificial service was not conducted – as far as we know – in Qumran, the original context of such songs should be in the Temple itself. In this respect the songs seem to express a mystical justification of the factual sacrificial cult.[70]

The content of the Songs of the Sabbath Sacrifice is similar to that of apocalyptic visions in many respects. A special feature in it is that angels seem to have a priestly function in heaven. The songs begin with an invitation to worship, but in the songs it is actually not the earthly congregation that praises God but the angels in heaven. The work describes a liturgy conducted in the heavenly temple.

According to this heavenly liturgy, for example in the seventh song, the kingship of the Lord is the object of joy and praise.

"Praise the God of the august heights, you august ones among the divinities of knowledge. May the holy ones of God make holy the king of glory, who makes holy with his holiness all the holy ones. The chiefs of the praises of all the gods, praise the God of magnificent

---

[67] In a certain vision even a heavenly sacrifice is mentioned. Cf. Himmelfarb, *Ascent*, 33-34.

[68] For the temple ideology of Qumran, see 1QS VIII, 5.

[69] According to Gärtner the obedience in keeping the law was believed to replace the service of the Temple of Jerusalem and the sacrifices. Gärtner, *Temple*, 20-21; cf. Vermes. *Qumran in Perspective*, 163.

[70] For the views of Qumran community, see above chapter 3.2., and Eskola, *Theodicy*, 87ff.

praises, for in the magnificence of the praises is the glory of his kingdom... For he is the God of the gods of all the chiefs of the heights, and king of king of all the eternal councils" (4Q403 1 i, 30-34; Martínez).

These songs preserve the mysticism of Jewish apocalyptic. There is a throne in heaven and angels and other heavenly beings are conducting a liturgy before it. It is located in the Holy of Holies which is the house of God appearing in flames of fire. The cherubim bow themselves before the throne singing songs of praise (cf. 4Q403 1 i, 36-37).[71]

In the twelfth song the actual *merkabah*-throne is in the centre of the heavenly worship.

"Praise the God of ...] ... The cherubim lie prostrate before him, and bless when they rise. The voice of a divine silence is heard, and their is the uproar of excitement when they raise their wings, the voice of a divine silence. They bless the image of the throne-chariot (which) is above the vault of the cherubim, and they sing [the splen]dour of the shining vault (which is) beneath the seat of his glory." (4Q405 20-21-22, 6-9; Martínez).

Such a mystical contemplation over the heavenly *debir* and the throne-chariot suits well the situation of high priests in the Temple of Jerusalem in the Second Temple period. It is easy to imagine that this kind of devout concentration on the heavenly temple has grown out of the prophetic tradition of e.g. the book of Ezekiel. The passage quoted above has several parallels to the vision of Ezekiel in Ezek. 1.[72] Moreover, there are parallels in the canonical Psalms, as we have seen earlier.[73]

Once again the unity of the temple cult and apocalyptic thinking is emphasized. The traditional, mainstream Jewish religious imagery had been attached to Temple cult, and the ark in the Holy of Holies had been identified as the throne of God. Now it seems probable that the Temple worship was justified with an apocalyptic scene which linked the earthly service to the heavenly realm. In addition to this, Levitical singers in the Second Temple period had an extraordinary status in Temple worship and were often considered as inspired seers and prophets.[74]

The Qumranic Songs serve as a model for a link between the earthly Temple and the heavenly sanctuary. There are several factors that support this kind of conclusion. Songs were sung in the Temple when the weekly Sabbath offering

---

[71] This kind of mysticism is well attested to also in later Jewish theology such as the second and third books of Enoch.

[72] See also Newsom, *Songs*, 313f.

[73] Cf. e.g. Ps. 103:19ff.

[74] For Levitical singers, see Tournay, *Hearing God*, 36f.

was performed.[75] The story of the restoration of the Temple worship by Hezekiah in 2 Chronicles is a proof of that:

"Then Hezekiah commanded that the burnt offering be offered on the altar. When the burnt offering began, the song to the Lord began also, and the trumpets, accompanied by the instruments of King David of Israel. The whole assembly worshiped, the singers sang and the trumpeters sounded; all this continued until the burnt offering was finished." (2 Chron. 29:27-28).[76]

As Newsom has noted, there is evidence for different types of liturgical cycles for the accompaniment of the daily and Sabbath whole offerings in Jewish writings.[77] Among the Dead Sea Scrolls we have a comment on king David and his compositions (11Q5, xxvii, previously called 11QPs^a, xxvii). David wrote "songs to be sung before the altar over the perpetual offering of every day, for all the days of the year: three hundred and sixty-four; and for the sabbath offerings: fifty-two songs" (11Q5, xxvii,5-8).

In Mishnah, however, we find a seven day cycle of biblical Psalms. In the "order of the daily whole offering in the liturgy of the house of our God" (mTamid 7:3) the Psalms that the Levites sing in the sanctuary are mentioned (mTamid 7:4). Here we have only seven biblical Psalms, but strictly taken, this is still in accordance with a larger cycle. These Psalms are sung during the week and only the last one of these is a Psalm for the Sabbath day. The list may well refer merely to one cycle out of 52. It is noteworthy that most of the Psalms mentioned in the Mishnah are so called Royal Psalms speaking of the kingship of the Lord (i.e. Psalms 24; 48; 93; 94). Furthermore, one of them is Psalm 82 speaking of God who is "a judge among the gods". There is an inner relationship between these biblical Psalms and the Qumran Songs of the Sabbath Sacrifice.

The Qumran Songs contain only thirteen compositions. The condition of certain manuscripts has been good enough to prove this amount final.[78] This means that the Songs represent only one quarter of the year. It is pure speculation, however, whether this cycle has been repeated during the year or whether it concerns only one season of festivals. The collection may be treated

---

[75] Already Strugnell suggested that the Songs do not present merely an angelic liturgy, but an earthly liturgy. In the Songs the heavenly Temple was portrayed on the model of the earthly one and a similar pattern of service may be detected in both of them. Strugnell, *VT Suppl. VII* (1960) 320. According to Schiffman the heavenly pattern of recitation of the qedushah is being imitated on earth. Schiffman, *Mystics*, 18.

[76] Cf. a similar scene concerning the high priest Simon in Sirach 50:1-21.

[77] Newsom, *Songs*, 18.

[78] Newsom, *Songs*, 5. This conclusion is confirmed by the analysis according to which the thirteen songs were organized around the seventh song which was the highlight of the cycle.

merely as one cycle of compositions written for the Temple liturgy of the Sabbath sacrifices.[79] These songs may not be part of the fifty-two songs for the sabbath offerings bearing the name of David, mentioned in 11Q5. However, they most probably served the same purpose. In an apocalyptic period, when for example Essene priests had some influence in Jerusalem, such songs must have had notable impact on the Temple worship.

In the Second Temple period the service in the temple was an honorary task and an extraordinary privilege for any priest. This is easily seen in the descriptions of the tractate Tamid in Mishnah, referred to above. Serving the Lord in the temple was no common thing. Those lucky ones chosen for the factual service were living a highlight of their life. In such a situation the liturgy focusing on the throne of the heavenly King also emphasized the unique religious moment that was taking place. Those brief descriptions that have been preserved for us in the Bible and the apocrypha,[80] confirm this revering attitude of devotional Jews towards the daily or weekly offering and towards God himself.

In a sense, the Qumran Songs of the Sabbath Sacrifice provide for us a missing link between the Old Testament priestly religion and later Jewish apocalyptic. They help us to explain why apocalyptic writings constantly return to traditional metaphors and use the language of the temple cult – a feature that we have seen in several occasions above when investigating selected apocalyptic writings. They also explain why Jewish apocalyptic remains theologically traditional, returning always to the kingship of God and constantly praising the enthroned Heavenly King.[81]

This survey on the nature of the Temple liturgy has been necessary because it reveals certain features of the cultic discourse prevailing in the Second Temple period. When cultic discourse is exploited, God's throne is presented in a new context. Now it is the centre of the heavenly liturgy. Also links to sacrificial conduct are evident. All this forms a relevant background for several New Testament descriptions, where Temple imagery becomes essential for the soteriological presentation.

The heavenly throne may also be the place for sacrificial atonement. In this way the cultic symbols of the Jerusalem Temple have apparently influenced

---

[79] Thus I do not agree with Newsom who concludes that the Sabbath Shirot should not be understood as a liturgical cycle for the weekly Sabbath offering. Newsom, *Songs*, 19f.

[80] Such as 2 Chron. 29; Sirach 50; see above.

[81] Following J. Maier, Himmelfarb has stated that it is most probably in priestly speculation about the heavenly correlate of the earthly temple "that we find the origins of that strand of apocalyptic literature concerned with the throne of God." Himmelfarb, *Ascent*, 28. Several passages in earlier Enochic literature point to that direction.

both the convictions of Jewish mysticism and the emergence of christological soteriology.

4.5. Throne in eschatological judgment descriptions

For a mainstream New Testament scholar the most obvious context for the enthronement theme would probably be that of the last judgment. Both the eschatological descriptions in the Gospels, and the common interpretation of early Christology in terms of futurist eschatology have been considered as proof of that. Scholars speak of Christ's eschatological enthronement in his parousia. In Jewish writings, however, the day of judgment rarely occurs in ascent stories.

Throne itself, though, appears frequently in Jewish eschatology. As a climax of the last days, the day of judgment is the moment when a heavenly judge enters upon the judgment seat and all humankind is taken before him. A throne is the center of the event, but an enthronement in the sense of an installation is never described.[82]

In Greek manuscripts, both the general word throne (θρόνος), and the word for the judgment seat (βῆμα) have been used in this kind of context. The Greek word θρόνος is depicted as a judgment seat for instance in 1 En. 9:4, where a judgment scene prevails.[83] A similar scene can be detected in TAbr. (A) 12:11. In the Testament of Abraham, however, also βῆμα denotes God's tribunal (TAbr. (A) 13:8).[84]

In the apocalyptic literature, the Danielic Son of Man may evidently be regarded as a prototypical figure for a heavenly enthronement. His enthronement, however, is not placed on the day of judgment in the book of Daniel itself. Rather, according to Daniel 7:14, his messianic power is presented as endless heavenly reign. In the book of Daniel, the day of judgment is not clearly described. Instead, the humankind is divided in the resurrection. "Many of those who sleep in the dust of the earth shall awake, some to everlasting life, and some to shame and everlasting contempt." (Dan. 12:2).[85]

In Enochic writings the figure of Son of Man is later exploited in contexts where the last judgment is also described. In the eschatology of the collection of 1 Enoch we find several straightforward descriptions of eschatological judgment. This document echoes the powerful proclamation of the Old

---

[82] See Dean-Otting, *Heavenly Journeys*, 276f.

[83] According to the Greek manuscript Codex Panopolitanus.

[84] The word in itself was a common word for the judgment seat also in non-religious texts, see Schneider, *ThWNT III* (1990) 445. It denoted the special judgment seat of judges.

[85] Cf. e.g. 2 Macc. 7:14.

Testament prophets and even goes beyond their visions. At the beginning of the book, in chapters 1-5, the last judgment is described as a horrible, cosmic event. The earth moves and people are horrified at meeting the Holy God.[86] There are different scenes for the revelation of God. In 1 Enoch 1 God is not seen on the throne of glory in heavens, but He "will come forth from his dwelling", instead (1 Enoch 1:3). God marches upon Mount Sinai and reveals himself in a flame (1:4-6).

In the previous analyses we have seen that, in Enochic eschatology, both God and the messianic figure are presented as judges on the day of wrath. In 1 Enoch 62 God enters upon the throne of glory.[87]

"The Lord of the Spirits has sat down on the throne of his glory, and the spirit of righteousness has been poured out upon him. The word of his mouth will do the sinners in; and all the oppressors shall be eliminated from before his face." (62:2).

According to 61:8 God places the Elect One on the throne of glory, "and he shall judge all the works of the holy ones in heaven above." In 62:5 the Elect One is identified as the Son of Man who sits on the throne. The image of the shared judgment thus reveals that also on the day of wrath a messianic figure was believed to take part in the judgment of humankind.[88]

In 1 Enoch the day of judgment is described as a meeting of a heavenly court. All people, good and evil, are gathered before the heavenly judge, and they will be sentenced according to their deeds. This kind of belief is common in Jewish writings, even when the throne itself is not highlighted. In the Psalms of Solomon, for instance, the difference between sinners and the righteous is emphasized.[89] In the descriptions of doom also the result of the judgment is painted in vivid colours. Faithful people will gain the glory of heaven as a reward:

"The Lord is faithful to those... who live in the righteousness of his commandments, in the Law... The Lord's devout shall live by it forever... they shall not be uprooted as long as the heavens shall last." (Ps.Sol. 14:1-4).[90]

The fate of sinners, in turn, is Hades, the kingdom of death, the place of their eternal punishment. "But not so are sinners and criminals... their

---

[86] These chapters are dated to the third century B.C. and they represent early apocalyptic of the Second Temple period. Nickelsburg - Stone, *Faith and Piety*, 122.

[87] Cf. 1 En. 98:10; 100:4-5.

[88] Cf. Bock, *Blasphemy*, 126.

[89] This also leads to the concept of judgment, see e.g. PsSol. 3:1-12. Schüpphaus, *Psalmen Salomos*, 92-93; Lührmann, *JSNT 36* (1989) 82; Winninge, *Sinners and the Righteous*, 42-43.

[90] Winninge, *Sinners and the Righteous*, 119.

inheritance is Hades, and darkness and destruction; and they will not be found on the day of mercy for the righteous." (Ps.Sol. 14:6-9).[91]

In the Sibyllines the judgment of God is a cosmic event where the collapse of the whole created world sets the scene for the punishment of sinners. "And God will speak... and judgment will come upon them from the great God, and all will perish at the hand of the Immortal. Fiery swords will fall from heaven on the earth" (Sib.Or. 3, 669-673). In the fourth book of the Sibyllines, too, the execution of the judgment is described in a vivid way (Sib.Or. 4, 40-43).[92]

"But when the judgment of the world and of mortals has already come, which God himself will perform, judging impious and pious at once, then he will also send the impious down into the gloom in fire."

Here we do not find a description of merkabah. God's throne is only implicit in the stories, providing the place for the judgment. In the second oracle, however, God's judgment seat has great significance for the presentation. All the souls of men are taken "to the tribunal of the great immortal God." (Sib.Or. 2:218-219; cf. 8:222.) According to the second oracle on the last day God "takes his seat on a heavenly throne" and the judgment begins. Here, however, as well as in Sib.Or. 8 later, the description is Christian and according to the passage Christ, "on the right of the Great One," will judge "at the tribunal." (Sib.Or. 2:238-244.)[93]

Therefore, on the basis of the extant material the exptected connection between the enthronement theme and the eschatological descriptions of the last judgment is not so obvious after all. The throne does appear in judgment descriptions, but the presentations are governed by judicial discourse. Under the influence of this discourse, the throne metaphor denotes God's judgment seat. Therefore, when explaining the details of the judgment event, one is not entitled to speak of an act of enthronement, but of entering upon the throne instead.

In this respect eschatological descriptions differ from other ascent descriptions. The idea of a messianic enthronement appears to be distinct from the explications of the final day of judgment. When messianic reign is referred to, the heavenly throne is a royal throne symbolizing eternal kingship. In eschatological passages, however, the throne is rather a tribunal of God himself and the Son of Man.

---

[91] On the nature of the Psalm, Schüpphaus, *Psalmen Salomos,* 60. Cf. PsSol. 15:10-13.

[92] Cf. Sib.Or. 3, 741-750; 4, 180-190; 4 Ezra 7:60; 9:15-25.

[93] See the analyses of the Christian passages later in chapter 9.2.

4.6. Conclusions

The analysis has proven that merkabah mysticism is a very potential source of influence for the Christology of the first Christians. There are several factors that must be taken into account. The symbolic universe of the traditional mainstream Second Temple Jewish theology has naturally had great effect on Jewish mysticism, and one may assume that it has also influenced the formation of early Christology. Basic Old Testament metaphors, and especially those of God as king and his heavenly dwelling as a palace with a throne of Glory, have a significant role also in the writings of apocalyptic Judaism as well. In the world view of the mystics the enthroned God is always in the centre of eschatological events.

However, different theories that have attempted to explain and explicate the nature of such influence have not always paid enough attention to the specific details of merkabah mysticism. The relation of Jewish mysticism and early Christology is not simple. Rather, we should begin our summary with certain restrictions and refutations as regards the interpretation.

As we consider the exaltation and enthronement of different heavenly figures, we need to note that there are several different categories of figures that occur in the apocalyptic exaltation descriptions. Even though we may speak of an ascent structure in merkabah mysticism, we cannot collect divine agents merely into one single category. Exalted patriarchs differ significantly from angels. Eschatological figures that belong mostly to the heavenly realm, such as the Son of Man, differ from both of these – not to mention the variations of more traditional messianology. All of these must be investigated separately and their comparison with christological material must be done likewise.

Moreover, we need to be cautious when speaking of the angelic or angelomorphic nature of a heavenly figure. There are naturally several extraordinary angels appearing in the writings, but the angelic identification of other beings is quite difficult. In the texts, different features have been used metaphorically when the exceptional appearance or status of an exalted being has been described. This does not necessarily imply that a metamorphosis or transformation of the being has taken place, even though we do have examples of that kind of procedure too in certain writings.

Furthermore, it is apparent that the enthronement theme is hardly ever applied to angels. AscIsa knows that angels have thrones in heaven and 2 Enoch places Gabriel beside God. These examples are too vague, however, in order to justify any far-reaching angelic interpretation when other kinds of passages are involved. The significance of the status of angels must be balanced with the concept of their function in heaven. Angels cannot be equated with enthroned patriarchs or other heroes who are enthroned in the highest heaven. They are not similar to the enthroned Davidide, either. They have a different function and the angelic interpretation must take that into account.

There are messianic figures in Jewish writings, but they rarely occur in the context of the ascent structure. The best example for our interests is in Qumran, where we find the expectation of an eschatological Davidide who will be enthroned and reign Israel in the end of days. Strictly speaking however, a heavenly enthronement is not presented in the passage. In other writings the figure of the Son of Man comes closest to a messianic figure, and he may be identified as a heavenly king sitting on the throne of Glory.

In addition to this the question concerning the messianology of Second Temple Judaism as such has turned out to be difficult. The concept of an eschatological Messiah is anything but clear. When one attempts to ask, where did the first Christians get their convictions about the messiahship of Jesus, one meets several open questions.

The basic features of early Christology would have further suggested that the theme of resurrection might have had more significance also in Jewish mysticism and in ascension stories. This, however, has not appeared to be the case. There are certain references to resurrection in the context of exaltation and even enthronement. It is at least implied that the enthronement of some of the patriarchs will take place after the general resurrection. In the enthronement passages themselves it plays hardly any role at all.

A further conclusion is interesting, as well. Since the enthronement itself does not refer to deification, it must have some other function. Merkabah mysticism knows well the tradition of the enthronement of a pious Jew. The ascension may thus reach even the throne of God, and the enthroned ones will function and judge as *synthronoi theou*, while remaining human beings. However, the enthronement theme does not threaten monotheism or alter theocracy. In all these descriptions God is the King of Israel and the King of the whole world.

Finally, as regards the eschatological passages describing the last judgment, one important distinction must be made. The concept of entering upon a throne before the event of the actual judgment is to be separated from an act of enthronement as an installation. In Jewish writings, the judgment day is not a coronation day. According to several writings, God himself enters upon the throne of Glory and performs the judgment. In some cases a messianic figure accompanies him in this task.

If these kinds of definitions are necessary in order to exclude certain bypaths in the interpretation, what then are the positive results of the analysis?

What kind of starting point does merkabah mysticism provide for the explanation of the emergence of Christology?

1. First we should pay attention to the general pattern that is present in all merkabah passages. Everything important takes place before the heavenly throne. The fate of humankind and the course of eschatology are destined in heaven, where the fiery throne of God, accompanied by the cherubim and the angels, is in the centre of action. This is a scene based on the traditional symbolic universe of Temple centered Second Temple Judaism. Already in Jewish passages, however, we have detected different kinds of discourses in the context of which the elements of the symbolic universe have been exploited. The enthronement discourse is not the only one that appears to be significant in this respect. The cultic discourse too has its place in Jewish descriptions, and further the aspect of the day of judgment brings to the fore a judicial discourse.

2. Merkabah mysticism also provides a model for the enthronement itself. Even though there are many different descriptions of enthronements in merkabah passages, the basic model is clear. Heavenly beings and eschatological luminaries are usually understood as enthroned beings. Their status is high in heaven. When first Christians needed to express the manner in which Jesus had been exalted there was a perfect model available in their Jewish tradition.

3. We might also add that according to certain writings, especially those from Qumran, the beings (angels) that resided in the heavenly Holy of Holies had an exceptionally high status. They were called sons of God. According to such a tradition the Holy of Holies in heaven was a restricted area and those entering it were quite privileged even among heavenly figures. However, the angels of the *debir*, that even had theophoric names such as "gods," remained inside a theocratic hierarchy and their main function was to worship God.

4. Certain heavenly figures even had a soteriological function. In some cases they had a priestly function providing atonement for the people. In other cases they were given a mission to deliver the oppressed Israel from the power of their enemies. The soteriological aspect becomes emphasized in the contexts where the cultic discourse is exploited. In these descriptions the place of atonement, in particular, is underlined and the heavenly Temple with its throne is described in a cultic setting.

5. What is furthermore important is that the expectation of an eschatological Davidide appears in merkabah passages too, as we noted above. Even though there is a diversity among the enthronement descriptions of different writings, at Qumran, in particular, we find an example where the pious awaited an eschatological enthronement of a Davidic Messiah.

Psalm 110, which has an exceptional function in early Christology, does not seem to have a special place in the exaltation descriptions of Jewish mysticism. The key expression of sitting "at the right hand" of God, does not explicitly exist in pre-Christian writings. In 11QMelch., there are royal and high priestly characteristics attached to the figure of Melchizedek. This is probably the most explicit example of the influence of Psalm 110, but in this fragment sitting "at the right hand" of God, or the enthronement itself, are not mentioned. The words do appear later in TJob 33, but even there they do not actually refer to the enthronement of Job.

6. Lastly, we need to remember that these features hardly ever occur together and are associated with only one heavenly figure. This is also the case as regards the Davidic Messiah. This fact poses a real challenge for the interpretation of early Christology where the exaltation and enthronement of Jesus Christ is described. But generally taken, these features evidently help us understand why, after the Easter events, the first Christians explained the meaning of Christ's resurrection by exploiting the idea of a heavenly enthronement.

III

The Messiah and the Throne in the New Testament Christological Discourses

§ 5 At the Right Hand of God *(Enthronement Discourse)*

In New Testament Christology the concepts of Messiah and throne appear together in several contexts and have different roles in different discourses. In general we might call the discourse under discussion an exaltation discourse, because all of these presentations are in one way or another associated with exaltation. In practice it is useful, however, to discern between different discourses, since the multiplicity of contexts justifies such discernment.

In previous chapters we have seen that in the Old Testament and in Second Temple Jewish theology the throne metaphor appeared in different contexts. It was an essential element in descriptions of heavenly journeys, and scholars investigating the ascent structure have constantly referred to it. It was especially connected with the idea of heavenly enthronements. In addition, a cultic feature could be discerned in certain texts. And finally, the throne played a central role in several eschatological passages. In most of these areas a heavenly figure, sometimes a messianic figure, also appeared.

Therefore, in the study of New Testament passages, special attention must be paid to the change of context and the change of discourse. In most of the relevant texts the idea of exaltation has been presented as the realization of an enthronement and as a realization of the resurrection. Furthermore, exaltation is an essential theme in the context of cultic discourse and in the context of judicial discourse.

This classification is more detailed than the one applied in the investigation of Jewish writings. There, for instance, discernment between a heavenly journey and the actual enthronement was sufficient for the needs of the analysis. New Testament Christology brings its own original features to this picture. Especially the role of resurrection is new, and this alters the conditions for the interpretation of certain details.

Probably the most interesting of the different discourses is the enthronement discourse. It is special since it constantly exploits Psalm 110. Therefore, this discourse provides rich material for intertextual investigation. In enthronement discourse the heavenly enthronement of Christ is in the focus of description.

Moreover, it soon becomes apparent that the features of merkabah mysticism were exploited in christological formulations. The crucial question is, how and to what extent did merkabah speculation affect the formation of early Christology? What we should expect to find in New Testament Christology, on the basis of Second Temple Jewish apocalyptic, is for the resurrected Christ to be described as a heavenly judge who reigns at the head of the heavenly hierarchy. He should, however, enjoy a theocratic relationship with God and he should apparently promote faith in God Almighty, the King of heaven and earth. In this theocratic scheme some kind of cultic function of the resurrected Christ would be quite obvious for Jewish theologians. In the New Testament there is, however, a Christology that goes far beyond the limits of Jewish theology.

In the New Testament we find the same symbolic world as in Jewish apocalyptic. The scene comprises a heavenly court, sometimes even a temple, and God's throne. There are several metaphors which are identical with those found in Jewish writings. In the New Testament they have been adopted in the service of Christology. While Jewish theology described ascensions and throne visions, in the New Testament Christ himself is at the centre of all these events. The New Testament writers refer to his ascension into heaven and to his sitting on the throne of glory.

From a methodological point of view this is a rather important point. It is apparent that the symbolic universe which directs the explication of Christology is closely linked to that of the Old Testament writers and Jewish theologians. Certain images are so powerful that several writers choose to employ them constantly when speaking of Christ, and especially of his resurrection.[1] Such metaphors may be regarded as key elements in New Testament Christology. In addition, there are certain Old Testament passages which are frequently quoted or alluded to, and these bring unity to the different writings. It is possible to analyze christological statements by concentrating on these features.

The christological passages of the New Testament contain some special features, as well. For example, the description of the actual throne seldom appears in the writings. Instead, we find associated sub-metaphors, such as the expression "at the right hand of God". It belongs evidently to an enthronement

---

[1] The benefits of such methodological approach have been stated in the introduction. The study of Christology should not be reduced to tracking down single Christological titles. Furthermore, the symbol of the throne must not be interpreted according to that kind of function. Instead investigation must concentrate on the symbolic world itself, and on the role of symbols in different christological discourses.

statement that alludes to Psalm 110, and with which Christ's ascension to the throne has been expressed.

In the following analysis we shall concentrate on the occurrence of these metaphors and sub-metaphors, as well as on different features of merkabah mysticism in the New Testament. Four different examples will be studied, namely the occurrence of the throne metaphor in the early Lukan traditions, the exploitation and confrontation of Jewish merkabah mysticism in Paul, enthronement language in the Letter to the Hebrews, and apocalyptic enthronement Christology in the Book of Revelation.

5.1. Psalm 110 in the Christology of the early Lukan traditions

There are several reasons why the survey should begin with the Book of Acts. Firstly, the Book of Acts contains traditional material and even a lot of homologies that must be considered very early. Secondly, these passages have had a key role in the investigation of early Christology. Thus it is interesting for us to see what is their relationship to the Jewish merkabah tradition.

Acts 2:22-36. The first of the passages to be examined, Peter's Pentecost speech, has always had a primary status in the study of Christology. Acts 2:22-36 is a passage which most probably contains early tradition material, intentionally describes the enthronement of Jesus, and also introduces a direct quotation from Psalm 110.

The passage as such has for a very long time been in the focus of scholarly debate. J. Weiss referred to it in his book *"Das Urchristentum"*. According to Weiss, it is one of the clearest passages where adoptionist Christology is present.[2] For R. Bultmann the passage was evidence for the idea that in the primitive Church "Jesus' messiahship dated from the resurrection."[3] The title κύριος, however, was parallel with the title "Son of God" and, according to Bultmann, both of these were given a "mythological sense" only later in Hellenistic Christianity. The former messianic interpretation must therefore have been dependent on an adoptionist idea based on Psalm 2.[4] E. Haenchen added one detail to this pattern of interpretation. While Luke himself apparently assumed that during his earthly life Jesus already possessed both his dignity as Son of God and the endowment of the Holy Spirit, he has here attempted to reconcile the received view and his own view.[5]

This German approach has strongly influenced the interpretation of this

---

[2] Weiss, *Das Urchristentum,* 85. We shall return to Weiss later in chapter 9.

[3] Bultmann, *Theology I,* 27.

[4] Bultmann, *Theology I,* 50; cf. 128f.

[5] Haenchen, *Acts,* 187.

passage. Furthermore, we should pay attention to later scholars such as O. Cullmann and F. Hahn. They lived and worked in a period when Christology was explained primarily in terms of Christological titles. Scholars attempted to discern the phase of tradition in which a particular title originated.[6] The phases were often classified according to an evolutionary pattern of the development of Christology. In this latter method Jewish Christianity was strictly separated from Hellenistic Christianity. Some titles were located in the former and others in the latter.

For instance, Hahn speculated primarily on this scheme when explaining the crucial passage of Acts 2:34ff. He considered it quite problematic, because it bears the features of (early) Jewish Christian Christology, referring to the exaltation of Christ in the resurrection. The passage, however, is closely linked to Kyrios-Christology and therefore Hahn, like Bultmann before him, located it in Hellenistic Christianity. The latter argument seems to have more weight in Hahn's final conclusion.[7]

The main difference between these interpretations and modern study is the new way of apprehending the history-of-religions approach. The emphasis was formerly on the Hellenistic environment which is now considered only a secondary element according to which the emergence of Christology should be evaluated. The focus has been shifted to Second Temple Judaism. This also changed the explanation of Acts 2:22-36. Furthermore, the significance of Psalm 110 has been given new weight. Its role has been noted before, as we saw above, but in the final analysis it has usually been neglected. In the new approach such a *sub-text* has a special role to play and therefore the main line of interpretation differs essentially from the previous ones.

Therefore, a new analysis is called for, and in this analysis we must pay special attention to those features that may be compared with Jewish merkabah mysticism. What, then, is the basic nature of the Christology presented in the passage? The whole passage 2:22-36 argues for the messiahship of Christ and explains the exaltation of Jesus as a Davidide. Every claim is further confirmed by quotations from the Old Testament.

It is naturally no novelty to state that in New Testament Christology there are well-developed intertextual strategies. Only the term is new. Most christological statements in the New Testament are linked to a particular Old

---

[6] See e.g. Hahn, *Hoheitstitel*, 11f., 74, 112f., 124-125. Cullmann does not follow Bultmann, though. He explains the title Lord as derived from its Jewish background, see Cullmann, *Christologie*, 213ff.

[7] See Hahn, *Hoheitstitel*, 116-117. He had evidently seen the problems of Bultmann's explanation, and therefore attempted to shift the focus to Hellenistic Christianity. Hahn too was perplexed by the exaltation Christology in this passage.

Testament passage. Acts 2:22-36 contains several such statements.[8] What is interesting here is the way the sub-texts are exploited. Can we detect changes in the discourses in which these texts occur?

In Acts 2:22-36 there are actually three references to different psalms, i.e. Psalms 16, 132, and 110. The intertextual strategy of the writer appears to be based on an associative combination of suitable passages in order to justify his exaltation statements. In these Old Testament passages both the throne or enthronement and the idea of life after death are emphasized, and in this speech the passages are most evidently associated with each other.[9]

Our attention is first drawn to a Psalm citation that serves as a Scriptural attestation for the resurrection of Jesus (2:24ff.). Psalm 16 contains two themes that are exploited in Peter's speech.[10] On the one hand, the passage is used as a proof-text for the bodily resurrection of Jesus. Ps. 16:10 is even repeated in the context: "For you will not abandon my soul to Hades, or let your Holy One experience corruption."[11] In Acts 2:31 this is rendered in a Christological form: "He was not abandoned". The conviction of the psalmist has become a promise that has been fulfilled in Christ. The basic content of the original text remains the same, however.[12]

On the other hand, the theme of "sitting at the right hand" is also exploited here. In Psalm 16:8 David sings, "I keep the Lord always before me; because he is at my right hand, I shall not be moved." In theory, this verse could also

---

[8] There are several studies on the use of the Old Testament in this passage. Holtz in his study examined especially the Old Testament text exploited by Luke, Holtz, *Untersuchungen*. Rese accepted a more hermeneutical position and emphasized the authority of David in the use of Psalm 110. Rese, *Motive*, 62f. For a more general treatment of the theme, see Barrett, *It is Written*, 231ff. The most detailed analysis is provided by Bock, *Proclamation*, 155ff., 181ff.; cf. Bock, *SBLSP* (1990) 494ff.

[9] Actually, in 2:24, the key text Ps. 16 is introduced by making allusions to 2 Sam. 22:6; Pss. 18:5 and 116:3. The idea of liberating Jesus from death highlights the idea of resurrection. On the complex nature of these allusions, see Bock, *Proclamation*, 171f.

[10] It should be noted that Psalm 16 is cited nowhere else in the New Testament except in Acts 13, where it has a somewhat similar function in the christological presentation. See Juel, *CBQ 43* (1981) 545.

[11] There are three changes concerning this passage between the MT and the LXX. The most important of these is that the LXX reads "corruption" for "pit". Rese suggests, however, that such interpretation is based on Hebrew semantics, where different verbal roots produce similar forms. Thus one does not need to conclude that the description in Acts 2 was necessarily derived from the Hellenistic Church. Rese, *Motive*, 57.

[12] Schneider calls it the "eschatological interpretation." Schneider, *Apostelgeschichte*, 273. Juel has suggested that the term "godly" (ὅσιος) was understood as a reference to the Messiah. This resulted in a christological interpretation of the psalm. Juel, *CBQ 43* (1981) 549. This is probable, and what is more important, such an interpretation is once again an example of a bold christological transformation of traditional Jewish themes.

have been interpreted in the sense that κύριος was "at the right hand" (ἐκ δεξιῶν) of God, but actually this is not the case in Acts 2. κύριος is now the Lord God himself and David is a type of Christ. For the writer it is not so significant who is at the right or at the left hand, as long as the term that forms a loose link with Psalm 110 later in verse 2:34 is preserved. The key expression "at the right hand" (ἐκ δεξιῶν) seems to be more important than the actual verbatim content of the Old Testament passage, because this expression was suitable for the enthronement description.[13]

In this respect we may conclude that the notion of being "at the right hand" existed even before in the Christology of the writer. Psalm 16 is a secondary tool in the explication of exaltation Christology. It could be applied to the enthronement discourse due to its special features, but it was certainly not the primary source of such Christology.

Thus, in Acts 2, it is the new David whose soul will not be abandoned to Hades. In Peter's speech this means, of course, "Jesus of Nazareth" (v. 22) whose "flesh will live in hope". He is the Holy One who will not experience corruption. In this respect Psalm 16 was perfectly suitable for the purposes of the writer, since there the exaltation terminology was connected with the idea of resurrection, and this was what the writer needed in his interpretation. The first David, in contrast, was dead and buried, and "his tomb is with us to this day" (v. 29).[14]

For the writer, the only logical and tenable interpretation of Psalm 16 is the messianic one.[15] But what is the purpose of this messianic interpretation? It is revealed in the following verses where a new passage from Psalm 132 is introduced:

"Since he was a prophet, he knew that God had sworn with an oath to him that he would put one of his descendants on his throne. Foreseeing this, David spoke of the resurrection of the Messiah" (Acts 2:30-31).

The messianic interpretation simply explains the enthronement of the Davidide.[16] This was naturally a proper Jewish interpretation of the theme under discussion. In his explanation the writer has exploited Psalm 132:11 in a straightforward manner.

---

[13] Cf. e.g. Pesch, *Apostelgeschichte*, 122: "eine Stichwortverbindung mit Ps 110,1."

[14] According to Bock, the hermeneutical logic of the writer is simple: "Since the text cannot apply in its fullest force to David, it must refer to his seed for whom he is speaking." Bock, *Proclamation*, 177.

[15] Cf. Carroll, *SBLSP* (1990) 521.

[16] A similar use of Psalm 16 is found later in Acts 13:16ff, esp. v. 35. For the connection of these two passages, see Lövestam, *Son and Saviour*, 82f.

"The Lord swore to David a sure oath from which he will not turn back: 'One of the sons of your body I will set on your throne' " (Ps. 132:11).

According to the writer of such early Christology these two Psalms belonged together. They had a similar message. When David as a prophet spoke of the "Holy One" who would not "experience corruption", he spoke of a descendant in his own family, who would be exalted and enthroned.[17] Resurrection and enthronement evidently both refer to the one and the same chain of events.

Such connecting of these kinds of Psalms is not self-evident, however. On the contrary, it may be considered rather problematic in the theology of that time. In the Old Testament we never find any reference to the resurrection of the Messiah or of a Davidide – apart from the rather vague example of Psalm 16. Resurrection is not a theme that would be associated with the idea of enthronement as such.[18] Instead, both in the Old Testament and in Jewish theological literature, we find a long tradition that centres around the theme of the enthronement of a Davidide. In fact, the hope of Judah is constantly based on this theme. In times of oppression this hope was expressed in terms of a certain promise tradition speaking of the exaltation of the seed of David.[19]

As regards the appellation Messiah, the problem is not a very difficult one. The idea of the enthronement of the Messiah is present in Psalm 132. In fact the aforementioned oath is preceded by a prayer for the continuation of the Davidic dynasty: "For your servant David's sake do not turn away the face of your anointed one" (Ps. 132:10).[20] Thus verses 10-11 in this Psalm speak explicitly about the enthronement of the "Messiah". This Psalm, however, makes no reference to resurrection or eternal life.

Such facts imply that, in the New Testament and in early Christianity even before the birth of the New Testament, enthronement discourse differed essentially from that of Old Testament writers and Jewish theologians. Therefore the solution of the above problem must lie in the combination of resurrection and enthronement. But how was such a combination supported in early Christology? What kind of discourse are we faced with?

First we must return to Psalm 132 and ask what was the "oath" of God to

---

[17] Cf. Bruce, *Acts*, 66. Such a connection is further confirmed by substituting "flesh" for the "holy one". This word does not appear in Psalm 16 but it underlines the idea of a bodily resurrection. See Bock, *Proclamation*, 178.

[18] This was quite apparent in the analysis of both Old Testament messianology and Jewish merkabah mysticism in chapters 2 and 3.

[19] The existence of a well-defined promise tradition has been suggested especially by Duling *NTS 19* (1973) 56f. For details of this theory see later chapters 9 and 10.

[20] This has been noted e.g. by Fitzmyer, *Acts*, 260.

David? There is little doubt that the famous prophecy of Nathan (2 Sam. 7:12-14) is behind this reference, even though the wording found in this passage refers to Psalm 132.[21] There is another allusion to 2 Sam. 7 in Acts 13:23, and it is directly quoted elsewhere in the New Testament, e.g. in Hebrews 1:5. In the prophecy of Nathan the Davidic dynasty is established by divine decree:

"I will raise up your offspring [seed (AV)] after you, who shall come forth from your body, and I will establish his kingdom. He shall build a house for my name, and I will establish the throne of his kingdom forever. I will be a father to him, and he shall be a son to me" (2 Sam. 7:12-14).

The significance of such a conception for different Old Testament writers is apparent, since there are several related traditions in the writings. In Psalm 2, for instance, the "decree" of God is sung to a new Davidide: "You are my son; today I have begotten you" (Ps. 2:7). The decree of the prophecy of Nathan is also referred to in Psalm 89, which is probably behind the wording of the passage in Acts: "I have sworn to my servant David: 'I will establish your descendants forever, and build your throne for all generations' " (Ps. 89:3b-4).[22] These examples prove that Psalm 132 is not a unique description of the special status of the Davidide.

Did such passages really form a factual promise tradition? This is quite possible. Duling has further suggested that certain elements of the prophecy of Nathan carried the tradition. He discerned, for example, the following three important elements: (1) the descent of the king from the seed of David; (2) the Father-son relationship between God and the king; (3) the promise of eternal reign on the throne of the kingdom of Israel.[23] Schweizer, in turn, spoke of "key words" that turn up time and again in later tradition whenever the Son of David is expected.[24] Even though the present investigation is not primarily interested in the Old Testament or Jewish traditions and their emergence, it is quite obvious that the writings that were available and authoritative for most Jewish theologians at the time of the early Church give the impression of an extant promise tradition. Therefore they evidently also applied such a conception in their own thinking and writing.

In the writings of Qumran, for instance, we find further confirmation for the existence of a promise tradition, or at least a belief that such a tradition existed.

---

[21] See e.g. Schweizer, *Studies*, 191; Hayes, *Interp* 22 (1968) 339; Schneider, *Apostelgeschichte*, 274; Dunn, *Acts*, 30-31.

[22] The link to 2 Sam. 7:14 is confirmed with a reference to the sonship of the Davidide: "He shall cry to me, 'You are my Father' " (Ps. 89:26).

[23] Duling *NTS 19* (1973) 56.

[24] Schweizer investigated key words such as throne, seed, kingdom of the son, house, and the relation of Father and son. Schweizer, *Studies*, 187f.

The famous 4QFlorilegium is a composition where the key passage 2 Sam. 7:10-14 is combined with excerpts from the messianic Psalms 1 and 2. As is well known, in the interpretation of this eschatological *pesher* the messianic Davidide, the "Shoot of David" is described.[25] The promise tradition centred around the expectation of the Davidide, as one would expect on the grounds of the prophecy of Nathan.

Such traditions seem to have been important for early Christian writers, as well. In Acts 2 we have the combination of Pss. 16, 132, and 110. At the beginning of Hebrews several passages are added to these, one of these being Psalm 2:7. Certain parallel New Testament passages also appear to have affected each other later in the copying process. For instance, in the version of D* of Acts 2, verse 30 is much longer than the original, and it mentions resurrection and a genealogical reference.[26]

Such concentration on the figure of the Davidide is significant as regards our interpretation. In early Christology the Davidic descent of Jesus is especially underlined. The exalted Christ is not an angelic figure or a mystical heavenly figure. He comes from the family of David. This means further that all possible features of merkabah mysticism that may be found in this passage must be adjusted to this general picture. The enthroned Jesus in heaven is the Davidic Messiah.

Another feature that is special here, when compared to Jewish merkabah mysticism, is the extraordinary significance of the resurrection. We may now return to the above verses, because the theological problem still awaits its solution. What is the exact relation between enthronement language and the resurrection of Jesus? How can the oath mentioning a throne be identified with the resurrection? There is most probably a semantic answer to this question.

It is probable that there is an inner logic between the words that denote resurrection and enthronement. Therefore the theological statement may be based on and constructed from a word-play. The actual Greek word for 'resurrection', ἀνάστασις, also appears in the Septuagint version of the prophecy of Nathan: ἀναστήσω τὸ σπέρμα σου μετὰ σέ (2 Sam. 7:12, LXX).[27] Here the word naturally means the "raising up" of a descendant and may well

---

[25] See e.g. the early remarks of Allegro, *JBL* 77 (1958) 350ff.

[26] It is echoed in the text of the AV based on certain later manuscripts: "that of the fruit of his loins, according to the flesh, he would raise up Christ to sit on his throne." There is a word for resurrection and further the phrase "according to the flesh" has been added. This κατὰ σάρκα has obviously been taken from Romans 1:3, which forms a close parallel to this passage, as we shall see later. All this emphasizes the close relationship between passages speaking of the Davidide. See Bruce, *Acts*, 126.

[27] See Betz, *NT* 6 (1963) 32 (and note 4); Schweizer, *Studies*, 190; Hayes, *Interp* 22 (1968) 342; Duling, *NTS* 19 (1973) 71.

refer to an enthronement. Therefore, on the level of Greek tradition such a connection between two theological ideas is well established.

What about the Hebrew/Aramaic tradition? Can we detect a word-play here as well? In the prophecy of Nathan a word for raising up or exaltation, *qûm*, is used (קום, hiph. הקים). In the Old Testament tradition of kingship ideology it is a "key word" often used for the enthronement of the Davidide (see e.g. Ezek. 34:23; Jer. 23:5).[28] This seems to indicate that there is a sound justification for the identification of resurrection and enthronement also in the Greek tradition building on a simple translation of the Hebrew original.

Actually, on this basis we might call the new Christian discourse a resurrection discourse, since the original feature in this passage is precisely resurrection. In this study, however, the conception of resurrection discourse has been reserved for such occasions where Psalm 110 has no explicit influence, and where the idea of resurrection prevails.[29] Therefore, the Christology of Acts 2 is treated as an example of enthronement discourse.

Thus, in the enthronement discourse of Acts 2, the passages taken from Psalms 16 and 132 play an essential role. They appear to dominate the first part of the passage and they evidently served as perfect Scriptural proof for the promises of the resurrection of Jesus. Resurrection was identified with exaltation and enthronement. These psalms are not, however, merely quoted in this passage. In fact, what is typical of the Christology of Acts 2 is the intertextual transformation that has been produced. Old Testament "promises" of the enthronement of a Davidide were interpreted as a prophecy of the resurrection of Jesus of Nazareth.[30]

There is one further interesting detail in this sequence. The exaltation "at the right hand" of God was supported by a proof-text from Psalm 16, even though the wording of that psalm was not as suitable for such purpose as the wording of Psalm 110, quoted a little later. Nevertheless, it was Psalm 16 that provided the crucial expression "at the right hand".

"This Jesus God raised up, and of that all of us are witnesses. Being therefore exalted at the right hand of God, and having received from the Father the promise of the Holy Spirit, he has poured out this that you both see and hear. For David did not ascend into the heavens..." (Acts 2:32-33).

---

[28] It is noteworthy that in 4Qflor., where 2 Sam. 7:12-14 and Amos 9:11 are parallelled, the verb *qûm* has replaced another word for raising up in Amos: "On that day I will raise up the booth of David that is fallen". This underlines the importance of the word. See especially van der Woude, *Qumran*, 173.

[29] See especially chapter 6.

[30] Cf. Carroll, according to whom Scripture "is not the basis for the christological argument but does serve to corroborate it." Carroll, *SBLSP* (1990) 521.

The parallelling and identification of David and Jesus is quite interesting from the point of view of our topic. It is easy to see that the enthronement of a known patriarch is not a pattern to be used here. "For David did not ascend into the heavens..." David is not the type of a person undertaking a celestial journey or of bodily resurrection. The passage actually denies the exaltation or heavenly enthronement of David himself. On the contrary, Jesus' resurrection and exaltation are unique. He is the only messianic candidate ever to have attained a high status through ascension.

Such polarization is emphasized by the statement that Jesus himself has dispensed the Spirit from heaven. According to some scholars, even this implies a divine Christology.[31] Jesus performs functions that belong to the functions of God himself. Such a change cannot be explained solely by referring to Christ's "intermediary" status in heaven.[32]

The pouring out of the Spirit thus becomes further proof for Christ's exaltation.[33] The one who is responsible for the experiences on the Pentecost day is the resurrected Jesus who sits at the right hand of the Father. He is an active Lord of the post-Easter community.

The messianic aspect is furthermore emphasized in verses 34-36 where the most essential one of all the mentioned sub-texts, namely Psalm 110:1, is introduced. According to these verses Jesus' resurrection has meant in particular his enthronement to a heavenly kingship. This idea was introduced already in v. 30 where the throne was mentioned, and now it is attested by a quotation from Psalm 110. "For David did not ascend into the heavens, but he himself says, 'The Lord said to my Lord, "Sit at my right hand"...'" (2:34). This famous enthronement Psalm introduces the very core of throne mysticism. In this passage Jesus is the κύριος who has been exalted "at the right hand" (ἐκ δεξιῶν) of God.[34] After the quotation the description climaxes in the explanation of the enthronement.[35]

---

[31] So e.g. Fletcher-Louis, *Luke-Acts*, 22. "Nowhere else in the OT, or in Judaism, does anyone other than God perform this function." Cf. Bock, *Proclamation*, 184.

[32] Dunn states that here the exalted Jesus is simply the intermediary in the bestowal of the Spirit. Dunn, *Christology*, 142. Such reasoning is evidently dependent on the general interpretation of the passage. The mention of the Father in this context does not diminish the originality of the description where Christ dispenses the Spirit.

[33] For this idea, see especially Gourgues, *A la Droite de Dieu*, 167.

[34] Cf. Hengel, *Studies*, 143, 217f.

[35] These clauses also appear to be built on earlier tradition. This is not justified merely by the notion that we have a short statement of homological nature, but also by the idioms. It has been noted that the expression "the entire house of Israel" is a "Septuagintismus". See Schneider, *Apostelgeschichte*, 122 footnote 122; Pesch, *Apostelgeschichte*, 124, especially footnote 33. This may be considered a sign of traditional language.

"Therefore let the entire house of Israel know with certainty that God has made him both Lord and Messiah (ὅτι καὶ κύριον αὐτὸν καὶ Χριστὸν ἐποίησεν ὁ θεός), this Jesus whom you crucified." (2:36).

In exaltation Christology there is no description of Christ's heavenly journey. The writer is simply indentifying the ascension with resurrection.[36] Resurrection as such is an ascension into the heavens. The metaphor "sit at my right hand" expresses the act of enthronement. Christ is given a heavenly throne, most probably God's throne, and he sits at the right hand of God. This parallels Jewish theology in two aspects. According to such Christology, Jesus is like a righteous person exalted on the throne of glory. He is also given a status at the top of heavenly hierarchy. In this sense he resembles Moses or Enoch in Jewish tradition. In this respect it is noteworthy that the motif of exalted patriarchs has not been used here.[37]

But Christ is not merely a righteous person here. God has made (ἐποίησεν) him both Lord and Messiah. This is a complex sentence and it has inspired vast discussion among scholars. At first some details should be mentioned. The word for making as such should not be considered as a too problematic one. As we remember, in Jewish tradition the exaltation and the enthronement did not mean the deification of the exalted persons, such as Abraham, Moses, Isaiah or even the angelic beings. Therefore no Jewish Christian preacher or listener would have thought that the "making" of a Messiah means any ontological change taking place in the act.[38]

This principle may be used in two opposite ways in the interpretation of this passage. On the one hand it could mean that the exalted Lord remains merely human in his enthronement. On the other hand it may as well mean that the divine exalted Lord must have been divine even before his exaltation. The adherents of the theory of adoptionist Christology have suggested the former alternative, as we have seen above.

According to adoptionist Christology verse 36 expresses that Jesus was not divine at all. If Jesus is merely "made" Lord and Messiah in the resurrection,

---

[36] Zwiep emphasizes that, "in the earliest preaching, the heavenly journey type of ascension is reserved for the Easter event." Zwiep, *Ascension*, 156.

[37] However, in this passage there is nothing that would justify an angelic interpretation which was suggested by Segal, *ANRW II 23.2* (1980) 1371. Hurtado considers this passage "clear evidence" for the fact that "Jesus' resurrection was understood by means of Jewish divine agency tradition." Hurtado, *One God*, 94. This seems to be too general a statement. Exalted Jesus in this passage is not a "divine agent", but simply a Davidide. The exaltation Christology of the passage should therefore be interpreted primarily in terms of messianology.

[38] Pesch suggests that the statement speaks of God's creative work in the event of exaltation. The enthroned Christ is God's ποίημα, as are the Christians in the end of days according to Eph. 2:10. See Pesch, *Apostelgeschichte*, 128.

does he not belong to the human line of the family of David? Isn't his ascension similar, for example, to the ascension of Enoch in the Enochic tradition? The theory of adoptionist Christology maintains that this indeed is the case. The adherents of this theory claim that in early Christology Jesus is described as an "earthly" Davidide who simply ascends as a human being to heaven. Thus the theocratic nature of the scene would be similar to that of Jewish apocalyptic. There are several difficulties in this explanation, as we shall see below, but the question is important and we shall return to it later.[39]

What is of further interest is the occurrence of the appellation Christ/Messiah in the context of Psalm 110. Why have the first Christians identified Lord with Christ? This is not self-evident on the basis of Psalm 110 while the appellation itself does not appear there. This means that the traditional methodology of detecting christological titles is completely useless here and rather leads one astray. The question becomes even more interesting when we note that the appellation Christ is primarily associated with the use of Ps. 110:1 in the New Testament traditions.[40]

It seems evident that the intertextual strategy of the first Christian thinkers provides a solution to this problem. The associative method of combining texts that are considered messianological has resulted in the conviction that the exalted one is the "Messiah". In Christian enthronement discourse the enthroned one is the Davidide, and the resurrection was considered the enthronement of the Davidide. Therefore, when the first Christians refer to Psalm 110 and state that Jesus has been "made" the Messiah, this means his installation to heavenly kingship. Resurrection day becomes a coronation day.[41]

The enthronement of the "Messiah" was naturally already stated in Psalm 132:10-11, as we saw above. The terminology was available for the early Christian theologians. In their associative method they only needed to combine these passages and thus bring the idea of exaltation as resurrection into the

---

[39] Dunn, however, is uncertain of the nature of the statement. On the one hand he says that Acts 2:34f. is proof for a confession of Jesus "in terms of divinity". But on the other hand he states that this is one of the passages in which the later adoptionist Ebionite Christology has its "firm anchor point." See Dunn, *Unity*, 53, 243. It is not completely clear whether Dunn understands adoptionist Christology in the same manner as his predecessors or not. It seems that he presupposes an ontological change of Jesus in the resurrection, which original adoptionist Christology never did. In his *Christology* Dunn concludes that, in the earliest Christian writings, the resurrection of Jesus was regarded as "of central significance in determinig his divine sonship." Dunn, *Christology*, 35.

[40] This has been pointed out by Loader, *NTS 24* (1978) 202ff.

[41] As regards terminology, in addition to Psalm 132, the appellation Messiah also appears in Psalm 2:2, where the installation of the Davidide as a Son of God is decreed (v. 7).

interpretation. One could also say that these concepts belonged to their new exaltation discourse.[42]

It is also useful to note that this is probably the most original meaning for "Messiah" (Χριστός). Jesus has been "anointed" king over the whole world.[43] The appellation itself does not provoke any question about the "messiahship" of Jesus before the exaltation. He may be considered a Messiah designate in his earthly life, if one chooses to use that category. The coronation day is simply the day of his anointment. For Luke himself this has naturally been clear from the very beginning. In the Christmas story Jesus is Χριστὸς κύριος already at his birth (Luke 2:11), not to mention the possession of the throne of David in Luke 1:32. Also according to Acts 2:22 Jesus was attested "by God with deeds of power, wonders and signs," and therefore his Messiahship as a Messiah designate was not questioned.[44]

Thus, in Acts 2:36, also the expression "made him Lord" is identical with the expression "made him Messiah". But what kind of "Lord" is the anointed king here? There has been a heated discussion over the question whether the appellation refers to God's own name or not.[45] How has Psalm 110 been interpreted in this Christology? First we should note that both on the level of Hebrew (*adonai*) and under the influence of the Septuagint (κύριος) an identification between God and the exalted Lord is possible.[46] Second, there is the testimony of other early traditional passages. In the hymn of Phil. 2 we have clear evidence of an identification of Christ with God expressly by using the appellation Lord, "the name that is above every name" (Phil. 2:9). This is confirmed by the following homology where exalted the Christ is confessed as the divine, heavenly Lord: "every tongue should confess that Jesus Christ is Lord" (Phil. 2:11).

---

[42] Conzelmann has erroneously suggested that the "Messiah title" was obtained from Psalm 16. Conzelmann, *Acts*, 21. This is a careless statement as he still supports the method of investigating separate christological "titles".

[43] Cf. Fitzmyer, *Acts*, 261. Hay, arguing for his thesis that references to Psalm 110:1 do not regularly denote Christ's present reign, suggests that we can also in the expressions of Acts 2 find "relative passivity" concerning Christ's kingship. In Lukan theology, Jesus' kingdom will begin only with the parousia. See Hay, *Glory*, 71. Hay apparently confuses the concepts of Jesus' Lordship and the eternal Kingdom. In Acts 2, and elsewhere, Christ the Lord is quite active in the present Church – while being enthroned at the right hand of God.

[44] So e.g. Rese, *Motive*, 58.

[45] As we have noted before, from the days of Bousset the "title" κύριος was located in Hellenistic environment. Cullmann, in his Christology, challenged this view and stated that in early Jewish Christianity the name Lord was considered the name "above every name", i.e. God's own name. Therefore, also in Acts 2:36, this view prevails. Cullmann, *Christologie*, 213ff., 224.

[46] Against Loader, *NTS* 24 (1978) 202.

The anointed king in Acts 2:36 is therefore most evidently presented as a divine Lord, who is worthy of devotion and who is also able to provide salvation to human beings. The radical re-interpretation of Joel 2:32 in the same context (Acts 2:21; cf. Rom. 10:13) confirms such a view: "Then everyone who calls on the name of the Lord shall be saved." The traditional reliance on God is changed to reliance on the exalted Christ.[47]

While the speech itself is primarily based on the interpretation of Joel 2, even the idea of Christ's pouring out of the Spirit supports such high Christology. In Acts 2:33 Christ's exaltation is the premise for the pouring out of the Spirit, and in Joel 2 both of these aspects are mentioned – namely the Spirit and the Lord. In the resurrection Jesus has been made "both Lord and Messiah", and therefore he is able to pour out the Spirit. In the new reality where the Spirit prevails, people may call on the name of this Lord.[48]

Luke has thus accepted and transmitted the basic content of early Christology. According to this teaching the resurrected Jesus has been exalted on the throne of Glory in heaven. He is called Lord and Messiah. As a new Davidide he sits at the right hand of God and reigns the world. He is a true Savior and faith in him brings human beings to new life. For the writer who has exploited very early Christian tradition in his teaching he is the Lord that was already mentioned in the same speech, verse 21: "Then everyone who calls on the name of the Lord shall be saved."

After the detailed analysis we need to consider similarities between Luke's description and merkabah mysticism. Do we really need merkabah mysticism for the interpretation of this passage? How do the discourses of Jewish mysticism and early Christology relate to each other?

1. First, in this passage there is an evident reception of Old Testament and Jewish metaphors. The exploitation of subtexts emphasizes this point of view. In a general sense the setting of the passage is similar to that of merkabah mysticism. Further, in some respect the reception of certain Old Testament metaphors is rather similar to that of Second Temple Jewish writings. A

---

[47] Haenchen did not note this, even though he admitted that Jesus was referred to in verse 21. According to him, that passage of Joel could be exploited in a christological sense only in the Hellenistic Church where the passage read Lord. Haenchen, *Acts*, 179, especially footnote 5. Later scholars, however, have paid attention to the identification of Jesus and God in this verse. So for instance Schneider, *Apostelgeschichte*, 276f. According to Capes this is one example how the Old Testament "Yahweh texts" have been applied to Jesus. See Capes, *Yahweh Texts*, 53; cf. also Fletcher-Louis, *Luke-Acts*, 21.

[48] Bock interprets the role of Psalm 110 in this context in a similar manner. "The resurrection/ascension and the distribution of the promise of the Spirit show that Jesus has taken up the role described in this Psalm." Bock, *Proclamation*, 185.

significant eschatological event takes place in heaven and the throne of God is once again the centre of everything. This is clearly an apocalyptical feature which is also identical with the ideas of merkabah mysticism, but we must admit that this remains a rather general statement. The description of the passage may also be based on the Old Testament. The quotations found in the passage are taken from "canonical" writings. We must remember that there also God's heavenly throne had a special function. Therefore, this feature, too, alone does not say much about the relationship that we are investigating.

2. The second point is more convincing, however. The passage speaks of a heavenly enthronement by exploiting Psalm 110 as a subtext, supported by Psalm 132. The enthronement is expressed by using a phrase that serves as a submetaphor for a throne, i.e. the sitting "at the right hand" of God. This point also confirms that the description of early Christology in Acts 2 is also dependent on the enthronement discourse. The exaltation of Jesus in his resurrection is interpreted as an act of enthronement, and the description exploits symbols that are associated with coronation. The pattern is similar to that of merkabah mysticism. The key person of the event is being enthroned on the throne of Glory. Therefore Jewish merkabah mysticism appears to be precisely the tradition that helps us understand why Jewish Christians considered such an enthronement necessary in their Christology. Even though Psalm 110 has once again been taken from the "canonical" writings, the setting of the scene with a heavenly palace and a heavenly throne is identical to that of merkabah mysticism.[49]

3. The exalted Christ is a Davidic Messiah. In this respect he differs from most other "heavenly agents" that appear in Jewish writings. In this passage Christ is neither an angelomorphic being nor an exalted patriarch. He is a heavenly king that has been enthroned above all other beings and who reigns in heaven. We have seen that especially the pious ones of Qumran anticipated the eschatological enthronement of a Davidide. The first Christians seem to have believed in the fulfilment of such an anticipation. This belief reveals an exploitation of both an ascent structure and merkabah speculation, since the exalted Davidide is presented as a heavenly ruler.

4. We should also note the obvious but in its own context quite astonishing feature that Davidic descendance and the ascent structure are linked to a historical event and applied to a historical person. In Jewish writings heavenly

---

[49] According to Hay the theme of Peter's speech in Acts 2 is not the work of the exalted Christ but "the vindication implied by his exaltation." Peter stresses that Jesus was condemned by men but glorified by God. Hay, *Glory*, 72. This, however, is too superficial an interpretation of the whole passage. Even though such polarization appears in the speech, the climax of the speech, which the exploitation of Psalm 110 underlines, is in the enthronement of Jesus and in his new Lordship that has soteriological significance.

agents are usually transcendent and eschatological. Not even the Teacher of Righteousness at Qumran was given such a status in the eschatology of the sect. It is true, however, that the anticipation of the exaltation of patriarchs in Jewish mysticism was quite realistic, and it was applied to individual persons. In early Christianity the ideas were different still. Early Christology speaks of the fulfilment and realization of eschatology. According to such belief, resurrected Jesus now sits on the throne of Glory and reigns as a heavenly king.

Such conception of the status of Jesus is emphasized by his relation to the Spirit. When Jesus is exalted to God's right hand he distributes the Spirit which God had promised beforehand. Therefore also the distribution of the Spirit is evidence for the extraordinary position of Jesus in heaven.[50]

5. The intertextual strategy of this passage is quite exceptional. According to the writer, or most probably according to the tradition that he exploited, the enthronement took place at the resurrection. These two eschatological events fall into one. Psalm 110 has been used as a proof-text for an exaltation in resurrection. Such intertextual transformation shows that early Christology exceeded the limits of merkabah mysticism. Even though resurrection as a theme also appeared vaguely in the context of merkabah passages in Jewish writings, it was never actually identified with enthronement. Now the act of raising Jesus up is simply identified as his enthronement. This reveals that the writer has brought traditional material into the context of a new enthronement discourse, where resurrection has a prominent function.[51]

6. The messianic aspect is further emphasized by the royal appellations that have been given to the enthroned one. The new titles reveal the unique status of the exalted Christ. Even Psalm 110 proves for early Christians that Jesus Christ is Lord, κύριος. The granting of new titles as such may be explained by referring to a general Old Testament tradition, but Psalm 110 transcends the scene. Jesus is κύριος on the heavenly throne where he reigns.[52] This is the best way to interpret the titles themselves. They are not independent entities according to which such passages should be interpreted. Instead, they are

---

[50] "The presence of the Spirit is evidence of Jesus' position of authority at the right hand of God. Psalm 110 describes this "co-regency" rule of Jesus. In fact, Joel calls upon people to call upon the Lord." Bock, *SBLSP* (1990) 504.

[51] For previous discussion on the significance and function of Psalm 110 in early Christology, see Marshall, *Christology*, 103f.

[52] In the context of history-of-religions approach initiated by Bousset, Bultmann stated that "the un-modified expression 'the Lord' is unthinkable in Jewish usage." Bultmann, *Theology* 1, 51. In the modern setting, however, it is exactly the identification of the risen Lord and God that appears to be typical of the earliest (Palestinian) christological formulations. See e.g. Fitzmyer, *Acts*, 260.

linked to the discourse in which the exaltation of the Messiah is under discussion. Furthermore, such titles are associated with the metaphors that form the ground for their proper interpretation.

Moreover, it is apparent that the concept of 'Messiah' denotes its original meaning in this context. In his resurrection Jesus has been anointed king over the whole world. Thus the coronation day of the 'Messiah designate' is the day of his anointment.

7. What is even more extraordinary in this passage is that the aspect of theocracy is changed here. In heaven Christ is given a throne "at the right hand" of God. He is now the Lord, and "everyone who calls on the name of the Lord shall be saved" (2:21). Christ is the Savior and baptism in the name of Jesus Christ brings men to salvation (2:38). Words such as these no longer conform to the theocratic ideal.[53] For example in the Ascension of Isaiah the seer was warned: "Worship neither throne, nor angel from the six heavens" (AscIsa 7:21). This is the basic reason to assume that verse 36 in Acts 2 cannot be separated from the rest of the text.[54] It is not an independent adoptionist statement that had been adapted into high Christology by Luke himself. This verse is actually the embodiment of the Christology based on Psalm 110, and the whole passage 2:22-36 intentionally argues for this Christology.[55]

8. How can we understand such a statement in the context of Jewish theology? Once again the analysis of Second Temple mysticism may help us. In Qumran writings the highest figures in the heavenly Holy of Holies were called gods. One can no longer make a strict distinction between those figures and God's functions or qualities.

Secondly, Philo, who presents an allegorical interpretation of the ark in the Holy of Holies, most probably exploits the old tradition according to which the cherubim on the ark are called God and κύριος. In Philo's interpretation the former represents the creative power of God and the latter his just ruling.

---

[53] Moule is rather cautious when stating that "there is little or no evidence for the actual *worship* of Jesus in early Palestininan traditions," even though he in the same occasion investigates the "transfer to Christ of passages in the Scripture originally relating to God." Moule, *Christology*, 41. He has not discussed the nature of the homological statements speaking of Christ's Lordship.

[54] Wilckens concluded that v. 36 is in agreement with Luke's view of salvation history. "Die Aussage bezieht sich auf das ganze christologische Geschehen von seiner Anfang an. Dann aber entfällt auch jede "adoptianische" Deutung des Satzes." Wilckens, *Missionsreden*, 173-174.

[55] This is naturally quite the opposite of what the adherents of the adoptionist interpretation say. According to Casey, for instance, the use of the resurrection as the point of entry into lordship, "was particularly suited to that stage of christological development which assumed that Jesus was not more than a man during his earhly life, however important his life might have been." Casey, *Jewish Prophet*, 106.

These details are significant in the sense that they apparently belong to the symbolic world of Second Temple Judaism.

I am not convinced, however, that we should attempt to find an actual "missing link" between Jewish mysticism and early Christology. High Christology in the Acts, according to which Jesus is made κύριος on the throne of Glory, is unique. What is interesting is the observation that such a Christology is not unnatural even in a Jewish context. Jewish theologians may well accept the conception of a divine κύριος "at the right hand" of God. The more difficult part is to accept the identification of Jesus with the enthroned κύριος, which is explicit in the kerygmatic tradition of Acts 2:36.

9. As regards soteriology, we have already seen that in Jewish theology, too, heavenly figures may have a soteriological function. Priestly figures provide an atonement for Israel. Messianic kingship, in turn, may be understood so that the eschatological Davidide will deliver Israel from the power of evil oppressors. In the theocratic setting of Jewish theology, however, these figures never became objects of faith. For the writer of the passage of Acts, resurrection Christology is simultaneously cultic soteriology. "Repent, and be baptized every one of you in the name of Jesus Christ so that your sins may be forgiven" (2:38). It was the crucified one who was resurrected (2:23, 36). In his name, i.e. κύριος, sins were forgiven. Christ thus had a cultic task and his work had produced a cultic benefit. Such a cultic nature of the resurrection Christology can also be seen elsewhere in early traditional formulas (especially Romans 4:25).[56] As the larger context of Peter's speech in Acts 2 appears to be that of baptism, it is justified to conclude that the speech contains traditional materials from that kind of setting. The exaltation statement itself may be a baptismal formula that has been exploited for kerygmatic purposes, as well.

10. One further remark should be made about the theocratic aspect. The Pentecost speech seems to question the adoptionist theory instead of affirming it. While in Jewish theology exaltation did not mean deification, neither would the idea of the "making" of the Messiah imply any ontological claims concerning the exalted one in the context of Jewish theology. This problem may also be approached from a reversed angle. If the enthroned one appears to have divine features, he must have possessed these even before the exaltation. There are no theological reasons why the exaltation would have produced them. Such a conclusion should not surprise us too much. It really conforms to what we know of Jewish Christianity. This is probably the reason why several scholars have abandoned the concept of adoption in their interpretation and

---

[56] Rom. 4:24-25: "to us who believe in him who raised Jesus our Lord from the dead, who was handed over to death for our trespasses and was raised for our justification".

speak of an enthronement instead.[57] The questions concerning the nature of early Christology in general and the theory of adoptionist Christology in particular are important. They greatly affect our understanding of the emergence of early Christology. Therefore they shall be examined later in a separate chapter.[58]

Acts 5:30-31. Later in the Acts we can find several passages where a similar Christology is presented. In the fifth chapter there is another description of the resurrection, and it repeats the idea of the Pentecost speech, even though the actual expressions are new.[59]

"The God of our ancestors raised up Jesus, whom you had killed by hanging him on a tree. God exalted him at his right hand as Leader and Savior (τοῦτον ὁ θεὸς ἀρχηγὸν καὶ σωτῆρα ὕψωσεν τῇ δεξιᾷ αὐτοῦ,) that he might give repentance to Israel and forgiveness of sins." (5:30-31).

Here the narrative is short and compact. It is a simple kerygmatic passion narrative where both crucifixion and exaltation are described. While Jesus' death is emphasized at first, his resurrection is evidently presented as the implicit cause of the exaltation even though it is not explicitly mentioned as such. Exaltation itself is not the actual issue of this passage but simply a premise for the message about salvation. The content of this formulation is soteriological. The enthroned Christ as a σωτήρ gives forgiveness of sins.[60]

While Psalm 110 has influenced the tradition that Luke exploits here ("at his right hand"), the reference appears to concern the whole Psalm with its cultic features. The exalted Christ is (implicitly) a new Melchizedek who has a priestly function providing atonement and forgiveness.

These notions prove that Psalm 110:1 was not exploited merely in the enthronement discourse of the Christian community. Thus we also have enthronement statements with a cultic function. The focus of the description is revealed when the statement is read in the context of cultic discourse, even though the basic expression "at his right hand" refers to enthronement discourse.

Acts 5:31 also suggests that the writer of these lines supports high

---

[57] Among scholars this kind of change has taken place as early as the 60's; see e.g. Schweizer, *Studies*, 187; Hayes, *Interp 22* (1968) 337ff.; cf. Duling, *NTS 19* (1973) 73.

[58] See chapter 9.

[59] For the comparison, see Schneider, *Apostelgeschichte I*, 395, also n.90.

[60] Loader is right when emphasizing this feature in the passage. Loader, *NTS 24* (1978) 203f. Hay, however, is persistent in his eschatological interpretation and also here states that the passage merely expresses "God's vindication of the Jesus whom men condemned to death." Hay, *Glory*, 73. Such an interpretation is bound to remain incomplete.

Christology. Christ as a σωτήρ has an extraordinary status. In Luke 1:47 the appellation has been used of God himself, as also often in the Old Testament (see e.g. 1 Sam. 10:19; Isa 45:15, 21).[61] Therefore this may well be another example of how Christ is being granted appellations that originally belong to God in the symbolic world of Second Temple Judaism.

How is it possible that such a well defined narrative has survived and found its way to the Acts? It seems probable that we have here an original formula that has been preached in the early Church.[62] The compact nature of the clauses and certain peculiar appellations argue for a tradition. This does not sound like a free composition which Luke had written for his own purposes, even though a similar structure can be found behind most of the speeches of the Acts. It seems far more consistent that the unity between these sermons is guided by kerygmatic tradition than by Luke's literary purposes.[63]

As a short summary we may note that, in Acts 5:30-31, exaltation Christology contains the same features as in Acts 2. In an evident kerygmatic passage exaltation is expressed with the help of Psalm 110, and the resurrected Christ is presented as an enthroned King of Heaven. The "titles" of Christ are different from those of Acts 2. He is now "Leader and Savior". This notion leads further to the cultic aspect of the formula. Savior is simultaneously the one who has atoned for sins and the one who gives forgiveness of sins to those who believe. The apparent features of enthronement discourse are now exploited in a cultic discourse, and evidently these two are not essentially separated from each other.

Acts 7:1-56. Among the exaltation narratives of the Acts we also have the speech of Stephen, which opens up quite a new aspect in resurrection theology. In the speech of Stephen the interesting question concerning the relationship of the Son of Man and the resurrected Christ is touched on.

The speech begins with Moses-typology. The rhetorical question in verse 27, "Who made you a ruler and a judge over us?", is answered later in 7:35: "It was this Moses... whom God now sent as both ruler and liberator (ἄρχοντα καὶ λυτρωτὴν)." Christ is presented as the new Moses who was expected to

---

[61] For such background, see Fitzmyer, *Acts*, 338.

[62] In this case I prefer the idea of fixed tradition, as did e.g. Wilckens, *Missionsreden*, 45; Pesch, *Apostelgeschichte I*, 213. Some commentators, like Dunn, consider that these verses merely "reflect Luke's awareness of various traditions from the early period." Dunn, *Acts*, 69.

[63] M. de Jonge suggests that there are "ancient elements" in the speeches of the Acts. "Among the constant elements we find a basic pattern in the preaching about Jesus' death and resurrection, in which the contrast between the acts of human beings and God's activity is stressed." de Jonge, *Christology*, 108.

come and liberate Israel.⁶⁴ A word-play on the word "raising" applies the Moses-typology to the exaltation discourse. The new Moses who after the promises of the Scriptures would be "raised" has now been exalted. "This is the Moses who said to the Israelites, 'God will raise up a prophet for you (Προφήτην ὑμῖν ἀναστήσει ὁ θεὸς) from your own people as he raised me up'." (Acts 7:37).⁶⁵

According to the writer, the exaltation of the new Moses is an eschatological event. In this respect the speech resembles Jewish eschatology prevailing at the Second Temple period. Temple criticism is explicit, e.g. in verses 47-49. "Yet the most high does not dwell in houses made with human hands; as the prophet says, 'Heaven is my throne...'." (7:48-49). Such Temple criticism relies on the basic message of apocalyptic Judaism. The real throne of God is in heaven. True piety adores the heavenly God and joins the heavenly worship that is performed before the throne. The earthly Temple of Jerusalem must be regarded merely as a metaphoric typos for the heavenly sanctuary. God "does not dwell in houses made with human hands".

At the end of the speech Stephen sees a throne vision. "I see the heavens opened and the Son of Man standing at the right hand of God!" (7:56).⁶⁶ This proclamation finally leads to the stoning of Stephen. The message of the writer is clear. The new Moses has been exalted.⁶⁷ Jesus is the Righteous One who has been betrayed and killed (v. 52). He has now been exalted to heaven and made the Lord of all heaven and earth. The Jews who heard Stephen could not accept such a message but rejected it as blasphemy.

There is also an interesting interpretative redaction in the speech. In verse 55 the writer explains the throne vision that he is going to present next in the story. "But filled with the Holy Spirit, he gazed into heaven and saw the glory of God and Jesus standing at the right hand of God." This should be considered one of the most important statements in the Christology of Acts. In this sentence Luke explains the relationship between Jesus' eschatological

---

⁶⁴ This equation, too, has been considered to derive from "primitive Christian apologetic". For the discussion, see Dunn, *Christology*, 138, especially footnote 46.

⁶⁵ In Acts 3:22 the same verse from Dtn. 18:15 has been used as a scriptural proof for the exaltation of Jesus. Schneider, *Apostelgeschichte*, 463.

⁶⁶ In this statement the "sitting" has been changed to "standing". This is evidently a result of the influence of Dan. 7:13-14. So Haencen, *Acts*, 292 footnote 4. For later discussion, see Bock, *Proclamation*, 222. The enthronement metaphor "at the right hand" has, however, been so strong that it has preserved its place in the exaltation description.

⁶⁷ The royal aspect is also evidently maintained in the Moses-typology. As Bock notes, in the speech the new Moses is a royal figure: "Once again Jesus is proclaimed from prophecy and pattern to be the prophet like Moses, a prophetic figure who delivers the nation like a king would." Bock, *Proclamation*, 221.

teachings and the exaltation Christology of the early Church. The vision apparently makes the identification between Jesus and Son of Man possible.[68]

Luke parallels the two main sentences in a way that cannot be misunderstood (Acts 7:55-56):

"I see...   the Son of Man   standing at the right hand of God"
"(he) saw...   Jesus   standing at the right hand of God"

In his Gospel Luke has naturally prepared the way for such an identification. For example in the prediction of Jesus' suffering (Luke 9:22) the resurrection of the Son of Man has been foretold, the reference being Ps. 110:1. In the eschatological speeches the parousia of the Son of Man is naturally described as a future event (21:27). In these narratives, however, enthronement is not the issue.

Another interesting detail in the Lukan gospel tradition is Jesus' debate with scribes over the son of David. This is a story where the key is in a word-play on Psalm 110. With a riddle concerning the son of David Jesus questioned the traditional Jewish concept of political messianism (Luke 21:40-44; and par., especially Mark 12:35-37). In Jewish eschatology the Davidic messiah was expected to be an ideal king who would restore the Davidic dynasty and destroy its enemies. The riddle was based on Psalm 110 where the Davidide is raised on the throne of glory: "The Lord says to my lord, 'Sit at my right hand until I make your enemies your footstool'." (110:1). The dynamic of the word-play is based on the word 'Lord'. "David thus calls him Lord; so how can he be his son?" (Luke 20:44; cf. Mark 12:37).The point of Jesus' speech is evident. The messiah cannot be merely a political earthly king. He must be a heavenly ruler who shall also be David's Lord, not his son and subordinate. Therefore, in this story too the Son of Man is actually identified with the son of David.

Finally in the Gospel of Luke there is a bridge that reaches up to the speech of Stephen in the Acts. When Jesus is brought before the council for a trial, his provocative answer to the chief priests summarizes his eschatological proclamation (Luke 22:69). "But from now on the Son of Man will be seated at the right hand of the power of God."[69] This is an enthronement statement par excellence. The Son of Man is enthroned "at the right hand" of God. For Luke, the awaited enthronement is even nearer ("from now on") than for Mark, who probably did not alter the traditional narration ("You will see the Son of Man seated...", Mark 14:62).

For Luke, and apparently for his tradition as well, the enthronement of the

---

[68] So e.g. Pesh, *Apostelgeschichte I*, 263.

[69] Fitzmyer, *Acts*, 392.

Son of Man takes place at the resurrection. This fact essentially alters the traditional scholarly view of futurist eschatology. The same concept of exaltation has already appeared to be the basic line of thought in several speeches of the Acts. In Acts 2, naturally, Jesus has been made the Lord and Messiah in the resurrection. In Acts 3 the reign of this Messiah is described. He "must remain in heaven until the time of universal restoration" (Acts 3:20-21).[70] For Luke, the time of the "Church" is the time of Christ's reign.

Therefore, in Stephen's speech too the basic structure of early exaltation Christology may be detected. As the new Moses the exalted Jesus is the leader of Israel, a heavenly king. He is a universal ruler who has been enthroned on the throne of Glory in his resurrection. As an enthroned leader Christ is simultaneously the promised Davidide. Even though such identification of different types may seem odd, we must note that early Jewish Christian thought did not make scholarly distinctions between such definitions. Such Christology appears to be associative. The writers freely combined suitable elements of tradition, whenever it helped to reach the goal. For Luke and evidently for several other early writers before him, the promised Davidide was actually the Danielic Son of Man, who was expected to have a unique status in heaven.

Thus in Lukan traditions there are certain interesting features that conform to the picture that we have seen in the merkabah mysticism of Jewish theology. In the descriptions of the resurrection of Jesus the conception of a throne vision is exploited. The visions of the enthronement of the Son of Man are identical with the visions of the resurrected Christ. Such descriptions can be understood only in the context of the apocalyptic tradition of Jewish mysticism.

Moreover, the status of the exalted Christ is explained with the aid of throne speculation. The Christology of Lukan traditions is based on the enthronement discourse. Resurrection is identified as an act of enthronement. The exalted Christ is a heavenly king, and he is given royal epithets, such as Messiah, Lord, Savior and Leader. As a heavenly king he is no doubt more than merely a heavenly judge who reigns at the top of the heavenly hierarchy. Here the theocratic relationship to God has been disturbed.

The unique status of Christ becomes even more emphasized as independent soteriological function is ascribed to him. This has been expressed at least in two ways in Lukan traditions. Firstly, according to the cultic interpretation of

---

[70] According to Bruce this kind of eschatology could well be described as "the most primitive eschatology of all". In other words it appears to be based on the early tradition which underlines exaltation Christology. Jesus is no longer a "Messiah designate" whose installation awaits his appearance from heaven. See Bruce, *Eschatology*, 60f.; against Robinson who stated: "Jesus is here still only the Christ-elect, the messianic age has yet to be inaugurated." Robinson, *Studies*, 144.

the (short) passion narrative Jesus has atoned for sins on the cross. In his name the forgiveness of sins has been granted. Secondly, the exaltation statements appear in homologies. This is a significant element in the early kerygmatic tradition. The ascension story is not merely an account of the enthronement of a righteous person. Early traditional formulas appear to be confessional statements where the exalted Christ at the right hand of God is the object of faith and the Savior of sinners.

5.2. Paul and merkabah mysticism

As we proceed to the letters of Paul some of the questions that we need to ask are similar to those posed to Lukan Christology and Luke's traditions. To what degree has Paul accepted and adapted exaltation Christology in his theology, and what role does early Christological tradition have in his letters? Do we find materials in which the influence of merkabah mysticism could be traced? Even a short survey of his letters reveals that there are several passages where the resurrected Christ is described as enthroned in heaven. There are also several passages where Psalm 110 has a primary significance. In what follows we must first investigate these passages.

There is, however, another point of view which is typical of Paul only. His interest in visions has led some scholars to ask if Paul himself was a merkabah seer. What is his relation to the Jewish apocalyptic tradition where heavenly journeys had an important role in the identity of the pious ones? This subject becomes even more important when we have reason to claim that Paul knew Jewish mysticism well and openly confronted it in his letters.[71] These subjects must be treated after the investigation of passages speaking of exaltation Christology.

1 Cor. 15:24-25. We shall begin the treatment of this subject by surveying Pauline passages reflecting on Psalm 110 and exaltation Christology. It is apparent that Psalm 110 also had great significance for his theology. On several crucial occasions we can find reference to it.

In such a significant exposition of the resurrection as 1 Cor. 15, one would expect to find a reference to traditional exaltation Christology. This chapter begins with a reference to a pre-Pauline homology, but this homology contains no reference to Psalm 110. During the exposition, however, the status of Christ becomes apparent, and finally in verse 25 the eschatological scene is

---

[71] The study on Paul's apocalyptic view has been a growing field for several years. For example Beker has suggested that the basic ideas of Paul's gospel are directed by apocalyptic premises, see e.g. Beker, *Paul*, 135ff. Segal in his *Paul the Convert* suggests that Paul was familiar with Jewish mysticism and that this tradition affected his theology. Segal, *Paul*, 34ff.

completed. "For he must reign until he has put all his enemies under his feet." (15:25). This expression implies that Christ has been enthroned in the resurrection and reigns in heaven. Only in the end of days "he hands over the kingdom to God the Father, after he has destroyed every ruler and every authority and power" (15:24).[72]

In 1 Cor. 15 Paul does not explicitly say that Christ's enthronement took place in the resurrection. In verses 4-5 he quotes an early Christian homology where the raising "on the third day" is mentioned. Then he says that Christ appeared to Cephas and several other Christians. In the following clauses he begins to make an apology for the resurrection. His apology climaxes in the verses quoted above, referring to Psalm 110.

What is clear, however, is that in 15:25 Paul is not speaking of an enthronement in parousia. Instead, Christ reigns "until he has put all his enemies under his feet". Christ's reign has begun at the resurrection and the final battle actually means the consummation of his reign.[73] This is also the purpose of the clear allusion to Psalm 110:1 (LXX: 109:1) in verse 25b. As we have seen in Lukan traditions, this eschatological pattern was common in the early Church (see Acts 3:21).[74]

Therefore, according to 1 Cor. 15, Paul's general conception of the resurrection appears to rest on the premise according to which Christ in his "raising from the dead" has been enthroned to heavenly power.[75] Resurrection is thus identified as the day of the inauguration of Christ's kingdom. He will reign until the day of the final judgment.

This view is further supported by Paul's resurrection theology. "But in fact Christ has been raised from the dead, the first fruits of those who have died. For since death came through a human being, the resurrection of the dead has also come through a human being." (15:20-21). The key event of eschatology, the resurrection of the dead has already taken place as far as Christ is

---

[72] In Philippians there is a similar allusion to the eschatological "power" of Christ. "He will transform the body of our humiliation that it may be conformed to the body of his glory, by the power that also enables him to make all things subject to him." (3:21).

[73] So also Conzelmann, *1 Corinthians*, 272 footnote 88; Loader, *NTS* 24 (1978) 208. Cf. Hengel, according to whom the reign of the Exalted and Coming One "begins with the resurrection and takes the place of the 'sitting at the right hand' in Ps. 110:1." Hengel, *Studies*, 164. Hay does not accept this kind of interpretation. He refers to "future messianic interim reign". Hay, *Glory*, 61. Such an explanation is hardly plausible, since Paul is clearly speaking of Christ's active kingship after resurrection.

[74] In Paul's early letters this seems to be the basic train of thought, even when he simultaneously emphasizes the significance of Christ's parousia. See 1 Thess. 1:10; 3:11-13; 4:14; 5:9-10. Cf. Holleman, *Resurrection*, 61ff.

[75] The aspect of resurrection in the enthronement is later emphasized in Eph. 1:20, which is usually considered a passage reflecting direct Pauline tradition.

concerned. In this eschatological climax he has been enthroned on a heavenly throne. There he will reign until the last day.[76]

While the so called interim period is a period of Christ's ruling, we may well call it the time of Christ's kingdom. According to Paul's eschatology, he is the Lord who reigns and combats "until he has put all his enemies under his feet". Thus the quotation of Psalm 110 in 1 Cor. 15 refers to the exalted Lord who is the king of heaven and earth.[77]

In Paul's exploitation of the Scriptural proof we once again witness a change of subject. In Psalm 110 (and Ps. 8:7) it is God who puts his enemies in subjection, but in Paul's interpretation this task is given to the enthroned Christ (1 Cor. 15:27-28).[78] This cannot be merely a sign of a free use of Scripture. Since it has appeared to be a constant feature in early Christology, it must be considered an intentional tool of christological description expressing high Christology. The enthroned Christ acts as a divine Lord on the throne of Glory.

In this respect Paul appears to have accepted the content of early Christian exaltation Christology. For him also Christ is a heavenly king who has been enthroned in his resurrection and Psalm 110 is an important scriptural proof for Christ's Lordship and heavenly power. Paul does not make essential alterations to such exaltation Christology, but exploits it in a self-evident way in his eschatology. This is apparent also in 1 Cor. 15:24-25 where Psalm 110 is referred to in an exegetical christological teaching. Paul clearly presupposes the exaltation and enthronement of Christ in his resurrection. The resurrected Jesus (1 Cor. 15:4), who is the subject of Paul's saving Gospel, is the enthroned Davidide at the right hand of God.

Rom. 8:34. Probably the most famous occurrence of the submetaphor "at the right hand" as a reference to Psalm 110:1 in Paul is found in Romans 8:34.

"It is Christ Jesus, who died, yes, who was raised, who is at the right hand of God (ὅς καί ἐστιν ἐν δεξιᾷ τοῦ θεοῦ), who indeed intercedes for us."

This short passage is a kerygmatic statement that most probably comes from

---

[76] Cf. Hay's famous statement: "It is, therefore, a serious mistake to claim that early Christian references to Psalm 110.1b regularly express convictions about Christ reigning as a royal lord in the present era." Hay, *Glory*, 91. The analysis of early traditions in this study evidence the opposite.

[77] As Orr and Walther remark, there is a bipolarity in Christ's victory. "Christ's rule is in process of controlling *all his enemies*, but the complete subjugation is still to come." Orr-Walther, *I Corinthians*, 333.

[78] For the change of subject, see e.g. Conzelmann, *I Corinthians*, 273; cf. Robertson-Plummer, *Corinthians*, 356.

early Christian tradition.⁷⁹ It is a crystallized statement including several important features. It mentions Christ's death and resurrection.⁸⁰ Exaltation is interpreted as enthronement "at the right hand", and the priestly function is obvious. The last one of these features connects the tradition with those found in the letter to the Hebrews.

The form of the expression "at the right hand" (ἐν δεξιᾷ) is interesting, since it is an independent rendering of the text of Psalm 110 and differs from the Septuagint Ps. 109 (ἐκ δεξιῶν).⁸¹ Therefore it most apparently originates in a Church where the Septuagint not yet influenced the formation of christological statements. In this case this is to be considered a sign of the occurrence of a traditional formula which originates in Aramaic Christianity.⁸²

Also several other elements support such conclusion. Firstly, this must be the shortest possible passion "narrative" having a formulaic ring and the content of a confession. Secondly, the use of Psalm 110 together with the cultic element that this Psalm carries along gather together almost all important features of early Christology.⁸³

The section may also be seen as a short ascent story. In this respect the statement appears to be a good example of early exaltation Christology. Also according to this passage Jesus in his resurrection has been enthroned on the heavenly throne. He is the awaited Davidide whose exaltation fulfilled the promises of Psalm 110. Furthermore, he appears to be the new Mechizedek who has a priestly function in the heavenly Temple (ὃς καὶ ἐντυγχάνει ὑπὲρ ἡμῶν). Thus both the messianic and the cultic element can clearly be seen in the

---

⁷⁹ Michel lists criteria such as short relative clauses and confessional style which together betray a liturgical tradition. Michel, *Römer (1978)*, 282. Dunn notes that these sentences have a "formulaic ring", even though the "balanced form of the statement" is more established than the particular wording. Dunn, *Romans*, 503.

⁸⁰ The short opening line Χριστὸς ['Ἰησοῦς] ὁ ἀποθανών resembles that of the kerygmatic formula in 1 Cor. 15:3. In my view such tradition has underlined the death of the Messiah. Thus the appellation Christ appears here in its original meaning denoting Jewish Messiah.

⁸¹ The form itself is possible, and it appears also in the Septuagint. In 1 Chr. 6:24, the singer Asaph sitting at the right hand of his brother; and in 1 Ezra 4:29, Apame sitting at the right hand of the king. For other occurrences in Greek literature, see Hengel, *Studies*, 141 footnote 52. In Christian tradition and in the New Testament this form, as well as the statement found in Rom. 8:34, has apparently had independent influence, as we can see in 1 Pet. 3:22, where almost an identical formulation may be found.

⁸² This has been pointed out e.g. by Hengel, *Studies*, 143.

⁸³ The sequential order of death, resurrection, enthronement, and intercession is remarkable. Cf. Gourgues, *A la Droite de Dieu*, 49f.

statement.[84] Christ's priestly function in this passage, however, is extraordinary.

As a heavenly high priest Christ is not *standing* before God's throne, as the high priest in Jerusalem did, or as the heavenly figures in Second Temple Jewish literature did.[85] Those characters were worshiping God who alone sat on the throne of Glory. In Rom. 8:34 Christ himself sat "at the right hand" of God and his ability to intercede for people was based on his exalted status.[86]

The context into which that piece of tradition has been placed also reveals something about its basic meaning. Paul is using it as a counterpoint in a judicial discourse where charges are brought against people and where condemnation is being threatened.[87] Furthermore, the great theme of justification is at issue (8:34).[88] The scene is skillfully created. The heavenly Temple is simultaneously a heavenly court and God is a judge. On the throne that now becomes identified as a judgment seat the divine judge is not sitting alone, however. Right in the heavenly court where charges should be brought the one who reigns is the crucified Lord "who indeed intercedes for us."[89]

Thus the traditional christological statement in Romans 8:34 confirms the picture that we have formulated concerning the nature of early Christology. Jesus' resurrection is interpreted as an act of enthronement. His exaltation is described by exploiting Psalm 110, and this Psalm enables early Christian theologians to combine the royal Messianic aspect with the priestly aspect. The Davidide will thus be identified with the Melchizedek figure. Both the

---

[84] Dunn has suggested that this statement may be an outworking of Paul's Adam Christology. Dunn, *Romans*, 504. Such a view, however, has little evidence for its support.

[85] "Rom. 8:34 is related to Hebrews through the fact that, in contrast to the heavenly cult and to the priestly sevice in the sanctuary or to courtly etiquette, Christ as intercessor does not *stand before* the throne of God but is the companion on the throne at the right hand of God." Hengel, *Studies*, 152 (italics his).

[86] As only God's throne is mentioned, this means that Christ sits on the throne of Glory itself. "He thus is given *the most immediate form of communion with God, which was comprehensible to a Jew based upon the texts of the Old Testament.*" Hengel, *Studies*, 149 (italics his).

[87] According to Michel such polarization in verses 33-34 is quite intentional. Michel, *Römer (1978)*, 282.

[88] Stuhlmacher emphasizes the judicial aspect in the interpretation of this passage. See Stuhlmacher, *Römer*, 127.

[89] This so called paraclete motif is connected with that of Heb. 7:25, where similarly Christ's high-priestly ministry of intercession on behalf of his own is described. Michel, *Römer (1978)*, 282; Moo, *Romans*, 585. Hay too suggests here an eschatological interpretation. "The time of intercession seems to be the last judgment." Hay, *Glory*, 131. This is not plausible because the passage is not eschatological but soteriological, like the one in Heb. 7.

sacrificial work of the crucified and the high-priestly ministry of intercession may easily be presented in one short statement. Paul has been well aware of such Christology and he has applied it in his letters, even though he seldom uses direct quotations of Psalm 110 in his letters.[90] The hermeneutical skill in which he applies such tradition in his theology proves that he has completely accepted the content of the tradition he exploits.

Col. 2:16-3:1. Another passage where Psalm 110:1 is referred to is Col. 3:1. The verse is actually a climax of a lenghty passage where Paul is having a bitter debate with his Colossian adversaries. This passage is famous for its complexity, and several theories about the "Colossian heretics" have been proposed. A growing interest in Jewish mysticism has also brought new aspects to the discussion over the nature of this passage.

Anyone approaching this passage is obliged to comment on two problems. The first one of these concerns Pauline authorship. Are we dealing with Paul's own letter and his own experiences, or do these lines come from the hand of his pupils? The second problem concerns Paul's abovementioned opponents. Was there a heretical group inside the Christian community, or was Paul (or the possible other writer) merely opposing for instance enthusiastic Jews or pagan Gnostics who were considered a threat for the ecclesia?

The discussion over the authorship is divided. The letter to the Colossians belongs to those shorter letters which are not unanimously considered Pauline. For some scholars, the vocabulary that somewhat differs from Paul's other letters, and certain theological views in the letter, especially that of Christology, point to the direction of post-Pauline authorship.[91] Other scholars, however, ascribe the exceptional vocabulary to exploited tradition. Apart from this, the language of the letter in general is considered Pauline. According to this view, the theological and christological conceptions in the letter are quite typical of Paul.[92]

---

[90] Loader opposes Hay, according to whom Paul is primarily concerned with the future. Hay, *Glory*, 59. Loader himself suggests that there was a development in early Christology concerning the conception of enthronement. At first Ps. 110 referred primarily to Jesus' enthronement "to be the Messiah to come at the end-time." Only later, like in Rom. 8:34, did the thought turn to the interim status and function of Jesus. Loader, *NTS 24* (1978) 205. According to our analysis this is not plausible. It appears to be the resurrection precisely that was at first interpreted as an act of enthronement.

[91] For the history of the discussion over the authorship, see e.g. Kümmel, *Introduction*, 340-346. The arguments for the negative view are presented and supported for instance by Vielhauer, *Urchristliche Literatur*, 126-200.

[92] Kümmel's conclusion is that the letter "is to be regarded as Pauline"; *Introduction*, 346.

The present study does not attempt to solve all the problems concerning authorship. One point of departure must be chosen, however. In what follows we shall first investigate the nature of the passage and its relation to Jewish mysticism. Only after that some comments on authorship will be made. For the sake of convenience, in the analysis, the author will simply be called "Paul", as this is the intention of the letter itself.

The second problem is in no respect easier than the first one. Whom is Paul opposing in this letter? The general idea has been that there was a heretic group inside the community, but this is not necessarily the case. There was a real threat, but it may have been outside the community.[93] The Colossian "philosophy" in itself naturally derived from outside the Christian group. Usually two main instances have been mentioned. The adversaries were either (Essene) Jews or adherents of a pagan mystery cult.[94] Also, a syncretistic group representing both of these beliefs has been proposed.[95] In order not to forget the complexity of the subject we should note that Gunther, in his study on Paul's opponents, listed forty-four different suggestions for the opponents of Paul at Colossae.[96]

Once again we need to remark that such a variety of ideas cannot be investigated in this study. What is interesting, however, is that in the discussion over Paul's opponents there has been a growing interest in Jewish mysticism. Therefore the following investigation will concentrate on the question how well does the hypothesis of Jewish mysticism solve the problems of the present discussion. As we saw above, Lightfoot had stated that the influence of Essene Judaism may be detected in the letter to the Colossians. Later for instance the influence of Qumranian Essenism has been suggested.[97] Finally, in 1962, Francis suggested that the Colossian ideas derived from Jewish Christian mystical asceticism.[98] As the study of Jewish merkabah mysticism has been growing, other detailed suggestions about the

---

[93] This has been proposed by Hooker, *Christ*, 329.

[94] For the Essene hypothesis with Gnostic overtones, see the views of Lightfoot, now printed in *Conflict*, 13ff., esp. 34f. The idea of a pagan mystery cult was introduced by Dibelius, now also available in *Conflict*, 61ff.

[95] According to Bornkamm the teaching that Paul opposed was a pronounced syncretistic religion. It belonged to the sphere of gnosticized Judaism, and had accepted Iranian-Persian elements and astrological influences. Bornkamm, *Conflict*, 125f., 132ff.

[96] See Gunther, *Opponents*, 3-4.

[97] So e.g. Lyonnet, who rejected the pagan Gnostic hypothesis and emphasized the Jewish nature of the teaching of the opponents. Lyonnet, *Conflict*, 147ff. See also Davies, *Scrolls*, 166f.; Gunther, *Opponents*, 173ff.; Stuckenbruck, *Angel Veneration*, 112ff.

[98] See Francis, *Conflict*, 163ff., 184f. His views have later been accepted e.g. by Bandstra, *New Dimensions*, 343, and O'Brien, *Colossians*, xxxvii, 141f.

relation between the Colossian "heresy" and Jewish apocalyptic ideology have been proposed.[99]

In Colossians 2:18 we find several details that make the abovementioned suggestion plausible. In his description of false teachers Paul refers to several elements that suit well the conceptions of Jewish mysticism. Even though this passage is linguistically rather complex, its basic content may be investigated by concentrating on its essential terminology.[100]

"Do not let anyone disqualify you, insisting on self-abasement (ἐν ταπεινοφροσύνῃ) and worship of angels (θρησκείᾳ τῶν ἀγγέλων), dwelling on visions (ἃ ἑόρακεν ἐμβατεύων)" (2:18).

The Colossian philosophy was considered especially dangerous since its followers would lose their "prize" in heaven. They would be led astray by tempting religious practices. The first one of these was "self-abasement". In the New Testament the Greek word ταπεινοφροσύνη usually means "humility" as a virtue (Phil. 2:3; 1 Pet. 5:5), but in this case that is hardly the basic message of the word, at least not in a positive sense. In such a context it must have a somewhat negative meaning, referring to the conduct of the opponents. Thus it does have the appearance of humility, but its function is not a gentle attitude towards one's neighbour. As the context is considered, it is also apparent that such "humility" has something to do with visionary practice. The analysis may show some relevant reasons for such a meaning for the word.

There are certain interesting parallels for the word in such contexts both in Christian and Jewish literature.[101] For instance in Hermas, ταπεινοφροσύνη is connected with fasting. When Hermas asks for revelation, he is told: "Every prayer should be accompanied with humility: fast, therefore, and you will obtain from the Lord what you beg." (Hermas, Vis., 10). Humility as fasting was obviously considered as means for obtaining visions.[102]

In Jewish literature fasting often belongs to heavenly precepts that are given to the seers that ascend to the heavens. Fasting and other bodily rigors are further presented as proper means for preparing oneself for revelations.[103] In

---

[99] See for instance the inspiring comments of Alexander in his introduction to 3 Enoch, Alexander, *Old Testament Pseudepigrapha I*, 246f.

[100] For a good overview of the history of the investigation of this verse, see Stuckenbruck, *Angel Veneration*, 111-119.

[101] In the Old Testament (LXX) this word for humility (self-abasement) is used in the context of the Day of Atonement. The Israelites must fast on the day when they shall be cleansed from all their sins (Lev. 16:29-31).

[102] Francis has given a thorough analysis of the word, Francis, *Conflict*, 167ff. He also refers to Tertullian, who in his Treatise on the Soul discusses similar means, 48.4.

[103] See e.g. ApcEzra 1:3-5; TIsaac 4:1f.; ApocAbr 9; AscIsa 2:7-11.

Colossians 2 it is useful to note that the reference to "humility" is preceded by comments on "food and drink" (v. 16). Below, in 2:23, such humility is defined as "severe treatment of the body", which fits well in the picture.

The reference to humility (self-abasement) evidently concerns the ascetic life-style of pious apocalyptics. This is quite familiar from general descriptions in Jewish sources, and it is especially well established in the writings of Qumran.[104] In his new freedom Paul opposes any asceticism that is built in favour of a person's own religious experience and not leading to Christ. Therefore, it is evident that the advocates of the Colossian philosophy "delighted in ascetic practices as a prelude to the reception of heavenly visions."[105]

The second feature concerns the opponents' angelology and interest in heavenly authorities. The expression θρησκείᾳ τῶν ἀγγέλων has usually been translated as an objective genitive, meaning the worship directed to the angels.[106] This alternative is possible and it is supported by the fact that syntactically the word is dependent on the preceding preposition ἐν. On the other hand, however, one should also take the following expression ἃ ἑόρακεν into account. It may well be a relative clause modifying the worship, denoting something that has been seen (in a vision). In that case the abovementioned expression could be translated as a subjective genitive, meaning the worship that the angels perform, and which has been seen in a vision.[107]

The angelic world was already described in the letter. According to 1:16 Christ is the head and creator of "things visible and invisible, whether thrones or dominions or rulers or powers." Such words are identical with the words for angels in apocalyptic literature, not to mention the metaphors describing the heavenly world, like the throne.[108] Overall in the letter Paul appears to contrast the apocalyptic view of Jewish mysticism with Christology.

The word for 'worship' itself usually denotes the worship of God. It may be used naturally of idolatry, as well, as is actually done in this chapter in verse 2:23. In this verse the opponents' worship is defined as self-chosen worship (ἐν ἐθελοθρησκίᾳ). In this respect it would be rather logical to assume that Paul is speaking of angelic worship here. The false teachers "claimed to have joined in the angelic worship of God as they entered into the heavenly

---

[104] See chapter 3.2. below.

[105] So O'Brien, *Colossians*, 142, summarizing Francis' views.

[106] For such a view, see e.g. Lohse, *Colossians*, 118f.; Scott, *Colossians*, 54; Gnilka, *Kolosserbrief*, 149f.

[107] This was suggested by Francis, *Conflict*, 164, 176ff. He was later followed e.g. by Carr, *Angels*, 71, O'Brien, *Colossians*, 143, and Dunn, *Colossians*, 180f.

[108] See Segal, *Two Powers*, 211.

realm and prepared to receive visions of divine mysteries."¹⁰⁹ This view is further supported by the fact that, in verse 3:1, the interest in heavenly mysteries is contrasted with the contemplation of the exalted Christ in heaven. Believers are encouraged to "seek the things that are above" in a proper way. The way of the philosophers, the Jewish mystics, is wrong. It is not the angelic worship that is significant in heaven. Believers concentrate on the exalted Christ.

Moreover, in Jewish writings the worship of angels is strictly prohibited. One could naturally claim that such prohibition would be unnecessary had there been no worship of angels taking place in the Jewish community. It is not plausible, however, that the vague expression in Colossians 2 would be a proper proof of the occurrence of veneration of angels in Colossae.¹¹⁰

It is possible that, according to the Colossian "philosophy," angels were regarded as mediators between God and man.¹¹¹ The contrasting of Christology and angelology in the letter might refer to such a view. On the other hand, however, it is also possible that the idea of a direct fellowship with angels points to another direction. It may be a sign of a belief that to achieve the mystical experience there was no need for a divine intermediary.¹¹² In this case the mediating role of the angels diminishes and the idea of direct heavenly wisdom becomes primary.

Therefore, merely the interest in heavenly hosts and their functions has no doubt been sufficient enough to arouse Paul's criticism, even if the worship of angels was not at issue. The vast speculation e.g. of Melchizedek at Qumran,

---

[109] O'Brien, *Colossians*, 143. For instance Lohse and Gnilka have pointed out that in v. 23 the "self-chosen worship" is perfomed by men, and therefore also the worship mentioned in v. 18 must have been performed by men. In this case that verse could not speak of an angelic worship. Lohse, *Colossians*, 119; Gnilka, *Kolosserbrief*, 149-150; Schweizer, *Kolosser*, 122. This is not necessarily true. For example the basic idea of the Qumranian heavenly liturgy in the Songs of the Sabbath Sacrifice evidently lies in the member's joining in the angelic heavenly worship.

[110] We have earlier noted that scholarship is divided in this question. Fossum was convinced that even pre-Christian Jewish apocalyptic had spoken of a divine angelic intermediary, and Fletcher-Louis shared his view. Stuckenbruck and Carrell, however, denied such a possibility. See Introduction above. It is rather interesting to note, however, that even Fletcher-Louis is uncertain of the role of Col. 2:18 in this question. See Fletcher-Louis, *Angels*, 6.

[111] So e.g. Alexander, *Old Testament Pseudepigrapha*, 246.

[112] This was the conclusion of Bandstra, *New Dimensions*, 339. Bandstra is right when stating that, for instance at Qumran, and especially in the Songs of the Sabbath Sacrifice, such immediate contact with the heavenly throne was described. Further, in the Apocalypse of Abraham, Jaoel was actually not a mediator between God and the human beings. *ibid.* 333-338.

and the detailed description of the figure of Metatron in Enochic tradition provide examples of such interest. Furthermore, the dividing line between speculation and adoration may have been rather vague. It is useful to note that it was the *danger* of venerating the angels in heaven that was the recurring theme in Jewish ascent stories, as we saw earlier. This does not mean the actual venerating of the angels, but rather a balancing on the dividing line.

In this respect the Colossian "heretics," i.e. Jewish teachers, may have been kindred souls of Qumran or Essene ascetics who possessed a rich angelology and based their faith in angelic liturgy.[113] Their description of the heavenly world was fascinating and offered great mystical experience. The concentration on heavenly luminaries lacked but one crucial element. According to Paul, Christ had no part in that contemplation.

Thirdly, we need to pay attention to the expression that has been translated as "dwelling on visions" (ἃ ἑόρακεν ἐμβατεύων). As such it looks like an explicit reference to the apocalyptic tradition. As we noted above, the literal meaning of ἃ ἑόρακεν is "which he has seen". The exact meaning of the whole expression is dependent on how one understands the relation of such seeing to the angelic worship on the one hand, and its relation to the following word ἐμβατεύειν on the other hand. The former question we have already treated above. It is logical to think that the seer has seen angelic liturgy in heaven. But another question remains. How does this interpretation relate with the rest of the expression?

The primary meaning of ἐμβατεύειν is "to enter".[114] Dibelius showed that in Greek mystical inscriptions the word has been used of the event of "entering" the mysteries.[115] In Colossians 2 there is no reference to initiation, however.[116] We are rather witnessing how the seer is entering the vision, or in more general terms, how he enters the heavens. Such idea of entering has appeared to be quite common in the writings of Jewish mysticism, as the analysis showed in chapter 3.

A classical example of such entering is found in the Testament of Levi. "And behold, the heavens were opened, and an angel of the Lord spoke to me:

---

[113] Cf. Lincoln, *Paradise*, 111; Dunn, *Colossians*, 181.

[114] For the semantics of the word, see e.g. O'Brien, *Colossians*, 143f.

[115] Studying the inscriptions of the Apollo sanctuary at Claros Dibelius suggested that the word would denote initiation into the mysteries. Dibelius, *Conflict*, 85ff. Such semantics is no longer acceptable. The occurrence of the word does not prove that similar mysteries had been referred to. It rather proves that such word was used for "entering" into mystical experience. In Jewish context the "entering" itself differs from the conceptions of Greek mysteries.

[116] Against Lohse who suggests that, in the circle of the philosophy, "cultic rites were performed." Lohse, *Colossians*, 120. There is nothing in the text to support the idea of cultic rites.

'Levi, Levi, enter!' And I entered the first heaven." (2:6-7).[117] The whole ascent structure is based on the idea that, in his vision, the chosen righteous one enters the heavens. This conception suits well the statement in Colossians 2:18. When entering the heavens the seer sees heavenly worship, the angelic liturgy, and through that liturgy and the mediation of the angels he is in contact with the heavenly world, God's reality.

These comments have led to a new translation of the verse 2:18 where the idea of the heavenly worship has been brought afore.[118]

"Let no one disqualify you, being bent upon humility and the worship of angels – which he has seen upon entering – being vainly puffed up by his mind of flesh."

Such translation has its advantages. It emphasizes the opponents' ascetic mysticism, and in this way Paul's criticism becomes understandable too. The interest in heavenly things without Christological reference is a product of the mind of flesh. It is self-chosen worship and as such opposes true knowledge of God. In their own mystical context such beliefs have the "appearance of wisdom", but in Paul's mind it is worst possible foolishness.

Another significant feature in the passage is the criticism against the legalistic nature of the "philosophy". This is a feature that has not always been easy to connect with ecstatic mysticism, and especially not with Gnosticism or Hellenistic mystery religion.[119] From the point of view of Jewish apocalyptic no such problem of interpretation emerges. Both the beliefs of the Qumran community and later Merkabah texts make it clear that apocalyptic mysticism can exist side by side with strict Torah-observant Judaism.[120]

"Therefore do not let anyone condemn you in matters of food and drink (ἐν βρώσει καὶ ἐν πόσει) or of observing festivals (ἐν μέρει ἑορτῆς), new moons (νεομηνίας), or sabbaths (σαββάτων)" (2:16).

These remarks are most evidently directed against purity regulations and food laws. Furthermore, a contrast with an interest in festival calendar like that

---

[117] Cf. e.g. 1 En. 14:8ff., 3 En. 1:1; 3 Bar. 2:2; AscIsa 7-8.

[118] Francis, *Conflict*, 166.

[119] Those supporting the idea of a syncretistic background are obliged to interpret the precepts of v. 16 separately from the traditional Jewish context. So e.g. Lohse: "the command to keep festival, new moon, and sabbath is not based on the Torah." Lohse, *Colossians*, 115.

[120] So Alexander, *Old Testament Pseudepigrapha I*, 246, especially in regards of Merkabah texts. He suggests that the opponents may also have demanded circumcision from converts (cf. Col. 2:11).

of the Qumran community is apparent.[121] Most of the features in this verse, however, could probably be ascribed to almost any Jewish group, beginning from Paul's "own" Pharisaic movement. The following of the festival calendar and the regulations for the keeping of the sabbath were obligatory for every pious Jew. However, in sectarian Judaism, and especially at Qumran the observance of the Sabbath and the festivals belonged to the special "knowledge" of the sect.[122]

Thus verse 2:16 serves as a significant context for verse 18. It places ascetic mysticism safely into rather traditional Judaism. This is no surprise. Most apocalyptic Jewish writings from the Second Temple period have appeared to preserve Torah-observance in a traditional way. It hardly ever drifts into conflict with mystical interests. This also appears to be the case with Paul's opponents at Colossae.

The discussion on the nature of Paul's opponents' beliefs is merely a prelude for the assessment of the most crucial detail of the passage, i.e. the reference to Psalm 110. As regards the topic of this study, the appearance of this reference in such a context is especially interesting. Why is it precisely exaltation Christology with Psalm 110 that is the counterpoint for the teachings of the Colossean philosophy?

We must begin with a more general treatment of Paul's answer. In several occasions in the letter he appears to build a confrontation with apocalyptic Judaism. The appeal to Christ's triumph serves well the purpose of resisting such mysticism (2:15).[123] As Jewish mysticism was searching for the core of heavenly worship, it is only natural that Paul replaces such worship with the worship of Christ. "For in him the whole fullness of deity dwells bodily, and you have come to fullness in him, who is the head of every ruler and authority." (2:9-10).

Christ is the embodiment of deity and all heavenly riches are to be found in him. There is no secret knowledge that should or could be attained through a

---

[121] Especially the study of the Qumran fragment MMT has proven that the accuracy of the festival calendar was no minor issue in sectarian Judaism. At Qumran it was a cornerstone of the identity of the emerging community. See Qimron-Strugnell, *Qumran Cave 4 (DJD X)*, 109f., 119f. For more general comments on the subject, see e.g. Stegemann, *Qumran*, 104ff., 166f.; VanderKam, *Dead Sea Scrolls*, 59ff.

[122] Cf. the comments of Davies, *Scrolls*, 167.

[123] Hooker appears to be right when stating that Paul's adversaries were not members of the community. Her other claim, however, namely that Paul's christological statement was not formulated in any attempt to combat false teaching, is not acceptable. Even though Hooker refers to Col. 1 instead of chapter 2, her view does not hold, since Paul's Christology seems to be intentionally directed against his adversaries throughout the letter. See Hooker, *Christ*, 329.

mantic or through a seer. Everything that is significant in heaven has already been revealed in Christ. Thus the "fullness" of God's wisdom is in Christ. If there are any authorities in heaven, and evidently there are such angelic figures even according to Paul, it is Christ who is "the head of every ruler and authority" in heaven.

Finally in chapter 3 the climax of the apology is reached. The Colossean Jewish mystics had relied on visions. They had sought the things that are above by conducting ascetic humility and joining angelic worship. For Paul, there was but one center in the heavenly Temple. It was the throne of Glory, and Christ, the Lord of the Church, was sitting enthroned on that throne.

"So if you have been raised with Christ, seek the things that are above, where Christ is, seated at the right hand of God." (3:1).

Paul is not abandoning the scene which forms the basis for the teachings of his opponents. Quite the contrary, he is confronting the Jewish sect by re-interpreting traditional Jewish mysticism while he places Christ on the heavenly throne.[124]

In this respect the Christology of Col. 3:1 is completely similar to that of the earliest kerygmatic statements. The resurrected Christ has been enthroned on the heavenly throne, and Psalm 110 is the scriptural proof for that.[125] Those believers who "have been raised with Christ"[126] as they entered his kingdom ("transferred us into the kingdom of his beloved Son," Col. 1:13) are now taught to seek only the enthroned Lord and leave other heavenly contemplations aside.[127]

The basic error of Paul's adversaries is not to be located inside the Christian community at Colossae. Paul is not dealing with converts that would have

---

[124] Several scholars assume that Paul continues the debate with his Colossean adversaries in this verse too. See e.g. Lohse, *Colossians*, 132. The analogy of Paul's Christology with Jewish mysticism has also been noted. Schweizer, *Kolosser*, 131f. However, the inner link between the opponent's teaching and early Christology has seldom been discussed. Dunn suggests that the danger of the Colossian mystics was in postulating too many heavenly powers. Dunn, *Colossians*, 204. We might go even further than that in reconstructing the relationship.

[125] Here also a tradition independent of the Septuagint, i.e. the tradition using the expression ἐν δεξιᾷ, is used. This forms an interesting link to Rom. 8:34. Cf. Hengel, *Studies*, 142.

[126] This is a typical Pauline reference to baptismal theology that is explicated in detail in Rom. 6:4.

[127] Hay states that this passage is "not joined to any statements about the power of activity of the one at God's right hand." Hay, *Glory*, 62. Quite the contrary, the whole train of thought in the passage 2:18-3:1 is based on the idea of Christ's universal power, and the enthronement statement is the highlight of that argument.

accepted the basic teaching about Christ's enthronement in his resurrection.[128] The adversaries were outside the community and attempted to persuade the converts to accept their conceptions about the heavenly world. Thus Paul's teaching in 3:1 is directed expressly against the Colossean philosophy.

Therefore, the investigated passage Col. 2:16-3:1 should be considered as one of the most significant examples of the emergence of early Christology. *Here exaltation Christology drifted into a conflict with such Jewish mysticism that had provided for the exaltation discourse exploited in the formation of exaltation Christology in the first place.*[129] This is probably the reason why the contrast was so deep. Such mysticism must have been a real threat to early communitites. It relied on similar structures as early Christology and presented a tempting opportunity to have a contact with the heavenly world – and all this in a good guidance of traditional Torah-observant Judaism. This may have been too difficult a temptation to be resisted by young converts at Colossae.

In a similar way as in Acts 2, also here the Jewish enthronement pattern has been re-interpreted by locating it into an eschatological context. For Paul, the only proper form of merkabah mysticism is the one where resurrected Christ is venerated as the enthroned Lord. Therefore, also Col. 3:1 in its original context, is a perfect example of early Christology that is based on enthronement discourse.

As an appendix to the actual analysis it is proper to comment on those two problems that were presented in the beginning. What can be said about the Colossean philosophy, and how can this analysis contribute to the discussion over the authorship of the letter? Firstly, there are some direct comments on the adversaries in the letter. In 2:8 Paul evidently refers to his opponents when saying:

"See to it that no one takes you captive through philosophy and empty deceit, according to human tradition, according to the elemental spirits of the universe, and not according to Christ."

---

[128] I cannot agree with Francis who suggests that the participants in the angelic liturgy would have sung their praise both to God and to him who sits at his right hand. The errorists must have questioned the fact that Christ had defeated heavenly powers and now sat on the throne of glory. See Francis, *Conflict*, 183f. The contrast between 2:18 and 3:1 is too strong to allow such a "positive" interpretation of the conflict.

[129] Lincoln has suggested that Paul is speaking of the "things above" in order to outclass his opponents on their own ground. Lincoln, *Paradise*, 122f., 131f. According to O'Brien the reference to Psalm 110 and to Christ's session at God's right hand is an attempt to define the realm above "which is to be the goal of the Colossians' striving." O'Brien, *Colossians*, 162. In addition to these suggestions the direct connection between Jewish mysticism and early exaltation Christology should also be noted. Paul combats his adversaries on their own ground and with their own weapons.

In the New Testament the word "philosophy" has been used of Epicurean and Stoic teachers in Acts 17:18. In the letter to the Colossians, however, it does not necessarily refer to Greek philosophers. Also in (Hellenistic) Jewish literature such epithet is common and it may refer for instance to Jewish sects (Josephus) or the Mosaic tradition (Philo).[130] While Paul is speaking here both of tradition and of the "elemental spirits" referring to the teachings discussed in vv. 2:16ff., such "philosophy" most probably denotes the beliefs of his opponents. But what were those beliefs?

Since the days of Dibelius Paul's adversaries were usually located in the sphere of Greek mystery religions. Also early Gnosticism has often been used as a criterion for explanation. It is true that, in Colossians, we meet the key word for gnosis, "wisdom" (1:9; 2:23). The occurrence of the word itself, however, is no surprise even in Jewish theology. In fact, apocalyptic Judaism in general was building on sapiential theology in the Second Temple period.[131]

The analysis made in this study strongly suggests that the beliefs of Paul's adversaries were essentially Jewish beliefs. Verse 2:16 refers directly to Torah-observant Judaism, and verse 21 later supports such a view. Probably also the circumcision was demanded (2:11). Further, verse 2:18 agrees largely with the kind of merkabah mysticism that was studied in chapter 3 above. In general, the picture of Paul's opponents is nicely summarized in 2:23. His adversaries appear to be ascetic Jewish apocalyptics who opposed Paul's gospel about the enthroned Christ.[132]

If this was the case, several ideas concerning the authorship emerge. Special terminology may well be ascribed to Paul's adversaries. Further, the answers given in the letter seem clearly Pauline. And lastly, the Christology of the letter agrees completely with that of 1 Cor. 15, Rom. 1:4, and Rom. 8:34. Therefore, the apostle Paul himself may well be the author of the letter.

If such a hypothesis is accepted, such perspective opens up several interesting questions about Paul's life and thought. How does Paul know this

---

[130] Josephus, for example, in his famous presentation of the sects writes: "The Jews, from the most ancient times, had three philosophies pertaining to their traditions, that of the Essenes, that of the Sadducees, and, thirdly, that of the group called the Pharisees." Jos.*Ant.* 18.11. For the references to Mosaic tradition, see Philo, *Leg.* 156; *Mut.* 223.

[131] See chapters 2 and 3 above. For such connections, see especially Hengel, *Judentum*, 330ff., especially 369ff.; cf. my analysis in Eskola, *Theodicy*, 36ff., 61ff.

[132] According to Davies such features betray the "predominantly Jewish character" of the sect. Davies, *Scrolls*, 166. In fact, several of those features that Bornkamm located in "syncretistic-gnostic" Judaizing movement fit well into merkabah mysticism that in no way needs to be considered syncretistic – at least not in this phase. Bornkamm, *Conflict*, 131f. Thus Francis' hypothesis about the Jewish character of the Colossian "heretics" has quite a strong evidence behind it. Francis, *Conflict*, 185.

sect so well? Why is he able to describe the habits of the sect in detail? Could it be that Paul himself had been one of these Jewish mystics before his conversion? It is possible that Saul the Pharisee had been engaged in the circles of Jewish mystics. In that case he has been familiar with self-abasement, angelic worship, and dwelling on visions, not to mention the food-laws and festivals. This could explain why Paul the convert is such an expert in opposing the influence of this tradition in emerging Christianity.

Such polarity would also explain why Paul saw Christ as an enthroned Messiah who reigns at the top of the heavenly hierarchy. It became a fulfillment of basic Jewish hopes. Christ is not merely "the end of the Law" or "righteousness for sinners". He is the new Davidide who has been made a reigning Messiah in his resurrection. The enthroned one has brought salvation for Israel and for the whole world. Those who remain in apocalyptic mysticism do not yet understand the fullness of Christ "at the right hand of God".

2 Cor. 12:1-5. Finally, we must shortly address the question of Paul's description of his own heavenly journey. In 2 Cor. 12:1-5 Paul speaks of "visions and revelations of the Lord".

"I know a person in Christ who fourteen years ago was caught up to the third heaven – whether in the body or out of the body I do not know; God knows – was caught up into Paradise and heard things that are not to be told, that no mortal is permitted to repeat." (12:2-4).

This intriguing passage has given birth to a vivid discussion on Paul's relation to Jewish mysticism. His personal relation to Ezek. 1-2 and mystical tradition has been studied, and the discussion has been accompanied by speculation on his own visionary experience.[133]

In this passage there are several features paralleling merkabah mysticism. Paul is speaking of three heavens in the manner of the Testament of Levi.[134] Furthermore he uses the word Paradise. This was a feature common to texts such as Jubilees and 2 Enoch. In addition to this, his vision is a revelation of the Lord.[135] It must evidently have contained the appearance of Christ, but perhaps this was precisely the secret "that no mortal is permitted to repeat".

---

[133] For a general overview on the subject, see Fossum, *Image*, 7-11. On the question of Paul as a visionary, cf. Lincoln, *Paradise*, 71ff.

[134] See TLev. 3:1-5. For the discussion on the number of heavens in Jewish literature, see Lincoln, *Paradise*, 78-79. There has been speculation, however, whether or not the third heaven mentioned here actually was the highest heaven, see Martin, *2 Corinthians*, 402. In Jewish parallels the Paradise was usually in the highest heaven, even though it would have been the seventh one.

[135] Against Schäfer, according to whom the genitive is a *genetivus auctoris*, and so the Lord is the origin and not the object of the revelation. Schäfer, *JJS 35* (1984) 21.

It is somewhat striking that Paul refers to "things that are not to be told." Usually in Jewish ascent stories the transmission of the heavenly message was the main purpose of the whole vision. Paul's description is also in contrast with his own call to preach the message of the Resurrected one. Thus the prohibition to say anything about the central vision emphasizes the originality of the vision itself.[136]

Paul does not proceed to any vision of a throne in this passage. In verse 9 the throne may be alluded to, but that is not certain. Visionary experience had been exploited to such purposes that a detailed description of the vision was not needed. It seems probable that Paul's opponents, the charismatic mystics had used their visions as legitimation for their authority. Actually Paul is also using his vision in this way here.[137] In contrast to that kind of "boasting" Paul, however, uses even his vision for the emphasizing of humility and weakness. True Christian visions do not lead to boasting, but to praising Christ.

"So, I will boast all the more gladly of my weaknesses, so that the power of Christ may dwell in me" (12:9).

It is possible that this kind of experience, at least together with the experience at the Damascus road, has become crucial for the Christology of Paul. Earlier in 2 Corinthians – which probably was an earlier letter – he writes about the "face" of Christ. "For it is the God who said, 'Let light shine out of darkness,' who has shone in our hearts to give the light of the knowledge of the glory of God in the face of Jesus Christ." (4:6). This may naturally be merely a metaphorical description, but on the other hand it may also refer to a vision of Christ.

Glory in itself is a significant term in Jewish mysticism. As Segal notes, it was actually a technical term for the human form of God (*kabod*) appearing in biblical visions.[138] Paul's astonishing statement is that the face of Christ is the *kabod*, the glory of God.[139] Christians who believe in Christ are in fact privileged to see God in him. The passage does not give enough information for us to conclude whether this conviction is dependent on Paul's vision at the Damascus road or not. The belief itself, however, is so important for Paul that it may well be based on his personal vision on some occasion.

Paul's experience reported in 2 Cor. 12, therefore, has been identified as a christocentric vision. Paul's vision may have been of the exalted Christ on the

---

[136] See Furnish, *II Corinthians*, 545.

[137] So e.g. Georgi, *The Opponents of Paul*, 281-282.

[138] Segal, *Paul*, 60.

[139] Cf. Segal, *Paul*, 61.

throne of Glory.[140] This is one of the reasons why this passage has been connected with Paul's experiences at his conversion.

Paul's vision at the Damascus road is naturally a key event in his personal history. For instance in Galatians he states that his conversion and call are completely dependent on that experience. At the Damascus road Paul experienced a vision where he saw Christ Jesus. He calls this vision ἀποκάλυψις, a revelation. God revealed his Son to Saul the Pharisee. Through this revelation Saul also received his gospel (δι' ἀποκαλύψεως Ἰησοῦ Χριστοῦ; Gal. 1:12). Could it be that Paul's experience was a merkabah vision?[141]

There are some arguments in the text for this kind of conclusion. First we must admit, however, that Paul's description does not give us much direct information. A throne or a chariot is not mentioned in Gal. 1, and the parallelling tradition in Acts 9 lacks such information, as well.[142] Paul saw a vision of Christ and we must draw our conclusions from this point of departure.

There is one detail, however, which may lead us further in this question. According to Galatians this event was especially a call (v.15) to evangelization. This call was given when the Son of God was revealed to Paul (ἀποκαλύψαι τὸν υἱὸν αὐτοῦ ἐν ἐμοί; v.16).[143] If we assume that the call vision of Ezekiel has affected Paul's interpretation of the experience, there may be a connection after all. In Ezekiel 1-2 the vision of a throne-chariot leads consistently to the call of the prophet in Ez. 2:3.[144]

A more convincing argument might be found in the way in which Paul/Saul presents Christ. Saul, who had persecuted the followers of Jesus now had a vision of Jesus as the Son of God. Even though he had evidently known that a belief in an enthroned Messiah was the essence of the faith of the alleged apostates he was persecuting ("the faith he once tried to destroy," v. 23), he had obviously believed that Jesus was merely a man that had been crucified in Jerusalem.

---

[140] So Chester, *Paulus*, 77. He admits, though, that such a conclusion "is already to go beyond the evidence."

[141] This question is discussed especially by Bowker, *JSS* 16 (1971) 157ff. See also Segal, *Paul*, 60ff.

[142] This is noted by Bowker, *JSS* 16 (1971) 171.

[143] The expression ἐν ἐμοὶ is a customary dative here and has to be translated "to me"; Blass-Debrunner-Rehkopf, *Grammatik*, § 220.1. Cf. Stuhlmacher, *Biblische theologie*, 173; against Longenecker, who presents the traditional interpretation "in me" corresponding to "Christ lives in me", Longenecker, *Galatians*, 32; and Schlier, *Galater*, 55.

[144] According to Bowker this might be the case, see Bowker, *JSS* 16 (1971) 172. The problem in this interpretation is that the wording in Gal. 1:15 refers probably to Isa 49:1 and to Jer. 1:5, but not to Ezek. 2.

Now this crucified Jesus appeared to him in a vision as the heavenly Son of God.[145] In Paul's vocabulary "Son of God" usually refers to the Davidic Messiah (Rom. 1:2-4; 1 Cor. 15:25-28; cf. 1 Thess. 1:10). Paul himself seems to have interpreted his experience as a vision of a Davidide who is a "Son of God in power" (cf. Rom. 1:4). At the beginning of Romans Paul uses similar terminology when arguing for his call and his mission, as well as for his gospel. Paul's gospel, which he according to the Galatians did not receive from a human source, was a message about the Davidic Messiah who had been enthroned in the resurrection.

On the basis of these considerations only one conclusion can be drawn. Whatever the actual vision of Saul may have been, he appears to have interpreted it as a merkabah vision. For Saul the vision was a crucial experience which both taught him the content of his gospel and gave him a prophetic call to mission. After having this vision Saul saw Christ as an enthroned Davidide who had become a universal ruler of heavens and earth. It seems apparent that Saul had already had a symbolic universe according to which his experience could be oriented. Therefore it seems probable that Saul himself had been familiar with merkabah mysticism.[146]

We have formerly been detecting how merkabah mysticism may have influenced the development of Christology. Paul adds an interesting chapter to this search. He may himself be an example of a Jewish mystic converted to Christ. If it had been common for Saul the Pharisee to speculate on visions and angels, it is quite understandable that Paul the convert was attached to the picture of Christ as an enthroned king of heaven. When the scheme was further confirmed by Psalm 110 which provided a Scriptural proof for the exaltation and enthronement of the Davidide, what could better serve the purposes of a devoted Jewish mystic who is enthusiastic to proclaim his new Messiah?

The study of Paul helps us to understand the relation between early Christology and merkabah mysticism from a new angle:

1. Firstly, Paul often describes the resurrected Christ as an enthroned Messiah in his Christology. He also exploits such kerygmatic or confessional statements that have been built on Psalm 110. The nature of these christological passages is quite similar to that of the Christology of Peter's Pentecost speech

---

[145] Cf. Stuhlmacher, *Biblische theologie*, 173. Stuhlmacher assumes that the crucified Christ revealed himself to Saul as possessing the Lordship of God. Segal remarks that in the context of Jewish theology the idea of a crucified Messiah was unique. Therefore a conviction of Jesus' enthronement after death and resurrection must be based on some kind of historical experience of the first Christians. Segal, *Paul*, 56-57.

[146] It is worth noting that in Gal. 1:8 Paul contrasts his own vision and gospel with heavenly angels and their message.

in Acts 2. Pauline materials thus confirm the picture that we have got before about the relation of merkabah mysticism and early Christology.

2. Thus in his christological descriptions Paul relies heavily on enthronement discourse. The basic scene for Christology is the heavenly court where Christ reigns on the throne of Glory. In conflict situations, that are often behind his letters, Paul emphasizes the essential content of his message. In such responses enthronement discourse has a primary status.

3. Furthermore, Paul's personal history appears to link him to some kind of visionary tradition. His vision of Christ at the Damascus road is crucial for his understanding of the gospel and for his commission. For Paul, Christ who appeared to him in a vision and gave him his call, is the Davidic Messiah who has been enthroned in heaven. Paul's mission is to call people from all nations to the new kingdom of this heavenly Lord. Paul also describes the enthroned Christ by using the terminology of Jewish mysticism. Especially the description of Jesus as the glory of God links Paul's exaltation Christology to merkabah tradition.

4. According to the letter to the Colossians Paul knows Jewish mystical tradition well. His polarized opposition to that tradition may also reveal his own close relationship with such a movement. It would be quite logical that one reason for the emergence of the Christological exaltation statements typical of Paul were in his engagement in mystical tradition. In this respect Paul may himself be one of those Christian teachers who have exploited merkabah mysticism in Christological formulations.

5.3. Reception of early enthronement Christology in the letter to the Hebrews and in the Revelation of John

In many respects the letter to the Hebrews is a perfect example of the use of enthronement Christology in New Testament letters. The letter belongs clearly to the tradition of Jewish Christianity. Even though the dating of the letter is uncertain and in any case not very early, the content is often parallel to those early traditional formulas found in other letters and in the Acts. The letter to the Hebrews is also unique for its great emphasis on Psalm 110.[147] It is not merely of literary value to say that this letter is actually a commentary on that psalm. Exaltation Christology appears to be the backbone of the theology of the writer.[148]

---

[147] For discussion, see e.g. Hay, *Glory*, 85ff., 143ff.; Loader, *Sohn*, 15ff.62ff.; Hengel, *Studies*, 145ff.

[148] Psalm 110 also appears in cultic contexts where Melchizedek-theology is presented, but those passages will be investigated below in a chapter of its own. Here we focus on the aspect of enthronement.

The description of Christology is quite clearly based on an ascent structure, and such pattern has often been noted in scholarship.[149] Under the influence of the history-of-religions-school, however, the structure was first interpreted in terms of gnosticism. According to Käsemann's famous interpretation the Christology of the Hebrews was built on the gnostic myth of the heavenly man. Both the motif of the Son as a creator and the motif of the enthronement "at the right hand" were considered gnostic. The idea of a heavenly journey was interpreted as a heavenly pilgrimage of the self.[150]

Later, however, on the grounds of Jewish apocalyptic and especially with respect to the Qumran scrolls, the Jewish nature of the Christology was suggested. In this phase attention was paid for instance to God's heavenly throne, God's majesty and holiness, the heavenly Temple, and heavenly worship. Following Williamson's earlier suggestions, Schenke finally identified such ideas as teachings of early Jewish merkabah mysticism.[151] Such a view did not become very popular in scholarship, though. The reason for this was mainly that merkabah texts were considered late. Therefore such views could not be regarded as a proper background for the letter to the Hebrews.[152] The fact that an ascent structure is clearly present in the Christology of the letter, and that the idea of a heavenly Temple is one of its cornerstones, demands a reassessment of the role of merkabah tradition in the teachings of the letter.

Heb. 1:3-4. The letter begins with a majestic statement where even an ascent structure can be detected:

"When he had made purification for sins, he sat down at the right hand of the Majesty on high, having become as much superior to angels as the name he has inherited is more excellent than theirs." (1:3-4).

The basic idea in this passage repeats the christologial conviction that we have found in early kerygmatic statements. Quite in the manner of the

---

[149] For the discussion concerning the background of thought of the letter, see especially Hurst, *Hebrews* (as regards exaltation Christology, see especially pp. 43ff., 67ff., 82ff.), and the introduction of Lane's commentary, Lane, *Hebrews 1-8*, civ ff.

[150] Käsemann, *Gottesvolk*, 61ff.; 71; 110ff. He has later been followed e.g. by Grässer, Hebräer I, 64ff.; cf. also Sanders, *Hymns*, 92-93.

[151] See Williamson, *ExpTim* 87 (1975-76) 234-236; Schenke, *Existenz*, 433.

[152] For a positive approach, see Hofius, *Christushymnus*, 87-88. The negative view is presented most clearly by Hurst, who admits merely the possibility of "pre-Merkabah" tendencies within Jewish apocalyptic. Hurst, *Hebrews*, 84-85; cf. Lane, *Hebrews 1-8*, cix. It is somewhat surprising, however, that even rather recent critics never refer to actual pre-Christian merkabah writings that have been given enormous weight for instance in the study of angelic Christology.

enthronement descriptions in Jewish merkabah mysticism Jesus is described as a Jewish Messiah who has been enthroned "at the right hand of God" after his resurrection.[153] The link to Jewish mystical tradition is even emphasized by the speculation over the status of angels (cf. 1 Peter 3:21-22).[154]

Once again the "sitting at the right hand" is expressed by using the form ἐν δεξιᾷ. This suggests that also the letter to the Hebrews relies on early Jewish Christian tradition that is not dependent on the use of the Septuagint. Actually the same form appears in the letter four times (8:1; 10:12; 12:2). In 1:3 the occurrence of that form is even more significant, since right below in verse 13, in the direct quotation of Psalm 110:1 the usual Septuagint form is given. Therefore, the opening lines of the letter appear to be influenced by a strong kerygmatic tradition deriving from Jewish Christian Church.[155]

The idea of the subordination of angels is so determined that one is tempted to interpret this passage from the point of view of Qumranian mysticism and bring the idea of the heavenly temple into the picture here. Christ who is exalted and enthroned "at the right hand" of God in the heavenly Holy of Holies has become superior to angels in the heavenly Temple and probably also the heavenly beings of the *debir*.[156] These must worship Christ as they previously worshiped only God. Such worship is further confirmed in verse 6 with a word that formally seems to come from Psalm 97, but that has an interesting history in itself: "Let all God's angels worship him" (97:7).[157]

This quotation refers originally to the "Hymn of Moses" in Deuteronomy 32 (v. 43). It is apparent that the sentence has been later adopted for liturgical use in the Temple, while it evidently appears in Psalm 97 and in the Septuagint

---

[153] The resurrection itself is not mentioned here, which is typical of christological hymns in general. Cf. Attridge, *Hebrews*, 46.

[154] "While there is no polemic against angels of angel worship, the fact that they were chosen as the first standard of comparison with the Son does indicate that the readers were interested in angelology." Gunther, *Opponents*, 182.

[155] See e.g. Hengel, *Studies*, 142. Also Loader notes such dependence on tradition, Loader, *Sohn*, 20. Jesus is not called κύριος in this passage, as Loader notes, but it is not plausible that the writer would have been unaware of such Christology, as he states. *ibid.*, 16. In the end of the Letter the writer calls the resurrected Jesus κύριος in a fine christological statement. Evidently the use of the priestly motif has superseded the κύριος motif in the letter.

[156] As we have seen, the conception of a heavenly temple and the idea of heavenly worship were the basic ideas in the Qumranian Songs of the Sabbath Sacrifice, see Newsom, *Songs*, 16f., 307f.; cf. Schwemer, *Königsherrshcaft*, 108ff.

[157] Lane, *Hebrews 1-8*, 28. Cf. later 12:22-24, where the new life is presented as participation to the worship that heavenly angels perform. There is no actual reference to liturgy here, even though Gunther in his interpretation mentions it, see Gunther, *Opponents*, 183.

where new Odes have been appended to the Greek Psalter. Actually, the form that is quoted in the Hebrews is identical with Ode 2:43: καὶ προσκυνησάτωσαν αὐτῷ πάντες ἄγγελοι θεοῦ. The older Greek version of Deut. 32:43 (LXX) speaks of the sons of God (υἱοὶ θεοῦ).[158]

The rendering of the Septuagint version of Psalm 96:7 (LXX) is close to that of the Odes, speaking of "his angels". The background of this form, however, is even more interesting. This verse is one of those passages where angels are called *elohim* in the Hebrew text (Ps. 97:7). There seems to be a connection with the angelology of Second Temple Jewish mysticism. As in the writings of Qumran, also here we find high rank angels called *elohim*. These may probably be the "gods" of the Holy of Holies mentioned several times in mystical writings.[159]

There are thus several possibilities to interpret the quotation given in Heb. 1:6. It may be that the writer has merely wanted to exploit a scriptural proof where the subordination of angels is attested. In this respect the quotation of the Odes seems sufficient. The evident reference to the Hymn of Moses, however, brings an important connotation to this verse. Also the writer of the Hebrews has exploited the method of changing the subject. The one with absolute authority is not God, but the enthroned Christ.[160]

Further it is possible that Psalm 97 (96 LXX) has carried a tradition of the highest angels that have been identified as the "gods" of the Holy of Holies. On the level of Greek tradition, naturally, the continuation of such a tradition is not very plausible. There is, however, one aspect that may support this kind of interpretation. The writer of the Hebrews associates such angels with the heavenly throne (v. 8). As interesting as this point of view may be, there is little evidence for its support.

There is obvious polarity between the angels and the divine Son in this passage. This becomes apparent when we consider the "pesher" on Psalm 45 in verse 8: "But of the Son he says, 'Your throne, O God, is forever and ever, and the righteous scepter is the scepter of your kingdom'." (on Psalm 45:7-8).[161] Through the metaphor of the throne the Son is identified as God himself.[162]

This astonishing statement could naturally be interpreted in two different

---

[158] For the details of such history and different renderings, see Lane, *Hebrews 1-8*, 28.

[159] See above, chapter 3.

[160] Cf. Bruce, *Hebrews*, 16; Grässer speaks of the writer's Messianic understanding of Scripture, Grässer, *Hebräer I*, 80-81.

[161] For an overview on the use of Psalm 45, see Allen, *Christ*, 220-242.

[162] "The writer does not hesitate to apply to Jesus, as the legitimate object of worship, a passage in which he is addressed as God. Lane, *Hebrews 1-8*, 29.

ways. If one wishes to maintain the distinction between Jesus and God one could say that only God's heavenly throne is meant when Psalm 45 is quoted. According to this interpretation Jesus as the Son of God is enthroned on the throne of glory and he is given a heavenly scepter that expresses his power.[163] The change of subject here, however, is similar to that of verse 6 above. Therefore the reader cannot avoid the impression that, in this passage, Jesus as the Son is identified as God.[164]

The christological message of the writer in chapter 1 is finally completed with a reference to Psalm 110. It's enthronement statement is the final argument for the writer and proves that no angel has been given such a promise (1:13). Christ on the throne is superior to angels and these worship him in the same manner as they worship "the Majesty".[165]

As in the hymn of the Philippians, so here the new throne-epithet of Christ is mentioned. As regards the angels, "the name he has inherited is more excellent than theirs." In Hebrews 1 that name is Son. The name Son is introduced in 1:2, and it is further confirmed with citations from Psalm 2:7 and the prophecy of Nathan, 2 Sam. 7:14. This raises a question of a possible promise tradition where certain Old Testament passages carry a Messianic tradition through history.[166]

It is actually quite essential to note that enthronement Christology in Hebrews is what Rissi calls "Sohneschristologie". The idea of Sonship becomes thus identified with kingship. The link to Old Testament Messianology is clear. In this kind of Christology the sonship of the historical Davidide is used as an essential element in christological development. Enthroned Christ is not called Son by accident, but on the basis of particular Old Testament passages that speak of a Davidic king.[167]

The opening section of the Letter to the Hebrews presents thus a

---

[163] Hay states that Hebrews "never represents the exalted Christ as ruler or judge". Hay, *Glory*, 86. This cannot be true. The enthronement pattern as such denoted the idea of ruling, not to mention the intention of Ps. 110:1.

[164] So de Jonge and van der Woude, *NTS 12* (1965-66) 315-316. See also Allen: "the double *ho theos* has a similar importance, and so is to be rendered in both cases as a vocative referring to Christ... The Son is unmistakably aligned with God as divine king over against the angels, who function in a subordinate role as messengers and ministers." Allen, *Christ*, 235.

[165] According to Gourgues the reference to Psalm 110 is actually an affirmation of Christ's divinity. Gourgues, *A la Droite de Dieu*, 103.

[166] Questions concerning a promise tradition will be discussed below, in chapter 6.

[167] Rissi, *Theologie*, 48f. As Attridge has noted, also in 1:6 there is a reference to royal ideology evidenced in Ps. 2 and 2. Sam 7. There the word "firstborn" is used. Attridge, *Hebrews*, 56. The reference itself, apparently, is made to Ps. 89:28.

christological statement that bears the marks of exaltation Christology known to us from several other early passages. Christ is here a Davidide that is enthroned to power in his resurrection. Christ's exaltation resembles a heavenly journey that leads to the holy throne of Glory in the heavenly Temple. Even in the beginning of the letter the Davidide is a priest-king who makes purification for sins before his entering upon the throne. In his description the *auctor ad Hebraeos* exploits several themes from Jewish mysticism. The most prominent of these is the theme of the subordination of angels which is used for the description of the extraordinary Sonship of Christ. The original Psalm pesher in Hebrews 1 supports the high Christology of the writer.

Heb. 8:1; 10:12. Psalm 110:1 occurs in other passages of the Hebrews, too. In 8:1 it appears as main argument ("the main point in what we are saying") for the Melchizedek-Christology that was developed in chapter 7. It solved the basic problem of the dispute that had risen from Jewish premises: "our Lord was descended from Judah, and in connection with that tribe Moses said nothing about priests." (7:14). Only the idea of a priest-king presents a solution that can be accepted also from the Jewish point of view.[168]

According to the writer, Christ is a heavenly high priest who is enthroned on the throne of glory: "[W]e have such a high priest, one who is seated at the right hand of the throne of the Majesty in the heavens." (8:1). The hermeneutical basis for this interpretation has been studied in earlier chapters and the exploitation of Ps. 110:4 is not surprising here. The language here is solemn, with its reference to the heavenly throne itself.[169]

The reception of Ps. 110 in Hebrews 7-8 is rather expected. Only the profoundness of the exploitation of the theme is astonishing. Exaltation Christology is not a minor aspect in the letter, but the main foundation on which the whole train of thought has been constructed. For the writer, the key event of eschatology is Christ's enthronement. His ascension has both cultic and royal features. It is apparent that, according to 8:1, the effectiveness of Jesus as the priestly intercessor and advocate is actually an expression of his participation in the dominion of God.[170]

It is further worth noting that the Son-Christology became completely

---

[168] In this respect de Jonge and van der Woude seem to be too cautious as they suggest that the writer does not try to prove that Jesus, born of Judah, had two offices, that of the high-priest and that of the future king, de Jonge and van der Woude, *NTS* 12 (1965-66) 322. Why then bother to mention the problem at all in v. 14? For the details of the expressions, see Lane, *Hebrews 1-8*, 182. In my view the whole speculation on Psalm 110 in itself treats the very same problem.

[169] Cf. Attridge, *Hebrews*, 217.

[170] So Hengel, *Studies*, 146.

identified with priestly Christology in the letter. They are both justified not only by the proof-text Psalm 110, as in 8:1, but also by the proof-text Psalm 2:7. The adoptional statement of Psalm 2 is in Hebrews 5:5 used as a justification for the exaltation of Christ to his office of high-priest.

In Hebrews 10 the royal aspect of the functions of the king-priest is emphasized. In general, the chapter still concentrates on Melchizedek-Christology, but the description has several features of a royal reign. In 10:12 there is almost a duplicate for 1:2-4. Christ offered a sacrifice for sins, and "sat down at the right hand of God." The cultic function of the ascension cannot and need not be separated from the enthronement itself.[171]

What is special in this passage is the reference to Ps. 110:1b, "until his enemies would be made a footstool for his feet." This is a short statement about Christ's heavenly status, and such reference reveals the influence of those elements that we have detected earlier in Pauline teaching and in the Acts. Paul presented the same idea in 1 Cor. 15, "For he must reign until he has put all his enemies under his feet" (15:25; cf. also Acts 3:21).

In Hebrews 8-10 the priestly function of the Anointed one is prominent. This does not mean, however, that the royal aspect would be completely absent. The enthroned Christ is rather a king-priest and Psalm 110 gives proper justification for such a conception. This feature shall be discussed later in detail in chapter 7.

Heb. 12:2. In 12:2 Psalm 110:1 is exploited for the last time in an exhortation and encouragement of believers in a similar manner as Paul did in Philippians 2. Here again the exemplary function of Christ's work becomes evident:

"let us run with perseverance... looking to Jesus the pioneer... who... endured the cross, disregarding its shame, and has taken his seat at the right hand of the throne of God" (Heb. 12:2).[172]

In this passage the pattern of humiliation and exaltation is presupposed, and it becomes a source of hope for all those believers that are presently living under threat and agony. An exaltation is promised in the future resurrection. Christ's suffering and enthronement are ideal proof for the fact that the oppressed also will "see the Lord" (12:14) in the end.

According to the writer, further, the throne may even be seen as the goal of the faithful believers. Christ is presented as a forerunner, who has entered the heavenly Temple and sat on the throne of Glory. Such a structure resembles

---

[171] According to Michel the enthroned Christ has rested "from all his works" just like God rested from his works after the creation. Therefore the (implied) "rest" is a sign of fulfilment and the "sitting" is a sign of Lordship. Michel, *Hebräer*, 340.

[172] See e.g. Attridge, *Hebrews*, 356.

the presentation of Revelation where the saved believers are called to share the throne with Christ (Rev. 3:21).[173]

Finally, the reference of Psalm 110 differs somewhat from previous instances. Here the definite character of Christ's session is emphasized. He "has taken his seat" in heaven. Such change probably underlines the hortatory nature of the passage.[174]

The letter to the Hebrews serves thus as a good example of how early Christology influenced later teaching of the early Church. It is understandable that these themes fascinated especially Jewish Christianity, of which this letter is clear proof. The main conclusions of the analysis are the following:

1. The reception of early enthronement Christology in the letter to the Hebrews is extensive. The basic themes according to which Christ in his resurrection has been enthroned on the throne of Glory in heaven, form the general outline of the whole letter. The writer has not merely exploited some selected features of early Christology in his letter, but he has rather put all his theological creativity in the service of that Christology. The whole letter is relying on apocalyptic cosmology and enthronement discourse. The key figure of the implied narrative is the new Melchizedek, the enthroned king-priest, whose enthronement takes place in the heavenly court.

One of the weaknesses of christological study, from the days of Käsemann onwards, was the presupposition that the interpretation of New Testament Christology demands a fixed figure in the past that would explain the christological statement. For Käsemann that kind of figure was the gnostic heavenly redeemer.[175] Later scholars have attempted to find a figure from the writings of Jewish mysticism. The emergence of christological statements, however, appear to rest on other kinds of premises. It is not the prototype or preceding figure that explains christological descriptions, but it is the setting inside which a christological transformation of tradition takes place that makes christological statements intelligible. We shall return to this kind of methodological discussion in chapter 11.

2. The Christology of the Hebrews reveals further several points of contact with Jewish merkabah mysticism and especially with the ascent pattern that we have detected in other passages containing early Christology. The basic structure of this Christology resembles that of Acts 2 and Pauline writings. Resurrected Jesus is a Davidic Messiah whose exaltation has been foretold e.g. in 2 Sam. 7 and Psalms 2 and 110. His resurrection is considered an act of

---

[173] For such connection, see Bruce, *Hebrews*, 354.

[174] Cf. Attridge, *Hebrews*, 358.

[175] Käsemann, *Gottesvolk*, 55.

enthronement as a fulfillment of Psalm 110:1. The idea of the heavenly court as well as descriptions of the heavenly throne are an essential part of the Christology.[176] It is further typical of the Hebrews to emphasize the humiliation and crucifiction of Christ before his exaltation. This theme is closely linked with the priestly interpretation that is primary in the letter.

3. What is interesting in the Christology of the letter is that it appears to derive from the independent tradition that may be ascribed to Jewish Christianity. Especially the expression ἐν δεξιᾷ suggests that the christological tradition is not dependent on the Septuagint. In this respect there is a close connection with Rom. 8:34.[177] This applies to the intercession motif, as well. Further, the idea of Christ's realized reign connects the tradition of the Hebrews to that of 1 Cor. 15:25, as well as Acts 3:21. We have earlier noted that this eschatological pattern was common in the early Church.[178]

4. The scheme of humiliation and exaltation produces a simple ascent structure in this Christology. The content of this ascent structure resembles the one in Jewish writings. Crucified Jesus is exalted to heaven after his death. In his resurrection he is enthroned on the throne of Glory.

5. The letter to the Hebrews has also an original feature in its Christology. The subordination of angels is an important theme for the writer. This intention is so evident that it resembles Paul's debate with his Colossian mystics. Also the writer of the Hebrews considers it necessary to make a distinction between Christ and heavenly angels. Apart from God, the enthroned Christ is the only heavenly Lord that may be worshiped in Christian devotion. Such restriction speaks against an angelic interpretation. In the Hebrews the enthroned Christ is not an angelomorphic figure who might be mixed up with other angels. He is a messianic Davidide under whom all angels and heavenly powers have been

---

[176] In this respect Hurst's pessimistic view proves to be based on an insufficient knowledge of merkabah texts. Behind the letter, there are not merely "pre-Merkabah" tendencies within Jewish apocalyptic, as he claims. See Hurst, *Hebrews*, 85. All evidence points to a well known and fixed tradition both within Judaism and within the early Church. One of the reasons for Hurst's view was that before him, for instance, Williams had investigated only late Jewish writings in his analysis. See Williamson, *ExpTim* 87 (1975-76) 233.

[177] I agree, therefore, with Hengel who has emphasized the significance of early Christian tradition that may be detected in the abovementioned passages. Hengel, *Studies*, 147.

[178] The neglect of the traditional background is probably one of the main reasons why Hay ends up denying the idea that, in the Christology of the Hebrews, the exalted Christ would be a ruler. He shares Käsemann's suggestion that the enthroned one is, at the most, destined to be ruler of the future world. Käsemann, *Gottesvolk*, 77; Hay, *Glory*, 86-87. Such a view is based on a too polarized view of early eschatology and runs into conflict with the texts themselves. The idea of an enthronement without an authorization to reign is hardly comprehensible.

subordinated. The assumed opponents of the writer, however, may well have had a tendency to interpret Christ's status with an angelic interpretation. The problem with such an explanation is that we cannot tell whether such hypothetical opponents were Jewish Christians or simply ordinary Jews.

6. The letter to the Hebrews confirms thus the hypothesis that merkabah mysticism has influenced the formation of early Christology. Even some of the terminology has survived and the speculation of angels is important. An ascent structure has its place in this Christology and the enthronement theme is exploited in the core of the explanation of the exaltation. Even though this kind of symbolic world has been exploited now in a rather traditional Mosaic context speaking of the Temple and priests, the basic structure of the Christology is hardly understandable without the context of Jewish mysticism.

Rev. 3:21. In the book of Revelation the reception of exaltation Christology is apparent, as well. In the beginning of the book Christ is "the firstborn of the dead" and "the ruler of the kings of the earth" (1:5). He is the firstborn of the general resurrection of the dead. As in Paul, also here the resurrection of the dead as an eschatological event is the centre of salvation history. As the Resurrected one Christ is further a heavenly king, who is the ruler of the whole world.

Also the enthronement of Christ has been explicated quite clearly: "I myself conquered and sat down with my Father on his throne" (3:21). This passage is special for the identification of Christ's throne with the throne of God. This, in fact, is also the case later in 7:17, according to which "the Lamb at the center of the throne will be their shepherd", and in 22:3, where "the throne of God and of the Lamb" stands in the middle of the new Jerusalem.[179]

Such Christology apparently builds on earlier enthronement tradition. The apocalypse partly describes and partly implies an ascension and an exaltation. Christ in his resurrection has been escorted to heaven and he has "sat down" on the throne of Glory. In Revelation short statement-like Christology has given room for a colorful narrative, where the heavenly enthronement in many respects forms the centre of the story.

The writer's scheme of salvation history, however, resembles that of earlier christological statements.[180] The faith of the persecuted Church is focused on the heavenly Messiah who is seated on God's throne. This enthroned Christ ensures the hope of the Church in the midst of eschatological upheavals. The enthronement statement is accompanied by a promise: "To the one who

---

[179] Revelation 3:21 is the only passage where Christ's sitting with the Father on the throne is explicitly mentioned. Hengel, *Studies*, 150.

[180] Cf. Aune, *Revelation*, 263.

conquers I will give a place with me on my throne" (3:21a). The writer of the Revelation exploits here the idea that Christians will reign with Christ in heaven.[181]

The term "at the right hand" does not appear in the book of Revelation. By exploiting narrative style the writer describes the heavenly throne in a more general sense. The basic content of the message, however, does not remain uncertain. The enthroned Messiah is a key figure in the eschatological story.

Rev. 4:1-9. In such an apocalypse one naturally expects to find traits of Jewish mysticism. The book of Revelation does not disappoint its reader's expectations in this matter. Revelation 4 begins directly with a vision of a heavenly journey. "After this I looked, and there in heaven a door stood open!" An angel addresses John: "Come up here, and I will show you what must take place after this." (4:1) One expects a journey through several heavens but instead of that the seer is instantly taken to the heavenly court.[182]

John does not proceed from outer to inner spheres of holiness.[183] A throne vision follows immediately, and it resembles those of other Jewish apocalyptic writings. "At once I was in the spirit, and there in heaven stood a throne, with one seated on the throne! And the one seated there looked like jasper and carnelian, and around the throne was a rainbow that looked like an emerald." (4:2-3). The appearance of a rainbow shows that the book of Ezekiel has infuenced the mind of the writer.[184]

The setting emphasizes the cultic nature of the heavenly world. Around the throne there are twenty four other thrones, and elders are seated on them. Their number, twenty four, apparently points to the twenty four divisions of priests in the Jerusalem temple.[185] The throne itself is surrounded by fire and flames.[186] "Coming from the throne are flashes of lightning, and rumblings and peals of thunder, and in front of the throne burn seven flaming torches, which are the seven spirits of God" (4:5).

---

[181] For the Jewish background, see e.g. 4Q521 (investigated in chapter 3.2.); for New Testament passages, see Matt. 19:28; 2. Tim. 2:12; cf. Rev. 1:6; 5:10; 20:4; 22:5.

[182] Gruenwald notes that there is not yet plurality of heavens in this book. Gruenwald, *Apocalyptic*, 62.

[183] For the differences between John's vision and 1 Enoch, see Halperin, *Chariot*, 88.

[184] See Ezek. 1:26-28; for the connection, see Halperin, *Chariot*, 89. Cf. e.g. Ezek. 1:4-5; 1. En. 71:5-7; ApAbr. 18. The description of the throne in Revelation, however, is much more detailed than for instance the one in TLev, 5:1.

[185] Gruenwald, *Apocalyptic*, 64.

[186] In 14:1, however, Mount Zion is identified as the throne of Glory. This is another example of how the temple imagery of Revelation conforms to that of Jewish apocalyptic (e.g. 1 Enoch 25).

The description of the throne includes several features that derive from the prophetic tradition. In front of the throne there is a "sea of glass, like crystal" (4:6). Around the throne there are four living creatures "full of eyes in front and behind". These creatures have the forms of a lion, an ox, a human face, and an eagle (4:7). These "living creatures" are obviously Ezekiel's *hayyot*.[187]

Also living creatures are connected with the heavenly liturgy. They sing a hymn to God "day and night without ceasing". The hymn is the *trishagion* that derives from Isaiah's tradition. And whenever the creatures give honor to God the elders join the praise and fall before the throne of God (4:9).[188]

In the apocalyptic scene of the Revelation the heavenly court is oviously identical with the heavenly temple.

"For this reason they are before the throne of God, and worship him day and night within his temple, and the one who is seated on the throne will shelter them" (7:15).

For the writer of the Revelation the throne is identified as the *hilastêrion*, the seat above the ark of covenant that the cherubim cover with their wings (cf. 11:19).

These examples show how especially Revelation 4 exploits the basic Jewish tradition about heavenly journeys. In this respect the book of Revelation is a perfect apocalypse. The ascent story is complete and it repeats most of the main features of respective stories of Jewish mysticism. The journey climaxes in the highest heaven where God's throne lies. There the seer joins the heavenly liturgy that is performed before the throne without ceasing.

Rev. 5:5-6. In Revelation the enthroned Christ is also a Davidide. After the description of John's heavenly journey, the "Lion of the tribe of Judah", "the Root of David" is introduced (5:5). In the vision John sees "between the throne and the four living creatures and among the elders a Lamb standing as if it had been slaughtered" (5:6). In the same manner as in Acts 2:34-36 and in Romans 1:3 the enthroned Christ is the Anointed one. He is the Anointed king from the family of David. Also in this respect the Christology of the book of Revelation resembles earlier homologies.

It is obvious that the Lamb appearing here is the apocalyptic ram, a figure known from Jewish sources. In 1 Enoch, for instance, David and Solomon are sheep before their crowning, and rams when they are enthroned (1. En. 89:45-

---

[187] See Halperin, *Chariot*, 90. The word *zóa* is the same as the LXX translators use for Ezekiel's expression.

[188] Cf. 7:9-10 where the heavenly hosts stand before the throne and sing praise to the heavenly King and the Lamb (7:9-10).

48).[189] In this respect also the character of the Lamb expresses the idea of messianic kingship. The character of the Lion, naturally, does this more evidently.[190] Therefore, these two characters do not seem to be sharply contrasted in this passage.

The reason for their parallelization and identification with one another is most probably the fact that the character of the Lamb was open to multiple interpretations. The slaughtering of the Lamb refers to the sacrificial death of Christ. Thus the double meaning of the character communicates the basic message of the passion kerygma of the early Church.

Christ's status in heaven also emphasizes his dignity. The Lamb stands in the middle of the throne, and the living creatures stand in the middle of the elders (5:6). As the elders apparently have a priestly function in the heavenly sanctuary, it is noteworthy that the location of the living creatures is separated from the location of the Lamb. This is a theological transformation of the basic conception which connects the living creatures with the throne itself.[191]

Later in 11:15 Christ is the Anointed one who has been enthroned and who shares the heavenly kingship with the Lord God. "The kingdom of the world has become the kingdom of our Lord and of his Messiah (Ἐγένετο ἡ βασιλεία τοῦ κόσμου τοῦ κυρίου ἡμῶν καὶ τοῦ Χριστοῦ αὐτοῦ), and he will reign forever and ever." Here the central theme of Old Testament faith, the kingship of God, has explicitly been connected with the kingship of the Anointed one. The appellation Christ, in this occasion, is not a title, but an appellation of an anointed king. Therefore this passage also links the Christology of the book of Revelation to that of the earlier christological statements.

In the book of Revelation references to the homology κύριος Ἰησοῦς are few. In the end of the book it appears in the final blessing (Rev. 22:21), but even there it appears in the form of an appellation.[192] In Revelation 17, however, the idea of the Lordship of Christ is apparent: "and the Lamb will conquer

---

[189] So Ford, *Revelation*, 88-89. The apocalyptic (Jewish) explanation supersedes the suggestions of the old history-of-religions school in which the connection was made with either Babylonian or Egyptian sources. For a critical discussion of these alternatives, see Aune, *Revelation 1-5*, 332-338.

[190] In the Old Testament, leaders were often compared to lions, see for instance Gad and Dan in Deut. 33:20-22. In 1. Macc. 3:4 this metaphor was attached to Judas Maccabeus.

[191] Halperin, *Chariot*, 92; Hengel, *Studies*, 151.

[192] The absence of the actual proclamation of the Lordship of Jesus has given room for the suggestion that the work would be of Jewish origin. See Ford, *Revelation*, 17. Such a view is rather strange, however, because the nature of the exaltation Christology of the book agrees completely with other essential christological statements of the New Testament. Christ is an enthroned Davidide who has atoned for the sins of men. He is the messianic ram who now reigns on the throne of Glory.

them, for he is Lord of lords and King of kings (κύριος κυρίων ἐστὶν καὶ βασιλεὺς βασιλέων)" (17:14; cf. 19:16).

Psalm 110 is not referred to in these connections. In this respect the explicit description of the book differs from early Christology. On the other hand, however, the narrative story of the book implies an exaltation Christology that builds on the idea of an exaltation of the Davidide. Therefore the difference concerning expressions is rather small.

In many respects the book of Revelation appears to be far more developed in its description of the heavenly temple than those short early statements that describe the exaltation of Christ in christological formulas. Even though the intention of Psalm 110, that is referred to in those formulas, evidently points to the same metaphorical scene, the details of the heavenly temple are not explicated in the same manner as in Revelation.

As an apocalyptical work Revelation exploits the mystical tradition of contemporary Jewish apocalyptic. It is clearly connected to the apocalyptical Jewish tradition of merkabah mysticism. In the book we find most of the features that appear in Jewish texts. There are the significant metaphors of heavenly court and the throne. The scene conforms to that of the great prophets, mentioning the creatures and the flaming chariot. The cultic aspect is also explicit.

In a general sense, however, Revelation is a perfect example of the reception of early Christian enthronement Christology. Even though the terminology of the book differs slightly from that of certain New Testament letters, the basic message is the same. The resurrected Christ is a Davidide who has been enthroned on the throne of Glory. In addition to that he is the suffering Messiah who has conquered and whose heavenly reign is unquestionable.

In Revelation the theocratic scene does not disqualify Christology in any sense. Christ is the one who brings salvation together with God. The multitude from every nation sings to both of them: "Salvation belongs to our God who is seated on the throne, and to the Lamb!" (7:10).

The character of the Davidic Messiah and the metaphor of throne are essential in early Christian enthronement discourse. Early Christology appears to be based on an ascent structure where the basic scene is similar to that of Second Temple Jewish mysticism. Christ's exaltation is considered a royal enthronement on a heavenly throne.

This kind of presentation may easily be detected for instance in Acts 2, several Pauline passages, and in the letter to the Hebrews. On several occasions we meet such Christology in short homologies or kerygmatic statements that bear marks of a fixed tradition. In Paul's theology, and in the letter to the Hebrews, however, the reception of the essential content of the Christology has led to a rich development of resurrection theology. The Revelation to John, lastly, gives us a clear view of how such conceptions have been planted into a colorful scene of Christian apocalyptic.

Such Christology no doubt exploits enthronement discourse, but there is a basic difference between Jewish description and early Christology. According to New Testament Christology, the enthronement took place in resurrection. These two eschatological events fall into one. Psalm 110 has been used as a proof-text for the idea of an exaltation in resurrection. In this respect early Christology exceeded the limits of merkabah mysticism.

What is common to several christological passages is the intertextual transformation that is typical of enthronement statements. New Testament descriptions interpret Old Testament passages boldly and the transformation is mainly christologically motivated. In this respect the traditional aspect of theocracy comes to new light on several occasions.

§ 6 Resurrection as Enthronement in Rom. 1:3-4
(resurrection discourse)

Even though the extraordinary christological passage in the prologue of Romans could well be investigated among the texts belonging to the enthronement discourse, there are reasons for giving it a separate treatment here. When compared with Acts 2:33-36 the prologue has several features of its own. In the latter, for instance, no throne is explicitly mentioned, and Psalm 110 that was crucial for the content of Acts 2 is not quoted or even alluded to. The following analysis will argue that this passage represents a special resurrection discourse, where resurrection terminology dominates enthronement description giving the passage its original features.[1]

6.1. Early tradition and the kerygmatic formula

Romans 1:3-4 has had a unique position in the study of Christology since, apart from the one in Acts 2, it has been considered one of the oldest pieces of tradition occurring in New Testament writings. Further, it is probably the most crucial one as regards early Christology, and no doubt one of the most debated ones. In the analysis of Acts 2 above we have seen how the relation between resurrection and enthronement was described and interpreted in a dynamic manner by early Christian writers. In Christology traditional Old Testament and Jewish messianology appears to have been interpreted in terms of Jewish merkabah mysticism. These notions enable us to proceed to the investigation of the present passage.[2]

In spite of certain differences, there are other features that link Romans 1:3-4 to a similar tradition as the one that lies behind Acts 2. In the prologue of Romans there are several submetaphors that fit well into an enthronement description. According to these verses Christ is a Davidide and the Son of God in power in the resurrection of the dead. As a Davidic Messiah he has been

---

[1] For the history of investigation, see e.g. Linnemann, *EvT 31* (1971) 264–275; Jewett, *Living Text*, 99–122. The following analysis is partly based on my dissertation "Messias ja Jumalan Poika" ["Messiah and Son of God"].

[2] Analyses on the passage are numerous. In addition to the abovementioned, see e.g. Boismard, *RB 60* (1953) 5-17; Schweizer, *EvTh 15* (1955) 563-571; Wengst, *Christologische Formel*, 114-117.; Wegenast, *Tradition*, 70-76; van Iersel, *'Der Sohn'*, 70-75; Schneider, *Bib. 48* (1967) 3659-387; Stuhlmacher, *EvTh 27* (1967) 374-389; Kramer, *Christos*, 105-108; Hahn, *Hoheitstitel*, 251-259; Burger, *Davidssohn*, 25-33; Schlier, *Geschichte*, 207-218; Hengel, *Sohn*, 93-104; Poythress, *ET 87* (1975) 180-183; Langevin, *Le Christ*, 277-327; Langevin, *ScEs 29* (1977) 145-177; Beasley-Murray, *TynB 31* (1980) 147-154; Froitzheim, *Christologie*, 101-104; de Jonge, *Jewish Eschatology*, 135-144; Pesch, *Christus*, 208-217; Scott, *Adoption*, 223-244; Whitsett, *JBL 119* (2000) 661-681.

exalted to power in the resurrection. All this is highly relevant in respect of the reception of Old Testament royal metaphors and the themes of Jewish messianic enthronement.

This is further a case where we benefit from the chosen methodological approach. The passage reflects the symbolic world of the first Christians. The secrets of this enigmatic piece of Christology will not be solved by tracing a Hellenistic "Sitz im Leben" of certain Christological titles. Such an enthronement passage needs to be located in the context of Jewish merkabah tradition which may help us explain the nature of the heavenly enthronement of Jesus described in this passage.

The crystallized Christological formulation in the prologue of Romans is a true *crux interpretum* in the history of Biblical studies. One can hardly find any consensus among scholars about the interpretation of the verses, even though they agree on some ideas and principles. It is a commonplace to find a traditional formula in the text of Paul. We are obviously dealing with early tradition, as we did in Acts 2. When discussing the form and nature of the formula, however, opinions differ significantly.

The explanation and interpretation of the passage is rather difficult since all attempts to explain the nature of the occurring Christology are dependent on the reconstruction that one has made of the underlying piece of tradition. The making of such reconstructions has proved to be complex, because the syntax of the clauses are also quite complex. Due to the nature of the passage we need to make a rather careful analysis of the text itself, even though the main interest of this study is in the nature of the early Christology that this passage represents. The complexity of these verses becomes evident for anyone approaching the text. This passage is almost impossible to translate. We are naturally familiar with the "standard" translation of the passage that goes as follows (with its context, 1:1-6):

"Paul, a servant of Jesus Christ, called to be an apostle, set apart for the gospel of God, 2 which he promised beforehand through his prophets in the holy scriptures, 3 the gospel concerning his Son, who was descended from David according to the flesh 4 and was declared to be Son of God with power according to the spirit of holiness by resurrection from the dead, Jesus Christ our Lord, 5 through whom we have received grace and apostleship to bring about the obedience of faith among all the gentiles for the sake of his name, 6 including yourselves who are called to belong to Jesus Christ."

There are several problems concerning the syntax in this passage. The "Son" who is coming (v. 3) is only "declared to be Son" in the next clause. Further, the twofold expression of the descendance, mentioning both seed and flesh, creates a problem present in every translation. And as regards Davidic descendance, AV reads "seed of David" as a verbatim translation, while other translations have neglected it. The information of this term may not refer merely to descendance. There have also been problems with the interpretation of the "appointment" of Jesus in verse 4. Does it mean merely designation, or an adoption to sonship, or perhaps installation to power? From the AV onwards a laudable solution for the translation of ὁρίζειν has been found in the verb "declare". We could also translate "designate" (RSV) or "destine", not to mention other alternatives.

There are also many alternatives to interpret the syntactical status of the words power and spirit. Above we had "Son of God with power", but NIV suggests "declared with power". One may further wonder what is the spirit of holiness and lastly, one may ask why English translations in general avoid the literal meaning of the resurrection of the dead (not just resurrection of Jesus).[3]

Translating the text, however, is not our primary problem. It is necessary to note these difficulties, but their message points to another direction. The complexity in itself may be seen as evidence for the use of some kind of traditional material. If the language in a passage is not fluent, the reason may be that fixed tradition has been exploited in the dictation of the letter. As we already noted above, scholars are quite convinced that Paul used earlier tradition in this passage.

There are several possibilities in defining the existence of earlier tradition and even the frames of an early formula.[4] Paul uses here a genetive structure (dependent on περὶ τοῦ) which covers both verses 3 and 4. Anything inside this structure may have belonged to earlier tradition.

According to form critical criteria the parallel use of participles and the occurrence of words without articles in fixed combinations should be seen as signs for tradition material.[5] In verses 3-4 both clauses begin with a participle. It is also evident that there are some very rare words in the passage. It is not typical of Paul to speak about the seed of David.

---

[3] Cf. Wilckens, *Römer*, 57f.; Dunn, *Romans*, 5f.; Fitzmyer, *Romans*, 230. The problems listed here will be treated in detail in the following chapter. Scott, however, has argued that the vocabulary itself is rather typical of Paul. Therefore he states that "it is no way certain" the passage contains a pre-Pauline creed. Scott, *Adoption*, 236; so also Whitsett, *JBL 119* (2000) 662, 679. Such an argument is not sufficient, though, because the linguistic problems of the passage are so prominent.

[4] For the criteria used in this context, see the summary of Jewett, *Living Text*, 100-102.

[5] See already Norden, *Agnostos theos*, 257; Stauffer, *Theologie*, 322. Wilckens and others are right when noting that ὁρίζειν in this form does not appear in the writings of Paul. Wilckens, *Römer*, 57. This alone would not be a significant feature, however, unless it wouldn't conform to the general nature of the passage. Paul, precisely, uses the same root in other words, and the closest example is in verse 1.

The word for declaring/designating (τοῦ ὁρισθέντος) is rare, likewise. And what is interesting enough, the term Spirit of holiness is a *hapax legomenon*.[6]

According to these notions the suggestion of tradition material is quite justified. We must, however, notice that there is a long way from these observations to the statement that the occurring material would be in a form of a *parallelismus membrorum*. This remark is important, since there have been many attempts to reconstruct a parallelism.

The discussion about the parallelistic nature of the passage is important in itself. If one could define a parallelism in the clauses, this would help to interpret many of the details of the passage. Should the Davidic descendance be considered as a Messianic statement or merely as a statement about Jesus' earthly life? Is there really an antithesis between flesh and spirit in the passage? Do different expressions with identical prepositions belong together? And finally, what is the relation between Jesus' Davidic descendance and his exaltation to power? We can answer these questions only after considering the reconstruction of tradition materials.

In principle there are several ways to define the parallelistic nature of the clauses. The "traditional" and most influential reconstruction comes from the commentary on Romans by O. Michel, who has organized the passage simply according to word order (A-B-C / A-B-C-D):[7]

1. τοῦ γενομένου   1. τοῦ ὁρισθέντος
2. ἐκ σπέρματος Δαυὶδ   2. υἱοῦ θεοῦ ἐν δυνάμει
3. κατὰ σάρκα   3. κατὰ πνεῦμα ἁγιωσύνης
                          4. ἐξ ἀναστάσεως νεκρῶν

We must pay attention to the fact that, in this reconstruction, the members of the paralleling clauses are not equal. The stichometric nature of the clauses differs from each other.[8] In addition to this the latter clause appears to have too many members.[9] In a strict *parallelismus membrorum* each unit should have a

---

[6] Cf. also Schweizer, *EvTh 15* (1955) 563; Wengst, *Christologische Formel*, 112; Dunn, *Romans 1–8*, 5.

[7] So Michel in his commentary, *Romans* (1955), 30; cf. Boismard, *RB 60* (1953) 7; Neufeld, *Confessions*, 50. The parallelism of this kind sounds more convincing in English than in Greek; see Barrett: "in the sphere of the flesh, born of the family of David; in the sphere of the Holy Spirit, appointed Son of God". Barrett, *Romans*, 18; he is being followed by Ziesler, *Romans*, 60.

[8] Against Neufeld, *Confessions*, 50, who claims that the antithesis is apparent, and that it is expressed by a series of three opposites. He places the resurrection statement in brackets, though.

[9] Against Smithals, *Römerbrief*, 49. According to Smithals the numbers 3 and 4 derived from the clauses have symbolic significance. Such a conclusion, however, presupposes too much as regards the structure of the tradition.

proper counterpoint in the next clause.[10] After this scholars began to discuss over the status of the flesh-spirit antithesis in the formula.

According to E. Schweizer's analysis it belonged to the original formula and expressed the basic difference between the earthly realm and God's heavenly realm. He constructed a two-stage Christology where the descendance of Jesus belonged to the "sphere of the flesh", and his resurrection life belonged to the "sphere of the spirit of holiness". Schweizer considered only the phrase "in power" a Pauline addition, made of theological reasons.[11] Thus his reconstruction was somewhat shorter than Michel's, and in Greek it would be as the following.

τοῦ γενομένου ἐκ σπέρματος Δαυὶδ κατὰ σάρκα /
τοῦ ὁρισθέντος υἱοῦ θεοῦ κατὰ πνεῦμα ἁγιωσύνης ἐξ ἀναστάσεως νεκρῶν.

Linguistic problems have not been solved in this reconstruction, however. The members of the first clause do not have a proper counterpoint in the second one. Therefore the parallelism of this kind sounds more convincing in English than in Greek. In his own proposal Barrett finished off the formula by leaving both the power and the resurrection out of the original parallelism.[12]

"in the sphere of the flesh, born of the family of David;
in the sphere of the Holy Spirit, appointed Son of God".

R. Bultmann, however, considered the flesh-spirit antithesis a Pauline construction and left it out from the original formula. He had noted that both clauses need a subject and therefore he added one in the beginning (A-B / A-B-C).[13]

ὁ υἱὸς τοῦ θεοῦ, ὁ γενόμενος ἐκ σπέρματος Δαυὶδ /
ὁ ὁρισθεὶς υἱὸς θεοῦ ἐν δυνάμει ἐξ ἀναστάσεως νεκρῶν.

The problems in reconstructing the original syntax cannot be reduced to the discussion over the alleged antithesis between flesh and spirit. As regards

---

[10] It is a little surprising that, for instance, Wilckens speaks of a *parallelismus membrorum* even though he follows Michel and parallels seed of David with Son of God. Apparently prepositions do not have syntactic significance in his reconstruction. Wilckens, *Römer*, 56. Dunn recognizes the problem but states, that "theological adequacy would be regarded as more important than stichometric consistency." Dunn, *Romans*, 5. The problem with such a statement is that when it is presupposed, one can no longer use a fixed parallelism as an argument in the reconstruction of the formula.

[11] Schweizer, *EvTh 15* (1955) 563f.; later also Wegenast, *Tradition*, 70f.; Kramer, *Christos*, 105; Hahn, *Hoheitstitel*, 252 (with the exception that "in power" is original).

[12] Barrett, *Romans*, 18; he is being followed by Ziesler, *Romans*, 60.

[13] Bultmann, *Theologie*, 52. So also Dahl, *Studia Paulina*, 90.

syntax, the prepositions have their role as well. This may be the reason why van Iersel applied another kind of criteria and made a new reconstruction proposing a form of A–B / A–B in a paratactic order instead. For this purpose he had to leave out both the flesh-spirit antithesis, and the reference to power.[14]

τοῦ γενομένου ἐκ σπέρματος Δαυὶδ /
τοῦ ὁρισθέντος υἱοῦ θεοῦ ἐξ ἀναστάσεως νεκρῶν.

Here the parallelism seems more beautiful, but even here the υἱοῦ θεοῦ is somewhat disturbing. It is apparent, that in this version the "Son" is the subject for both clauses. Therefore the parallelism is not regular. Furthermore, the reconstruction implies certain difficult presuppositions. The words κατὰ σάρκα, ἐν δυνάμει and κατὰ πνεῦμα ἁγιωσύνης are considered here as Pauline insertions.[15] Of these the "spirit of holiness" was a *hapax legomenon* which, according to other criteria, was one of the reasons why one should expect the occurrence of tradition materials in the first place. We meet the same problem in Bultmann's reconstruction.

In either case the members of the clauses do not have real correspondence typical of parallelism in general. In this respect the presented alternatives must be considered too artificial for such a purpose. While a parallelism is usually defined by a strict correspondence of the members as regards words and syntax, our clauses do not seem to fit into this kind of scheme. Further, it is impossible to find any metrical correspondence, even by eliminating words. In every reconstruction the result is far from the clarity of the simple Greek parallelisms that can found for instance in 1 Tim. 3:16 and 1 Pt. 3:18.[16] It is apparent that one has to handle the material quite freely in order to arrange it into the form of a parallelism.[17]

The paradox between these two competing reconstructions is so remarkable, that Schneider finally suggested a hypotethical parallelism in a chiastic order A–B(–C–D) / D–C–B–A. While the expressions with prepositions appear to be parallel in a backward order, he suggested that "Son of God" and "in power"

---

[14] See van Iersel, *'Der Sohn'*, 72. Actually he considered also the last clause of the Lordship of Christ original. He is being followed by Fuller, *Christology*, 165; Schlier, *Geschichte*, 213.

[15] Cf. the mediating view of Wilckens, *Römer*, 56, and Froitzheim, *Christologie*, 102, who consider the expression "in power" a Pauline insertion.

[16] Cf. e.g. 1 Tim. 3:16: ἐφανερώθη ἐν σαρκί / ἐδικαιώθη ἐν πνεύματι.

[17] Hunter has suggested, on the basis of a later Peshittah translation, that there were originally three clauses, the last one of which spoke about the resurrection of Jesus Christ. Hunter, *Paul*, 25. Even though such a solution is artificial it shows that the complexity of the passage leaves room for several different explanations.

must have had antithetical counterpoints in the original formula, as well. Therefore he added [C] "in weakness" (of the flesh; 2 Cor. 13:4; 1 Cor. 15:43) to oppose the latter, and [D] "Son of Man" (Rom. 5:18-19; Heb. 2:6) to oppose the former.[18] Such hypothesis is interesting, but purely fictional.

Linnemann attempted to solve the problem by correcting Bultmann's reconstruction and by paying attention to the fact that the "spirit of holiness" is a *hapax legomenon*. She regarded only κατὰ σάρκα a Pauline addition, and claimed that the κατὰ preposition in the latter clause was Pauline for the sake of an *ad hoc* parallelism. According to Linnemann the original expression was "in power of the spirit of holiness".[19]

According to Fuller there are different layers in the formula and this explains the conceptual confusion in the final text. Following Hahn he suggested that the flesh-spirit antithesis derives from the Hellenistic Church (Hellenistic Jewish Christianity).[20] As the expression "in power" was further considered a Pauline addition, Fuller thought that it would be possible to reconstruct an antithetical formula of Palestinian origin (similar to that of van Iersel's above).[21]

γενομένου ἐκ σπέρματος Δαυὶδ /
ὁρισθέντος υἱοῦ θεοῦ ἐξ ἀναστάσεως νεκρῶν.

Fuller is able to answer the questions he himself has posed, but one may wonder, why such a formula should be considered antithetical. For instance Zimmermann has concluded that Hellenistic theologians exploited Jewish Christian messianology, but he states that the writers used two independent homologies in their formula. According to Zimmermann the message of both of these homologies was originally quite identical. Only in the Hellenistic Church they were contrasted with each other and this also created the problems found in the passage.[22]

---

[18] Schneider, *Bib. 48* (1967) 362.

[19] Linnemann, *EvT 31* (1971) 273f.

[20] Interpretation appears to be dependent also on the view of the history of early Church. According to Bultmann the theology of the formula was a contradiction to Hellenistic Christology. Bultmann, *Theologie*, 53. Fuller has turned the view around and considers the formula an example of Hellenistic Christology. The key to this shift is Hahn's idea of Hellenistic Jewish Christianity that must be placed between early Jewish Christianity and later Hellenistic Christianity of pagan origin. Hahn, *Hoheitstitel*, 252ff. In this case evidently the root of the Christology is Jewish but the context Hellenistic. Such a hypothesis is rather impossible to prove by any extant evidence.

[21] Fuller, *Christology*, 165.

[22] Zimmermann, *Neutestamentliche Methodenlehre*, 201. In this way he actually finally placed the formula right in the Hellenistic Church, against Bultmann, see above.

There are certain important conclusions that can be drawn from this analysis. Firstly, this passage does not contain a *parallelismus membrorum*. Whatever the reconstruction of earlier tradition, it is in reality made on theological grounds, not on linguistic grounds alone. Some reconstructions attempt to solve the problem of adoptionist Christology, others concentrate on the flesh-spirit antithesis. A few scholars wish to explain both of these problems.

In addition to this there is another quite astonishing feature in scholarship. It is not possible to find one detailed analysis of the syntax of the clauses, as regards the participles and their relation to the subject of the sentence. The theological tension in this passage is apparently so great that scholars have passed a cool analysis of the clauses and rushed to the explanation of the content.

This must be the reason why several scholars and most translations treat the passage as if it read "declared to be Son of God" (as the NRSV does), or "appointed/ installed Son of God." Such a translation would imply that υἱός were a predicate complement for the participle. This, naturally, is impossible. The translations referred to above must therefore rest on a theological hypothesis.

As we analyse the passage where the introductory 3a is excluded, there is only one subject in these clauses. It is υἱός, the "Son" in verse 4. Both participles are attributes to this subject. The passage speaks of the coming of the Son and – if we here agree on using the most general lexical meaning of ὁρίζω for the sake of convenience – the designation of the Son, and both of these actions have been completed in the past.

While the subject is located in verse 4, verse 3 necessarily forms a subordinate sentence for the second clause. The writer speaks of the realized coming (aorist participle) of the "Son" from the seed of David. Rhetorical weight is, however, on the latter clause. Here we have the actual subject and another aorist participle. If we once again use the general meaning "designate", the latter clause says: "the designated Son of God." On the basis of syntax one should further expect that this expression were a bridge that covers the gap between the subject and the preceding attribute in verse 3. The Son who had come is the Davidide whose coming and exaltation had been designated before.

There is no other way to translate the latter clause (despite the fact that ὁρίζω may be translated by some other word). The aorist participle is an attribute to the subject. The syntax of this clause corresponds with the syntax of Acts 10:42 where the participle is connected to a verb.

οὗτός ἐστιν ὁ ὡρισμένος ὑπὸ τοῦ θεοῦ κριτὴς ζώντων καὶ νεκρῶν (Acts 10:42)

According to Acts 10, Christ has been decreed beforehand to be a judge in the last day. We may make a test and apply this structure also to Romans 1 in order to compare the syntactic structures. In the formula such a structure would produce the following:

[οὗτός ἐστιν ὁ ὁρισθεὶς υἱὸς θεοῦ ἐν δυνάμει]

With the main verb εἰμί the participle is a predicate complement as one should expect.[23] This does not change the status of the word "Son" in the sentence. Also in this case we must translate: this is the one who had been designated Son of God in power.

How does this alter the traditional translation of verse 4? It is apparent that God's action (*passivum divinum*) towards the Son, which is described by ὁρίζω, has not taken place in the present moment but in the past, instead. This notion will help us later in defining the exact meaning of ὁρίζω in this context. ὁρίζω does not refer directly to the present exaltation, i.e. the resurrection, but to an earlier decree concerning the resurrection. Therefore, ὁρίζω refers to the whole idea of "raising" the Davidide. The interpretation of the word must thus also take verse 3 into account.

The analysis made above has brought up certain new principles for the explanation of verses 3 and 4 in the prologue of Romans. As we already noted above, we cannot speak of a *parallelismus membrorum* in the strict sense of the term.[24] The syntactic nature of the passage is complex. It is no longer possible to make a reconstruction of earlier materials on linguistic grounds alone. Every reconstruction is dependent on theological premises.

Secondly, a simple analysis shows that the participles in the clauses are attributes for one and the same subject "Son" in the latter clause. Therefore the clauses must also be kept together in the interpretation of the content. The closer explanation of details, such as the precise meaning of ὁρίζω, must be left to the theological analysis.

Because we cannot use the idea of a parallelism as an argument when defining the traditional formula behind Paul, structural observations have no primary value in the process of theological analysis. The questions concerning the content and theological motives must in this case have more weight also in the form critical analysis.

This does not mean, however, that we should abandon the hypothesis

---

[23] Cf. Bornemann-Risch, *Grammatik*, § 242.

[24] The idea of a parallelismus is doubted also by Zimmermann, *Neutestamentliche Methodenlehre*, 200, where this passage is presented as a test-case for the tradition history of early formulas; Burger, *Davidssohn*, 29, and Poythress, *ET* 87 (1975) 180–181.

concerning tradition materials. Quite the contrary, the complexity of the passage confirms that Paul must have exploited earlier tradition, oral or written, when dictating the Christological opening for his important letter to Rome. Even though we are not able to use a linguistic method for a strict reconstruction of the alleged formula, we must take the presence of tradition for granted.[25] Most scholars agree on the basic point of departure. After introducing his great theme of the gospel of the Son in verse 3a, Paul exploits earlier tradition in the clauses beginning with participles in verses 3b-4.[26] Whether the final Kyrios-statement in v. 4b should be included in the formula or not is a matter of dispute, and we shall treat the question later.[27]

Why should one, then, conclude that the tradition material exploited by Paul is early? On the one hand, usually the tradition-hypothesis has already produced this view without any detailed argumentation behind it. As we have seen, according to many scholars the formula was a fixed one and in earlier scholarship fixed formulas were considered results of a long development. In German scholarship after von Harnack fixed formulas were identified as dogma and there had to be a long period of time between "living Christianity" and dogma. Therefore the reasoning usually went as follows: if one can find any pre-Pauline Christological formula in Paul's letters, its content must originate from a very early period.

On the other hand, the content of the prologue of Romans has for a long time been linked to the content of Acts 2. The Christology of both of these passages has been identfied as adoptionist Christology, and therefore it has been convenient to date it early. According to such a scheme adoptionist Christology predates high Christology, and it must be early already by definition.[28]

Both of the abovementioned arguments have lost their weight during the last decades of scholarship. This means that we must re-open the question of the

---

[25] According to Poythress we have here merely Paul's free composition using a number of traditional expressions and ideas. Poythress, *ExpT 87* (1975) 182. This, however is an unnecessary conclusion. A theological analysis does not need to separate different expressions from each other.

[26] See e.g. Schweizer, *EvTh 15* (1955) 563; Kramer, *Christos*, 105; Hahn, *Hoheitstitel*, 252; Burger, *Davidssohn*, 26; Linnemann, *EvT 31* (1971) 274; Wengst, *Christologische Formel*, 112.

[27] One naturally expects that some kind of presentation of the subject of the statement should be included either before the participial construction or after it. Bultmann in his reconstruction placed words "Jesus Christ" in the beginning of the clauses. Bultmann, *Theologie*, 52. He is being followed later e.g. by Wegenast, *Tradition*, 70.

[28] For Käsemann, for example, adoptionist Christology was evidence for the diversity of Christological thinking precisely in the early Church. Käsemann, *Exegetische Versuche I*, 215; cf. later Dunn, *Unity and Diversity*, 243.

dating of the passage. There are certain facts for the investigation, however, that we do not need to question. We are dealing with tradition that predates Paul's letter to the Romans. The age of this tradition is unknown to us, but any date approximately between 30 and 50 is possible in principle. Moreover, this may be a piece of tradition that unites Paul and his readers. While it appears in the beginning of the letter, it serves well the purpose of making a trustworthy introduction convincing Roman Christians about Paul's gospel.[29] If we are to believe the greetings in the end of the letter to the Romans, the common faith should include the Jewish Christian preachers who "are prominent among the apostles," and who have been "in Christ" before Paul (Rom. 16:7). These apostles, who have also been in prison with Paul, can give their testimony to the whole congregation (all house churces) in Rome about Paul's message. Therefore it is quite possible that the tradition material used in the letter conforms with the Christology of apostolic Jewish Christianity of the first two Christian decades.[30]

In this analysis we have met with the problems that are typical of the explanation of Romans 1:3-4. The passage is complex and quite many factors point in the direction of tradition material behind Paul's writing. The frames of the exploited material, however, are not easily defined. The parallelism is not regular and different expressions, apart from the participles, do not have an unambiguous counterpoint in the paralleling clause. Certain facts refer to the possibility that we are dealing with early tradition material here, probably even with Jewish Christian Christology. The basic problem with all this is that the final conclusion must be made on the grounds of the content of the passage. Therefore the only possibility to get forward in this situation is to analyse the Christology of the passage and to attempt to apply different form-critical alternatives to that analysis.

6.2. The formula and the symbolic world of Jewish Christianity

The understanding of the content of the formula is dependent on the reconstruction of the symbolic world of the original writer of the formula. We need to know what is the function of the "seed of David" in Jewish tradition. We have to find motivation for the description of the exaltation of the Messiah, and we must attempt to explain why early writers thought that resurrection is able to make the Davidide a Son of God in power.

In this search links to Old Testament writings have a primary value. One

---

[29] This has been a common argument in scholarship, see Michel, *Römer* (1955), 30; Wegenast, *Tradition*, 75; Schneider, *Bib 48* (1967) 359; Dunn, *Romans*, 5.

[30] Also later a similar homology, probably dependent on this passage of Romans, has been considered essential, see Ign.Eph. 20:2; Ign.Sm. 1:1.

should not forget the rather self-evident fact that in all paralleling Christological passages in the New Testament certain Old Testament sections are quoted or alluded to. In Acts 2 there were references to 2 Sam. 7 and Ps. 110, and in Acts 13 references to 2 Sam. 7 and Ps. 2. In the beginning of the letter to the Hebrews all these three passages are quoted. It is justified to expect that these Old Testament sections have influenced early exaltation Christology, and that there may be traits of this influence also in the prologue of the Romans.

Such an approach is not arbitrary in the interpretation of Romans 1, because there is an explicit justification for it even in Paul's own text. The gospel of the Son which Paul teaches in the opening lines of the letter is a gospel that God "promised beforehand through his prophets in the holy scriptures" (1:2). He seems to be aware of the connection between Old Testament writings and the tradition he uses in his letter.

It is clear that in the prologue of the Romans there are no explicit quotations of the Old Testament. There are allusions to the "seed" of David and the "power" of the Son of God, however. These features have lead most scholars to look for Old Testament connections. Therefore, in the study of Christology, this passage has been rather unique since the deciphering of Christological titles has not been the only method used in the interpretation. It has been applied to the search for the Old Testament background of the passage. For decades the Christology of Rom. 1:3-4 has been connected with the abovementioned Old Testament passages speaking about the Davidic dynasty (2 Sam. 7:12–14; Ps. 2:7). Even the first authors of the theory of adoptionist Christology, D.F. Strauss and J. Weiss concentrated on these texts.[31]

This general observation has led many scholars into the area of Davidic Royal ideology, i.e. in the study of related texts concerning the Davidic dynasty. In this respect we need to return to the themes that were treated already when Acts 2 was analysed. Usually the connection between Romans 1 and the Royal ideology has been seen on the level of theological motives.[32] At first glance there seems, especially, to be similarities with Nathan's prophecy, which we need to quote once more (2 Sam. 7:12–14).

"When your days are fulfilled and you lie down with your ancestors, I will raise up your offspring [AV: seed] after you, who shall come forth from your body, and I will establish his

---

[31] See Strauss, *Leben Jesu*, 478f.; Weiss, *Urchristentum*, 86. Cf. later chapter 10.

[32] Some scholars think that the connections with 2 Sam. 7:14 can be seen as such. According to Boismard the main motive is enthronement which can be seen in Psalm 2 and Nathan's prophecy. "En faveur de cette idée d'une intronisation du Roi–Messie, déclaré alors Fils de Dieu, on peut citer aussi II Sam., vii, 14." Boismard, *RB 60* (1953) 14. Legrand makes note of the notion that in Nathan's prophecy as well as in the prologue the title Son of God is connected with an idea of a messianic descendant of David. Legrand, *RB 70* (1963) 181.

kingdom. He shall build a house for my name, and I will establish the throne of his kingdom forever. I will be a father to him, and he shall be a son to me."

In the prologue of Romans we find the descendant of David and the word "seed" which is used in Nathan's prophecy. Exalted Christ is further a Son of God, as was the Davidide in the Old Testament. As regards the Septuagint text of 2 Samuel, a connection may even be seen between the words raising and resurrection (ἀνάστασις). This connection is not limited to Greek connotation, but the link may be detected in Hebrew, as well, as we shall see below. In this case there would be a literal dependence between these passages.[33]

Also Psalm 2 has been suggested to have a special relation to Romans 1.[34] Psalm 2 is speaking of the "decree" of the Lord, which refers to the sonship of the anointed king. This relation is mainly theological, not based on literal dependence. Here again the Davidide is an enthroned Son of God and he gains his position through God's special decree.

We have earlier referred to the theory of a Jewish promise tradition that may have influenced early Christology. This theory needs to be considered already in this instance.[35] Several texts confirm the idea that the themes of the exaltation of a Davidide, his adoptional sonship to God, the dynasty's eternal royal covenant and covenantal grace are constant features in Old Testament theology.[36] According to the theory the Davidic ideology contained certain structural components, often metaphors, representing the Davidic descendant. The title Son of David as such is not primary in this tradition, but the descendant is described as the seed of David, or the Shoot of David, by a father-son relationship, by an enthronement, or by a promise of eternal reign.

One may assume that these kinds of elements have been significant in the symbolic world of both Second Temple Judaism and early Christianity. The

---

[33] According to several scholars links between the prologue and the prophecy of Nathan are direct. For instance van Iersel thinks that the words υἱός, ἀνάστασις, σπέρμα and the name David come directly from the book of Samuel. He uses here the text of Septuaginta. van Iersel, *'Der Sohn'*, 73. The same kind of observations are being made by Betz. He says that the literary connection between the texts is clear. "Die beiden alten, parallelen Bekenntnissätze sind bewusst nach dem Nathanspruch geformt." Betz, *Jesus*, 65. Betz is being followed by Hengel, *Sohn*, 101, and alluded to by Haacker, *NT 20* (1978) 14 note 51, though the interpretation of Haacker is nearer to that of Legrand, see Haacker, ibid., 13.

[34] Boismard thinks that the obedience to the faith of the nations is an allusion to Psalm 2 where Son of God is the ruler of the nations. Boismard, *RB 60* (1953) 15.

[35] This has been worked out in detail e.g. by Duling and Schweizer. Schweizer, *Studies*, 186ff. Duling, *NTS 19* (1973) 55-77. Cf. Whitsett, *JBL 119* (2000) 675ff., who has suggested that Paul himself exploited the promise tradition in this passage.

[36] See e.g.: Ps. 2; Ps. 89; Isa. 11; 55; Jer. 23; Ezek. 34; PsSal. 17; 4Qflor.; TLev. 18; 1 Enoch 46; 62; 4 Ezra 12.

anticipated Messiah was a Davidide, "from the seed of David". A key eschatological event would be the "raising", i.e. the enthronement of this Davidide. As a Davidide he would be called the Son of God who reigns on his eternal throne. Indeed, these are elements that conform to those found in the exaltation Christology of Acts 2. The details of this kind of presentation in Romans 1 must now be investigated in order to be able to draw justifiable conclusions about the Christology itself.

In the interpretation of verse 3 the problems of methodological discussion must also be treated shortly. In previous studies deriving from the beginning of this century scholars attempted to investigate whether the "son of David" was an absolute Messianic title in Jewish theology or not.[37] Such a question is, however, rather fruitless as regards the explanation of verse 3. In this verse there is no appellation whatsoever. The verse speaks only about the descendance of the Davidide. One may naturally ask if the statement is meant to be Messianic. Some scholars speak only of the earthly life of Jesus or of his genealogical qualification for Messiahship.[38] The general opinion, however, has emphasized the theological sense of the clause and considers the statement Messianological as such.[39]

Several scholars have suggested a comparison with the prophecy of Nathan, and this turns out to be rather illuminating in this question. The most obvious similarity between the texts (Rom. 1:3 and 2 Sam. 7:12) is the expression ἐκ σπέρματος Δαυὶδ. The key word σπέρμα has heuristic value. The word may naturally bear a general meaning of descendance but the occurrence of the name David reveals a close relationship between the passages.[40]

It is worth mentioning that in Romans 1 verse 3 the "seed" itself is not said to be exalted as was the case in the Septuagint text of 2 Sam. 7:12 (ἀναστήσω τὸ σπέρμα σου μετὰ σέ). The "coming" of the seed is thus seen as a fulfillment of an earlier decree or promise.[41] When the text says that the king will come

---

[37] See e.g. Sanday-Headlam, *Romans*, 6-7; Bousset, *Christos Kyrios*, 4; Lietzmann, *Römer*, 25.

[38] So e.g. the old commentary by Zahn, *Römer*, 36; cf. Althaus, *Römer*, 6; van Unnik speaks of the genealogy, van Unnik, *NTS 8* (1962) 108f.; cf. Wengst, *Formel*, 114.

[39] According to Kuss this cannot be merely a genealogical statement, Kuss, *Römerbrief*, 5; see also Burger, *Davidssohn*, 26; Cranfield, *Romans*, 58; van der Minde, *Schrift*, 41; Dunn, *Romans*, 12; Stuhlmacher, *Römer*, 22.

[40] Both texts use the word 'seed', so also LXX. See the comments of van Iersel, *Sohn*, 73, and Betz, *Jesus*, 65.

[41] Burger writes: "Die Rede vom 'Samen' als der Nachkommenschaft eines Mannes ist zwar griechisch wie hebräisch möglich. In der Verbindung mit dem Namen Davids entspricht sie aber genau der alttestamentlichen Verheissung und der traditionellen Sprache jüdischer Erwartung". Burger, *Davidssohn*, 28.

"from the seed of David" he becomes identified with the descendant of David of whom it is said: "I will set up thy seed after thee" (AV: 2. Sam. 7:12). This leaves further room for an unorthodox exploitation of the LXX word raising (ἀναστήσω) as we shall see later.

The basic Messianological interpretation in the alleged formula resembles thus the Qumran pesher 4Qflor. on 2 Sam. 7:12-14.

"...'YHWH de[clares] to you that he will build you a house. I will raise up your seed after you and establish the throne of his kingdom [for ev]er. I will be a father to him and he will be a son to me.' This (refers to the) 'branch of David', who will arise with the Interpreter of the law who [will rise up] in Zi[on in] the last days..." (4Qflor. I, 10-12).

For Qumran theologians the Messianic character of the metaphor "seed" was self-evident. In their ideology the Davidide was expected to be a political Messiah who would defeat foreign rulers and free Israel from their oppression.[42]

In Romans we have a parallel interpretation, but with a new intention. Jesus is a Davidide whose enthronement has already taken place. Christian theology might paraphrase the text of Florilegium hypothetically: he *has risen* in the last days. The formula has been written from the point of view of this kind of conviction. Jesus is the one who "has come" (γενόμενος) and he reigns on David's throne. This interpretation, dependent naturally on the suggestion that 2 Sam. 7 is behind the train of thought, makes the statement in Rom.1:3 completely messianological. The exact relation of this clause to verse 4, however, may be defined only after the second clause has been investigated.

In verse 4 we meet one of the most difficult details of the whole passage. What is the meaning of the Greek word ὁρίζω? According to the traditional adoptionist interpretation it means appointment to sonship. In his enthronement Jesus has been made the Son of God.[43] As a reaction against this interpretation some scholars have explained the word to mean "predetermination" or "designation", mostly on theological grounds.[44] Most scholars, however, think that the meaning of the word must refer to appointment or even to

---

[42] For a recent analysis, see e.g. Collins, *Scepter*, 49ff.

[43] This may be seen already in Weiss, *Urchristentum*, 86. The comment of Bultmann has also been influential: "the earliest Church called Jesus Son of God (messianic) because that was what the resurrection made him. However, unlike the later Hellenistic Church it did not regard the earthly Jesus as a Son of God (mythological)". Bultmann, *Theology I*, 50.

[44] See for instance Sanday-Headlam, *Romans*, 7f. Fuller in his *Christology*, 166, suggested an eschatological interpretation: "predetermined from the time of (ἐξ) the resurrection to be the eschatological Son of God at the parousia." His explanation of the preposition ἐκ in the expression concerning resurrection, however, is not very convincing.

installation.[45] None of these scholars think, however, that the expression would actually mean the "making" of the Son, as we will see below.

Translations normally use the word declare, "declared to be Son of God" (NRSV), as we have seen earlier, but this sounds more like a compromise than a justified translation. In order to find out the best possible solution we need to get three different aspects together. The interpretation of ὁρίζω must treat firstly the lexical meaning of the word, secondly the word's use in the sentence, and thirdly the theological context in which the word occurs.

Our first task is to attempt to define the lexical content of the word. Even with regards to this question there has been considerable disagreement among scholars. In Liddell-Scott the semantic field of ὁρίζω comprises words such as ordain and determine. It has to do with defining objects. An idea of installation is not in fact in the scope of this semantic field. As regards the idea of the ordaining of people, the word designate might be proper.

New Testament occurrences of the word usually conform to that field. In the Acts, for instance, Jesus is "the one ordained by God as judge of the living and the dead." (Acts 10:42). Such designation to an eschatological ministry occurs also in Acts 17:31: "he has fixed a day on which he will have the world judged in righteousness by a man whom he has appointed, and of this he has given assurance to all by raising him from the dead." Here the actual installation is not yet meant.

Therefore, these passages do not describe Jesus' realized installation to an eschatological ministry. He is rather designated to be a judge in the future, in the last day. An idea of a designation may be applied to the prologue of Romans too, even though there the judgement is not the issue. In the formula the crucial event is resurrection. As regards the lexical level, ὁρίζω may well have a similar meaning as in the abovementioned passages of Acts, and denote designation to an enthronement in resurrection.

This is actually the way that the translator of the Vulgate has understood the meaning of the word in the prologue of Romans (ὁρισθεὶς υἱὸς θεοῦ): *qui praedestinatus est Filius Dei*. According to the Vulgate the formula refers to a divine decree according to which the exaltation has taken place.[46] In the Vulgate the word has been identified as προ-ὁρίζω. This is not necessarily a theological rendering. Even though in Romans there is no prefix in the verb,

---

[45] See e.g. Michel, *Römer* (1955), 31; Dunn, *Romans*, 13. Legrand attempts to avoid the theological problem by using καλέω as a synonym (both allegedly coming from Heb. *kara*). Thus ὁρίζω would mean the vocation of the Son. Legrand, *RB 70* (1963) 14. This alternative does not connect the word with kingship ideology.

[46] Michel excludes this alternative in the explanation of Romans 1, however. Michel, *Römer* (1955), 32.

the meaning of the word is the same in principle. The word refers to a designation or decree that has been given in the past.

For instance in the Acts ὁρίζω and προ-ὁρίζω are used in an identical function.⁴⁷ In Acts 4:25-28 the rulers, such as Herod and Pilate, who acted "against the Lord and against his Messiah" (cf. Ps. 2:1-2), did only what God's "plan had predestined (προ-ὁρίζω) to take place" (Acts 4:28). According to Acts 2:23, however, Jesus was handed over to those who condemned him "according to the definite plan (ὁρίζω) and foreknowledge of God."⁴⁸

In addition to this semantic investigation it is important to notice that the use of the word in its context and its syntactic status in the passage support this kind of translation. In Romans 1:4 the participle ὁρίζω is an attribute of the subject "Son".⁴⁹ According to syntax the participle gives new information about the designation that has taken place before. Furthermore, the expression in question (ὁρισθεὶς υἱὸς θεοῦ) is clearly a *passivum divinum* denoting the active designation by God himself.⁵⁰ It refers to God's decree that he has given in the past.

In this respect the Christology of the formula may well be parallel to that of Acts 2 that we investigated earlier. There the "oath" to David had great significance for the exaltation Christology presented (Acts 2:30). The oath was considered God's promise of the enthronement of a descendant of David, and there were evident links to 2 Sam. 7:12. This kind of view also fits well into the messianological nature of the formula of Romans. The crucial statement in the prophecy of Nathan (2 Sam. 7:12),

"I will raise up your seed" (והקימתי את-זרעך),

has been understood and treated as a promise of the exaltation and enthronement of the future king, the Messiah (cf. "I will establish the throne [כסא] of his kingdom", 7:13).⁵¹

In 2 Sam. 7:12 God's promise is expressed with the verb *qûm*, which evidently leaves room for the connotation of ἀνάστασις, resurrection (from the dead). This aspect is even more clear on the level of Greek tradition (ἀναστήσω τὸ σπέρμα σου μετὰ σέ), even though the word play works also in Hebrew.

---

⁴⁷ Allen, *NTS 17* (1971) 105f.

⁴⁸ Cf. Lk 22:22, "For the Son of Man is going as it has been determined [or: decreed]."

⁴⁹ See the analysis in previous chapter.

⁵⁰ Cf. Hengel, *Sohn*, 97.

⁵¹ The verb *qûm* has a central position in the promise tradition (Jer. 23:5; Ez. 34:23; 4Qflor). Quite many texts use this word when speaking about the exaltation/appointment of a king from the dynasty of David. And when the Aramaic tradition is considered, the verb also appears there meaning enthronement (Dan 5:21).

Therefore the writer of the Christological formula believed that God's "decree" (*praedestinatus est*), i.e. his divine designation, has been the statement that he will raise the seed of David and establish his throne.[52] As we saw earlier, this interpretation fits well the syntax of the clauses where both participles are attributes of the same subject "Son".

It would be tempting to suggest that the actual word decree mentioned in Psalm 2:7 (*hôq*) had something to do with the decree mentioned in Romans.[53] It is indeed a decree of the enthronement of the Son of God.

"I will tell of the decree of the Lord: He said to me, 'You are my son; today I have begotten you'." (Ps. 2:7).

In this case the abovementioned Old Testament passages would together form the background for the original formula. This is possible in principle, because Psalm 2:7 and 2 Sam. 7:12 appear together both in Acts 13:33f. and in Heb. 1:5 (cf. Heb. 5:5-6, where Ps. 2:7 appears with Ps. 110:4).[54] In early Christianity these passages had a similar function and they were connected simply because of their similar content. If they have together influenced the Christological formula in Romans, it would thus present an independent rendering of *hôq* when using ὁρίζω.[55]

We have thus analysed some features of the symbolic world that has directed the Christology of the formula. It seems apparent that an unknown Jewish Christian preacher or prophet has exploited this kind of messianology in the same manner as did the tradition that has been used in Acts 2 and Hebrews 1. God has fulfilled his promises when raising Jesus from the dead. Jesus' resurrection has also served as an act of enthronement, where the "seed of David" has been installed to power. Jesus is the Davidide who had been

---

[52] For this view see already Betz, *NT 6* (1963) 32; ibid. *Jesus*, 66; cf. Hengel, *Sohn*, 100; Haacker, *NT 20* (1978) 14 footnote 51; Schweizer, *Studies*, 190; Hayes, *Interp. 2.* (1968) 342; Duling, *NTS 19* (1973) 71. Scott has rejected this interpretation, because he believes that Paul bases his Christology here on the Damascus-Road Christophany. Scott, *Adoption*, 243. This, however, lessens neither the value of the linguistic argument nor the value of the theological argument presented above.

[53] This has been suggested already by Boismard, *RB 60* (1953) 14; and explicated in detail later by Allen, *NTS 17* (1971) 104ff. See also Poythress, *ExpT 87* (1975) 181.

[54] In 4Qflor. we have a pesher on 2 Sam. 7:10-14, and in the end of the fragment Ps. 2:1-2 is treated. We have therefore evidence for the occurrence of a relevant catena, but no exact evidence of the joining of 2 Sam. 7 and Ps. 2:7.

[55] There is no other linguistic evidence for this view. The Septuagint does not support this translation. In 4Qpatr., however, we have a Hebrew word-play on the ruler's "staff" (Gen. 49:10). The staff (מחקק) has been interpreted as a pass. part. of חקק. In the pesher the staff thus represents a Davidide who has been decreed to be installed to power in the eschatological future. See van der Woude, *Die messianischen Vorstellungen*, 170; Lövestam, *Son*, 66; Allen, *NTS 17* (1971) 104.

decreed to be enthroned, in other words, to be exalted as the Son of God in power in the resurrection.

This view helps us further to answer the question concerning the moment when Jesus was designated to his eschatological Messiahship. Most scholars would answer that Jesus was appointed Son of God in his resurrection.[56] In this alternative the appointment actually becomes identical with installation, and ὁρίζω should be translated: "the installed Son of God". The word ὁρίζω would not only refer to resurrection through an ancient decree, but it would actually mean the enthronement of Christ in his resurrection – or, as Fuller has suggested, his predetermination "from the time of the resurrection" to be the Son of God in power at the parousia.[57]

Does ὁρίζω refer directly to the resurrection statement? This has often been presupposed since the understanding of verse 3 heavily suggests it. The participle and the following preposition *ek* seem to belong together.[58] Therefore also in verse 4 the appointment was connected with the expression ἐξ ἀναστάσεως νεκρῶν. This, however, is not a good solution.

We have above abandoned the possibility of using a hypothesis of a *parallelismus membrorum* in the explanation of the passage. Therefore we must not let it affect our explanation here. As regards the content of the passage, it is not the appointment that is taking place in the resurrection, but the enthronement, the "raising" of the seed of David. In verse 4 *ek* cannot mean the moment of resurrection in a temporal sense "from the time of resurrection". As in several other exaltation passages it simply means the act of resurrection. The expression itself is complex and it will be dealt with below.

As the whole formula is considered, the abovementioned solution solves best the problems of interpretation. There must be one divine decree that is behind the expectations of the formula. That decree was given when the "raising of the seed of David" was promised. The suggestion given here, following several predecessors, is that the decree has consciously been identified as 2 Sam. 7:12 (ἀναστήσω τὸ σπέρμα σου μετὰ σέ). The Septuagint text of that passage suits well our purposes in the analysis, even though we have already seen that the same reasoning is also possible in Hebrew.

The promise in 2 Sam. 7:12 speaks of the raising of the "seed" of David. In Romans 1:3 γίνομαι already begins to fulfill that expectation. Verse 4 only

---

[56]This is the way, for instance, those who accept the theory of two-stage Christology think, see e.g. Schweizer, *Studies*, 186. However, cf. also Michel, *Römer* (1978), 74.

[57] See comments on Fuller above. For the quotation, see Fuller, *Christology*, 166. Cf. later the discussion on the theory of polarized eschatology, chapter 8.3.

[58] For a temporal interpretation of ἐκ, apart from Fuller above, see Lietzmann, *Römer*, 25; Schweizer, *EvTh 15* (1955) 563; Kramer, *Christos*, 107.

confirms the fulfillment. The promise concerned the enthronement of a future Davidide. Therefore it is logical to conclude that ὁρίζω serves here as a linguistic bridge and refers to the ancient decree. There has been an act of installation, as the decree determined. In the formula this installation is expressed with the reference to resurrection.[59] The Christological consequences of this solution will be considered later.

All this leads to a novel hypotheses concerning the interpretation of verses 3 and 4 in the prologue of Romans. *Actually the statement in verse 3 needs to be interpreted with the help of verse 4. Therefore, the inference moves backwards in the passage. God's divine "appointment" or decree mentioned in verse 4 refers both to the seed of David mentioned in verse 3 and to resurrection mentioned in verse 4.* We shall return also to the details of this interpretation below.

A proper translation for the core of the formula - before the discussion concerning the status of flesh and spirit, and the resurrection theme - should emphasize the connection between the clauses:

"from the seed of David [...],
the designated Son of God in power [...]."

Such a translation rightly emphasizes the Son as the subject of the sentence. For the sake of clarity one could even replace the word designated by the word promised. This would be a dynamic, theological translation, since God's decree, given in the past, has usually been called a promise both in Jewish theology and Christian teaching. Therefore the dynamic meaning of the formula may be seen in the translation:

"from the seed of David [...],
the promised Son of God in power [...]."

From the point of view of this translation scholars following Schweizer are quite right when stating that the alleged opposition between flesh and spirit is the main reason why Paul's writing in this passage sounds antithetical. Apart from this "antithesis" the clauses belong syntactically together and communicate a similar message. In this respect the content of the hypothetical formula does not seem to fit into the final composition. This has evidently been seen by some scholars, since their abovementioned reconstructions have attempted to avoid the problems created by such antithesis. Poythress and Zimmermann even concluded that the original tradition comprised merely

---

[59] Cf. e.g. Hengel, *Damaskus*, 168-169: "Der Text sagt nicht, dass der ganz gewöhnliche Mensch Jesus erst durch die Auferstehung zum Sohn Gottes wird, sondern der aus dem Geschlecht Davids stammende (gekreuzigte) Messias Jesus ist seit der Auferstehung als Sohn Gottes in Macht und verklärter Gestgestalt von Gott eingesetzt."

separate clauses or expressions.[60] The complexity of the formula was thus a result of joining expressions that somewhat disagree with each other.

What is the relation of κατὰ σάρκα and κατὰ πνεῦμα? Do these expressions really oppose each other, or should they be explained separatedly in their close context? The present reader of the passage naturally opposes these expressions, especially due to the connecting preposition. We must question this impression, however. Is such antithesis intentional, or is it merely accidental, dependent on features that originally do not oppose each other? Or should we consider the opposition secondary and a result of redaction?

We must begin with the expression κατὰ σάρκα in verse 3. As we have noted above, the clause in verse 3 gives the impression of repetition. The first statement "coming from the seed of David" as such is quite capable of expressing the descendance of Jesus. The words κατὰ σάρκα after this statement sound excessive. There are several possibilities to solve this problem.

1. It is possible that the first clause already contains a parallelism. If the formula is of Aramaic origin, such a possibility is even more likely. In 2 Sam. 7:12 the raising of the seed was actually expressed by using a parallelism: "I will raise up your offspring [AV: seed] after you, who shall come forth from your body [AV: out of thy bowels]." The descendant in flesh and blood (σάρξ) is the representative of the family.

There is one interesting text variant that may support this kind of interpretation. In the analysis of Acts 2 above we became acquainted with a reading where both the "loins" and the "flesh" are mentioned. D* reads Acts 2:30: " that of the fruit of his loins, according to the flesh (ἐκ καρποῦ τῆς ὀσφύος αὐτοῦ τὸ κατὰ σάρκα) he would raise up Christ." The writer of this specification has identified the fruit of the loins and σάρξ. If this identification was originally based on a general understanding of the similarity of the expressions, there would be evidence for the parallelity of those two expressions also in Romans 1:3.

This explanation would be in agreement with the analysis made above, according to which the clauses in verses 3 and 4 belong together under the same subject. In this case the κατὰ σάρκα in verse 3 would be merely a part of an expression describing the Davidic descendance of the Messiah, and the opposition of the expression with κατὰ πνεῦμα would be accidental. However, I do not reckon this the best explanation for the passage.

2. Should κατὰ σάρκα be seen as the counterpoint of κατὰ πνεῦμα? The argumentation growing out of the idea of a *parallelismus membrorum* in the

---
[60] Zimmermann, *Neutestamentliche Methodenlehre*, 200; Poythress, *ExpT 87* (1975) 180-181.

formula is far from being clear. There are several alternatives to interpret such parallelity.

In the New Testament flesh and spirit are often anthropological terms. In the interpretation of the formula such an alternative is rather impossible. How could only Jesus' spirit be connected with the resurrection? This necessarily implies a dualistic anthropology and it cannot be regarded a relevant feature for a Jewish Christian formula.[61]

Actually the term πνεῦμα ἁγιωσύνης is not an anthropological spirit of holiness in a general sense. It appears to be a substantive form of the term Holy Spirit, i.e. "Spirit of Holiness".[62] It has its background in a Hebrew original. The Septuagint uses only the adjective form "Holy Spirit", το πνεῦμα το ἅγιον (Dan. 5:12; 6:4; SapSol. 1:5). In spite of this we must remember that the word for Holy, *qâdôsh,* is both adjective and substantive in Aramaic and in Hebrew.[63] This is evidently the reason why in TLev. 18:11 we have the substantive form πνεῦμα ἁγιωσύνης in Greek.[64] Therefore, as regards the tradition history of the term, πνεῦμα ἁγιωσύνης in Romans is not neccessarily a plain translation of an Aramaic term. It may have been exploited in the formula since it is a well known term in Hellenistic Jewish eschatology.

Therefore the interpretation of the parallelity of the clauses, if there is any, must take semantics into account. If the parallelism is considered antithetical, flesh and the Holy Spirit must oppose each other. In this case they apparently represent two different realms. One may refer to Paul himself, who uses κατὰ σάρκα in this sense in Romans 9:3.[65] According to this alternative the first clause would be a genealogical statement. But what is the nature of the second clause? The Spirit of Holiness should be interpreted in its own context. The opposition for flesh would in this case be the "Pauline" thought of a spiritual resurrection existence. Quite like Paul in 1 Cor. 15, the formula would oppose, rather, neutral created flesh with the resurrection body, "spiritual body". This conception in 1 Cor. 15 is based on Christology. The one who has a spiritual body is Christ, the "second man" who is "from heaven" (1 Cor. 15:44-47). The problem with this interpretation is that the formula does not use this

---

[61] The old Sanday-Headlam commentary has proposed an anthropological interpretation, but the writers have had to reject the idea of the polarity of the clauses, see *Romans*, 7.

[62] So e.g. Black, *Romans*, 37; Dunn, *Romans*, 15; Ziesler, *Romans*, 63; Stuhlmacher, *Römer*, 21.

[63] In Aramaic the word occurs both as an adjective holy and a substantive (the latter in Dan. 4:10, 14, 20). This could explain the sustantive form in Greek.

[64] The substantive form is found also in an old Greek amulet, see Peterson, E., *Frühkirche, Judentum und Gnosis*, 249-351.

[65] Cf. flesh denoting descendance in Gen. 37:27.

language. The mere occurrence of the name Holy Spirit in this context does not yet communicate the idea of a spiritual body.

Usually the antithetical position of the terms is said to refer to the opposition of sinful flesh and the sphere of the Holy Spirit. This was one of the main arguments for the interpretation of a two-stage Christology. According to this alternative we should translate "in the sphere of flesh" and "in the sphere of the Spirit of Holiness".[66] According to Paul Christ no doubt appears in the form of sinful flesh (Romans 8:1ff.), but can we ascribe such theology to a pre-Pauline Jewish Christian formula? Schweizer is right when noting that already in Jewish theology "flesh" had a negative connotation of sinfulness. In the explanation of the formula, however, it is exactly this interpretation that creates most problems.

If the messianic statement in verse 3 is claimed to refer to the existence of sinful flesh, it no longer has anything to do with the second clause. If it had, the antithesis would have no significance. Also the "sphere of the Spirit of Holiness" is a difficult conception. It has meaning in the sense of 1 Cor. 15, but when this passage is exploited, it brings the same problems that we discussed above. Therefore, the idea of a two-stage Christology does not seem to be a relevant argument for a consistent interpretation of the formula. All of the explanations where the intentional antithesis is suggested appear to rest on weak justification.

3. Lastly, there is the possibility that the opposition in the final formula is secondary. Could κατὰ σάρκα be Paul's own theological insertion to the original formula? There is some justification for this view. Firstly, it recognizes that πνεῦμα ἁγιωσύνης as a *hapax legomenon* belongs to the tradition. Secondly, several scholars have noted that the flesh and spirit antithesis as such looks "suspiciously Pauline".[67] The evidence for similar language has most often been taken from Paul's letters, not from Second Temple Jewish writings. In Paul's theology the antithesis does serve his intentions in Christology (Rom. 8:1ff.; 9:3; 1 Cor. 15:35ff.). Thirdly, in this way we are able to explain why there is tension between the basic message of the passage and the extant antithetical position of the clauses.

Therefore, a proper solution for the basic problem of the antithesis seems to be that the occurring opposition in the formula is secondary. It must be regarded as Paul's redaction.[68] The expression κατὰ σάρκα may be Paul's insertion, or it may be that Paul has exploited an expression concerning

---

[66] See especially Schweizer, *EvTh 15* (1955) 569.

[67] The expression of Poythress, *ExpT 87* (1975) 180.

[68] In this I agree with Linnemann, *EvT 31* (1971) 273.

descendance so that it gives the impression of belonging to the realm of flesh. The mentioning of the Spirit of Holiness, i.e. God's Spirit, belongs to the original formula. The Holy Spirit has acted in the exaltation. This, naturally, was a view that Paul also would subscribe to.[69]

This kind of messianology derives clearly from Second Temple Jewish eschatology. In the area of Jewish messianology the ocurrence of the words power and Spirit in such context is common. Both of them are well known attributes of the Messiah in the Old Testament and Jewish writings (Isa. 11:2; TLev. 18:11; PsSol. 17:37).

As regards the term ἐν δυνάμει, its position has also appeared to be rather complex. According to the syntax it can be explained as an attribute either for the Son, or the designation, unless it is considered instrumental then it should be connected with the Spirit. According to the present explanation the word is rather senseless if it is considered an attribute for a designation in the past. The instrumental interpretation is weak, as well, because one would expect quite another kind of syntax if that were the purpose of the writer.[70] Therefore the word must be connected with the Son. This solution is also best in agreement with the theological content of the expression. The exalted Jesus is a "Son of God in power."

Next we must return briefly to the expression meaning resurrection (ἐξ ἀναστάσεως νεκρῶν).[71] This expression has also disturbed scholars. If the original writer were speaking of the resurrection of Jesus, he should most evidently have written ἀνάστασις ἐκ νεκρῶν.[72] In this case the expression would speak merely of Jesus' resurrection and underline the event of resurrection at Easter.

When taken literally, however, the expression is speaking about the resurrection of the dead (ἀνάστασις νεκρῶν).[73] Jesus' resurrection has been

---

[69] For instance in Romans 8:11 the Spirit is an agent of resurrection both for Jesus and for believers, and furthermore the guarantee of the coming resurrection for the latter on the basis of the former.

[70] See e.g. Linnemann, who has suggested the instrumental interpretation. In her reconstruction even the Greek has been changed when she translates the new clause "by the power of the Spirit of Holiness." Linnemann, *EvT 31* (1971) 274.

[71] For a general overview, see especially Hooke, *NTS 9* (1963) 370ff.

[72] A problem noted e.g. by Sanday-Headlam, *Romans*, 10. Already Lietzmann considers the extant form merely a shortening of a longer original possessing also the latter *ek*. Lietzmann, *Römer*, 25. So also Hahn, *Hoheitstitel*, 255f.

[73] This alternative is accepted e.g. by Nygren, *Romarbrevet*, 57; Michel, *Römer* (1955), 32; Bartsch, *ThZ 23* (1967) 333; Hooke, *NTS 9* (1963) 371; Langevin, *ScEs 29* (1977) 163; Wilckens, *Römer*, 65; Dunn, *Romans*, 34; Froitzheim, *Christologie*, 103; Schmithals, *Römerbrief*, 50; Stuhlmacher, *Römer*, 22.

described in terms of an eschatological resurrection. Such an expression fits well in with early Jewish Christianity and we can assume that the conception of resurrection had been taken from Second Temple Jewish eschatology. In Jewish theology resurrection was the crucial event that preceded divine judgment in the end of days.[74]

In Acts 26 we find a similar conception. Christ who has suffered is the first one who has been raised in the resurrection of the dead (Acts 26:23):

πρῶτος ἐξ ἀναστάσεως νεκρῶν.

In the description of the formula from Romans we are therefore in the middle of an eschatological discourse where the theme of the resurrection of the dead is being brought among the themes of messianology. What kind of connection can be found between the Davidic dynasty, the resurrection of the dead and the easter experience of the followers of Jesus? The formula maintains that the enthronement of the messianic Davidide has taken place in the eschatological event of the resurrection of the dead. The resurrection of Jesus was not merely an exaltation to heaven or a raising to a new life. It marked the beginning of the eschatological resurrection of the dead.[75]

Paul himself appears to be quite familiar with this kind of theology. For instance in 1. Cor. 15 and Rom. 8 he regarded Jesus' resurrection precisely as the beginning of the general resurrection of the dead. We might thus state that Paul's letters are good evidence for the reception of this kind of early Christian eschatology. The prologue of the Romans happens to reveal the historical roots of that eschatology through the short expression that we have investigated here.[76]

Therefore we can state that there is a clear apocalyptic scene behind the Christology of the formula. The anticipated messianic Davidide has come, and God has raised him to power. He sits enthroned on a heavenly throne. This event marks the beginning of the last age. The eschatological covenant promised to David has come true under the reign of the new Davidide (Isa. 11:1-10; 55:3-5).[77]

Finally we must treat the closing sentence of the sequence. It should not be excluded from the analysis without discussion. There are formal as well as

---

[74] Cf. Isa 26:19; Dan. 12:2; 1 En. 102-103; PsSol. 2:30f., 3:11f., 14:6f.

[75] So e.g. Kegel, *Auferstehung*, 31f.

[76] Hill actually believes that the expression is one proof for the pre-Pauline origin of the formula. Hill, *Greek Words*, 280. Unfortunately, the argument may as well be used as evidence for a Pauline origin of the expression. On theological grounds, however, it should not be considered Paul's insertion.

[77] See Bartsch, *ThZ 23* (1967) 335; Jewett, *Living Text*, 115.

theological reasons for this. Firstly, the mentioning of Jesus here again is an unnecessary repetition when the content of Paul's theme is considered. Therefore the exclamation may belong to the original formula. Secondly the clause is formular. This does not, of course, automatically mean that such a common formulation should have been a part of the original formula. On the other hand, however, it does not rule out the possibility that it did.

On theological grounds we can say that the epiteths used here fit well in the Royal messianology exploited in the formula. Jesus is Messiah as well as *Kyrios* when he is being exalted to the universal kingship. According to Psalms 2 and 110 these are the epiteths or metaphors for the Davidide who shall fulfill the eschatological expectations of God's kingdom.

During the analysis we have thus reached certain conclusion that affect the reconstruction of the formula and its interpretation. The most important of these are the following.

1. The "seed of David" is a Messianic metaphor.

2. The participles are attributes for the subject υἱός, and thus the clauses belong closely together. There is no strict *parallelismus membrorum* between the clauses.

3. The simplest way of translating ὁρίζω appears to be also the best one. In this context the word denotes designation in the past.

4. The words Son of God and power belong together. In his enthronement the Davidide has become a king in power.

5. While the clauses belong together, γίνομαι already in verse 3 refers to the fulfillment of the ancient decree in the exaltation. When Jesus has come "from the seed of David" he is precisely the Messiah whose raising (*qûm*) had been decreed in the Scriptures.

6. The Spirit of Holiness denotes the Spirit of God, i.e. the Holy Spirit.

7. The resurrection of the dead should be read literally as it is. The writer means the eschatological resurrection that inaugurates the last events.

8. The raising of the Davidide has come true in the eschatological resurrection of the dead, in which Jesus as the first fruits has been exalted to be the Son of God in power.

9. Thus the whole formula describes the enthroned Davidide whose exaltation has been promised beforehand. The first clause does not explicitly refer to the genealogical descendance of Jesus, even though it naturally implies it. Therefore the antithetical nature of the passage must be regarded as secondary, and κατὰ σάρκα is to be held as a Pauline insertion.

The third clause has most probably belonged to the original formula, as it describes Jesus as Kyrios in the same manner as the paralleling passages e.g.

in the Acts. It also provides a necessary subject for the descriptive participial clauses.[78]

A dynamic translation, parts of which have already been suggested above, must therefore be completed in the following manner:

"From the seed of David,
the promised Son of God in power,
according to the Holy Spirit, through the resurrection of the dead,
Jesus the Messiah, our Lord."

During the analysis we have thus arrived at a new interpretation concerning the passage. Firstly, the analysis confirms the suggestion that verses 3 and 4 cannot be explained satisfactorily by means of linguistic methodology. The parallel nature of the clauses does not help us explain the details of the passage. Secondly, a detailed analysis of the clauses brings up a new hypothesis as regards the dynamics of the Christological statement. It seems evident that the act of interpretation must work backwards between verses 3 and 4. The statement in verse 3 of the Davidic descendance of Jesus needs to be interpreted with the help of verse 4, where God's divine designation is mentioned. We must remember that the descriptive participial clauses describe the new status of Christ. They are not active expressions describing some kind of process.[79]

If ὁρίζω means designation, the original writer must have been thinking of a special decree that can be found in the Scriptures. Therefore the γίνομαι in verse 3 as such refers to the fulfillment of that decree. It seems quite consistent to explain such an idea of fulfillment in the context of early Christology, where 2 Sam. 7:12-14, in particular, is used as a Scriptural proof for Davidic Messianology. When Jesus has come "from the seed of David" he is exactly the Messiah whose raising (*qûm*) had been decreed in the Scriptures. This raising has come true in the eschatological resurrection of the dead, in which Jesus as the first fruits has been exalted as the Son of God in power.

---

[78] This kind of new approach to the passage does not justify, however, the idea that we could ascribe the original formulation of the clauses to Paul himself. Whitsett is right when stating that several features in the prologue of Romans are similar to the themes that Paul discusses during the letter. Whitsett, *JBL 119* (2000) 664ff., 681. He has not, however, paid proper attention to the linguistic problems of the formula. Paul exploits traditional materials even here, but he does so in his own personal manner.

[79] Against e.g. Scott, *Adoption*, 239f. He states that even though there is no antithetical parallelism in the section, one can find a climatic parallelism here. "For the second clause echoes the first in terms of formal structure, but adds to it an element which carries forward the sense to its culmination: the son of David was 'appointed Son of God in power'." Scott still seems to believe in the strict formal structure of the passage, and what is more important, he states that a process is described in these participial clauses.

Most details in the passage reveal a close relationship between the symbolic world of both Old Testament messianology and Second Temple Jewish mysticism. The exaltation of the Davidide is a transcendent exaltation that takes place in the resurrection of the dead. In his resurrection Jesus is enthroned on a heavenly throne, assumedly in the heavens where God resides. As an enthroned king he is a Son of God in power. Such an idea of a universal rule is common in the enthronement descriptions of Jewish mysticism. In the next section we will attempt to analyse the content of this kind of Christology and also to locate it in the context of Second Temple Jewish thinking.

6.3. Enthronement theme in the context of resurrection discourse

Even though most of the passages where the enthronement of the Davidide is described could be included in enthronement discourse, in a passage like Romans 1:3-4 the aspect of resurrection is dominant. Therefore, it is justified to explain it as part of a special resurrection discourse. The aspect of enthronement is merely implied here, because the throne or a corresponding submetaphor are not explicitly mentioned.

The idea of an enthronement, however, belongs essentially to the Christology of the passage.[80] The analysis made earlier has shown that the writer of the original Christology has been dependent on the symbolic world of early Jewish Christianity. In this passage we find therefore a reference to the implied enthronement of a Davidide, a description of the Son of God in power, and a reference to an enthronement in resurrection. These elements alone connect this formula with other significant texts of early Christology.[81]

Despite the general similarities as regards passages that belong to the sphere of enthronement discourse, the prologue of Romans contains several features typical of a special resurrection discourse. The most prominent ones of these are the word-play on resurrection and the reference to the resurrection of the dead. The word-play especially reveals the intertextual level that lies behind the present expression.

As regards the explanation of the word-play, one needs to return to the tradition history of the passage. The Old Testament background, common to

---

[80] To state this is no novelty in scholarship, though. See for instance Blank: "The text does not speak about an 'adoption' but about an 'enthronement'; this is an enthronement formula." Blank, *Paulus und Jesus*, 253. Cf. also Thüsing, *Per Christum in Deum*, 145. A quite detailed interpretation was given by Hayes. "The earliest Christology was based on an interpretation of the Resurrection as Jesus' enthronement as the Messiah in the heavenly sphere at the right hand of God... Such an interpretation was dependent upon an eschatological, messianic exegesis of certain Old Testament passages (especially Pss 110.1; 2.7 and 2 Sam 7) which reflected the Davidic royal theology." Hayes, *Interp.* XXII (1968) 345.

[81] Cf. e.g. Beasley-Murray, *TynB 31* (1980) 152; Froitzheim, *Christologie*, 102.

most key passages of early Christology and referring to the Septuagint passage of 2 Sam. 7 (ἀναστήσω τὸ σπέρμα σου μετὰ σέ), would imply that enthronement and resurrection should be identified also in the formula. They were clearly considered identical in Acts 2:33-36, and in Hebrews 1 the situation was the same. In this respect the formula appears to belong to a similar tradition. In the passage the Davidide is a Son of God in power for the sake of the resurrection. Raising becomes thus the act of the enthronement of the "seed".[82]

Such Christology is most evidently based on a word-play between raising and resurrection. This word-play works both on the level of Hebrew (*qûm*) and Greek (ἀνίστημι) as we have seen earlier. The Old Testament decree concerning the raising, i.e. the enthronement, of a Davidic king has been interpreted as the resurrection of Jesus as a Davidide. The raising means resurrection – therefore the resurrection means enthronement.[83] The "sense" of such a word-play comes from the intertextual reality.

This notion is quite important for the identification of the Christology of the formula. Even though a throne is not mentioned here, and Psalm 110 is not referred or alluded to, an enthronement is evidently described in these verses.[84] Through the resurrection Jesus is a Davidic Messiah who has been enthroned on a heavenly throne and now he reigns in power. Therefore the key elements of the Christology of the passage are identical with the Christology of Acts 2 and Hebrews 1, where resurrection was also identified as enthronement.

Resurrection discourse must further be the reason why there is an explicit mentioning of the resurrection of the dead in the formula. As we noted above, Jesus' resurrection has been described in terms of an eschatological resurrection (cf. Acts 26:23). The formula of Romans is therefore an eschatological description where the theme of resurrection of the dead is being brought among the themes of messianology. The formula maintains that the enthronement of the messianic Davidide has taken place in the eschatological

---

[82] See already Michel and Betz: "Das ἀναστήσω liess sich mit der ἀνάστασις verbinden, und so ist es wohl möglich, dass die alte christologische Formel, die Paulus eingangs des Römerbriefes zitiert, an II Sam 7:12ff. orientiert ist." Michel-Betz, *Judentum*, 6.

[83] Hayes still thought that both terminological and eschatological concepts existed "ready at hand" to be used by the early Church. Hayes, *Interp. XXII* (1968) 343. We should rather pay attention to the transformation that is made in the Christology of the formula, since the word-play was not yet exploited in pre-Christian Jewish writings.

[84] Duling remarks that the formula does not mention a throne or a kingdom. All the elements of the promise tradition are thus not present in the formula. Therefore one is entitled to speak of enthronement only in a metaphorical sense. Duling, *NTS 19* (1973) 73. The analysis has proved, however, that an implied enthronement is necessarily behind the train of thought here.

event of the resurrection of the dead.[85] In this respect, the Christology of Romans 1:3-4 differs in detail from the Christology of those passages belonging to the enthronement discourse. The difference is not remarkable, however. It is rather a question of different emphasis, even though the main content remains the same. The making of a distinction between the discourses is helpful, though, since it helps one to discern the significance of certain details in this passage.

But what about merkabah mysticism? Does merkabah mysticism fit in with the interpretation of this passage as it did in the interpretation of Acts 2:33-36? Certain comparisons will clarify the question.

1. In a general sense the Christology of Romans 1 conforms to the ideas of Jewish merkabah mysticism. The passage is clearly speaking of a transcendent heavenly rule. As in the presentations of Jewish mysticism, here also Christ is presented as a heavenly king. The motif of the enthronement of an earthly king is thus functioning as a metaphor which is expressing the significance of the new status Jesus has received. In Acts 2 we had a significant eschatological event that took place in heaven and the throne of God was the centre of everything. In Romans 1 the throne as such is not mentioned. Therefore one cannot identify the place of the enthroned one as God's throne. The idea of heavenly enthronement, however, is identical with the teachings of Jewish merkabah mysticism.

2. As regards the enthronement the description differs from that of Acts 2. Since Psalm 110 is not referred to, we do not find the expression "at the right hand". Christ is simply a Son of God in power. This is due to the changed discourse. The explicit wording of the formula does not follow the lines of usual enthronement discourse. The "mystical" nature of the enthronement, however, is identical both in Acts 2 and Romans 1. The enthronement takes place in the resurrection. The Davidide is enthroned on a heavenly throne. The throne itself may be the throne of glory or Messiah's own throne.[86]

3. In both of these writings the exalted Christ is a Davidic Messiah. In this respect there is no difference between the passages. Christ is neither an angelic being nor an exalted patriarch. He is a heavenly king that has been enthroned

---

[85] According to Casey the formula merely "dates Jesus' sonship from the resurrection." Casey, *Jewish prophet,* 111. This kind of view ignores the aspect of enthronement.

[86] Burger suggested that in Jewish tradition the son of David would as such be simultaneously the son of God. In this respect he concludes that in the formula there is another kind of conviction. Jesus is the Son of God only after his resurrection. Burger, *Davidssohn,* 26-27. This cannot be true, however. In Jewish tradition the Davidide becomes a son of God on the coronation day. In this respect, there are no essential differences between these two traditions.

above all other beings and who reigns in heaven.[87] Therefore the eschatology of the formula in Romans 1 is also based on an anticipation of the eschatological enthronement of a Davidide. As we already noted in respect of Acts 2, an interpretation concerning the fulfillment of such an anticipation implies both an ascent structure and merkabah speculation, since the exalted Davidide is a heavenly ruler.[88]

In the analysis we ended up with a conclusion that the parallelism in verses 3 and 4 must in fact be read backwards. God's divine "appointment" or decree mentioned in verse 4 refers both to the seed of David mentioned in verse 3 and to resurrection mentioned in verse 4. The Resurrected One is the promised one who has already come (γενόμενος). This has been an appropriate way to emphasize that the enthroned Jesus is *the* Davidide.

4. In the formula of Romans the exalted Christ is called Son of God. On the one hand this appellation belongs to Old Testament royal ideology, where it is often attached to the Davidide. On the other hand, however, we may see here another link to Jewish mysticism. As we saw above, in Qumran writings the highest figures in the heavenly Holy of Holies were called gods. In the interpretation of Acts 2 we doubted, however, the idea of a "missing link" between Jewish mysticism and early Christology. The same must be done here. It does not seem probable that the Qumranian idea was the reason for the high Christology in the formula. Jesus was not simply considered a God in the heavenly *debir* because his exaltation resembles the pattern. We need to approach the subject from another angle.

As Jewish Christian theologians accepted the identification of Jesus with the exalted Son of God, the rest was consistent with their earlier beliefs. The heavenly Son of God was not an angelic figure. He was a messianic Davidide, a *Kyrios* on the heavenly throne. This conception connected such Christology to Jewish messianology.

5. In Acts 2 exaltation Christology was *Kyrios*-Christology. This is most probably true also in Romans 1. The *Kyrios*-statement in verse 4b is an

---

[87] There has been discussion about the significance of the appellation 'Messiah' as regards both Second Temple Judaism and early Christianity. According to Charlesworth, for instance, one should not overemphasize the title 'Messiah' in the last clause of the formula, since there is the danger of becoming "blind to the many other titles attributed to Jesus." Charlesworth, *Judaisms*, 253. He states that the confession is really about the celebration of the identity of 'God's Son.' One should not, however, forget that God's Son in this passage is precisely the messianic Davidide.

[88] According to Merklein such exaltation Christology about the appointment of Jesus in a messianic ministry implies a theological theme similar to that of the Son of Man Christology. Jesus as an enthroned king in heaven is identified with an eschatological judge who will enter upon the last judgment. Merklein, *ZNW 72* (1981) 20.

essential part of the description. According to most scholars the participial clauses in verses 3-4 must also have referred to an explicated subject.[89] The statement in 4b "Jesus Christ our Lord" may therefore have belonged already to the original formula. If this is so, this formula speaking of the enthronement of a messianic Davidide has also been part of the *Kyrios*-Christology of the early period. This is naturally possible, because not all Christological statements mentioning *Kyrios* in the New Testament refer to Psalm 110. The content of the formula fits in the abovementioned construction. Jesus is *Kyrios* only on the heavenly throne where he reigns.

Further, and here again in the same manner as in Acts 2, the "seed" of David in his resurrection is Χριστός, the Anointed One. The resurrection day has become a coronation day, and the Davidide has been anointed into kingship. This point of view confirms our hypothesis that the first clause does not speak of a Messiah designate. It refers to the enthronement and the actual installation of the Davidide.

6. There is further one aspect that demands our attention, and it is probably more clearly seen in the investigation of Romans 1 due to the resurrection discourse. According to both passages the enthronement took place in resurrection. These two eschatological events fall into one. In Jewish writings resurrection was never actually identified with any heavenly enthronement. When combining the themes of enthronement and the resurrection of the dead, the writer of the formula has in fact combined two such eschatological themes which have no immediate causal relationship to each other. The conception of resurrection in Romans 1 is even more informative than the one in Acts 2. The formula speaks of the resurrection of the dead. This must necessarily mean the general Jewish conception of an eschatological resurrection.[90] The original writer of the formula has thus believed that the general resurrection of the last days has begun in the resurrection of Jesus.[91]

This conception opens up a new horizon for the interpretation of the Christology of the formula. The theme of the resurrection of the dead functions here as a watershed between two ages of salvation history. According to the

---

[89] See the analysis above.

[90] In agreement with Kegel, *Auferstehung*, 31-32, and against Hahn and Becker who speak merely of Jesus' resurrection. See Hahn, *Hoheitstitel*, 255. Becker states that the resurrection from the dead has no apocalyptic meaning in this context. Becker, *Auferstehung*, 30.

[91] Hahn thinks that the joining of the enthronement and resurrection results in a change in the enthronement theology of the early Church. The enthronement no longer leads directly to the judgment of God. Hahn, *Hoheitstitel*, 257. It might be better to speak of realized eschatology. Jesus' reign has begun and eschatological reality has begun. The judgment is still to come. Cf. Schade, *Christologie*, 32-33.

writer the day of salvation has come. The promised Davidide has been enthroned on his heavenly throne. The resurrection of the dead has begun. The days of divine grace are here. It is apparently no coincidence that Paul uses this kind of eschatology also in 1 Cor. 15 when teaching about resurrection (1 Cor. 15:20-25). The risen Christ is the "first fruits of those who have died" (v. 20).[92] There is, however, a crucial difference between Jesus' resurrection and the resurrection of his followers. Believers shall be resurrected only "at his coming" (v. 23).

If this idea of salvation history is taken further in the interpretation, we might even speak of an implicit theme of new covenant behind the formula. Jesus' enthronement may now be explained as the inauguration of a new Davidic covenant, the promised covenant of grace (Is. 55:3).[93] Exalted Christ reigns in the new kingdom which is constructed on the eschatological reality of resurrection.[94]

7. This explanation alters the traditional interpretation of the passage significantly. In Schweitzer's two-stage interpretation the clauses were separated from each other. The first clause was said to describe the earthly stage of Jesus' mission, and the second clause was believed to describe his resurrection to heavenly realm.[95]

In the light of the analysis made here this kind of explanation misses the point of the early writer. The only scheme in the passage is that of salvation history. God has decreed something in the past, and now it appears to have been fulfilled. It is a message of the enthronement of a Davidide. The writers of early Christology did not concentrate on the earthly "stage" of Jesus' ministry, nor did they contradict it with his exaltation. The Davidic descendance of Jesus expresses his Messiahship as the enthroned one whose

---

[92] Cf. Acts 26:23.

[93] For this kind of interpretation, see e.g. Bartsch, *ThZ 23* (1967) 332, 335; Jewett, *Living Text*, 115.

[94] Cf. Bartsch: "Die Totenauferstehung und Jesu Auferstehung wurden ursprünglich einfach gleichgesetzt, und die Heidenmission war die notwendige Folgerung, die Öffnung der Tempels für die Völker der apokalyptische Topos, der sie veranlasste. Nur in einem Punkte herrschte Klarheit: Jesu Tod und Auferstehen wurden auf den Einbruch des verheissenen Gottesreiches bezogen, mit diesem Ereignis hatte die Erfüllung eingesetzt." Bartsch, *ThZ 23* (1967) 335.

[95] In addition to the previously mentioned literature, see Schweizer, *Studies*, 187; Hahn, *Hoheitstitel*, 254. In modern study of Christology for example de Jonge, *Christology*, 49; and Pesch, *Christus*, 215.

resurrection and exaltation had been promised beforehand.[96] As we noted above, the latter clause in fact refers to the former, and thus the alleged "scheme" of the formula turns into its opposite.[97]

8. The final conclusion from these details is that the formula in Romans 1:3-4 belongs indeed to the context of early Christology that has exploited Jewish merkabah mysticism and which is constructed on the world view and symbolic world of Jewish mysticism. In this early formula we find a description of an ascension in the eschatological resurrection and an enthronement of the Davidide as the Son of God in power. The interpretation of the content of the formula is not intelligible unless we assume that there is an implied ascent structure behind the train to thought. The original writer of the formula has described the heavenly enthronement of the Messiah in his homology.

---

[96] So also Becker, *Auferstehung*, 27. Theobald calls the vanishing of the aspect of political Messianology "Entpolitisierung". As Schweitzer underlined a dichotomy between Jewish and Christian Messianology inside the formula, Theobald locates the dichotomy in the background of the formula. Theobald, *Kontinuität*, 384.

[97] In a later article de Jonge changed his explanation and suggested that the clauses present merely two different viewpoints; de Jonge, *Jewish Eschatology*, 143. According to the present analysis, this kind of explanation also misses the original nature of the formula.

§ 7 Throne as a Place for the Atonement (*cultic discourse*)

In the second part of this study we suggested that the link between Old Testament priestly religion and Second Temple apocalypticism could be found in the sacral mysticism attached to Temple cult. Such mysticism transcended the conception of the throne, and the relation between heavenly reality and the earth, between the heavenly shrine and Jerusalem Temple became essential for Temple liturgy. In Second Temple Jewish theology, therefore, one can detect a cultic discourse that was applied to different subjects.

Such cultic discourse is familiar to us also from merkabah mysticism. In ascent stories seers saw and sometimes even joined heavenly worship in the Temple above. In this kind of discourse God's dwellings are described as a Temple where priestly figures, other than human, perform cultic actions. These figures apparently have a hierarchy in their organization, as well. Thus the priestly ministry also has its metaphorical counterpoint in the heavenly Temple.

Also in the New Testament a similar cultic discourse can be detected. Already in the preceding chapters we have seen some traits according to which there is a connection between enthronement statements and New Testament cultic soteriology. The cultic aspect in exaltation Christology is rather strong. In cultic interpretation the throne of God is, in particular, the mercy seat of the Holy of Holies, the *debir*. It is obvious that the images of the symbolic world, common to enthronement discourse, have now been applied to a new discourse. Therefore the meaning of the terms, as well as the meaning of christological statements, have been changed.

7.1. The throne as a mercy seat

In the letter to the Hebrews heavenly Temple and Jerusalem Temple are strictly contrasted. Previous shrines, both the Mosaic place of worship in the wilderness and the Temple in Jerusalem are dismissed by one essential argument. The earthly shrine is a "sanctuary made by human hands". It is merely a "copy of the true one" (Heb. 9:24).[1] The heavenly Temple is the true Temple of God.

This view does not resemble traditional schismatic Jewish Temple criticism. We have earlier seen how for instance at Qumran the Covenanters resisted Jerusalem because the sanctuary had been defiled by a false high priesthood. According to Qumran eschatology the aim of the sect was to seize the Temple and reform its worship.[2] In addition to this, however, the functions of the

---

[1] Cf. Isaacs, *Early Christian thought*, 149.

[2] See e.g. Cross, *Qumran*, 100ff., Milik, *Discovery*, 44ff.

Temple had also been transferred. Qumran sectarians believed that the community itself was actually a new Temple. Therefore, it could also provide atonement for its members.

The idea of a new Temple was embodied in the council of the community. There was an atonement for sins in the community, but it was acquired in the manner of Second Temple sapiential theology.[3] Atonement was linked to obedience. The council of this priestly community was considered the "holy of holies for Aaron" (1QS VIII, 5-8) and its strict asceticism and perfect life atoned for the sins of the members.[4]

In Hebrews there is no reference to a defilement of the Jerusalem Temple. It was the whole covenant that had to be changed (Heb. 8:13). When this change was described the idea of a heavenly Temple became essential. It was a logical counterpoint for the earthly Temple and its worship.

There are actually two different ways in which the writer of the Hebrews exploits the idea of the heavenly Temple. Firstly, there is what one could call an apocalyptic notion of an actual Temple in heaven.[5] It is described as a heavenly building where different priestly functions are performed. According to Hebrews 8 Christ is "a minister in the sanctuary and the true tent that the Lord, and not any mortal, has set up." (Heb. 8:2).[6]

Secondly, though, in Hebrews 9 there is another kind of conception of a temple-structured universe. Here the earthly shrine as a whole is compared to the "first tent" (9:8). According to the writer, the way into the sanctuary "has not yet been disclosed as long as the first tent is still standing." Only Christ as a new high priest has now entered the factual Holy of Holies, i.e. heaven.[7]

"For Christ did not enter a sanctuary made by human hands, a mere copy of the true one, but he entered into heaven itself, now to appear in the presence of God on our behalf." (9:24).

It is apparent, however, that the former view dominates the theology of the writer. As we have noted earlier, such a view most probably derives from a Jewish *pargod* (curtain) speculation.[8] According to that mystical view the heavenly palace is depicted as a Temple and the throne itself is identified as the

---

[3] See my analysis elsewhere, Eskola, *Theodicy*, 87ff.

[4] See e.g. 1QS III, 6-9. For such a view, cf. Gärtner, *Temple*, 20f., Klinzing, *Umdeutung*, 105; Janowski, *Sühne*, 264; Vermes, *Qumran in Perspective*, 163.

[5] Cf. TLev. 3:4; see the analysis in chapter 3.2.

[6] For the discernment of different conceptions of the heavenly Temple, see MacRae, *Semeia* 12 (1987) 187; cf. Buchanan, *Hebrews*, 132ff.; Rissi, *Theologie*, 36ff.

[7] So MacRae, *Semeia* 12 (1987) 187; against Hofius, *Der Vorhang*, 61.

[8] See 3.1. and Hofius, *Der Vorhang*, 4ff., 17f., 71.

mercy seat.⁹ In the letter to the Hebrews such a background explains the meaning that is given to the heavenly throne. It is located in the context of cultic discourse, and therefore it also has a new function. In the heavenly Temple and especially in the Holy of Holies the throne, ἱλαστήριον, is now explicitly the cover of the ark. This is evident while the *debir* on earth (9:5) is presented as a model for the heavenly Holy of Holies (9:12). On that ἱλαστήριον sacrifice is given and atonement is made by sprinkling blood upon the mercy seat (Lev. 16:15f.).

The identification of the ark with God's throne is evident already on the grounds of the reference to the "cherubim of glory" (9:5).¹⁰ As we have seen in 1 Sam. 4:4, the Lord was assumed to be "enthroned on the cherubim". Elsewhere in Hebrews the ark is called for instance the "throne of grace" (4:16) which believers can approach.¹¹ Above all it is the place of God's presence and revelation.¹²

Temple symbolism is thus explicit in Hebrews, but it has been exploited for the needs of Christology. Ministry of a high priest is the metaphor that has been applied to the resurrected Christ. The ἱλαστήριον is important since it brings forth the symbolism of the Day of Atonement. Jesus is now the high priest who enters the Holy of Holies with blood. The interpretation is brave, but in the context of Jewish theology it is however quite consistent. The centre of Jewish cultic soteriology has become the centre of Christian soteriology.

As we saw above, the enthronement scene of the letter was of cultic nature already in the first lines of the work: "When he had made purification for sins, he sat down at the right hand of the Majesty on high" (1:3-4). Thereafter, temple symbolism is prominent throughout the letter. In his death Jesus has entered the inner shrine behind the curtain (6:19), the heavenly sanctuary "to appear in the presence of God" (9:24).

The sacrificial ritual becomes then the main theme of the letter. "Christ... through the eternal Spirit offered himself without blemish to God" (9:14). Actually it was the blood that was offered as a perfect sacrifice, expressed here simply with an adjective ἄμωμον, to God (τὸ αἷμα τοῦ Χριστοῦ, ὃς διὰ πνεύματος

---

⁹ According to Loader the idea of atonement in Hebrews implies the concept of a heavenly sanctuary. He does not accept, however, the view that there would be two different concepts of the heavenly temple in Hebrews. Loader, *Sohn*, 182f. His criticism remains unconvincing, since the idea of a temple-structured universe appears to be a distinctive feature in the letter, even though it is not a dominating one.

¹⁰ See Attridge, *Hebrews*, 238. Cf. Lev. 16:2; Ezek. 1:10.

¹¹ For the new meaning of the throne, see e.g. Michel, *Hebräer*, 124.

¹² "Die Kapporet ist der eigentliche Ort der Gegenwart Gottes, seiner Offenbarung, Sühnstätte im eigentlichen Sinn." Michel, *Hebräer*, 303.

αἰωνίου ἑαυτὸν προσήνεγκεν ἄμωμον τῷ θεῷ). Like a high priest Christ entered the shrine: "[H]e entered once for all into the Holy Place, not with the blood of goats and calves, but with his own blood, thus obtaining eternal redemption" (9:12).[13]

This passage is a Christological pesher on the cultic text of Leviticus (16:15). The blood of Christ is a central element in this symbolism since it was also the blood of the sacrifice that was taken to the shrine according to Leviticus: "sprinkling it upon the mercy seat and before the mercy seat". The blood of a goat was sprinkled upon the ἱλαστήριον. For the writer of the Hebrews, then, the death of Christ meant the slaughtering of the sacrifice. In his resurrection Christ then acted as a high priest and entered the heavenly shrine with atoning blood.[14]

As in the Old Testament, also in Hebrews the throne of God is on the ark of the covenant. This throne is the place where atonement is obtained. It is not merely a place of devotion and worship. The blood of a sacrifice must be taken on that throne which, through the atonement, becomes a throne of grace. This description of Hebrews is thoroughly Jewish, while it naturally is simultaneously thoroughly christological. It belongs to the Jewish Christianity of the first century.

In his letters Paul too refers to that kind of conception. He has made good use of several traditional formulas that were known to him from the teaching of the first leaders of the early Church. These traditional formulas provide evidence for the fact that the cultic interpretation of easter events was constructed quite early. One of the most interesting of these passages is in first Corinthians.[15] "Christ died for our sins in accordance with the scriptures" (1 Cor. 15:3). Here the death of Jesus is interpreted as a cultic event. Jesus has given a sacrifice that has atoned for sins.

This formula, which in the context is connected to the first apostles, unites Paul with the transmission of a common easter message. It shows that Paul's theological roots lie in the same Jewish Christian tradition where the writer of the Hebrews also lived and worked.[16] In addition to this, Paul speaks often about sacrifice, blood, and even the ἱλαστήριον in his letters.

---

[13] The term denotes the absence of defects in a sacrificial animal; Num. 6:14 LXX. For the occurrence of the conception in Judaism, see Lane, *Hebrews 9-13*, 240.

[14] Cf. Lane, *Hebrews*, 238. The separation of the atonement from Christ's death has given birth to some theological discussion, see Bruce, *Hebrews*, 200ff. The basic idea of the cultic discourse here, however, seems to be evident. Atonement is linked with resurrection.

[15] For the analysis and the early dating of the formula, see e.g. Barrett, *I Corinthians*, 337ff., Conzelmann, *1 Corinthians*, 251-255.

[16] Cf. Hengel, *Anfänge*, 51.

Paul himself describes the death of Jesus as a sacrifice to God. In Romans 5 Paul uses Temple metaphors when speaking about the death of Jesus. According to Paul, the death of Christ is a sacrifice "for us" (ὑπὲρ ἡμῶν), and our justification is in "his blood" (v. 9). Furthermore, we are "reconciled to God through the death of his son" (κατηλλάγημεν τῷ θεῷ διὰ τοῦ θανάτου τοῦ υἱοῦ αὐτοῦ). By this obedience of Christ "the many will be made righteous" (διὰ τῆς ὑπακοῆς τοῦ ἑνὸς δίκαιοι κατασταθήσονται οἱ πολλοί; v. 19). Similarly in Romans 8:32, God "did not withhold his own Son, but gave him up for all of us" (ὑπὲρ ἡμῶν πάντων παρέδωκεν αὐτόν).

In these passages Christ acts as a high priest obtaining atonement by sprinkling his blood before God. Paul is simply describing a sin offering. This is a perfect act of reconciliation and in this sacrifice sinners will be made righteous. In the presentation of Romans 3 all this is even more clearly brought to the fore:

"all... are now justified by his grace as a gift, through the redemption that is in Christ Jesus, whom God put forward as a sacrifice of atonement [a place of atonement] by his blood" (Rom. 3:23-25).

According to this tradition, through his sacrifice Christ himself has become the ἱλαστήριον, the mercy seat (ὃν προέθετο ὁ θεὸς ἱλαστήριον διὰ [τῆς] πίστεως ἐν τῷ αὐτοῦ αἵματι 3:25).[17] This is not quite explicit any more in the translation of this verse. The tradition that Paul uses here is similar to the tradition of the Hebrews. The cover of the ark, the ἱλαστήριον, i.e. the throne of God, has now become a mercy seat. Jesus himself will be met on the place of atonement, when one seeks the presence of God.

The ἱλαστήριον serves in a way as a double metaphor here.[18] The throne is not merely the place where blood is sprinkled. Jesus as a person has become a ἱλαστήριον for all sinners who need atonement.[19] In addition to that Jesus' blood is emphasized as the reason for the redemption. Like in Leviticus, also here it is only blood that can obtain atonement.

---

[17] Michel suggests that the terms redemption and mercy seat have had a close relation to the liturgy of eucharistia. Michel, *Römer*, 92.

[18] The cultic term ἱλαστήριον has been exploited in a metaphoric sense also in Jewish theology. In 4 Macc. 17:22 the death of a martyr is described by using the same metaphor. Dunn is right, however, when commenting that this thought has no direct relation to the theology of Paul. Despite that, it is a good example of how the term was also exploited in Jewish tradition. Dunn, *Romans*, 171.

[19] I agree with Wilckens who remarks that there is no disagreement between the images of Jesus' blood and the ἱλαστήριον (Kapporät). "Sofern nun Gott Christus als Kapporät 'öffentlich hingestellt' hat, hat er den Gekreuzigten zum Ort erlösender Sühne für alle Glaubenden gemacht, an dem er selber gegenwärtig ist." Wilckens, *Römer*, 192.

It is probably no wonder that temple symbolism is prevalent also in the book of Revelation, in which we have previously detected traces of the influence of Jewish merkabah traditions. According to the writer, heaven is explicitly a temple and in the centre of that temple there is a throne (e.g. Rev. 4:2; 5:11; 7:9, 15; 11:16; 19:4; 20:11). These heavenly visions are rather similar to those found in the Songs of the Sabbath Sacrifice in Qumran. They both describe the heavenly Temple in detail.[20]

The throne itself is once called the ark of the covenant (11:19). The imagery seems to be evident. In that passage the seer is allowed to look into the heavenly Holy of Holies and he sees the "true" ark, which once served as an archetype for the construction of the ark in the earthly tabernacle.[21]

According to Revelation, the salvation at the end of time may be described as an endless worship before the throne of God:

"For this reason they are before the throne of God, and worship him day and night within his temple, and the one who is seated on the throne will shelter them." (7:15).[22]

Cultic soteriology is present in Revelation even from the beginning of the work. In the opening lines we meet a eulogy where the sacrificial blood of Christ not only frees from sins but also makes the believers priests serving the heavenly God. This aspect is also near the presentation of Qumran.

"To him who loves us and freed us from our sins by his blood, and made us to be a kingdom, priests serving his God and Father, to him be glory and dominion forever and ever." (Rev. 1:5-6).

In one of the opening visions of Revelation the cultic aspect is linked to Davidic messianology. Jesus is the "Lion of the tribe of Judah" and "the Root of David" (5:5). This Davidide, whose messiahship is the reason for an enthronement, is simultaneously the one who gives his sacrifice. In the vision John sees "between the throne and the four living creatures and among the elders a Lamb standing as if it had been slaughtered" (5:6).

These passages taken from several New Testament writings reveal

---

[20] Already 4:2 may be seen as parallel for instance to TLev. 5:1, even though the Temple itself is not mentioned here. In chapter 4, however, the Temple imagery with the heavenly liturgy is explicit. Aune speaks here merely of heavenly throne rooms (modelled after those of earthly kings), Aune, *Revelation 1-5*, 284. Ford states that the throne room "takes the place of the sanctuary." Ford, *Revelation*, 81. The writer apparently went farther than that and based his presentation on the conception of an apocalyptic Temple in heaven – a conception that was also held by the author of Hebrews.

[21] So Aune, *Revelation 6-16*, 677.

[22] Here also Aune admits that the presence of a temple in heaven is frequently mentioned in Revelation. On the basis of Jewish literature it is, furthermore, logical to present the heavenly temple as the location of the throne of God. Aune, *Revelation 6-16*, 475-476.

interesting features in early Christology. The use of cultic terminology in early soteriology is inventive and it also reinterprets Jewish tradition in a radical way. Christological theology of redemption differs from all earlier patterns of soteriology. In Qumran we saw a pattern of soteriology that was constructed in the context of temple criticism. In that situation, however, atonement was not based on a new sacrifice or sacrificial act in the community. Instead, atonement was provided by an atoning acting of the community and its council. On the other hand, the soteriology of Qumran was not directed against the Temple itself. According to the eschatology of the community a new era was anticipated, and a future messianic priest from the community was expected to renew the sacrifices of the Temple. For the Jewish Christian identity of Jesus' followers such an interpretation of soteriology was not sufficient enough.[23]

In Hebrews and in Pauline traditions temple and sacrifices were considered from a new point of view. The heavenly Temple was a prototype for the earthly Temple – but what is more, earthly worship was only a metaphor referring to the true heavenly ministry of the Messiah. When Christ acted as a high priest in the heavenly Temple, earlier worship was reduced to the status of a simple metaphor, and its primary meaning was no longer relevant for believers. Such a view is not only critical towards the Temple, but its attitude is basicly against the Temple of Jerusalem. The sacrifices of the old covenant may even threaten the unique significance of the redemption in Christ, if they are kept side by side with the sacrifice of Christ. Thus the Temple worship was replaced by faith in Christ whose blood atoned for sins.

In the cultic discourse of New Testament Christology several ideas from merkabah mysticism have been exploited. The description of heavenly things and events is not, however, identical with the conceptions of Jewish ascent structure. In ascent stories seers saw and sometimes even joined heavenly worship in the heavenly Temple. In New Testament Christology the resurrected Christ enters the heavenly Holy of Holies alone and takes the place of a high priest. Nevertheless, in exaltation Christology traditional symbols maintain their meaning. There is an ark in the heavenly Holy of Holies, and it becomes identified with God's throne. In this respect the relation between this kind of Christology and Jewish merkabah mysticism remains close. What is of special interest in this scene is that, in the cultic soteriology of the New Testament, the resurrection is the basic event for the atonement – not merely

---

[23] Contra Dunn, *Partings of the Ways*, 57-59, who claims, arguing on the basis of the first chapters of Acts, that first Christians maintained a Jewish conception of the temple and didn't even speak of the death of Jesus as a redemptive act. Such a view ignores both the passages investigated above and the cultic features of the traditions of Acts, see e.g Acts 2:36-38; 5:30-31.

the death of Jesus. Thus there is no tension between the themes of the sacrificial death of Jesus and the obtaining of atonement before the heavenly throne. But how was such unity of exaltation and atonement explained?

7.2. The unity of exaltation and atonement

A special feature in the cultic discourse of New Testament Christology is that Psalm 110 is also a key text here. Particularly in the letter to the Hebrews it plays an essential role. Through this Psalm Jesus' exaltation and his priestly ministry that obtains atonement were joined together.

In this Psalm the enthronement of the Davidide is identified with his priestly ministry according to a new order of priesthood (Psalm 110:1, 4):

"The Lord says to my lord, 'Sit at my right hand until I make your enemies your footstool.'... The Lord has sworn and will not change his mind, 'You are a priest forever according to the order of Melchizedek'."

Certain features are evident in this Psalm. Firstly, the Messianic figure is a Davidide, as we have seen in previous analyses. Furthermore, he is a priest-king who has a special status in the history of Israel. The Davidide king actually appears here as the heir of the Canaanite priest-king who had authority over Abraham.[24] From the point of view of Jewish theology such an invention was necessary when non-Aaronic priesthood needed to be justified.

The fact that Psalm 110 was exploited in the letter reveals the writer's intention. This concerns primarily the christological premise. He wished to present the resurrected Christ as a heavenly priest who offers a sacrifice for sins. In this respect there is also a link to the high-priest's ministry on the Day of Atonement. As Isaacs has noted, Hebrews works "within a system which assumes that sacrifice is the *sine qua non* of entry into the presence of God (9.22), since it removes the barrier of sin which divides the sacred from the profane."[25]

The Psalm as such no doubt served as a good starting point for such a presentation. The letter appears to be really a commentary on Psalm 110.[26] As we saw above, the letter begins with an exaltation statement, according to which Jesus is enthroned "at the right hand" of God (1:3), and this is later confirmed with a direct quotation of our Psalm (1:13). The leading theme of the letter, i.e. the high priesthood of Christ, is introduced by the help of that

---

[24] Cf. Delcor, *JSJ 2* (1971) 121.

[25] Isaacs, *Early Christian thought*, 152.

[26] For the special significance of Psalm 110 for the author, see Attridge, *Hebrews*, 23f., Lane, *Hebrews 1-8*, cxiii-cxvii. Buchanan called the letter actually "a homiletical midrash based on Ps 110." Buchanan, *Hebrews*, xix. Cf. the negative estimation of Lindars, *Theology*, 26.

Psalm (5:6). The priesthood of Christ has begun in resurrection, for which Psalm 110 is proof (6:20). After this notion there is a section where the priesthood of Melchizedek is described (7:1-28). Furthermore, as a Davidide promised in Psalm 110 Jesus has been enthroned "at the right hand" of God, where his royal messiahship is fulfilled in his priestly ministry, again according to Psalm 110. "[W]e have such a high priest, one who is seated at the right hand of the throne of the Majesty in the heavens." (8:1).

As a heavenly King Christ reigns and, according to the writer, also waits "until his enemies would be made a footstool for his feet." (10:12-13). Finally, at the end of the letter, Christ who has "endured the cross" and taken his seat "at the right hand" of God is the object of faith. The readers of the letter are encouraged to look "to Jesus the pioneer and perfecter of our faith." (12:2).

Such an emphasis on one sole text is remarkable. It is apparent that Psalm 110 has some feature that essentially discloses the writer's basic intention. This feature, quite evidently, is the combining of the exaltation and Christ's priestly function. The great purpose of the writer is to explain eternal atonement with the help of exaltation Christology.

In scholarly discussion, however, there has been one hermeneutical problem. In protestant biblical criticism the death of Jesus has usually been emphasized in soteriology. This has evidently been done for dogmatic reasons. Christ who "endured the cross" is the one who is the justification for sinners. Such a view does not, however, cover the whole spectrum of early christological soteriology. Exaltation Christology interpreting Psalm 110 combined the sacrifice and enthronement with the help of the idea of Christ's high priestly ministry. It would be a mistake to contrast these two aspects on the level of the premises of the investigation. Jesus' death needs to be related with the cultic scene that implies that the blood must be taken to the shrine before the throne of God.[27]

For the writer of Hebrews, Psalm 110 was perfectly suitable for a cultic interpretation where priesthood is a significant metaphor for heavenly ministry. In resurrection God exalted Christ to heaven. Within the symbolism of the temple cult this meant entering the heavenly shrine. The function of the exalted Christ is priestly. He takes his own blood into the Holy of Holies and sprinkles it on the ἱλαστήριον, the cover of the ark of covenant, i.e. the throne of God. This is regarded as a priestly ministry according to the order of Melchizedek, and it obtains redemption for the whole of humankind.

---

[27] Hegermann attempts to solve the tension by stating that the writer is merely describing different functions of the Christ-event. Therefore the use of different images was possible. Hegermann, *Anfänge*, 348. Such an existentialist explanation, however, ignores the aspect of exaltation Christology in the interpretation of Psalm 110.

The aspect of royal messianism will not be reduced by this priestly scene, however. In his exaltation Christ is indeed a Davidide who is seated "at the right hand" of God.[28] Psalm 110 contains both of these aspects and this must be the reason why it became so popular in early Christology. This scene is quite explicitly expressed in Hebrews: "But when Christ had offered for all time a single sacrifice for sins, 'he sat down at the right hand of God,' and since then has been waiting 'until his enemies would be made a footstool for his feet'." (10:12-13). An eschatological event renews the priesthood so that the Davidide may minister as a priest according to the order of Melchizedek, and simultaneously function as a messianic ruler.[29]

Hengel is probably right when suggesting that such priestly exaltation Christology connecting Psalm 110:1 and 4 was not created by the author of the Hebrews at a relatively late date, but is much older and was already known to Paul.[30] A similar message appears to form the core of the tradition that Paul uses in Romans 8:34.[31] There the death of Christ is linked to his priestly ministry. "It is Christ Jesus, who died, yes, who was raised, who is at the right hand of God, who indeed intercedes for us." The cultic soteriology of the passage has already been referred to above. The resurrection of Jesus means here quite simply the beginning of his priestly ministry on the basis of Psalm 110.[32] Therefore Christ reigns "at the right hand" of God and simultaneously intercedes as a heavenly priest.[33]

The intercession of the exalted Christ is done "for us" (ὑπὲρ ἡμῶν). This is a short formula describing the priestly ministry of Jesus. On other occasions in the New Testament such a formula is attached to the act of obtaining

---

[28] See Hengel, *Anfänge*, 47.

[29] This aspect is missing in the presentation of Buchanan who states that the son of David theology is not important for the description of Christ's priestly function. Buchanan, *Hebrews*, 167.

[30] Hengel, *Studies*, 147.

[31] In verse 34 Paul uses earlier material. Certain scholars suggest that it is based on a confessional statement that would resemble the short formula in 1 Thess. 4:14, see Wilckens, *Römer (2)*, 174 footnote 782. Either Paul or his predecessor has probably expanded it with the theme of intercession, see Schlier, *Römerbrief*, 278. We have above seen, however, that the theology of redemption linked to Psalm 110, as well as the idea of exaltation may well have belonged already to the original tradition.

[32] Cf. Hengel, *Anfänge*, 46.

[33] Wilckens sees the similarities with the theology of the Hebrews and suggests that the tradition which Paul has used may lead us to the sources of the Christology of Hebrews. Wilckens, *Römer (2)*, 174 footnote 784. Dunn, who applies Adam-typology as far as possible, is even more cautious. He thinks that a priestly Christology may be "latent" behind the passage. Dunn, *Romans*, 504. As regards the history of tradition it seems clear that a formula building on Psalm 110 belongs to the early period of New Testament history.

atonement. Paul presents it in such a context in the traditional formula of 1 Cor. 15:3. Furthermore it occurs in the context of eucharistia, where the cultic content is even emphasized (1 Cor. 11:24; Mark 14:24par.).

It is quite obvious that the unity of exaltation and atonement, or the unity of the themes of royal enthronement and priestly ministry have their rationale in the conception that the ark is actually God's throne. The narrative story according to which early Christology is presented exploits the potential meanings of the throne in an ingenious way. According to the story, the Davidic priest-king enters the heavenly Temple as a high priest *par exellence*. He offers a sacrifice for sins and sprinkles blood upon the mercy seat. After this the priest-king is enthroned on the very same seat, God's throne of Glory in the heavenly Holy of Holies.[34]

Such uniting of two different discourses is evident in several passages, but especially in 8:1: "we have such a high priest, one who is seated at the right hand of the throne of the Majesty in the heavens." Here it is explicitly the high priest who is enthroned in the manner of a Davidide "at the right hand" of God. The justification for this kind of presentation came naturally from Psalm 110, where the enthronement statement concerned simultaneously the new Melchizedek.

But why Melchizedek? What was the purpose for making a Canaanite priest-king the model for a Davidic Messiah? A simple answer would be that in Jewish speculation every argument derived from the Scriptures was valid. Aaronic priesthood naturally had a primary status in Temple worship, but the Scriptures presented also another alternative. In a very special moment, as in the one in the original story about Abraham and Melchizedek, God could choose an unorthodox way to act.

Certain aspects in Hebrews point to this kind of reasoning. The Old Testament story itself shows that Melchizedek has an extraordinary status in the eyes of God. "It is beyond dispute that the inferior is blessed by the superior." (Heb. 7:7). Melchizedek was superior to Abraham as far as God's criteria are regarded.[35] This kind of priority became then the basis for the justification for the change in the priesthood later. Now Psalm 110 is a divine

---

[34] Loader has stated that, in the letter to the Hebrews, it was actually the death of Jesus that was presented as the decisive act of atonement – not his heavenly ministry. He thinks that the writer merely speaks of Jesus' entering into the heavenly Temple without the idea of an atoning act. Loader, *Sohn*, 185f. This kind of view, however, does not take the image of the mercy seat/throne properly into account. The atonement takes place when the blood is sprinkled upon the throne.

[35] There is probably even a contrast between law and promise in this passage. Abraham with his promise and blessing is contrasted with Levites who collected tithes according to the law. See Michel, *Hebräer*, 267f., Lane, *Hebrews*, 169.

proof-text for God's salvation history. Perfection was not attainable through the levitical priesthood. Therefore there was a need to "speak of another priest arising according to the order of Melchizedek" (7:11).[36]

In this respect the exploitation of the Melchizedek figure may simply be justified by the writer's purpose to argue for the change in the priesthood. Eschatological perfection could not be attained through the traditional priesthood. A model for another kind of priesthood was found in the Old Testament tradition about Melchizedek, a God-chosen priest.[37] This kind of explanation has its faults, however. It seems obvious that in priestly Christology Psalm 110 precedes the original Old Testament story. Therefore the basic intention of the Christology cannot be explained merely by referring to Genesis. Rather, the abovementioned reasoning must be considered a secondary one that has grown out of the primary one based on Psalm 110.

There have been also other kinds of explanations. The use of the figure of Melchizedek has been explained by referring to the influence of Jewish mysticism. Already in the original story Melchizedek may actually be an angelic figure, the archangel Michael who blessed Abraham. We have earlier seen that particularly in Qumran writings, in 11QMelch., Melchizedek is actually identified as Michael who furthermore is a heavenly high-priest and has a primary status in heaven.[38]

There is no doubt certain justification for the angelic interpretation in the letter to the Hebrews, as well. In chapter 7 there is a thorough speculation on the King Melchizedek himself. His name means "king of righteousness". Furthermore, as a king of Salem, he is a "king of peace".[39] He has no genealogy and no father: "having neither beginning of days nor end of life, but

---

[36] A speculation over the Levite priesthood can be detected also in the Testament of Levi, where the priestly figure from Judah contests the Levite priesthood; TLev. 8:14; 18:1ff. These passages may naturally reflect Christian theology where the idea of a new priesthood has been brought into a work originally emphasizing the primacy of the tribe of Levi. Cf. Michel, *Hebräer*, 269f.; Hagner, *Hebrews*, 106.

[37] Lane emphasizes that the writer is not insensitive to Old Testament tradition. "While developing these comparisons, the writer is careful not to dissolve redemptive history into timeless categories. It is crucial to his argument for the superiority of the priest like Melchizedek that the oracle proclaiming a new act of God was promulgated after the law (7:11-19, 28). That God announced a different and superior priesthood in the OT was itself indicative that the Levitical priesthood had been insufficient and was obsolete." Lane, *Hebrews*, 196-197.

[38] See chapter 3 above. Cf. Milik, *JJS 23* (1972) 95ff., Hurtado, *One God, One Lord*, 79.

[39] It is possible that the logic of argumentation has turned here. Rissi has suggested that the description of Melchizedek is actually dependent on a christological hymn. Therefore, in the presentation of the author, Melchizedek has been made to look like Christ in order to underline Christ's superiority to him. See Rissi, *Theologie*, 86-90.

resembling the Son of God, he remains a priest forever." (7:2-3). Such a superhuman figure evidently resembles a mighty angel. He could easily be identified with archangel Michael as the head of the heavenly hosts.

If the writer was thinking of such a figure, Melchizedek would probably be an example of a heavenly being installed to eternal priesthood. The writer would thus refer to Melchizedek as a heavenly high-priest who appeared to Abraham and blessed him.[40] In this case the intention of the writer would probably be to claim that Christ has taken the place of the archangel Michael in heaven.[41] We must note, however, that in Hebrews, the possible angelic nature of Melchizedek is never explicitly stated.[42]

This kind of explanation has its advantages, but we must also note the differences between 11QMelch. and Hebrews. In 11QMelch. Melchizedek is evidently an eschatological savior. According to Qumran teaching Melchizedek will bring an age of peace. This, however, does not happen through a sacrificial act. Qumran theology was directed by a rather typical Jewish view of predestination. Sin would be punished in the end of time and Melchizedek had a role in this.[43] The age of peace would follow only after the last judgment.[44]

In New Testament soteriology Christ-Melchizedek is first sacrificed on the cross. Only after this he is resurrected, and as a new priest according to the order of Melchizedek he brings the blood of sacrifice on the mercy seat in the heavenly shrine. This Melchizedek is simultaneously a Davidide, a heavenly King "at the right hand" of God.[45] He, too, has a kingdom of peace, and he reigns in mercy. Every one who approaces this King, finds peace.

---

[40] De Jonge and van der Woude have proposed this kind of solution for the interpretation of the passage. They suggest that the mentioning of the Son of God here seeks to emphasize the subordination of the angel Melchizedek to the pre-existent, heavenly Son of God; see *NTS 12* (1965-66) 321.

[41] This is how Schenke explains the use of the figure of Melchizedek. Schenke, *Existenz*, 430.

[42] Kobelski remarks that the author in all probability regarded Melchizedek as a heavenly being, but that his angelic status is never exploited in the comparison with the priesthood of Jesus. Kobelski, *Melchizedek*, 126.

[43] This is noted e.g. by Kobelski, *Melchizedek*, 127, and Hagner, *Hebrews*, 104-105.

[44] Flusser has suggested that in 11Q Melch. the figure of Melchizedek is identified with the Son of Man of Daniel. According to Flusser Psalm 110 must have given the reason for the uniting of these features in Qumran, and he refers to the teachings of the letter to the Hebrews. Flusser, *Origins*, 189. One must be cautious, however, when interpreting the priestly aspect in this connection.

[45] In this respect the difference between the writings of Qumran and the letter to the Hebrews cannot be over-emphasized. According to Qumran writings the Davidic Messiah could never have priestly functions. The high esteem of Zadoqite priesthood in that priestly sect prevented such an alternative. Cf. Hagner, *Hebrews*, 84.

Angelic interpretation cannot reach the final focus of the message of the Hebrews. It does not seem to be the Melchizedek analogy, but the "order of Melchizedek" that is under speculation. Christ is not a new angelic leader in heaven. He is a Davidic king who also has a priestly ministry. Whoever the Canaanite Melchizedek may originally be, the point is in the change in the priesthood. The Scriptures give sound justification for the belief that the Davidic Messiah is a priest-king.

Therefore, there are evident traces of Jewish merkabah mysticism in the teaching of Hebrews, but the angelic interpretation of the figure of Melchizedek is not one of them. Once again the main source of influence appears to be found in the central metaphors on which the teaching is constructed. In the letter to the Hebrews these metaphors have been exploited in an extraordinary manner. As a God-chosen high priest Christ enters the heavenly Temple and performs the sacrificial ritual. The narrative is constructed on the idea of a temple-structured universe. Christ leaves the "first tent," i.e. the earth, and enters the heavenly Holy of Holies behind the cosmological curtain. The unity of exaltation and atonement is justified by the help of the metaphor that is most central to them all, the throne of Glory. Resurrection is a necessary precondition for Christ's entering into the heavenly sanctuary and for the atonement that is made by sprinkling the blood of sacrifice on the mercy seat.

7.3. The emergence of the cultic interpretation

One problem still remains, as regards the construction of early Christology. What was the basic reason for the usage of cultic images in this connection? How did the cultic interpretation emerge? Why was the cultic discourse considered relevant for expressing certain features of Christology?

In the Old Testament there were two themes that were essential for the concept of God's kingship. Firstly, the theocratic reign of God was expressed by the image of a throne that was located in the Holy of Holies. God could be met with on earth, and the place for that was before the ark of the covenant in the Temple of Jerusalem.

"The Lord is king; let the peoples tremble! He sits enthroned upon the cherubim; let the earth quake! The Lord is great in Zion; he is exalted over all the peoples... Extol the Lord our God; worship at his footstool. Holy is he!" (Ps. 99:1, 2, 5).

Secondly, the throne of God was simultaneously considered transcendent.[46]

"The Lord has established his throne in the heavens, and his kingdom rules over all. Bless the Lord, O you his angels, you mighty ones who do his bidding, obedient to his spoken word. Bless the Lord, all his hosts, his ministers that do his will." (Ps. 103:19-21).

---

[46] See chapter 2 above.

These two aspects point to the scene that is of utmost importance for us. The place where God can be encountered was the Temple. Therefore the theocratic ideology of Israel implied a Temple cult that formed the basis for all the peoples' worship. God the King could be approached, but there were strict rules for this. The Holy of Holies could be entered only once a year, and the high priest who was privileged to do this could not enter without the help of sacrifices (Lev. 16:11-16).

The throne of God was thus also a place for the atonement. People's sins prevented them from approaching God whenever they like. In order to make an approach, a blood sacrifice had to be offered. This condition emphasized God's holiness and his majesty. The atonement was obtained by sprinkling the blood of the sacrifice on the mercy seat, the throne of God itself.

The restriction that was produced by God's holiness did not prevent Israelites from worshiping the heavenly King whenever they liked, though. We have seen that apocalyptic groups made good use of sacrificial songs that had been taken from the temple liturgy. In the Qumran Songs of the Sabbath Sacrifice we have fine evidence for a devout worship where the praising of God is expressed quite in the manner of bringing sacrifices to him.[47]

As we have seen earlier, these Songs really belong to a context of temple songs of Sabbath sacrifice. They express the mystical piety that was attached to the ministry of priests in the Temple. As the songs were sung in the Temple when the weekly Sabbath offering was performed, these songs emphasized the Kingship of God in a remarkable way. This was seen for example in the twelfth song of the Songs of the Sabbath Sacrifice. There the *merkabah*-throne of God was the focus of the heavenly worship.

"Praise the God of ...] ... The cherubim lie prostrate before him, and bless when they rise... They bless the image of the throne-chariot (which) is above the vault of the cherubim, and they sing [the splen]dour of the shining vault (which is) beneath the seat of his glory." (4Q405 20-21-22, 6-9; Martínez).

The cosmic scene of these songs is identical with apocalyptical mysticism. There is a throne in heaven and angels and other heavenly beings are conducting a liturgy in front of it. Furthermore the throne is located in the *debir*, the Holy of Holies, which is described as a house of God appearing in flames of fire. Also the cherubim bow themselves before the throne singing songs of praise (cf. 4Q403 1 i, 36-37).

There are certains aspects in these songs that still deserve our attention. These songs are linked to the weekly Sabbath offering in the Temple – at least

---

[47] Therefore, the apocalypticists' view of devout worship is an essential element in the development of the Christology of the New Testament. See Eskola, *Theodicy*, 87ff.

in a metaphorical sense. As we have seen, there is also other kinds of evidence for the existence of such songs. In the "order of the daily whole offering in the liturgy of the house of our God" (mTamid 7:3) the Psalms that the Levites sing in the sanctuary are mentioned (mTamid 7:4). The context of weekly Sabbath offering links these songs to sacrifices, even though the Day of Atonement is not meant here.[48]

The transcendent scene of the Songs is interesting, as well. The singers of such songs have been convinced – quite in the manner of canonical Psalmists – that the "real" throne of God exists actually in the heavens. Israel's earthly worship is symbolic and through the praises and prayers of the worshipers it is united with the factual liturgy of the cherubim before God's heavenly throne.[49]

How can these traditions help us to understand the emergence of the cultic interpretation of exaltation Christology in the New Testament? First of all, it is rather easy to understand why the aspect of atonement and the idea of bringing sacrificial blood occur in soteriological passages. God's heavenly palace was seen as a temple and there was also priestly ministry in heaven. Jewish writings do not mention blood in the contexts of heavenly sacrifices, though, and in this sense the New Testament description is unique.[50]

The transcendent scene, however, is similar. Both in Hebrews and in the Pauline traditions temple and sacrifices were considered heavenly. Quite in the manner of Jewish belief, the heavenly Temple was the archetype for the earthly Temple. In such a context it was easy to exploit the figure of the high priest when the entering of the heavenly temple was described. Thus the earthly worship was used as a metaphor for the heavenly ministry of the priestly Messiah.[51]

This was what the writer of Hebrews wished to present. Exalted Jesus has entered the inner shrine behind the curtain, the heavenly sanctuary, "to appear in the presence of God" (9:19-24). The ministry of Christ was a ministry of a

---

[48] Newsom suggest that at Qumran the songs were part of "something like communal mysticism." Newsom, *Songs*, 19. Therefore, the link to factual sacrifices is metaphorical.

[49] "Der himmlische Kult der 'Priesterengel' ist das Urbild des irdischen Kultes, das galt nach qumranischen Verständnis nicht mehr für den Jerusalemer Tempel, aber sehr wohl für die eigene Gemeinschaft." Schwemer, *Königsherrschaft*, 65.

[50] Loader states that there is a contrast between the Old Testament image of bringing the blood of animals and the New Testament description of Jesus bringing his own blood to the temple. This is the reason why, according to Loader, the letter to the Hebrews speaks merely in a figurative sense about Christ taking his own blood to the heavens. Loader, *Sohn*, 190. As regards the present study, this sort of idea is unable to explain the emergence of the cultic interpretation as such.

[51] I agree with Isaacs according to whom the barrier dividing the sacred from the profane had to be removed; cf. above, Isaacs, *Early Christian thought*, 152.

high priest, but in a symbolic manner: "Christ... through the eternal Spirit offered himself without blemish to God" (9:14).[52] Similarly, in Romans 3:23-25, blood was brought before God, but the throne was not merely a mercy seat upon which blood was sprinkled. Jesus as a person had become a ἱλαστήριον for all sinners who need atonement.

Cultic interpretation was thus constructed by exploiting the metaphorical figure of the high priest. The blood of Jesus, however, was the starting point for the whole procedure. Jesus had been "slaughtered" on the cross. He had been "handed over" as a sacrifice. Therefore, in this narrative scene, he factually had the sacrificial blood that was to be sprinkled upon the mercy seat in heaven. Priestly ministry was merely used as an instrument in the description of the act of atonement.[53]

In addition to this, the cosmology of Jewish mysticism was essential for the presentation. There is an ascent structure in the description of the exaltation of the new Melchizedek. Christ ascends into the heavenly Temple and enters the Holy of Holies behind the Temple curtain. These images were available already in Second Temple Jewish mysticism.[54]

It is naturally important to note that atonement was obtained only in the Holy of Holies, and not at the moment when the sacrifice was slaughtered. This is why the scene of early exaltation Christology is consistent to detail. Here we see also why Psalm 110 was exploited in the cultic intepretation. In resurrection God exalted Christ to heaven. Christ entered the heavenly shrine and took his own blood into the Holy of Holies. There he obtained atonement by sprinkling the blood on the ἱλαστήριον.[55]

This is what the Pauline tradition states in Romans 4:25. Also according to this short parallelism Jesus was "slaughtered" on the cross. He was "handed over to death for our trespasses". Jesus was a sin offering for the trespasses of Israel. In addition to that, there had to be the priestly ministry. This is stated in the latter part of the parallelism. In the resurrection Jesus "was raised for our justification". His priestly ministry obtained justification for sinners.

The priestly aspect of exaltation Christology is understandable and

---

[52] Cf. Löhr, *Königsherrschaft*, 194.

[53] Cf. Rissi, *Theologie*, 73.

[54] Hofius maintained that the writer of the letter to the Hebrews was well aware of the Jewish concept of a heavenly Temple that is separated from this world, and that the image of the Temple curtain had an essential role in this description. Hofius, *Vorhang*, 95; cf. MacRae, *Semeia 12* (1978) 187.

[55] Therefore Loader's construction, where the atonement is attached to the moment of Christ's death, remains unconsistent as regards the exploitation of the basic idea of the heavenly Temple. See Loader, *Sohn*, 192.

consistent. When the exalted one entered the heavens and approached the throne of God, he approached the Holy God. Therefore it is also suitable for him to minister as a priest before God. There are, however, two interesting questions arising from this scene. Firstly, why did Christ have to make atonement instead of experiencing only an enthronement? And secondly, why didn't the enthroned patriarchs, about whose enthronement Jewish writings speak so much, have a priestly ministry?

We have seen that the priestly aspect in no way disturbed the enthronement scene of the enthronement of a Davidide. For example in Hebrews 10 they occurred together:

"But when Christ had offered for all time a single sacrifice for sins, 'he sat down at the right hand of God,' and since then has been waiting 'until his enemies would be made a footstool for his feet'." (10:12-13).

A similar scene was provided in the traditional passage of Romans 8:34. Instead of a tension we see that, according to the message of Psalm 110, the exalted Davidide ministers as a priest according to the order of Melchizedek, and he also reigns as a messianic ruler.

But the question remains, why did the exalted one have to make a sin offering? In Jewish mysticism there were several patriarchs and other figures that were enthroned or promised a throne in heavens. They never had a priestly function, though. They were able to approach the heavenly throne of glory without the help of sacrifices. Where does the cultic interpretation come from?

Jesus surely did not need to make atonement for his own behalf, as the family of Aaron needed to do in Leviticus 16. No New Testament writer would state such a thing. According to those New Testament passages that we have investigated, Jesus gave himself as a sacrifice for sinners, for "us". "Christ died for our sins" (1 Cor. 15:3). This simply means that the easter events, as a whole, were given a cultic intepretation. The cultic interpretation of exaltation must thus be based on an idea of a suffering messianic figure.[56] So the death of the Messiah must have a special meaning. Only an independent theological motif explains why priestly symbolism was attached to the enthronement theme.[57]

This uniting of such themes must have taken place quite early. We find the cultic interpretation of the death of Jesus in early Christian formulas that must have been used in the Church long before e.g. Paul recorded them in his

---

[56] Cf. Stuhlmacher, *Biblische Theologie*, 192ff.

[57] Lindars remarks that, according to the writer of the Hebrews, the reconciliation, once achieved, should be permanent. Therefore there is "the contrast between the limitations of the old covenant and the lasting condition of the new." Only the sacrifice of the new covenant was able to achieve this. Lindars, *Theology*, 90-91.

letters. Once it was done, however, there was no lack of scriptural proof on its behalf. As we have seen several times, Psalm 110 provided a complete scene for the priestly function and heavenly ministry of the exalted Davidide. This was further confirmed by the concept of heavenly ministry prevalent in Jewish mysticism. God's temple in the heavens was a suitable place for heavenly ministry and God's throne was indeed the mercy seat upon which the blood of the sacrifice was to be sprinkled.

The influence of merkabah mysticism is evident also in the cultic interpretation of exaltation Christology. Christ's exaltation was considered a heavenly journey where the God-chosen king-priest was exalted before God's throne in the heavenly Temple. Such a presentation has several original features of its own, however.

Psalm 110 has been exploited in cultic discourse and this has resulted in new aspects in exaltation Christology. Throne, in this context, is the mercy seat, the ἱλαστήριον in the heavenly Holy of Holies. Therefore it becomes a place for atonement in the manner of the original mercy seat in the Jerusalem Temple.

In cultic discourse Christ's exaltation is presented as a cultic act. Christ himself is a high priest who in his resurrection is exalted to God's heavenly shrine. As a king-priest he performs sacrificial ritual in the Holy of Holies. Therefore, also in the context of this discourse, we still have both the Davidic Messiah and the heavenly throne, but they are both given new meanings. The throne is God's ark in the Holy of Holies, and the Davidide is a heavenly high priest according to the order of Melchizedek.

In the letter to the Hebrews, especially, the exaltation narrative is based on the idea of a temple-structured universe. Christ dies in the sphere of the "first tent". This metaphor represents now the complete old covenant. In his resurrection he is exalted to the place behind the heavenly curtain, and thus he enters the divine Holy of Holies as an eternal high-priest. The act of atonement that he performs in the heavenly *debir* legitimizes a new covenant.

What is special about this new discourse is that the imagery as such is capable of producing such interpretations without misrepresenting the original symbols. God's ark is simultaneously the throne of Glory and, according to Psalm 110, the Davidide is the new Melchizedek. Therefore, in early Christology and especially in the theology of Hebrews, both aspects of these symbols may be presented side by side. Exalted Christ is also the new Davidide who is enthroned on God's throne and who reigns over the whole world. Angels and other creatures are subjected to his power.

§8 The Centre of the Last Judgment *(judicial discourse)*

After investigating the occurrence of the throne metaphor in the context of enthronement discourse, resurrection discourse, and cultic discourse, we must finally comment on the eschatological interpretation which has probably been the most common context for the explanation of the theme of Messiah and the throne in the past. In the study of New Testament Christology a polarized futurist eschatology has prevailed. According to the basic scheme Christ will be enthroned on the last day and perform judgment over the whole world.[1]

It is easy to understand how such a view has emerged. It is based on certain passages in the gospels where the throne of the Son of Man is introduced. In the climax of eschatology all the nations will be gathered before the Messiah for a final judgment. The concept of Messianic enthronement has been interpreted in terms of this presentation. Already during the overview of Jewish eschatology we noted that the enthronement theme does not actually appear in the context of the day of judgment. Therefore, relevant New Testament passages will also need to be investigated anew.

In addition to this one should pay attention to the fact that in eschatological descriptions we encounter a new discourse. The meanings of different details are dependent on the particular discourse where the judicial aspect prevails. Therefore, the aspect of enthronement must also be investigated and explained in the context of this new discourse.

8.1. Son of Man and his throne

As far as gospel stories are regarded, the Son of Man is linked to the throne in descriptions of the end of the world.[2] The Son of Man is a heavenly ruler who will come "in clouds with great power and glory" (Mark 13:26-27).[3] He is a universal judge who will gather all mankind before him:

---

[1] This has been an influential pattern already from the days of J. Weiss and his theory of "consistent eschatology"; see Weiss, *Predigt Jesu*, 1892, 51-54. The pattern was accepted and promoted especially by Bultmann, *Theologie*, 27, 31f., 52. In the study of Christology one of the most influential books in this tradition was Tödt, *Menschensohn*, see esp. pp. 266f.

[2] For a general overview on the subject, see Nickelsburg, *ABD VI* (1992) 137-150. Review articles have been provided e.g. by Marshall, *EvQ 42* (1970) 67-87; Walker, *CBQ 45* (1983) 584-607; and Donahue, *CBQ 48* (1986) 484-498.

[3] The investigation of Son of Man Christology as such is not the task of the present study. Here the problem concerning the relation of the Son of Man figure and the heavenly throne is treated in respect of different discourses. The nature of the Christology itself is a debated subject, and scholars constantly disagree on their conclusions. See e.g. Tödt, *Menschensohn*, 265ff.; Theisohn, *Der auserwählte Richter*, 161ff., Kim, *Son of Man*, 99ff.; Lindars, *Jesus*, 29ff.

"When the Son of Man comes in his glory, and all the angels with him, then he will sit on the throne of his glory. All the nations will be gathered before him, and he will separate people one from another..." (Matth. 25:31-32).

The basic features of such a description differ essentially from those of the previous discourses. There is no reference to resurrection here. Psalm 110 is not referred to, either. The messianic figure is rather a Danielic Son of Man who acts as a heavenly judge at the end of the world.[4]

Again in this narration the throne is a "throne of his glory". In an eschatological context the throne is evidently identified as a judgment seat. In this respect the content of the saying resembles that of 1 En. 9:4 where θρόνος was the centre of a judgment scene. Also in Matthew 25 the Son of Man acts as a heavenly judge.[5]

This kind of description is naturally closely linked to Jewish merkabah mysticism. In addition to the Danielic Son of Man there were several figures in different writings who acted as heavenly judges. Above we have referred to Melchizedek in 11QMelch., the archangel Michael, who had the role of a judge in heaven. Also in the end of the 4Q491 fragment there is a reference that may also refer to a judge: "And who can deal with the issue of my lips? Who shall summon me to be destroyed by my judgment?" (4Q491 fr. 11, 17).[6]

In the Exagoge of Ezekiel Moses was promised a great throne and he was said to be a judge and a leader of the whole of humankind. This passage is not eschatological, however, in the sense that the day of judgment is not explicitly referred to. Only Moses' status reminds us of that of the Son of Man.[7]

There were also already other elements linked to the day of judgment in pre-Christian writings. In the Book of Watchers Enoch's ascent had the primary purpose of explaining some of the great evil on earth while confirming that both the suffering of the righteous and the success of sinful forces would be righted hereafter. Such a purpose also justifies well the conception that is

---

[4] For the essential significance and influence of Daniel 7 for Son of Man descriptions in both Jewish and Christian writings, see Nickelsburg, *ABD VI* (1992) 137f.; cf. also Hagner, *Matthew 14-28*, 741-742.

[5] Scholars usually note that the throne of Glory in this passage is God's throne, but they do not emphasize the aspect of the judgment seat in this particular case. See e.g. Gnilka, *Matthäusevangelium 2*, 371; Hagner, *Matthew 14-28*, 742.

[6] As we have noted earlier, the identification of this figure as a Davidic Messiah is not evident, however. For discussion, see Collins, *Scepter and the Star*, 147-148.

[7] Ex.Ez. 6, 15-19. See chapter 3.2. Due to the vast number of heavenly figures some scholars suggest that there was no well defined Jewish concept of a heavenly Son of Man at all in the Second Temple period. For the discussion, see Walker, *CBQ 45* (1983) 585ff. This is an overstatement, even though one must be cautious when explaining the relation between Jewish presentations and their Christian transformations.

presented in Jubilees. According to Jubilees Enoch takes part in the last judgment and will "report every deed of each generation in the day of judgment." (Jub. 10:17).

In this respect it is consistent that later in Enochic writings the "Elect One" takes part in the judgment itself. In the Similitudes the Elect One was apparently identified as the Son of Man. "On that day, my Elect One shall sit on the seat of glory and make a selection of their deeds." (1 En. 45:3).[8] We have earlier accepted the view that this kind of description is based on Jewish theology and is not primarily dependent on Christian theology in spite of the dating and provenance of the writings. Even the eschatological passage in 1 En. 51:1-3, that parallels those of Matthew quoted above, is most probably not a duplicate of the gospel tradition but a reminiscent of Daniel 7 instead.[9]

Therefore, in Enochic writings, the description of the event of an eschatological entrée of God himself, or the Elect One, is to be discerned and separated from the enthronement theme. The entering upon a throne in the end of days is not part of the exaltation narrative. It is an act where God sets himself as a judge for the Last Judgment. It does not resemble a description of an enthronement that takes place in resurrection.

In this sense also in Matthew the Son of Man's entering upon the throne of Glory on the day of judgment is an eschatological event leading to the judgment of all humankind. This is in no sense a description of a heavenly coronation day, or an enthronement to Lordship.[10] The discourse that is exploited here is completely different. The exalted Christ is here a heavenly judge who has the extraordinary task of bringing eternal righteousness.

The concept of a Messianic judge also occurs in another kind of context. In chapter 3 we have noted that the theme of heavenly judges was common in Jewish writings. Already according to Daniel the judgment "was given for the holy ones of the Most High" (Dan. 7:22). In the book of Zechariah the high priest Joshua was promised a heavenly reign: "If you will walk in my ways and keep my requirements, then you shall rule my house and have charge of my courts" (Zech. 3:7). In the Wisdom of Solomon the righteous were promised a heavenly office: "They will govern nations and rule over peoples"

---

[8] Collins finds the clearest allusions to Daniel 7 in 1 Enoch 46:1 and 47:3f., where the function of the Son of Man figure is speculated on. Collins, *Scepter and the Star*, 177.

[9] See above, chapter 3.3.

[10] This view, however, has been a matter of dispute. Under the influence of the so called theory of consistent eschatology (see analysis below, in chapter 8.3. where the problem of polarized eschatology is discussed) Matt. 25:31 has been interpreted in terms of an exaltation-enthronement theme. So e.g. Albright and Mann, *Matthew*, 306f. Later scholars have mostly abandoned this kind of interpretation, though. Cf. Gnilka, *Matthäusevangelium 2*, 370f.; Hagner, *Matthew 14-28*, 741f.

(SapSol. 3:8). A similar idea may be seen in 1 En. 1:9, the passage that is later quoted in Jude 14-15. According to the Sibyllines the prophets "are judges of men and righteous kings" in the eschatological kingdom (Sib. 3:781-782). The Qumran Covenanters also anticipated this kind of future: "by means of his chosen ones God will judge all the nations" (1QpHab. V, 4).

In Jewish eschatology this theme has also been combined with the great post-exilic theme of the restoration of the twelve tribes.[11] On the one hand, certain groups anticipated the glorious future of the tribes at the times of the Messiah (Ps.Sol. 17:26, 44; TBenj. 9:2; TJud. 25). On the other hand, the leading role of the renewed tribes would be unquestionable. According to TAbr. (A) 13:6 the wicked "will be judged by the twelve tribes of Israel."[12]

A similar hope may be detected in the New Testament, where the disciples were promised a glorious future with their Messianic leader.[13]

"Truly I tell you, at the renewal of all things, when the Son of Man is seated on the throne of his glory, you who have followed me will also sit on twelve thrones, judging the twelve tribes of Israel" (Matt. 19:28).

The difference between this passage and the eschatological speech in Matthew 25:31 investigated above is that here the Son of Man is not "coming" in his glory, but he is "seated" on the throne of his glory. The aspect of sitting assumedly changes the focus of the statement. Here the final judgment is not described in detail. Instead of that, the leading role of the twelve tribes is emphasized by introducing the judicial offices of the disciples. Therefore, the day of judgment is not necessarily referred to.[14] The offices of heavenly judges granted to the twelve disciples may be honorary offices. In this case the disciples judge "the twelve tribes of Israel" in heaven, in the new world, which is a token of the restoration of Israel.[15]

The moment of the event is apparently the same in these two passages. It is called the moment of "the renewal of all things." The focus of the presentation

---

[11] In Old Testament prophetic tradition this theme was based on passages such as Isa 49:6; Ezekiel 37:19-24; and Psalm 122:3-5; cf. Sirach 36:11; 48:10.

[12] See Evans, *Jesus*, 461. For the appearance of the theme at Qumran, see Grappe, *Trône de Dieu*, 206f.

[13] Cf. 1 Cor. 6:2; Rev. 20:4.

[14] In agreement with Evans, *Jesus*, 472: "It seems probable, then, that the saying, both in its original sense, and in its later adaptation by the evangelists Matthew and Luke, connotes the sense of rule, and not the sense of punitive judgment."

[15] Most scholars agree on this view, see Albright and Mann, *Matthew*, 234; Hagner, *Matthew 14-28*, 565; Blomberg, Matthew, 301; Mounce, *Matthew*, 185. Some scholars suggest, however, that the passage refers to the judgment day itself, see e.g. Filson, *Matthew*, 211; Gnilka, *Matthäusevangelium 2*, 171.

is different, however. As Matthew 25 appears to look at the judgment day, Matthew 19 seems to look at the heavenly realm after the judgment day. In this respect the Son of Man's entering upon the throne refers to his unique status in the heavenly kingdom.

What is special about the passage is the intertextual reality that highlights the relation between the Son of Man and his throne. Matthew 19:28 exploits the tradition of the restoration of the twelve tribes partly in order to emphasize the Lordship of the Son of Man. An evident identification is postulated in the presentation. As the twelve disciples are promised their thrones in the world to come, the highest throne is reserved to their rabbi and leader, Jesus of Nazareth. In this respect the throne becomes a symbol for Jesus' Lordship in the kingdom of heaven.[16]

Even a short analysis shows that judicial discourse presents Christ's appearing on a throne in a completely different way than other discourses. Even though the central metaphor remains the same, it has a new function in the story that is developed here. The day of judgment is at hand. The Messiah enters upon the throne of Glory in order to perform judgment on the whole of humankind.

8.2. The reception of early judgment descriptions in Paul

Even though Paul has exploited early exaltation traditions profoundly in his letters, judgment descriptions also have a significant role in his teaching. In this respect, Pauline letters serve as a good example of how resurrection Christology and judgment descriptions were related in the proclamation of the early Church.

In Paul's eschatology the throne is first of all described as God's judgment seat. As a heavenly judge God naturally has a judgment seat, and all people will be brought before it. "For we will all stand before the judgment seat of God (πάντες γὰρ παραστησόμεθα τῷ βήματι τοῦ θεοῦ)... each of us will be accountable to God." (Rom. 14:10-12). The mention of the judgment seat brings us to a heavenly court of law where legal processes are being conducted.

God's seat mentioned here, βῆμα, is not actually a royal throne. The precise

---

[16] In this respect the intertextual approach may be rather helpful also for the study of Son of man Christology as such. Walker still focused on the question whether the concept or even a title Son of Man existed during first-century Judaism. Walker, *CBQ* 45 (1983) 585ff. Further, Lindars stated that Jesus used the definite form of the expression merely "idiomatically," and therefore it cannot be considered as an exclusive self-reference. See Lindars, *Jesus*, 17-24. From the point of view of the intertextual approach such "linguistic" ponderings are rather useless since the point of Jesus speech is in the intertextual transformation of Daniel's message.

denotation of the word is a judgment seat.[17] This is also the meaning for the word in an everyday sense in the New Testament.[18] The word is often used with regards to the judgment seats of earthly rulers (see Matt. 27:19; John 19:13; Acts 18:12, 16; 25:6, 10, 17). Both Jewish theology and the New Testament teach that God has this kind of seat.[19] In the context of judicial discourse God's throne of glory becomes thus identified as a public judgment seat. The seat, however, lies in the heavenly court. The basic significance for it still comes from the fact that it is God's holy throne. The new association merely adds one aspect to the original metaphor.[20]

The judgment seat of God is, according to Paul, also simultaneously the judgment seat of Christ.[21] Even the same word βῆμα, is used.

"For all of us must appear before the judgment seat of Christ, so that each may receive recompense for what has been done in the body, whether good or evil." (2 Cor. 5:10).

According to Paul's Christocentric treatment, Christ accompanies God in the execution of the last judgment. This feature also occurs in the second chapter of Romans: "God, through Jesus Christ, will judge the secret thoughts of all" (Rom. 2:16b). This view is so typical of Paul that it appears several times in his letters (1 Cor. 4:5; 1 Thess. 2:19).[22]

Judicial discourse no doubt adds a new aspect to the soteriology of the early Church. Metaphors taken from legal terminology concerning processes in the court of law emphasize the juridical nature of God's eschatological judgment. Judgment is unavoidable because of the transgressions. The ungodliness of the people will arouse the wrath of God and lead to a just judgment. Only the final judgment and the revealing of God's wrath can renew this world which has been corrupted by sin. This message is the counterpoint of cultic discourse, where Christ entered the heavenly Holy of Holies with sacrificial blood in his hands, removing the barrier of sin which divides the sacred from the profane.

In Paul's theology, however, there is no contradiction between the

---

[17] See e.g. Michel, *Römer (1978)*, 428, esp. footnote 27.

[18] For the occurrences in the Old Testament and Jewish literature, see chapter 4.5. above.

[19] Concerning Jewish theology see Or.Sib. 2:218; 8:222, 242. Paul's theology was later developed in Polycarp 6:2.

[20] An etymological interpretation thus misses the point. Dunn has suggested that the seat is "a raised place or tribune for delivery of speeches in public assembly... and hence the tribunal of a magistrate or judge." Dunn, *Romans 9-16*, 809. For Dunn this is the reason why the seat is believed to be in a public place. It is not etymology, however, that gives the word its final meaning. The use of the word fits well into the judicial discourse, but it does not change the basic meaning of God's throne.

[21] Cf. Dunn, *Romans 9-16*, 809.

[22] For the occurrence of this theme in Paul, see Furnish, *II Corinthians*, 275, 304f.

eschatological idea of entering upon the throne and exaltation Christology. They depend on separate discourses and complete each other. In 1 Thessalonians the eschatological hope of believers is based on the heavenly Son of God who is the seal of salvation for every one that puts his/her trust in him: "to wait for his Son from heaven, whom he raised from the dead – Jesus, who rescues us from the wrath that is coming." (1 Thess. 1:10).

Most of the central features of early exaltation Christology can be found in this short statement. Resurrected Jesus is the Son of God who has been exalted to heaven. In his parousia he will rescue believers from the wrath of God on the day of judgment. The stress is on salvation. Christ is not presented as a judge, even though the expression itself implies his judicial function in the parousia.

In Romans the day of wrath is the day when "God's righteous judgment will be revealed" (Rom. 2:5). A reminiscent of 1 Thessalonians follows then in chapter 5, where again salvation is underlined: "Much more surely then, now that we have been justified by his blood, will we be saved through him from the wrath of God." (Rom. 5:9).

It is probably worth noting that in Acts, in traditions attached to Paul, Christ's resurrection is in fact a premise for his eschatological entrée. When Paul is in front of the Areopagus in Athens, he proclaims:

"he has fixed a day on which he will have the world judged in righteousness by a man whom he has appointed, and of this he has given assurance to all by raising him from the dead." (Acts 17:31).

It seems obvious that this passage refers to Christ as a heavenly judge who has gained his extraordinary position in the resurrection. According to this text an eschatological (future) enthronement will not fulfil Christ's eschatological office, but resurrection is the crucial event as regards Christ's universal power. In this respect the passage in Acts 17 agrees with Pauline conceptions about the relation between the idea of an enthronement in the resurrection and the idea of entering upon a throne on the day of judgment.

As we have seen before, especially in 1 Cor. 15:25-28 Paul emphasized the difference between the enthronement in the resurrection and the final judgment. Christ reigns "until he has put all his enemies under his feet". Christ's reign has begun at the resurrection and the final battle actually means the consummation of his reign.[23] This was also the purpose of the clear allusion to Psalm 110:1 (LXX: 109:1) in verse 25b.[24]

For Paul, therefore, Christ's enthronement in the resurrection is a necessary

---

[23] In agreement e.g. with Conzelmann, *1 Corinthians*, 272 footnote 88; Loader, *NTS 24* (1978) 208; Hengel, *Studies*, 164.

[24] In chapter 5, also an evident link with Lukan traditions in Acts 3:21 has been noted.

precondition for his heavenly power. Only the heavenly Lord is able to "put all his enemies under his feet" and to act as an eschatological judge on the day of wrath.[25]

This overview shows that Paul was well aware of a Christology that emphasized Christ's role as a heavenly judge on the day of judgment. Such a view in fact guided his conception of the parousia. In his descriptions of the last judgment he exploits judicial discourse and it clearly directs his Christology in this connection. Such descriptions, however, do not contradict his view of Christ as an enthroned Davidide who has been exalted to power in the resurrection. Why was it then that several scholars claimed to find a contradiction between these two christological presentations? The answer lies in the concept of a polarized eschatology.

8.3. Judicial discourse and the problem of polarized eschatology

How do the eschatological view and exaltation Christology relate to each other? The symbolic world seems to be common to both of them. They both speak of an eschatological Messiah who reigns enthroned on a mighty heavenly throne. Is it possible that merely a change of discourse could explain the differences in these descriptions?

Several christological passages have created problems for scholars, and there have been different methodological solutions with which they have attempted to solve those problems. We have above referred to the polarized view that for a long time was a criterion according to which christological statements were dated. From the days of the history-of-religions school a pattern of polarized eschatology has prevailed, speaking one-sidedly of the future enthronement of the Son of Man. While this view was considered to agree with the eschatological message of Jesus, it has been ascribed to the first Jewish Christian Church, as well. According to the explanation, the first Christians spoke only of the future enthronement of Jesus in the parousia.[26]

The simplest answer was thus that every statement disagreeing with that kind of Christology could not belong to the early Jewish Christian community. They must have been constructed later in some other kind of context. Since all christological statements did not fit this pattern – and especially those essential statements that have been studied in the present investigation – there emerged a need to explain differences by some other kind of criteria. Such a need produced a methodological principle according to which different christological statements were located in the sphere of different groups in the early Church.

---

[25] This point of view has been emphasized especially by Stuhlmacher, *Biblische Theologie*, 308.

[26] For the discussion, see references given in 8.1.

Already Baur had divided early Christian history rather strictly into two phases, namely into earlier and in some way "authentic" Jewish Christianity and later, essentially different Hellenistic Christianity.[27] According to Heitmüller, another influential German scholar who wrote almost a century later, the evolutive scheme ("Entwicklungsreihe") went as follows: Jesus – Early Church – Hellenistic Christianity – Paul.[28] This scheme affected strongly the discernment and interpretation of Christological themes.[29]

The contribution of Bousset was that he underlined the importance of Hellenistic mystery religions in the evolutive development of Christological conceptions. Christology was to be studied by concentrating on the different titles of Jesus.[30] The content of those titles was explained by the help of mystery religions. It was actually the pagan religions under whose influence, for instance, the conviction of Christ's deity evolved. The argumentation concerned especially the interpretation of the title "Son of God". Hellenistic pagan mysticism was further seen as the very source from which the title Kyrios was taken.[31]

Therefore, the most prominent theory concerning the eschatology of first Christians has for a long time been that of a strict polarization. It was based mainly on the picture of the Son of Man in the Gospels. Since the Jewish Christian group was waiting for the more or less imminent parousia of their Savior, their hope must have been focused on the end of days. They must have thought that the Lordship of Christ would only be disclosed on the Day of Judgment.

Such futurist eschatology was contrasted with Hellenistic versions, according to which Jesus was considered divine, and his resurrection was interpreted as an exaltation to heavenly power. This kind of polarized view has prevailed in scholarship despite the fact that there has been vast discussion concerning the premises underlying it. In Germany, Hahn exploited the scheme of history in his *Christologische Hoheitstitel*. Hahn accepted the basic

---

[27] For a short introduction to Baur's theory, see Kümmel, *New Testament*. 127-132.

[28] Heitmüller. *ZNW 13* (1912) 330.

[29] It is easy to see its influence for example in Bultmann's *Theologie des Neuen Testaments*, which of course has been a standard for decades. Even the outline of the work follows the evolutive pattern, Bultmann, *Theologie*, xiii-xix. For a later example, see e.g. Casey, *Jewish prophet*, 41.

[30] Cf. the discussion on methodology in chapter 1.3.

[31] Bousset, *Kyrios Christos*, 57, 99; concerning Paul, see 75ff. Bousset still seems to be important for example to Hahn, see Hahn, *Hoheitstitel*, 120. Hurtado analyses the significance of Bousset's influence on the study of Christology in Hurtado, *TS 40* (1979), especially 306-307.

scheme, but added Hellenistic Jewish Christianity after Jewish Christianity.[32] In the discussion over Hahn's monograph Vielhauer questioned the consistency of the evolutive scheme of history.

According to Vielhauer it is not justified to separate Hellenistic Jewish Christianity from Jewish Christianity. The division had been made according to theological themes, but according to Vielhauer one cannot date the tradition merely on the basis of the content. The inference should proceed from the other direction. Historical analysis should show the context into which different presentations belong. On the other hand, in the non-Jewish Christian churches the teaching and Christology was so widely based on Jewish materials that it is not possible to explicate dramatic contrasts between them.[33]

These are no doubt valid notions in the discussion over methodology. In spite of that, however, it is useful to note that the abovementioned criteria were factually applied in the interpretation of early Christology. As regards content, the Pentecost speech in Acts 2 would serve as a good example for that, but in the history of interpretation it has not produced enough explanations suitable for our purposes. It's exaltation Christology is no doubt difficult for those who accept the pattern of polarized eschatology, but the passage has been most often used merely as an example of adoptionist Christology.[34] While it is not easy to locate the Christology of Acts 2:36 in Hellenistic Christianity as such, there have been other solutions. For instance Hahn located it in Hellenistic Jewish Christianity. This he considered justified in two respects. On the one hand, the "adoptionist" tone of the passage did not fit Hellenistic Christianity, where Jesus was considered divine. On the other hand, according to Hahn's theory, the combining of exaltation Christology with Messianic statements and especially the use of the title Kyrios were results of Hellenistic Jewish Christian theology.[35] All this informs us well of a classifying exegesis done on the basis of a strict evolutive scheme of history, but it provides little help for the present discussion.

While the christological passage of Acts 2 did not prove to be heplful, we need another example. The prologue of Romans (Rom. 1:3-4), analysed as a test case already in previous chapters, also serves well as an example here. It's history of interpretation has produced almost all possible variations of interpretative models in eschatology.

---

[32] Hahn, *Hoheitstitel*, 251, 292. He was later followed e.g. by Fuller, *Christology*, 17.

[33] Vielhauer, *EvTh 25* (1965) 26. Cf. the criticism presented by Balz, *Methodische Probleme*, (especially) 23-24. For a later discussion, see Kramer, *Christos Kyrios*, 9; Hengel, *Geschichte*, 60; Keck, *NTS 32* (1986) 368f.; Hurtado, *TS 40* (1979) 99.

[34] For the discussion on adoptionist Christology, see especially chapter 10 below.

[35] Hahn, *Hoheitstitel*, 115-117.

The Baurian evolutive scheme has had enormous effect also on the interpretation of the christological formula of Romans. As Bousset focused his analysis on christological titles, he was interested in the titles "Son of God" and "Kyrios". While the former, according to Bousset, never appeared as a fixed title in Jewish theology, it had to come from Hellenistic religions.[36]

In the circles of the history-of-religions school, however, the scheme of history affected the interpretation of Christology more than the use of christological titles. For example Bultmann interpreted the formula by referring to two different stages of tradition. He regarded the original formula (Rom. 1:3-4) archaic and located it in Jewish Christianity.[37] In that context, according to Bultmann, christological titles found in the formula, i.e. son of David and son of God, denoted simply the messianic king of Israel. This was changed in Hellenistic Christianity, to which Paul was thought to belong. In the Hellenistic Church the political messianology of the formula was interpreted in quite another way. Due to the influence of Hellenistic mystery religions the title son of God was understood to mean the divine nature of Christ. In contrast to this, Bultmann thought the title Son of David had begun to mean the earthly life of Jesus.[38]

As we saw above, Hahn adopted the evolutive scheme of history of the history-of-religions school, but he added Hellenistic Jewish Christianity after Jewish Christianity. Hahn further considered the earliest form of eschatology of the early Church futurist eschatology, a view that we have called polarized eschatology. On the one end of the scheme there was the Jesus of history, proclaiming the future Son of Man. On the other end there was the Son of David, the royal Messiah who would be enthroned in parousia. As Jesus in the formula is the Son of David already in humiliation, the formula did not fit in the earliest theology of Jewish Christianity. It had to be located in the sphere of Hellenistic Jewish Christianity.[39]

There was also another feature in the formula that, according to Hahn, confirmed the classification of the formula as a representative of Hellenistic Jewish Christian theology. Christ's exaltation was said to take place in the resurrection. This meant a significant change in the futurist eschatology of the early Church. As exaltation replaced the idea of parousia, such a view could

---

[36] Bousset, *Kyrios Christos*, 57, 99. As regards the interpretation of the prologue of Romans he was ambivalent, however, since he was aware of the background of kingship ideology in the Old Testament.

[37] See Bultmann, *ThR 8* (1936) 11.

[38] Bultmann, *Theologie*, 52f., 132.

[39] Hahn, *Hoheitstitel*, 253.

never find its home in early Palestinian Jewish Christianity.[40] The conception of enthronement as such was based on Jewish theology, but it was no longer placed in parousia. Now enthronement was believed to take place in resurrection, and this had to be a form of Christology that belonged to Hellenistic Jewish Christianity. Hahn calls it the "de-eschatologizing" ("Enteschatologisierung") of the enthronement theme.[41]

It is easy to see that Hahn's explanation is dependent on his fixed view of eschatological convictions in the early Church. He exploits those conceptions when constructing a convincing development in Christology according to his new scheme of history. He cannot avoid criticism, however. Hahn is making his conclusions merely by the help of the classification of theology that he has constructed. No other arguments are available. His hypothesis of a separate Hellenistic Jewish Christianity rests on the assumption that certain theological themes may be ascribed to such a group. This kind of assumption is supported only by the premise that Jewish Christianity as such taught futurist eschatology.

A hypothesis such as that falls when the view of the teaching of early Christianity changes. We have earlier seen that confessional formulas in the New Testament center on exaltation Christology. Thus, the evidence of the earliest phase of tradition does not support Hahn's hypothesis or premises. The conception of the theology of the first Christians must be reconsidered. Was there really a tension between exaltation and parousia – or are they merely complementary themes of the apocalyptic eschatology of Second Temple Jewish Christianity? It would be rather logical to conclude that a heavenly dominion of Christ was considered as a necessary premise for an idea of parousia.[42]

Hahn's solution did not completely displace the polarized view in the interpretation of Romans 1:3-4, however. For instance R.H. Fuller followed Hahn in many details but he attempted to maintain the futurist eschatology in the interpretation of the formula. He first reconstructed the earliest form of the formula by removing both the flesh-spirit dualism (as Hellenistic redaction) and the reference to power (as an expression of Paul's theology). What was

---

[40] Hahn, *Hoheitstitel*, 288, 292.

[41] Hahn, *Hoheitstitel*, 257.

[42] For example Thüsing does not see these themes as opposites in early Christian eschatology. Thüsing, *Erhöhungsvorstellung*, 91. Schade, in turn, parallels the prologue of the Romans with 1 Thess.1:9f., where the idea of parousia is explicit, and concludes that the themes of enthronement and Lordship connect these descriptions. Therefore it is not justified to contrast them. Schade, *Christologie*, 32–33. On the other hand, some scholars have thought that the formula of Romans is incomplete in the present form since it does not mention parousia, see Beasley–Murray, *TynB 31* (1980) 148.

left was a short formula: "Born of the seed of David; appointed Son of God from the resurrection of the dead".[43]

Fuller's main thesis was that the word ὁρίζω means predestination instead of appointment or installation ("declared to be" NRSV). Christ has been predestined to be our eschatological judge in the end of days: "predetermined from the time of the resurrection to be the eschatological Son of God at the parousia." This interpretation was confirmed by parallel occurrences of the word in Acts.[44] The occurrences in Acts no doubt support such a conclusion, but there are two weaknesses in Fuller's explanation. Even though one could explain the formula in the reduced form he has given, one could not treat Jesus' resurrection merely as an occasion when a predestination has been decreed. Christ's resurrection is the beginning of the eschatological resurrection from the dead and thus, as a special event, it is a special moment in history. Further, the formula does not speak of some vague seed of David that is destined to be a heavenly king, but refers rather to a distinct Davidide who is decreed to kingship in the resurrection. Early Christology, in general, agrees with this kind of explanation, and this we cannot say about the futurist eschatology. In addition to this it is hardly worth mentioning that the formula lacks any reference to parousia.

It seems that Fuller, too, has been biased in his explanation. He attempted to adjust the formula into futurist eschatology even by force. Even though the formula fits in the early Jewish Christian Church in many ways, it is in no way incompatible with the eschatological concept of parousia. The content of the formula, therefore, probably is incompatible with the idea of a polarized eschatology but, according to the present study, that is an inevitable result of comparing early Christology with Jewish mysticism. The formula, rather, expressed living eschatology where believers experienced eschatological reality in their own lives. They believed that the last days had already begun in the resurrection of the Davidide, and that they themselves now lived under the kingship of their Lord.

The solution for the problem of polarized eschatology seems thus evident. No real polarization ever existed. *In the context of the eschatological notion of the parousia there was no conception of Christ's future enthronement, a messianic installation that would take place only on the day of judgment.* The judicial discourse presents the event in another way.[45] Christ's entering upon the throne on the last day is an act that expresses his office as the supreme judge who will gather all people before him.

---

[43] Fuller, *Christology*, 165.

[44] Cf. above especially Acts 17:31.

[45] Cf. e.g. Schade, *Christologie*, 32f.

Resurrection Christology, presented in terms of enthronement discourse, does not contradict that view. Its expressions are different, naturally, but it's intention agrees with that of judicial discourse. In his resurrection Christ as a Davidic Messiah has been enthroned on the throne of Glory. In him the promises of Psalm 110 have been fulfilled. As a heavenly Lord he reigns "until he has put all his enemies under his feet".[46]

Therefore, the idea of a "de-eschatologizing" ("Enteschatologisierung") of the enthronement theme apparently presents the historical development of early Christology in a completely wrong way. The conception of enthronement in resurrection is the earliest form of exaltation Christology.[47] It is a belief that is constructed on the symbolic world of Second Temple Judaism. As an expression of Christian enthronement discourse it further represents innovative intertextual transformation of Jewish views. In this respect there is nothing that would prevent us from ascribing such Christology even to the first Jerusalem community.[48]

Judicial discourse, in turn, is a world of its own. It belongs to early Christian eschatology concentrating on God's day of wrath and the last judgment. Also it must be dated early – especially while it appears to derive from the teachings of Jesus himself. There is no reason to doubt that it has existed side by side with early enthronement Christology.

Judicial discourse differs somewhat from the previous two discourses that have been treated above. Even though many features common to apocalyptic Jewish mysticism have been exploited here, Psalm 110 has no relevant function in these passages. In eschatological descriptions the enthroned Christ is a heavenly judge who performs God's final judgment.

Therefore, the throne in judicial discourse is often βῆμα, the judgment seat of God – even though the term itself does not differ essentially from the

---

[46] This was Paul's notion in 1 Cor. 15:25.

[47] This was the conclusion of Schlier, as well. Since in his reconstruction the flesh and spirit antithesis belonged to the second phase of tradition (Hellenistic Jewish Christianity), the original formula contained no antithesis at all. Schlier, *Geschichte*, 215f.

[48] In many respects the new approach to earliest Christology, promoted e.g. by Hengel and Stuhlmacher as reviewed above, has altered the situation of interpretation. It is no longer useful to be content with an unreflective reception of the views presented e.g. by Bultmann and Tödt. According to Bultmann, the "earliest Church" was confused with its conceptions concerning eschatology. The "imminent dramatic End" controlled the consciousness of the Church, and "Jesus' advent and ministry was not yet clearly recognized as eschatological occurrence." Bultmann, *Theology I*, 43. The analysis of earliest traditions refers to the opposite direction. Earliest Christology was well organized and it was centered around the idea of Jesus' eschatological enthronement that justified both his Lordship and his office as an eschatological judge.

common words for throne. It is evidently God's throne and not some special throne made for that distinct purpose, and in certain passages this is also explicitly stated. The discourse, however, governs the formation of its meaning. In these descriptions the throne is, in particular, a place for judgment.

These descriptions also differ from other christological statements in the sense that Christ's resurrection has no role here. They describe rather his entering upon the throne – an image that emphasizes the inauguration of an eschatological climax.

In Jewish merkabah mysticism we have found several examples of different figures that take part in the final judgment. It seems to be an honorary task granted to several patriarchal characters or other heavenly figures. The straightforward typological application, however, remains insufficient here. We witness rather the intertextual transformation where Christ's exceptional status is brought to the fore.

Judicial discourse presents Christ as a heavenly judge who performs eschatological judgment on the last day. This description has often been falsely confused with enthronement statements and interpreted with the help of a strictly polarized pattern. Therefore, it is necessary to emphasize that, in early Christology depending on judicial discourse, Christ's Messianic enthronement is not the essential content of the description. This line of Christology does not compete with exaltation Christology referring to resurrection. It rather speaks of Christ's entering upon the judgment seat for the performing of the divine judgment.

§ 9 The History of Influence: Enthronement in Jewish Christian Pseudepigrapha

In New Testament writings exaltation discourse appears to have essential significance in the formation of early resurrection Christology. Such Christology has further an interesting history of influence. In Jewish Christian Pseudepigrapha there are several writings that originally derive from the sphere of Jewish mysticism or that are based on Jewish traditions, but which have later undergone remarkable Christian editing and re-writing. Some of these pseudepigraphic works contain merkabah speculation, and what is even more significant, the re-written parts speak of Christ's heavenly enthronement. Such descriptions directly reveal the relationship between Jewish mysticism and early Christology in a context which most probably belongs to Jewish Christianity.

9.1. Exalted Christ in the Ascension of Isaiah

The main evidence for an intentional reception of early enthronement Christology in an apocalyptic work is the pseudepigraphic writing the Ascension of Isaiah.[1] As we have seen earlier in chapter 3 of this study, this writing presents precisely what it promises, a story of an ascension. The vision in AscIsa chapters 6-11 describes Isaiah's heavenly journey through seven heavens. The story in itself sounds rather traditional. It is quite an ordinary Jewish apocalyptic writing depending on an ascent structure. In the story, however, the description of separate heavens is interrupted when Isaiah reaches the seventh heaven. The focus of the narration is shifted on the life, suffering, and resurrection of Jesus. Such a change creates a problem concerning the origin of the writing.

Earlier in this study it was suggested that, in the course of the tradition process, a traditional Jewish merkabah vision has probably been replaced by Christian message. Instead of a vision of God's throne the manuscript contains several descriptions of the history of Christ. The other alternative is that this is originally a Jewish Christian work that exploits ascent stories of Jewish mysticism. It is not essential to solve this problem,[2] however, because the

---

[1] The work itself is rather late, and in the present form it sounds mainly Christian. However, as we have noted earlier, the text evidently has a long prehistory. Several features in the text, especially the description of the heavenly journey, may well derive from Jewish apocalyptic. See Knibb, *Old Testament Pseudepigrapha I*, 147ff.

[2] This question is left open also by Himmelfarb in her *Ascent*, even though she had previously supported the idea of a Jewish original behind the Christian work. Himmelfarb, *Ascent*, 58. For the discussion, see Hall, *JBL 113* (1994) 464.

basic point of departure is clear. In this work Christ's ascension is described in terms of Jewish ascent structure.[3]

The story in itself is quite consistent. Isaiah ascends to the seventh heaven in order to hear a prediction concerning the Beloved one, who is to be called Christ. In the seventh heaven Isaiah hears the story of Christ, beginning from his descent and birth, and ending with the passion story and resurrection. The resurrection leads to ascension and finally to enthronement (9:6-18).

In chapter 9 there is a carefully structured description of trinitarian worship that takes place in the seventh heaven.[4] It begins with the worship of Christ. The righteous ones worship him and Isaiah joins them. Then the angels worship Christ (9:28-32). Next the Holy Spirit is worshiped. Here again the righteous ones worship first and Isaiah joins them (9:33-36; here an angelic interpretation, v. 36: "Worship him, for this is the angel of the Holy Spirit who has spoken in you and also in the other righteous."). Finally, in 9:40-10:6, both Christ and the angel of the Holy Spirit worship the Lord, and other beings join their worship. God is depicted as the "Most High of the high ones" (10:6).

In regard to this passage an angelic intepretation of the Christology has also been suggested. According to 9:30 (the Ethiopian text), Christ "was transformed and became like an angel." This has been seen as proof for transformational Christology.[5] The text may be corrupt here, and the passage has probably referred to Isaiah's transformation.[6] Furthermore, the angelic interpretation is in contradiction with the explicit prohibition of the worshiping of angels in the writing. Christ, evidently, is the object of worship in the trinitarian passage, and therefore, according to the writer, he cannot have an angelic function in the heavenly world.[7]

Next Isaiah wittnesses the event when Christ is commissioned to his ministry in the world: "Go out and descend through all the heavens." (10:8).

---

[3] The first part of the work, the Martyrdom, is evidently quite old. Nickelsburg has suggested that it is related to traditions well known in the Second Temple period. He has even compared it with the writings of Qumran and found plausible parallels. The theme concerning the throne vision in AscIsa is connected with the visions of the prophets Micah and Isaiah himself. See Nickelsburg, *Jewish Literature*, 143f. Such references show that apocalyptic writers preferred traditions that were able to prove continuity between their own work and history. From such a point of view we may date the traditions behind AscIsa quite early.

[4] For the analysis of the structure, see Bauckham, *NTS* 27 (1980) 333-334.

[5] So Gieschen, *Christology*, 236-237.

[6] Himmelfarb refers to the Latin and Slavonic renderings that speak of Isaiah's transformation, Himmelfarb, *Ascent*, 56, see esp. 135 footnote 33: "there is no reason for Christ to be transformed into a being of lesser status before Isaiah worships him."

[7] For the aspect of worship, see e.g. Bauckham, *NTS* 27 (1980) 323, 333.

A more detailed story of Christ's descent, life and ascension follows.[8] There are several overlappings in the story, so that the speaker returns to the event of crucifixion from time to time. For example in chapter 11 Jesus' death and resurrection are summarized in a short, almost homological sentence (11:20-21):[9] "I saw how they crucified him on a tree, and likewise (how) after the third day he rose".

Jesus' exaltation is predicted already in chapter 10, and thus it is included in the commissioning: "but in glory you shall ascend and sit at my right hand" (10:14). The exaltation pattern is similar to those found in canonical writings and especially in traditional and homological statements. The sitting "at the right hand" of God, taken from Psalm 110, once again serves as the basic (sub)metaphor which expresses the act of enthronement. The occurrence of the submetaphor in this kind of context is not surprising, however, since we have found similar constructions, for instance, in Lukan traditions.[10]

In the extensive passage AscIsa 10:17-11:33 we actually find a short apocryphal gospel. Christ's descent through the heavens is described in detail and the story also serves the purpose of preparing a punishment for fallen angels.[11] The story of the miraculous birth with its gynegological interest (11:9) bears the marks of a rather late tradition. Jesus' life is referred to only briefly, and the passion story appears to have more significance for the writer. The ascension, however, is the main theme of the work.[12]

The highlight of the narration comes finally in the end of the book. After his resurrection the Lord ascends through seven heavens. All the angels of the firmament, including Satan, worship Christ during the journey. The worship is repeated in each heaven. Finally, in the seventh heaven there follows a majestic scene of Christ's enthronement.

---

[8] Rowland is evidently right when assuming that the descent pattern in the story is not particularly Jewish. Rowland, *Open Heaven*, 262. Actually, it may refer to a Gnostic reworking of the text. See Gruenwald, *Merkavah Mysticism*, 62. In general, however, AscIsa does not appear to contain Gnostic overtones.

[9] Cf. e.g. the early homology in 1 Cor. 15:3-5; and the kerygmatic statements in Acts 2:23-24; 3:15; 4:10; 5:30-31.

[10] Cf. above chapter 5.1., and Luke 7:55; Acts 2:34f.

[11] The theme of punishing the angels was also significant in the traditions of 1 Enoch, see e.g. 1 En. 14:1ff. In the cosmology of the writing the lowest heaven is the place for the "angels of the air". These creatures resemble demons, and they are most probably referring to fallen angels. See Carr, *Angels*, 145f.

[12] We might compare this structure with the short description of Christ's ascension in Eph. 4:10, that could in a restricted sense be called a story of his heavenly journey. "He who descended is the same one who ascended far above all the heavens, so that he might fill all things."

"And I saw how he ascended into the seventh heaven, and all the righteous and all the angels praised him. And then I saw that he sat down at the right hand of that Great Glory, whose glory I told you I could not behold. And also I saw that the angel of the Holy Spirit sat on the left." (11:32-33).

Such an extensive description of Christ's ascension is rather unique in early Christian literature. In the New Testament the beginning of the book of Hebrews is somewhat comparable to this passage, and only certain sections of the book of Revelation provide a similar scene.[13]

The writer of the final version of AscIsa has applied the complete ascent structure to Jesus' exaltation. Christ ascends to the seventh heaven, he sits down "at the right hand" of God on the throne of Glory, and he is being praised and worshiped by the angels and all the righteous. It seems evident that the rejection of the worship of angels (7:21) serves the purpose of focusing the worship not only on God, but on Christ and the Holy Spirit, as well.[14]

Here early resurrection theology has been explicated in terms of Jewish mysticism. It has been placed in a story about a vision and a heavenly journey. The main feature that has been exploited in the "Christian merkabah" is the throne in the highest heaven. There are several different thrones in AscIsa. Also Isaiah himself is promised a throne. Christ's throne is unique, however. It is actually the throne of Glory, and therefore Psalm 110 has suited perfectly this enthronement statement.

Therefore, the Christology of AscIsa is quite similar to that of early homologies in the New Testament. AscIsa is a beautiful example of exaltation Christology that has been constructed on a precise ascent structure in the context of a heavenly journey. All the main elements of Jewish mysticism are present in the story. One could not find a more expressive example of early Christology in its natural theological context.[15]

Such a text proves that the core of exaltation Christology fits well into an actual story of a heavenly journey. Merkabah speculation is a most suitable

---

[13] Cf. Heb. 1:3; Rev. 3:21; 5:6-12: 7:15-17. Later in Christian pseudepigrapha the submetaphor of sitting at the right hand has been preserved in different contexts. In the Apocryphon of James (Nag Hammadi) the ascension is referred to: "today I must take (my place at) the right hand of the Father." (ApocJas 14:30.) In the Apocalypse of Peter, however, the idea of Christ's parousia governs the context: "And all will see how I come upon an eternal shining cloud, and the angels of God who will sit with me on the throne of my glory at the right hand of my heavenly Father." (ApocPet. 6.)

[14] Cf. Stuckenbruck, *Angel Veneration*, 100.

[15] In addition to the discussion on the problem of transformation in 9:30, certain references to angels, and especially to the angel of the Holy Spirit, might suggest an angelic intepretation of the Christology of AscIsa. This, however, is not plausible. As Bauckham has noted, there is a "rigorous differentiation" between Christ and the angels in this passage (see e.g. 9:32). Bauckham, *NTS 27* (1980) 334.

environment for the description of Christ's heavenly enthronement. In a sense AscIsa infers backwards the dynamics of the emergence of early Christology. The writer places exaltation Christology into the context to which it originally belonged.[16]

Therefore, even as a late text, AscIsa becomes strong evidence in the search for the nature of early Christology. It is an example of a Jewish Christian reception of New Testament Christology, understood as a part of the larger corpus of Second Temple Jewish writings. For the writer, Jewish apocalyptic and early Christology belonged together. He did not see any essential difference between them. Yet in AscIsa, however, the intertextual transformation typical of early Christological descriptions may be detected. The enthroned Christ is more than merely a fulfilment of some kind of prototype found in Jewish tradition. He is the Son of God who reigns on the throne of Glory.

The Ascension of Isaiah thus confirms the conclusion that has been drawn during the analysis of the New Testament. The writings of Jewish mysticism were exploited in the construction of early Christology. The symbolic world of the first Christians comprised the ideas of ascension and enthronement. God's throne was constantly a key symbol for theologians. Also Psalm 110 and the submetaphor "at the right hand" preserved their status as significant signs for the central message of exaltation Christology. When the Christian enthronement discourse was later applied to a Jewish writing such as AscIsa, all the pieces fit together. A Jewish merkabah vision was easily turned into a vision of the enthroned Christ.

9.2. Enthroned Davidide in the Sibyllines

The Sibyllines is a collection of various different eschatological writings, some of which are of Jewish origin, others of Christian origin. In this collection we most probably also have such Jewish writings that have later undergone a Christian redaction and re-writing. The enthronement theme is clearly seen in several oracles, and these passages are referring to Jesus' resurrection.

In the first book of the Sibylline Oracles there is a Christian passage on the

---

[16] The idea of an intentional exploitation of a Jewish original seems to suit best the interpretation of AscIsa. Hall has stated, however, that the work was not written primarily to reveal what Christ accomplished. Therefore the function of the Beloved one in the story has been misinterpreted. According to Hall, the Vision of Isaiah is a book about how Isaiah attains a heavenly throne. Therefore he considers it a consistent *Christian* work. Hall, *JBL* *113* (1994) 476-477. It is difficult to imagine, however, that Christ's ascent and enthronement could be merely side points in an early Christian writing.

incarnation and life of Christ.[17] In the end of the passage resurrection and exaltation are described.

"But when he comes to light again in three days and shows a model to men and teaches all things, he will mount on clouds and journey to the house of heaven leaving to the world the account of the gospel." (SibOr. 1, 379-382)

Jesus in this Christian passage is called Christ and "the son of the great God" (324, 331). In the exaltation passage he is also identified as the "shoot" after whom Christians are named. In this sense he is probably identified as a Davidide, even though this is not explicitly stated in the section.

The resurrected Christ is further mounting "on clouds". This may be a reference to Acts 1:9, but we must note that the statement does not remain without an explanation. Christ's exaltation on clouds means a "journey to the house of heaven". Thus the event of exaltation is interpreted in terms of an ascent structure. First of all, it is a heavenly journey. Secondly, the exaltation reaches the house of heaven.[18]

The writer most probably refers to the heavenly Temple or palace where God resides. It is the only meaningful "house" that can be found in the heavens. In the symbolic world of the writer this must further be the house from which Christ has descended in the incarnation (1, 324f.). The house is not mentioned in that context, but the pattern of descending to the earth is clearly described.

Thus these few words actually reveal a complete ascent structure behind the train of thought. In his resurrection Christ the "Shoot" is exalted to the highest heaven and he enters the house of God in heaven. The exaltation pattern is quite similar to that of AscIsa, and the narration is more clearly related to Jewish heavenly journeys than any New Testament passage (apart from the descriptions of an enthronement "at the right hand" of God).

In the second book of the Sibylline Oracles Jesus appears as a heavenly judge who performs the final judgment. The enthronement scene describes the entering upon the throne in the last day. Christ in this passage is the Son of Man in the manner of Gospel tradition.

"When Sabaoth Adonai, who thunders on high, dissolves fate and raises the dead, and takes his seat on a heavenly throne, and establishes a great pillar, Christ, imperishable himself, will come in glory on a cloud toward the imperishable one with the blameless angels. He will sit on the right of the Great One, judging at the tribunal the life of pious men and the way of impious men." (SibOr. 2, 238-244).

---

[17] According to Collins, the first book is primarily a Jewish work provided with an extensive Christian redaction, see Collins, *Old Testament Pseudepigrapha I*, 331-333.

[18] This passage, evidently, refers to a bodily exaltation, not a visionary ascension. In this respect the setting differs essentially from e.g. that of TLev. 2:5-8, or 1En. 14:8ff.

The enthronement itself is not described. Only the basic metaphor "on the right of the Great One" reveals that the enthroned Christ is a Davidide who is judging people in this eschatological climax. The influence of Psalm 110 is strong, even though the tradition as such may have carried this theme in its proper context.[19]

In the sixth book of the Sibylline Oracles we have a hymn to Christ that is completely Christian, but that also exploits Jewish tradition in great deal.[20]

"I speak from my heart of the great famous son of the Immortal, to whom the Most High, his begetter, gave a throne to possess before he was born, since he was raised up the second time according to the flesh, when he had washed in the streams of the river Jordan, which moves with gleaming foot, sweeping the waves." (SibOr. 6, 1-5)

Here Christ's throne is predestined to him even before his birth. It is probable that the description of the promise derives from the Similitudes of 1 Enoch.[21] Furthermore, there is much weight on Jesus' baptism here, even though the Christology of the section is not adoptionist. "He will escape the fire and be the first to see delightful God coming in the spirit on the white wings of a dove." (6-7).[22] In the poetic description of this oracle Christ is again a Davidide who will appear enthroned on the day of the final judgment.

"From one wallet men will have surfeit of bread when the house of David brings forth a shoot. In his hand are the whole world and earth and heaven and sea. He will flash like lightning on the earth as the two begotten from each other's sides once saw him when he first shone forth." (SibOr. 6,15-19).

According to the sixth oracle the enthroned Christ is a universal ruler who reigns on his heavenly throne until the last day. Even though the background of the description is evidently Jewish, it is proper to note that the "figure" appearing here is Christ. The "son of the Immortal" is not a Jewish figure that has been exploited in a Christian context.[23]

---

[19] Therefore, this passage is more closely linked to gospel tradition. It is probable that the Son of Man logions have been exploited, even though the term Son of Man in itself does not appear here. Cf. Matt. 19:28; 25:31ff.

[20] For the Christian nature of the sixth book, see Collins, *Old Testament Pseudepigrapha I*, 406.

[21] So Hengel, *Studies*, 188-189, who emphasizes that in this passage God gives the pre-existent one his own throne.

[22] There has been discussion about the nature of the Christology of this passage, and it has been paralleled with the beliefs of the Ebionites. Collins is right, however, when remarking that features of SibOr. 6 are not essentially sectarian. Collins, *Old Testament Pseudepigrapha I*, 406.

[23] For instance Bock does not make such a distinction very carefully, see Bock, *Blasphemy*, 158 footnote 134.

In the seventh book of the Sibylline Oracles we find finally a perfect description of the ascension and enthronement of the Davidide. The oracle in itself contains a prediction of the time of destruction. This prediction is interrupted by a fine description of the messianic Davidide who will come and bring salvation to the elect.

> "For one day that time will come to pass when once for all men will beseech God, but will not stop fruitless troubles. But all will be fulfilled through the house of David. For God entrusted and gave a throne to him. The angels will sleep under his feet – those who cause fires to gleam and those who pour forth rivers, those who protect cities and those who send out storm winds. A difficult life will come upon many men, entering souls and changing hearts of men. But when a young shoot puts forth eyes from the root [Isa 11:1] which once distributed abundant nurture to all branches..." (SibOr. 7, 29-39).

This passage provides important evidence about the process of how Old Testament royal tradition survived in Jewish Christian tradition. The promise to David regarding the throne of his successor has a key role in this description.[24] David's throne is simultaneously the throne of the Messianic figure, the "Shoot" of David (Isa 11:1). The writer exploits similar Old Testament passages as does the Gospel tradition. Enthronement itself is not described. The throne is simply "given" to the Davidide.[25] On his throne the new David has a unique status, however. He is exalted above the angels. This tradition resembles the one in the letter to the Hebrews.[26]

Angels have an important role in this description. The angels under Christ's feet are angels of the elements. Such angels appear often in apocalyptic writings. Already in Jubilees 2:2 we find for instance the angels of the spirits of the winds, and the angels of the spirits of fire. In Enochic literature similar conceptions constantly appear.[27]

The writers of Sibylline Oracles, and escpecially the writer of the seventh oracle, still exploit enthronement discourse in their Christology. The resurrected Christ is primarily a Davidide who has been exalted on his heavenly throne in his ascension. The ascent structure is evident behind these descriptions. These oracles differ from the narration of the Ascension of Isaiah, however.

The Old Testament royal tradition appears to have influenced these descriptions greatly. This is probably the reason why the content of the oracles

---

[24] Cf. 2 Sam. 7:12-16, Ps. 132:11 and 89:36; for the tradition itself, see the analysis in 6.1.

[25] "The house of David is summed up in an individual figure, presumably Christ, who is enthroned above the angels." Collins, *Old Testament Pseudepigrapha I*, 409.

[26] Cf. 5.3. above.

[27] See e.g. 1 En. 60:12-22; 82:10-14; 2 En. 4-6; 19:4.

is closer to the New Testament than Jewish apocalyptic writings, even though several passages exploit Jewish materials.

Thus, these oracles also serve as evidence for the reception of early Christian exaltation Christology in later Jewish Christian thinking. The apocalyptic scene has remained unchanged. Several themes of early Christology have been applied to Jewish tradition so that the details differ clearly from New Testament teaching. The content of the Christology, however, repeats the themes of both Gospel tradition and the Christology of early homologies.

9.3. Paul and merkabah in the Apocalypse of Paul

The apocryphal writing called the Apocalypse of Paul, dating earliest in the second century A.D., describes the heavenly journey of Paul himself. It is easy to understand that one of the main reasons for the exploitation of such a theme is Paul's notion in 2 Cor. 12. When Paul spoke of "a person" who "fourteen years ago" was "caught up to the third heaven" (12:2-4), he inevitably set expectations for speculation over mysticism.

"And after that I saw one of the spiritual beings beside me and he caught me up in the Holy Spirit and carried me up to the third part of Heaven, which is the third heaven." (ApcPl 11).

In the third heaven Paul met several exalted patriarchs, such as Enoch (20). In the city of Christ he saw further many of the prophets (25) and David (29). There was also a paradise (cf. 2 Cor. 12), but the tree of life was not identified as the throne (45). Paul's vision here is similar to visions of Jewish apocalypticism in many respects. The archangel Michael leads Paul before the heavenly throne (43). Also the scene of heavenly liturgy is quite familiar in many respects.

"And I looked and I saw heaven move as a tree shaken by the wind. And they suddenly threw themselves on their faces before the throne; and I saw the 24 elders and the 4 beasts worshiping God, and I saw the altar and the veil and the throne, and all were rejoicing" (44).

In addition to the idea of the heavenly journey the Apocalypse of Paul thus brings forth the image of four beasts worshiping God before the throne. This theme has been connected with the feature of 24 elders who also appear before the throne.[28] Once again, the heavenly court is simultaneously a heavenly temple.

The heavenly Temple is carefully described. There is an altar and a veil. Therefore, the main purpose of the passage becomes evident. The throne of

---

[28] This passage is evidently influenced by Revelation 4 since the 24 elders are mentioned. Gruenwald, *Merkavah Mysticism*, 71. The basic scene, however, agrees completely with that of Jewish mysticism.

God is located in the Holy of Holies. It becomes identified as the Holy Ark behind the veil. This, naturally, is the identification that has been made even before, and which is quite consistent with the tradition that we have investigated throughout the study.[29]

In the concluding passage an angel brings Paul back to the Mount of Olives. There Paul meets the apostles and makes everything known to them. In this passage the description reminds us of the vision of Ezekiel in that the traditional theme of the chariot recurs. "While the apostles were talking with us the Savior Christ appeared to us out of the chariot of the cherubim."

This, in fact, is an extraordinary statement mentioning Christ's chariot. The writer of the Apocalypse of Paul has united the appearance of the Resurrected with traditional theophanies. He is thus using metaphors with which the resurrection of Jesus Christ has been identified and interpreted as an enthronement. This has not been done by using common images of early Christology or Pauline theology, but by exploiting metaphors taken from Jewish apocalypticism.

These examples show that the reception of early Christian exaltation Christology was wide and the enthronement theme had significant influence on the theology of the apocrypha. Especially in the Ascension of Isaiah we find a remarkable Christian reworking of a Jewish apocalyptic writing. The vision of a heavenly journey is climaxed in the enthronement of Christ. In this description the aspects of the enthronement theme of early Christology are exploited in a creative manner.

In addition to this, several books of the Sibylline Oracles and the Apocalypse of Paul show that enthronement discourse has maintained its influence in apocryphal literature. These writings imitate Jewish style in their presentation, even though the direct connection to Jewish tradition may be rather vague. The resurrected Christ is described as an enthroned Davidide whose reign aims at an apocalyptical consummation of the ages.

---

[29] Gruenwald is somewhat puzzled with such an identification. "What, however, is the throne of God doing in the heavenly Temple?", he asks. He admits that already Isaiah 6 refers to such identification, and that the idea of a heavenly Temple is clear in TLev. 5. Nevertheless, he remains ambivalent in his final conclusions. Gruenwald, *Merkavah Mysticism,* 72. The analysis made in the present study shows, however, that the identification of the Ark and God's throne is most suitable and solves many problems in the interpretation of both Jewish mysticism and early Christology.

IV

The Nature of Early Enthronement Christology

§ 10 Some Problems with the "Theocratic" Theory of Adoptionist Christology

It is not so easy to define the nature of early Christology. One might suppose that, after analysing both the tradition of Jewish merkabah mysticism and the main features of early enthronement Christology, it would be unproblematic to suggest some new insights for the explanation of the teachings of the early Church. There are certain obstacles, however, that must first be dealt with before new hypotheses can be introduced. Any scholar approaching the subject encounters the problem concerning the nature of the earliest Jewish Christianity. And, as we know, this is a field of heated discussion.

In scholarship there have been several influential models of interpretation that have given their own solution to the problems of early Christology. Jewish Christianity has been considered legalistic and traditionalistic. Circumcision is considered as one of its characteristic features. In respect of the present study, however, the main peculiarity was the alleged low Christology that has been detected in several patristic writings. Earliest, Jerusalem centered Jewish Christianity is said to have generated the so called adoptionist Christology.

In earlier chapters we have seen that, in the study of Jewish mysticism, there was vivid discussion concerning the deification of certain heavenly beings or even patriarchs enthroned on a heavenly throne. The problem concerning adoptionism as a scholarly question is quite the opposite though. The line of thought is basically simple. According to the theory, the first Christians and apostles thought that, as regards the nature of Jesus, he was not a true Son of God but that he only became a "son" in the resurrection.[1] Jesus was no more than a Jew and a prophet, and analoguously the early Palestinian Church was a thoroughly Jewish community – with strict monotheism excluding all "ontological" views of the divinity of Jesus Christ. This theory has formed the basis for the concept of progressive development in the making of Christology.

---

[1] For example, Käsemann relies rather strongly on this feature in his famous article on the coherence of early theology, 'Begründet der neutestamentliche Kanon die Einheit der Kirche?', *Exegetische Versuche I*, 214-223, see esp. 215. Dunn, writing on unity and diversity in the New Testament, considers adoptionist Christology a significant example of Christological diversity. See e.g. Dunn, *Unity and Diversity*, 243. In the debate in England over the theme of the "Myth of God Incarnate", likewise, adoptionist Christology was used as a weighty argument in defining the nature of early Christology for instance by Goulder, *The Myth of God Incarnate*, 77-78.

Building on the Old Testament theme of the enthronement of the Davidic king, the adoptionist theory attempted to explain how the ideas of adoption and enthronement were exploited in early exaltation Christology. Therefore, for a long time, this theory has provided an influential explanation for the subject that is the very topic of the present study: the heavenly enthronement of the Davidide in resurrection.

The theory itself actually originated quite early in the history of biblical criticism. The first task for our analysis is the investigation of the earliest arguments that were used in the development of the theory. Secondly, however, we must concentrate on the so called Ebionite hypothesis that has later been the main argument in the explanation of the teachings of Jewish Christianity.

10.1. The theory of theocratic adoptionism in scholarship

The first scholars to use the concept of adoptionism were the great figures of early biblical criticism, D.F. Strauss and J. Weiss. They made use of the idea of adoption when characterizing the nature of the Christology in passages such as Rom. 1:3–4 and Acts 2:36. We must remember, of course, that Strauss and Weiss did not work together. They belonged to different times and different generations. Bearing this in mind we can explicate the first occurrences of this interpretation.

In his book *Das Leben Jesu* (1835–1836) Strauss defined theocratic Christology as a Son of God Christology which speaks of Jesus as a king.[2] He thought that the reason for this kind of expression could be found only in the idea of adoption in the Old Testament. The king of Israel was called Son of God, as can be seen in passages such as 2 Sam. 7:14 and Psalms 2:7 and 89:28. God adopted the king of Israel as his son. In this way the theocratic status of the king was expressed and it also legitimized his reign. Strauss thought that this theocratic sense is the original meaning of the term Son of God in Messianology. Thus he also assumed that this was the way Jesus himself might have used the term.[3]

In a later monograph Strauss applied this theory to the prologue of Romans, in particular to verses 3 and 4 which we have investigated above. Strauss says that the description of Jesus, on the one hand, as a human being in the lineage of David and, on the other hand, as the Son of God in power after the

---

[2] According to Strauss, in the New Testament there are at least four types of Son of God Christology: a physical one (the conception by the Holy Spirit, Luke 1:35), a metaphorical one (the relationship of father and son, Matthew 5:45), and a metaphysical one (John 10:30). In addition, the term is a Messianic title, synonymous with Christ. The latter sense, says Strauss, can be seen in the theocratic interpretation. Strauss, *Leben Jesu*, 478.

[3] Strauss, *Leben Jesu*, 479.

resurrection is a clear example of theocratic Christology. Those who knew Jesus as the son of Joseph could well call him the Son of God in a theocratic sense.[4]

After Strauss, Weiss in his famous book *'Das Urchristentum'* [*Early Christianity*], followed the same line of interpretation, even though he did not share Strauss' theological views.[5] In the new context of the theory of "consistent eschatology" Weiss wrote that Jesus, as a radical Jewish rabbi, had awaited his eschatological exaltation according to the expectations concerning the Son of Man and Son of David.[6] Later this thought also found a place in the early Jewish-Christian party. This can be seen in passages such as Acts 2:36 and Rom. 1:4.[7]

Thus Weiss also refers to the passages that have been crucial in the present study where the relation of Jewish merkabah mysticism and early Christology has been investigated. Consistent eschatology was not Weiss' only interpretation concerning these passages, however. In *'Das Urchristentum'* he took these ideas one step further. The adoption of the Israelite king was a normal feature in Jewish teaching. The adoption took place in the act of enthronement. According to Weiss, this was the reason why Jesus too must be an adopted Son, since he was exalted to the right hand of God.[8]

In Weiss' explanation there is a sharp contradiction between exaltation Christology and the Christology of pre-existence. His main argument in this question was the content of Acts 2:36. The idea of adoption excludes the concept of natural sonship. The only conclusion can be that, according to this line of theology, Jesus was not the Messiah or Son of God from the very beginning, but became one by the appointment of God.[9] According to Weiss, in the prologue of Romans these two views collide: "the Son of God from the very beginning (Paul), and Jesus, who has been exalted in the resurrection as

---

[4] "The Psalm about the Son of God who had been born... could be applied to Jesus by those who saw him as a son of Joseph and at the same time understood this divine begetting and sonship in a Theocratic sense... When we read what the Apostle Paul writes about Jesus in the prologue of Romans (1:3)... so we see how little these two points of view exclude each other." D.F. Strauss, *Das Leben Jesu für das deutsche Volk bearbeitet II*, 14.

[5] Weiss is famous for his "consistent eschatology", which has nothing to do with Strauss.

[6] Weiss, *Die Predigt Jesu*, 51, 54.

[7] Weiss, *Die Predigt Jesu*, 54–55.

[8] Weiss, *Das Urchristentum*, 86.

[9] "Adoption is used here as an opposite to the natural Sonship which one gains by birth. This is why we have here the idea that Jesus was not a Messiah... or a Son of God from the beginning, but that he only became one by a certain... act of God." Weiss, *Das Urchristentum*, 85.

the "Son of God in power", which means a royal ruler of the world (the early Church)".[10]

This interpretation of Weiss's is so carefully defined and detailed that it is actually he who is regarded as the "father" of the theory of adoptionism, not Strauss. It is easy to see that the expositions of Strauss and Weiss were quite similar. In both cases the arguments for the idea of adoptionism rely on the concept of the theocratic adoption of the Davidide.

Without being thoroughly examined or questioned by scholars, the adoptionist theory gradually became a standard one in the field of biblical studies. It was popular, for example, in the critical tradition of the school of the History of Religion. In his book *Kyrios Christos* Bousset described the two early forms of Christology as pneumatic and adoptionist.[11] Bultmann in turn explained the origin of the Son of God Christology on the basis of the same premises. In the context of exaltation terminology the Son of God Christology is Jewish in nature. According to Bultmann, the theology of incarnation, by contrast, was later and Hellenistic.[12]

As a standard theory, adoptionism later gained many adherents. In post-Bultmannian existentialism it became an essential premise for the explanation of the development of Christology, as we saw above.[13] For the critical voices one should mention E. Schweizer, who commented on the accepted interpretation with a remark that the early Church must have already considered the earthly ministry of Jesus as Messianic.[14] O. Michel in turn introduced the theory of Bultmann as expounded above, but pointed to another interpretation in line with the kenotic Christology of Phil 2.[15]

In this way the theory of adoptionist Christology as formulated by Strauss and Weiss gradually entered the field of biblical studies. According to the theory early exaltation Christology refers not merely to enthronement but also to adoption. Therefore the ontological question becomes relevant. It is important to note that the theory does not mean that Jesus would become

---

[10] See Weiss, *Das Urchristentum*, 85.

[11] Bousset, *Kyrios Christos*, 263–264.

[12] Bultmann, *Theologie*, 53.

[13] See footnote 1 above. For instance in the interpretation of the prologue of Romans, adoptionism was accepted by Knox, *Romans*, 382; Robinson, *Kerygma und historischer Jesus*, 69 n. 2; Wengst, *Christologische Formel*, 107; and later e.g. Jewett, *Living Text*, 114; Schmithals, *Römerbrief*, 51.

[14] Schweizer, *EvTh 15* (1955) 563–564.

[15] See Michel, *Römer (1955)*, 30–31, and Kuss, *Römerbrief*, 6–8. In a later edition of his commentary Michel rejects the adoptionist theory quite clearly, *Römer (1963)*, 38–39.

ontologically the Son of God in the resurrection.[16] It states that Jesus was merely a man and was raised as a man into heaven. Many scholars accepted the adoptionist interpretation in this form.

Later this view met with criticism but it seems that adoptionism was often misunderstood. Many commentators seem to oppose the theory because they think that adoptionism refers to an ontological change in the resurrection.[17] As we have seen, this is not the case in the ideas of Strauss and Weiss. In this theory there are features, however, that raise several questions. The main problem concerns the conception of adoptionism itself. Is there a real connection between early exaltation Christology and later "heretical" adoptionism, or should we strictly separate these conceptions from each other?

10.2. Adoptionism and the Ebionite theory

The basic idea in Strauss' and Weiss' theory was the conviction that earliest Jewish Christianity maintained its monotheistic beliefs and presented the status of the exalted Christ in terms of Old Testament political messianism. This kind of view became later quite popular among scholars and it was justified with the so called Ebionite theory. According to this interpretation the teaching and Christology of earliest Jewish Christianity was similar to that of Jewish Christian Ebionites of the patristic period. The Ebionites were considered pure adoptionists.

The application of the term "adoptionism" as such already shows that even Weiss at least implicitly identified apostolic teaching with a later dogmatic heresy, even though he never mentioned special groups or the Ebionites. Later such identification was made openly and with definite purpose. Ebionites were regarded as an early Christian group and, according to the theory, its roots were found in the earliest Jerusalem centered Jewish Christianity.[18]

There are, therefore, several questions that need to be answered. Could there be a direct connection between biblical adoptionism and dogmatic adoptionism? Was the dogmatic concept of adoptionism connected with biblical passages concerning resurrection, as scholars have suggested? And finally:

---

[16] Only H.W. Schmidt seems to speak of an ontological change in this context. He thinks that in the resurrection Jesus became divine by the Holy Spirit he was given. This is why the term "Son of God" would also refer to the nature of Christ. Schmidt, *Römer*, 18.

[17] See Boismard, *RB 60* (1953) 6; Barrett, *Romans*, 20.

[18] For instance Dunn based his identification of earliest "Palestinian" (Jewish) Christianity completely on his reconstruction of Ebionite Christology. He was convinced that Jewish Christianity as such held to the adoptionist view, and he also suggested that Ebionites were the heirs of the traditional line of Jewish Christianity led in the beginning by James in Jerusalem. Dunn, *Unity and Diversity*, 237-245.

what do we know about the Ebionites and their Christology? Earliest post-biblical writings can hardly help us answer the question.

From the very beginning for instance the prologue of Romans was used as an argument in favour of the Christology of incarnation. This is evident especially in the writings of the Apostolic Fathers (see for example Ignatius, I Sm. 1:1; I Trall. 9:1; I Eph. 18:2).[19] In these writings the enthronement theme did not have a central part as regards theological disagreement. The point of weight was on Christ's Davidic descent. According to this evidence the prologue of Romans does not seem to have been part of any alleged controversies concerning adoptionist Christology among early Christian communities, and the same must be said about Peter's speech in Acts 2.[20]

This much we can learn from earliest post-biblical writings. It is apparent that, according to these examples, a disagreement over exaltation Christology was not the key subject that would explain the alleged complex and tense relations between different local Churches. The Ebionite theory does not rest on this kind of evidence, however. Ebionites are mentioned in the heresiologies of later Church Fathers, and these writings have always been essential for the theory.[21]

Among western Fathers the first one to write about the Ebionites is Irenaeus, around 200 C.E. He must be dependent on earlier documents, but they are no longer extant. According to Irenaeus, the Ebionites was an early Jewish Christian sect that was known for its observance of the Jewish law and some legalistic practices, such as the rite of circumcision (e.g. AH 1.26.2.).[22]

The appellation itself has been taken from Hebrew, meaning "poor". A link to early Jewish Christianity has been suggested since, in the New Testament, the term denoted the humble identity of the community, probably reflecting their life-style (Gal. 2:10; Rom. 15:26).[23] Also Qumran has been mentioned in

---

[19] A similar use can be found in Irenaeus, where the problem is Gnostic docetism, Adv. haer. 3.16.3; 3.22.1.

[20] As we have seen, the idea of the designation of Jesus in Rom 1:4 inspired the discussion of the Fathers. There is, however, no evidence that any group would have actually used this verse as an argument in favour of adoption. The Fathers only deny the possibility of the dangerous interpretation this verse makes possible. See especially Schelkle, *Paulus Lehrer der Väter*, 22–23.

[21] In the investigation of this question I have had the pleasure of using a recent dissertation on the Ebionites by S. Häkkinen, *"Köyhät kerettiläiset"* [The Poor Heretics. Ebionites in Patristic Texts.] published in Finnish. References to this book will be limited because of the language problem. On relevant occasions his views will be described to some length, however.

[22] Goranson, *ABD II* (1992) 261; Simon, *Verus Israel*, 247.

[23] Cf. Kelly, *Doctrines*, 139-140.

this connection, because poverty was one of the main characteristics of the Dead Sea community. In general one could conclude that the appellation evidently referred to a rather ascetic life-style of the sect, typical of Second Temple Jewish sectarianism.[24]

As regards Christology, however, the evidence is somewhat disturbing. Irenaeus does explicitly state that the Ebionites held to a low Christology and taught for instance that Jesus was "begotten by Joseph" (AH 3.21.1.), and this was considered as the "old leaven of the natural birth" (AH 5.1.3.). Therefore, they did not believe in the Virgin birth.[25] But the question of adoptionism is not clear at all. When Irenaeus speaks of the exact nature of heretical Christology, he does not refer to Jewish Christianity. He does not describe Ebionite teaching or even mention their name but takes up two new names. Irenaeus presents actually the thoughts of Cerinthus and Carpocrates.

Cerinthus and Carpocrates were second century Gnostics.[26] Their Christology was based on mystical cosmology and dualistic anthropology. Irenaeus describes first the teaching of Carpocrates. The key event is Jesus' baptism. A power descended upon Jesus from the Father, and made him able to "destroy" the passions which dwell in men. Therefore, in this belief system, Jesus becomes an example of a perfect ascetic. Also his followers can accomplish the same results. According to Irenaeus, some of them even declare themselves similar to Jesus. (See AH 1.25.1-3.)

The system of Cerinthus was more developed. He taught that Jesus was born according to the ordinary course of human generation. The key event here again is Jesus' baptism. After the baptism of Jesus the man, "Christ descended upon him from that Principality that is above all in the form of a dove. And then he proclaimed the unknown Father and performed miracles." The rationalistic anthropology is quite consistent in the story. Before Easter events Christ "flew away again from Jesus," and Jesus the man suffered and rose again. (See AH 1.26.1-2.)[27]

Therefore, it seems evident that the identification that has been made on the basis of Irenaeus' writings must be erroneous. Irenaeus himself did not intend

---

[24] Cf. Goranson, *ABD II* (1992) 261.

[25] According to Wilson Irenaeus has recorded all essential information about the Ebionites. "Later writers add little that is substantial to this list. Tertullian is the first to express the heresiologists' penchant for connecting all heresies with a founder by mistakenly supposing that theirs was a man called Ebion." Wilson, *Related Strangers*, 148.

[26] Cockerhill, *ABD I* (1992) 885; Wilson, *TRE XIII* (1984) 543.

[27] For the translation, see Klijn and Reinink, *Patristic Evidence*, 105.

to say that the beliefs of Cerinthus and the Ebionites were exactly identical.[28] Already the teachings of Cerinthus and Carpocrates differ from each other. One can find certain common features in them, but their actual christological patterns differ from each other. And what is most important: the ideas of the Ebionites are not descibed at all. Irenaeus merely remarks that their opinions are "similar" to those of Cerinthus and Carpocrates (if we are to believe the corrected reading of AH 1.26.2.).[29] Such identification, however, has made several scholars maintain that their beliefs must have been completely identical.[30]

Irenaeus also states that there are differences between Ebionites and Cerinthus and Carpocrates. In a later passage where he writes that the Ebionites prefer the Gospel of Matthew, he also refers to "Those again who distinguish between Jesus and Christ and say that Christ cannot have suffered but that actually only Jesus suffered, which means those who prefer the Gospel according to Mark." Here, evidently, the christological convictions of Ebionites and Cerinthus are considered quite different.[31] The distinguishing feature is precisely the idea that Christ has descended on Jesus.

If the Ebionites that Irenaeus knew held merely to the "old leaven of the natural birth," and therefore apparently regarded Jesus as a Jewish prophet, the two docetic Gnostic systems described by Irenaeus do not at all agree with that kind of teaching.[32] Especially the dualistic Christology of Cerinthus is far from "traditional" theocratic Judaism. The similarity between the Ebionites and

---

[28] Klijn and Reinink note this problem. "From these passages it appears that according to the Ebionites Jesus was the son of Joseph and Mary (III 21 1), but nothing is said about Christ descending on Jesus." Klijn and Reinink, *Patristic Evidence*, 20.

[29] Actually, the present text says "not similar" (*non similiter*) AH 1.26.2. This, however, is considered problematic while Hippolytus quoting Irenaeus says merely "similar". For the discussion over the problem, see Klijn and Reinink, *Patristic Evidence*, 19. This problem needs not to be solved here, because the question concerning the relationship between these groups may well be discussed by the help of other passages describing their beliefs.

[30] Ireaneus' text, naturally, is easily understood as a complete identification of these two groups. For instance Simon concludes that Irenaeus makes Jewish Christianity merely "a doctrinal variant of the heresy of Cerinthus." Simon, *Verus Israel*, 242. This, however, may not be the whole truth of Irenaeus' thoughts, as we shall see below.

[31] So Klijn and Reinink, *Patristic Evidence*, 20, referring to Irenaeus AH 3.11.7. (translation Klijn and Reinink, *Patristic Evidence*, 105-106).

[32] Simon remarks that the Christology of Jewish Christianity was "radically different from that of the two docetic gnostic systems to which it is claimed to be related. Simon, *Verus Israel*, 242. He further notes that, in traditional Judaism or Jewish Christianity, God can never be an "unknown Father." Such a view is not compatible with the "perfectly orthodox theodicy with which the same authors credit the Ebionites." Simon, *Verus Israel*, 250.

Cerinthus in the writings of Irenaeus is, therefore, mainly in the fact that both of them rejected the Virgin birth. The identification of those sects, however, made several later writers consider the Ebionites as adoptionists.[33]

It is no wonder, then, that Hippolytus, Irenaeus' pupil, also connected Ebionites with Cerinthus and Carpocrates. In his *Refutatio omnium haeresium* he described both the Ebionites as a sect, and "Ebion" as a person like Cerinthus. The teaching of the sect is described in the manner that resembles Irenaeus' description of the teaching of Carpocrates. As a legalistic Jewish group the Ebionites believe that a perfect follower of the law can himself become a "Christ" (Ref. 7.34). The person Ebion is further connected with Cerinthus and the "school of Gnostics." Ebion's teaching is then identified with the Christology of a certain Theodotus, whose dualistic Christology resembles that of Cerinthus (Ref. 7.35).

Theodotus is an interesting figure, because his history is most probably known. He was excommunicated in Rome by bishop Victor around 190 C.E.[34] It is therefore probable that Hippolytus knew the heresy of Theodotus rather well and was able to describe it properly. Further, it is possible that this fact has affected the description of the teachings of Cerinthus and the Ebionites (or "Ebion"). The docetic Gnostic dualism appears to be especially a feature typical of the heretical Christology at the end of the second century.[35]

The Gnostic identification is evident also in the text of Irenaeus. Cerinthus and Carpocrates are grouped together with Basilides, whose Gnostic cosmology was based on the idea of emanation. Basilides' Christ, according to Irenaeus, is the "Nous" (mind) of the unborn father. He was an uncorporeal power who could transfigure himself "as he pleased". According to this docetic view Christ did not suffer death. Simon bore the cross in his stead, and as Christ transfigured himself into Simon's form, also Simon was transfigured by him. Then Christ, before his ascension to father, laughed at the ignorance of human beings as he watched Simon's crucifixion while he was in Simon's form (Irenaeus, AH 1.24.3-7.).

We have good evidence that this kind of tradition has also been popular later in Gnostic circles. This has become apparent through Nag Hammadi texts. In the dualistic Christology of the so called Sethian Gnosticism, namely, a similar

---

[33] Häkkinen writes that it must be precisely the christological conviction rejecting the Virgin birth that was the reason for Irenaeus to identify the Ebionites with Cerinthus and other heretics that taught Jesus' natural birth. This identification was fateful as it made later writers consider the Ebionites as adoptionists. Häkkinen, *Köyhät kerettiläiset,* 100.

[34] This is told e.g. by Eusebius in his Church History, HE 5.28.6.

[35] Häkkinen considers the historical information rather trustworthy because Theodotus was the contemporary of Hippolytus in Rome, Häkkinen, *Köyhät kerettiläiset,* 110-111.

pattern prevails.[36] In the Second Treatise of the Great Seth VII.51-56 Christ is again depicted as one "from above." He is clearly described as distinct from the "earthly man" whose form he has taken, or whom he has possessed (VII.51.30f.). The story in this Treatise follows the one presented by Basilides. Christ does not suffer death, but Simon dies on the cross in his stead. The heavenly Christ, once again, laughs at the ignorance of his persecutors.[37]

"But I was rejoicing in the height over all the wealth of the archons and the offspring of their error, of their empty glory. And I was laughing at their ignorance." (VII.56.14-20.)

A dualistic docetism is evident in this Gnostic tradition. Moreover, it has a rationalistic overtone. The divine Christ cannot suffer or die, and therefore there must be another earthly person that dies in his stead. In the story, the divine Christ acts with an air of superiority and treats his enemies with arrogant contempt. These features show that there is nothing "Jewish" in this christological pattern.

In western tradition, therefore, the first trustworthy notions of groups or sects called Ebionites come from Irenaeus. It is propable that Irenaeus has exploited earlier heresiologies when writing about the Ebionites. Also his knowledge about Cerinthus and other Gnostics who had lived several decades before his birth evidently rests on earlier documents. But why did Irenaeus parallel Ebionites with the Gnostics? The most probable reason for that seems to be that both sects denied Virgin birth.

It is naturally also possible that at Irenaeus' time there was a sect calling itself Ebionites and teaching dualistic docetism. The problem with this alternative is that there is no clear evidence of it in the extant documents. The so called "adoptionist" Christology is always described under the name of a distinct Gnostic. Therefore, it is more likely that the "Ebionites" Irenaeus referred to merely taught the "old leaven of the natural birth," i.e. that Jesus was begotten by Joseph – not Gnostic dualism.

Eastern tradition seems to confirm this kind of conclusion. In the light of the writings of Origen it seems evident that several Jewish Christian groups were called Ebionites in the second century. According to Origen there were two parties among the Ebionites, one confessing that Jesus was born of a virgin, and the other holding that he was merely a man (Contra Celsum 5.61.).

---

[36] I have chosen to use the term Sethian Gnosticism for practical reasons, even though I am aware that some of my colleagues do not count the Second Treatise of the Great Seth among proper Sethian texts as Seth is not mentioned in the text itself. Here this question is not that important, however.

[37] A similar view prevails also in another Nag Hammadi writing, i.e. in the Apocalypse of Peter VII. 81.3-24.

Therefore, in the eastern tradition, the appellation Ebionite as such does not refer to a "heretical" Jewish Christian group that denied the Virgin birth.

Origen did know a "heretical" Jewish Christian sect that did not accept the Virgin birth, but he did not identify this group as the original Palestinian Jewish Christian Church that would be the heir of the Jerusalem community. Heretical Ebionites were rather a small sect that had drifted into conflict with other Jewish Christian groups. Furthermore, the Christology of Origen's Ebionites is in no respect docetic or dualistic as is the adoptionism of the western Gnostics.[38]

It is, therefore, quite evident that the reconstructed hypothesis of early Ebionites as a single Jewish Christian group with adoptionist Christology is false. There was no specific group of Ebionites that would have carried on the Jewish Christian tradition of the apostolic Jerusalem community. There must have been several Jewish Christian groups that identified themselves as Ebionites.[39] Certain groups under that name had adopted low Christology, and their relation to groups with high Christology was tense. The concept of dualistic Ebionite adoptionism is a product of unintentional or careless connection of certain Ebionite groups with second century Gnostics in the writings of the western Fathers. Once the identification was made, it was exploited as the justification of the theory of Ebionite adoptionism.[40]

Later, in the writings of Epiphanius (around 370 C.E.) these themes were united and developed into a system that has greatly attracted New Testament scholars. According to Epiphanius the distinctive christological belief of the Ebionites was a distinction between Jesus and Christ. Christ was not "born of God the Father but that he was created as one of the archangels... and that he is Lord over the angels." (Epiph. Pan. 30.16.4.).[41]

The dualism of Cerinthus has been applied into angelology. Jesus the man and Christ the archangel were considered completely separate persons. For the

---

[38] See for instance Origen's sermons on Matthew, 16.12. This is also how Eusebius later describes the Ebionites. He appears to prefer the information of Origen and presents different Jewish Christian groups with different beliefs. See the Church History, HE 3. 27.1-6.

[39] Wilson even calls this the "Ebionite cluster." Wilson, *Related Strangers*, 152.

[40] According to Simon the error is the result of the writings of the Fathers. "Anxious to express the affinities and connections of their families of doctrines in a concrete way, they made Ebion a disciple of Cerinthus, himself a disciple of Carpocrates. This blatant misrepresentation of the chronological relationships turned the direct heirs of primitive Palestinian Christianity into latter-day sectarians of the third remove." Simon, *Verus Israel*, 242.

[41] For the translation, see Klijn and Reinink, *Patristic Evidence*, 183. It is proper to note that Dunn also notes this feature. Dunn, *Unity and Diversity*, 242. For some reason, however, it does not affect his interpretation.

justification of a kind of adoptionism the event of Jesus' baptism was still indispensable. The Gnostic pattern of Cerinthus can be seen clearly in Epiphanius' presentation. When the distinction between Jesus and Christ had first been made, the act of adoption was located in Jesus' baptism. In baptism the Christ-Spirit descended upon Jesus.

"Christ they call the prophet of truth and 'Christ, the Son of God' on account of his progress (in virtue) and the exaltation which descended upon him from above... They want him to be only a prophet and man and Son of God and Christ and mere man, as we said before, who attained by a virtuous life the right to be called Son of God." (Epiph. Pan. 30.18.5-6.).[42]

The so called Ebionite Gospel of Matthew had also added this feature into the account of the baptism of Jesus. According to their text the Holy Spirit in the form of a dove came down "entering into him" (Epiph. Pan. 30.13.7.).[43] This may also be a simple modification made on the basis of Mark 1:10 that reads "into" (εἰς). The motivation for such change, however, may well be in the dualistic conviction of the sectarian that made the redaction on the Gospel.

Also Epiphanius records that there were different Ebionite groups. It is no longer possible to date their views, however, because he may refer to any syncretistic group before 370 C.E. Some groups identify the heavenly Christ as a Spirit that has possessed Jesus, as it had earlier possessed several great patriarchs such as Abraham and Jacob. Some groups simply taught: "the spirit who is Christ came upon him and took the boy of him who is called Jesus. " (Epiph. Pan. 30.3.1-7.).[44]

This view that is mainly identical with the teaching of Cerinthus, is quite extraordinary. *It does not actually describe an adoption of the human Jesus, but rather the possession of Jesus by a heavenly person, Christ.*[45] Jesus the Jew has in fact merely a minor role in the christological narrative of the Gnostic "Ebionites". It is the angelic Christ who had the key role in such soteriology.

In this respect Epiphanius' Ebionite Christology appears to be a rare example of an extreme angelic interpretation in sectarian Christology, Christ being an angelic figure and "Lord over the angels". Even though the Gnostic features of that kind of construction are prominent, it is proper to ask if it has

---

[42] Translation in Klijn and Reinink, *Patristic Evidence,* 187-189.

[43] Cf. Hipp. Ref. 7.35.2.

[44] Translation in Klijn and Reinink, *Patristic Evidence,* 179. Pelikan has summarized this Christology as follows: "born as other men are. Jesus was elected to be the Son of God, and... at his baptism Christ, an archangel, descended on him, as he had on Adam, Moses and other prophets." Pelikan, *Christian Tradition,* 24. A similar belief is probably behind the Ebionite Epistula Petri, part of the pseudo-Clementine homilies. The spirit of God is manifested in several incarnations, changing his forms and his names, from Adam onwards. Clem. Hom. III 20.

[45] The so called possessionist feature has been noted e.g. by Goulder, *Paul,* 110-112.

anything to do with Jewish mysticism. For instance Pelikan has suggested that Ebionite Christology may reflect Essene teaching, the Ebionites being possibly descendants of the Essenes who remained Christian after the year 70.[46] Unfortunately this is merely a hypothesis and he does not present any evidence to justify his claim. But the hypothesis is, nevertheless, interesting. Even though the distinction between Jesus and Christ resembles the ideas of various Gnostic Christian systems, Pelikan considered a connection to Second Temple Judaism also possible.

On the grounds of Second Temple Jewish theology investigated in part II above it is not easy to conclude what could serve as a starting point for this kind of development. In different writings there were certain messianic figures, some of which were identified as angelic beings. Melchizedek in 11QMelch. is a perfect example of these. We don't have a model for any incarnation or human manifestation of these figures, however. They remain heavenly angelic figures even when they have soteriological functions.

On the other hand, when certain pious Jews were endowed with the Spirit of God, such endowment never produced an identification with some angel. The blessed righteous ones at Qumran, for instance, were simply human beings. In this respect Epiphanius' "Ebionite" Christology is *sui generis*. In Enochic tradition there was a model for the transformation of Enoch into an angelic being, but in this tradition, however, the human Enoch is not united with any distinct heavenly or angelic figure.

According to Epiphanius' records, the angelic Christ-Spirit dwelled in Jesus and made him the Son of God. Even though the angelic/angelomorphic interpretation has been quite popular among scholars as regards the study of New Testament Christology, this kind of pattern for the nature of early Christology has seldom been presented.[47] The dualistic anthropology in Irenaeus' and Epiphanius' records is different. It's only point of contact with angelomorphic interpretation is in the idea that Jesus is considered a prophet and a mere man.

According to angelic or angelomorphic interpretation the exalted Christ was described in a similar manner as the angels. In the Ebionite interpretation Jesus is possessed by an angelic Christ. So even the human aspect is different in these two. Therefore, the best one can suggest is that Irenaeus' and Epiphanius' Ebionite Christology may serve as evidence for the *influence* of

---

[46] Pelikan, *Christian Tradition*, 24.

[47] Gieschen, however, comments on Epiphanius and suggests: "This form of Angelomorphic Christology, which presents the True Prophet as the Chief Archangel, probably grew out of the more fundamental identification of Christ with the ancient Angel of the Lord traditions." Gieschen, *Christology*, 210.

Jewish mysticism on Gnostic thinking.[48] Recent scholars have been quite aware of the fact that these writers' view of Ebionite Christology resembles Gnostic thinking in many respects. This concerns especially the dualistic nature of that Christology. Therefore, it can hardly be a result of the influence of Second Temple Jewish theology as such. As we saw above, it resembles the teaching of Basilides, and further, it is quite similar to the later docetic possessionism of Sethian Gnosticism.[49]

The most important result of the analysis, however, is that the idea of a so called Ebionite Christology in itself is a construction. It is possible that around 200-300 C.E. there have been syncretistic groups that have taught dualistic adoptionism under the name Ebionite. In the second century, however, the dualistic ideas were actually ascribed to Gnostic teachers, and Ebionite groups were accidentally identified with these groups.

Certain essential conclusions can be drawn from the analysis:

1. The appellation "Ebionites" apparently refers to Jewish Christians.

2. In the second century there were several different Jewish Christian groups that used that appellation.

3. There is no necessary link between the appellation itself (i.e. the groups it represents) and low Christology.

4. According to Irenaeus and Origen there were some Ebionites who did not accept the Virgin birth. Others, however, had adopted high Christology.

5. When Irenaeus and Hippolytus referred to Ebionites and described the dualistic teaching ascribed also to certain Ebionite groups, they actually described second century docetic Gnostic dualists, such as Cerinthus. This kind of teaching is well known from the tradition of Sethian Gnosticism.

6. The view that the Ebionites also taught a sort of adoptionist Christology is most probably a literary invention and a false construction – unless it is based on information about syncretistic heretics around 200 C.E. and later.

7. Ebionite/Gnostic Christology in patristic writings has nothing to do with

---

[48] Goulder has attempted to locate the possessionist pattern in the earliest Christianity. "The Ebionites are plainly Jewish Christians, and close to the positions which we have ascribed to the Jerusalem mission." Goulder, *Paul*, 109. He refers to the baptism story in Mark 1:10 where the Spirit descends into Jesus and states that it must evidence the possessionist view of the earliest Church. Therefore, for Goulder, the possessionist Ebionite Christology "is not the invention of the late second century. It was the creed of the Jerusalem church from early times." Goulder, *Paul*, 130, 134. It is, however, hardly possible to identify Mark's Spirit with the Gnostic heavenly Christ.

[49] It is worth noting that such Gnostic tradition is never referred to either in Dunn's Ebionite theory, or in Goulder's possessionist interpretation. Dunn simply spoke of Jewish Christian Christology, and Goulder treated Cerinthus as a Jewish Christian Ebionite.

New Testament exaltation Christology. Its key passages, such as Acts 2:36, or Rom. 1:3-4, are never referred to.

8. Ebionite/Gnostic Christology does not present a monotheistic view of the alleged adoption of Jesus as a political Messiah in the heavenly realm. The patristic reconstruction, therefore, has nothing in common with Weiss' hypothesis.

9. Therefore, the main argument used in biblical criticism when discussing adoptionism appears to be erroneous. Early Christology was supposed to present the adoption of Jesus the Jew (in the resurrection) without any ontological change into divinity, and patristic evidence was believed to confirm the existence of this kind of adoptionism in the "original" Jewish Christian Ebionite community. There is no evidence whatsoever for such postulations. Ebionite/Gnostic Christology rests on dualistic Gnostic anthropology and a bizarre ontology.

10. In patristic writings, Ebionite/Gnostic Christology, strictly speaking, is not even a version of adoptionism. It is a docetic Gnostic system with strong dualism. Christ is considered a heavenly spirit or angelic figure who possesses the human Jesus for a time, and departs from him before his suffering.

10.3. Defining early Jewish Christianity

How to define the nature of early Jewish Christianity and its teaching? The analysis made above has shown that one of the main theories of explanation rests on false presuppositions and insufficient evidence. Early Jewish Christianity cannot be identified simply as a form of Ebionism, teaching adoptionist Christology.[50] According to patristic evidence, several Jewish Christian groups held to high Christology. Certain groups were divided in the christological question, but the subject was mainly that of the Virgin birth.[51]

Further, the ideas of "heretical" Ebionism in the writings of the Church Fathers do not resemble Weiss' reconstruction of adoptionist Christology at all. In no writing is the "adoption" of Jesus located in his resurrection. The short references to Ebionite teaching found in the writings of the Church Fathers all emphasize the baptism of Jesus. Therefore also the suggestion of Dunn, presented above, seems to be problematic. According to Dunn the adoptionist Christology of the Ebionites had "a firm anchor point in the earliest

---

[50] Cf. for instance Simon's conclusion: "It is very likely that the syncretistic sects, which combined a Judaizing practice with a gnostic analysis of the biblical revelation, proposed a Docetic dichotomy of the person of Jesus Christ. But it is safe to assert that a system of this sort can hardly have sprung from the Palestinian Ebionites as the term is usually understood." Simon, *Verus Israel*, 250.

[51] So also Klijn and Reinink, *Patristic Evidence*, 42-43.

Christian attempts to express faith in Jesus the Christ."[52] He referred to exaltation Christology in passages such as Acts 2:36, Rom. 1:3f., Heb. 5:5, and Phil. 2:9-11. As we have seen above, none of these passages has been cited or commented on in the extant references to Ebionite teachings. It seems apparent that the Weissian theory of adoptionist Christology and the Ebionite theory have been united into one theory of explanation, but this connection has been done on the basis of poor evidence.

The result of the analysis concerning Ebionite theory was therefore inevitable. The patristic Ebionite/Gnostic possessionism has nothing in common with Weiss' idea of theocratic adoptionism. Weiss' theory cannot be justified with later patristic evidence. Only if it has some relevance on the grounds of its own internal arguments, can it have value in the investigation of early Jewish Christianity. We shall return to Weiss below.

It seems apparent that many of the problems found in the Ebionite theory derive from the adopted approach. Most scholars have attempted to define Jewish Christianity with the help of post-70 C.E. writings, i.e. writings that have been written or compiled after the destruction of Jerusalem. Even the pattern for the development of New Testament Christology followed that division to a great extent, high Christology being considered a late Hellenistic development, and low Christology being considered an "original" Jewish Christian teaching. In addition to this, patristic 200-400 C.E. writings had an essential role in the theory.

In this respect a considerable change in scholarship has taken place during the last three or four decades. The study of Second Temple Judaism has grown significantly, and Second Temple writings have become the main source of evidence in the investigation. Therefore, the point of weight is in the pre-70 C.E. writings and in the setting of Second Temple Judaism in Israel during the first decades of the Common Era.[53]

Such a change is especially significant as regards our view of Judaism.[54] In the pattern presented repeatedly from Weiss to Dunn, the view of Judaism was simple and unproblematic. Judaism at the time of the Jerusalem Jewish Christian community was considered theocratic, rabbinic Judaism, holding to

---

[52] Dunn, *Unity and Diversity*, 243.

[53] It is still worth while mentioning that one of the most influential factors in this change was Hengel's monumental investigation *Judentum und Hellenismus*, which altered essentially our view of Jewish thinking at that period.

[54] The change that has taken place in scholarship needs little apology as such. See for instance the collection of Hengel, *Studies in Early Christology*, or Sander's theses concerning the nature of Second Temple Judaism in his *Paul and Palestinian Judaism*, 2-6, 33-34. For the discussion after Sanders, see Eskola, *JSJ 28* (1997) 390ff.

nomistic beliefs that we usually ascribe to the Sadduceans rather than the Pharisees. If there was some eschatology involved, it was considered purely futurist eschatology fitting well into the picture of "main stream" Judaism.

This is hardly what the Second Temple writings evidence. The diversity among different groups was apparent. Second Temple Judaism is known for its apocalyptic groups and its mystics, as well as nomists and almost apostate Hellenists. There were groups from priestly Sadduceans to Qumran Essenes. Quite many traditions were apocalyptic, and early Christianity seems to have adopted many of their teachings.[55]

In the present study early Christology has been studied in the context of Jewish merkabah mysticism. Therefore the approach differs essentially from the one adopted for instance by Käsemann or Dunn. Throne mysticism is regarded as a prominent feature in Second Temple Jewish thinking among several different groups. In this respect the view of Jewish Christianity will also be different.

How can we determine the teachings of early Jewish Christianity? The study of late patristic writings is hardly a proper way to accomplish such a task. The theology of the early Jerusalem community and the nature of apostolic teaching is, rather, detected in the homological statements found in the New Testament writings, especially in the letters.

As we have seen, most of the relevant passages for the present study have usually been considered quite early, and several of them have been located in the Jewish Christian community. This general view raises the question of the dating of confessional material and Christological statements. In scholarship there have been different approaches for such dating. Many scholars assume that early homologies must have been short. This is due to some kind of evolutionist presupposition behind the explanation. Their focus was on christological statements such as "Jesus is Lord" (1 Cor. 12:3), "Jesus is the Christ" (1 John 2:22), or "Jesus is the Son of God" (Acts 8:37, according to the western text E). For example according to Cullmann, this kind of formula developed only gradually into larger confessions.[56]

There were also certain rules defined for the development. These short formulas were extended for example by contrasting different things in separate clauses. Christ was described on one hand "in flesh" and on the other hand "in spirit" (Rom. 1:3), or as humiliated and exalted (Phil. 2:6ff.). In addition to that there were different kinds of confessions being transmitted in the tradition,

---

[55] For the question over the diversity of Second Temple Judaism, see e.g. Kraft, *Christianity*, 188-191, Talmon, *Jewish Civilization*, 16, and Porton, *Early Judaism*, 57.

[56] Cullmann, *Glaubensbekenntnisse*, 36.

such as the formula in the beginning of 1 Cor. 15.[57] This kind of evolutive view soon became a standard in New Testament study.

Later Dunn, for example, dated the short homologies as early. He considered even some Christological epithets' homologies, such as the "Son of Man", "Messiah", and "Son of God". The most important one in Pauline churches was, according to Dunn, "Jesus is Lord".[58] It is obvious that the premise concerning the form of early homologies is crucial as regards the hypotheses one is to make about the status and function of the homologies in the early Church. If one considers the earliest homologies as short, an evolutive pattern is unavoidable. They are usually separated from more developed confessions and dated much earlier.

An evolutive pattern as such does not imply that the homologies would be stereotypical in a negative sense, but it surely rests on a presupposition of schematism and formalism. In some cases it probably preserves the presumption of a degeneration taking place in the early Church.[59] In addition to this, there is also an interesting presupposition concerning length. Short homologies are regarded old and in some way authentic. Longer confessional statements are automatically pronounced young and dated late in the tradition. This is actually not what seems to happen in the course of tradition in general. There is rather a tendency of shortening and reducing taking place.[60]

Already A. Seeberg, however, made a distinction that is essential for the understanding of the nature of early homologies. He suggested that a descriptive confession should not be identified with an acclamation. There were even form critical differences supporting such distinction. The acclamation was a short homology confessing subjective faith, not a description of any particular content of faith in general. Seeberg's distinction is so informative that it needs to be rehabilitated and exploited when the nature of early confessions is defined.

The basic distinction makes a difference as regards the interpretation of the short homologies that, for example, Cullmann analyzed. According to Seeberg such statements should not be classified as confessions but as acclamations, because they are not precise descriptions of the content of faith. Instead of that, they are personal and subjective, and they should be regarded as responses to a

---

[57] Cullmann, *Glaubensbekentnisse*, 36.

[58] See Dunn, *Unity and Diversity*, 35ff., 50. For a similar conviction concerning the titles, see Frankemölle, *Glaubensbekentnisse*, 19ff.

[59] This was rather typical of the post-Bultmannian approach, see for instance Käsemann, *Exegetische Versuche 1*, 215f.; cf *Exegetische Versuche 2*, 101f.

[60] For the views on the nature of tradition see Hengel, *Geschichtsschreibung*, 16ff.

confession.[61] Seeberg was further wise enough not to identify the confessional description merely as a liturgical formula. He thought that it had also lived in the teaching and proclamation of the Church.[62]

According to modern linguistic methods this kind of distinction between statements and acclamations is important. Acclamations cannot be understood merely by themselves. They imply a christological narrative that provides meaning for the short acclamation. Sometimes this is also the case with short statements with specific content. A couple of words cannot carry a wider meaning just in themselves. They are merely short indicators that refer to schemes and narratives that express the whole train of thought. In early Christology acclamations serve well as such indicators.

Did early Jewish Christianity produce, adopt, and use such resurrection statements? We have noted the fact that several of the passages under discussion express resurrection Christology or enthronement Christology. In this respect it is quite natural to locate exaltation Christology in the Jewish Christian community where the influence of Jewish merkabah mysticism is natural and expected.

There is further one passage in the New Testament where the confessional unity between Pauline Christianity and Jerusalem Jewish Christianity is expressed explicitly. As Paul speaks of the confessional formula in the beginning of 1 Cor. 15 he refers to apostolic tradition. Already when introducing the formula, Paul explicitly says that he is speaking of a transmitted tradition. The text itself follows a clear schema.[63]

"Christ died for our sins in accordance with the scriptures, and that he was buried, and that he was raised on the third day in accordance with the scriptures, and that he appeared to Cephas." (1 Cor. 15:3-5).

This confession presents a cultic interpretation of Jesus' death, and places his resurrection in an eschatological frame. The theological content of the passage is interesting as such, as the short formal statement presupposes a good deal of cultic convictions combined with resurrection statements. Further, the hermeneutical view appears to be that of the history of salvation. God's promises are believed to have been fulfilled in Easter events. What is special of the creed, however, for the purposes of the present study, is the connection

---

[61] See Seeberg, *Katechismus*, 152ff., 182. Later for example W. Kramer has used a similar classification in his *Christos Kyrios Gottessohn*, 15ff., 61.

[62] Seeberg, *Katechismus*, 152ff., 168ff. See later also Neufeld, *Confessions*, 42, 50, 62.

[63] This passage has been essential in the study of confessions, see Kelly, *Creeds*, 17; Schlier *Christologie*, 27. For the problems of reconstruction see e.g. Conzelmann, *1 Corinthians*, 251-254.

that Paul makes between himself and other apostles. The exceptional feature in the passage is the linking of the formula with apostolic tradition. Cephas, James, and the twelve, as well as "all the apostles" are being brought behind the confessional statement (1 Cor. 15:5-7).[64] The confession may thus be justifiably called the "Jerusalem confession". "Whether then it was I or they, so we proclaim and so you have come to believe" (v. 11). According to Paul, thus, the confession was even a criterion that directed proclamation.[65]

There is, therefore, no reason to doubt that exaltation statements were already generated in the Jewish Christian community. They may be regarded as expressions of early theological reflection on the experiences of the followers of Jesus. This is not yet the answer to our main question, however. Even though exaltation traditions may be considered early, and the pattern of Ebionite "adoptionism" has appeared to be unsuitable for the explanation of Jewish Christology, the theory of theocratic adoptionism has not yet been investigated.

Could it be that early exaltation Christology reflects such theocratic adoptionism that has occurred only in the beginning and has left no clear traces in Christian writings thereafter? Did first Jewish Christian writers interpret Jesus ascent according to an Old Testament concept of theocratic "adoption"? Should we follow Strauss and Weiss and state that in a Jewish context a Davidide was always considered an adopted Son of God when being enthroned to power?

As we return to the treatment of Weiss' theory, we necessarily need to make certain positive comments on some arguments exploited in the explanation. Even according to the present analysis the link to Old Testament imagery is evident. When the first Christians interpreted Jesus' resurrection in their theological reflection, they described it as the enthronement of the promised Davidide. This must have been a crucial theme in early Christian proclamation.

The theocratic emphasis found in Jewish theology and in the Old Testament naturally supports the idea that the exaltation of the "seed" should be understood as an act of adoption. In Israel the king himself was not worshiped as a God. He was not considered divine in nature, as the the leaders among the neighbouring nations were. The king's relationship to the supreme King, Israel's God, was theocratic. This must have given identity to Davidic kings,

---

[64] When Paul writes "they," he presumably refers, as Barret remarks, to "other apostles, as referred to in the list of resurrection appearances, and possibly, whether or not by their own choice, ranged in some sense as rivals to Paul." Barrett, *I Corinthians*, 346; cf. also Fee, *I Corinthians*, 736.

[65] Conzelmann concludes that the expression points back to the creed in vv 1-3. "Once again it is plain that the authority and the content of the creed are not disputed in Corinth." Conzelmann, *I Corinthians*, 260.

who were enthroned by God's decree and who were considered mediating figures in God's theocratic reign.[66]

During the analysis of Jewish mysticism we have further noted that the nature of visions and their interpretations was intentionally theocratic. Jewish mystics wished to preserve the core of the theocratic ideal of First Temple Judaism. God is still the King of Israel. The eschatological hope of righteous Jews had not been altered. The adoration of the enthroned God in the Jerusalem Temple is identical with the adoration of the heavenly God on the *merkabah*-throne. This was confirmed with descriptions of heavenly journeys. Seers were escorted to heaven, in order to meet God. Such faith maintains essential traditional features of Temple piety. The identity of Jewish faith is preserved only as far as the Enthroned One is praised and worshiped as the heavenly King.[67]

The essential question in this situation is whether Jesus, as an enthroned Davidide, stays under the hierarchic structure of theocracy. Did the first Christians believe that the exalted Christ was merely a human Davidide who has ascended to heaven, or did they ascribe to him divine features that reach beyond the theocratic hierarchy? It is apparent that the answer is dependent on one's view of the relation between Jewish mysticism and early Christology.

The proponents of the adoptionist theory interpreted the historical exaltation of the Davidic king precisely as a prototype of the exaltation of Christ. Through adoption the king gained a special status in relation to God. He became a mediator between God and Israel. The king carried out God's theocratic rule on the earth. When the Old Testament background was applied to the "appointment" of Jesus, he was said to have received theocratic status in the heavenly court. The term "Son of God" now became evidence for this theocratic interpretation. According to the adoptionist theory, Jesus was merely an ordinary Jewish man or perhaps a prophet in his resurrection to power.[68]

Previous analysis of theocratic adoptionism pointed out that the theory interpreted Christology in terms of political messianology. Jewish political messianology was the pattern with which Jesus' exaltation was compared.

---

[66] See chapter 2.4. above.

[67] I happily agree with Scholem who stated years ago: "From the interpretation of the throne-world as the true centre of all mystical contemplation it is possible to deduce most of the concepts and doctrines of these ancient mystics." Scholem, *Major Trends*, 44.

[68] Weiss equated the exaltation of the king with the raising of a prophet up to heaven, as we have seen above. Weiss, *Das Urchristentum*, 88. In his monograph on Christology M. Casey also uses the idea of raising a prophet up to heaven when defining the nature of early Christology. Casey, *Jewish Prophet*, 102. This line of thought is problematic since nowhere in the Old or New Testaments has anyone maintained that a prophet might become a king or a heavenly ruler. The focus is always on the dynasty of David.

This is the reason why the theory made no distinction as to whether it is the historical Davidide who is raised as the king of Israel or Jesus who is raised from the dead in order to be a universal heavenly king.

This kind of reasoning does not explain the transcendent feature in early Christology. How should we explain the exaltation of the Davidide to a heavenly throne, and furthermore, the throne of Glory? Some scholars have suggested that Jesus was identified as a heavenly agent or an angelic figure, as we have seen before. In this case the royal enthronement would thus have been interpreted by exploiting a new principle which has been taken from another imagery.

In the writings of Jewish mysticism there are several examples of theocratic enthronements. In this respect even the adoptionist theory might be supported by this kind of interpretation. The nature of different descriptions of enthronements is usually theocratic. No exalted figure is presented as divine in heaven.[69] Certain figures, such as patriarchs or prophets, are indeed exalted high in the heavenly hierarchy. Their position remains below God, however, and no person claims to have a divine nature in Jewish writings. The same applies to angelic figures. They may even have theophoric names, but their status remains under the theocratic hierarchy. Therefore this kind of interpretation does not essentially change the premises of the abovementioned adoptionist interpretation.

Some scholars have attempted to avoid the problematic definition of early Christology by introducing the idea of functional Christology. According to these scholars the act of adoption must be separated from the act of enthronement. Early formulas that describe the heavenly kingship of Christ do not refer to his nature but to his function as a king. The benefit of this explanation was that it was able to bring forth the functional element in the presentation of exaltation. Jesus as a cosmological ruler is a king, but his kingship is not comparable with the kingship of the historical dynasty of David. The only problem with the functional theory is that it does not fulfill its own promises. It does not actually change the premises of the theocratic interpretation.

The adherents of the theory noted several important details, though. It is true that exaltation Christology seems to imply much more than a mere exploitation of Old Testament royal ideology and the image of adoption. Further, scholars such as Weiss had evidently been too greatly indebted to the

---

[69] There was disagreement on this question, as we saw in chapter 4 above, but there is no convincing evidence for the view that any Second Temple Jewish writing would have threatened traditional monotheism. The view of the heavenly hierarchy was strict in these writings.

christological controversies of the first centuries. After presenting this kind of criticism for example Kramer wrote that the seemingly adoptional terminology in central christological passages of the New Testament does not refer to the nature of Christ before the resurrection.[70] Hahn in turn stated that the theme of adoption should not be understood in the light of the later Christological debates, but in the light of Jewish theology and the Old Testament. Therefore one should not speak about the "Son of God" in a physical sense in these contexts.[71] Hahn too stated that the change that took place in the resurrection concerned only Jesus' status and function (Würde und Funktion).[72]

According to this new explanation the exaltation was thus interpreted as a mere enthronement, not as an adoption.[73] Scholars probably thought that the symbol itself, the enthronement, had to be separated from its origin. If the purpose of christological statements is to describe Jesus' enthronement in his resurrection, the metaphor does not refer to the "making" of a Son. The purpose must have been to describe Christ's function in his eschatological ministry.[74] This kind of reasoning may be the reason why after 1960 most monographs and commentaries have spoken of functional Christology.[75]

A functional element is evident in the central passages of early Christology, but we must still ask whether it actually excludes the adoptional interpretation. Is not the functional interpretation of Old Testament royal ideology still a theocratic concept? Firstly, we have earlier observed that in the descriptions of

---

[70] Kramer, *Christos*, 107. For him, the appointment of a Son of God was a juridical procedure.

[71] Hahn, *Hoheitstitel*, 254.

[72] Hahn, *Hoheitstitel*, 254. Similar thinking was common during that decade, e.g. Betz, *NT VI* (1963) 20–48, esp. 32; Legrand, *RB* 70 (1963) 161-192, esp. 181.

[73] So for instance Blank, *Paulus und Jesus*, 253; Thüsing, *Per Christum in Deum*, 145; and Hayes, *Interp. XXII* (1968) 345.

[74] Some scholars also changed their views during the course of this discussion. For example Schweizer later dropped the concept of adoptionism and spoke of the functional character of the terms. "The description as adoptional Christology ... is actually not correct, because it connects the contrast to another concept which is not meant here... The right way to say it is that the title Son of God describes the function of Jesus, since verse 4 [i.e. in Rom 1] says plainly that at Easter Jesus has begun his office as a Messianic King ruling his Church." Schweizer, *ThWNT VIII* (1969) 368. Dunn, however, is quite ambivalent. The adoptionist theory is usually a basic principle in his interpretation of early Christology and Rom 1 (see Dunn, *Unity and Diversity*, 45, 243; and later the second edition, 1990, likewise). In his commentary on Romans, however, Dunn rejects adoptionism in the interpretation of Rom 1:3-4. Dunn, *Romans*, 14.

[75] A review of modern studies makes this evident, e.g. Wilckens, *Römer I*, 65; Beasley–Murray, *TynB 31* (1980) 152; Theobald, *Kontinuität*, 387; Froitzheim, *Christologie*, 102; Pesch, *Römerbrief*, 25.

Jewish mysticism the enthronement as such does not effect deification. There may be the idea of some kind of metamorphosis in certain writings, but those passages speak of a change from a human figure to an angelic figure. Therefore, merely on the basis of Jewish mysticism, one should not expect any deification to take place in the exaltation. In this respect the reference to functional Christology does not answer the basic question. Christology may be called functional, but Weiss may still be right in his adoptionist interpretation.

Secondly, the basic image that is exploited is still that of an earthly Davidide. As long as we attempt to produce exaltation Christology according to the idea of theocratic kingship, we are bound to end up with an adoptionist pattern. In this respect we must say that the efforts to substitute a functional Christology for adoptionist Christology have been made in vain. If Jesus merely has a task and a function in Christology, he can always be considered a servant of God who was adopted into this functional status by Almighty God – even though Christological statements themselves would not make explicit claims of his ontological status.[76]

The same applies to the hypotheses concerning so called divine agents, such as personified wisdom, as typological tools in the making of Christology. Implicitly they too maintain a functional perspective in their interpretation.[77] The agents are merely members of the heavenly hierarchy. As we saw above, in Jewish mysticism they rather belong to the theocratic system of Jewish thought.

But do the actual statements of early Christology express the theocratic status of the risen Christ? How does exaltation Christology relate to the ascent stories of Jewish mysticism? We do know the symbols and images that have been exploited in the relevant descriptions. Kingship, throne, and heavenly palace are essential elements of both Jewish mysticism and early Christology. We also know the narratives. In this respect Jewish descriptions and christological descriptions differ from each other.

There are some common elements, though. For instance the pattern of a heavenly enthronement on the throne of Glory is one of these. There were Jewish ascent stories describing such ascents. In this respect Christian ascent stories have not altered the narrative tradition essentially. It has been exploited in christological presentation, even though the application has not necessarily followed the Jewish pattern in detail.

The cultic interpretation found in several New Testament passages is exceptional, however. According to Jewish sources the Davidide was not

---

[76] One must bear in mind that the idea of an ontological change was never a part of the so called adoptionist theory.

[77] This applies for instance to the view of Hurtado, *One God*, 91.

expected to die, or to provide atonement in a cultic sense. Further, the soteriological intention of exaltation Christology is unique in Second Temple Judaism. The latter aspect needs to be studied more carefully.

In the descriptions of early Christology Jesus does not have angelic features and he does not act like a heavenly agent in the sense of the presented theories. If we consider the most common one of the christological patterns, Christ is simply described as a Davidic Messiah who has a special status in heaven. Christ ruling as a king and as Son of God in heaven does not act as a mediator in a theocratic context. He is not a human regent of God, and he does not lead people as a new Israel to pure theocracy. Christ is the eschatological ruler himself. This kind of change appears to be essential for the writers of early Christology. For them, Christ is the object of faith, and thus also the object of the confessional homologies of the Church.

Several observations made on the basis of the key texts of early Christology support this view. According to the passages that we have investigated, Jesus has become superior to angels in the heavenly hierarchy (Heb. 1:4). God has exalted him so that "every knee should bend" as before a God (Phil. 2:10). His name is "above every name" (Phil. 2:10). In his resurrection he has been made the Lord and the Messiah (Acts 2:36). This divine name has become the source of salvation. Therefore the acclamation κύριος Ἰησοῦς is identified as the "calling on the name of the Lord", i.e. as calling on the name of the YHWH, King of Israel (Rom. 10:9-13).[78]

Several scholars have noted that these passages sound liturgical. They have the form of some kind of confession, and some of them express liturgical praise. Therefore, they express the worship of Jesus that as a phenomenon is quite unique in a Jewish context.[79] As the context for such high Christology is liturgical, it is located in the core of early Christian devotion. Thus it has essential value when estimating the role of high Christology in the teaching and life of the early Jewish Christian community.[80]

Further, there is an example of the history of influence of that kind of

---

[78] Cf. Kreitzer, *Jesus and God*, 168f.

[79] See e.g. Bauckham, *NTS* 27 (1980-1) 335; France, *Christ*, 24ff.

[80] Segal discusses such devotion when investigating his "two powers" theory in respect of early Christology. He states, however, that the "title of God was applied to Jesus more quickly in liturgical contexts than in narrative or epistolary literature." For Segal this is a token of "ambiguities in Christian traditions." Segal, *Two Powers*, 215. This can hardly be a proper explanation of the general nature of Gospel tradition or other New Testament materials. Our analysis has shown that homological material covers several layers and lines of tradition. Therefore there are no good arguments for the "ambiguities" of early traditions. Rather, the liturgical aspect proves that high Christology had an essential meaning for the identity of first Jewish Christians.

devotion. As we have noted before, the worship of angels was strictly prohibited and Jewish writings contain warnings against it. In the writings of Jewish mysticism the so called divine agents never had such position in heaven where they would have been considered objects of faith.

In the Ascension of Isaiah there is a perfect description of the worship of Christ, and this presentation is expressed in an identical context as the christological statements of the New Testament. Jesus, who is worshiped in the story, is the enthroned Davidide on his throne in the heavenly Temple, and he is the object of faith for the writer of the description (AscIsa 9:28-32).[81]

Therefore, both in early christological tradition, in the New Testament, and in some later Christian writings the worship of Jesus is explicit and intentional. Jesus is the Messiah who brings salvation. He is the one whom the first Christians adore. Together with God the father Jesus is the object of devotion.[82]

This aspect of worship is the main reason why we cannot follow Strauss and Weiss and state that the Davidide was considered an adopted Son of God also in early christological formulations. We must agree on the notion that the exalted Christ was indeed a messianic Davidide who was enthroned on the throne of Glory. His factual status, however, is unique in respect of Jewish messianology. He is revered as God on his throne, and he is the source of salvation for those who call upon his name.

As early Christology transforms the theocratic concepts of Second Temple Judaism, it may further be regarded as an intertext. It does exploit the writings of the Old Testament, as well as other Jewish traditions. The dynamics of such intertextuality will be discussed later, after the narrative elements of early Christology have been investigated.

We may finally draw certain conclusions as regards the theocratic theory of adoptionist Christology.

1. The Old Testament and Jewish theocratic concept concerning the status of a Davidic king may be defined as adoptionist in the sense that an exceptional relationship between God and king is postulated in several writings.

2. Early Christology no doubt exploits the key passages of that kind of Davidic idealism in its descriptions.

3. Such a view does not have, however, any connection with later patristic debates concerning "adoptionist Christology". The so called Ebionite theory has appeared to be a theory concerning dualistic Gnostic possessionism which has nothing in common with New Testament Christology.

---

[81] For the view of AscIsa, see Bauckham, *NTS* 27 (1980-1) 334-335.

[82] Also according to Hurtado the aspect of worship is an essential feature in early hymns and prayers, *One God*, 102-104.

4. Interpretations such as functional Christology, or divine agent theory, do not essentially change the premises of an adoptionist interpretation.

5. The main problem with the theory of adoptionist Christology is that it presupposes a theocratic pattern in the explanation of Christology. In early Christology, however, it is precisely the theocratic pattern that is changed. Jesus has been exalted on the throne of Glory and now he is considered the divine Savior of the world. As a Davidic Messiah he is the one who brings salvation. Therefore he is worshiped together with God the Father.

6. As the adoptionist theory cannot explain the confessional nature of early Christology, its only benefit seems to be in the explication of the Davidic typology behind exaltation Christology. The Christology itself must be interpreted according to the apocalyptic world-view that is implicit in old formulas, and in the devotional context that expresses a change in the traditional theocratic view.

These conclusions raise certain questions that must be answered below. The most important one of these concerns the dynamics behind the making of the Christology. How and why did first Christians connect the messianic tradition with apocalyptic images and high Christology? How did the Davidide become a divine ruler of the world? These questions will be discussed in the following chapters.

§ 11 Main Factors in the Emergence of Christology

It is quite apparent that the thinking of the first Christians was guided by a symbolic world that was comprised of different conceptions of heavenly figures, thrones, and enthronements. The analysis has shown that first Christians in many respects shared the symbolic world of Second Temple Judaism. These elements formed the material that was used when Jesus' resurrection was interpreted an described in christological statements. But how did the final exaltation Christology emerge?

Approximately at the time of the New Testament there were several Jewish writings where the eschatological enthronement of Adam, Enoch, Noah, Abraham, and other noticeable patriarchs was anticipated, as we have seen above. On the other hand, certain apocalyptics awaited the Son of Man who would be enthroned in the last days and act as a heavenly judge. In Qumran a belief in the enthronement of messianic figures was commonplace. How do these conceptions relate to early Christology? Should we attempt to apply some kind of typological interpretation where the typos primarily explains the christological statement?

The analysis shows that in these writings we have a common scene for an eschatological enthronement. It is justified to speak even of an exaltation discourse. According to this discourse everything important takes place in the heavenly palace where God's throne is located. Descriptions relying on an ascent structure sometimes lead to an act of enthronement even in Jewish writings. Therefore, the idea of a transcendent throne is the first apparent element common both to Jewish writings and the New Testament. This, however, does not yet mean that both Jewish descriptions and statements of early Christology belong to the same discursive formation. The problem of continuity and discontinuity between these two will be treated below.

It is not easy to explain the relation between Jewish conceptions and distinctive features of Christology. As we have already seen in the Introduction, there have been three main theories explaining this relation. The theory of divine agency emphasized a pattern of exalted figures in general. Angelic interpretation identified the figures as angels. The more general messianic interpretation underlined the thematic content of early Christology. In what follows, we must estimate how these theories solve the basic problem concerning the originality of early Christology. What kind of theory can explain the essential transformation that has taken place in christological exaltation statements? How should we estimate the shift from Jewish ascent stories to descriptions of a resurrected Lord?

11.1. Divine agents and angels?

The theory of divine agents put emphasis on patterns in Jewish theology. The basic idea of the theory was that a Jewish prototype is a key to the meaning of a christological statement, and it also explains the emergence of such formation. In this kind of explanation there is not much room for the idea of transformation in early Christology. In fact, an idea of transformation weakens the very explanatory power of the theory.

There are several methodological problems in this theory. Hurtado, who introduced the divine agent theory, made an extensive analysis of Second Temple Jewish writings but, in the end, he was not able to exploit this analysis in his final explanation. His methodological principles prevented him from making a consistent theory of explanation. In spite of his critisicm against the methodology of previous christological study, Hurtado seems to be dependent on the tradition that concentrates on christological titles. He no longer emphasized the titles themselves, but changed them to heavenly figures. This is too small a step in order to change the view essentially. Hurtado investigated different figures, God's "chief agents" that appear in Jewish writings. Then he attempted to use these agents as models or types for Christ in Christology.

An example for such an agent is the chief angel Michael:

"Great power that he is, this angel characteristically delivers a revelation to some Old Testament worthy or guides him through the heavenly strata to a vision of the divine and, sometimes, to a heavenly exaltation. That is, God's chief servant, second only to God in heavenly authority, is ordered by God to act as the personal guide of a patriarchal figure, whose vision, ascent, and exaltation assure and prefigure the hope of the elect."[1]

Hurtado hopes to justify his position by a reasoning which he ascribes to Jewish theologians but nevertheless, his explanation sounds rather rationalistic. According to Hurtado God employs chief agents to deliver his message, or to bring eschatological deliverance, because this is a more sophisticated view of God's operations than the one where God is doing everything himself. It is further essential that the one who appears is none less than God's chief agent, the highest-ranking member of the heavenly hierarchy.[2]

There are several different divine agents in Jewish writings, and Hurtado treats them all in an identical way.[3] Since he is interested only in heavenly figures, both patriarchs and divine figures fall into the same category.

---

[1] Hurtado, *One God*, 90f.

[2] Hurtado, *One God*, 91.

[3] Capes is right in his criticism when he notes that, for instance, a manifestation of YHWH is not actually intended to be understood as a separate person. Capes, *Yahweh Texts*, 169.

"But the more fundamental idea that God has a 'chief agent,' whether principal angel, exalted patriarch, or some divine attribute described in personified language, was nevertheless an important development."[4]

The idea of divine agents then became the basic argument according to which Hurtado interpreted New Testament Christology. He made a survey over important Christological passages such as Acts 2:33-36, Romans 1:1-4, 1 Thessalonians 1:9-10, and Philippians 2:5-11. For him these passages indicated that "the earliest christological conviction was that the risen Jesus had been made God's chief agent."[5]

Typological idealism and pattern-application are explicit in this solution. The idea of a chief agent is the category that is presented as the heuristic tool for the identification of the nature of a christological statement. On this level the theory does not allow for any transformation of conceptions.

The weaknesses of this line of interpretation are evident. When divine agents are made some kind of prototypes for the exalted Christ, there should be a useful parallelism and sufficient identity between these two. Hurtado is, however, obliged to refrain from making detailed comparisons in the end. Actually, he doesn't even mean that Jesus is merely God's chief agent, even though he explicitly stated so. This may be seen in some of Hurtado's most crucial statements.

Apparently Hurtado has not been able to complete his theory without taking the idea of transformation into account. Therefore he made a distinction between the presentation of the exalted Christ in the New Testament and the presentation of divine agents in Jewish writings. He calls the difference a Christian mutation that has taken place in such tradition. Christian theologians actually changed Jewish concepts. This is where the explanatory force of the theory becomes questionable. What use is it to refer to such figures if they are not in fact exploited in the interpretation? The essential element that remained in this procedure was the enthronement scene itself. But this, for some reason, was not emphasized by Hurtado in his explanation.[6]

In other words, Hurtado has not made a conscious distinction between different discourses where an exalted figure occurs. He has simply identified all descriptions where some kind of exaltation takes place. After this his theory runs into problems, when the necessity of a distinction becomes inevitable.

---

[4] Hurtado, *One God*, 91.

[5] Hurtado, *One God*, 95. In his summary Hurtado writes: "At the earliest stages, Christian experience of and reflection upon the risen Jesus were probably influenced by and drew upon the divine agency category. Jesus was experienced and understood as exalted to the position of God's chief agent." p. 123.

[6] For the Christian mutation, see Hurtado, *One God*, 99ff., 114.

Therefore his reasoning remains on a too general level in order to be able to explain the factual emergence of christological thinking.

Even though Hurtado does investigate and make some use of the idea of enthronement, it is superseded by his interest in divine agents. This may also be the reason why he does not examine messianic enthronement passages in Jewish literature or the messianic nature of early exaltation statements in the New Testament. This should probably be considered his greatest weakness. He has presumably consciously excluded that subject from the area of his study.[7] Nevertheless, he makes conclusions about the enthronement passages in the New Testament. Thus he is not able to avoid the situation where his explanations overlap with the messianic intentions of early Christology and makes statements of its original meaning.[8]

In the New Testament Jesus is not an exalted patriarch. A similar problem concerns the angelic interpretation. However, it has admittedly been a better attempt at explaining early Christology. In Jewish writings angelic figures often have a mediating position between God and humankind. Some angels may even have a cultic ministry in heaven, and so the idea of atonement has been attached to the heavenly figure. And furthermore, as we have seen in several passages, many angels are high in the heavenly hierarchy and have a ruling position in heaven.[9]

Therefore, one may easily agree with Segal's notion that in a general sense also Christ's status in New Testament Christology resembles the one of those angels. He has "a considerable status" in heaven.[10] However, in this phase, there is already one difficult anomaly. In christological passages Christ is never described as a heavenly figure who worships God before the throne of Glory. In this respect, there is no exact identification of Christ with the angels even as regards their heavenly functions.

In addition to this, there is another problem that cannot be avoided. In his angelic interpretation Segal stated that Jesus as a divine figure is a fulfilment of Ps. 110 and Dan. 7:13. This fulfilment had come true on the basis of Jesus'

---

[7] Hurtado, *One God*, 18.

[8] In the beginning of his work Hurtado suggested that the concept he uses may have been giving early Christology a "conceptual framework" into which exaltation statements such as those speaking of Jesus "at the right hand" of God could be fit. (p. 21). In the end of his work that concept is no longer a framework but the core of the explanation itself.

[9] Capes attempts to find a solution to Hurtado's problems by referring to the figure of the angel of Yahweh. According to Capes this figure, unlike other angelic figures, represents the manifestation of God. Even he himself has to admit, however, that angelic figures in Second Temple texts are not clearly defined and the aspect of manifestation is not that evident. Capes, *Yahweh Texts*, 170.

[10] Segal, *ANRW* 23.2. (1980) 1371. See also chapter 1.1.c. above.

ascension to heaven and his identification with the "Lord".[11] Here Segal has identified two quite different traditions. Those Old Testament passages are naturally linked with Davidic traditions, not with angelic descriptions.[12]

Should Jesus as an enthroned Davidide really be associated with the angel of YHWH who is superior to all angels? Such a conclusion would not be consistent. As we have seen in the analysis, exalted Christ is almost without exception a Davidic Messiah, quite as Segal himself has noted. New Testament writings describe the ascension and exaltation of the Davidide. This means the royal enthronement of the Messiah of Israel. All of the exploited words and metaphors belong to the same semantic field. According to this description, the enthroned Christ is a heavenly king who reigns over the heavens and earth. This conviction is accompanied by the belief that the enthroned Christ is "Lord".[13]

Therefore, it is hardly plausible that the "fulfilment of Ps. 110 and Dan. 7:13" could be regarded as an identification of Jesus as an angelic figure, as Segal emphasizes. It is also apparent that in Segal's interpretation two quite separate discourses, or at least different symbols or metaphors, have been identified without sufficient evidence. A "considerable status" cannot be considered a sufficient argument for the identification of angelic figures with the exalted Christ. As we pointed out above, Segal himself, when mentioning the enthronement of the Davidide, has provided essential counter-arguments that make his explanation unconvincing.[14]

As we have seen earlier in this analysis, there were attempts to modify the angelic interpretation to a more general form. Rowland and his followers wished to redefine the original point of departure. As regards Christology they made a new distinction between angel Christology and angelomorphic Christology. Angel Christology means here an explicit identification of Christ as an angel.[15] Such a strict view was abandoned since angelic form, function, or terminology does not of necessity imply created ontology. The occurrence

---

[11] Segal, *ANRW* 23.2. (1980) 1371.

[12] The identification must therefore have been made on the basis of a very general comparison of patterns. This, however, does not take properly the nature of these traditions into account.

[13] This criticism applies also to the angelic interpretation of Gieschen that was treated in detail above in chapter 4.3.

[14] Segal probably has a better justification for his view when he later suggests that Paul has exploited angelic traditions in his Glory Christology. Here, however, Segal himself admits that the angelic figure in these traditions is actually associated with God's appearances. See Segal, *Death, Ecstasy,* 99ff.

[15] See above chapter 4; for the views, see e.g. Gieschen, *Christology,* 28; following Rowland, *JSNT 24* (1985), 100.

of those features does not prove that Christ would have been identified entirely with the created order. Therefore Christology was defined merely as "angelomorphic".

We have already earlier questioned such a distinction. It evidently helps one to use angelic interpretation without a necessary commitment to an ontological principle, but its benefits are limited. If Christ in early Christology has features of angelic form and function, he has merely been described by using such metaphors. We should emphasize that this kind of interpretation is no longer "angelic", since Christ is not identified as an angel. Therefore, one is not allowed to treat it later as a kind of angelic interpretation, but merely as an interpretation based on a general comparison.

Considering all this criticism it seems evident that the theory of messianic enthronement has been able to explicate best the essential content of early exaltation Christology. According to this theory, heavenly agents did not have a crucial role in the explanation of Christology. In Jewish writings there were several divine agents who acted in the heavenly sphere, but in the final comparison they could never serve as a complete parallel to christological statements. The disciples of Jesus claimed, as Hengel wrote, that a historical person, who was put to death in a disgraceful fashion in Jerusalem as a leader of the people, was "enthroned as the companion of God on the throne in accordance with Ps. 110:1."[16]

According to the theory of messianic enthronement one cannot explain the nature of early Christology unless the royal figure of the new Davidide is placed in the center of the Christology. During the analysis it has become quite apparent that neither the theory of divine agents nor the theory of angelic/angelomorphic Christology are able to do so. Therefore, the final process of defining the nature of early Christology must pay attention to the theory of messianic enthronement.

During the discussion in the present chapter we have once again met the problem concerning intertextual transformation, i.e. the transformation of ideas. Theories that depend on the idea of investigating typological causalities between Jewish mysticism and early Christology appear to be tied up with their premises. Their explanatory force depends completely on the preceding prototype itself.

If an angelic figure is taken as a prototype, the explanation is consistently dependent on the typological relation. If that relation is weakened during the explanation, a great deal of the explanatory force of the theory is also lost. Therefore, any attempt to bring a new conception for the actual interpretation of the nature of Christology inevitably changes the premises of the whole theory.

---

[16] Hengel, *Studies*, 203.

In this respect the premises of an explanatory theory should already be reassessed.

The present analysis has shown, however, that typological theories are not very fruitful in the interpretation of early Christology. The relation between Jewish merkabah mysticism and early Christology seems to be firm, though, and therefore its potential must not be abandoned in the investigation. What needs to be done in the next chapter is the discerning of "mystical" features in early Christology.

11.2. Possible features of a Christian merkabah tradition

How should we then attempt to define the point of departure for the emergence of early Christology? The fruitful part of the abovementioned theories has been the concentration on the ascent stories of Jewish mysticism. As far as the symbolic world is considered, it is quite evident that the images that are used in early Christology are taken from Jewish apocalyptic. Ascent stories appear to be based on a general exaltation discourse where the scene of events is rather uniform. In this respect we might well also speak of a Christian merkabah discourse where similar conceptions prevail.

The essential pattern that appears to have been accepted from the Jewish apocalyptic and mystical tradition, is the basic ascent structure with its special enthronement scene. This view does not imply that the resurrected Christ in early christological statements would be identical with the figures appearing in Jewish writings. The main postulation is that the so called apocalyptic imagination of the first Christian theologians has produced Christology in the framework of merkabah speculation that was typical of Jewish theology at that time.

During the study we have analyzed different aspects of Jewish merkabah tradition. It seems to provide a fitting background for the descriptions of early Christology. They both speak of heavenly thrones and even kingship – in a somewhat different manner, though. In Lukan traditions Christ is an enthroned Davidide, whose installation has taken place on the day of the resurrection. In Pauline theology the eschatological aspect of the resurrection of the dead is emphasized. In the letter to the Hebrews Christ's ascent is a fulfilment of Psalm 110.

On the basis of the investigation it is possible to attempt to discern certain plausible features of a Christian merkabah tradition. In the christological passages of the New Testament there are certain features that suit well such a conception.

Firstly, *the throne is presented as a central metaphor for the new status of Christ.* In Jewish mysticism the throne was a unique metaphor in two respects.

On one hand, there was the throne of Glory, God's throne. All heavenly worship centered before that throne. On the other hand, there were several thrones in heaven, prepared for pious Jews, especially for famous patriarchs. We must not forget the aspect of heavenly hierarchy, either. In Jewish theology throne is usually a metaphor expressing the highest rank of the hierarchy. As the status of Christ is described by the help of the throne-metaphor, Jewish hearers have instantly understood the message. The resurrected Jesus, "at the right hand" of God, has received the highest possible status in heaven.[17]

Secondly, in New Testament Christology, *resurrection is regarded as an act of enthronement*.[18] There is an interesting feature in the way in which early Christians have interpreted the relationship of resurrection and the Old Testament enthronement language. Enthronement statements of the royal ideology have been interpreted as prophecies about the resurrection of Jesus. Resurrection was thus identified with exaltation, and exaltation was simultaneously regarded as enthronement.

In Jewish mysticism we find several descriptions of the enthronement of different pious Jews. These acts of enthronement are not identical with the heavenly journeys that some seers experience. Jesus' exaltation is not described as a heavenly journey, either. Since the exaltation takes place in resurrection, his enthronement is eschatologically motivated. Jesus' enthronement on the throne of Glory is a highlight of soteriological eschatology.

The latter aspect is further a reason for the fact that Jesus' enthronement is not precisely a parallel to those enthronements described in Jewish writings. In Jewish mysticism Moses, Enoch, or some angelic figure may be enthroned as a heavenly judge on a heavenly throne. They are like the apostles who are promised a throne in the end of days, and who shall judge the tribes of Israel. In the christological merkabah mysticism of the early Church the enthroned *Christ has a universal power over all of humankind as a Savior*.[19] In the exaltation of Jesus the eschatological resurrection of the dead has begun. It also inaugurates a new era of salvation.

---

[17] This feature is hardly contested. It is in fact emphasized by all of the main theories presented and discussed in this study. See e.g. Segal, *ANRW* 23.2. (1980) 1371; Hurtado, *One God*, 121f.; Hengel, *Studies*, 133ff.

[18] For instance, even Gieschen in his angelomorphic interpretation refers several times to this feature, see Gieschen, *Christology*, 301, 321f. Probably the most extensive analysis of this feature is found in Hengel, *Studies*, 137ff.

[19] This one, naturally, is one of the most studied features in early Christology in the previous investigation; see especially chapter 8 above. Therefore, it should not be forgotten when the relation of Christology to Jewish mysticism is investigated.

Christ's universal power is most often expressed with the epithet Lord. As a Lord he is a "Leader and Savior" (Acts 5:31) of those who believe in him. Christological merkabah speculation is thus a part of soteriology. The enthroned one is not merely a judge. He has other, even more important, functions. On the throne Christ has a cultic function. He serves as a priest in the heavenly Temple and gives forgiveness of sins.

The soteriological aspect leads finally to the last important feature in christological merkabah tradition. *On the throne of glory the Lord Christ is an object of devotion.*[20] The Christology of early confessional formulas and kerygmatic statements is no longer of a theocratic nature in the traditional sense of the word. It is Christ on whose name people shall call in order to be saved. Christ is also praised in the same manner as God himself.

This is a very interesting factor in early Christology. It links the christological merkabah tradition with the original merkabah speculation of the Old Testament and Jewish theology. In the latter God himself was always the object of adoration and worship. Now a clear shift in the scheme has taken place. The resurrected Christ sits enthroned on the throne of Glory and he is the object of devotion and worship.[21] In this sense the christological merkabah tradition seems to exploit the very core of Jewish merkabah speculation, instead of only the apocalyptic scheme that provides for the setting of different heavenly descriptions.[22]

There are thus several factors in early Christology that may be defined as parts of a new discourse that may be called Christian merkabah mysticism. According to this tradition, Christ sits on the throne of glory in the heavenly Temple and he is the Leader of humankind. The believers' worship is linked with heavenly worship before the divine throne where Christ is. Furthermore, this throne is the place from which God's mercy is delivered to this world. It is no longer merely the throne of the Holy God, but the throne of Christ. Therefore, it is a mercy seat that brings salvation.

---

[20] This feature was discussed above, see chapter 10.3. A detailed analysis of this feature is given in Hurtado, *One God*, 101ff.

[21] Capes emphasizes – against Hurtado – that, in early Christology, Christ is not merely worshiped alongside God, but he is worshiped as God. Capes, *Yahweh Texts*, 172. This is apparently true, even though I am not convinced that the reason for this could be found in the way Jewish texts describe the angel of Yahweh, as Capes suggests.

[22] Fletcher-Louis develops his angelomorphic interpretation in the opposite direction. "Our expectation that angelomorphic traditions would bear fruit in the search for a simpler and more precise history-of-religions explanation of an early Christology, in which a fully human Jesus is worshiped alongside the one Jewish God, has indeed been fulfilled." Fletcher-Louis, *Angels*, 254. According to the present analysis, the intention of the early Christian merkabah Christology is precisely the worshiping of the divine Son of God on the throne of Glory.

It is hardly possible to understand early Christology without the scene of apocalyptic merkabah speculation. Without it, one would remain quite unaware of why enthronement language should be exploited precisely in the context of resurrection. It would further be difficult to understand why the throne is the central metaphor for Christology. As the general description of the christological merkabah tradition has been given, we shall proceed in estimating its value in the methodology of explaining the emergence of Christology.

11.3. Merkabah tradition and the search for a "missing link"

Above we noted that the theories that depend on the idea of investigating typological causalities between Jewish mysticism and early Christology are tied up with their premises. They cannot give proper attention to the transformational process that appears to be quite explicit in the formation of Christology. Those theories seem to run into problems right in the crucial point where their explanatory ability would have been needed. This seems to highlight the fact that the basic nature of early exaltation Christology is very original and exceptional. It cannot be explained merely by exploiting the categories of Jewish apocalyptic.

During the analysis we have already noted several of those exceptional features. The merkabah discourse in the New Testament is quite limited and it is focussed on one central figure. Most such descriptions where the identity of the exalted one can be discerned point in one direction. The relevant pattern to be used seems to be that of the enthronement of a Davidide. The only exception is that of the heavenly high priest occurring in the cultic discourse but even there, at least as regards the letter to the Hebrews, we find the king-priest who is actually a Davidide fulfilling the priesthood of Melchizedek (Psalm 110).[23]

The exceptional feature of Christology, in comparison to Jewish mysticism, is the connecting of that messianological pattern or theme with the apocalyptic ascent structure. Jesus as a Davidide has been exalted on the throne of Glory in the heavenly Holy of Holies in his resurrection. For this kind of messianology we have no exact parallel in Jewish theology.[24] Some descriptions of the anticipated Davidic Messiah in the Dead Sea Scrolls, though, come close. In those descriptions, however, the ascent structure is not clear. In this respect the conception found in early Christology is unique. It reveals a new discourse where terms and expressions that have been taken from the symbolic world of Jewish theology have been given a new meaning.

---

[23] See especially chapter 7.2. above.

[24] For instance Charlesworth has pointed out that the concept of 'Messiah' was not simple and self-evident in the first-century Judaism. Charlesworth, *Judaisms*, 228ff.

In christological statements we may note both conceptual and intertextual transformation. There is first of all a transcendental shift that locates the reign of the Davidide in the heavenly realm. The universalistic intention is clear, too, even though it cannot be considered a very original feature since traits of that have occurred also in certain Jewish writings. Further, the status of the exalted one in christological statements is unique, as we shall see later.

From the point of view of methodology this means that we must make a distinction between the symbolic world that has been exploited in early Christology and the discursive formation in the terms of which that Christology has been expressed. As we have seen before, the symbolic world is mostly common to both Jewish apocalyptic and early Christology. This, however, does not yet mean that the essetial meaning of Christology could be derived completely from that Jewish background – even though most methods have rested on such a premise.

In a general sense we may naturally say that there is an exaltation discourse prevailing in Second Temple Jewish theology, and that it also influences Christology. In a more precise sense, as far as semantics are considered, we must speak of a discursive formation that is typical of early Christology only. As we noted earlier in the Introduction, it is actually the discourse that makes it possible to construct the topic in a certain way. Early Christology constructs the actual description of the risen Christ in a way that is quite foreign to earlier Jewish writings.

These observations lead further to a re-assessment of christological investigation. It is apparent that the theory of divine agents, as well as that of angelic interpretation, have rested on a fixed presupposition. These theories have been attempts to find a "missing link" between Jewish theology and early Christology.[25] Scholars have attempted to discern a divine agent or an angelic figure that might serve as a prototype for the exalted Christ in Christology. According to those scholars, only such *typos* could explain how the first Christians were able to present the resurrected Christ as a heavenly being. This sort of goal leads us astray, however.

In pre-Christian Judaism there is no exact typos for Christ that could serve

---

[25] Even though Capes criticized Hurtado for his tendency of referring to divine agents that actually do not explain the typological relation between Jewish theology and early Christology, he himself proposed merely a new kind of typology by introducing the idea of the angel of Yahweh that should be understood as a manifestation of God. Capes, *Yahweh Texts*, 168ff. Capes attempted to justify his theory with the idea that, already in the Old Testament, Yahweh is presented as a corporate person. As the Israelites conceived of their one God as having plural manifestations, it was possible for early Christians to consider Messiah Jesus to be a manifestation of Yahweh. Capes, *Yahweh Texts*, 173-174. In the New Testament, however, Christ is evidently more that merely a manifestation of God.

as a "missing link" for the interpretation of his exalted status as a Lord on the heavenly throne. It seems that such typological idealism has rested on an implicit "evolutionist" presupposition.

Scholars have attempted to maintain the continuity of messianology from Jewish theology to early Christology by substituting a typos that has enough functions to reach in both directions. This, however, is not what a discourse demands. Quite the contrary, a discourse gives its own meanings to the symbols that are being exploited. Even though the context provides the continuity of tradition, the new discourse itself aims at a new identity of ideas.[26]

It is rather easy to see why the missing link was sought after. The first Christian theologians have connected traditions that did not yet belong together in Second Temple Judaism. The ascent structure and the idea of heavenly enthronements belonged to the world of "divine agents" – if one chooses to use that epithet. It is true that there were exceptional angelic figures in Jewish writings. Therefore the abovementioned scholars were rather consistent when attempting to connect these figures with the risen Christ. In this way, as regards the coherence of their theory and conditions, they were able to find a reason for the "angelic" heavenly status of the Davidide. The only problem in this construction is that those descriptions in Jewish writings have practically nothing to do with early Christology.[27]

Christological descriptions in early kerygmatic statements, homologies, and hymns are quite unique. They present Christ as a Davidic Messiah who has been enthroned on the heavenly throne "at the right hand" of God. The Davidide is no longer an earthly figure. He is messianic, though, and as a heavenly king and Lord he reigns on the throne. He is the head of heavenly hosts and he is being worshiped as the divine Son of God. He is not like an angel, he is like a king.[28] The descriptions are not angelic or angelomorphic. They are royal and messianic.

---

[26] As regards methodology, a distiction between the sign itself and its use is essential for the present view of the relation between Jewish theology and early Christology. See chapter 1.3.

[27] This was, actually, what, for instance, Hurtado himself admitted. In his study, as we have seen already above, he emphasized the "Christian mutation" of Jewish ideas. According to Hurtado one should note "the most significant difference between earliest Christianity and other contemporary religious groups: the place of the exalted Christ in the religious life, devotion, or piety of its adherents." Hurtado, *One God*, 99. When such a notion is taken seriously, the premises of explanation must change – more than Hurtado has done.

[28] One should probably repeat that the main problem with typological explanation is the fact that the assumed *typos* has no factual counterpoint in early Christology. The typological identification does not work in practice.

What, then, does the messianic aspect mean in enthronement Christology? When Christ is exalted on the throne of glory he is not merely installed as a heavenly judge as the enthroned patriarchs were in Jewish apocalyptic writings or the apostles in the Gospel tradition. It is naturally true that, in the Old Testament, a king of Israel also acted as a judge. In spite of this, early Christology is not content with that kind of description. Instead, royal epithets are used of the exalted Jesus.[29] According to earliest formulations Jesus has been made "both Lord and Messiah". *This combining of messianic tradition and merkabah speculation is rather unique in Jewish theology.* We will pay special attention to it later.

As regards the explanation of the dynamics of the formation of Christology, some further comments are needed. The interpretation of the nature of early Christology is not dependent on earlier types, but on the symbolic world of Second Temple Judaism.[30] First Christians the use same symbols as their predecessors, such as the kingly figure and the throne. There are even heavenly servants and a transcendent temple liturgy. All of these symbols have been exploited when Jesus' new status in heaven is being described.[31]

When explaining different details of early Christology we do not need to bring the types of Jewish theology into the Christology itself. For instance in the case of the appellation Son of God it is sufficient to be reminded of the symbols of Old Testament royal ideology. We do not need to make any new effort to revive the method of Christological titles, even though there were also interesting new aspects in that area.

It is true that in Qumran Songs of the Sabbath Sacrifice the highest figures in the heavenly *debir* were called gods. Also the special priestly figure in 4Q491 anticipated to be "reckoned with gods". Such a view, however, cannot

---

[29] Gieschen in his concluding statements maintained that angelomorphic traditions played a significant role when Christ was described as the "visible manifestation of God." He further stated that a "gigantic" step was taken when the earliest Christians made the confession "Jesus is Lord." Gieschen, *Christology*, 349-350. It is apparent that even in his final conclusions Gieschen confused royal themes with his angelomophic interpretation. Such a conclusion should rather question the relevance of any angelomorphic theories. Cf. the criticism of Carrell, *Jesus*, 228.

[30] This is a crucial difference also with regard to the traditional methodology of Christology. In the introduction the investigation of christological titles was abandoned, and the abovementioned result justifies such decision on its part.

[31] As regards methodology Hay is still somewhat ambiguous in this question. On the one hand he states that Psalm 110 was used to support particular christological titles. On the other hand, however, he notes that only particular ideas of heavenly position, vindication etc. were exploited in early Christology. Actually Christian exegesis "took a new path" by referring the psalm to Jesus. See Hay, *Glory*, 155, 161.

be the precise reason why Jesus is called the Son of God on the throne.[32] Such a view can only help us to explain the reception of royal messianology in the early Church. Believing Jews may have found it easy to understand how Christ can be a Son of God in the heavenly Holy of Holies. In spite of such an interesting connection the messianic presentation cannot be reduced to angelology. According to apocalyptic messianology the Davidide was to be a Son of God on the throne. The conviction of the writers of early Christology was based on this anticipation. This had become true in Jesus' enthronement.

The same applies to the understanding of the appellation Lord. In Philo the cherubim on the ark were called God and *Kyrios*. If we assume that such a conception was more widely known in the Jewish community, it was probably easy for many Jews to understand that the Son of God "at the right hand" of God was the Lord. This was the place for the Lord, defined in an excellent and influential way in Psalm 110. Christ, however, was no cherub in the descriptions of early Christology. He was rather paralleled with God's manifestation on the heavenly ark. He was the risen Jesus who had been enthroned in the heavens and who now was the Lord of all the world.

Typological idealism may further be detected in the idea of "transformational mysticism" that has been popular in recent studies.[33] The mystical tradition presents an idea of the transformation of the mystic's body into a heavenly figure. There no doubt is certain evidence for such a process in some mystical writings, as we have seen during the analysis.[34] In the explanation of early Christology, however, the pattern is still that of typology.

After these considerations we may conclude that the emergence of early Christology was dependent on the symbolic world of Second Temple Judaism on the one hand, and on the unique belief in an exaltation in the resurrection on the other hand. Early Christology was not dependent on heavenly agents or figures that would serve as typological predecessors for the risen Christ. Quite the contrary, the elements of Jewish mysticism were exploited when a new theme, the heavenly enthronement of the resurrected Davidide, was introduced.

---

[32] Collins has attempted to connect the exalted figure of 4QM both with "traditions associated with Moses, that envisaged deification by enthronement," and with the assumedly messianic figure of 1QH 3. In this respect he wishes to reconstruct a situation in Jewish theology where the pattern of deification by enthronement could be associated with a Davidic messianic figure – in order to explain "the milieu in which Christianity developed." Collins, *Death, Ecstasy*, 54-55. This can be considered an ultimate example of typological idealism, but its explanatory force is as weak as in other typological theories.

[33] See for instance Himmelfarb, *Ascent*, 41f., 45-46.

[34] Morray-Jones speaks of an "ancient tradition of transformational mysticism," according to which "the vision of God's Glory transforms the visionary into the likeness of that Glory and invests him with the divine Name." Morray-Jones, *JJS 43* (1992) 30.

11.4. Semiosis in early Christian theology

We may also outline certain methodological factors that enable us to understand why the search for a "missing link" is unnecessary in the explanation of early Christology. Those methodological aspects that we discussed in the introductory part of the present study, lead finally to the investigation of the *semiosis*, i.e. the process where meaning is constructed, that has taken place in the earliest Jewish Christian community.[35]

Semiosis has to do with signs and with meanings that are given to particular signs. During the study we have paid attention to the symbolic world that has prevailed in the Second Temple period. Both Jewish writings and the New Testament exploit similar images and metaphors. On the level of the symbolic world there is an explicit continuity of tradition observed in these writings.[36]

These separate images may be regarded as signs that have been exploited in Jewish mystical presentations or in Christian christological descriptions. As regards methodology, however, the semiosis concerning different signs must always be investigated in their primary context. The process of constructing meaning cannot be generalized to the extent that its results would cover all belief-systems and religious groups of the Second Temple period.

In a general sense the approach presented in the previous chapter needs to be repeated again here. Words get a new meaning when they are exploited in a new discourse. A more detailed semiotic analysis of the construction of meaning leads us even further, however. There is a distinct way in which meaning is constructed in the semiosis of Second Temple groups. The most common pattern in the construction of meaning seems to be that signs are connected with particular narratives that link the sign to a larger context. Thus, for example, words such as "king" or "throne," are given their proper meaning in the context of descriptions of heavenly enthronements. The narrative provides a scene where the sign finds its logical place and where it also has a significant function.

When New Testament writers exploit traditional images – signs taken from the symbolic world of Second Temple Judaism – in their Christology, they do not exploit or produce exactly the same narratives as their predecessors. Rather, they are constructing Christocentric narratives where the actualization

---

[35] For the theory of semiosis, see e.g. Eco, *Semiotics*, 32ff.; Hawkes, *Structuralism*, 123, 133f.; Culler, *Pursuit of Signs*, 18ff.

[36] In the methodological part of the study we have pointed out that words in a language-system are signs that merely have a lexical meaning. They may thus be regarded as signs that may be used in a process of semiosis. Only when they are used in a discourse do they get a referential meaning. Therefore, the units of the symbolic world of Second Temple Judaism do not have a universal meaning that could as such be transferred to the interpretation of Christology. See chapter 1.3.a.

of tradition produces something completely new. Christian narratives exploit traditional material and traditional features, but they also create a new scene where previous tradition is transformed into someting unique.[37] The so called Christian merkabah tradition differs from the merkabah traditions and from the ascent structure of Jewish mysticism.

In this respect Christian theologians present us new mental pictures of things in heaven. They provide new interpretation of traditional signs referring to heavenly things and events, and new schemes of the conduct of the Messiah after his resurrection. In literary analysis we prefer to call these schemes narratives, since that is a proper term to be used in the study of written documents. Christological narratives provide us with a sequence of events that are essential and meaningful for the subject that is being presented.

During the analysis we have seen several examples of this kind of procedure. Early Christian enthronement narratives surpass the ascent structure presented in Jewish writings. New Testament cultic interpretation transforms the Melchizedek-theology of Second Temple writers. The process of signification depends essentially on the presented narrative, on the scheme that gives a significant context for the sign.

Therefore, one of the most important tasks of christological study is to discern different narratives that serve as the source of meaning for different christological presentations. Some features of the nature of Christology will also be revealed when the function of disctinct signs – units of the common symbolic world – in these narratives is investigated. In the following sections these subjects will be treated in detail. First the elements of symbolic world will be discerned, and then all relevant christological narratives concerning exaltation Christology will be studied.

In the beginning of this study we have further noted that the dynamics of the process of signification may also be approached from the point of view of intertextualism. New Testament Christology exploits the "texts" of Jewish mysticism. The investigation of the intertextual relationship is analoguous to the investigation of early Christian semiosis. Now the point of weight is on the textual relationship and in the intertextual transformation of previous texts. This kind of relationship will also be studied when different christological narratives concerning exaltation Christology will be investigated below.

---

[37] Therefore, the idea of semiosis in early Christology, is necessarily dependent on the idea of intertextuality, discussed earlier in chapter 1.3.c.

§ 12 Theocracy, Exaltation Discourse, and Christology

Did Jewish merkabah mysticism influence the formation of early Christology? In the analyses of this work we have investigated both the central elements of merkabah mysticism in Second Temple Jewish writings and different aspects of early Christian exaltation Christology. We have studied the symbolic world that was essential for Old Testament faith, as well as selected metaphors and their function in the discourses of New Testament Christology. In what follows it is time to attempt to construct main lines in early Christology on the grounds of these analyses, and as well to define the nature of the Christology found in the old kerygmatic statements and homologies and that in the letters and other books of the New Testament.

The question about the nature of 'influence' is not very simple, however. During the study a distinction has been made between the role of the symbolic world that appears to have common features throughout the Second Temple period, and the role of different discourses in the context of which theological conceptions, and especially Christology, have been presented. The flaws of simple typological explanations of influence have been noted in the previous chapter. The appearance of an exalted figure in a Jewish writing does not actually explain the meaning of a christological description found in the New Testament.

Influence, thus, may be assumed to work on two levels. On the level of the symbolic world one may easily detect the exploitation of different figures and characters, as well as the adoption of a whole scene like the one speaking of a heavenly Temple. Such elements no doubt direct the thinking of the writer. In respect of meaning, however, the problem of influence appears on a new level. An analysis of the background of a New Testament discourse is not exactly a matter of genealogy. The continuity of tradition is not based on an evolutive scheme where the essential elements of a discourse were dependent on earlier occurrences of similar elements in the manner of etymology.

The so called influence is rather a matter of intertextual process where earlier elements and texts have been exploited and merged into new descriptions. The new text may assimilate, echo, re-assess, or even contradict earlier material. The final meaning is dependent on the new discourse where the revised elements play an integral part. Signs get their final meaning in the context of the narrative in which they occur. Therefore, christological titles as such do not have heuristic value in the present study. They do not serve as autonomous indicators of relgous convictions. Instead of that we must concentrate on the christological discourse itself – or rather on the selection of discourses and respective narratives extant in early Christology.

12.1. Three enthroned figures

On the level of individual symbols it is easy to note that several traditional Jewish figures have been exploited in christological description. In fact, most modern christological investigations have concentrated on these figures. The main stream study centering on christological titles is a perfect example of this. No one would deny that the symbolic world of Second Temple Judaism has given its terminology to early Christology.

As regards the elements of early Christology, one must first investigate how Christ is presented and described as an enthroned figure in heaven. In the analysis we have noted that a messianic figure appears mainly in the context of three different discourses. In enthronement discourse that figure is the messianic Davidide, the eschatological king from the family of David. In cultic discourse he is the new Melchizedek, a heavenly high priest. In judicial discourse, in turn, he is something like the Son of Man, a heavenly judge who participates in the final judgment of the whole of humankind.

In the symbolic world of the first Christians these are the symbols that are exploited in the formation of Christology. The messianic figure itself appears to change from discourse to discourse. What unites these figures is the fact that they are all enthroned figures. All of these discourses thus have a common point of departure that appears to be the ascent structure that has been applied to all of them. The throne, however, apart from the fact that it appears in all of these descriptions, is given a different meaning in each context.

a. Messianic Davidide on the throne of Glory

In the enthronement discourse, of which the resurrection discourse must in this case be considered a part, the messianic figure is the royal son of David, the ideal king who is expected to reign over Israel in eschatological times.[1] The Christology of the enthroned Davidide exploits those two elements on which we have concentrated in this study. There is the metaphor of the throne and there is the idea of the exaltation of the Messiah. These features also comprise

---

[1] The concept of Messiah, however, is ambivalent in Second Temple Judaism, as Neusner, Green, et.al., have pointed out in their collection "Judaisms and Their Messiahs." The term itself was not widely used, and in different contexts it refers to quite different subjects (e.g. Israelite king, foreign king, high priest, patriarch). Green, *Judaisms*, 2f. In this respect the term is a good example of a sign that may be exploited in different discourses. The approach of Neusner, Green, et.al, therefore, is invaluable. One should remember, however, that in the descriptions of Davidic dynasty and its expected future, the term is not problematic, as Green himself admits. Green, *Judaisms*, 3. In this respect the collection under discussion is in danger of reducing the subject to triviality, which does no justice to the significance of the theme in the New Testament. A further problem with the collection is the titular emphasis. Writers investigated merely the occurrence of the title *christos*, and separated it from Jewish eschatology in general.

the elements of the so called Christian merkabah speculation that we are attempting to reconstruct. In early Christology they are being combined in the basic belief that Jesus' resurrection is considered an act of enthronement.

The Davidide, on the one hand, is the king of Israel. In Jewish tradition king has constantly been a useful metaphor for the expression of transcendent, universal power. Jesus as a Davidide is an eschatological king who is linked to the history of Israel. In Second Temple writings the messianic idea was often maintained by the help of a distinctive promise tradition, as we have seen.[2] The idea of a Davidic kingship brings with it the idea of the Davidic covenant, that has often been understood as a covenant of grace.[3] The identification of Jesus as a Davidide provides thus several features that can be exploited in the formation of Christology.

The throne, on the other hand, has appeared to be one of the key elements in the symbolic universe of Jewish merkabah mysticism. The throne itself is a metaphor that was taken from Old Testament history. The writings of Jewish mysticism evidence thus the reception of Old Testament metaphors in a new context. Therefore, the content of the conception is often similar to that of Old Testament beliefs. When for example the throne of Glory is mentioned, it is always a throne in a heavenly palace where God is the King of heaven and earth.[4]

Royal epithets seem to be constant in apocalyptic descriptions and that is why it is justified to conclude that the heavenly court is a palace. What was interesting in Jewish tradition was that the cultic context was easily attached to the royal one. The royal palace was simultaneously the Temple of God. Just as there was the ark in the Temple of Jerusalem, there was also a royal throne in the heavenly Holy of Holies. So the heavenly palace may easily be described as a Temple, as it is done in several writings. In the heavenly Temple there is a liturgy being performed before the divine throne. This is why the religious liturgical aspect is present in almost every description of the heavenly palace.

In the writings of Jewish mysticism the throne has appeared to be a fundamental metaphor for heavenly power. According to the analysis, this is practically true in all of the investigated visions. The throne not only expresses power but also serves as a true metaphor for the Lordship of God. The

---

[2] In addition to the interest in distinct metaphors, Duling emphasized the covenantal idea, see Duling, *NTS* 19 (1973) 56.

[3] For instance in Sirach there is the idea of the everlasting covenant of Davidic kingship, see Sirach 47:11; cf. PsSol. 17:4, 21. See von Rad, *ThLZ* (1947) 215; Allen, *NTS* 17 (1971) 104.

[4] For instance, according to Dean-Otting the Temple setting preserves the orginal motif in its "purest" outline. Dean-Otting, *Heavenly Journeys*, 264.

metaphorical relationship is based on a general conception of earthly kings who perform sovereign reign over their subservients. The dynamics of metaphors teach us that the power of God looks similar to such reign, but in reality it is a much greater reign over the whole world.[5]

This kind of background gives us some relevant material for the explanation of the symbol of throne in christological descriptions. The sitting "at the right hand" is evidently a metaphor for heavenly power. According to the passages referring to a heavenly enthronement Christ has participated in God's Lordship on a heavenly throne.[6]

In Jewish mysticism the use of the throne metaphor was rather complex, however. As we have seen, there were several different thrones in the heavens. God's throne had a central status, but in addition to that several patriarchs and righteous ones had thrones of their own. It is justified to speak of a tradition of the enthronement of patriarchs. We have also noted that, in the case of multiple heavens, each heaven may have a throne of its own that is occupied by an angel (AscIsa).[7]

The throne is thus one symbol belonging to the symbolic universe of Jewish theologians in the Second Temple period. In itself it was not necessarily a metaphor for the enthronement of the Messiah, however. In fact, it was not always attached to messianic descriptions. The throne must rather be seen as a useful metaphor that could be exploited in different descriptions of heavenly events. In most passages, nevertheless, the throne is depicted as the throne of Glory on which God himself sits.

Furthermore, in Jewish theology, the description of the exaltation of the Davidide on a throne remains on such a metaphorical level that almost nothing is said about the person himself. Usually his kingship can be understood in earthly terms. Even if his reign could be interpreted as an eschatological reign, as in the case of the Qumran passage, the Son of David is not an earthly person who would ascend to heaven before his enthronement. This fact has produced a puzzle that has remained unsolved, especially among those searching for a typological solution.

This is not to deny that in Jewish theology there was a tradition about the eschatological enthronement of a Davidic Messiah. This was seen especially in

---

[5] Cf. Hengel, *Studies*, 175ff.; Dean-Otting, *Heavenly Journeys*, 286; Himmelfarb, *Ascent*, 28; Collins, *Death, Ecstasy*, 45ff.

[6] Already Gourgues treated the "sitting at the right hand" as a "symbol" for an invisible state of affairs. In his explanation this symbol represented especially Christ's heavenly power. Gourgues, *A la Droite de Dieu*, 220f. For the idea of participating in God's reign, see pp. 223ff.

[7] Cf. Gruenwald, *Merkavah Mysticism*, 60f.

the Dead Sea Scrolls. In the Isaiah Pesher (4Q161) the idea of an enthronement was rather clear, in spite of the fragmentary and somewhat corrupt nature of the manuscript (Frags. 8-10, col. III, 18-21, Vermes):

> "[Interpreted, this concerns the Branch] of David who shall arise at the end [of days]... God will uphold him with [the spirit of might, and will give him] a throne of glory..."

There is some resemblance between this description and the passage of the enthronement of the Son of Man in 1 Enoch. In 4Q161, however, the Davidic genealogy of the king is more emphasized. In fact, in this passage political kingship is given an eschatological interpretation.[8] Isaiah's prophecy is interpreted as a promise of the enthronement of the Messiah.

Therefore, in this Qumranian passage Jewish messianic tradition has not actually been combined with merkabah speculation. On the one hand the enthronement language in the pesher is similar to that of Old Testament royal ideology. Davidic kings were always expected to be exalted on a divine throne, at least in a metaphorical sense. Their royal power was often described in a pleonastic manner. On the other hand there was a clear line of apocalyptic merkabah mysticism extant in the community of Qumran, and it has not been exploited here.[9]

In many respects the Isaiah pesher of Qumran is quite close for instance to the Christological formulas in Romans and in Acts. In the formula of Romans the Davidic lineage of Jesus is quite emphasized.

> "[T]he gospel concerning his Son, who was descended from David according to the flesh and was declared to be Son of God with power according to the spirit of holiness by resurrection from the dead, Jesus Christ our Lord" (Rom. 1:3-4).

According to our analysis, the clauses are subordinate to the subject "Son", and therefore the first clause already refers to the exaltation.

Thus the special feature in this formula is the idea that messianic expectation does not receive its fulfillment in the Davidic descent of Jesus, but in the enthronement of Jesus as a Davidic king in heaven. In this respect there is little difference in regard to the Isaiah pesher of Qumran: "[Branch] of David who shall arise... God will... [... give him] a throne of glory." The focus in both of these passages lies on the enthronement of the Davidide.

---

[8] Talmon speaks of a "millenarian-messianic" idea at Qumran: "The expected *New Aeon* will unfold as an age in which terrestrial-historical experience coalesces with celestial-spiritual utopia... The New Order to be established by the Anointed is not otherworldly but rather the realization of a divine plan on earth... Qumran Messianism reflects the political ideas of the postexilic returnees' community." Talmon, *Judaisms*, 131.

[9] Also Collins notes that the figure of the Davidic Messiah in the writings of Qumran is an ideal king. He will restore Davidic dynasty and he has a role in the eschatological war, but his heavenly reign is not described. Collins, *Scepter*, 67.

We must note, however, that the occurrence of elements of the same symbolic universe does not yet confirm that the Christian description had been formulated in the context of a similar discourse. Christological discourse emphasizes that Jesus of Nazareth is the awaited Davidide. The person himself is already known to the compilers of the description. Furthermore, the enthronement is linked to resurrection. This is naturally exceptional for Second Temple Jewish literature. Also Jesus' Lordship is a feature that has no counterpoint in earlier writings.[10]

Therefore, it is apparent that the so called messianic symbol, the figure of the Davidide, is given new exact meaning in terms of the new discourse. The symbol as such is familiar to most Jewish thinkers, but the new interpretation is based on a particular transformation of earlier ideas. We shall return to this question below.

This new description of the exalted Davidide appears frequently in christological statements. As we have seen in the analyses, the throne or a corresponding submetaphor is constantly attached to the exalted Christ in New Testament Christology. In numerous passages Christ is a Davidide whose enthronement has taken place at Easter (Acts 2:22-36; 5:30-31; 7:52-56; 1 Cor. 15:25; Rom. 8:34; Col. 3:1; Eph. 1:20; Hebr. 1:3-4; 10:12; 12:2; 1 Peter 3:21-22; Rev. 3:21; 5:5-6).

It is especially noteworthy that Psalm 110 ("sitting at the right hand of God") that has largely been the focus of interest in the present study, refers also to an eschatological Davidic king. In this respect one could say that Jesus' Davidic messiahship is implied in a vast number of christological passages in the New Testament.[11]

As regards the messianic feature itself, therefore, there is hardly disagreement about the key symbol of early Christology. In the symbolic world of the first Christians Christ was first and foremost an enthroned Davidide. He was depicted as a kingly Messiah. The content of Christology was constructed on this basis. Whatever the discourse was in which this term was exploited, the point of departure was clear. Christ is not an exalted angel. He is not merely a divine agent. He is a messianic Davidide in heaven.

---

[10] It seems apparent that the major theme of Davidic descendence serves as a justification for the messianic interpretation. Cf. Hengel, *Studies*, 217; Chester, *Paulus*, 77.

[11] Already Segal noted that the interpretation of Psalm 110 was crucial for early Christian exaltation Christology. Segal, *ANRW* 23.2. (1980) 1371. We have earlier maintained that this view created problems for his angelic interpretation. It is further noteworthy that Hurtado, in his theory of divine agents, was not able to combine the information gained from Jewish writings with information gained from early Christology. In his explanation of earliest exaltation Christology he does not investigate Christ's role as an exalted Davidide. See e.g. Hurtado, *One God*, 99ff.

b. New Melchizedek on the mercy seat

In the context of the cultic discourse the enthroned figure was described in terms of cultic terminology. He was a high priest, a new Melchizedek who had a cultic function in the heavenly Temple. Even though the elements of the symbolic world are now different, the elements that provide premises for the new christological transformation are similar to those functioning in the preceding discourse. Here also the exaltation is based on resurrection. Further, the enthronement takes place on the cherub-throne that is located in the heavenly Holy of Holies. And finally, Psalm 110 is often exploited in the presentations of Christology.

Also the cultic discourse derives from the Jewish background. The point of departure for such descriptions is naturally the Temple worship in Jerusalem, that has provided for the exploited terminology. The high priest figure was taken from the Old Testament, but the presentation of the figure is exceptional here. The high priest is Melchizedek, a priest-king who also has political power.[12]

In addition to this, mystical transcendentalism of the apocalyptic constructed a scene of heavenly worship, and this became essential for Second Temple writings. The Qumran Songs of the Sabbath Sacrifice described a throne in heaven, and angels and other heavenly beings that conducted a liturgy in front of it. The throne was located in the Holy of Holies. The cherubim before the throne sung songs of praise. It is worthwhile repeating here the description of the twelfth song: "Praise the God of ...] ... The cherubim lie prostrate before him... They bless the image of the throne-chariot (which) is above the vault of the cherubim..." (4Q405 20-21-22, 6-9; Martínez).

As noted already earlier, such mystical contemplation over the heavenly Holy of Holies and the throne-chariot suited well the justification of the situation of high priests in the Temple of Jerusalem in the Second Temple period. There evidently was a unity of temple cult and apocalyptic thinking.[13] The traditional, mainstream Jewish religious imagery had been attached to Temple cult, and the ark in the Holy of Holies had been identified as the throne of God. Now the apocalyptic scene linked the earthly service to the heavenly worship. In this respect, the Qumran Songs of the Sabbath Sacrifice seem to rest on the Old Testament priestly religion. They help us to explain why Jewish

---

[12] Here the differences are as significant as the uniting factors. One should not be too hasty in identifying the role of the risen Christ with the function of the priests of the Jerusalem Temple. He is particularly a heavenly high-priest Melchizedek whose identity is open to new interpretations that differ essentially from those of the Jerusalem priests.

[13] I agree especially with MacRae who spoke of an apocalyptic notion of a heavenly Temple, see MacRae, *Semeia 12* (1987) 187.

apocalyptic remained theologically traditional, returning always to the kingship of God and praising the enthroned Heavenly King.[14]

This is the scene also for the cultic Christology of the New Testament. Soteriological events take place in a heavenly Temple. It is expected that in the context of this discourse the throne itself is given a precise meaning. In the cultic discourse it is the mercy seat that is the centre of the rite of atonement. Especially in the letter to the Hebrews, but also in Pauline traditions, this aspect is exploited in the soteriological intepretation of the exaltation event.

It must be the basic metaphor itself, however, i.e. that of God's throne in the theocratic Old Testament tradition, which enables the first Christians to unite the royal aspect with the cultic aspect. Christ as a heavenly Melchizedek is basicly a priest-king whose actions are not limited to Temple cult. Therefore, above all in the letter to the Hebrews, Melchizedek's enthronement is described as a genuine coronation of an eschatological Messiah.[15]

The identification of Jesus as Melchizedek links him once again to the divine history of Israel. This time the identification is somewhat striking, however. Christ is depicted as a God chosen priest outside the Mosaic covenant. We have earlier seen that there may be several reasons for making a Canaanite priest-king the model for the Davidic Messiah. Aaronic priesthood had naturally had a primary status in Temple worship, but in a very special moment, as in the one in the original story about Abraham and Melchizedek, God could choose an unorthodox way to act. The Old Testament story itself shows that Melchizedek has an extraordinary status in the eyes of God. "It is beyond dispute that the inferior is blessed by the superior." (Heb. 7:7). Melchizedek was superior to Abraham as far as God's criteria are regarded.[16]

In New Testament soteriology, however, the historical Melchizedek is then merely a God-chosen high priest. The original Old Testament person has nothing to do with Jesus' work. In this respect the "sign" and it's use must be separated from each other. In the New Testament, Christ-Melchizedek is first sacrificed on the cross. Only after this he is resurrected, and as a new priest according to the order of Melchizedek he brings the blood of sacrifice to the mercy seat in the heavenly shrine.

Whoever the Canaanite Melchizedek may originally be, the point exploited in New Testament Christology is the change that has taken place in the

---

[14] Cf. Himmelfarb, *Ascent*, 28; Himmelfarb, *Death, Ecstasy*, 126. It is not sufficient to explain the Christology of the Hebrews merely by referring to the Old Testament background or Psalm 110, as Loader has done. See Loader, *Sohn*, 148ff.

[15] Cf. also Rissi, *Theologie*, 88-89.

[16] This was evidently a valid argument for any Jew on the basis of Torah itself, see Lane, *Hebrews*, 169.

priesthood. God has chosen a new way for the atonement. As a priest-king Jesus has entered the heavenly Temple and approached the mercy seat. The imagery is completely governed by Temple terminology, but the message is dramatically contrasted with traditional Temple worship.

c. Son of Man on the judgment seat

In the context of the third discourse the elements are new again. The enthroned one is now a heavenly judge. He is a figure that mostly resembles the Son of Man in the gospel tradition. The throne itself is apparently also God's throne here, but in accordance with the new discourse it is defined as a judgment seat.[17] The heavenly Temple changes into a heavenly court where the royal figure acts as a judge.[18]

In judicial discourse legal terminology is striking. Metaphors taken from legal terminology concerning processes in the court of law emphasize the juridical nature of God's eschatological judgment. For instance Paul spoke of Christ's tribunal (βῆμα): "For all of us must appear before the judgment seat of Christ" (2 Cor. 5:10). The background for this feature can obviously be found in the Old Testament where the king acted also as a judge.[19]

In Gospel tradition the enthroned one is usually the Son of Man, but later in early Christianity and especially in Paul's writings the appellation is simply Christ. One may assume that a messianic idea is behind this appellation also in this context since, juridically, a messianic king was a judge.

The uniting element between this discourse and the previous ones is now primarily the throne. The divine throne in heaven is still the centre of eschatological events. This point of view underlines the importance of Old Testament imagery. In a theocratic context the image of God's throne cannot be ignored but it remains as a constituent part of the description.

---

[17] We have earlier seen that this kind of distinction has not always been made in the investigation of judicial passages. In respect of defining the meaning of the throne-image, however, it is essential. See chapter 8.1. above.

[18] One should bear in mind that the discernment of "signs", i.e. the figures that appear in christological narratives, is not the same task as the discernment of the so called christological titles. For instance Moule has still spent much time in discussing the problem of the "title" Son of Man. He assumes that the interpretation of Son of Man Christology depends mainly on the decision whether a definite article justifies the titular use of the expression. Moule, *Christology*, 12ff. From the point of view of semiotics and intertextualism the situation is different. It is not any alleged title that defines an interpretation, but rather the narrative in the context of which different signs have been exploited.

[19] In Pauline scholarship the judicial nature of the throne has been noted. See e.g. Michel, *Römer (1978)*, 428; Dunn, *Romans 9-16*, 809. The reason for this is the fact that Paul exploits words that denote the judicial aspect.

Another feature worthwhile mentioning is that resurrection is not usually mentioned in these descriptions. These descriptions differ from the previous ones in that they are not describing the coronation day of the Davidide. In New Testament Christology they represent another kind of tradition. Christ's Lordship is rather a necessary condition for the judgment. [20]

This kind of conclusion was inevitable for instance as regards Acts 17 where Paul in Athens proclaimed:

"he has fixed a day on which he will have the world judged in righteousness by a man whom he has appointed, and of this he has given assurance to all by raising him from the dead." (Acts 17:31).

It is evident that this passage refers to Christ as a heavenly judge who has gained his extraordinary position in the resurrection. Resurrection is the crucial event as regards Christ's Lordship, and it is also a condition for the future entering upon the throne for the last judgment.

In this respect judicial eschatological Christology, or the Son of Man Christology, is not actually a typical form of early exaltation Christology. Even though some of the exploited metaphors are similar, and the scene presents a heavenly royal court, it is not exaltation that leads to the event of judgment. Judicial discourse is used when the eschatological climax is described and Christ is presented as a messianic judge who sits on his glorious throne and judges all of humankind.

12.2. Four narratives – four ascent stories

In the contexts of different discourses the figures and characters of the symbolic world attained different meanings. The character of the enthroned one changed from occasion to occasion. Also the meaning of the throne metaphor appeared to be different in different descriptions. These figures are not separate or individual elements in christological descriptions, however. They are integral parts of narratives, elements in consistent stories expressing christological convictions.

As regards the interpretation of New Testament discourses that have been defined during the study, we may therefore apply the idea of narrative syntax and define different christological narratives that express different modes of Christology in respective discourses. As there were four discourses defined and exploited in the analysis, we may discern also four christological narratives. In respect of the background of Jewish mysticism we may even speak of four different ascent stories. They all express one form of "Christian merkabah tradition" and describe the risen Christ from a new point of view.

---

[20] The lack of resurrection statements is a significant feature in judicial Christology, and we shall return to this problem below.

Instead of discerning christological titles, or of grouping different divine agents, we attempt to investigate the narrative reality of the early Church.[21] This enterprise implies a premise according to which christological descriptions can be classified according to the nature of the Christian ascent story.[22] The diversity of christological descriptions will be explained by the occurrence of different discourses.

This is further another tool for assessing the relation between Jewish merkabah mysticism and early Christology. As the compiling of a christological narrative in the early Church has been a matter of text production, it simultaneously has been a matter of intertextuality.[23] This aspect underlines the historicity of the new text. Therefore, this assessment provides materials for the estimation of the originality of christological descriptions in relation to Jewish theology. In this respect the interest lies in the christological transformation that may be detected in the new text.

a. The heavenly enthronement of the seed of David

During the Second Temple period, the Davidic Messiah was a well known character for instance to the readers of Ezekiel, for the followers of the sapiential tradition of ben Sira, for the writers and readers of the Psalms of Solomon, and for the Qumran covenanters. He was considered an ideal king who would lead Israel to a new glory.[24] In early Christology this character was also exploited, but not in a traditional political sense.

It seems apparent that Jewish mysticism provided the scene for the

---

[21] One must admit, however, that the investigation of titles has not always followed the formal Boussetian lines. For instance Cullmann in his magisterial work on Christology treated different titles as indicators of distinct functions in the descriptions of different Christologies. Cullmann, *Christologie*, 6. In his work, thus, the titles were in fact treated as signs that have been incorporated in a narrative. Cf. Hengel who writes: "It is the peculiarity, indeed uniqueness, of earliest Christianity that the development of christology and its titles remained inextricably bound to the offence of the crucified Jesus of Nazareth." Hengel, *Studies*, 363.

[22] This is the methodological conclusion made in the beginning of the present study, see the methodological discussion in the Introduction.

[23] This kind of principle is identical with the one presented by Green in the study of Second Temple messianology. Green stated, with a reference to Foucault, that the origin of the Christian concept of Messiah cannot be found simply by postulating a uniform messianic concept in preceding Jewish theology. Green, *Judaisms*, 1. Green's interest was mainly in the diversity of Jewish conceptions, but his presumption is similar to that made in the present study. What is special about early Christology, are not its common features with Jewish thinking, but rather the dynamic transformation of earlier ideas.

[24] This feature is hardly denied in the modern study of Jewish messianology, even though some scholars would like to emphasize the diversity of Jewish conceptions. For a positive approach, see e.g. Talmon, *Messiah*, 91ff.

descriptions where the messianic enthronement was located in heaven. Early Christology is presented in the form of an ascent story. Jesus the Jew is exalted on a heavenly throne, and the messianic reign of this new Davidide begins there.

What is exceptional in early Christology, however, with regard to Jewish theology, is the christological transformation of traditional messianism. The new Davidide will not reign in David's city, Jerusalem. The first Christians presented a transcendental interpretation of the enthronement of the Davidide. His power is heavenly power and his reign is eternal reign in the kingdom of God.[25]

This kind of view was expressed by a Christian ascent story that denoted the coronation celebration. The Davidide approaches the royal throne in the heavenly court, and he is exalted at the right hand of the heavenly King of Israel. He is given throne-names, such as the Lord, and he reigns over the whole world.[26]

The dynamic text production exploits the symbolic world of Second Temple mysticism. It adopts the cosmic scene on which all events take place. In this respect the narrative sounds like an apocalyptic Jewish ascent story. The result of the writer's theological convictions differs from Jewish views, however. Christian writers speak of a transcendent Davidide whose reign is eternal reign in heaven. His throne is the throne of Glory in God's heavenly palace.

This procedure is something quite different from the simple typological exploitation of the so called christological titles. Transformational features in Christology must be regarded as even more important than the uniting features that have been taken from the symbolic world of Second Temple Judaism. Jesus from Nazareth has evidently been identified as the "seed of David" who will fulfil the promises of the past, but this is not the whole truth.

The way these promises are fulfilled, however, is unexpected. Jesus' resurrection from the dead is interpreted in early Christology as an installation

---

[25] This new interpretation should not be considered too easy and simple, however. This kind of danger in explanation may be seen for instance in the solution of Chester, who sees no problems in connecting Jewish beliefs with Christology. Chester approaches the question from the point of view of typological explanation. He states that the concepts and traditions of mediatorial figures were "available" already when for instance Paul wrote his letters. Paul just made these concepts apply "directly to the figure of the Messiah." In this way the Messiah was "interpreted by means of heavenly or transcendental categories." Chester, *Paulus*, 76. According to our analysis, these kinds of "concepts" were in fact not available for the first Christians who formulated early Christology. The resurrection and ascension of the Davidide was not a widespread conviction in Judaism.

[26] This kind of story is behind several of the passages that were investigated in this study, e.g. in Acts 2:35-36; 5:30-31; Phil. 2:9-11; Col. 3:1; Hebr.1:3-4, and implied e.g. in Rom. 1:3-4; 1 Cor. 15:24-25; Rev. 3:21.

to heavenly power and as an enthronement to the heavenly throne.[27] It is remarkable that in this new setting the traditional Jewish interpretation of Psalm 110:1 is significantly altered.

In Old Testament kingship ideology the justification of the earthly kingship was expressed by the conviction that the Davidide was believed to sit metaphorically "at the right hand" of the heavenly King. In the mystical reality of Christian merkabah speculation this passage became an expression of Christ's actual ascent in his resurrection.[28]

The intertextual strategy appears to be primarily that of actualization. The enthronement statement was considered a realistic description of Christ's exaltation. This contrasted the new interpretation with traditional Jewish beliefs. The realistic approach towards the features of Psalm 110:1 transformed both the exaltation statement and the idea of Lordship to an extent that was no longer acceptable to most adherents of monotheistic Judaism.[29]

Such conclusions once again bring up the problems of typological interpretation. Exalted Jesus is not a typical member of the Davidic dynasty. Rather, he is a unique Davidide on the heavenly throne. The "typos" is merely a metaphor for the enthroned Son of God who reigns as a king in heaven. Early Christology cannot be reduced to the alleged "meaning" of the preceding typology, or to the "meaning" of selected titles. The meaning of Christology must be formulated on the basis of christological descriptions, not on the basis of Old Testament or Jewish descriptions.

We may further note certain features of the narrative nature of such Christology. The story itself implies certain polarizations that may be rather easily detected. For instance, another kind of state must necessarily precede the

---

[27] Charlesworth has formulated this kind of view in detail in regard to messianology: "Jewish messianology does not flow majestically into Christian christology." Charlesworth, *Judaisms*, 255. The same is true in the explanation of resurrection Christology. The essential content of earliest Christology does not become comprehensible merely by investigating the signs and symbols of Jewish theology. It's leading principle is in the explanation of Jesus' resurrection.

[28] Cf. Hengel, *Studies*, 220-221. Also Hay pays attention to this polarization. "Originally the psalm was a confession of faith that a particular Jerusalem monarch governed with the power and authority of God... Early Christian exegesis of the psalm was conditioned by a general confidence that it was Jesus in whom all the promises of the Jewish scriptures had their eschatological fulfillment." Hay, *Glory*, 161.

[29] According to Segal early Christology may be explained according to the intentions of the early community only. "It is the Christian community itself that unites all the different Jewish possibilities of mediatorship into one single myth, because it sees Jesus as a unique and definitive mediator." Segal, *ANRW 23.2*. (1980) 1371-1372. Even though he referred to early Christology in a somewhat more general sense, exaltation Christology was also meant here.

exaltation. It is a state where the Davidide as a Messiah designate is not yet a king. Such a polarization appears to have produced the Christology, in particular, in the hymn recorded in Phil. 2. In this hymn Jesus' state before the resurrection is described explicitly as humiliation (Phil. 2:7-8).

Secondly, there is an opposition between death and resurrection. Exaltation is strictly combined with resurrection in early Christology both in exaltation discourse and in resurrection discourse. This is a feature that we shall investigate further in the next section.

As regards different characters, the enthronement story often mentions only two of them, namely the Davidide and God himself (see e.g. Acts 2:36; Rom. 1:3-4, *passivum divinum*). In certain passages the subordination of angels or enemies is emphasized (Heb. 1:3-4; in 10:12 the "enemies").[30] In addition to this the exalted status of Christ brings him authority. In this respect all the world is subordinated to him (Phil. 2:10; Eph. 1:21).

The first narrative about the heavenly enthronement of the seed of David is thus a good example of the text production of the early Church. Christological transformation of Jewish themes is evident. These two apparently share the same symbolic world, but the actual explication of the enthronement event is new. The Christological interpretation contrasts Jesus' enthronement in resurrection with traditional enthronement descriptions by exploiting mystical cosmology. Also the interpretation of the essential Old Testament passage Psalm 110:1 is governed by the new text production. The ideas of earthly enthronement and Lordship are transformed into expressions of divine power on the throne of Glory. The role of the main features of Jewish merkabah mysticism here is allegedly quite important. Jesus' enthronement is described as an ascent story where the messianic figure, in his resurrection, approaches the throne of Glory. In an act of installation he is enthroned at the right hand of God, and he becomes the Lord of the whole universe.

b. Prince of life conquers death

In the context of the resurrection discourse, where certain elements of the exaltation discourse are given new emphasis, the christological narration is also somewhat different. The point of weight is naturally in the resurrection itself. Therefore, as regards the narrative dynamics of the story, the opposition of death and resurrection governs the message.

The scene is still the same as in the previous narrative. Heaven is the place for God's sanctuary and the ascent is heading towards God's dwellings. There is certain originality, however, in the New Testament idea that the heavenly

---

[30] Here Pauline criticism against Colossian mystics and their angelology should also be noted, see Col. 2:18; cf. chapter 5.2. above.

enthronement of the messianic Davidide takes place in the resurrection. Once again text production is dependent on christological transformation. Already during the analysis we have noted that in no Jewish writing is the resurrection considered a premise for the enthronement of the Shoot of David.

When Christian theologians combined the themes of enthronement and resurrection, and explicitly the idea of the resurrection of the dead, they in fact connected two such eschatological themes which have no immediate causal relationship to each other in the traditional Jewish messianological discourse. In Jewish writings the raising of the dead is not usually mentioned in the context of the descriptions of enthronement. For the first Christians, however, such an eschatological context was important.[31]

For instance in Acts 2:32-36 the identification of resurrection with enthronement is evident, and Psalm 110 which we have referred to several times was used when proof was given. The act of enthronement was completed by giving the enthroned one great royal epithets. Seated at the right hand of God, the resurrected and exalted Jesus is "Lord and Messiah". According to Romans 1, in turn, the exaltation takes place in the eschatological resurrection of the dead.

These christological patterns apparently rest on eschatological premises. Enthronement statements of the Old Testament royal ideology have been interpreted as prophecies about the resurrection of Jesus, as the analysis has shown. We have above treated the combining of messianic tradition and merkabah speculation from the point of view of the exaltation. As we here consider the same event from the point of view of the promises given to the family of David, the result is quite similar. The installation of the Davidide is comprehensible only as an apocalyptical and eschatological heavenly enthronement.[32]

This is where we actually see the unique transformational nature of exaltation Christology. *First Christians located the enthronement of the Messiah in the eschatological event of the resurrection of the dead.* This procedure had several theological consequences.

1. Two different and somewhat illfitting traditions were identified with each other. Traditional messianology was planted into resurrection discourse and interpreted in terms of resurrection theology. Exaltation, resurrection and

---

[31] The Jewish character of the belief in the eschatological resurrection of the dead is evident, however. As Zeller has pointed out in a recent study, the Greek-Roman world had not adopted such a view. This made even the reception of Christian proclamation difficult in the Roman empire. See Zeller, *Von Jesus zum Christus,* 90.

[32] Against Frankemölle who has pursued the view that the exaltation Christology of earlierst Christian resurrection statements was not apocalyptic at all. See Frankemölle, *Von Jesus zum Christus,* 67ff.

enthronement became thus identical.[33] This is an example of a new formulation of messianology. The main reason for this kind of formulation was evidently the Easter experience which is consistently the point of departure for most descriptions of early Christology.[34]

2. Resurrection was considered an act of enthronement. Therefore the only suitable place for the enthronement was the transcendent throne which was in the heavenly Temple where God resides. Here the mystical cosmology of Second Temple Judaism is also implied.

3. Messianology became apocalyptical. In this kind of Christology the enthronement of the Messiah took place in heaven, and the exalted Davidide became a universal ruler on the throne of Glory.

4. Christology was formulated in terms of merkabah mysticism. In Second Temple Judaism there was a tradition that was able to provide a symbolic world that suited the description of Jesus' enthronement in resurrection. The Messiah was presented as a heavenly ruler whose reign is transcendent. This solution created the problem which several scholars have attempted to solve. How can the enthroned Davidide be described as a heavenly being which we encounter primarily in the angelology of mystical writings?

The compilers of early Christology did not give the figures of Jewish mysticism a primary status in their theology. Jesus was not described as an angel or as a divine agent. The first Christians approached the subject from another point of view. They were describing the enthronement of the Davidide in a historical situation where their thinking was guided by Jesus' followers' experiences of the resurrection of their Lord. Therefore they exploited the symbolic world and cosmology of Jewish mysticism in their Christology.[35]

---

[33] In general, resurrection does not appear to be a significant subject in all of the investigated traditions of interpretation. For instance most scholars speaking of an angelic/angelomorphic interpretation do not pay attention to the resurrection itself. They merely presuppose that, in order to speak of Christ's heavenly life, a resurrection must have taken place. See e.g. Fletcher-Louis, *Angels*, 251f., Gieschen, *Christology*, 349f. Hurtado, who speaks of the Christian mutation of the Jewish divine agency tradition, does the same, and he does not give resurrection a decisive role in the "mutation." Hurtado, *One God*, 100ff. Only Hengel, who supports a messianic interpretation, pays much attention to the subject of resurrection. Hengel, *Studies*, 214ff.

[34] It is noteworthy that Segal, who mainly promoted the angelic interpretation, noted the combining of messianology and resurrection. "The combination of the events of Jesus' death as a martyred messianic pretender and the conviction that he was resurrected (justifying the messianic title) is expressed by the use of selected biblical texts reunderstood as prophesies about crucified Messiah." Segal, *ANRW 23.2.* (1980) 1370-1371.

[35] For instance according to Hengel, the "present experience of the appearances of the Resurrected One" had a significant role in the "eschatological-missionary enthusiasm" of the early Church. Hengel, *Studies*, 219.

It is no wonder that such an eschatological scheme was also interpreted in terms of cosmic history. We have earlier concluded that the theme of the resurrection of the dead in such Christology functioned as a watershed between two ages of salvation history.[36] In the context of the Davidic promise tradition the enthronement was explained as the confirmation of the Davidic covenant, the covenant of grace (Isa. 55:3). The idea of "ruling over the nations" was now comprehended as a special feature of the office of the Enthroned One. Christ's reign inaugurated the age of the covenant of grace under the new David.

The opposition of death and resurrection may further be seen as one motivation for the fact that, in early Christology, the participation of Christ in humankind is emphasized. He is a Davidide, a descendant in the family of David. Christology is stating the resurrection of this human figure. Other kinds of explanations do not fit well in this kind of scheme. In Jewish thought, for instance, the idea of resurrection of angels would be quite incomprehensible.[37]

This notion creates problems for the angelic interpretation. An angelic/angelomorphic interpretation could not provide a theological explanation for the main event, the resurrection itself. It might be useful only if the idea of transformation could be demonstrated in early Christology.[38] As this is not possible, angelomorphic interpretation must be content with more modest conclusions. It is bound to exploit merely angelomorphic analogies in its explanation.[39]

Scholars may discern selected features that seem angelomorphic and state that, in early Christology, the exalted Christ is described by exploiting such

---

[36] Cf. Hengel, *Studies*, 216: "His resurrection was – as anticipation – the beginning of the general resurrection and the period until his coming to judgement was a period of grace to permit the repentance of the people of God."

[37] When Gieschen finally in the Conclusion of his study assesses the usefulness of his angelomorphic interpretation, he somewhat strikingly proposes an adoptionist interpretation. He states that the confession "Jesus is Lord" enabled first Christians "to link one or more of the unnamed angelomorphic figures intimately identified with YHWH (i.e., the Angel, the Glory, the Name, the Word, Wisdom) to the fleshly Jesus who had ascended and was now enthroned." Gieschen, *Christology*, 350. As Gieschen was unable to exploit the idea of resurrection in his angelomorphic interpretation, he reduced the "angelomorphic" material to certain metaphorical labels that could be attached to the enthroned, "fleshly" Jesus.

[38] One must admit that the idea of a heavenly transformation is possible in principle. Especially in later Jewish mysticism, investigated above in chapter 3.3., we have examples of earthly beings that are transformed into angelic beings in the heavenly realm. See e.g. Morray-Jones, *JJS 43* (1992) 8ff. According to the present analysis, however, there are not traits of such a belief in early Christology.

[39] For instance Fletcher-Louis in his angelomorphic interpretation ends up in emphasizing Luke's resistance against docetic Christology in respect of other "contemporary views of the angelic life." Fletcher-Louis, *Angels*, 252.

features. The interpretation itself, however, is not able to exploit the main typology it has formerly presupposed.

In Christology, thus, there is polarity between the mortal nature of Jesus and the resurrection life of the Risen One. This, naturally, is expected since Christology expands the passion story where we find polarity between the cross and the empty tomb, between Good Friday and Easter morning.

The story, in this respect, has certain polarities, but it also has a hero. We should not attempt to reduce the Easter story merely to one theme that may be detected in it. The crucial fact is that there are two elements in exaltation Christology. The description of resurrection has been combined with the theme of enthronement. In the interpretation of this scheme, therefore, both of these factors must be taken into account.

Exaltation Christology presents thus a story of how death is defeated. Christ is the hero of this event. The story itself is quite unusual. The hero is not a warrior who achieves his goal by masterful action. This is rather a story of a suffering Messiah, whose exaltation is completely grounded on God's action. Such a presentation implies the polarization between humiliation and exaltation, that we mentioned above. One cannot exist without the other. The idea of an enthronement in resurrection raises a serious question. Why did the prince have to die? One easily understands the enthronement of a *Messias designatus*, but the death of such a Messiah is more difficult to understand. A pattern of humiliation and exaltation must be implied in the story.

Therefore the natural Jewish course of narration: anticipated king - enthronement - universal power, is not the whole story.[40] Neither do we find an eschatological hero defeating enemies and rescueing the oppressed, even though in New Testament soteriology such a pattern has also evidently been developed – despite the fact that it, too, is based on the pattern of humiliation and exaltation.[41] The lacking part must be added. The story must include resurrection.

In early Christology we find an ascent structure combined with an enthronement theme, and both of these appear in an eschatological context. The hero is a dead prince, the anticipated Davidide, whose exaltation is based on his resurrection from the dead in an extraordinary eschatological event. Only resurrection leads to his enthronement to universal power, or simply becomes an act of enthronement itself. This is how he becomes the "prince of life" (Acts 3:15).

---

[40] Most stories in the messianological discourse of Jewish theology produce exactly this kind of plot.

[41] In Jewish theology even some angelic passages describe such a hero, see for instance the nature of the Melchizedek figure in Qumran (especially in 3.2.).

The second one of the narratives of early Christology may thus be constructed on these conditions. In the context of resurrection discourse it is a narrative of a prince from the family of David who has a cosmic mission.

The prince dies, but through an eschatological renewal, the appearance of the resurrection of the dead, he is enthroned on the throne of Glory and given dominion over the whole world.

The story denotes the new life and extraordinary ruling power of the hero, Jesus Christ. It naturally also implies soteriology, the renewal of all subservients of this Messiah in the general resurrection of the dead, as well as the idea of an eternal kingdom of the Davidide, but these implications must be distinguished from the primary message.

The second narrative about the defeating of death brings to the fore the eschatological scene of the resurrection of the dead. Here again the transformational nature of exaltation Christology is evident. As the first Christians located the enthronement of the Messiah in the eschatological event of the resurrection of the dead, they emphasized the aspect of eschatological renewal. In this narrative, Christ becomes the prince of life, a Davidide who has a cosmic mission. His resurrection is proof of the fact that death has been defeated. Therefore the dominion of the enthroned one is a life-giving dominion in the realm of the new creation. In this narrative, the influence of Jewish merkabah mysticism can be detected more in the background of the presentation. The basic scene is similar in these two, and the resurrection may be regarded as a heavenly journey. The actualizing interpretation of the eschatological resurrection of the dead that governs the Christian narrative, however, belongs to the transformational features of early Christology.

c. Eternal high priest enters the debir

The christological narrative emerging in cultic discourse differs somewhat from that of enthronement discourse and resurrection discourse. In cultic discourse resurrection still plays a significant role and this perspective is not the one where the differences may be sought for. Further, as we noted above, even in the cultic discourse, especially in the letter to the Hebrews, we find the king-priest who is actually a Davidide fulfilling the priesthood of Melchizedek (Psalm 110).

In cultic discourse the function of the throne is different, even though the enthronement itself also remains as a fundamental factor in this discourse. Now the throne is a place for atonement. It is the mercy seat in the heavenly Holy of Holies. In this respect Temple imagery has been especially emphasized. Such emphasis is not artificial, however. The cultic aspect as such has already been significant in Jewish writings.

The story, at least in the letter to the Hebrews, has been formulated after the actions of the high priest in the Temple. If we still take the new Melchizedek to be a prince from the family of David, however, there is a close connection with the story of the enthronement discourse. In the letter to the Hebrews, naturally, that story is also prominent. Christ, after his resurrection and priestly service, is enthroned on the throne of Glory and given dominion over the whole world.[42]

The new narrative emphasizes the role of the high priest. In this story Jesus' death also has a special place, since it is interpreted as a sacrifice. The blood that was offered, in particular, was the actual sacrifice. After this the scene changes to heaven. Resurrection has taken place. Like a high priest Christ enters the shrine:

"[H]e entered once for all into the Holy Place, not with the blood of goats and calves, but with his own blood, thus obtaining eternal redemption" (Hebr. 9:12).[43]

This description was also working on a subtext. The abovementioned statement is a christological pesher on the cultic text of Leviticus (16:15). The blood of Christ is a central element in this symbolism since the blood of the sacrifice was also taken to the shrine according to Leviticus: "sprinkling it upon the mercy seat and before the mercy seat". Further, the throne metaphor is present in this description. The blood of a goat was sprinkled upon the mercy seat.[44]

In particular, in the letter to the Hebrews the cultic narrative has been constructed on the basis of a cosmological idea of a temple-structured universe. Christ leaves the "first tent," i.e. the earth, and enters the heavenly Holy of Holies behind the cosmological curtain. The unity of exaltation and atonement is justified by the help of the metaphor that is most central of them all, the throne of Glory. Resurrection is a necessary precondition for Christ's entering into the heavenly sanctuary and for the atonement that is made by sprinkling the blood of sacrifice on the mercy seat. The first part of the Temple metaphor represents in a sense the complete old covenant. In his resurrection Jesus has

---

[42] Christ, in the cultic discourse of the New Testament, is a priest-king unlike the Messiah's of the Qumran community. In this respect the royal aspect, therefore, is of special importance in the interpretation of the New Testament message even though it has a minor role in the christological narrative itself. Cf. e.g. Hagner, *Hebrews*, 84.

[43] Against Loader who thought that the writer of the Hebrews merely spoke of Jesus' entering into the heavenly Temple without the idea of an atoning act. Loader, *Sohn*, 185f. The narrative is not complete unless one presupposes that the priestly service factually takes place in heaven.

[44] As Michel noted, the mercy seat is the actual place for the atonement. Michel, *Hebräer*, 303. Therefore, the narrative apparently locates the sacrifice in the heavenly shrine.

been exalted behind the heavenly curtain, and thus he enters the divine Holy of Holies as an eternal high-priest. The act of atonement that he performs in the heavenly *debir* legitimizes a new covenant.

In Hebrews, therefore, the intertextual interpretation adapts Temple imagery to Christology in a bold way. Christ is both the sacrifice and the priest. The function of the priest remains the same, however. This narrative is simply a description of a sacrificial act before the throne of Glory and before God's face. *The narrative, therefore, is a story of a transcendent high priest, a king-priest Melchizedek, who has a cultic mission. Through his death and resurrection he enters the holy of holies in the heavenly Temple and with his own blood obtains eternal redemption.*[45]

In Jewish theology the throne also appeared in a cultic setting, and this must be the rationale for connecting the cultic mission with enthronement. In Jewish theology, however, a messianic figure never appeared directly in a cultic context. This is apparently the reason why the priestly order of Melchizedek was exploited in this Christology.

The figure of Melchizedek also occurred naturally in Psalm 110. Therefore we do not need to work merely with the character of Melchizedek found in Genesis. This fact makes the whole figure rather abstract. For the writer of the Hebrews, for instance, the order of Melchizedek seems to be more important than the actual figure (Hebr. 5:6). The figure is simply that of a high priest and this image identifies Christ with the high priests of the Jerusalem Temple.

In this respect the actual "subtext" for sacrificial Christology is the complete sacrificial Temple cult. The exploited images or Old Testament passages are merely in service of the main purpose. In this ascent story Christ is exalted as an extraordinary high priest, and his heavenly journey aims at the heavenly Holy of Holies. As a priest-king Melchizedek he enters the heavenly Temple and approaches the mercy seat. The christological transformation is astonishing. Christ's journey is contrasted with traditional Temple worship.[46]

In the mystical tradition of Jewish apocalyptic the idea of a heavenly temple as such was a commonplace. In this respect the mere adaptation of Jewish

---

[45] One should note that Cullmann, for instance, who in his interpretation still emphasized Jesus' earthly work and his death, already pointed out that the priestly Christology of Hebrews focuses on resurrection and thus it must be exaltation Christology. Cullmann, *Christologie*, 100f. His explanations were, however, dependent on the investigation of the "functions" of different christological titles, and therefore he did not yet pay attention to the problem of how a royal messianic figure could have a cultic mission. Cf. Cullmann, *Christologie*, 88f.

[46] Such an intertextual position has in fact been presupposed in those descriptions of New Testament theology where the sacrificial cult of the old covenant has been contrasted with Christ's high-priestly service of the new covenant. See e.g. Lindars, *Theology*, 90-91.

imagery does not contrast Christology with more traditional Judaism. The exploitation of the priestly figure, however, underlines that a change has taken place in the priesthood. Here the contrast is sharp. According to the writers of this narrative, God has chosen a new way for the atonement.[47]

The sacrificial narrative constructs cultic Christology. The discourse is, as postulated, completely cultic. Exalted Christ gives his sacrifice for the whole of humankind. His ascent reaches the Holy of Holies in the heavenly Temple. In this respect, the third christological narrative also resembles the ascent stories of Jewish mysticism. As a priest-king Melchizedek, however, Christ is simultaneously a messianic figure. After the sacrificial atonement the heavenly liturgy turns into a coronation celebration. The heavenly Melchizedek is exalted on the mercy seat, on the throne of Glory, and he reigns forever at the right hand of God. Such christological transformation of Jewish traditions threatens the status of earthly Temple worship, and evidently approaches even religious apostasy.

d. Eschatological entrée of the messianic judge

As we move to the area of judicial discourse, the cosmology of Jewish merkabah mysticism still appears to be an integral part of the christological description. The throne is the centre of events and it is depicted as the heavenly throne of Glory. In judicial discourse, however, the exact definition of the throne has changed. God's throne is an eschatological judgment seat.[48]

Judicial discourse governs the terminology, and Paul, for instance, speaks consistently about Christ's tribunal, the βῆμα. The description refers clearly to the last judgment. Christ on his throne is a judge who judges human beings according to their deeds. The messianic figure, whom we have previously chosen to call the Son of Man, is apparently a heavenly king even though he acts as a judge. In Jewish writings the appellation Son of Man can be found, and in the Gospels he is the prevailing figure in this context. In later New Testament writings, usually, simply Christ is mentioned. This is a reminder of the fact that narrative has a primary signification in the interpretation of

---

[47] For instance Anderson, investigating the intellectual background of the Christology of Hebrews, still seeks for a "missing link" (see chapter 12.3. above) in his explanation. He refers to the Exagoge of Ezekiel and suggests that "a tradition somewhat similar to that in the Tragedian's account of Moses' vision may lie vaguely in the background of Hebrews." Anderson, *Messiah*, 530. Actually he doesn't finally claim this, though, because Christ's exaltation is a widely known feature in the New Testament, and because there is nothing priestly about the figure of Moses. The method behind his inference is evident, however. He still believes that a uniting factor could best explain the identity of New Testament Christology.

[48] See chapter 8.1. above.

Christology, and that the appellations or titles are subordinated under the narratives and respective discourses.

The christological narrative itself, on which those descriptions are based, is not, however, a traditional ascent story. In judicial christological descriptions no ascent or resurrection is referred to.[49] This was true also as regards relevant passages in Jewish writings. The main purpose of the narrative is to describe Christ's entering upon the throne, the judgment seat, before the actual judgment.

The implied narrative, therefore, is a story of the eschatological entrée of a messianic judge. Christ is presented as an ominpotent ruler who judges all the world. All the living and the dead are escorted before his throne and their destiny is sealed by a righteous judgment.

Due to the special nature of judicial Christology the intertextual point of view also differs from that of other narratives. The status of the heavenly judge is quite similar both in Jewish writings and in New Testament descriptions. In this case one could probably even speak of a typological relationship. Especially as regards the Jewish Son of Man figure (a royal judge on a heavenly throne), the similarity is striking.

Another common feature is the similar eschatological emphasis. Both in Jewish writings and in early Christology the messianic judge enters upon his throne in the end of days when the last judgment is at hand. In respect of the eschatological interpretation one does not need to search for differences between these traditions.

A certain dependence on Jewish merkabah traditions, however, remains. The uniting feature, once again, is the throne metaphor. The throne is a symbol of power and universal rule, and ultimate theocracy is also realized through the throne in these descriptions. The heavenly court is probably not that much of a Temple but a palace, but as we have seen, that symbolism was also common in Jewish writings.

We have earlier discussed the interpretation of judicial Christology in the history of investigation. The pattern of polarized eschatology used to be popular, and the idea of eschatological enthronement governed the explanation of judicial passages.[50] According to our analysis, however, no real polarization ever existed. In the context of the eschatological notion of the parousia there was no conception of Christ's future enthronement, a messianic

---

[49] In the identification of judicial Christology this feature is quite significant. Resurrection has no christological role in this narrative as it had in all the other narratives that have been treated here. Enthronement narrative or cultic narrative were not conceivable without the idea of Christ's resurrection. In judicial discourse, however, the point of weight is somewhere else.

[50] See for instance Hahn, *Christologische Hoheitstitel*, 46.

installation that would take place only on the day of judgment. Christ's entering upon the throne on the last day was rather seen as an act that expressed his office as the supreme judge who will gather all people before him.[51]

It is true that the idea of a *sessio*, the sitting "at the right hand" of God, also appeared in certain judicial passages where the aspect of judgment prevailed. These passages, however, did not speak of an enthronement in resurrection. Therefore, here the narrative also governs the details. The exalted Christ "at the right hand" of God is the Son of Man who shall execute judgment on the last day.[52]

The fourth story, therefore, is a narrative of the eschatological entrée of a messianic judge. It is implied in several New Testament descriptions of the last judgment. According to this narrative Christ is a heavenly judge who gathers all the world before his tribunal. The special feature in such Christology is its essential difference from other exaltation narratives. Christ's entering upon the throne of Glory is not an eschatological enthronement, and the day of judgment is not a coronation day. Rather, Christ the Exalted King is the one who is able to enter upon his own throne and execute the judgment when the last day arrives.

12.3. Intertextual aspect: Christ as the reigning God on the throne of Glory

Finally, we must investigate the aspect of intertextuality on a very general level, the intertext being the christological idea of Christ's exaltation, and the subtext being the traditional Jewish monotheism that is expressed in Temple worship. During the study we have suggested that certain Christian transformations of earlier Jewish tradition seem to alter even some basic beliefs of Second Temple Judaism. How do the traditional monotheistic theocracy and the new Christian merkabah tradition fit together?

If we apply the same question to the subjects that have been investigated in the present study, we need to ask what is the relation of the Christian description of Christ at the right hand of God on the throne of Glory to the

---

[51] See chapter 8.3. above. As Paul, for instance, wrote about Christ's parousia in his early letters (esp. 1. Thess. 1) he actually implied resurrection Christology in his presentation. Therefore Paul, in his early days, did not see any contradiction between exaltation Christology and eschatological notions. See especially Riesner, *Paul's Early Period*, 399-400.

[52] It is worth mentioning that certain scholars investigating Son of Man Christology explain the Danielic tradition as an expression of the vindication and exaltation of a faithful pious Jew, and therefore no longer see exaltation Christology and Son of Man Christology as conflicting or contradictory. See e.g. Moule, *Christology*, 24f., de Jonge, *Christology*, 58f., 171, 203.

greatest symbol of Old Testament faith, i.e. to the idea of God as Israel's enthroned King in heaven. As this subject belongs to the sphere of exaltation discourse we will concentrate on that in what follows. The interest of the investigation lies in the application and adaptation of previous symbols, ideas, and texts in christological formulations.[53]

Exaltation narrative soon reveals the relevance of the abovementioned subject for our study. According to the story, the Davidic prince was exalted in the resurrection of the dead and enthroned "at the right hand" of God in the Holy of Holies of the heavenly Temple (Psalm 110). The place for the throne is most evidently the heavenly Temple, and exaltation is being performed by God the King himself, who invites the Davidide to sit "at his right hand".

All of these details are connected with the core of Old Testament faith. The Davidic prince is exalted to the place where God the King resides. He is escorted to the throne that is God's throne. He is seated on the throne that, in the writings of the Old Testament, as well as in later Jewish theology, is considered the most holy place of all in this world. Only one conclusion is possible in this situation. The enthroned Christ sits where the King of Israel should be sitting.[54]

This should raise some problems. What did the first Christians mean when constructing such a story of the exalted Christ? What is the relation between God and his Messiah in this structure? How does the Israelite's faithfulness to God relate to the confessing of the enthroned Christ? And in a more technical sense, how do the descriptions of early Christology function as intertexts in such a situation?

In Jewish descriptions of enthronements the theocratic ideal of First Temple Judaism was always preserved. The kingship of God was in fact emphasized. The message of most apocalyptic writings was that God is still the King of Israel. Thus the eschatological hope of righteous Jews had not been altered. The adoration of the enthroned God in Jerusalem Temple was identical with apocalypticists' devotion, the adoration of the heavenly God on the *merkabah*-throne.

This is why the theocratic ideology appears in a rather simple form in apocalyptical writings. For example seers are accompanied to heaven and before God's throne. The conviction of the writers is crystal clear. The identity of Jewish faith is preserved only as far as the Enthroned One is praised and

---

[53] There are parallels for this kind of transformation of tradition in Jewish writings. See e.g. Collins' analysis of the transformation of Exodus traditions in Hellenistic Egypt. Collins, *For a Later Generation*, 62.

[54] This is the crucial point where one should "remember the obvious," as we postulated in the beginning of the analysis in chapter 2. As the focus of events is God's heavenly throne, the intertextual problem is evident and unavoidable.

worshiped as heavenly King. It is no wonder that some of the ascending visitors were further given a message about this kingship, and they should deliver it to the fallen Israel after their return to the earth.[55]

But what is the relation of early Christology to the theocratic ideal? During the analysis we have seen that in early Christology there were features in which the theocratic view and the christocentric view were mixed with each other. Old Testament passages and ideas were given a christocentric rendering. Furthermore, Christ was revered as a divine being on the throne.

The investigation on the context of resurrection homologies proved that the sociological situation for enthronement formulas was usually that of becoming a Christian. The "Sitz im Leben" of the formulas was in missionary proclamation and most probably also in baptismal ceremonies. Exaltation Christology was thus used in situations where faith in Christ was confessed. Also the form of the formulations betrays homological nature. A key expression in this respect is the acclamation *Jesus is Lord*. In this acclamation the new status of the enthroned Davidide is revered.

Therefore, such Christology inevitably presents a new interpretation of theocracy in its classical Jewish sense. In fact, this view raises the question of the deity of Christ. It is hard to believe that those Christians who believed that Christ is sitting on the throne of Glory as a universal ruler, and who confessed their faith in him as a κύριος would not have considered him divine.[56]

Both in early formulas and in Paul we find a strict concentration on christological soteriology. Only those who call upon the name of Jesus will be saved. Therefore the core of the saving message was the easter message about the resurrected Jesus who had been "made" Lord and Messiah on the heavenly throne.

In such a soteriological context Jesus' enthronement cannot be merely an honorary enthronement. Instead, according to Psalm 110, it was considered as the fulfilment of the kingship of God. Therefore it became the content of a saving gospel.[57] Salvation no longer meant merely the confessing of the kingship of God. It comprised the confessing of the kingship of Christ, as well. For example for Paul such confession was the "word of faith" that alone was sufficient for salvation (Rom. 10:9).[58] According to his gospel, only

---

[55] Cf. especially the Enochic descriptions in chapter 3.3.

[56] For instance Capes noted that one reason for Paul's use of κύριος as a christological title was to apply to Jesus concepts and functions originally reserved for Yahweh in the Old Testament. Capes, *Yahweh Texts*, 89.

[57] Cf. Stuhlmacher, *Theologie*, 161, 168f., 184, 202f., 248.

[58] For the Christocentric element in New Testament soteriology, see France, *Christ*, 24, 34; Kreitzer, *Jesus*, 168-169; Hurtado, *One God, One Lord*, 102-104.

those who confessed the Lordship of Christ belonged to the kingdom of salvation.

But how should we address the question of the deity of Christ? We have seen that the discussion about the relation of Jewish theology and New Testament Christology has often been focused on two significant themes, the problem of deification and the question concerning adoptionist Christology. The latter one of these was argued on the basis of Old Testament royal ideology. As the king from the family of David was considered an adopted son of God in his reign, so also all messianic figures must have lived in an adoptional relationship to God. This was naturally consistent in a religion where theocracy was the main premise both in cult and in politics.

In such a context, according to the theory, also the nature of early Christology was considered adoptionist. As we have seen above, according to the adoptionist theory, the first Christians – and especially the apostles – regarded Jesus merely a devout Jewish preacher, probably a prophet or a rabbi, but nothing more. His status had to fit in the theocratic system of Israel. Divinity was reserved for God only. Therefore all ideas about deification must derive from the non-Jewish, i.e. Hellenistic world.[59]

It is understandable that the problem of deification was later one of the main themes in the Christological speculation of the history-of-religions school. The adherents of this paradigm from Bousset to Bultmann exploited both the Baurian pattern of history and the theory of adoptionist Christology. In Christology, they argued, all divine attributes of Christ have been adopted from Hellenistic mystery religions. Among these religions there was said to prevail a general belief in divine figures, the divine men, who descend on the earth through a miraculous birth, and who live an astonishing life as gods or at least semi-gods.[60]

As regards modern scholarship, the pattern of history has been completely changed and even replaced by the question of the Hellenization of Judaism in the Second Temple period. Further the premises of the theory of adoptionist Christology have turned out to be invalid (see chapter 9 above). As regards the theory of the divine men, New Testament scholarship has proceeded essentially and abandoned the conclusions of the history-of-religions school.[61]

---

[59] This view is prevalent also in some modern studies, see e.g. Dunn, *Unity*, 242f.; Casey, *Jewish Prophet*, 110-111.

[60] This is the reason why such views have been widely accepted also in the existentialist tradition.

[61] See e.g. the criticism of Colpe, *Die religionsgeschichtliche Schule*, 194-195; cf. also Berger, *Exegese*, 90f., 99f. For the historical problems of the theory, see Koskenniemi, *Apollonios*, 64ff.

Such development in investigation explains why scholars turned to Jewish writings. This new approach, however, got attached to typological idealism. The main method was to attempt to find a Jewish prototype for a divine heavenly being. Adherents of the angelic interpretation suggested that the heavenly being should be considered an angel. For instance Fossum attempted to prove that both in Samaritan and Jewish writings there occurred an idea of a second power in heaven, that was identified as the Angel of the Lord. This angel shared God's name and was considered divine. According to this pattern both apocalyptic writers and first Christians formulated later their conceptions of exalted and enthroned divine beings in heaven.[62]

Fossum apparently attempted to find a pre-Christian conception of a divine angelic intermediary. As we have seen, Fletcher-Louis followed Fossum with only the exception that according to Fletcher-Louis there was no direct angel-Christology in early Christian thought. One can detect merely angelomorphic identity in Christological statements.[63]

The problem with these explanations is, as already stated before, that New Testament texts do not confirm their hypotheses. There is no evidence that the resurrected Jesus would have been described according to the pattern of some general heavenly being or divine angelic intermediary.[64] Actually the opposite is true in certain passages. Exalted Jesus is explicitly separated from angels. Therefore explanations relying on the conception of exalted beings appear to be primarily dependent on typological idealism, i.e. on the intention of finding a divine prototype for Christ's divinity on a heavenly throne.[65]

This kind of intention was detected further in the works of those scholars who emphasized the significance of exalted patriarchs. Meeks suggested that

---

[62] Fossum, *Name*, 333; cf. also 292f. Already in the discussion over the angeli interpretation, however, some scholars abandoned the idea that angelic beings would have been considered divine in Jewish theology. See Introduction, and e.g. Stuckenbruck, *Angel Veneration*, 200ff.

[63] Fletcher-Louis, *Angels*, 251f.

[64] Cf. Hengel, who admits that an angel Christology was "a real possibility" since in Jewish writings there were several exalted characters that were brought into close relationship with the angels. According to New Testament evidence, however, his conclusion remains negative. "In the oldest and christologically most significant texts in the New Testament we find no traces of an angel christology." Hengel, *Studies*, 221.

[65] One should probably repeat that the angelomorphic interpretation cannot escape the abovementioned problems. The exploitation of selected angelic features in the interpretation (e.g. Gieschen, *Christology*, 350) cannot prove that early Christology was essentially angelomorphic, because analogies do not reveal the meaning of christological statements. There are no doubt certain analogies on that level, but they cannot explain either the resurrection and enthronement of a royal Davidide, or the cultic ministry of the heavenly Melchizedek.

Philo would speak of the deification of Moses, and also van den Horst proposed that there would be a description of the deification of Moses in the Exagoge of Ezekiel.[66] Of these scholars Meeks was dependent on the views of the history-of-religions school. He stated that in Philo the concept of Moses' implicit or even explicit divine status originates in a "usual" Hellenistic conception of the "divine man". Therefore his claims must be submitted under the abovementioned – quite severe – criticism against that theory.

Both of these scholars were unable, however, to give proof of any change in the theocratic pattern as regards the status of Moses. Moses may have been revered as an extraordinary human being, but his alleged divinity has no devotional consequences in any extant writing. In the Exagoge of Ezekiel Moses' enthronement to a heavenly throne results in his extraordinary status in heaven, but here too the scene remains theocratic. There is a strict hierarchy in the palaces of the heavenly court and the enthroned ones are merely given a high status in that hierarchy. In New Testament Christology everything appears to be different.[67]

What, then, could explain the emergence of the belief in Jesus as the divine Son of God in power? In what follows we will argue that the developing of such belief did not need any concept of divine prototype in Jewish theology. *The conception of Jesus as a divine Son of God is grounded on Christian merkabah speculation working on subtexts such as Psalm 110.* It is simply a result of the original feature of early Christology, namely of the combining of the theme of Messiah's enthronement and the eschatological event of the resurrection of the dead.[68]

The enthronement story based on exaltation discourse as such implies the idea of the deity of Christ.[69] According to the story the Davidic prince, in his transcendent post-resurrection enthronement has become κύριος on the throne of Glory. Now he reigns in the kingdom of God as a Lord. While faith in him

---

[66] Meeks, *Essays*, 369ff.; van den Horst, *Essays*, 67.

[67] See chapter 3.2. above.

[68] Hay maintains that early Christian conceptions of Jesus' heavenly glory at God's right hand "probably went beyond the limits of what most Jewish exegesis could tolerate just because these conceptions moved in the direction of affirming the full divinity of Christ." Hay, *Glory*, 161.

[69] Already Segal noted that, for instance, in the exaltation Christology of Philippians 2, Pauline predicates of the exalted Christ are divine in character. These are "biblical references referring to God used in Jewish liturgy as doxologies." Segal, *ANRW 23.2.* (1980) 1373; cf. Capes, *Yahweh Texts*, 158ff. For the connection between Phil. 2 and Isa 45:21-25 see Hofius, *Christushymnus*, 41ff; and Laato, *Star*, 351: "The christological hymn in Phil 2:5-11 suggests that monotheism was seen as glorified in the confession 'Jesus Christ is Kyrios.' This confession glorified the name of Yhwh according to Isa 45:21-25 because everyone must confess that only Yhwh can give righteousness."

means confessing him as Lord, he is proven to be the object of faith. Therefore the deity is implied already on this basis, without referring to any other premise.[70]

This view is confirmed by the eschatologial perspective. The enthronement of the Davidide is placed in the eschatological event of the resurrection of the dead. This is no accident. The kingdom of the heavenly king is a new creation. It is based on the resurrection of the Messiah himself. Therefore the soteriological status of Christ as a universal ruler produces new reality. Every one who confesses this Lord is saved to this kingdom of the new creation.[71]

Psalm 110 as a subtext has provided material for the new interpretation. It is a text of enthronement, and of granting a great name, the name Lord itself. In early Christology (e.g. Acts 2:34-36) it becomes a text of eschatological change, referring to resurrection. The intertextual adaptation is bold. Messianic enthronement is an event of cosmic climax, the realization of the resurrection of the dead.[72]

With such a soteriological aspect of exaltation Christology we have finally reached the culminating point and highlight of early Christian teaching. The royal reign of the divine Davidide becomes a principle of intepretation of Jewish tradition. According to this principle, exaltation Christology re-interpreted the core of traditional Jewish theology, the basic idea of theocracy, i.e. meeting with God.[73]

This is an example of a proper intertextual procedure. Previous tradition is re-interpreted in a new situation. Old Testament faith is not abandoned,

---

[70] Chester has noted that "the imposing of transcendent categories on Jewish messianic hope is a secondary development rather than being an integral or important part of messianism as such." Chester, *Paulus*, 46. He does not, however, refer to the aspect of deity.

[71] It is important to bear in mind the view of the modern study of Jewish messianism. For instance Charlesworth has repeatedly maintained that Second Temple Jewish messianology was not uniform, and few Jews expected in the near future a Messiah. Charlesworth, *Judaisms*, 250. Therefore, the concept that great eschatological events should be connected with a historical messianic figure – i.e. Jesus – is quite unique among the beliefs of Second Temple Judaism.

[72] For instance Capes notes the intertextual reality in early Christology. In respect of Paul he writes that Paul's christological use of Yahweh texts indicates that he "considered his Lord Jesus to be equal with God." Capes, *Yahweh Texts*, 182. Due to his emphasis on the idea of divine manifestations, however, he did not recognize the significance of Psalm 110 in this connection. He rather treated it merely from the point of view of traditional titular explanation. See Capes, *Yahweh Texts*, 58.

[73] Davis, who investigated the so called triple pattern of mediation (past, present, future) in Jewish writings concluded that, "the ascription of a triple pattern of mediation did note ensure that the mediator became an object of worship." Davis, *JTS* 45 (1994) 498. Therefore, Davis also admits that an essential change must take place in the Christian interpretation. The intertextual approach is able to outline the essence of that kind of a change.

however. It is merely adapted into the exaltation discourse of early Christology.

The purpose of Old Testament cultic theology was to maintain Israel's good relationship with God. In the New Testament, theocracy is expected to be realized in a new way. Here the exalted Lord is the object of faith together with God. People needing atonement and salvation are not directed to the Temple but to Christ. They are told to believe in the Resurrected.

The Lordship of Christ became thus a principle according to which the whole Temple cult and thus also the idea of theocracy were re-interpreted:

The kingship of YHWH was seen to be realized and fulfilled in the Lordship of Christ who sits on the throne of Glory. Obedience to God was now primarily obedience of faith to Christ and it became realized in the Church. In the New Testament theocracy became Christocracy.[74]

While the basic "subtext" in this case is the theocratic "text of Jewish faith," the belief in God as a King on his throne of Glory, the new intertextual interpretation transforms traditional beliefs. Heavenly kingship is seen in a new light. Heavenly reign is given a new meaning. Veneration is understood in terms of the new situation. Theocracy is interpreted under new conditions. Therefore, the concept of monotheism is also transformed and given a new meaning. It no longer needs the images of theocratic subordination.[75] Quite the opposite, the reign of the enthroned Davidide now realizes the traditional faith.[76]

Such a transformation is most clearly detected in the conceptions of early Christian soteriology, as we stated above. Early Christology is not dogmatic but pragmatic. It is completely in the service of soteriology. Exaltation statements investigated in this study occur mainly in missionary speeches or in the context of exhortation to conversion. In addition to this, the scene of

---

[74] Stuckenbruck is right when emphasizing that, in early Christology, the exalted status of Christ as an object of worship alongside God "was not intended as a breach of monotheism." Stuckenbruck, however, still seems to expect Jewish ideas to "flow majestically into Christian Christology" (see the notions of Charlesworth above) when he concludes that there must be a Jewish analogy that explains the reconciliation of venerative attitudes to monotheism. "Perhaps the closest analogy to the veneration of an independent figure coupled with an express retention of a monotheistic framework is evident in some of the sources in which angels are honored alongside God as aligned and yet subordinate beings." Stuckenbruck, *Angel Veneration*, 272. The intertextual aspect reveals rather a radical transformation both of the concept of veneration and the concept of monotheism.

[75] The eschatological subordination described e.g. in 1 Cor. 15 is no longer theocratic subordination. It does not change the relation between Christ and human beings.

[76] This is where we need to "remember the obvious." In intertextual assessment one must not forget the main narrative of Old Testament faith. Enthronement Christology must be related to the conception of God as King of Israel on his throne of Glory. See chapter 2.2.

christological statements was that of salvation history. Jesus' death and resurrection were interpreted as preparation for redemption, and as the inauguration of the age of salvation. This must be the reason why one part of the message was expressed in terms of cultic discourse. In this context the priestly ministry of the Resurrected One in the heavenly shrine was emphasized. In his exaltation Jesus entered the heavenly Holy of Holies, and as a heavenly high priest he sprinkled his own sacrificial blood on the mercy seat thus obtaining atonement for sins.[77]

New Testament exaltation Christology was simultaneously atonement Christology. No sacrifice was needed any more, since Christ's sacrifice was sufficient. Therefore, early exaltation Christology is completely soteriological. The enthroned Lord is also a Savior who has atoned for the sins of humankind. This formed the foundation for the age of salvation.

Without their conception of redemption first Christians would have been in a similar situation as the community of Qumran. Atonement should have been acquired either in a traditional way like in sapiential theology, i.e. by a perfect and eager conduct of life and a commitment to the law of Moses, or by a belief in the redemptive power of the council of the community. In the early Church the community did not have this kind of status. We find instead the exalted Christ, who in all kerygmatic statements and confessions is the salvation of sinners.

The soteriological aspect may further be the theological reason for the uniting of priestly symbolism with the enthronement theme – a question that we discussed in chapter 6. There we saw that the priestly aspect did not disturb the enthronement scene of the enthronement of a Davidide. This is clear, for example, in Hebrews 10:

"But when Christ had offered for all time a single sacrifice for sins, 'he sat down at the right hand of God,' and since then has been waiting 'until his enemies would be made a footstool for his feet'." (10:12-13; cf. Rom. 8:34; 4:25).

It is probably the salvation history, in other words the context of soteriology itself, that implied the redemption theme.[78] As a new Davidide the enthroned Christ has inaugurated the age of salvation. Such a "new covenant" needed to be based on atonement, since in Second Temple Jewish theology salvation was also based on it. Therefore New Testament writers proclaim that Jesus gave

---

[77] Karrer in his large monography on Christology describes the resurrected Jesus mainly as σωτήρ. The evident defect in this explanation is that exaltation is given only a minor role in early resurrection Christology. See Karrer, *Jesus Christus*, 45ff., esp. 58.

[78] We have seen above that the formulas containing cultic soteriology that Paul used is in accord with later Jewish Christian writings, such as the letter to the Hebrews.

himself as a sacrifice for sinners. "Christ died for our sins" (1 Cor. 15:3).[79] When such a context was available, there were plenty of themes that could be, and in fact also were, attached to it.

Psalm 110 provided for a complete scene for the priestly function and heavenly ministry of the exalted Davidide.[80] This was further confirmed by the concept of heavenly ministry prevalent in Jewish mysticism. God's temple in the heavens was a suitable place for heavenly ministry and God's throne was indeed the mercy seat upon which the blood of the sacrifice was to be sprinkled. As an exalted Davidide Christ ministered as a high priest according to the order of Melchizedek. The obtaining of atonement was a unique event. After that Christ reigns "at the right hand" of God, until the end of time.

The first Christians thus believed that the salvation that came through Christ was real and present. The one who confessed the Lordship of Christ was certain that there is an antonement for his sins and that through his confession he has entered the kingdom of mercy. As regards the past, the age of the Temple had been passed. The new faith was the fulfilment of God's covenant.[81]

Therefore, the identity of first Christians also confirms the principle of interpretation and intertextual reality that we have presented here. *The confessing of Christ as Lord realizes simultaneously the core of Jewish devotion – faith in and faithfulness to God as a heavenly King.* This is an original intertextual move. From the point of view of traditional Judaism it is quite daring.[82]

---

[79] It is justified to conclude that we are here facing the earliest tradition of Christianity. One should remember that the so called pre-Pauline period cannot have been very long. Hengel has noted that the relative short period of time between the death of Jesus and the conversion of Paul was "two, three or at most four years" long. Hengel, *Studies*, 214.

[80] Also the application of Psalm 110 to resurrection Christology has been considered very early, see Gourgues, *A la Droite de Dieu*, 210.

[81] Contra e.g. Dunn, who thinks that in the early Church there was nothing that could not fit the convictions of a pious Jew. Dunn, *The Partings of the Ways*, 185. According to Dunn one should not read into early conceptions "too much too soon" (p. 184). Early conceptions of Jesus' resurrection did not yet mean any identification of God with Jesus. For Dunn the confession "Jesus is Lord" merely meant that God has shared his Lordship with the exalted Christ, pp. 190-191.

[82] For instance Kreitzer noted that in several New Testament passages a "conceptual overlap" existed between God and Christ. Kreitzer, *Jesus*, 156-169. The intertextual aspect is able to explain such "overlap." As the symbols or "signs" of kingship and throne are exploited in Christology, they apparently re-interpret the belief in the Enthroned One. Capes, who suggested that Jesus was conceived of as a manifestation of Yahweh, also draws a similar conclusion about the realization of faith, even though his premises are different. Capes, *Yahweh Texts*, 166-167.

Such new interpretation did not threaten traditional Jewish concept of God as King, however. The status of God himself had not changed.[83] What is new is the unique status of Christ who has been identified as a divine Ruler on God's throne. This, naturally, may easily be seen as a threat to traditional Jewish monotheism, and it is no wonder that it is treated as one from the very beginning.

Our analysis in this study has confirmed the view that the metaphor of throne has a special significance for exaltation descriptions both in the Old Testament, the writings of Jewish mysticism, and early Christology. As the relation of Jewish merkabah mysticism to early Christology was studied on the level of exaltation descriptions, certain important conclusions were made during the analysis.

1. How did Jewish mysticism influence Christology? An essential distinction needs to be made between separate signs and explicate narratives. Meaning cannot be investigated merely by the help of individual signs and metaphors. Rather, influence appears to work on two levels. On the level of the symbolic world one may easily detect the exploitation of different figures and characters, as well as the adoption of a whole scene like the one speaking of a heavenly Temple. with regard to meaning, however, the problem of influence appears on a new level. An analysis of the background of a New Testament discourse is not a matter of genealogy. The continuity of tradition is not based on an evolutive scheme where the essential elements of a discourse were dependent on earlier occurrences of similar elements in the manner of etymology. The so called influence is rather a matter of intertextual process where earlier elements and texts have been exploited and merged in new descriptions. The new text may assimilate, echo, re-assess, or even contradict earlier material.

2. It is quite apparent that, in New Testament exaltation statements, there are at least three distinctive enthroned figures. They all differ from each other. The main character is the royal Davidide, who appears in several passages. In addition to that we find the priestly figure Melchizedek, whose throne has been transformed into a mercy seat. In eschatological passages there is further the heavenly judge on the judgment seat, whom we have chosen to call the Son of Man.

These figures may be investigated on the level of individual signs. The

---

[83] As de Jonge has put it, the view did not "endanger the worship of the one God of Israel." de Jonge, *Christology*, 230. New Testament writers and especially Paul, however, saw no contradiction between traditional faith and the new Christology. For Paul, for instance, God and Jesus were united "in one saving action." de Jonge, *Christology*, 231.

images have been taken from the Old Testament or from Jewish writings. Their christological meaning, however, is dependent on the christological narrative in which they have been exploited – not on the Jewish background. Therefore, it has been necessary to outline four narratives that express early exaltation Christology.

The most common of these narratives is the one describing the heavenly enthronement of the seed of David. The first Christians presented a transcendental interpretation of the enthronement of the Davidide. His power is a heavenly power and his reign is an eternal reign in the kingdom of God. When eschatological reality was emphasized, Jesus' resurrection was placed as the focus of the presentation. In the narrative where the prince of life conquers death, first Christians located the enthronement of the Messiah in the eschatological event of the resurrection of the dead. Traditional messianology was placed in resurrection discourse and interpreted in terms of resurrection theology. Exaltation, resurrection and enthronement became identical.

The narrative about the heavenly Melchizedek is a story of a transcendent king-priest who has a cultic mission. Through his death and resurrection he enters the holy of holies in the heavenly Temple and with his own blood obtains eternal redemption. In Jewish theology the throne also appeared in a cultic setting, and this must be the rationale for connecting the cultic mission with enthronement. In Jewish theology, however, a messianic figure never appeared directly in a cultic context. This is apparently the reason why the priestly order of Melchizedek was exploited in this Christology.

The cultic narrative has its special features. The exalted Christ gives his sacrifice for the whole of humankind. His ascent reaches the Holy of Holies in the heavenly Temple. In this respect, the narrative also resembles the ascent stories of Jewish mysticism. As a priest-king Melchizedek, however, Christ is simultaneously a messianic figure. After the sacrificial atonement the heavenly liturgy turns into a coronation celebration. The heavenly Melchizedek is exalted on the mercy seat, on the throne of Glory, and he reigns forever at the right hand of God. It is no longer possible to explain such Christology on typological grounds. It is rather an example of a radical transformation of Jewish traditions.

Finally, there is a narrative about the eschatological entrée of the messianic judge. It is implied in several New Testament descriptions of the last judgment. According to this narrative Christ is a heavenly judge who gathers all the world before his tribunal. The special feature in such Christology is its essential difference from other exaltation narratives. In judicial christological descriptions no ascent or resurrection is referred to. Christ's entering upon the throne of Glory is not an eschatological enthronement, as the adherents of the theory of polarized eschatology have maintained. In early Christology, the day of judgment is not a coronation day. Rather, Christ the Exalted King is the one who is able to enter upon his own throne and execute the judgment when the last day arrives. The scene, therefore, is still that of the heavenly court, and the exploited images and metaphors are similar to those in other narratives. The basic narrative here, however, is new. It should not be confused with those expressing convictions about the actual exaltation.

3. The intertextual reality was further studied on a very general level, where the Old Testament theocratic idealism was taken under consideration. In this case the intertext is the christological idea of Christ's exaltation, and the subtext respectively the traditional Jewish monotheism that is expressed in Temple worship. In this study we have concluded that the developing of a belief in the deity of Christ did not need any presupposition of a divine prototype in Jewish theology. The conception of Jesus as a divine Son of God is grounded on Christian merkabah speculation working on subtexts such as Psalm 110. It is simply a result of the original feature of early Christology, namely of the combining of the theme of Messiah's enthronement and the eschatological event of the resurrection of the dead

The enthronement story based on exaltation discourse as such implies the idea of the deity of Christ. According to the story the Davidic prince, in his transcendent post-resurrection enthronement has become κύριος on the throne of Glory. Now he reigns over the kingdom of God as a Lord. Faith in him means confessing him as Lord and in this way he is proven to be the object of faith.

The Lordship of Christ became thus a principle according to which the whole Temple cult and thus the idea also of theocracy were re-interpreted. The kingship of YHWH was seen to be realized and fulfilled in the Lordship of Christ who sits on the throne of Glory. Obedience to God was now primarily obedience of faith to Christ and it became realized in the Church. In the New Testament theocracy became Christocracy. This is where we see intertextuality in its full force. The confessing of Christ as Lord realizes simultaneously the core of traditional Jewish devotion – faith in and faithfulness to God as a heavenly King.

4. We have been pursuing the question, "In which manner has Jewish merkabah speculation affected the formation of early Christology?" Was it that it gave the symbolic world, metaphors, and the settings for the christological scene, with which the story could be formulated? During the study we have noted numerous similarities. In fact, early Christology is rather incomprehensible without the background of Jewish mysticism. As regards christological narratives and especially the Christian resurrection discourse,

however, merkabah mysticism did not direct Christology. Merkabah discourse, or rather discourses, of Second Temple Judaism do not yet give the interpretative point of departure for early Christology. The exploited terminology is similar, while both parties are dependent on the same symbolic world. Exaltation discourse in early Christianity, however, is quite unique and contains features that are completely new in the Jewish tradition of the Second Temple period.

In order to state that Christ has been enthroned on the divine throne-chariot in heaven one has evidently had to presuppose the cosmology and imagery of Jewish merkabah mysticism. Once this identification was made, the field was open to any application where God's throne plays a significant role. Jesus the son of David is Christ the Lord who sits as a king "at the right hand" of God on the throne of Glory. He is a heavenly high priest who enters the heavenly debir and approaches the mercy seat. He is the glorified king-priest who is exalted above the cherubim. Further, this seat is the eschatological throne-chariot on which Christ shall also return to this world and gather all the world before his tribunal. As a theological construction such Christology has appeared to be a radical intertextual transformation where tradition is completely in the service of the new message.

Conclusion

The relation between Jewish merkabah mysticism and early Christology has turned out to be a complex subject where several different factors affect the results and the conclusions that are to be drawn from the extant evidence. Throughout the study we have pursued the question, "Did Jewish merkabah mysticism influence the emergence and formation of the earliest exaltation Christology?" The analysis has shown that many of the earlier attempts, for instance that of the traditional investigation concentrating on christological titles, and those typological explanations referring to the exaltation of angelic figures or patriarchs, have been insufficient in explaining the original nature of early Christian Christology.

In the present study, a new approach has been suggested. The nature of early Christology can be detected through the exploitation of linguistic and literary methods. The content of Christology is rather easily defined by investigating the narrative structure of christological statements, and the implied narratives that make even short confessions comprehensible. These narratives are dependent on respective discourses that give a "language" for the presentation. The images exploited in these narratives, i.e. the elements of the symbolic world where the images are taken from, must be regarded merely as signs that gain their proper meaning only when they are used, in other words when they are placed in a narrative.

This methodology makes it possible to discern between the symbolic world that we also know from the texts of Jewish merkabah mysticism, and the christological statements that express the convictions of the first Christians. Further, the relation of Jewish mysticism and early Christology is an intertextual relation. Therefore christological statements may be treated as intertexts that exploit earlier elements for their own purposes. The new text may assimilate or re-assess earlier material. The study of earliest Christology has been carried out by exploiting this kind of methodology.

The kingship of God and heavenly enthronements

In a study on the theme of kingship and on the throne metaphor one should not ignore the key symbols of Old Testament faith: the kingship of God and the extraordinary place of his majestic presence, the throne of Glory. This is what we have called "remembering the obvious." Already in Old Testament writings the throne is a special symbol for divine kingship, and earthly power is constantly related to the kingship of God.

This essential point of departure has turned out to be significant in the interpretation of the ascent structure of Jewish mysticism found in several Second Temple writings. Our analysis has confirmed the view that earliest Jewish mysticism was throne-mysticism that concentrated on the heavenly reign of God the King.

Following the visionary tradition of Old Testament prophetic writings Jewish mysicism produced stories of heavenly visions that describe a journey of a chosen one who is called to visit the heavens. The ascent structure comprises visions of the heavenly palace or temple, as well as visions of God on his glorious throne. The purpose of such journeys is usually an announcement of a special message for humankind. Quite many of the investigated writings concentrate on the problem of theodicy. The chosen people are in danger and God is silent. In such a situation a solution is desperately needed. One basic solution was to remind the readers of God's universal and eschatological power. Seers have seen the Lord who reigns. The heavenly King is going to say the last word.

As we consider the descriptions of heavenly journeys, they seem to express especially the transcendence of God. In Jewish writings these journeys may be short, through three heavens (1 Enoch; TLev.), or long and filled with interesting details of even seven or ten separate heavens (e.g. AscIsa; ApAbr; 3 Baruch). The emphasis on transcendence as such is not necessarily a sign of Temple criticism, but may as well express the "transcendent" justification of Temple cult. Temple terminology has been transferred to the heavenly realm. This feature, however, could be seen already in certain biblical writings, as in the Psalms.

The cultic aspect is sometimes expressed in terms of *pargod* speculation, where the Temple veil serves as a significant symbol and indicator for the heavenly Holy of Holies that lies behind the veil. All this shows that the symbolic universe of traditional Old Testament religion has maintained its relevance in the writings of Jewish mysticism. Heavenly journeys are described in terms of theocratic theology, and the cultic nature of the encounter with God is evident. Communication with God is constantly linked to heavenly liturgy.

What is special about the visions are the descriptions or promises of heavenly enthronements. There seems to be a special relation between God's throne of Glory and other heavenly thrones. The throne in Jewish apocalyptic may be a place for judgment, and different characters are exalted into a position of heavenly judges. Throne is also an honorary place that is promised to several righteous people, especially to patriarchs and prophets. According to apocalyptic writings, there are several different thrones in heavens. In different writings for instance Adam, Abel, Enoch, Noah, Shem, Abraham, Isaac, Jacob, Moses, Isaiah and Job are being promised a heavenly throne of their own. This kind of tradition is similar to that of the promising of the twelve thrones for the disciples of Jesus. In addition to this we have for instance the descriptions of the enthronement of the Son of Man figure in 1 Enoch, as well as the enthronement of the "shoot" of David in the Isaiah Pesher of Qumran (4Q161).

The most obvious question that arises on the basis of New Testament Christology concerns the resurrection of a Davidide. According to the analysis there is practically nothing in apocalyptic Jewish writings that would resemble such an idea. In no writing is the resurrection considered a premise for the enthronement of the Shoot of David. The description of the exaltation of the Davidide on the throne of glory remains on such a metaphorical level that almost nothing is said about the person himself. Usually his kingship can be understood in earthly terms. Even if his reign could be interpreted as an eschatological reign, as in the case of the Qumran passage, the Son of David is not presented as an earthly person who would ascend to heaven before his enthronement.

Merkabah mysticism and Christology

As the transition from merkabah mysticism to early Christology was investigated, certain essential conclusions were drawn. Firstly, there were several different categories of figures that occurred in apocalyptic exaltation descriptions. Even though one may speak of an ascent structure in merkabah mysticism, one cannot collect divine agents merely into one single category. Exalted patriarchs differ significantly from angels. Eschatological figures that belong mostly to the heavenly realm, such as the Son of Man, differ from both of these – not to mention the variations of more traditional messianology. All of these must be investigated separatedly and their comparison with christological material must be done likewise.

Secondly, one needs to be cautious when speaking of the angelic or angelomorphic nature of a heavenly figure. There are naturally several extraordinary angels appearing in the writings, but the angelic identification of other beings is quite difficult. In the texts, different features have been used metaphorically when the exceptional appearance or status of an exalted being has been described. This does not necessarily imply that a metamorphosis or transformation of the being would have taken place, even though we also have examples of that kind of procedure in certain writings. Further, it is apparent that the enthronement theme itself is hardly ever applied to angels.

Thirdly, there are messianic figures in Jewish writings, but they rarely occur in the context of the ascent structure. The best example for our interests is in Qumran, where we find the expectation of an eschatological Davidide who will be enthroned and reign over Israel in the end of days. Strictly speaking, however, a heavenly enthronement is not presented in the passage. In other writings the figure of the Son of Man comes closest to a messianic figure, and he may be identified as a heavenly king sitting on the throne of Glory.

In addition to this the question concerning the messianology of Second Temple Judaism as such has turned out to be difficult. The concept of an eschatological Messiah is anything but clear. When one attempts to ask, where did the first Christians get their convictions about the messiahship of Jesus, one meets several open questions.

These observations suggested that a new approach was needed when the relation between Jewish mysticism and early Christology was investigated. Therefore, in the actual analysis of New Testament Christology, linguistic and literary methods as well as the intertextual approach were exploited in order to find a new way to explain the abovementioned relation.

New Testament exaltation Christology

In New Testament Christology the concepts of Messiah and throne appear together in several contexts and have different roles in different discourses. Therefore, New Testament materials were investigated according to four categories, i.e. four different discourses, enthronement discourse, resurrection discourse, cultic discourse, and judicial discourse. The idea of exaltation is common to all of them, but the detailed descriptions differ essentially from each other.

In the New Testament we find the same symbolic world that prevailed in Jewish apocalyptic. The scene comprises a heavenly court, sometimes even temple, and God's throne. There are several metaphors which are identical with those found in Jewish writings. In the New Testament they have been taken in the service of Christology. While Jewish theology described ascensions and throne visions, in the New Testament Christ himself is in the centre of all these events. Writers speak of his ascension to the heavens and of his sitting on the throne of glory.

For instance in Acts 2:22-36 the writer speaks of a heavenly enthronement by exploiting Psalm 110 as a subtext, supported by Psalm 132. The enthronement is expressed by using a phrase that serves as a submetaphor for a throne, i.e. the sitting "at the right hand" of God. This point confirms further that the description of early Christology in Acts 2 is dependent on enthronement discourse. The exaltation of Jesus in his resurrection is interpreted as an act of enthronement, and the description exploits symbols that are associated with coronation. The pattern is similar to that of merkabah mysticism. The key person of the event is being enthroned on the throne of Glory.

The character of the Davidic Messiah and the metaphor of throne are essential in early Christian enthronement discourse. This kind of presentation may also easily be detected in several Pauline passages, and in the letter to the Hebrews. On several occasions we meet such Christology in short homologies or kerygmatic statements that bear marks of a fixed tradition. In Paul's theology, and in the letter to the Hebrews, however, the reception of the essential content of the Christology has led to a rich development of resurrection theology.

The analysis has further confirmed the view that the apostle Paul was well acquainted with Jewish mysticism. Already Paul's personal history appears to link him to some kind of visionary tradition. In his christological descriptions Paul relies heavily on enthronement discourse. He describes the resurrected Christ as an enthroned Messiah in his Christology. He exploits kerygmatic or confessional statements that have been built on Psalm 110. Pauline materials thus confirm the picture that we have gained regarding the relation between merkabah mysticism and early Christology. It is also noteworthy that in Col. 2:16-3:1 (Pauline, or Pauline tradition) exaltation Christology drifted into a conflict with such Jewish mysticism that had provided for the exaltation discourse exploited in the formation of exaltation Christology in the first place. The polarized opposition to that tradition may also reveal Paul's own close relationship with such a movement. Paul may himself be one of those early Christian teachers who have exploited merkabah mysticism in Christological formulations.

The Revelation to John, finally, gives us a clear view of how the investigated conceptions have been placed in a colorful scene of Christian apocalyptic. Such Christology no doubt exploits enthronement discourse, but there is a basic difference between the Jewish description and early Christology. According to New Testament Christology, the enthronement took place in resurrection. These two eschatological events fall into one. Psalm 110 has been used as a proof-text for the idea of an exaltation in resurrection. In this respect early Christology exceeded the limits of merkabah mysticism.

The famous christological passage Romans 1:3-4, in turn, is a perfect example of exaltation Christology that expresses resurrection discourse. The passage exploits quite early tradition and it is rather difficult to explain. We have suggested here that the parallelism in verses 3 and 4 must be read backwards. God's divine "appointment" or decree mentioned in verse 4 refers both to the seed of David mentioned in verse 3 and to resurrection mentioned in verse 4. The Resurrected One is the promised one who has already come (γενόμενος). This has been a proper way to emphasize that the enthroned Jesus is *the* Davidide.

The formula itself is based on a word-play on ἀνάστασις. It exploits the Old Testament/Jewish tradition of "raising" the seed of David. This is the reason why resurrection could be identified as the enthronement of the Davidide. It seems apparent that an unknown Jewish Christian preacher or prophet has exploited this kind of messianology in the same manner as did the tradition that has been used in Acts 2 and Hebrews 1. God has fulfilled his promises when raising Jesus from the dead. Jesus' resurrection has simultaneously been an act of enthronement, where the "seed of David" has been installed to power. Jesus is the Davidide who had been decreed to be enthroned, in other words, to be exalted as the Son of God in power in the resurrection.

The Christology of Romans 1 further conforms to the ideas of Jewish merkabah mysticism. The passage is clearly speaking of a transcendent heavenly rule. As in the presentations of Jewish mysticism, here also Christ is presented as a heavenly king. As regards the enthronement the description differs from that of Acts 2. Since Psalm 110 is not referred to, we do not find the expression "at the right hand". Christ is simply a Son of God in power. This is due to the changed discourse. The explicit wording of the formula does not follow the lines of usual enthronement discourse. The "mystical" nature of the enthronement, however, is identical in both Acts 2 and Romans 1. The enthronement takes place in the resurrection. The Davidide is enthroned on a heavenly throne.

When combining the themes of enthronement and the resurrection of the dead, the writer of the formula has in fact combined two such eschatological themes which have no immediate causal relationship to each other. The conception of resurrection in Romans 1 is even more informative than the one in Acts 2. The formula speaks of the resurrection of the dead. This must necessarily mean the general Jewish conception of eschatological resurrection.

In cultic discourse Christ's exaltation is presented as a cultic act. Christ himself is a high priest who in his resurrection is exalted to God's heavenly shrine. As a king-priest he performs sacrificial ritual in the Holy of Holies. Therefore, in the context of this discourse also, we have both the Davidic Messiah and the heavenly throne, but they are both given new meanings. The throne is God's ark in the Holy of Holies, the mercy seat, and the Davidide is a heavenly high priest according to the order of Melchizedek.

What is quite special about this new discourse is that the exploited imagery as such is capable of producing such interpretations without misrepresenting the original symbols. Now God's ark is simultaneously the throne of Glory and, especially according to Psalm 110, the Davidide is the new Melchizedek, the king-priest.

Judicial discourse differs somewhat from the previous two discourses that have been treated. Even though many features common to apocalyptic Jewish mysticism have been exploited here, Psalm 110 has no relevant function in these passages. In eschatological descriptions the enthroned Christ is a heavenly judge who performs God's final judgment. Therefore, the throne in judicial discourse is often βῆμα, the judgment seat of God – even though the term itself does not differ essentially from the common words for throne.

These descriptions also differ from other christological statements in the sense that Christ's resurrection has no role here. They describe rather his entering upon the throne – an image that emphasizes the inauguration of an eschatological climax. Judicial discourse presents Christ as a heavenly judge who performs eschatological judgment on the last day. This description has often been falsely confused with enthronement statements and interpreted with the help of a strictly polarized pattern. Therefore, it is necessary to emphasize that, in early Christology depending on judicial discourse, Christ's messianic enthronement is not the essential content of the description. It rather speaks of Christ's entering upon the judgment seat.

In addition to the New Testament evidence early Christology has also had a significant history of influence (admittedly through New Testament tradition) in different kinds of Jewish writings. In Jewish Christian Pseudepigrapha there are several writings that derive originally from the sphere of Jewish mysticism or that are based on Jewish traditions, but which have later undergone Christian editing and re-writing. Some of these pseudepigraphic works contain merkabah speculation, and what is significant still, the re-written parts speak of Christ's heavenly enthronement. Especially in the Ascension of Isaiah we find a remarkable Christian reworking of a Jewish apocalyptic writing. The vision of a heavenly journey is climaxed in the enthronement of Christ. In this description the aspects of the enthronement theme of early Christology are exploited in a creative manner.

Further, several books of the Sibylline Oracles and the Apocalypse of Paul show that enthronement discourse has maintained its influence in apocryphal literature. These writings imitate Jewish style in their presentation, even though the direct connection to Jewish tradition may be rather vague. The resurrected Christ is described as an enthroned Davidide whose reign aims at an apocalyptical consummation of the ages.

On defining earliest Jewish Christian Christology

The nature of the earliest Christology of the Jewish Christian community has traditionally been interpreted in terms of a theocratic theory of adoptionist Christology. D.F. Strauss and J. Weiss made use of the idea of adoption when characterizing the nature of the Christology in passages such as Rom. 1:3–4 and Acts 2:36. The adoption of the Israelite king was a normal feature in Jewish teaching. The adoption took place in the act of enthronement. According to Weiss, this was the reason why Jesus too must be an adopted Son, since he was exalted to the right hand of God. The basic idea in this interpretation was that earliest Jewish Christianity maintained its monotheistic beliefs and presented the status of the exalted Christ in terms of Old Testament political messianism.

This kind of view became later quite popular among scholars and it was justified by the so called Ebionite theory. According to this interpretation the teaching and Christology of earliest Jewish Christianity was similar to that of Jewish Christian Ebionites of the patristic period. The Ebionites were considered pure adoptionists.

In the analysis we have noted that early Christology no doubt exploited the key passages of Davidic idealism in its descriptions. This, however, doesn't explain the meaning of such Christology. What is important in the assessment of these theories, is that such a view has no connection with later patristic debates concerning "adoptionist Christology". As regards the Ebionite theory, its interpretations have often been erroneous. In the analysis Ebionite theology has appeared to be dualistic Gnostic possessionism which has nothing in common with New Testament Christology, but which is rather related to the so called Sethian Gnosticism, well known in extant writings.

The main problem with the theory of adoptionist Christology is that it presupposes a theocratic pattern in the explanation of Christology. In early Christology, however, the theocratic pattern, precisely, is changed. Jesus has been exalted to the throne of Glory and now he is considered the divine Savior of the world. As a Davidic Messiah he is the one who brings salvation. Therefore he is worshiped together with God the Father.

As the adoptionist theory cannot explain the confessional nature of early Christology, its only benefit seems to be in the explication of the Davidic typology behind exaltation Christology. The Christology itself must be interpreted according to the apocalyptic worldview that is implicit in old formulas, and in the devotional context that expresses a change in the traditional theocratic view. As regards the aspect of typology, however, new difficulties emerge.

Another feature that has been criticized in several theories of explanation is the typological idealism on which they depend. The basic idea in several theories is that a Jewish prototype is a key to the meaning of a christological statement, and that it also explains the emergence of such a formation. In this kind of explanation not much room is left for the idea of transformation in early Christology. In fact, an idea of transformation weakens the very explanatory power of the theory.

Theories that depend on the idea of investigating typological causalities between Jewish mysticism and early Christology appear to be tied up with their premises. Their explanatory force depends completely on the preceding prototype. If an angelic figure is taken as a prototype, the explanation is consistently dependent on the typological relation. If that relation is weakened during the explanation, a great deal of the theory's explanatory force is lost. Therefore, any attempt to bring a new conception for the actual interpretation of the nature of Christology changes the premises of the whole theory.

One should rather concentrate on the transformational process that reveals the final meaning of Christian convictions and beliefs. It is apparent that the theory of divine agents, as well as that of angelic interpretation, rested on a fixed presupposition. These theories attempted to find a "missing link" between Jewish theology and early Christology. Scholars attempted to discern a divine agent or an angelic figure that might serve as a prototype for the exalted Christ in Christology. According to those scholars, only such *typos* could explain how first Christians were able to present the resurrected Christ as a heavenly being. According to the analysis, however, there is no exact typos in pre-Christian Judaism that could serve as a "missing link" for the interpretation of Christ's exalted status as a Lord on the heavenly throne.

It seems that such typological idealism rested on an implicit "evolutionist" presupposition. Scholars attempted to maintain the continuity of messianology from Jewish theology to early Christology by substituting a typos that has enough functions to reach both directions. We have also suggested an explanation for the fact that a missing link was sought after. The first Christian theologians had connected traditions that did not yet belong together in Second Temple Judaism. The ascent structure and the idea of heavenly enthronements belonged to the world of "divine agents." It is true that there were exceptional angelic figures in Jewish writings. Therefore scholars were rather consistent when attempting to connect these figures with the risen Christ. In this way they were able to find a reason for the "angelic" heavenly status of the Davidide. The only problem with this construction is that those descriptions in Jewish writings have practically nothing to do with early Christology.

Christological descriptions in early kerygmatic statements, homologies, and hymns are quite unique. They present Christ as a Davidic Messiah who has been enthroned on the heavenly throne "at the right hand" of God. The Davidide is no longer an earthly figure. He is messianic, though, and as a heavenly king and Lord he reigns on the throne. He is the head of heavenly hosts and he is being worshiped as the divine Son of God. He is not like an angel, he is like a king.

The Christian merkabah tradition

In order to explain the emergence of this kind of Christology we have concentrated on the relation between Jewish merkabah mysticism and early Christology, and proposed a construction of "Christian merkabah tradition," where Christology is interpreted in terms of a messianic figure's heavenly enthronement on the throne of Glory. We have further suggested selected features that should be ascribed to such a Christian merkabah tradition.

1. The throne is presented as a central metaphor for the new status of Christ.

2. Resurrection is regarded as an act of enthronement.

3. The enthroned Christ has a universal power over all of humankind as a Savior.

4. On the throne of glory the Lord Christ is an object of devotion.

There are thus several factors in early Christology that may be defined as parts of a new discourse that may be called Christian merkabah mysticism. According to this tradition, Christ sits on the throne of glory in the heavenly Temple and he is the Leader of humankind. The believers' worship is linked with heavenly worship before the divine throne where Christ is. And furthermore, this throne is the place from which God's mercy is delivered to this world. It is no longer merely the throne of the Holy God, but the throne of Christ. Therefore, it is a mercy seat that brings salvation.

Such a tradition transforms the ideas of Jewish merkabah mysticism and presents a new Christian interpretation. It also explains why enthronement language was exploited precisely in the context of resurrection. Without this kind of background it would be difficult to understand why the throne is the central metaphor for early Christology.

The relationship between Jewish theology and early Christology has further been defined by the help of a semiotical analysis. By semiotical approach we mean especially the investigation of the *semiosis*, i.e. the process where meaning is constructed, that has taken place in the earliest Jewish Christian community. Semiosis has to do with signs and with meanings that are given to particular signs. During the study we have paid attention to the symbolic world that has prevailed in the Second Temple period. Both Jewish writings and the New Testament exploit similar images and metaphors. On the level of the symbolic world there is an explicit continuity of tradition observed in these writings.

These separate images may be regarded as signs that have been exploited in Jewish mystical presentations or in Christian christological descriptions. As regards methodology, however, the semiosis concerning different signs must always be investigated in their primary context. The process of constructing meaning cannot be generalized to the extent that its results would cover all belief-systems and religious groups of the Second Temple period.

As regards New Testament Christology, on the level of the symbolic world one may easily detect the exploitation of different figures and characters, as well as the adoption of a whole scene like the one speaking of a heavenly Temple. Such elements no doubt direct the thinking of the writer. In respect of meaning, however, the problem of influence appears on a new level. An analysis of the background of a New Testament discourse is not exactly a matter of genealogy. The continuity of tradition is not based on an evolutive scheme where the essential elements of a discourse were dependent on earlier occurrences of similar elements in the manner of etymology.

The so called influence is rather a matter of intertextual process where earlier elements and texts have been exploited and merged in new descriptions. The new text may assimilate, echo, re-assess, or even contradict earlier material. The final meaning is dependent on the new discourse where the revised elements play an integral part. Signs get their final meaning in the context of the narrative in which they occur.

When New Testament writers exploit traditional images – signs taken from the symbolic world of Second Temple Judaism – in their Christology, they do not exploit or produce exactly the same narratives as their predecessors. Rather, they are constructing Christocentric narratives where the actualization of tradition produces something completely new. Christian narratives exploit traditional material and traditional features, but they also create a new scene where previous tradition is transformed into someting unique.

Exalted figures and christological narratives

As the "meaning" of christological descriptions was investigated, a distinction was made between exploited images (Davidide, high-priest etc.) and the christological narrative to which these traditional images are being attached. In the analysis we noted that a messianic figure appears mainly in the context of three different discourses.

In enthronement discourse that figure is the messianic Davidide, the eschatological king from the family of David. In cultic discourse he is the new Melchizedek, a heavenly high priest. In judicial discourse, in turn, he is something like the Son of Man, a heavenly judge who participates in the final judgment of the whole of humankind. The throne metaphor, respectively, is understood in a slightly different way in different contexts. In the enthronement discourse it is the royal throne of the heavenly Messiah. In cultic discourse it is the mercy seat in the heavenly debir. And finally, in the judicial discourse, the throne is Christ's tribunal on the day of the last judgment.

We have further discerned four different narratives which all express one form of "Christian merkabah tradition." In respect of the general nature of New Testament christological statements, the most important one of these narratives is the one describing the heavenly enthronement of the seed of David. The first Christians presented a transcendental interpretation of the enthronement of the Davidide. His power is a heavenly power and his reign is an eternal reign in the kingdom of God.

When eschatological reality was emphasized, Jesus' resurrection was placed as the focus of the presentation. In the narrative where the prince of life conquers death, the first Christians located the enthronement of the Messiah in the eschatological event of the resurrection of the dead. Traditional messianology was planted in resurrection discourse and interpreted in terms of resurrection theology. Exaltation, resurrection and enthronement became identical.

The narrative regarding the heavenly Melchizedek is a story of a transcendent king-priest who has a cultic mission. Through his death and resurrection he enters the Holy of Holies in the heavenly Temple and with his own blood obtains eternal redemption. In Jewish theology the throne also appeared in a cultic setting, and this must be the rationale for connecting the cultic mission with enthronement. In Jewish theology, however, a messianic figure never appeared directly in a cultic context. This is apparently the reason why the priestly order of Melchizedek was exploited in this Christology.

The cultic narrative has its special features. The exalted Christ gives his sacrifice for the whole of humankind. His ascent reaches the Holy of Holies in the heavenly Temple. In this respect, the narrative also resembles the ascent stories of Jewish mysticism. The cosmology of Jewish mysticism also supports this view. The concept of a temple-structured universe explains why the "first tent" was identified with the earth and everything on it, and heaven itself was identified with the heavenly Holy of Holies behind the cosmic curtain.

As a priest-king Melchizedek, however, Christ is simultaneously a messianic figure. After the sacrificial atonement the heavenly liturgy turns into a coronation celebration. The heavenly Melchizedek is exalted on the mercy seat, on the throne of Glory, and he reigns forever at the right hand of God. It is no longer possible to explain such Christology on typological grounds. It is rather an example of a radical transformation of Jewish traditions.

Finally, there is a narrative about the eschatological entrée of the messianic judge. It is implied in several New Testament descriptions of the last judgment. According to this narrative Christ is a heavenly judge who gathers all the world before his tribunal. The special feature in such Christology is its essential difference from other exaltation narratives. In judicial christological descriptions no ascent or resurrection is referred to. Christ's entering upon the throne of Glory is not an eschatological enthronement, and the day of judgment is not a coronation day. Rather, Christ the Exalted King is the one who is able to enter upon his own throne and execute the judgment when the last day arrives.

These kinds of narratives cannot be read word by word in the writings of the New Testament. They must rather be postulated as implied narratives according to which different kinds of christological statements have been constructed. Sometimes the expressions may be quite extensive, as is the case in the letter to the Hebrews. In other cases a narrative may be expressed merely by a couple of words that form a coherent unity and still convey the implied narrative.

During the study we have maintained that in early Christology the narrative reality prevails. The nature of Christology should not be investigated by concentrating on the so called christological titles. That line of study has over-emphasized the significance of individual titles at the cost of the holistic view, the story that also factually gives meaning to different appellations. It should also be noted that the so called titles do not always even occur in crucial christological passages. Focusing on narratives helps one to cover the evidence more accurately.

Further, we hope to have been able to point out that several of the traditional problems of christological study have been dependent on the selected approach. Thus, for instance, the history-of-religions approach, the idea of polarized eschatology, the theory of adoptionist Christology, typological idealism, and the investigation of christological titles have produced scholarly problems that are relevant only to the respective theories. When the premises of the theories have been abandoned, the problems of early Christology also appear in a new light. In this respect the new approach that has been exploiting methods from semiotics and narratology to intertextualism, represents a new paradigm in the investigation.

From the present point of view, the main feature of exaltation narratives has appeared to be an essential transformation of Old Testament and Jewish ideas. There are several uniting features and most images and metaphors were taken from these traditions, as we saw above, but the christological statements themselves apply the tradition in a completely new way. As a Davidide Jesus is the king of Israel, but his reign is actually a universal, transcendent reign. He is a cosmic king who has inaugurated the eschatological resurrection of the dead. He is also a high priest, but as a heavenly Melchizedek he is a God-chosen king-priest whose priesthood replaces that of the first covenant.

All of these christological descriptions may be defined as different modes of resurrection Christology. Even though the narratives are slightly different, the main emphasis is similar in all of them. The locating of the act of enthronement in the resurrection of the dead, therefore, did not mean any "Enteschatologisierung" of an alleged "original" futurist concept of messianic enthronement, as some scholars have suggested. Exaltation Christology expressing Jesus' heavenly enthronement was resurrection Christology already in the earliest christological formulations that may be detected in the New Testament.

The basic coherence of resurrection Christology is further the reason why respective passages should not be investigated as expressions of Son of God Christology, Son of David Christology, or Melchizedek Christology. They are not completely unrelated christological expressions, but there is a close unity between them. This can be seen in several uniting features that have been investigated during the study. Only the narratives are different, and therefore they must not be confused in the explanation of individual narratives.

Exaltation Christology as an intertext

As the aspect of intertextuality was investigated on a very general level, also the Old Testament theocratic idealism was taken under consideration. In this case the intertext was the christological idea of Christ's exaltation, and the subtext respectively the traditional Jewish monotheism that is expressed in Temple worship. During the study we concluded that the developing of a belief in the deity of Christ did not need any presupposition of a divine prototype in Jewish theology. In this respect the attempts that have been made in order to find a pattern of deification already in Jewish writings have little relevance for the interpretation of early Christology.

According to certain scholars it is probable that the concept of divinity was vague already in Second Temple Jewish writings. This, however, is not a decisive notion for the understanding of Christology. The conception of Jesus as a divine Son of God is, rather, grounded on Christian merkabah speculation working on subtexts such as Psalm 110. It is simply a result of the original feature of early Christology, namely of the combining of the theme of the Messiah's enthronement and the eschatological event of the resurrection of the dead. The enthronement story based on exaltation discourse as such implies the idea of the deity of Christ. According to the story, the Davidic prince in his transcendent post-resurrection enthronement, has become κύριος on the throne of Glory. Now he reigns in the kingdom of God as a Lord. Faith in him means confessing him as Lord and in this way he is proven to be the object of faith.

The Lordship of Christ became thus a principle according to which the whole Temple cult and also the idea of theocracy were re-interpreted. The kingship of YHWH was seen to be realized and fulfilled in the Lordship of Christ who sits on the throne of Glory. Obedience to God was now primarily obedience of faith to Christ and it became realized in the Church. In the New Testament theocracy became Christocracy. This is where we see intertextuality in its full force. The confessing of Christ as Lord realizes simultaneously the core of traditional Jewish devotion – faith in and faithfulness to God as a heavenly King.

Messiah and the throne

It is not, therefore, an essential problem in the interpretation of early Christology that there is no clear and simple figure of the Messiah found in Second Temple Jewish writings. Nor is it alarming that angelic figures or heavenly intermediaries cannot provide a firm background for the development of Christology. The interpretation of early Jewish Christian Christology is not dependent on typological explanation, even though it does have some evident typological features. It is not dependent on finding independent absolute titles in Jewish writings, either, in order to justify the use of absolute titles in Christology – even though the writers appear to have also used fixed appellations.

Jesus' new status after the resurrection has been expressed by new narratives that merely exploit the material taken from the tradition. The narratives themselves are independent and they reflect convictions that have emerged only after easter, and after the unique experiences of Jesus' followers in their community. Signs have been given new meanings in new contexts.

The investigated narratives share the basic idea of exaltation, but the outlook and nature of a narrative changes according to the discourse in the context of which it has been constructed. In early Christology, Christ is no doubt a royal Messiah. He is an anointed Davidide *par excellence* that has been enthroned on the heavenly throne. His heavenly power is unquestionable.

In order to state that Christ has been enthroned on the divine throne-chariot in heaven one has evidently had to presuppose the cosmology and imagery of Jewish merkabah mysticism. Once this identification was made, the field was open to any application where God's throne plays a significant role. Jesus the son of David is Christ the Lord who sits as a king "at the right hand" of God on the throne of Glory. He is a heavenly high priest who enters the heavenly Holy of Holies and approaches the mercy seat. He is the glorified king-priest who is exalted above the cherubim. Further, this seat is the eschatological throne-chariot on which Christ shall also return to this world and gather all the world before his tribunal.

As a theological construction, however, such Christology has appeared to be a radical intertextual transformation where tradition is completely in the service of the new message. The earliest exaltation Christology is not comprehensible without the background of Jewish merkabah mysticism – but it is comprehensible only as a uniquely Christian example of a transformation of Jewish ideas. Christ is not merely an exalted patriarch, prophet, or pious king, whom God vindicated through the exaltation. He is the Son of God, and faith in him realizes faith in the Lord of Israel.

Bibliography

1. Sources, texts

Allegro. J.H. (ed.), *Qumrân Cave 4: I (4Q158-4Q186)*. DJD 5. Oxford: Clarendon. 1968.
Baillet. M. (ed.), *Qumrân Grotte 4: III (4Q482-4Q520)*. DJD 7. Oxford: Clarendon. 1982.
Baillet, M. - Milik, J.T. - Vaux, R. de (eds.), *Les 'Petites Grottes' de Qumrân. Exploration de la falaise. Les grottes 2Q, 3Q, 5Q, 6Q, 7Q à 10Q. Le rouleau de cuivre.* DJD 3. Oxford: Clarendon. 1962.
Barthélemy, D. - Milik, J.T. (eds.), *Qumrân Cave 1.* DJD 1. Oxford: Clarendon. 1955.
Biblia Hebraica Stuttgartensia, Ediderunt K. Elliger et W. Rudolph. Textum Masoreticum curavit H.P. Rüger. Masoram elaboravit G.E. Weil. Stuttgart. 1977.
Biblia sacra iuxta vulgatam versionem, Recensuit et brevi apparatu instruxit Robertus Weber osb. Tomus II. Stuttgart. 1969.
Brock, S.P. (ed.), *Testamentum Iobi.* PsVTGr II. Leiden: Brill. 1967.
Burrows, M. (ed.), *The Dead Sea Scrolls of St. Mark's Monastery.* 2 vols. New Haven: ASOR. 1950/1951.
Charlesworth, J.H. (ed.), *The Old Testament Pseudepigrapha. Volume 1. Apocalyptic Literature and Testaments.* New York: Doubleday. 1983.
Charlesworth, J.H. (ed.), *The Old Testament Pseudepigrapha. Volume 2. Expansions of the "Old Testament" and Legends, Wisdom and Philosophical Literature, Prayers, Psalms, and Odes, Fragments of Lost Judeo-Hellenistic Works.* New York: Doubleday. 1985.
Charlesworth, J.H. (ed.), *The Dead Sea Scrolls. Hebrew, Aramaic, and Greek Texts with English Translations. Vol. 1. Rule of the Community and Related Documents.* The Princeton Theological Seminary Dead Sea Scrolls Project. Tübingen: Mohr (Siebecl Louisville: Westminster. 1994.
Charlesworth, J.H. (ed.), *The Dead Sea Scrolls. Hebrew, Aramaic, and Greek Texts with English Translations. Vol. 2. Damascus Document, War Scroll, and Related Documents.* The Princeton Theological Seminary Dead Sea Scrolls Project. Tübingen: Mohr (Siebeck) / Louisville: Westminster. 1995.
Colson, F.H., *Philo in Ten Volumes (and Two Supplementary Volumes).* LCL. Cambridge Mass.: Harvard/ London: Heinemann. 1932ff.
Danby, H., *The Mishnah. Translated from Hebrew with Introduction and Brief Explanatory Notes.* Oxford: University Press. Repr. 1980.
Feldman, L.H., *Josephus. Jewish Antiquities, Books XVIII-XIX.* LCL IX. Cambridge Mass.: Harvard/ London: Heinemann. 1965.
Fischer, J.A., *Die Apostolischen Väter. Griechisch und Deutsch.* 9., durchgesehene Auflage. München: Kösel. 1986.
Geffcken, J., *Die Oracula Sibyllina.* GCS 8. Leipzig: Hinrichs. 1902.
Hennecke, E. - Schneemelcher, W., *New Testament Apocrypha I-II.* Philadelphia: Westmister. 1963.
Holm-Nielsen, S., *Hodayot: Psalms from Qumran.* AThD 2. Aarhus: Universitetsforlaget. 1960.
Jonge, M. de (ed.), *Testamenta XII Patriarcharum. Edited According to Cambridge University Library MS Ff I.24 fol. 203a-262b. With Short Notes.* PVTG 1. Leiden: Brill. 1964.

Kittel, B., *The Hymns of Qumran. Translation and Commentary*. SBL diss. 50. Scholars Press. 1981.
Knibb, M.A., *The Qumran Community*. CCWJCW 2. Cambridge: Cambridge University Press. 1987.
Kurfess, A., *Sibyllinische Weissagungen*. Berlin: Heimeran. 1951.
Lohse, E. (hrsg.), *Die Texte aus Qumran*. München: Kösel. 1986.
Neusner, J., *The Mishnah. A New Translation*. New Haven/ London: Yale University Press. 1988.
Maier, J., *The Temple Scroll. An Introduction, Translation & Commentary*. JSOTS 34. Sheffield: JSOT Press. 1985.
Martinez, F.C., *The Dead Sea Scrolls Translated. The Qumran Texts in English*. ET: W.G.E. Watson. Leiden: Brill. 1994
Nestle - Aland (26), *Novum Testamentum Graece*. Post Eberhard Nestle et Erwin Nestle communiter ediderunt K. Aland, M. Black, C.M. Martini, B.M. Metzger, A. Wikgren. 26. Auflage, nach dem 7. revidierten Druck. Stuttgart: Deutsche Bibelgesellschaft. 1983.
Nestle - Aland (27), *Novum Testamentum Graece*. Post Eberhard et Erwin Nestle communiter ediderunt B. Aland, K. Aland, J. Karavidopoulos, C.M. Martini, B.M. Metzger. 27. revidierte Auflage. Stuttgart: Deutsche Bibelgesellschaft. 1993.
Newsom, C., *Songs of the Sabbath Sacrifice. A Critical Edition*. Harvard Semitic Studies. Atlanta : Scholars. 1985.
Picard, J.-C. (ed.), *Apocalypsis Baruchi Graece*. PsVTGr II. Leiden: Brill. 1967.
Qimron, E. - Strugnell, J. (eds.), *Qumran cave 4. V. Miqsat ma^{c}a'se ha-torah*. DJD X. Oxford: Clarendon. 1994.
Rahlfs, A. (ed.), *Septuaginta id est Vetus Testamentum graece iuxta LXX interpretes*. 2 vols. Stuttgart: Deutsche Bibelgesellschaft. 1979.
Roberts, A. - Donaldson J., *Ante-Nicene Fathers. The Writings of the Fathers Down to A.D. 325*. Peabody: Hendrickson. 1994.
Robinson, J.M., *The Nag Hammadi Library*. 3rd Edition. San Francisco: Harper and Row. 1988.
Sanders, J.A. (ed.), *The Psalms Scroll of Qumrân Cave 11 (11QPs^a)*. DJD 4. Oxford: Clarendon. 1965.
Smend, R., *Die Weisheit des Jesus Sirach: Hebräisch und Deutsch*. Berlin: Reimers. 1906.
Thackeray, H.St.J., *Josephus. The Jewish War*. LCL. Cambridge, Mass./London: Harvard University Press. Repr. 1989.
Thackeray, H.St.J. - Marcus, R. - Wikgren, A. - Feldman, L.H., *Josephus. Jewish Antiquities*. LCL. Cambridge, Mass./London: Harvard University Press. Repr. 1991.
Vaux, R. de - Milik, J.T. (eds.), *Qumrân Grotte 4: II. Tefillin, Mezuzot et Targums (4Q128-4Q157)*. DJD 6. Oxford: Clarendon. 1977.
Vermes, G., *The Dead Sea Scrolls in English*. Revised and Extended Fourth Edition. Sheffield: Sheffield Academic Press. 1995.
Violet, B., *Die Esra-Apokalypse (IV. Esra)*. GCS 18. Leipzig: Hinrichs. 1910.
Whiston, W., *The Works of Josephus. Complete and Unabridged*. New Updated Edition. Peabody, Massachusetts: Hendrickson. 1987.

2. Subsidia

Aland, K. - Werner, H., *Computer-Konkordanz, Zum Novum Testamentum Graece von Nestle-Aland*, 26. Aufl. und zum Greek New Testament 3rd Edition. Herausgegeben vom Institut für Neutestamentliche Textforschung und vom Rechenzentrum der Universität Münster, unter besonderer Mitwirkung von H. Bachmann, W.A. Slaby. Berlin/New York: de Gruyter. 1980.

Balz, H. - Schneider, G. (hrsg.), *Exegetisches Wörterbuch zum Neuen Testament*. 3 vols. Stuttgart: Kohlhammer. 1980/1981/1983.

Bauer, W., *Griechisch-deutsches Wörterbuch*. 6., völlig neu bearbeitete Auflage. Hrsg. K. Aland und B. Aland. Berlin/New York: de Gruyter. 1988.

Blass, F. - Debrunner, A. - Rehkopf, F., *Grammatik des neutestamentlichen Griechisch*. 15. durchgesehene Auflage. Göttingen: Vandenhoeck & Ruprecht. 1979.

Botterweck, G.J. - Ringgren, H. (hrsg.), *Theologisches Wörterbuch zum Alten Testament*. Stuttgart: Kohlhammer. 1970ff.

Brown, F. - Driver, S.R. - Briggs, C.A. - Gesenius, W., *The New Hebrew and English Lexicon*. Peabody, Mass.: Hendrickson. 1979.

Davidson, B., *The Analytical Hebrew and Chaldee Lexicon*. London. 1970.

Denis, A.-M., (ed.), *Concordance Grecque des Pseudépigraphes d'Ancien Testament*. Louvain-la-Neuve: Université Catholique de Louvain (Institut Orientaliste). 1987.

Fitzmyer, J.A., *The Dead Sea Scrolls: Major Publications and Tools for Study*. SBLSBS 8. Missoula: Scholars. 1975.

Hatch, E. - Redpath, H.A., *A Concordance to the Septuagint and other Greek Versions to the Old Testament (Including the Apocryphal Books)*. 2 vols. Oxford: Clarendon. 1897. (= Grand Rapids: Baker 1987).

Kittel, G. - Fiedrich, G. (hrsg.), *Theologisches Wörterbuch zum Neuen Testament*. 10 vols. Stuttgart: Kohlhammer. 1933-1979.

Kuhn, K.G., (hrsg.) *Konkordanz zu den Qumrantexten*. Göttingen: Vandenhoeck & Ruprecht. 1960.

Koehler, L. - Baumgartner, W., *Hebräisches und Aramäisches Lexicon zum Alten Testament*. Dritte Auflage. 2. vols. Leiden: Brill. 1967/1974.

Koehler, L. - Baumgartner, W., *The Hebrew and Aramaic Lexicon of the Old Testament I-II*. Rev. by W. Baumgartner and J.J. Stamm. Leiden: Brill. 1994/1995.

Liddell, H.G. - Scott R., *A Greek-English Lexicon*. Revised and Augmented throughout by H.S. Jones. With a Supplement. New (ninth) edition. Reprinted. Oxford. 1973.

Metzger, B.M., *A Textual commentary on the Greek New Testament*. London/New York: United Bible Societies. 1975.

Reicke, B. - Rost. L. (hrsg.), *Biblisch-historisches Handwörterbuch*. 4 vols. Göttingen: Vandenhoeck & Ruprecht. 1962-1979.

Roth, C. - Wigoder, G. (eds. in chief), *Encyclopaedia Judaica* 1-16. Jerusalem: Keter. 1971-.

Stemberger, G., *Der Talmud. Einführung - Texte - Erläuterungen*. München: Beck. 1982.

Strack, H.L. - Billerbeck, P., *Kommentar zum Neuen Testament aus Talmud und Midrasch*. 1-6. München: Beck. ^{6}1986.

3. General bibliography

Albright, W.F. - Mann, C.S., *Matthew. Introduction, translation, and notes.* AncB 26. New York: Doubleday. 1987.
Alexander, P., 3 (Hebrew Apocalypse of) Enoch. A New Translation and Introduction. *OTP I.* 223-315. 1983.
- Enoch, Third Book of. *ABD 2* (1992) 522-526.
Allegro, J.M., Fragments of a Qumran Scroll of Eschatological Midrash. *JBL* 77 (1958) 350-354.
Allen, L.C., Psalm 45:7-8 (6-7) in Old and New Testament Settings. - *Christ the Lord.* 220-242. FS D. Guthrie. Ed. H.H. Rowden. Downers Grove, IL: Inter-Varsity Press. 1982.
Althaus, P., *Der Brief an die Römer.* NTD 6. Göttingen. 1932.
Andersen, F.I., 2 (Slavonic Apocalypse of) Enoch. A New Translation and Introduction. - *OTP I.* 91-221. 1983.
Anderson, H., The Jewish Antecedents of the Christology in Hebrews. - *The Messiah. Developments in Earliest Judaism and Christianity.* The First Princeton Symposium on Judaism and Christian Origins. 512-535. Ed. J.H. Charlesworth, J. Brownson, M.T. Davis, S.J. Kraftchick, and A.F. Segal. Minneapolis: Fortress. 1992.
Attridge, H.W., *The Epistle to the Hebrews.* Hermeneia. Philadelphia: Fortress. 1989.
Aune, D., *Revelation 1-5.* WBC 52a. Dallas: Word. 1997.
- *Revelation 6-16.* WBC 52b. Nashville: Nelson. 1998.
Bakhtin, M., *Problems of Dostoevsky's Poetics.* Theory and History of Literature 8. Manchester: Manchester University Press. 1984.
Balz, H.R., *Methodische Probleme der neutestamentlichen Christologie.* WMANT 8. Neukirchen-Vluyn: Neukirchener. 1967.
Bandstra, A.J., Did the Colossian Errorists Need a Mediator? - *New Dimensions in New Testament Study.* 329-343. Ed. R.N. Longenecker and M.C. Tenney. Grand Rapids: Zondervan. 1974
Barr, J., *The Semantics of Biblical Language.* Oxford: Oxford University Press. 1967.
Barrett, C.K., *A Commentary on the Epistle to the Romans.* BNTC. 2d ed. London: Black. 1967.
- *A Commentary on the First Epistle to the Corinthians.* Second Edition. Black. London: Black. 1971.
- Luke-Acts. - *It is Written: Scripture Citing Scripture. Essays in Honor of Barnabas Lindars.* 231-244. Ed. D.A. Carson and H.G.M. Williamson. Cambridge: Cambridge University Press. 1988.
Barthes, R., From Work to Text. - *Textual Strategies. Perspectives in Post-Structuralist Criticism.* 73-81. Ed. J.V. Harari. Ithaca, New York: Cornell University Press. 1979.
Bartsch, H-W., Zur vorpaulinischen Bekenntnisformel im Eingang des Römerbriefes. *ThZ 23* (1967) 329-339.
Bauckham, R., The worship of Jesus in apocalyptic Christianity. *NTS* 27 (1981) 322-341.
Beasley-Murray, P., 'Romans 1:3f: An Early Confession of Faith in the Lordship of Jesus', *Tyndale Bulletin* 31 (1980) 147-154.
Becker, J(oachim)., *Messianic Expectation in the Old Testament.* Edinburgh: Clark. 1980.

Becker, J(ürgen).. *Untersuchungen zur Entstehungsgeschichte der Testamente der zwölf Patriarchen.* AGAJU 8. Leiden: Brill. 1970.
- *Auferstehung der Toten im Urchristentum.* SBS 82. Stuttgart: Katholisches Bibelwerk. 1976.
Beker, J. Chr., *Paul the Apostle. The Triumph of God in Life and Thought.* Philadelphia: Fortress. 1980.
Benveniste. E., *Problems in General Linguistics.* Miami Linguistics Series 8. Coral Gables: University of Miami Press. 1971.
Berger, K.. *Exegese und Philosophie.* SBS 123/124. Stuttgart: Katholisches Bibelwerk. 1986.
Berger, P.L. and Luckmann, Th., *The Social Construction of Reality. A Treatise in the Sociology of Knowledge.* London: Penguin. 1971.
Betz, O.. 'Die Frage nach dem messianischen Bewusstsein Jesu', *NT VI* (1963) 20–48.
- *Was wissen wir von Jesus.* Stuttgart: Kreuz-Verlag. 1967.
Black, M., *Models and Metaphors. Studies in Language and Philosophy.* Ithaca: Cornell University Press. 1962.
- More about Metaphor. - *Metaphor and Thought.* 19-43. Ed. A Ortony. Cambridge: Cambridge University Press. 1979.
Blank, J., *Paulus und Jesus. Eine theologische Grundlegung.* StANT XVIII. München: Kösel. 1968.
Blomberg, C.L., *Matthew.* NAC 22. Nashville: Broadman. 1992.
Bloom, H.. *The Anxiety of Influence. A Theory of Poetry.* London and Oxford and New York: Oxford University Press. 1975.
- *A Map of Misreading.* Oxford and New York and Toronto and Melbourne: Oxford University Press. 1980.
Bock, D.L., *Proclamation from Prophecy and Pattern. Lukan Old Testament Christology.* JSNTS 12. Sheffield: JSOT. 1987.
- The Use of the Old Testament in Luke-Acts: Christology and Mission. *SBLSP* (1990) 494-511. Ed. D.J. Lull. Atlanta, GA: Scholars.
- *Blasphemy and Exaltation in Judaism and the Final Examination of Jesus. A Philological-Historical Study of the Key Jewish Themes Impacting Mark 14:61-64.* WUNT 2. Reihe 106. Tübingen: Mohr (Siebeck). 1998.
Boismard, M-E., 'Constitué fils de Dieu (Rom.,I, 4)', *RB* 60 (1953) 5-17.
Bornkamm, G., The Heresy of Colossians. - *Conflict at Colossae. A Problem in the Interpretation of Early Christianity Illustrated by Selected Modern Studies.* 123-146. Rev. Ed., Ed. F.O. Francis and W.A. Meeks. SBS 4. Missoula: Scholars. 1975.
Bousset, W., *Kyrios Christos.* 3d ed. Göttingen: Vandenhoeck & Ruprecht. 1926.
Bowker, J.W., "Merkabah" Visions and the Visions of Paul. *JSS 16* (1971) 157-173.
Brettler, M.Z., *God is King. Understanding an Israelite Metaphor.* JSOTS 76. Sheffield: Sheffield Adacemic Press. 1989.
Brooke, G.J., Melchizedek (11QMelch). *ABD IV* (1992) 697-688.
Bruce, F.F., *The Epistle to the Hebrews.* NICNT. Grand Rapids: Eerdmans. 1964.
- Eschatology in Acts. - *Eschatology and the New Testament. Essays in Honor of George Raymond Beasley-Murray.* 51-63. Ed. W.H. Gloer. Peabody: Henrickson. 1988.
Brueggemann, W., *Theology of the Old Testament. Testimony, Dispute, Advocacy.* Minneapolis: Fortress Press. 1997.

Buchanan, G.W., *To the Hebrews. A New Translation with Introduction and Commentary.* AncB 36. New York: Doubleday. 1972.
Bultmann, R., Neueste Paulusforschung. *ThR* 8 (1936) 1-22.
– *Theologie des Neuen Testaments.* 8th ed. [1st ed. 1953]. UTB 630. Augsburg: Mohr. 1980.
– *Theology of the New Testament.* Volume One. London: SCM. 1983.
Burger, C., *Jesus als Davidssohn: eine traditionsgeschichtliche Untersuchung.* FRLANT 98. Göttingen: Vandenhoeck & Ruprecht. 1970.
Capes, D.B., *Old Testament Yahweh Texts in Paul's Christology.* WUNT 2. Reihe 47. Tübingen: Mohr (Siebeck).1992.
Carr, W., *Angels and Principalities. The background, meaning and development of the Pauline phrase hai archai kai hai exousiai.* Cambridge: Cambridge University Press. 1981.
Carrell, P.R., *Jesus and the angels. Angelology and the christology of the Apocalypse of John.* SNTS.M. 95. Cambridge: Cambridge University Press. 1997.
Carroll, J.T., The Uses of Scripture in Acts. *SBLSP* (1990) 512-528. Ed. D.J. Lull. Atlanta, GA: Scholars.
Casey, P.M. *From Jewish Prophet to Gentile God. The Origins and Development of New Testament Christology.* Worcester: Clarke/ Westminster/John Knox. 1991.
Charlesworth, J.H., From Jewish Messianology to Christian Christology. Some Caveats and Perspectives. – *Judaisms and Their Messiahs at the Turn of the Christian Era.* 225-264. Ed. J. Neusner, W.S. Green, E.S. Frerichs. Cambridge: Cambridge University Press. 1987.
– From Messianology to Christology: Problems and Prospects. – *The Messiah. Developments in Earliest Judaism and Christianity.* The First Princeton Symposium on Judaism and Christian Origins. 3-35. Ed. J.H. Charlesworth, J. Brownson, M.T. Davis, S.J. Kraftchick, and A.F. Segal. Minneapolis: Fortress. 1992.
Chatman, S., *Story and Discourse. Narrative Structure in Fiction and Film.* Ithaca and London: Cornell University Press. 1978.
Chester, A., Jewish Messianic Expectations and Mediatorial Figures and Pauline Christology. – *Paulus und das antike Judentum. Tübingen-Durham Symposium im Gedanken an den 50. Todestag Adolf Schlatters (19. Mai 1938).* 17-90. Hrsg. Hengel, M., Heckel, U. WUNT 58. Tübingen: Mohr (Siebeck).
Cockerhill, G.L., Cerinthus. *ABD I* (1992) 885
Cohn, D., *The Distinction of Fiction.* Baltimore and London: John Hopkins University Press. 1999.
Collins, J.J., – Sibylline Oracles. A New Translation and Introduction. – *OTP I.* 318-472. 1983.
– Apocalyptic literature. – *Early Judaism and its Modern Interpreters.* 345-370. Ed. R.A. Kraft and G.W.E. Nickelsburg. The Bible and Its Modern Interpreters 2. Atlanta: Scholars Press. 1986.
– Was the Dead Sea Sect an Apocalyptic Movement? – *Archaeology and History in the Dead Sea Scrolls.* The New York University Conference in Memory of Yigael Yadin. Ed. L. Schiffman. Worcester. JSOT/ASOR Monograph Series 2. / JSPS 8. 25-51. 1990.
– *Apocalyptic Imagination.* An Introduction to the Jewish Matrix of Christianity. New York: Crossroad. 1992.

- Dead Sea Scrolls. *ABD II* (1992) 85-101.
- Early Jewish Apocalypticism. *ABD I* (1992) 282-288.
- The Son of Man in First-Century Judaism. *NTS 38* (1992) 448-466.
- *Daniel: A Commentary of the Book of Daniel.* Hermeneia. Minneapolis: Fortress. 1993.
- *The Scepter and the Star: The Messiahs of the Dead Sea Scrolls and Other Ancient Literature.* The Anchor Bible Reference Library. New York: Doubleday. 1995.
- A Throne in the Heavens: Apotheosis in pre-Christian Judaism. – *Death, Ecstasy, and Other Worldly Journeys.* 43-58. Eds. J.J. Collins, M. Fishbane. New York: State University of New York Press. 1995.
- *Seers, Sybils and Sages in Hellenistic-Roman Judaism.* JSJ supplements 54. Leiden: Brill. 1997.
- Reinventing Exodus: Exegesis and Legend in Hellenistic Egypt. – *For a Later Generation. The Transformation of Tradition in Israel, Early Judaism, and Early Christianity.* 52-62. FS G. Nickelsburg. Ed. R.A. Argall, B.A. Bow, R.A. Werline. Harrisburg: Trinity. 2000.

Colpe, C., *Die religionsgeschichtliche Schule. Darstellung und Kritik ihres Bildes vom gnostischen Erlösermyhus.* FRLANT 78. Göttingen: Vandenhoeck & Ruprecht. 1961.

Conzelmann, H., *1 Corinthians. A Commentary on the First Epistle to the Corinthians.* Hermeneia. Philadelphia: Fortress. 1975.

Cooke, G., *The Book of Ezekiel.* ICC. Edinburgh: Clark. 1936.
- The Israelite King as Son of God, *ZAW* 73 (1961) 202-225.

Craigie, P.C., *Psalms 1-50.* WBC 19. Waco: Word Books. 1983.

Cranfield, C.E.B., *The Epistle to the Romans.* Volume I. (With corrections.) ICC. Edinburgh. 1982.

Cross, F.M., *The Ancient Library of Qumran.* 3rd Edition. The Biblical Seminar 30. Sheffield: Sheffield Academic Press. 1995.

Culler, J., *The Pursuit of Signs. Semiotics, Literature, Deconstruction.* Ithaca, New York: Cornell University Press. 1981.

Cullmann, O., *Die ersten christlichen Glaubensbekenntnisse.* Theologische Studien 15. Zürich: Zollikon. Zweite Auflage. 1949.
- *Die Christologie des Neuen Testaments.* 2. Auflage. Tübingen: Mohr (Siebeck). 1958.

Dahood, M., *Psalms I. 1-50. A New Translation with Introduction and Commentary.* AncB 16. New York: Doubleday. 1986.
- *Psalms II. 51-100. A New Translation with Introduction and Commentary.* AncB 17. New York: Doubleday. 1986.

Dahl, N.A., Die Messianität Jesu bei Paulus. – *Studia Paulina in honorem J. de Zwaan Septuagenarii.* Haarlem. 1953.

Davies, W.D., Paul and the Dead Sea Scrolls: Flesh and Spirit. – *The Scrolls and the New Testament.* 157-182. Ed. K. Stendahl and J.H. Charlesworth. Christian Origins Library. New York: Crossroads. 1992.

Davis, P.G., Divine Agents, Mediators, and New Testament Christology. *JTS 45* (1994) 479-503.

Dean-Otting, M., *Heavenly Journeys. A Study of the Motif in Hellenistic Jewish Literature.* Judentum und Umwelt 8. Frankfurt am Main: Peter Lang. 1984.

Delcor, M., Melchizedek from Genesis to the Qumran texts and the Epistle to the Hebrews. *JSJ 2* (1971) 115-135.

Dibelius, M., The Isis Initiation in Apuleius and Related Initiatory Rites. – *Conflict at Colossae. A Problem in the Interpretation of Early Christianity Illustrated by Selected Modern Studies.* 61-122. Revised Edition. Ed. F.O. Francis and W.A. Meeks. SBS 4. Missoula: Scholars. 1975.
Donahue, J.R., Recent Studies on the Origin of "Son of Man" in the Gospels. *CBQ 48* (1986) 484-498.
Duling, D.C., 'The Promises to David and Their Entrance into Christianity – Nailing Down a Likely Hypothesis'. *NTS 19* (1973) 73-77.
Dumbrell, W.J., *Covenant and Creation. An Old Testament Covenantal Theology.* Exeter: Paternoster. 1984.
Dunn, J.D.G., *Christology in the Making. A New Testament Inquiry Into the Origins of the Doctrine of the Incarnation.* Philadelphia: Westminster. 1980.
– *Unity and Diversity in the New Testament. An Inquiry into the Character of Earliest Christianity.* Trowbridge: SCM. 1977.
– *Unity and Diversity in the New Testament. An Inquiry into the Character of Earliest Christianity.* Second Edition. London: SCM. 1990.
– *Romans 1–8, 9–16.* Word Biblical Commentary 38a, 38b. Dallas: Word Books. 1988.
– *Jesus, Paul, and the Law.* Studies in Mark and Galatians. Louisville, Kentucky: Westminster/ John Knox Press. 1990.
– *The Partings of the Ways. Between Christianity and Judaism and their Significance for the Character of Christianity.* London: SCM / Philadelphia: TPI. 1991.
– *The Epistles to the Colossians and to Philemon. A Commentary on the Greek Text.* NIGTC. Grand Rapids: Eerdmans. 1996.
Eagleton, T., *Literary Theory. An Introduction.* Oxford: Blackwell. 1989.
Eco, U., *A Theory of Semiotics.* Thetford: Indiana University Press. 1976.
Eissfeldt, O., *The Old Testament. An Introduction including the Apocrypha and Pseudepigrapha, and also the works of similar type from Qumran.* ET P.R. Ackroyd. Oxford: Blackwell. 1974.
Eskola, T., *Messias ja Jumalan Poika. Traditiokriittinen tutkimus kristologisesta jaksosta Room. 1:3,4.* [Messiah and Son of God. A Tradition-Critical Study of the Christological Clauses in Romans 1:3,4. English Summary.] SESJ 56. Helsinki: Suomen eksegeettinen seura. 1992.
– Paul, Predestination and "Covenantal Nomism". Re-assessing Paul and Palestinian Judaism. *JSJ 28* (1997) 390-412.
– *Theodicy and Predestination in Pauline Soteriology.* WUNT 2. Reihe 100. Tübingen: Mohr (Siebeck). 1998.
Eslinger, L.M., *Kingship of God in Crisis. A Close Reading of 1 Samuel 1-12.* BiLiSe 10. Sheffield: JSOT Press/Almond. 1985.
Evans, C.A., The Twelve Thrones of Israel. Scripture and Politics in Luke 22:24-30. – *Jesus in Context. Temple, Purity, and Restoration.* 455-479. Eds. B. Chilton, C.A. Evans. AGAJU 39. Leiden/New York/Köln: Brill. 1997.
Fabry, H.-J., *kissê'. TDOT VII* (1995) 232-259.
Fairclough, N., *Discourse and Social Change.* Cambridge: Polity. 1996.
Fee, F.D., *The First Epistle to the Corinthians.* NICNT. Grand Rapids: Eerdmans. 1987.
Filson, F.V., *A Commentary on the Gospel According to St. Matthew.* BNTC. London: Black. 1971.

Fitzmyer, J.A., *Romans. A New Translation with Introduction and Commentary.* AncB 33. New York: Doubleday. 1993.
- *The Semitic Background of the New Testament. Combined Edition of Essays on the Semitic Background of the New Testament and A Wandering Aramena: Collected Aramaic Essays.* The Biblical Resource Series. Grand Rapids: Eerdmans. 1997.
Fletcher-Louis, C.H.T., *Luke-Acts: Angels, Christology and Soteriology* WUNT 2. Reihe 94. Tübingen: Mohr (Siebeck). 1997.
Flusser, D., The Dead Sea Sect and Pre-Pauline Christianity. – *Judaism and the Origins of Christianity.* 23-74. Jerusalem: Magnes Press. 1988.
- Melchizedek and the Son of Man. – *Judaism and the Origins of Christianity.* 186-192. Jerusalem: Magnes Press. 1988.
Fohrer, G., 'υἱός B. Altes Testament', *ThWNT* VIII (1969) 340-354.
Ford, J.M., *Revelation. Introduction, Translation and Commentary.* AncB 38. New York: Doubleday. 1975.
Fossum, J.E., *The Name of God and the Angel of the Lord. Samaritan and Jewish Concepts of Intermediation and the Origin of Gnosticism.* WUNT 36. Tübingen: Mohr (Siebeck). 1985.
- Introduction: The New Testament and Early Jewish Mysticism. – *The Image of the Invisible God. Essays on the influence of Jewish Mysticism on Early Christology.* 1-11. NTOA 30. Göttingen: Vandenhoeck & Ruprecht. 1995.
Foucault, M., *The Archaeology of Knowledge.* London: Routledge. 1995.
France, R.T., The Worship of Jesus: A Neglected Factor in Christological Debate? – *Christ the Lord.* 17–36. FS D. Guthrie, ed. H.H. Rowdon. Leicester: Inter-Varsity. 1982.
Francis, F.O., Humility and Angelic Worship in Col 2:18. – *Conflict at Colossae. A Problem in the Interpretation of Early Christianity Illustrated by Selected Modern Studies.* 163–195. Revised Edition. Ed. F.O. Francis and W.A. Meeks. SBS 4. Missoula: Scholars. 1975.
Frankemölle, H., *Glaubensbekenntnisse. Zur neutestamentlichen Begründung unseres Credos.* Düsseldorf: Patmos. 1974.
- Auferweckung Jesu – (nur) ein Zeichen apokalyptischer Endzeit? Ein Zwischenruf. – *Von Jesus zum Christus. Christologische Studien.* 45-69. FS P. Hoffmann. Hrsg. R. Hoppe und U. Busse. Berlin/ New York: W. de Gruyter. 1998.
Freundlieb, D., Foucault and the Study of Literature. *Poetics Today 16* (1995) 301-344.
Froitzheim, F., *Christologie und Eschatologie bei Paulus.* FzB 35. Würzburg: Echter. 1982.
Fuller, R.H., *The Foundations of New Testament Christology.* London: Lutterworth. 1965.
Furnish, V.P., *II Corinthians. Translated with Introduction, Notes, and Commentary.* AncB 32A. New York: Doubleday. 1984.
Garnet, P., *Salvation and Atonement in the Qumran Scrolls.* WUNT 2. Reiche 3. Tübingen: Mohr (Siebeck). 1977.
- Qumran Light on Pauline Soteriology. – *Pauline Studies.* FS F.F. Bruce. 19-32. Eds. D.A. Hagner, M.J. Harris. Exeter: Paternoster/ Eerdmans. 1980.
Gärtner, B., *The Temple and the Community in Qumran and the New Testament. A Comparative Study in the Temple Symbolism of the Qumran texts and the New Testament.* SNTS.MS. 1. Cambridge: Cambridge University Press. 1965.
Gaylord, H.E. Jr., 3 (Greek Apocalypse of) Baruch. A New Translation and Introduction. – *OTP I.* 653-679. 1983.

Genette, G., *Palimpsestes. La littérature au second degré.* Paris: Èditions du Seuil. 1982.
Gese, H., *Zur biblischen Theologie.* Tübingen: Mohr (Siebeck). 1989.
Georgi, D., *The Opponents of Paul in Second Corinthians.* Philadelphia: Fortress. 1986.
Gieschen, C.A., *Angelomorphic Christology. Antecedents and Early Evidence.* AGAJU 42. Leiden, Boston, Köln: Brill. 1998.
Gnilka, J., *Der Kolosserbrief.* HThK X, 1. Freiburg: Herder. 1980.
- *Das Matthäusevangelium II. Teil. Kommentar zu Kap. 14,1 - 28,20 und Einleitungsfragen.* HThK I, 2. Freiburg: Herder. 1988.
Goranson, S., Ebionites. *ABD II* (1992) 260-261.
Goulder, M., 'The Two Roots of the Christian Myth' - *The Myth of God Incarnate.* 64-86. Ed. J. Hick. London: SCM. 1977.
- *St. Paul versus St. Peter. A Tale of Two Missions.* Louisville: Westminster John Knox. 1995.
Gourgues, M., *A la Droite de Dieu. Résurrection de Jésus et Actualisation du Psaume 110:1 dans le Nouveau Testament.* EtB. Paris: Lecoffre. 1978.
Gray, G.B., *A Critical and Exegetical Commentary on the Book of Isaiah. I-XXVII. Vol I.* ICC. Edinburgh: Clark. 1980.
Grappe, C., Le logion des douze trônes. Exlairages intertestamentaires. - *Le Trône de Dieu.* 204-212. Éd. M. Philonenko. WUNT 69. Tübingen: Mohr (Siebeck). 1993.
Grässer, E., *An die Hebräer (Hebr 1-6).* EKK XVII/1. Zürich: Benziger/ Neukirchen Vluyn: Neukirchener. 1990.
Green, W.S., Introduction: Messiah in Judaism: Rethinking the Question. - *Judaisms and Their Messiahs at the Turn of the Christian Era.* 1-13. Ed. J. Neusner, W.S. Green, E.S. Frerichs. Cambridge: Cambridge University Press. 1987.
Greenberg, M., *Ezekiel 1-20. A New Translation with Introduction and Commentary.* AncB 22. New York: Doubleday. 1986.
Greimas, A.J., Narrative Grammar: Units and Levels. *Modern Language Notes* 86 (1971) 793-806.
- *Structural Semantics. An Attempt at a Method.* Lincoln and London: University of Nebraska Press. 1983.
Gruenwald, I., *Apocalyptic and Merkavah Mysticism.* AGAJU 14. Leiden / Köln: Brill. 1980.
Gunther, J.J., *St. Paul's opponents and their background. A study of Apocalyptic and Jewish sectarian teaching.* NTsuppl. 35. Leiden: Brill. 1973.
Haacker, K., Exegetische Probleme des Römerbriefs. *NT 20* (1978) 1-21.
Haenchen, E., *The Acts of the Apostles. A Commentary.* Philadelphia: Westminster. 1971.
Hagner, D.A., *Hebrews.* NIBC 14. Peabody: Hendrickson. 1990.
- *Matthew 14-28.* WBC 33b. Dallas: Word Books. 1995.
Hahn, F., *Christologische Hoheitstitel. Ihre Geschichte im frühen Christentum.* FRLANT 83. Göttingen: Vandenhoeck & Ruprecht. 1963.
Hall, R., The *Ascension of Isaiah:* Community Situation, Date, and Place in Early Christianity. *JBL 109* (1990) 289-306.
- Isaiah's Ascent to See the Beloved: An Ancient Jewish Source for the *Ascension of Isaiah? JBL 113* (1994) 463-484.
Hall, S., The West and the Rest: Discourse and Power. - *Formations of Modernity.* 275-320. Ed. by S. Hall and B. Gieben. Oxford: Blackwell. 1992.

Halperin, D.J., *The Faces of the Chariot. Early Jewish Responses to Ezekiel's Vision.* TSAJ 16. Tübingen: Mohr (Siebeck). 1988.
Hanson, P.D., *The Dawn of Apocalyptic. The Historical and Sociological Roots of Jewish Apocalyptic Eschatology.* Revised Edition. Philadelphia: Fortress. 1979.
Harris, R., *Reading Saussure. A critical commentary on the Cours de linguistique générale.* London: Duckworth. 1987.
- Language as Social Interaction: Integrationalism versus Segregationalism. – *The Foundations of Linguistic Theory. Selected Writings of Roy Harris.* 197-209. Ed. by N. Love. London & New York: Routledge. 1990.
Hartman, L., *Asking for a Meaning. A Study of 1 Enoch 1-5.* CB.NT 12. Lund: Gleerup. 1979.
Hasel, G., *Old Testament Theology: Basic Issues in the Current Debate.* Revised and Expanded Fourth Edition. Grand Rapids: Eerdmans. 1991.
Hawkes, T., *Structuralism and Semiotics.* Berkeley and Los Angeles: University of California Press. 1977.
Hay, D.M., *Glory at the Right Hand. Psalm 110 in Early Christianity.* SBL.MS 18. Nashville/New York: Abingdon. 1973.
Hayes, J.H., 'The Resurrection As Enthronement and the Earliest Church Christology', *Interp.* XXII (1968) 333-345.
Hays, R.B., *The Faith of Jesus Christ. An Investigation of the Narrative Substructure of Galatians 3:1-4:11.* SBL.DS 56. Chico, CA: Scholars. 1983.
Hegermann, H., Christologie im Hebräerbrief. – *Anfänge der Christologie.* FS F. Hahn. 337-351. Hrsg. Breytenbach und Paulsen. Göttingen: Vandenhoeck & Ruprecht. 1991.
Heitmüller, D., Zum Problem Paulus und Jesus. *ZNW* 13 (1912) 320-337.
Hengel, M., Christologie und neutestamentliche Chronologie. – *Neues Testament und Geschichte: historisches Geschehen und Deutung im Neuen Testament.* 43-67. FS. O. Cullmann. Hrsg. H. Baltensweiler, B. Reicke. Zürich: Theologischer Verlag. 1972.
- *Der Sohn Gottes. Die Entstehung der Christologie und die jüdisch-hellenistische Religionsgeschichte.* Tübingen: Mohr. 1975.
- The Son of God. – Hengel, M. *The Cross of the Son of God.* 1-90. London: SCM. 1976.
- Qumran und der Hellenismus. – *Qumrân. Sa piété, sa théologie et son milieu.* Ed. M. Delcor. BEThL XLVI. Paris-Gembloux: Duculot/ Leuven University Press. 1978.
- *Zur urchristlichen Geschichtsschreibung.* Stuttgart: Calwer. 1979.
- *Judentum und Hellenismus.* 3., durchgesehene Auflage. WUNT 10. Tübingen: Mohr (Siebeck). 1988.
- Psalm 110 und die Erhöhung des Auferstandenen zur rechten Gottes. – *Anfänge der Christologie.* FS F. Hahn. Hrsg. Breytenbach und Paulsen. 43-73. Göttingen: Vandenhoeck & Ruprecht. 1991.
- Der vorchristliche Paulus. – *Paulus und das antike Judentum.* Hrsg. M. Hengel, U. Heckel. Tübingen-Durham-Symposium im Gedenken an den 50. Todestag Adolf Schlatters (19. Mai 1938). Tübingen: Mohr (Siebeck). 177-293. 1991.
- 'Sit at My Right Hand!' The Enthronement of Christ at the Right Hand of God and Psalm 110:1. – Hengel, M., *Studies in Early Christology.* 119-225. Edinburgh: Clark. 1995.
- Christological Titles in Early Christianity. – Hengel, M., *Studies in Early Christolc* 359-389. Edinburgh: Clark. 1995.

Hengel, M. – Schwemer, A.M. (hrsg.), *Königsherrschaft Gottes und himmlischer Kult im Judentum, Urchristentum und in der hellenistischen Welt*. WUNT 55. Tübingen: Mohr (Siebeck). 1991.

Hengel, M. – Schwemer, A.M., *Paulus zwischen Damaskus und Antiochien*. WUNT 108. Tübingen: Mohr (Siebeck). 1998.

Hill, D., *Greek Words and Hebrew Meanings. Studies in the Semantics of Soteriological Terms*. SNTS.MS. 5. Cambridge: Cambridge University Press. 1967.

Himmelfarb, M., *Ascent to Heaven in Jewish and Christian Apocalypses*. New York: Oxford University Press. 1993.

– The Practice of Ascent in the Ancient Mediterranean World. – *Death, Ecstasy, and Other Worldly Journeys*. 123-137. Eds. J.J. Collins, M. Fishbane. New York: State University of New York Press. 1995.

Hirsch, E.D., *Validity in Interpretation*. New Haven and London: Yale University Press. 1973.

Hofius, O., *Der Vorhang vor den Thron Gottes*. WUNT 14. Tübingen: Mohr (Siebeck). 1972.

– *Der Christushymnus Philipper 2,6-11. Untersuchungen zu Gestalt und Aussage eines urchristlichen Psalms*. WUNT 17. Tübingen: Mohr (Siebeck). 1976.

– *Paulusstudien*. WUNT 51. Tübingen: Mohr (Siebeck). 1989.

Holladay, C.R., *Fragments from Hellenistic Jewish Authors. Volume II: Poets. The Epic Poets Theodotus and Philo and Ezekiel the Tragedian*. SBL. Texts and Translations 30. Pseudepigrapha Series 12. Atlanta: Scholars Press. 1989.

Hollander, H.W. – de Jonge, M., *The Testaments of the Twelve Patriarchs. A Commentary*. SVTP 8. Leiden: Brill. 1985.

Holleman, J., *Resurrection and Parousia. A Traditio-Historical Study of Paul's Eschatology in 1 Corinthians 15*. NTsuppl. 84. Leiden: Brill. 1996.

Holtz, T., *Untersuchungen über die alttestamentliche Zitate bei Lukas*. TU 104. Berlin: Akademie Verlag. 1968.

Hooke, S.H., The Translation of Romans I. 4. *NTS* 9 (1963) 370-371.

Hooker, M.D., Were there False Teachers in Colossae? – *Christ and Spirit in the New Testament. Studies in honour of Charles Francis Digby Moule*. 315-331. Ed. B. Lindars and S.S. Smalley. Cambridge: Cambridge University Press. 1973.

Horst, P.W. van den, Moses' Throne Vision in Ezekiel the Dramatist. – *Essays of the Jewish world of Early Christianity*. 63-71. NTOA 14. Freiburg Schweiz/Göttingen: Vandenhoeck & Ruprecht. 1990.

Hunter, A.M., *Paul and his Predecessors*. London. 1961.

Hurst, L.D., *The Epistle to the Hebrews. Its background of thought*. SNTSMS 65. Cambridge: Cambridge University Press. 1990.

Hurtado, L.W., New Testament Christology: A Critique of Bousset's Influence. *TS* 40 (1979) 306-317.

– *One God, one Lord: early Christian devotion and ancient Jewish monotheism*. London: SCM. 1988.

Häkkinen, S., *Köyhät kerettiläiset. Ebionit kirkkoisien teksteissä*. STKSJ 223. Helsinki: Suomalainen teologinen kirjallisuusseura. 1999.

Iersel, B.M.F. van, *'Der Sohn' in den synoptischen Jesusworten*. NT.S. vol. III. Leiden: Brill. 1961.

Isaac, E., 1 (Ethiopic Apocalypse of) Enoch. A New Translation and Introduction. – *OTP I*. 5-89. 1983.
Isaacs, M.E., *Sacred Space. An Approach to the Theology of the Epistle to the Hebrews*. JSNTS 73. Sheffield: JSOT Press. 1992.
– Hebrews. – *Early Christian thought in its Jewish Context*. 145-159. FS M. Hooker. Ed. J. Barclay and J. Sweet. Cambridge: Cambridge University Press. 1996.
Jacobson, H., Mysticism and Apocalyptic in Ezekiel's Exagoge. [Illinois Classical Studies] *ICS* 6 (1981) 272-293.
– *The Exagoge of Ezekiel*. Cambridge: Cambridge University Press. 1983.
Jakobson, R., Sign and System of Language. A Reassessment of Saussure's Doctrine. – *Verbal Art, Verbal Sign, Verbal Time*. 28-33. Ed. K. Pomorska and S. Rudy. Oxford: Blackwell. 1985.
– Two Aspects of Language and Two Types of Aphasic Disturbances. – *Language in Literature*. 95-114. Ed. K. Pomorska and S. Rudy. Cambridge, Mass. and London: Harvard University Press. 1987.
Janowski, B., *Sühne als Heilsgeschehen: Studien zur Sühnetheologie der Priesterschrift und zur Wurzel KPR im Alten Orient und im Alten Testament*. WMANT 55. Neukirchen-Vluyn: Neukirchener. 1982.
Jenny, L., The Strategy of Form. – *French Literary Theory Today. A Reader*. Ed. T. Todorov. 34-63. Cambridge: Cambridge University Press/ Paris: Maison des Sciences de l'Homme. 1982.
Jewett, R., 'The Redaction and Use of an Early Christian Confession in Romans 1:3–4'. – *The Living Text*. 99–122. FS E.W. Saunders. Ed. D.E. Groh and R. Jewett. Lanham/New York: University Press of America. 1985.
Jonge, M. de., *Christology in Context. The Earliest Christian Response to Jesus*. Philadelphia: Westminster. 1988.
– Jesus, Son of David and Son of God. – *Jewish Eschatology, Early Christian Christology and the Testaments of the Twelve Patriarchs*. Collected Essays of M. de Jonge. 135-144. Ed. H. de Jonge. NT.S. LXIII. Leiden: Brill. 1991.
Jonge, M. de. – Woude, A.S. van der, 11QMelchizedek and the New Testament. *NTS* 12 (1965-66) 301-326.
Juel, D., Social Dimensions of Exegesis: The Use of Psalm 16 in Acts 2. *CBQ* 43 (1981) 543-556.
Karrer, M., *Jesus Christus im Neuen Testament*. GNT 11. Göttingen: Vandenhoeck & Ruprecht. 1998.
Käsemann, E., *Das wandernde Gottesvolk. Eine Untersuchung zum Hebräerbrief*. Göttingen: Vandenhoeck & Ruprecht. 1939.
– Begründet der neutestamentliche Kanon die Einheit der Kirche? – *Exegetische Versuche und Besinnungen I*. 214–223. Göttingen: Vandenhoeck & Ruprecht. 1960.
– Die Anfänge christlicher Theologie – *Exegetische Versuche und Besinnungen II*. 82–104. Göttingen: Vandenhoeck & Ruprecht. 1964.
– *An die Römer*. HNT 8a. Tübingen: Mohr (Siebeck). 1973.
Keck, L.E., Toward the Renewal of New Testament Christology. *NTS* 32 (1986) 362–377.
Kee, H.C., Testaments of the Twelve Patriarchs. A New Translation and Introduction. *OTP I* (1983) 775-828.

Kegel, G., *Auferstehung Jesu - Auferstehung der Toten. Eine traditionsgeschichtliche Untersuchung zum Neuen Testament.* Gütersloh: Mohn. 1970.
Kelly, J.N.D., *Early Christian Doctrines.* Revised Edition. San Francisco: Harper & Row. 1978.
- *Early Christian Creeds.* Third Edition. New York: Longman. 1991.
Kim, S., *"The 'Son of Man'" as the Son of God.* WUNT 30. Tübingen: Mohr (Siebeck). 1983.
Klijn, A.F.J. - Reinink, G.J., *Patristic Evidence for Jewish-Christian Sects.* NT.S. 36. Leiden: Brill. 1973.
Klinzing, G., *Die Umdeutung des Kultus in der Qumrangemeinde und im Neuen Testament.* SUNT 7. Göttingen: Vandenhoeck & Ruprecht. 1971.
Knibb, M.A., Martyrdom and Ascension of Isaiah. A New Translation and Introduction. - *OTP II.* 143-176. 1985.
Knox, J., *The Epistle to the Romans.* IntB IX. New York/Nashville: Abingdon-Cokesbury. 1954.
Kobelski, P.J., *Melchizedek and Melchiresha^c.* CBQ. Monographic series 10. Washington: The Catholic Biblical Association of America. 1981.
Koskenniemi, E., *Apollonios von Tyana in der neutestamentlichen Exegese.* WUNT 2. Reihe 61. Tübingen: Mohr (Siebeck). 1994.
Kraft, R.A., The Multiform Jewish Heritage of Early Christianity. - *Christianity, Judaism and Other Greco-Roman Cults.* 175-199. FS M. Smith, ed. J. Neusner. Part III, Judaism before 70. SJLA 12/3. Leiden: Brill. 1975.
Kramer, W., *Christos Kyrios Gottessohn.* AThANT 44. Zürich: Zwingli. 1963.
Kraus, H-J., *Die Königsherrschaft Gottes im Alten Testament. Untersuchungen zu den Liedern von Jahwes Thronbesteigung.* BHTh 13. Tübingen: Mohr (Siebeck). 1951.
- *Psalmen I. 1-59.* BKAT XV/1. Neukirchen-Vluyn: Neukirchener. 1978.
- *Psalmen II. 60-150.* BKAT XV/2. Neukirchen-Vluyn: Neukirchener. 1960.
Kreitzer, L.J., *Jesus and God in Paul's Eschatology.* JSNTS 19. Worcester: Sheffield Academic Press. 1987.
Kristeva, J., *Revolution in Poetic Language.* New York: Columbia University Press. 1984.
Kuss, O., *Der Römerbrief.* Regensburg: Pustet. 1957.
Kümmel, W.G., *The New Testament. The History of the Investigation of its Problems.* London: SCM. 1978.
- *Introduction to the New Testament.* Revised Edition. London: SCM. 1984.
Laato, A., *Who is Immanuel? The Rise and the Foundering of Isaiah's Messianic Expectations.* Diss. Åbo. 1988.
- *History and Ideology in the Old Testament Prophetic Literature. A Semiotic Approach to the Reconstruction of the Proclamation of the Historical Prophets.* CB.OT 41. Stockholm: Almqvist & Wiksell. 1996.
- *A Star is Rising. The Historical Development of the Old Testament Royal Ideology and the Rise of the Jewish Messianic Expectations.* University of South Florida International Studies in Formative Christianity and Judaism 5. Atlanta: Scholars Press. 1997.
Lakoff, G. - Johnson, M., *Metaphors We Live By.* Chigago: University of Chigago Press. 1980.
Lane, W.L., *Hebrews 1-8.* WBC 47a. Dallas: Word. 1991.

– *Hebrews 9-13.* WBC 47b. Dallas: Word. 1991.
Lang, B., Kipper. *TDOT VII* (1995) 288-303.
Langevin, P-É., Une confession prepaulinienne de la "seigneurie" du Christ. – *Le Christ hier, aujourd'hui et demain.* Publié par R. Laflamme, M. Gervais. 277-327. Quebeck. 1976.
– Quel est le "Fils de Dieu" de Romains 1,3-4. *ScEs XXIX/2* (1977) 145-177.
Legrand, L., L'arrière-plan néo-testamentaire de Lc, I, 35. *RB 70* (1963) 161-192.
Lietzmann, H., *An die Römer.* HNT 8a. Dritte Auflage. Tübingen. 1928.
Lightfoot, J.B., The Colossian Heresy. – *Conflict at Colossae. A Problem in the Interpretation of Early Christianity Illustrated by Selected Modern Studies.* 13-60. Revised Edition. Ed. F.O. Francis and W.A. Meeks. SBS 4. Missoula: Scholars. 1975.
Lincoln, A.T., *Paradise now and not yet. Studies in the role of the heavenly dimension in Paul's thought with special reference to his eschatology.* SNTS 43. Cambridge: Cambridge University Press. 1981.
Lindars, B., *Jesus Son of Man. A Fresh Examination of the Son of Man Sayings in the Gospels.* Grand Rapids: Eerdmans; London: SPCK. 1983.
– *The Theology of the Letter to the Hebrews.* New Testament Theology. Cambridge: Cambridge University Press. 1994.
Linnemann, E., Tradition und Interpretation in Röm. 1,3f. *EvT 31* (1971) 264-275.
Loader, W.R.G., Christ at the Right Hand – Ps. CX in the New Testament. *NTS 24* (1978) 199-217.
– *Sohn und Hoherpriester. Eine traditionsgeschichtliche Untersuchung zur Christologie des Hebräerbriefes.* WMANT 53. Neukirchen-Vluyn: Neukirchener. 1981.
Lohse, E., *Colossians and Philemon. A Commentary on the Epistles to the Colossians and to Philemon.* Hermeneia. Philadelphia: Fortress. 1971.
Longenecker, R.N., *The Christology of Early Jewish Christianity.* SBT 2. ser. 17. London: SCM. 1970.
– *Galatians.* WBC 41. Dallas: Word. 1990.
Lunt, H.G., Ladder of Jacob. A New Translation and Introduction. – *OTP II.* 401-411. 1985.
Lührmann, D., Paul and the Pharisaic Tradition. *JSNT 36* (1989) 75-94.
Lyonnet, S., Paul's Adversaries in Colossae. – *Conflict at Colossae. A Problem in the Interpretation of Early Christianity Illustrated by Selected Modern Studies.* 147-162. Revised Edition. Ed. F.O. Francis and W.A. Meeks. SBS 4. Missoula: Scholars. 1975.
Löhr, H., Thronversammlung und preisender Tempel. Beobachtungen am himmlischen Heiligtum im Hebräerbrief und in den Sabbatopferliedern aus Qumran. – *Königsherrschaft Gottes und himmlischer Kult im Judentum, Urchristentum und in der hellenistischen Welt.* 185-205. Hengel, M. und Schwemer, A.M. (hrsg.). WUNT 55. Tubingen: Mohr (Siebeck). 1991.
Lövestam, E., *Son and Saviour. A Study of Acts 13,32-37. With an Appendix: 'Son of God' in the Synoptic Gospels.* CNT XVIII. Lund: Gleerup. 1961.
MacRae, G.W., Heavenly Temple and Eschatology in the Letter to the Hebrews. *Semeia 12* (1978) 179-199.
Marshall, I.H., The Divine Sonship of Jesus. *Interp. XXI* (1967) 87-103.
– The Son of Man in Contemporary Debate. *EQ 42* (1970) 67-87.

- *The Origins of New Testament Christology.* Leicester: Inter-Varsity. 1990.
Martin, R.P., *2 Corinthians.* WBC 40. Waco: Word. 1986.
McNicol, A.J., "The Heavenly Sanctuary in Judaism: A Model for Tracing the Origin of an Apocalypse." *JRS 13* (1987) 66-94.
Meeks, W.A., *The Prophet-King. Moses Traditions and the Johannine Christology.* NT.S. 14. Leiden: Brill. 1967.
- Moses as God and King. - *Religions in Antiquity. Essays in memory of E.R. Goodenough.* 354-371. Ed. J. Neusner. Studies in the History of Religions 14. Leiden: Brill. 1968.
Merklein, H., Die Auferweckung Jesu und die Anfänge der Christologie (Messias bzw. Sohn Gottes und Menschensohn). *ZNW* 72 (1981) 1-26.
Mettinger, T.N.D., *King and Messiah. The Civil and Sacral Legitimation of the Israelite Kings.* CB.OT 8. Stockholm: Almqvist & Wiksell. 1976.
- *The Dethronement of Sabaoth. Studies in the Shem and Kbod Theologies.* ConBOT 18. Stockholm: Almqvist&Wiksell. 1982
Michel, O., *Der Brief an die Römer.* KEK IV. 10. Auflage. Göttingen: Vandenhoeck & Ruprecht. 1955.
- *Der Brief an die Römer.* KEK IV. 12. Auflage. Göttingen: Vandenhoeck & Ruprecht. 1963.
- *Der Brief an die Römer.* KEK IV. 14. Auflage. 5., bearb. Aufl. dieser Auslegung. Göttingen: Vandenhoeck & Ruprecht. 1978.
- *Der Brief an die Hebräer.* KEK XIII. 14. Auflage. Göttingen: Vandenhoeck & Ruprecht. 1984.
Michel, O. - Betz, O., Von Gott gezeugt. - *Judentum Urchristentum Kirche.* Festschrift für Joachim Jeremias, hrsg. W. Eltester. 3-23. Berlin. 1960.
Milik, J.T., *Ten Years of Discovery in the Wilderness of Judaea.* Studies in Biblical Theology. London: SCM. 1959.
- Milkî-ṣedeq et Milkî-reʿšaᶜ dans les anciens écrits juifs et chrétiens. *JJS 23* (1972) 95-144.
- *The Books of Enoch. Aramaic Fragments of Qumrân Cave 4.* With the Collaboration of M. Black. Oxford: Clarendon. 1976.
Minde van der, H.-J., *Schrift und Tradition bei Paulus.* Paderborner Theologische Studien, Band 3. München: Schöningh. 1976.
Montgomery, J.A., *A Critical and Exegetical Commentary on the Book of Daniel.* ICC. Edinburgh: Clark. 1950.
Moo, D.J., *Romans 1-8.* The Wycliffe Exegetical Commentary. Chigago: Moody. 1991.
Morray-Jones, C.R.A., Transformational Mysticism in the Apocalyptic-Merkabah Tradition. *JJS 43* (1992) 1-31.
Moule, C.F.D., *The Origin of Christology.* Cambridge: Cambridge University Press. 1978.
Mounce, R.H., *Matthew.* NIBC 1. Peabody, Mass.: Hendrickson. 1991.
Neufeld, V.H., *The Earliest Christian Confessions.* NTTS 5. Leiden: Brill. 1963.
Newman, C.C., *Paul's Glory-Christology. Tradition and Rhetoric.* NovTsuppl. 69. Leiden: Brill. 1992.
Newsom, C., *Songs of the Sabbath Sacrifice: A Critical Edition.* Harvard Semitic Studies 27. Atlanta: Scholars. 1985.
Nickelsburg, G.W.E., *Resurrection, Immortality, and Eternal Life in Intertestamental Judaism.* HThS XXVI. Cambridge: Harvard University Press. 1972.

- *Jewish Literature Between the Bible and the Mishnah. A Historical and Literary Introduction*. London: SCM. 1981.
- Salvation without and with a Messiah: Developing Beliefs in Writings Ascribed to Enoch.
- *Judaisms and Their Messiahs at the Turn of the Christian Era*. 49-68. Ed. J. Neusner, W.S. Green, E.S. Frerichs. Cambridge: Cambridge University Press. 1987.
- Son of Man. *ABD* VI (1992) 137-150.

Nickelsburg, G.W.E. - Kraft, R.A., Introduction: The Modern Study of Early Judaism. - *Early Judaism and its Modern Interpreters*. 1-30. Ed. Kraft and Nickelsburg. (The Bible and its modern interpreters 2) SBL. Atlanta: Scholars. 1986.

Nickelsburg, G.W.E. - Stone, M.E., *Faith and Piety in Early Judaism. Texts and Documents*. Philadelphia: Trinity Press International. 1991.

Norden, E., *Agnostos theos*. Leipzig. 1913.

Nygren, A., *Romarbrevet*. Tolkning av Nya testamentet VI. Stockholm. 1944.

O'Brien, P.T., *Colossians, Philemon*. WBC 44. Waco: Word. 1982.

Orr, W.R. - Walther J.A., *1 Corinthians. A New Translation. Introduction with a Study of the Life of Paul, Notes, and Commentary*. Anchor Bible 32. New York: Doubleday. 1976.

Osborne, G., Christology and New Testament Hermeneutics: A Survey of the Discussion. *Semeia 30* (1985) 49–62.

Patte, D., *What is Structural Exegesis?* Guides to Biblical Scholarship. Philadelphia: Fortress. 1976.
- *Structural Exegesis for New Testament Critics*. Guides to Biblical Scholarship. Minneapolis: Fortress. 1990.

Pelikan, J., *The Christian Tradition. A History of the Development of Doctrine. 1. The Emergence fo the Catholic Tradition*. Chigago and London: University of Chigago Press. 1971.

Pesch, R., *Römerbrief*. Die Neue Echter Bibel 6. Würzburg: Echter. 1983.

Peterson, E., *Frühkirche, Judentum und Gnosis*. Freiburg. 1959.

Phelan, J., *Narrative as Rhetoric. Technique, Audiences, Ethics, Ideology*. Chelsea: Ohio State University Press. 1996.

Philonenko, M. (ed.), *Le Trône de Dieu*. WUNT 69. Tübingen: Mohr (Siebeck). 1993.

Plöger, O., *Das Buch Daniel*. KAT 18. Gütersloh: Mohn. 1965.

Pokorny, P., *Der Gottessohn*. ThSt(B) 109. Zürich. 1971.
- *Die Entstehung der Christologie*. Stuttgart. 1985.
- *The Genesis of Christology. Foundations for a Theology of the New Testament*. Clark: Edinburgh. 1987.

Porton, G.G., Diversity in Postbiblical Judaism - *Early Judaism and its Modern Interpreters*. 57-80. Ed. Kraft and Nickelsburg. (The Bible and its modern interpreters 2) SBL. Atlanta: Scholars. 1986.

Poythress, V.S., Is Romans 1. 3–4 a Pauline Confession After All? *ET* 87 (1975) 180–183.

Propp, V., *Morphology of the Folktale*. Second Edition Revised and Edited with a Preface by L.A. Wagner. New Introduction by A. Dundes. Austin: University of Texas Press. 1994.

Rad von, G., Das judäische Königsritual. *ThLZ* (1947) 211-216.
- *Theologie des Alten Testaments*. Band 1. 9. Aufl. München: Kaiser. 1987.
- *Theologie des Alten Testaments*. Band 2. 4. Aufl. München: Kaiser. 1965.

Rehm, M.D., Levites and Priests. *ABD 4* (1992) 297-310.
Rengstorf, K.H., Old and New Testament Traces of a Formula of the Judean Royal Ritual. *NT V* (1962) 229-244.
Rese, M., *Alttestamentliche Motive in der Christologie des Lukas.* StNT 1. Gütersloh: Mohn. 1969.
Ricoeur, P., *Interpretation Theory. Discourse and the Surplus of Meaning.* Fort Worth: Texas Christian University Press. 1976.
– *The Rule of Metaphor. Multidisciplinary Studies of the Creation of Meaning in Language.* Toronto: University of Toronto Press. 1977.
Riesner, R., *Die Frühzeit des Apostels Paulus. Studien zur Chronologie, Missionsstrategie und Theologie.* WUNT 71. Tübingen: Mohr (Siebeck). 1994.
– *Paul's Early Period. Chronology, Mission Strategy, Theology.* Grand Rapids: Eerdmans. 1998.
Rimmon-Kenan, S., *Narrative Fiction: Contemporary Poetics.* London and New York: Methuen. 1983.
Ringgren, H., *The Faith of Qumran. Theology of the Dead Sea Scrolls.* Expanded Edition with a New Introduction by J.H. Charlesworth. New York: Crossroad. 1995.
Rissi, M., *Die Theologie des Hebräerbriefs. Ihre Verankerung in der Situation des Verfassers und seiner Leser.* WUNT 41. Tübingen: Mohr (Siebeck). 1987.
Robertson, A. - Plummer, A., *A Critical and Exegetical Commentary on The First Epistle of St. Paul to the Corinthians.* ICC. Edinburgh: Clark. 1986.
Robinson, J.A.T., *Twelve New Testament Studies.* SBT 34. London: SCM. 1962.
Robinson, J.M., *Kerygma und historischer Jesus.* Zürich/Stuttgart: Zwingli. 1960.
Rowland, C., *The Open Heaven. A Study of Apocalyptic in Judaism and Christianity.* New York: Crossroad / London: SPCK. 1982.
– *Christian Origins. An Account of the Setting and Character of the Most Important Messianic Sect of Judaism.* London: SPCK. 1985.
– The Second Temple: Focus of Ideological Struggle? – *Templum Amicitiae. Essays of the Second Temple presented to Ernst Bammel.* Ed. W. Horbury. 175-198. JSNTS 48. Sheffield: JSOT Press. 1991.
Sanday, W. - Headlam, A.C., *Critical and Exegetical Commentary on the Epistle to the Romans.* 5th ed. ICC. Edinburgh: Clark. 1950.
Sanders, E.P., *Paul and Palestinian Judaism.* Philadelphia: Fortress. 1977.
– Testaments of the Three Patriarchs. Introduction. – *OTP I.* 868. 1983.
Sanders, J.T., *The New Testament Christological Hymns.* SNT.SMS 15. Cambridge: Cambridge University Press. 1971.
Saussure de, F., *Course in General Linguistics.* Translated and annotated by Roy Harris. London: Duckworth. 1983.
Schade, H-H., *Apokalyptische Christologie bei Paulus. Studien zum Zusammenhang von Christologie und Eschatologie in den Paulusbriefen.* GTA 18. Göttingen: Vandenhoeck & Ruprecht. 1981.
Schelkle, K.H., *Paulus Lehrer der Väter. Die altkirchliche Auslegung von Römer 1-11.* 2. ed. Düsseldorf: Patmos. 1959.
Schenke, J.-M., Erwägung zum Rätsel der Hebräerbriefes. – *Neues Testament und christliche Existenz.* 421-437. FS H. Braun. Ed. H.D. Betz and L. Schrottroff. Tübingen: Mohr (Siebeck). 1973.

Schiffman, L.H., Merkavah Speculation at Qumran: The 4Q Serekh Shirot ᶜOlat ha-Shabbat.
- *Mystics, Philosophers, and Politicians. Essays in Jewish Intellectual History in Honof of A. Altmann.* 15-47. Eds. J. Reinharz and D. Swetschinski. DMMRS 5. Durham: Duke University Press. 1982.
- *From Text to Tradition. A History of Second Temple & Rabbinic Judaism.* Hoboken, New Jersey: Ktav. 1991.
- Messianic Figures and Ideas in the Qumran Scrolls. - *The Messiah. Development Earliest Judaism and Christianity.* The First Princeton Symposium on Judaism and Christian Origins. 116-129. Ed. J.H. Charlesworth, J. Brownson, M.T. Davis, S.J. Kraftchick, and A.F. Segal. Minneapolis: Fortress. 1992.
- *Reclaiming the Dead Sea Scrolls. The History of Judaism, the Background fo Christianity, the Lost Library at Qumran.* Philadelphia and Jerusalem: Jewish Publication Society. 1994.

Schlier, H., *Der Brief an die Galater.* KEK 7. Göttingen: Vandenhoeck & Ruprecht. 1971.
- Die Anfänge des christologischen Credo. - *Zur Frühgeschichte der Christologie.* 13-58. Hrsg. B. Welte. QD 51. Freiburg: Herder. 1970.
- Zu Röm 1,3f. - *Neues Testament und Geschichte, historisches Geschehen und Deutung im Neuen Testament.* 207-218. FS O. Cullmann, hrsg. H. Baltensweiler und B. Reicke. Zürich: Theologischer Verlag. 1972.
- *Der Römerbrief.* Dritte Auflage. HThK VI. Freiburg: Herder. 1987.

Schmidt, H.W., *Der Brief des Paulus an die Römer.* ThHk VI. 3d ed. Berlin: Evangelische Verlagsanstalt. 1972.

Schmithals, W., *Der Römerbrief: ein Kommentar.* Gütersloh: Mohn. 1988.

Schneider, B., κατὰ πνεῦμα ἁγιωσύνης (Romans 1,4). Bib. 48 (1967) 359-387.

Schneider, C., κάθημαι. *ThWNT III* (1990) 443-447.

Scholem, G.G., *Major Trends in Jewish Mysticism.* First Schocken Paperback Edition. Reprinted from the Third Revised Edition. New York. 1961.

Schüpphaus, J., *Die Psalmen Salomos. Ein Zeugnis Jerusalemer Theologie und Frömmigkeit in der mitte des vorchristlichen Jahrhunderts.* ALGHJ 7. Leiden: Brill. 1977.

Schürer, E., *The History of the Jewish People in the Age of Jesus Christ (175 B.C. -. A.D. 135).* I-III. Revised and edited by G. Vermes, F. Millar and M. Black. Edinburgh: Clark. 1987.

Schweizer, E., Röm. 1,3f. und der Gegensatz von Fleisch und Geist vor und bei Paulus. *EvTh 15* (1955) 563-571.
- *Erniedrigung und Erhöhung bei Jesus und seinen Nachfolgern.* AThANT 28. Zürich. 1962.
- The Concept of the Davidic "Son of God" in Acts and Its Old Testament Background. - *Studies in Luke-Acts.* 186-193. Ed. L.E. Keck, J.L. Martyn. Nashville. 1966.
- Zum religionsgeschichtlichen Hintergrund der "Sendungsformel" Gal 4,4f. Rm 8,3f. Joh 3,16f. 1 Joh 4,9f. *ZNW 57* (1966) 199-210.
- 'υἱός', *ThWNT VIII* (1969) 364-395.
- *Der Brief an die Kolosser.* EKK XII. Zürich: Benziger/ Neukirchen-Vluyn: Neukirchener. 3. Auflage. 1989.

Schwemer, A.M., Gott als König und seine Königsherrschaft in den Sabbatliedern aus Qumran. - *Königsherrschaft Gottes und himmlischer Kult im Judentum, Urchristentum und in der hellenistischen Welt.* 45-118. Hengel, M. und Schwemer, A.M. (hrsg.). WUNT 55. Tubingen: Mohr (Siebeck). 1991.

Schäfer, P., New Testament and Hekhalot Literature: The Journey into Heaven in Paul and in Merkavah Mysticism. *JJS 35* (1984) 19-35.
- *Hekhalot-Studien.* TSAJ 19. Tübingen: Mohr (Siebeck). 1988.
Schäfer, P. - Herrmann, K., *Übersetzung der Hekhalot-Literatur I §§ 1-80.* In Zusammenarbeit mit U. Hirschfelder und G. Necker. TSAJ 46. Tübingen: Mohr (Siebeck). 1995.
Scott, E.F., *The Epistles of Paul to the Colossians, to Philemon and to the Ephesians.* Moffatt. London: Hodder and Stoughton. 1958.
Scott, J.M., ΥΙΟΘΕΣΙΑ. *An Exegetical Investigation Into the Background of Divine "Adoption as Sons" In the Corpus Paulinum.* Dissertation. Evangelisch-theologischen Fakultät, Eberhard-Karls-Universität, Tübingen. 1988.
- *Adoption as Sons of God. An Exegetical Investigation into the Background of* ΥΙΟΘΕΣΙΑ *in the Pauline Corpus.* WUNT 2/48. Tübingen: Mohr (Siebeck). 1992.
Searle, J.R., Metaphor. - *Metaphor and Thought.* 92-123. Ed. A Ortony. Cambridge: Cambridge University Press. 1979.
Seeberg, A., *Der Katechismus der Urchristenheit.* TB 26. München: Kaiser. 1966.
Segal, A.F., *Two Powers in Heaven. Early Rabbinic Reports about Christianity and Gnosticism.* Studies in Judaism in Late Antiquity 25. Leiden: Brill. 1977.
- Heavenly Ascent in Hellenistic Judaism, Early Christianity and their Environment. *ANRW II.23.2* (1980) 1333-1394.
- *Paul the Convert: The Apostolate and Apostasy of Saul the Pharisee.* New Haven: Yale University Press. 1990.
- Paul and the Beginning of Jewish Mysticism. - *Death, Ecstasy, and Other Worldly Journeys.* 95-122. Eds. J.J. Collins, M. Fishbane. New York: State University of New York Press. 1995.
Selden, R., Widdowson, P., Brooker, P., *A Reader's Guide to Contemporary Literary Theory.* Fourth Edition. London et al.: Prentice Hall/ Harvester Wheatsheaf. 1997.
Seow, C.L., Ark of the Covenant. *ABD I* (1992) 386-393.
Seybold, K., *melek.* IV. Theological Usage: Yahweh as King - Yahweh mlk. *TDOT 8* (1997) 365-374.
Simon, M., *Verus Israel. A study of the relations between Christians and Jews in the Roman Empire (135-425).* The Littman Library of Jewish Civilization. Oxford: Oxford University Press. 1986.
Sjöberg, E., *Der Menschensohn im Äthiopischen Henochbuch.* Lund: Gleerup. 1946.
Slingerlander, H.D., *The Testaments of the Twelve Patriarchs. A Critical History of Research.* SBL.MS. 21. Missoula: Scholars. 1977.
Smith, M., Ascent to the Heavens and Deification in 4QM[a]. - *Archaeology and History in the Dead Sea Scrolls.* 181-188. The New York University Conference in Memory of Yigael Yadin. Ed. L. Schiffman. Worcester. JSOT/ASOR Monograph Series 2. / JSPS 8. 1990.
- Two Ascended to Heaven - Jesus and the Author of 4Q491. - *Jesus and the Dead Scrolls.* 290-301. Ed. J.H. Charlesworth. The Anchor Bible Reference Library. New York: Doubleday. 1992.
Soggin, J.A., *Judges. A Commentary.* OTL. Philadelphia: Westminster. 1981.
Soskice, J.M., *Metaphor and Religious Language.* Oxford: Clarendon. 1985.
Stauffer, E., *Die Theologie des Neuen Testaments.* ThW. Stuttgart: Kohlhammer. 1941.

Stegemann, H., *The Library of Qumran. On the Essenes, Qumran, John the Baptist, and Jesus.* Grand Rapids: Eerdmans/ Leiden: Brill. 1998.
Stinespring,W.F., Testament of Isaac. A New Translation and Introduction. – *OTP I.* 901-911. 1983.
Stone, M.E., Questions of Ezra. A New Translation and Introduction. – *OTP I.* 591-599. 1983.
– Apocalyptic Literature. – *Jewish Writings of the Second Temple Period. Apocrypha, Pseudepigrapha, Qumran Sectarian Writings, Philo, Josephus.* 383-441. Compendia Rerum Iudaicarum ad Novum Testamentum II. Ed. M.E. Stone. Assen: Van Gorcum / Philadelphia: Fortress. 1984.
– The Question of the Messiah in 4 Ezra. – *Judaisms and Their Messiahs at the Turn of the Christian Era.* 209-224. Ed. J. Neusner, W.S. Green, E.S. Frerichs. Cambridge: Cambridge University Press. 1987.
Strauss, D.F., *Das Leben Jesu, kritisch bearbeitet.* Erster Band. Tübingen: Osiander. 1835.
– *Das Leben Jesu, kritisch bearbeitet.* Zweiter Band. Tübingen: Osiander. 1836.
– *Das Leben Jesu für das deutsche Volk bearbeitet.* Erster Theil. Leipzig: Kröner. 1864.
– *Das Leben Jesu für das deutsche Volk bearbeitet.* Zweiter Theil. Leipzig: Kröner. 1864.
Strugnell, J., The Angelic Liturgy at Qumran. 4Q Serek Sirôt ᶜOlat Hassabbât. *Vetus Testamentum Supplements 7.* 318-345. Leiden: Brill. 1960.
Stuckenbruck, L.T., *Angel Veneration and Christology. A Study in Early Judaism and in the Christology of the Apocalypse of John.* WUNT 2. Reihe 70. Tübingen: Mohr (Siebeck). 1995.
Stuhlmacher, P., *Gerechtigkeit Gottes bei Paulus.* FRLANT 87. Göttingen: Vandenhoeck & Ruprecht. 1965.
– Theologische Probleme des Römerbriefpräskripts. *EvTh* 27 (1967) 374–389.
– *Das paulinische Evangelium. I Vorgeschichte.* FRLANT 95. Göttingen: Vandenhoeck & Ruprecht. 1968.
– Paul's Understanding of the Law in the Letter to the Romans. *SEÅ 50* (1985) 87-104.
– *Der Brief and die Römer.* NTD 6. Göttingen: Vandenhoeck & Ruprecht. 1989.
– *Biblische Theologie des Neuen Testaments.* Band 1. Göttingen: Vandenhoeck & Ruprecht. 1992.
Szikszai, S., Theocracy. *IDB 4* (1962) 617-618.
Talmon, S., Waiting for the Messiah: The Spiritual Universe of the Qumran Covenanters. – *Judaisms and Their Messiahs at the Turn of the Christian Era.* 111-137. Ed. J. Neusner, W.S. Green, E.S. Frerichs. Cambridge: Cambridge University Press. 1987.
– The Internal Diversification of Judaism in the Early Second Temple Period. – *Jewish Civilization in the Hellenistic-Roman Period.* 16-43. Ed. S. Talmon. Philadelphia: Trinity Press International. 1991.
Taranovsky, K., *Essays on Mandelstam.* Harvard Slavic Studies 6. Cambridge, Mass. and London: Harvard University Press. 1976.
Tate, M.E., *Psalms 50-100.* WBC 20. Dallas: Word Bookd. 1990.
Theisohn, J., *Der auserwählte Richter. Untersuchungen zum traditionsgeschichtlichem Ort der Menschensohngestalt der Bilderreden des Äthiopischen Henoch.* SUNT 12. Göttingen: Vandenhoeck & Ruprecht. 1975.
Theobald, M., "Dem Juden zuerst und auch dem Heiden". – *Kontinuität und Einheit.* 376–392. FS F. Mussner. Ed. P–G. Müller and W. Stenger. Freiburg: Herder. 1981.

Thiselton, A.C., Semantics and New Testament Interpretation. – *New Testament Interpretation. Essays on Principles and Methods.* 75-104. Ed. I.H. Marshall. Exeter: Paternoster. 1979.

Thüsing, W., *Erhöhungsvorstellung und Parusieerwartung in der ältesten nachösterlichen Christologie.* SBS 42. Stuttgart: Katholisches Bibelwerk. 1969.

– *Gott und Christus in der paulinischen Soteriologie. Band I. Per Christum in Deum. Das Verhältnis der Christozentrik zur Theozentrik.* 3., verbesserte und um hermeneutisch-methodische Vorüberlegungen zum Gesamtwerk sowie um einen Anhang erweiterte Auflage. Münster: Aschendorff. 1986.

Todorov, T., *The Poetics of Prose.* New York: Cornell University Press. 1977.

– *Literature and Its Theorists. A Personal View of Twentieth-Century Criticism.* London: Routledge & Kegan Paul. 1988.

Tödt, H.E., *Der Menschensohn in der synoptischen Überlieferung.* Gütersloher: Mohn. 1959.

Tournay, R.J., *Seeing and Hearing God with the Psalms. The Prophetic Liturgy of the Second Temple in Jerusalem.* JSOTS 118. Sheffield: JSOT Press. 1991.

Trocmé, E., "C'est le ciel qui est mon trône." La polémique contre le Temple et la théologie des Hellénistes. – *Le Trône de Dieu.* 195-203. Éd. M. Philonenko. WUNT 69. Tübingen: Mohr (Siebeck). 1993.

Unnik, W.C. van, Jesus the Christ. *NTS* 8 (1962) 101-116.

VanderKam, J.C., *The Dead Sea Scrolls Today.* Grand Rapids: Eerdmans/SPCK. 1994.

– Messianism in the Scrolls. – *The Community of the Renewed Covenant. The Notre Dame Symposium on the Dead Sea Scrolls.* 211-234. Ed. by E. Ulrich and J. VanderKam. CJAS 10. Notre Dame: University of Notre Dame Press. 1994.

– *From Revelation to Canon. Studies in the Hebrew Bible and Second Temple Literature.* JSJ supplements 62. Leiden: Brill. 2000.

Vermes, G., *The Dead Sea Scrolls. Qumran in Perspective.* Revised Edition. London: SCM. 1994.

Veijola, T., *Das Königtum in der Beurteilung des deuteronomistischen Historiographie.* AASF B 198. Helsinki. 1977.

– *Die ewige Dynastie.* STAT B 193. Helsinki. 1975.

– *Verheissung in der Krise.* STAT B 220. Vammala. 1982.

Vielhauer, Ph., Ein Weg zur neutestamentlichen Christologie. *EvTh* 25 (1965) 24-72.

– *Geschichte der urchristlichen Literatur. Einleitung in das Neue Testament, die Apokryphen und die Apostolischen Väter.* Berlin: de Gruyter. 1975.

Volz, P., *Jesaia II. Übersetzt und erklärt.* KAT IX. Leipzig: Scholl. 1932.

Walker, W.O.Jr., The Son of Man: Some Recent Developments. *CBQ* 45 (1983) 584-607.

Watts, J.D.W., *Isaiah 1-33.* WBC 24. Waco: Word Books. 1985.

Wegenast, K., *Das Verständnis der Tradition bei Paulus und in den Deuteropaulinen.* WMANT 8. Neukirchen: Neukirchener. 1962.

Weiss, J., *Die Predigt Jesu vom Reiche Gottes.* Göttingen: Vandenhoeck & Ruprecht. 1892.

– *Das Urchristentum.* Göttingen: Vandenhoeck & Ruprecht. 1917.

Wengst, K., *Christologische Formel und Lieder des Urchristentums.* StNT 7. Gütersloh: Gütersloher. 1972.

Whitsett, C., Son of God, Seed of David: Paul's Messianic Exegesis in Romans 2:3-4. *JBL* 119 (2000) 661-681.

Wilckens, U., *Die Missionsreden der Apostelgeschichte. Form- und Traditionsgeschichtliche Untersuchungen.* WMANT 5. Neukirchen: Neukirchener. 1961.
- *Der Brief an die Römer. 1. Teilband. Röm 1–5.* 2., verbesserte Auflage. EKK VI/1. Neukirchen – Vluyn: Benziger/Neukirchener. 1987.
- *Der Brief an die Römer. 2. Teilband. Röm 6–11.* 2., verbesserte Auflage. EKK VI/2. Neukirchen – Vluyn: Benziger/Neukirchener. 1987.
Wildberger, H., *Jesaja. I Teilband. Jesaja 1-12.* BKAT X/1. Neukirchen-Vluyn: Neukirchener. 1972.
Williamson, R., The Background of the Epistle to the Hebrews. *ExpT* 87 (1975-76) 232-237.
Wilson, R. McLachlan, Gnosis/Gnostizismus II. Neues Testamnet, Judentum, Alte Kirche. *TRE XIII* (1984) 535-550.
Wilson, S.G., *Related Strangers. Jews and Christians 70-170 C.E.* Minneapolis: Fortress. 1995.
Winninge, M., *Sinners and the Righteous. A Comparative Study of the Psalms of Solomon and Paul's Letters.* CB.NT 26. Stockholm: Almqvist & Wiksell International. 1995.
Wintermute, O.S., Jubilees. A New Translation and Introduction. *OTP II* (1985) 35-142.
Witherington (III), B., *Paul's Narrative Thought World. The Tapestry of Tragedy and Triumph.* Louisville: Westminster/John Knox. 1994.
Woude van der, A.S., *Die messianischen Vorstellungen der Gemeinde von Qumran.* Assen. 1957.
Zahn, T., *Der Brief des Paulus an die Römer.* KNT VI. Leipzig. 1910.
Zeller, D., Hellenistische Vorgaben für den Glauben an die Auferstehung Jesu? – *Von Jesus zum Christus. Christologische Studien.* 71-91. FS P. Hoffmann. Hrsg. R. Hoppe und U. Busse. Berlin/ New York: W. de Gruyter. 1998.
Ziesler, J.A., *Paul's Letter to the Romans.* TPI New Testament Commentaries. London: SCM / Philadelphia: Trinity. 1989.
Zimmerli, W., *Ezechiel.* 1 Teilband. BKAT 13. Neukirchen: Neukirchener. 1969.
Zimmermann, H., *Neutestamentliche Methodenlehre.* Stuttgart: Katholisches Bibelwerk. 1968.
Zwiep, A.W., *The Ascension of the Messiah in Lukan Christology.* NTsuppl. 87. Leiden: Brill. 1997.

Index of Ancient Sources

1. Old Testament

Genesis
5:21-24	72
5:24	72, 120
6:2-4	83, 141
15	105
18:2	66
21:18	66
22:11	66
26:4	88
28:11-22	107
28:11-17	66
31:11-13	66
34	
37:9	88
49:10	85, 234

Exodus
3:2	66
4:16	89, 90
7:1	89, 90
15:11	83
15:17	53
15:17-18	46
19:16-18	66
23:21	106, 140
24:10	66, 87
24:15ff.	57
25	57
25:17-22	55
25:20-22	50
25:22	50
26:33	68
32:13	88
32:20-21	106
40:34	68

Leviticus
16	268
16:2	253
16:11-13	56
16:11-16	265
16:15	254, 357
16:15-16	56
16:15f.	253
16:29-31	189

Numbers
6:14 (LXX)	254
10:35-36	51

Deuteronomy
4:11-15	66
18:15	179
32:43	204, 205
33:20-22	214

Judges
8:23	45

1 Samuel
2:1-10	70
2:7-8	70
2:10	70
4:4	50, 253
8	58
8:5	58
8:6	58
8:7	45, 58
10:19	178

2 Samuel
7	60, 209, 228, 229, 244, 245
7:10-14	166, 234
7:12	166, 230, 231, 233, 234, 235, 237, 245
7:12-14	59, 86, 165, 167, 228, 231, 243
7:12-16	292
7:13	233
7:14	165, 206, 296
22:6	162
22:12	68

1 Kings
22:17-23	48
22:19	66

2 Kings
2:11	66
19:15	50

1 Chronicles
6:24	185
28:2	51
29:23	59, 92, 131
29:25	59

2 Chronicles
29	150
29:27-28	149

Ezra
4:29	185

Job
1:6-12	48
2:1-6	48
26:9	68
36	101
36:6-7	70
36:7	101

Psalms
1	166
2	61, 166, 209, 228, 229, 242
2:1-2	233, 234
2:2	170
2:6	59
2:7	59, 165, 166, 206, 208, 228, 234, 244, 296
2:8	60
5:3	46
5:6	259
8:4	7
8:7	184
9:7	53
10:4 (LXX)	68
11:4	52, 68, 119
16	162, 163, 166, 167, 171
16:8	162
18:5	162
18:10	119
18:10-11	68
22:3	53
22:27-28	47
24	46, 149
24:2	51
24:7	51
24:8-9	51
27:4	52
32	162
33:13-14	53
45:6	53
45:7-8	205
45:8	205
47:9	47, 50
48	149
48:1-3	46
61:6-7	59
67:18 (LXX)	118
68:17	66, 75
68:24	75
74:12	48
80:1-2	52
82	149
82:2	129
89	165, 229
89:3-4	165
89:7	83, 141
89:14	53
89:28	296
89:36	292
89:45	52
93	149
93:1	47
93:1-2	48, 53
94	149
95:2-3	47
96:7 (LXX)	205
96:10	47
97:1	47
97:1-3	48
97:2	68
97:7	204, 205
97:8	205
98:1ff.	49
98:6	47
99:1	47, 51, 52, 264
99:2	52, 264
99:5	51, 52, 264
102:12	52
103:19	68, 119, 148

103:19-21	53, 264	11:1-10	241
109 (LXX)	185	11:2	240
109:1 (LXX)	276	14:13	52
109:3 (LXX)	60	24:21	48
110	7, 78, 79, 85, 101, 130, 131, 134, 157, 160, 162, 163, 166, 167, 170-175, 177, 178, 180, 182-187, 194-196, 201, 202, 206, 208, 209, 215, 216, 217, 228, 242, 245, 246, 248, 258, 259, 260, 261, 262, 267, 268, 269, 271, 283, 287, 288, 289, 325, 326, 328, 331, 334, 335, 343, 344, 345, 352, 356, 358, 362, 363, 366, 367, 370, 373, 378, 379, 380, 381, 388	24:23	48, 50
		26:19	134, 241
		40-55	93
		40:9-10	49
		41:21	46
		42:10f.	49
		43:15	46
		44:6	46, 49
		45:15	178
		45:21	178
		45:21-25	366
		49:1	200
		49:6	273
		52:7	49, 129, 140
		55	229
		55:3-5	241
		55:3	249, 354
110:1	12, 61, 69, 88, 163, 168, 170, 171, 177, 180, 183, 184, 187, 204, 206, 208, 210, 244, 258, 260, 276, 327, 349, 351	*Jeremiah*	
		1:5	200
		3:16-17	54
110:3	60	10:10	46
110:4	79, 207, 234, 258, 260	14:21	54
116:3	162	17:12	54
122:3-5	273	22:30	52
132	163, 165, 166, 167, 170, 173, 378	23	229
		23:5	233
132:7	51	23:5	133, 167
132:10	164	33:15	133
132:10-11	170		
132:11	163, 164, 292	*Ezekiel*	
146:4 (LXX)	88	1	107, 148
149:2	46	1-2	198, 200
		1:4-5	67, 212
Greek Odes (LXX)		1:6-10	67
2:49	205	1:6-12	106
		1:10	253
Isaiah		1:15	67
6	110, 294	1:22	72
6:1	48	1:23	106
6:1-2	66	1:26	67
6:3	67	1:26-28	212
6:5	48	1:27	68
10:34-11:1	85	1:28	68
11	229	2	200
11:1	133, 292	2:3	200
11:1-5	85		

8	107	3:8	133
8:2-4	67	6:12	133
9:3	53	14	46
10:1-2	54		
10:9-17	67		
10:18	54	## 2. Jewish Literature	
34	229		
34:23	167, 233	### A. Apocrypha	
37:12	134		
37:19-24	273	*1 Maccabees*	
		3:4	214
Daniel		14:41	79
4:10	238		
4:14	248	*2 Maccabees*	
4:20	238	7:9	134
4:34	46	7:14	135, 151
5:12	238		
5:21	233	*Sirach*	
6:4	238	4:12	135
7	87, 92, 93, 271, 272	17:28	135
7:9	69	36:11	273
7:9-10	73	47:11	92, 340
7:10	69	48:10	273
7:13	7, 325, 326	50	150
7:13-14	179	50:1-21	149
7:14	69, 151		
7:22	89, 272	*Wisdom of Solomon*	
8:13	118	1:5	238
12:2	134, 135, 151, 241	2:19-20	135
		3:8	83, 89, 273
Daniel (LXX)		4:7-11	135
3:54-55	69	5:1ff.	135
		5:15-16	135
Joel		9:10	54
2:32	172		
		### B. Pseudepigrapha	
Amos			
9:11	167	*Apocalypse of Abraham*	
		ApcAbr	126, 376
Micah		1:8	212
2:13	46	9	189
Zephaniah		10:3	105, 140
3:15	46	10:8	105, 140, 141
		15	105
Haggai		17:1-21	106, 140
2:22	52	17:8-9a	106
		17:13	106
Zechariah		18:3	106
3:1-5	48	18:12-13	106
3:7	89, 272	21:6-7	107

Index of Ancient Sources

Apocalypse of Ezra	
1:3-5	189
Ladder of Jacob	
1:4	107
2:7-9	107
2:15	108
2:17-18	108
5:16-17	108
Apocalypse of Moses	
19:2	112
22:3	112
22:4	112
28:4	113, 135
32:2	112
39	116
39:1-3	113
39:2-5	112
39:3	135
41:3	102, 113, 135
Life of Adam and Eve	
12-17	113
13:1-15:3	138
14:2	143
25:2-3	112
47:3	113
Testament of Abraham (A)	
10:1	114
11:4	114
11:5-11	114
11:9	114
12:4	114
12:5	114
12:11	151
13:1	114
13:2	114
13:3	114
13:8	151
20:11-12	115
Ascension of Isaiah	
AscIsa	126, 127, 136, 341, 376
1-5	108
6-11	285
2:7-11	189
3:13-4:18	108
4:2f.	109
6-11	108
7-8	193
7:21	110, 143, 175, 288
7:22	110
8:7	109
9:6ff.	110
9:6-18	286
9:7-10	111
9:9	111
9:17-18	111
9:24-26	111
9:27ff.	110
9:28-32	286, 320
9:30	286, 288
9:32	288
9:33-36	286
9:36	286
9:40-10:6	286
10:6	286
10:8	286
10:14	287
10:17-11:33	287
11:9	287
11:20-21	287
11:32-33	288
2 Baruch/Apocalypse of Baruch	
59:3-4	87
3 Baruch	126, 376
2:1-2	117
2:2	193
6:14	117
9:3	117
11:2	117
1 Enoch	126, 146, 212, 376
1-5	152
1:3	152
1:4-6	152
1:9	273
9:4	72, 151, 271
10:12	129
14	72-75; 95, 142, 147
14:1	74
14:1ff.	287
14:8ff.	193, 290
14:8-9	72
14:10	72
14:16	72

14:18-20	73	20:3 (J)	104
14:21	73, 141	20:4	104
14:24-25	73	21:1-22:10	139
18:8-9	74	22:1 (J)	104
24:3	74	22:10 (J)	104
24:5	74	24:1 (J)	104, 142
25	212	24:1 (A)	142
25:3	74	30	104
25:4-5	75	30:11	105
26:1	76	71:33-34	104
37-71	91-96		
38:2	93	*3 Enoch*	
45:3	91, 272	1:1	193
46	229	1:1-2	120
46:1	91, 272	3-15	95
46:2	91	4:3	120
47:3f.	272	4:5	121
51	93	7	120
51:1-3	92, 272	10:1	122
51:3	88, 130	10:3	121, 122
53:6	93	12:5	121, 140
55:4	93	16:3-4	122, 143
60:12-22	292	17:1-3	120
61:8	93, 130, 152	18	120
62	229	18:1-2	120
62:2	94, 152	18:3	120
62:5	152	45	68, 121
62:5b	94	48D:1	89, 140
62:13-14	94	48C:4	121, 122
71:3	95		
71:5-7	95, 212	*Exodus of Ezekiel*	
71:10	95	6,15	82
71:14	95	6,8-10	87
71:14-17	93	6,15-19	87, 271
71:17	96	7,3-7	88
82:10-14	292	7,9	83, 88
89:45-48	213, 214	9, 8	90
91-93	129		
98:10	152	*4 Ezra*	
100:4-5	152	7:33-34	100
102-103	241	7:60	153
		7:89-91	99
2 Enoch		7:97	100
1:1	103	8:20-25	99
4-6	292	8:48	135
8:1-3 (J)	103	8:48-55	100
8:8 (J)	103	9:15-25	153
9:1	103	12	229
19:4	292	12:32-33	100
20:3	104	12:32f.	61, 133

Index of Ancient Sources

Jubilees
2:2	292
4:16	75
4:18	76
4:19	76
4:21	76
4:23	76
4:25	76
8:19	76, 118
10:17	76, 272
31:11	75

Psalms of Solomon
2:30-31	135, 241
3:1-12	152
3:11-12	135, 241
14:1-4	152
14:6-9	153, 241
14:6-10	135
15:10-13	153
15:12-13	135
17	229
17:4	340
17:21	61, 133, 340
17:26	133, 273
17:37	240

Joseph and Aseneth
15:12	142

Prayer of Joseph
A, 1	108
A, 2-3	98
A, 6	141

4. Maccabees
17:18	102
17:22	255

Pseudo-Philo
11:5	87
18:5	105

Sibylline Oracles
1,324	290
1,331	290
1,379-382	290
2,218-219	153
2,218	275
2,238-244	153, 290
3,1	118
3,11-12	119
3,669-673	153
3,741-750	153
3,781-782	89, 273
4,40-43	153
4,180-190	153
6,1-5	291
6,6-7	291
6,15-19	291
7,29-39	292
8,222	153, 275

Testament of Job
TJob	157
33	88, 101, 102
39	101
39:11-12	101
43:7	103
52:8	102
52:11	102
53:8	102

Testament of Abraham
13:6 (A)	273
20:11-12	102

Testament of Isaac
2:7	116, 128
4:1f.	189
6:4-5	115
6:26-27	116
7:1	116

Testaments of the Twelve Patriarchs
TLevi	126, 146, 376
2:5-8	290
2:6-7	77, 193
2:10	78
3:1-5	198
3:4	252
3:6	78
5	294
5:1	212, 256
5:1-2	78
5:3-5	78
5:5-6	142
8:3	78
8:14	262

18	62, 229	*1QH*	
18:1ff.	262	3	335
18:2	79	3, 21-22	82
18:2-3	61		
18:10	79	*1QM*	
18:10-11	135	12, 1	81
18:11	238, 240	15, 4	83

TJudah		*1QS*	
22:3	133	III, 6-9	252
24	136	IX, 3-6	147
25	136, 273	VIII, 5	147
25:1	135	VIII, 5-8	252

TNaphtali		*1QSa*	
8:2-3	62	II	94
		II, 17-21	62, 132
TBenjamin			
9:2	273	*1QSb*	
10:3	101	3, 25ff.	84, 130
10:6	101, 128	4, 25ff.	84
		4, 25-26	83
Questions of Ezra		5, 20ff.	85
A, 1	119		
A, 19	119	*1QapGen*	
A, 21	119	19:8	76
A, 29	120		

4Q405 Songs of the Sabbath Sacrifice

Apocalypse of Paul		SSS	146
11	293	1, 31-32	83, 141
20	293	1, 44-45	83, 141
25	293	20-21-22,6-9	148, 265, 344
29	293	22, 8	80
43	293		
44	293	*1QpHab*	
45	293	5, 4	89, 273

Hellenistic Synagogue Prayer		*4QAaronA*	62
(AposCon 7)			
4:1	118	*4QFlor (4Q174)*	
4:8-10	118	4Qflor.	166, 229, 231, 233, 234
4:11-12	118	1-3, I, 10-11	85
4:15	118	1-3, I, 10-12	231
4:22	118	1-3, I, 11	61

C. Dead Sea Scrolls

		4QMMT	194
CD			
16,3-4	75	*4QPatr*	234
34-38	75	3	61

4Q161	84, 377	**D. Josephus**	
8, III, 8-10	61, 342		
8, III, 18-21	85, 342	*Antiquities*	
		18.11	197
4Q204	80		
4Q213	80	**E. Philo**	
4Q252	85	*Commentary on Genesis*	
		1, 26	96
4Q285	85		
		Vita Mosis	
4Q385		I, 155-159	89, 97
4, 5-6	80	II, 99-100	97, 141
4Q403		*De Praemiis et poeniis*	
1i, 30-34	148	43f.	96
1i, 36-37	148, 265		
1i, 44	90	*De Confusione Linguarum*	
		146	98
4Q427			
VI	83	*Questions on Exodus*	
VII	141	40	97
4Q471b	83, 141	*De Legatione ad Gaium*	
		156	197
4Q491 (4QM^a)	88, 90, 92, 130, 141, 142,		
	334, 335	*De Mutatione Nominum*	
11, I, 12-13a	81	223	197
11, I, 13-14	82		
11, I, 17	83, 271		
11, I, 18	82	**F. Rabbinic**	
4Q503 (13-16)		mTamid	
VI, 4-10	80	7:3	149, 266
		7:4	149, 266
4Q511			
35	83	**3. New Testament**	
4Q521	212		
2, 7	85	*Matthew*	
		5:45	296
11QBer	142	19	274
		19:28	89, 128, 212, 273, 291
11QMelch	84, 129, 130, 157, 262,	24:30	94
	263, 271, 307	25	274
		25:31-32	271
11Q5 (11QPs^a)		25:31	272, 273
XXVII	149, 150	25:31ff.	291
XXVII, 5-8	149	27:19	275

Index of Ancient Sources

Mark
1:10   308
12:35-37   180
12:37   180
13:26-27   270
14:24   261
14:62   180

Luke
1:32   171
1:35   296
1:47   178
2:11   171
7:55   287
9:22   180
20:44   180
21:40-44   180
22:22   233
22:30   89
22:69   180

John
10:3   296
19:13   275

Acts
1:9   290
2   201, 209, 215, 217, 218, 226, 228, 230, 233, 234, 245, 246, 247, 248, 279, 300, 378, 380
2:22-36   160-177
2:22-36   161, 162, 175, 343, 378
2:21   172, 175
2:22   163, 171
2:23   176, 233
2:23-24   287
2:24ff.   162
2:29   163
2:30   166, 168, 233, 237
2:30-31   163
2:31   162
2:32-33   167
2:32-36   352
2:33   172
2:33-36   217, 245, 246, 324
2:34   163, 168
2:34ff.   161, 170, 287
2:34-36   168, 213, 367
2:35-36   349

2:36   169, 171, 172, 175, 176, 279, 296, 297, 309, 310, 319, 351, 382
2:38   175, 176
3:15   287, 355
3:20-21   181
3:21   183, 208, 210, 276
3:22   179
4:10   287
4:25-28   233
4:28   233
5:30-31   177-178, 287, 343, 349
5:31   177, 330
7:1-56   178-182
7:27   178
7:35   178
7:37   179
7:47-49   179
7:52   179
7:52-56   343
7:55   179
7:55-56   180
7:56   179
8:37 (E)   311
9   200
10:42   224, 225, 232
13   162, 228
13:16ff.   163
13:23   165
13:33f.   234
13:35   163
17:18   197
17:31   232, 276, 347
18:12   275
18:16   275
21:27   180
25:6   275
25:10   275
25:17   275
26:23   241, 245, 249

Romans
1:1-4   324
1:1-6   218
1:2   228
1:2-4   201
1:3   166, 213, 218, 219, 224, 225, 226, 230, 231, 235, 236, 237, 239, 243, 247, 296, 297, 311, 379

1:3-4	217-250; 217, 219, 226, 227, 228, 244, 246, 248, 279, 280, 281, 296, 309, 310, 317, 342, 349, 351, 379, 382	15:20	249
		15:20-21	183
		15:20-25	249
		15:23	249
		15:24	183
1:4	197, 201, 219, 224, 225, 231, 233, 235, 236, 237, 243, 247, 296, 297, 300, 317, 379, 380	15:24-25	184, 349
		15:25	182, 183, 208, 210, 283, 343
		15:25b	276
2:5	276	15:25-28	201, 276
2:16b	275	15:27-28	184
3:23-25	255	15:35ff.	239
3:25	255	15:43	223
4:24-25	176	15:44-47	238
4:25	176, 267, 369		
5:9	255, 276	*2 Corinthians*	
5:18-19	223	4:6	199
5:19	255	5:10	275, 346
6:4	195	12	199
8	241	12:1-5	198-202
8:1ff.	239	12:2-4	198, 293
8:11	240	12:9	199
8:32	255	13:4	223
8:33-34	186		
8:34	184-187; 184, 185, 186, 187, 195, 197, 210, 260, 268, 343, 369	*Galatians*	
		1	200
		1:8	201
9:3	238, 239	1:12	200
10:3	172	1:15	200
10:9-13	319	1:16	200
10:9	363	1:23	200
14:10-12	274	2:10	300
15:26	300		
16:7	227	*Ephesians*	
		1:20	183, 343
1 Corinthians		1:21	351
4:5	275	2:4-6	102
6:2	89, 273	2:9-11	310
11:24	261	2:10	169
12:3	311	4:10	287
15	197, 238, 239, 241, 312, 313, 368		
		Philippians	
15:1-3	314	2	298, 366
15:3	185, 254, 261, 268, 370	2:3	189
15:3-5	287, 313	2:5-11	324, 366
15:4	184	2:6ff.	311
15:4-5	183	2:7-8	351
15:5-7	314	2:9	171
15:11	314	2:9-11	349

2:10	319, 351	5:5-6	234
2:11	171	5:6	358
		6:19	253
Colossians		6:20	259
1	194	7	262
1:9	197	7-8	207
1:13	195	7:1-28	259
1:16	190	7:2-3	263
2:8	196	7:7	261, 345
2:9-10	194	7:11	262
2:11	193, 197	7:11-19	262
2:16-3:1	187-198; 195, 196, 379	7:14	207
2:15	194	7:25	186
2:16	193, 194, 197	7:28	262
2:18	143, 189, 191, 193, 196, 197, 351	8-10	208
		8:1	204, 207-208, 259, 261
2:23	190, 191, 197	8:2	252
3	197	8:13	252
3:1	187, 191, 195, 196, 343, 349	9:5	253
		9:8	252
		9:12	253, 254, 357
1 Thessalonians		9:14	253, 267
1	361	9:19-24	266
1:9f.	281, 324	9:22	258
1:10	183, 201, 276	9:24	251, 252, 253
2:19	275	10	208
3:11-13	183	10:12	204, 207-208, 343, 351
4:14	183, 260	10:12-13	259, 260, 268, 369
5:9-10	183	12:2	204, 208-209, 259, 343
		12:14	208
1 Timothy		12:22-24	204
3:16	222		
		1 Peter	
2 Timothy		3:18	222
2:12	212	3:21-22	204, 343
		5:5	189
Hebrews			
1	245, 380	*1 John*	
1:2	206	2:22	311
1:2-4	208		
1:3	204, 258, 288	*Jude*	
1:3-4	203-207; 203, 253, 343, 349, 351	14-15	273
1:4	319	*Revelation*	
1:5	165, 234	1:5	211
1:6	205, 206	1:5-6	256
1:13	204, 206, 258	1:6	212
2:6	223	3:21	209, 211-212, 288, 343, 349
4:16	253		
5:5	208, 310	4	293

4:1	212	*Hermas*	
4:1-9	212-213	9:9-10:1	
4:2	256	10	189
4:2-3	212		
4:5	212	*Polycarp*	
4:6	213	6:2	275
4:7	213		
4:9	213		
5:5	213, 256	## 5. Church Writings	
5:5-6	213-215, 343		
5:6	213, 214, 256	*Irenaeus*	
5:6-12	288	*Against Heresies*	
5:10	212	1.24.3-7	303
5:11	256	1.25.1-3	301
7:9	256	1.26.1-2	301
7:9-10	213	1.26.2	300, 302
7:10	215	3.11.7	302
7:13-15	102	3.16.3	300
7:15	213, 256	3:21.1	301, 302
7:15-17	288	3.22.1	300
7:17	211	5.1.3	301
11:15	214		
11:16	256	*Hippolytus*	
11:19	213, 256	*Refutatio omnium haeresium*	
14:1	212	7.34	303
17	214	7.35	303
17:14	215	7.35.2	306
19:4	256		
19:10	110	*Eusebius*	
19:16	215	*Preparatio Evangelica*	
20:4	89, 212, 273	IX, 28-29	86
20:11	256		
22:3	211	*Church History*	
22:5	212	3.27.1-6	305
22:9	110	5.28.6	303
22:21	214		
		Origen	
## 4. Early Christian		*Contra Celsum*	
		5.61	304
Ignatios			
IgnEph.		*Sermons on Matthew*	
18:2	300	16.12	305
20:2	227		
		Tertullian	
IgnSm.	227	*Treatise on the Soul*	
1:1	300	48.4	189
IgnTrall.		*Epiphanius*	
9:1	300	*Panarion*	
		30.3.1-7	306

30.16.4	305	*Apocalypse of Peter*	
30.18.5-6	306	6	288
30.13.7	306	7.81.3-24	304

Pseudo-Clementine Homilies
III.20 306

Second Treatise of the Great Seth
VII.51-56 304
VII.51.30f. 304
VII.56.14-20 304

6. Nag Hammadi

Apocryphon of James
14:30 288

Index of Authors

Albright, W.F., 272, 273
Alexander, P., 95, 120, 131, 189, 191, 193
Allen, L.C., 205, 206, 233, 234, 340
Allegro, J.M., 166
Althaus, P., 230
Andersen, F.I., 103
Anderson, H., 359
Attridge, H.W., 204, 206, 207, 208, 209, 253, 258
Aune, D., 211, 214, 256
Bakhtin, M., 34, 35, 36
Balz, H.R., 38, 40, 41, 279
Bandstra, A.J., 188, 191
Barr, J., 21, 22
Barrett, C.K., 162, 220, 221, 254, 299, 314
Barthes, R., 35, 36
Bartsch, H-W., 240, 241, 249
Bauckham, R., 8, 110, 286, 288, 319, 320
Baur, F.C., 278, 280
Beasley-Murray, P., 217, 244, 281, 317
Becker, J(oachim), 60
Becker, J(ürgen), 62, 248, 250
Beker, J. Chr., 182
Benveniste, E., 20, 21
Berger, K., 39, 364
Berger, P.L., 28
Betz, O., 59, 166, 229, 230, 234, 245, 317
Black, M., 26, 27, 238
Blank, J., 244, 317
Blomberg, C.L., 273
Bloom, H., 36
Boccaccio, G., 30
Bock, D.L., 14, 76, 93, 94, 95, 104, 106, 108, 110, 114, 120, 142, 152, 162, 163, 164, 168, 172, 174, 179, 291
Boismard, M-E., 217, 220, 228, 229, 234, 299
Bornkamm, G., 188, 197
Bousset, W., 38, 39, 40, 41, 171, 174, 230, 278, 280, 298, 348, 364

Bowker, J.W., 6, 200
Brettler, M.Z., 28, 45, 46, 52, 53, 54, 61, 62
Brooke, G.J., 129
Brooker, P., 30, 32, 36
Bruce, F.F., 164, 166, 181, 205, 209, 254
Brueggemann, W., 45, 47
Buchanan, G.W., 252, 258, 260
Bultmann, R., 18, 39, 160, 161, 174, 221, 223, 226, 231, 270, 278, 280, 283, 298, 364
Burger, C., 217, 225, 226, 230, 246
Capes, D.B., 14, 172, 323, 325, 330, 332, 363, 366, 367, 370
Carr, W., 190, 287
Carrell, P.R., 15, 142, 191, 334
Carroll, J.T., 163, 167
Casey, P.M., 39, 175, 246, 278, 315, 364
Charlesworth, J.H., 132, 134, 247, 331, 350, 367
Chatman, S., 22, 32
Chester, A., 13, 85, 98, 104, 105, 111, 113, 115, 200, 343, 349, 367
Cockerhill, G.L., 301
Cohn, D., 33
Collins, J.J., 62, 69, 74, 75, 78, 79, 81, 82, 83, 84, 93, 96, 106, 114, 118, 131, 132, 133, 140, 231, 271, 272, 290, 291, 292, 335, 341, 342, 362
Colpe, C., 39, 364
Conzelmann, H., 171, 183, 184, 254, 276, 313, 314
Cooke, G., 53, 59, 60, 67
Craigie, P.C., 46, 51, 52
Cranfield, C.E.B., 230
Cross, F.M., 251
Culler, J., 31, 34, 336
Cullmann, O., 161, 171, 311, 312, 348, 358
Dahood, M., 46

Dahl, N.A., 221
Davies, W.D., 188, 194, 197
Davis, P.G., 10, 11, 367
Dean-Otting, M., 125, 127, 151, 340, 341
Delcor, M., 258
Dibelius, M., 188, 192
Donahue, J.R., 270
Duling, D.C., 59, 132, 164, 165, 166, 177, 229, 234, 245, 340
Dumbrell, W.J., 60
Dunn, J.D.G., 39, 165, 168, 170, 178, 179, 185, 186, 190, 192, 195, 219, 220, 221, 226, 227, 230, 232, 238, 240, 255, 257, 260, 275, 295, 299, 305, 308, 309, 310, 311, 312, 317, 346, 364, 370
Eagleton, T., 29
Eco, U., 336
Eissfeldt, O., 75, 77, 109
Eskola, T., 74, 99, 147, 197, 217, 252, 265, 310
Eslinger, L.M., 58
Evans, C.A., 273
Fabry, H.-J., 50
Fairclough, N., 23, 24, 25, 34
Fee, F.D., 314
Filson, F.V., 273
Fitzmyer, J.A., 129, 164, 171, 174, 178, 180, 219
Fletcher-Louis, C.H.T., 14, 83, 91, 129, 138, 139, 140, 142, 145, 168, 172, 191, 330, 353, 354, 365
Flusser, D., 263
Fohrer, G., 60
Ford, J.M., 214, 256
Fossum, J.E., 14, 113, 142, 191, 198, 365
Foucault, M., 22, 23, 24
France, R.T., 319, 363
Francis, F.O., 188, 189, 190, 193, 196, 197
Frankemölle, H., 312, 352
Freundlieb, D., 23
Froitzheim, F., 217, 222, 240, 244, 317
Fuller, R.H., 222, 223, 231, 235, 279, 281
Furnish, V.P., 199, 275
Garnet, P., 129
Gärtner, B., 147, 252

Gaylord, H.E. Jr., 117
Genette, G., 35, 37
Gese, H., 50, 55, 57
Georgi, D., 199
Gieschen, C.A., 14, 83, 95, 109, 129, 137, 138, 139, 140, 141, 142, 143, 145, 286, 307, 326, 329, 334, 353, 354, 365
Gnilka, J., 190, 191, 271, 272, 273
Goranson, S., 300, 301
Goulder, M., 295, 306, 308
Gourgues, M., 168, 185, 206, 341, 370
Gray, G.B., 48, 66, 67
Grappe, C., 12, 273
Grässer, E., 203, 205
Green, W.S., 339, 348
Greenberg, M., 67
Greimas, A.J., 18, 30
Gruenwald, I., 3, 4, 66, 73, 74, 103, 106, 109, 110, 121, 212, 287, 293, 294, 341
Gunkel, H., 47
Gunther, J.J., 188, 204
Haacker, K., 229, 234
Haenchen, E., 160, 172, 179
Hagner, D.A., 262, 263, 271, 272, 273, 357
Hahn, F., 11, 39, 40, 161, 217, 221, 223, 226, 240, 248, 249, 278, 279, 280, 281, 317, 360
Hall, R., 108, 109, 110, 285, 289
Hall, S., 22
Halperin, D.J., 5, 67, 73, 80, 105, 106, 112, 120, 127, 142, 212, 213, 214
Hanson, D.D., 2
Harris, R., 19
Hartman, L., 74
Hasel, G., 44
Hawkes, T., 20, 29, 30, 336
Hay, D.M., 79, 101, 171, 173, 177, 183, 184, 186, 187, 195, 202, 206, 210, 334, 350, 366
Hayes, J.H., 165, 166, 177, 234, 244, 245, 317
Hays, R.B., 17
Headlam, A.C., 230, 231, 238, 240
Hegermann, H., 259

Heitmüller, D., 278
Hengel, M., 6, 7, 10, 11, 12, 13, 40, 69, 81, 84, 87, 90, 91, 92, 101, 121, 130, 134, 144, 168, 183, 185, 186, 195, 197, 202, 204, 207, 210, 211, 214, 217, 229, 233, 234, 236, 254, 260, 276, 279, 283, 291, 310, 312, 327, 329, 341, 343, 348, 350, 353, 354, 365, 370
Herrmann, K., 120, 121
Hill, D., 241
Himmelfarb, M., 73, 78, 104, 111, 121, 126, 147, 150, 285, 286, 335, 341, 345
Hirsch, E.D., 32
Hofius, O., 68, 203, 252, 267, 366
Holladay, C.R., 86, 87, 88, 90
Hollander, H.W., 62, 77
Holleman, J., 183
Holtz, T., 162
Hooke, S.H., 240
Hooker, M.D., 188, 194
Horst, P.W. van den, 88, 89, 90, 144, 366
Hunter, A.M., 222
Hurst, L.D., 203, 210
Hurtado, L.W., 9, 10, 38, 39, 40, 92, 93, 95, 97, 128, 136, 140, 142, 169, 262, 278, 279, 318, 320, 323, 324, 325, 329, 330, 332, 333, 343, 353, 363,
Häkkinen, S., 300, 303
Iersel, B.M.F. van, 217, 222, 230
Isaac, E., 95
Isaacs, M.E., 251, 258, 266
Jacobson, H., 86, 87, 88, 90
Jakobson, R., 19, 20, 24, 32
Janowski, B., 56, 57, 252
Jenny, L., 36
Jewett, R., 217, 219, 241, 249, 298
Johnson, M., 27
Jonge, M. de., 62, 77, 178, 206, 207, 217, 249, 250, 263, 361, 371
Juel, D., 162
Karrer, M., 369
Käsemann, E., 203, 209, 210, 226, 295, 311, 312
Keck, L.E., 38, 40, 41, 279

Kee, H.C., 77
Kegel, G., 241, 248
Kelly, J.N.D., 300, 313
Kim, S., 270
Klijn, A.F.J., 301, 302, 305, 306, 309
Klinzing, G., 252
Knibb, M.A., 108, 109, 111, 285
Knox, J., 298
Kobelski, P.J., 129, 263
Koskenniemi, E., 364
Kraft, R.A., 311
Kramer, W., 217, 221, 226, 235, 279, 313, 317
Kraus, H–J., 47, 49, 51, 53, 59, 60
Kreitzer, L.J., 319, 363, 370
Kristeva, J., 35, 36
Kuss, O., 230, 298
Kümmel, W.G., 187, 278
Laato, A., 37, 45, 50, 60, 61, 85, 366
Lakoff, G., 27
Lane, W.L., 203, 204, 205, 207, 254, 258, 261, 262, 345
Lang, B., 57
Langevin, P-É., 217, 240
Legrand, L., 228, 229, 232, 317
Lieberman, S., 121
Lietzmann, H., 230, 235, 240
Lightfoot, J.B., 188
Lincoln, A.T., 192, 196, 198
Lindars, B., 258, 268, 270, 274, 358
Linnemann, E., 217, 223, 226, 239, 240
Loader, W.R.G., 170, 171, 177, 183, 187, 202, 204, 253, 261, 266, 267, 276, 345, 357
Locke, J., 19
Lohse, E., 190, 191, 192, 193, 195
Longenecker, R.N., 200
Luckmann, Th., 28
Lunt, H.G., 107, 108
Lührmann, D., 152
Lyonnet, S., 188
Löhr, H., 11, 12, 267
Lövestam, E., 163, 234
MacRae, G.W., 78, 252, 267, 344
Maier, J., 150
Mann, C.S., 272, 273

Marshall, I.H., 174, 270
Martin, R.P., 198
McNicol, A.J., 5
Meeks, W.A., 88, 97, 144, 365, 366
Merklein, H., 247
Mettinger, T.N.D., 46, 51, 53, 54, 60
Michel, O., 59, 185, 186, 208, 220, 221, 227, 232, 235, 240, 245, 253, 255, 261, 262, 275, 298, 346, 357
Milik, J.T., 251, 262
Minde van der, H.-J., 230
Montgomery, J.A., 69
Moo, D.J., 186
Morray-Jones, C.R.A., 121, 335, 354
Moule, C.F.D., 175, 346, 361
Mounce, R.H., 273
Mowinckel, S., 47
Neufeld, V.H., 220, 313
Newman, C.C., 13, 14, 18, 31, 73, 93
Newsom, C., 6, 80, 89, 90, 148, 149, 150, 204, 266
Nickelsburg, G.W.E., 72, 75, 91, 95, 100, 131, 135, 152, 270, 271, 286
Norden, E., 219
Nygren, A., 240
O'Brien, P.T., 188, 190, 191, 192, 196
Orr, W.R. - Walther J.A., 184
Osborne, G., 38
Patte, D., 18
Peirce, C.S., 20, 37
Pelikan, J., 306, 307
Pesch, R., 163, 168, 169, 178, 180, 217, 249, 317
Peterson, E., 238
Phelan, J., 32
Philonenko, M., 11
Plöger, O., 69
Plummer, A., 184
Pokorny, P., 39
Porton, G.G., 311
Poythress, V.S., 217, 225, 226, 234, 237, 239
Propp, V., 30
Qimron, E., 194
Rad von, G., 49, 60, 340
Rehm, M.D., 56

Reinink, G.J., 301, 302, 305, 306, 309
Rengstorf, K.H., 59
Rese, M., 162, 171
Richards, I.A., 26
Ricoeur, P., 20, 21, 22, 24, 26, 27
Riesner, R., 361
Rimmon-Kenan, S., 30
Ringgren, H., 129
Rissi, M., 206, 252, 262, 267, 345
Robertson, A., 184
Robinson, J.A.T., 181
Robinson, J.M., 298
Rowland, C., 4, 5, 8, 9, 14, 66, 67, 70, 72, 78, 104, 107, 126, 137, 138, 142, 287, 326
Sanday, W., 230, 231, 238, 240
Sanders, E.P., 113, 310
Sanders, J.T., 203
Saussure de, F., 18, 19, 20, 31
Schade, H-H., 248, 281, 282
Schelkle, K.H., 300
Schenke, J.-M., 203, 263
Schiffman, L.H., 5, 6, 80, 85, 86, 132, 149
Schlier, H., 200, 217, 222, 260, 283, 313
Schmidt, H.W., 299
Schmithals, W., 220, 240, 298
Schneider, B., 162, 165, 168, 172, 177, 179, 217, 223, 227
Schneider, C., 151
Scholem, G.G., 2, 65, 125, 315
Schüpphaus, J., 152, 153
Schürer, E., 56
Schweizer, E., 165, 166, 177, 191, 195, 217, 220, 221, 226, 229, 234, 235, 239, 249, 298, 317
Schwemer, A.M., 11, 12, 81, 204, 266
Schäfer, P., 6, 120, 121, 198
Scott, E.F., 190
Scott, J.M., 217, 219, 234, 243
Searle, J.R., 27
Seeberg, A., 312, 313
Segal, A.F., 3, 7, 8, 14, 72, 73, 74, 78, 91, 96, 99, 102, 105, 106, 113, 121, 127, 138, 169, 182, 190, 199, 200, 201, 319, 325, 326, 329, 343, 350, 353, 366

Selden, R., 30, 32, 36
Seow, C.L., 51, 57
Seybold, K., 45, 47, 48, 51
Simon, M., 300, 302, 305, 309
Sjöberg, E., 95
Slingerlander, H.D., 77
Smith, M., 82
Soggin, J.A., 46
Soskice, J.M., 26, 27
Stauffer, E., 219
Stegemann, H., 80, 194
Stinespring, W.F., 115
Stone, M.E., 72, 92, 93, 116, 119, 133, 152
Strauss, D.F., 228, 296, 297, 298, 320, 382
Strugnell, J., 5, 149, 194
Stuckenbruck, L.T., 14, 15, 106, 142, 143, 145, 188, 189, 191, 288, 365, 368
Stuhlmacher, P., 11, 49, 186, 200, 201, 217, 230, 238, 240, 268, 277, 283, 363
Szikszai, S., 45
Talmon, S., 132, 311, 342, 348
Taranovsky, K., 35, 37
Tate, M.E., 47, 49
Theisohn, J., 270
Theobald, M., 250, 317
Thiselton, A.C., 21, 22
Thüsing, W., 244, 281, 317
Todorov, T., 30, 35
Tödt, H.E., 270, 283
Tournay, R.J., 52, 148
Trocmé, E., 12
Unnik, W.C. van, 230

VanderKam, J.C., 76, 85, 194
Vermes, G., 81, 147, 252
Veijola, T., 46, 58
Vielhauer, Ph., 38, 40, 41, 187, 279
Volz, P., 49
Walker, W.O.Jr., 270, 271, 274
Walther J.A., 184
Watts, J.D.W., 48
Wegenast, K., 217, 221, 226, 227
Weiss, J., 160, 228, 231, 270, 296, 297, 298, 309, 310, 314, 315, 320, 382
Wengst, K., 217, 220, 226, 230, 298
Whitsett, C., 217, 219, 229, 243
Widdowson, P., 30, 32, 36
Wilckens, U., 175, 178, 219, 221, 222, 240, 255, 260, 317
Wildberger, H., 48, 67
Williamson, R., 89, 203, 210
Wilson, R. McLachlan, 301
Wilson, S.G., 301, 305
Winninge, M., 152
Wintermute, O.S., 76
Witherington (III), B., 17
Wittgenstein, L., 26
Woude van der, A.S., 62, 85, 167, 206, 207, 234, 263
Zahn, T., 230
Zeller, D., 352
Ziesler, J.A., 220, 221, 238
Zimmerli, W., 54
Zimmermann, H., 223, 225, 237
Zwiep, A.W., 169

Index of Subjects

Aaron, 66
Abel, 88, 110, 111, 114, 115, 128
Abraham, 10, 66, 88, 93, 96, 101, 105, 106, 115, 128, 135, 261, 262, 263, 306, 322, 345
- burial, 115
- exaltation, 114
Adam, 88, 110, 112, 113, 128, 139, 322
- burial, 113
- exaltation, 112
Adoption, 59, 60, 208, 219, 296
Adoptionist Christology, 160, 177, 223, 226, 228, 231, 279, 296, 304, 309, 315, 317, 320, 321, 364, 382
- and the Church Fathers, 300-303, 306
Angel Christology, 7, 9, 137, 307
Angelic interpretation, 7-9, 14, 137-146, 154, 166, 211, 286, 306, 307, 319, 325-327, 333, 354, 365
Angelic liturgy, 5, 192
Angel of God, 66,
Angelology, 4, 8, 104, 105, 106, 190, 205, 263, 292
Angelomorphic Christology, 14, 137, 138, 154, 307, 326, 327, 354, 377
Angel veneration, 142, 190-192, 195
Anointment, 171, 172, 175
Apocalyptic
- literature, 3,
- theology (Jewish), 8, 67, 68, 69, 89, 99, 135, 189, 194
- Christology, 8, 13, 173, 194, 195, 353
Aramaic Christianity, 185
Archaeology of knowledge, 23
Ark (of the Covenant), 50, 51, 52, 54, 57, 63, 70, 97, 119, 175, 213, 253, 254, 261, 264, 340
Ascent story, 347, 372
Ascent structure, 3, 5, 75, 79, 86, 109, 110, 111, 122, 202, 288, 333, 355, 376
Atonement, 55, 57, 63, 129, 150, 156, 253, 254, 255, 267-268, 369
Atonement and resurrection, 259-261, 268

Baal, 46
Baruch, 116, 117
Basilides, 303
Belial, 140
Binary oppositions, 30
Bogomil, 71, 105

Carpocrates, 301, 302, 303
Cerinthus, 301, 302, 303, 304, 305, 306
Change in the priesthood, 262, 345
Cherubim, 50, 54, 92, 141, 265, 266
Cherub-throne, 51, 54, 56, 67, 68, 98, 112, 118, 294, 344
Christ, 171
- resurrection, see: Christology, resurrection
- enthronement, 110, 170, 174, 181, 185, 201, 209, 242, 244, 245, 261, 329, 349
- parousia, 151, 180, 183, 276, 277
Christ and the kingship of God, 368, 370
Christ and Spirit, 172
Christ as the object of faith, 368, 370
Christ's heavenly journey, 285, 286
Christology
- method, 38-42, 278-281, 375
- and discourse, 41, 158
- formulas, 218, 220, 222, 223, 236
- emergence of, 159, 170-174, 196, 228, 243, 318, 319, 322, 331, 338, 353, 363, 366
- resurrection, 16, 162, 183, 229, 235, 236, 240, 241, 244, 245, 260, 313, 349, 351, 355
- exaltation, 162-163, 168, 177, 185, 194, 195, 201, 207, 209, 224, 287, 290, 319, 349, 362
- Savior, 177, 178, 330
- Leader, 177, 330
- judge, 151, 152, 153, 272, 276, 284, 290, 359
- High Priest, 252, 255, 259, 260, 266, 267, 356, 357, 358, 370, 380
- titles, 38, 40, 170, 174, 178, 228, 230, 280, 350

Index of Subjects

- worship of Jesus, 320, 330, 363, 367, 368
- "missing link", 176, 247, 331-335
- enthroned figures, 339, 344, 346
- Christological narratives, 347, 348, 351, 356, 359, 372, 385, 386, 387
- Christological predestination, 232, 233
- Christian merkabah tradition, 328-330, 337, 347, 366, 384, 386
- Colossians, letter to the
- authorship, 187, 196-198
- Communication theory, 20, 32
- Consistent eschatology, 297
- Crucifixion, 177, 200, 259, 287, 303
- Cultic discourse, 177, 251, 257, 269, 356, 358, 378, 380
- Cultic soteriology, 253, 258, 261, 263, 267-268, 318, 345, 359, 369

- David, 10
- Davidic covenant, 354
- Davidic kingship, 58, 59, 60,
- Davidic Messiah, see: Messiah
- Day of atonement, 55, 56,
- Day or Wrath, 276
- Dead Sea Scrolls, 5, 79
- Death and resurrection, 354, 355
- Deep structure, 31
- Deification, 82, 97, 106, 142, 143, 144, 155, 176, 318, 363, 364, 373
- Designation, 231, 232
- Dialogism, 34
- Discourse, 21-24, 25, 34, 37, 158, 324, 330, 338, 375
- Discourse analysis, 23
- Discursive formation, 22, 24, 332
- Discursive practice, 24
- Divine agent theory, 9-11, 13, 91, 128, 136, 173, 321, 323-325, 377
- Dream visions,

- Ebion, 303
- Ebionites, 299
- the appellation, 300
- and Qumran, 301, 307
- and Virgin birth, 301, 304, 305
- and Gnosticism, 301, 303, 304, 305, 307
- Ebionite theory, 299, 321, 382
- dualistic anthropology, 301, 307
- dualistic Christology, 303, 304, 305, 306
- docetism, 302, 304
- ascetism, 301
- possessionism, 306, 309, 320
- and angelology, 307
- Ebionites and Jewish Christianity, 305, 308, 309, 310
- Egyptian religion, 60
- Elect One, 91, 92, 93, 272
- Enoch, 9, 72, 75, 76, 101, 103, 110, 111, 120, 128, 142, 272, 322
- seer, 76
- priest, 76
- Son of Man, 95
- Metatron, 95, 120
- Enthronement, 7, 8, 11, 15, 61, 70, 83, 91, 102, 103, 110, 121, 132, 151, 156, 164, 180, 181, 195, 209, 213, 231, 242, 246, 259, 290, 292, 316, 342, 352, 362, 368, 378
- Enthronement and the deity of Christ, 366-368, 388
- Enthronement and resurrection, 167, 180, 181, 183, 196, 217, 232, 235, 244, 246, 317, 329, 352-353, 366, 380
- Enthronement discourse, 43, 156, 158, 167, 173, 177, 181, 202, 216, 244, 283, 294, 343, 378
- Enthronement in the parousia, 277, 280, 281, 282
- Enthronement of the patriarchs, 101, 110, 111, 114, 127, 128, 130, 134, 155, 174, 322, 329
- Enteschatologisierung, 248, 283
- Entpolitisierung, 250
- Epicureans, 197
- Eschatological entrée, 94, 153, 155, 272, 276, 359, 360, 361, 372
- Eschatology
- Judaism, 2, 49, 92, 94, 111, 151
- Paul, 241, 249
- Essenes, 188
- Eve, 111
- Exaltation and atonement, 258-264
- Exaltation discourse, 179, 322
- Exalted patriarchs, 138, 139, 154, 365
- see also: Enthronement of the patriarchs
- Exodus, 86

- Fall, 111,
- Flesh and Spirit, 221, 236, 237-240
- Functional Christology, 316, 317, 318, 321

Futurist eschatology, 181, 277, 278, 282

Gabriel, 104, 142, 154
Gerizim, 34
German idealism, 39, 40
Glory, 199
Gnosticism, 4, 7, 71, 193, 203, 209, 301, 303, 304, 305, 307
- heavenly redeemer, 203, 209
God
- king, 2, 43, 44-49, 54, 63, 125, 150, 154, 265, 315, 362, 368, 375
- warrior, 46
- shepherd, 46
- lordship, 52
Gods of the Holy of Holies, 82, 130, 141, 156

Hagar, 66
Heavenly court of law, 274, 275
Heavenly journey, 5, 72, 77, 78, 87, 91, 95, 103, 109, 112, 114, 115, 116, 119, 120, 123, 127, 169, 192, 212, 285, 290, 376
Heavenly liturgy, 6, 53, 67, 69, 76, 80, 103, 106, 110, 118, 120, 147, 148, 150, 192, 193, 213, 265, 266
Heavenly palace, 46, 63, 72
Heavenly Temple, 68, 72, 73, 78, 107, 119, 123, 251, 252, 254, 257, 265, 266, 290, 293, 340, 345, 351
Hebrews, letter to the
- and gnosticism, 203
- and Jewish apocalyptic, 203, 205, 209
- enthronement Christology, 203, 204, 206, 209, 345, 357
- cultic Christology, 208, 253, 260, 264, 266, 267
- Priest-king, 207, 208, 262, 264, 344, 345
- Temple symbolism, 252, 345, 357, 358
- atonement, 253, 254, 261, 357
- angels, 205, 206, 210
Hekhalot literature, 4
Hellenism, 39
Hellenistic Christianity, 40, 161, 278, 279
History-of-religions school, 39, 40, 161, 203, 277, 280, 364, 366, 387
Holy of Holies, 50, 53, 55, 56, 67, 73, 121, 141, 156, 253, 356
Homologies, 182, 311, 312
- and acclamations, 312, 313

Humility (self-abasement), 189, 199
Humiliation and exaltation, 208, 210, 355
Hymnic tradition, 5
Hymn of Moses, 204, 205

Individuation, 36
Intertextual criticism, 34-38
Intertextuality (see also: sub-texts), 162, 338, 348, 361, 367, 373, 385
Intertextual strategy, 350
Intertextual transformation, 42, 216, 274, 289, 324, 327, 332, 343, 361, 367, 368, 370, 374, 385, 388
Isaac, 102, 115, 128, 135
- exaltation, 116
Isaiah, 88, 109, 110, 111, 128

Jacob, 66, 96, 102, 107, 108, 128, 135, 306
Jacob's ladder, 66, 107
Jaoel, 8, 89, 105, 106, 107, 139
Jesus, 9, 122
- see also: Christ
Jewish Christianity, 202, 227, 279, 310, 314
Jewish mysticism, 1, 2, 43, 188
Job
- ascension, 102
- exaltation, 101, 128, 157
Joseph, 88
Joshua, 272
Judaism
- Premonarchic period, 45
Judges
- holy ones, 83, 89, 272
- twelve tribes, 273
- Jesus' disciples, 128, 273
Judgment
- eschatological, 93, 100, 133, 135, 151, 152, 153, 270, 346
- final judgment, 48, 92, 93, 100, 271, 272, 275, 282, 361
Judgment seat, 151, 346, 359
Judicial discourse, 186, 270, 274, 275, 283, 347, 359, 360, 378, 381

King (of Israel), 58, 62
Kingship-of-Yahweh psalms, 47,
Kyrios, 9, 131, 169, 226, 242, 247, 279, 335, 363
Kyrios-Christology, 161, 242, 247, 248

Langue, 18, 20, 21
Levi, 75, 77, 96
Levitical singers, 148, 149
Literary theory, 17, 375
Liturgical celebration of Yahweh's kingship, 46, 47
Liturgical cycles, 149, 150
Logos, 9, 98
Lord, 97, 170, 171, 180, 214, 326, 363

Maccabees, 134
Marcionism, 204
Melchizedek, 8, 84, 96, 104, 129, 130, 140, 157, 177, 186, 191, 207, 258-264, 271, 307, 331, 337, 344, 345, 356, 357, 358, 370, 371
Mercy seat, 55, 57, 63, 70, 251, 255, 358, 374
Merkabah (throne), 2, 12, 65, 68, 80, 105, 110, 116, 125, 146, 148, 315, 362, 374, 389
Merkabah literature, 24
Merkabah mysticism, 1, 2, 5, 9, 15, 37, 48
- and Christology, 172, 173, 175, 181, 188-196, 201, 202, 207, 209, 213, 215, 246, 250, 257, 269, 288, 289, 328, 330, 334, 336, 366, 371, 373-374, 377-378, 388, 389-390.
Merkabah visions, 6,
Messiah, 61, 62, 84, 90, 92, 155, 169, 171, 214, 334
- eschatological atonement, 253, 255
- exaltation of, 127, 132, 156
- priestly Messiah, 61, 84, 130, 186, 207, 208, 253, 258, 259, 344, 356
- king, 92
- judge, 151, 152, 153 272, 276, 284, 290, 359
- and resurrection, 136, 174
- see also: Son of David (the Davidide)
- see also: Son of Man
Messianic enthronement, 11-13, 327, 334, 335, 377
Messias designatus, 171, 175, 351, 355
Metaphor, 25-29, 49, 74, 125, 172, 229, 242
- live metaphors, 27
Metaphor-as-myth, 27
Metatron, 95, 120-122, 192
Michael (archangel), 9, 11, 81, 115, 117, 262, 271, 323
Monotheism, 10,
Moses, 9, 10, 51, 66, 86, 87, 88, 93, 128, 178
- enthronement, 88
- problem of deification, 89, 90, 97, 144, 145
- ascension, 96
Moses-typology, 178, 179
Mount Qater, 76
Mount Sinai, 66, 74, 87, 96
Mount Zion, 46
Mystery religions (Hellenistic), 193, 197, 278, 280, 364, 366
Mystical ascension, 96

Narrative, 348, 358, 360, 375
Narrative discourse, 22
Narrative syntax, 30, 31, 33, 347
Narratology, 29-33
Nero, 109
New history of religions school, 16
Noah, 128, 322

Pantextualism, 34, 35, 38
Parallelismus membrorum, 220, 221, 222, 223, 224, 225, 235, 237, 242
Pargod speculation, 68, 119, 123, 376
Parole, 18, 20, 21
Paul
- Christology, 182, 194, 197, 199, 201, 216, 219
- and Judaism, 188
- and merkabah mysticism, 182, 198, 201, 202, 242, 246, 379
- and early Christian tradition, 218, 219, 226, 242
- visionary experience, 198-201
- Damascus road, 199, 200
- Colossian heretics, 187-196
- pagan mystery cult, 188, 193
- judgment descriptions, 274, 275
- theology of the law, 198
- boasting, 199
- persecution, 200
- resurrection body, 238
Paul's heavenly journey, 293
Pharisees, 194
Polarized eschatology, 277-283, 360, 373

Prince of life, 355, 356, 372
Promise tradition, 165, 229, 236

Qumran community
- apocalyptic, 82
- eschatology, 85, 132, 147
- messianology, 84-86, 132
- priesthood, 67, 79, 84, 89, 216
- salvation, 132
- Teacher of Righteousness, 81, 83, 174
- Temple, 80
- Temple symbolism, 80, 147, 252, 265
- atonement, 147, 252
- throne visions, 79, 81

Resurrection,
- of the dead, 100, 113, 135, 240, 241, 245, 329, 352
- of the body, 162
- and raising up, 233, 234, 235
- semantics, 166-167
- see also: Christology
Resurrection discourse, 217, 244, 248, 351, 356, 378
Revelation, book of
- Christology, 211, 215
- Lamb, 213, 214
- Lion, 213, 214
- enthronement, 212
- heavenly Temple, 212, 256
- cultic soteriology, 256
- and Jewish apocalyptic, 212, 213, 214
Royal metaphors, 124, 125, 218, 340

Salvation history, 354
Semantic fields, 26
Semantics, 17, 19, 21
Semiosis, 336-337, 384
Semiotics, 17, 18, 19, 336
Seth, 102
Sethian Gnosticism, 303, 304
Shem, 128
Shiloh, 50
Signified, 18
Signifier, 18
Sociology of knowledge, 278
Sola fide, 107
Son of David (the Davidide), 61, 84, 85, 86, 92, 95, 131, 132, 133, 156, 157, 164, 165, 166, 173, 176, 180, 201, 207, 213, 215, 228, 229, 230, 241, 258, 261, 292, 318, 326, 339, 342, 343, 348, 370, 379
Son of Man, 69, 70, 91, 94, 130, 151, 152, 153, 154, 270, 271, 272, 297, 346, 347, 359, 360
Sonship, 59, 206, 207
Spirit of holiness, 222, 223, 238, 239, 242
Spirit of Light, 11
Stephen, 178, 179, 180
Stoicism, 197
Structuralism, 18, 29-33
Submetaphors, 28, 184
Subtexts, 35, 43, 161, 166, 168, 172, 173, 184, 205, 358, 366, 373
Symbolic universe, 28, 154, 156, 159, 341
Symbolic world, 63, 211, 218, 227, 242, 250, 283, 289, 332, 335, 336, 339
Synagogue liturgy, 117

Temple criticism, 126, 146, 179, 251-252
Temple cult, 55-57, 146, 252, 254, 257
Temple liturgy, 51, 52, 148, 149, 150, 266
Temple structured universe, 252, 253, 269
Textual surfaces, 35, 36
Theocracy, 45, 49, 57, 58, 63, 125, 131, 175, 215, 315, 318, 362, 367
Theocratic adoptionism
- theory, 295, 296, 308, 309, 320
- history, 296-298
- and early Christology, 296, 309
- see also: Ebionite theory
Theodicy
- in apocalyptic, 99, 108
- problem of, 126
Theodotus, 303
Theophany, 4, 5,
Throne, 48, 50-54, 63, 71, 87, 117, 118, 127, 151, 169, 213, 253, 264, 291, 340-341
- place for the atonement, 265
- judgment seat, 151, 274, 275
Throne of Glory, 44, 99, 107, 121, 169
Throne visions, 3, 4, 65, 66, 69, 73, 87, 95, 99, 105, 106, 115,
Transformational mysticism, 335
Transtextuality, 35
Triple pattern of mediation, 10,
Typological interpretation, 25, 324, 332, 333, 335, 350, 365, 383, 387
Two-stage Christology, 221, 239, 249

Victor (bishop of Rome), 303
Wicked Priest, 62
Wrath of God, see: God

Yahweh, see: God

Zaphon, 46

www.ingramcontent.com/pod-product-compliance
Lightning Source LLC
Chambersburg PA
CBHW052052110526
44591CB00013B/2173